British Crime Writing

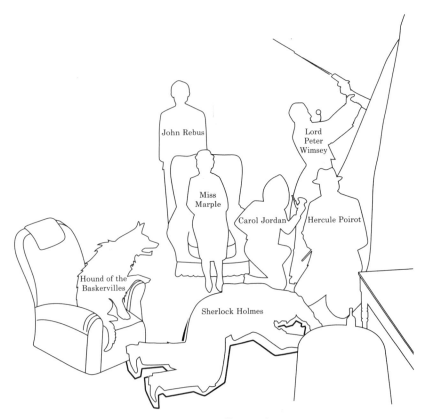

John Rebus

Lord
Peter
Wimsey

Miss
Marple

Carol Jordan

Hercule Poirot

Hound of the
Baskervilles

Sherlock Holmes

Key to cover illustration.

British Crime Writing

An Encyclopedia

Volume I: A–H

Edited by Barry Forshaw

Greenwood World Publishing
Oxford / Westport Connecticut
2009

First published by Greenwood World Publishing 2009

1 2 3 4 5 6 7 8 9 10

Copyright © Greenwood Publishing Group 2009

This book is sold subject to the condition that it shall not, by way of trade or otherwise, be lent, resold, hired out, or otherwise circulated without the publisher's prior consent in any form of binding or cover other than that in which it is published and without a similar condition being imposed on the subsequent publisher

Greenwood World Publishing
Prama House
267 Banbury Road
Oxford OX2 7HT
An imprint of Greenwood Publishing Group, Inc
www.greenwood.com

British Library Cataloguing-in-Publication Data: a catalogue record for this book is available from the British Library

Library of Congress Cataloging-in-Publication Data

British crime writing : an encyclopedia / [edited by] Barry Forshaw.
    p. cm.
   Includes bibliographical references and index.
   ISBN 978-1-84645-022-8 (set: alk. paper); ISBN 978-1-84645-030-3 (vol. 1: alk. paper);
ISBN 978-1-84645-031-0 (vol. 2: alk. paper)
   1. Detective and mystery stories, English – Encyclopedias.   2. Crime writing – Great Britain – Encyclopedias.   3. Authors, English – Biography – Encyclopedias.   I. Forshaw, Barry.

   PR19B67   2009
   823'.087209003 – dc22   2008030713

· ISBN 978-1-84645-022-8 (set)
ISBN 978-1-84645-030-3 (vol. 1)
ISBN 978-1-84645-031-0 (vol. 2)

Designed by Fraser Muggeridge studio
Pictures researched by Zooid Pictures
Typeset by TexTech International
Printed and bound by South China Printing Company

Contents

Acknowledgements

In addition to my appreciation of the inestimable industry and scholarship of the contributors (notably Mark Campbell, Russell James and Geoff Bradley, who provided much added value), I owe a special debt of gratitude to two Mikes, Ashley and Ripley, whose knowledge of the crime genre is prodigious. In fact, Mike Ashley's contribution to the encyclopedia has – in many ways – been nonpareil. Simon Mason at Greenwood has been a constant source of inspiration and literary erudition, while Liane Escorza has provided invaluable liaison expertise. Finally, my thanks to Judith Forshaw for her invaluable administrative help.

Alphabetical List of Entries

Guide to Related Topics

Golden Age Crime Fiction

Allingham, Margery (1904–1966)
Bentley, E[dmund] C[lerihew]
  (1875–1956)
Blake, Nicholas (1904–1972)
Charteris, Leslie (1907–1993)
Cheyney, Peter (1896–1951)
Creasey, John (1908–1973)
Crispin, Edmund (1921–1978)
Crofts, Freeman Wills (1879–1957)
Dickinson, Peter (b.1927)
Dudley, Ernest (1908–2006)
Freeman, R. Austin (1862–1943)
Golden Age Crime Fiction
Goodchild, George (1888–1969)
Graeme, Bruce (1900–1982)
Heyer, Georgette (1902–1974)
Hornung, E.W. (1866–1921)
Household, Geoffrey (1900–1988)
Iles, Francis (1893–1971)
Knox, Ronald (1888–1957)
Marsh, Ngaio (1895–1982)
Mason, A[lfred] E[dward] W[oodley]
  (1865–1948)
Mitchell, Gladys (1901–1983)
Morland, Nigel (1905–1986)
Rohmer, Sax (1883–1959)
Tey, Josephine (1896–1952)
Vickers, Roy (1889–1965)
Wallace, Edgar (1875–1932)
Wentworth, Patricia (1878–1961)
Wheatley, Dennis (1897–1977)
Whitechurch, V[ictor] L[orenzo]
  (1868–1933)

Thrillers

Archer, Geoffrey (b.1944)
Bagley, Desmond (1923–1983)
Child, Lee (b.1954)
Creed, John (b.1961)
Davidson, Lionel (b.1922)
Egleton, Clive (1927–2006)
Follett, Ken (b.1949)
Forsyth, Frederick (b.1938)
Fullerton, John (b.1949)
Gadney, Reg (b.1941)
Harris, Robert (b.1957)
Higgins, Jack (b.1929)
Innes, Hammond (1913–1998)
Leather, Stephen (b.1956)
Lyall, Gavin (1932–2003)
McLaren, John (b.1951)

McNab, Andy (b.1959)
Ryan, Chris (b.1961)
Seymour, Gerald (b.1941)
Thrillers: Novels of Action
Williams, Alan (b.1935)

Academic Crime

Academe, Death in
Blake, Victoria (b.1963)
Dexter, Colin (b.1930)
Innes, Michael (1906–1994)
Stallwood, Veronica

Espionage

Allbeury, Ted (1917–2005)
Ambler, Eric (1909-1998)
Canning, Victor (1911–1986)
Childers, Erskine (1870–1922)
Clifford, Francis (1917–1975)
Cumming, Charles (b.1971)
Deighton, Len (b.1929)
Espionage Fiction
Fleming, Ian (1908–1964)
Freemantle, Brian (b.1936)
Gardner, John Edmund (1926–2007)
Haggard, William (1907–1993)
Leasor, James (1923–2008)
le Carré, John (b.1931)
Le Queux, William (1864–1927)
MacLean, Alistair (1922–1987)
Markstein, George (1929–1987)
Mitchell, James (1926–2002)
O'Donnell, Peter (b.1920)
Oppenheim, Edward Phillips (1866–1946)
Porter, Henry (b.1953)
Price, Anthony (b.1928)
Rimington, Stella (b.1935)
Trevor, Elleston (1920–1995)

Comic Crime

Brahms, Caryl (1901–1982)
Brookmyre, Christopher (b.1968)
Caudwell, Sarah (1939–2000)
Edwards, Ruth Dudley (b.1944)
Fforde, Jasper (b.1961)
Guttridge, Peter (b.1951)
Humour and Crime Fiction
Lindsay, Douglas (b.1964)
Porter, Joyce (1924–1990)
Pryce, Malcolm (b.1960)
Ripley, Mike (b.1952)

Film

Beat Girl (film, 1960)
Brighton Rock (film, 1947)
Bulldog Jack (film, 1935)
Criminal, The (film, 1960)
Dead Man's Shoes (film, 2004)
Film and Crime: Page to Screen
Frenzy (film, 1972)
Frightened City, The (film, 1961)
Gangster No. 1 (film, 2000)
Get Carter (film, 1971)
Gumshoe (film, 1971)
Hell Drivers (film, 1957)
Hell Is a City (film, 1960)
It Always Rains on Sunday (film, 1947)
League of Gentlemen, The (film, 1960)
Lock, Stock and Two Smoking Barrels
    (film, 1998)
Long Good Friday, The (film, 1980)
Mona Lisa (film, 1986)
Murder on the Orient Express (film, 1974)
Night and the City (film, 1950)
No Orchids for Miss Blandish (film, 1948)
Performance (film, 1970)
Sexy Beast (film, 2000)
Tiger in the Smoke (film, 1956)
Villain (film, 1971)

Television

The Bill (television series, 1984–)
Brother Cadfael (television series, 1994–1998)
Cracker (television series, 1993–2006)
Cribb (television series, 1980–1981)
Dalgliesh, Adam
Dalziel & Pascoe (television series, 1996–)
Frost, Inspector
Hazell (television series, 1978–1980)
Holmes on TV
Inspector Morse (television series, 1987–2000)
Marple, Jane
Police Procedurals
Prime Suspect (television series, 1991–2006)
Rebus, Inspector
The Saint on Television
Sharman (television series, 1995–1996)
TV Detectives: Small-Screen Adaptations
Wexford, Inspector
Wimsey, Lord Peter
Wire in the Blood (television series, 2002–)

Introduction

There are few genres in popular fiction that have such a hold on readers' affections as has crime fiction, and however accomplished the American titans of the genre (past and present), the amazing flowering of talent in Great Britain (since the genesis of the genre in the nineteenth century) has no equal. Hardly surprising, given that Charles **Dickens** and Wilkie **Collins** were the progenitors of the genre, producing (*inter alia*) its key elements: dogged detective, complex plotting and surprising revelations. Although it has to be said that Arthur Conan **Doyle** modelled Sherlock **Holmes** on the American Edgar Allan Poe's super-intelligent detective Auguste Dupin, he added in the process rich layers of the eccentric characterisation and accoutrements that have made Holmes one of the best-loved figures in fiction.

Coordinating an encyclopedia such as this is a daunting task, given the range of British crime fiction across the centuries. Remarkably, this range is broad, despite the apparent geographical limitations of the British Isles compared to the vast canvas of the United States. But perhaps the very parochialism of much British crime fiction is precisely what imbues it with its customary sharpness, particularly when murderous secrets confined in British suburban spaces are set free. And then, there is the received perception of the British love of order (although such stereotypes are in flux at present); crime novels are particularly satisfying in that we are invited to relish the chaos unleashed by the crime and criminals before the status quo is re-established – a process that has a particular resonance for the British character (more so than for, say, Americans – the barely contained pandemonium of the large American city is never really tamed). Of course, when (as mentioned earlier) Charles Dickens and Wilkie Collins introduced several of the key tropes of crime fiction (in such classics as *Bleak House* (1853) and *The Moonstone* (1868)), neither author had any thoughts of creating a genre (although it is instructive to remember that their books, while massively popular, lacked the literary gravitas in their day that later scholarship dressed them with; this was the popular fare of the day, dealing in the suspense and delayed revelation that was later to become the *sine qua non* of the genre). In generic fiction, the violin-playing denizen of 221b Baker Street and his celebrated creator are, of course, the single most important factors in terms of generating an army of imitators – notably Agatha **Christie**'s Hercule **Poirot** (although Holmes clones continue to surface to this day, dressed in contemporary garb rather than deerstalker and Inverness cape but still demonstrating impressive ratiocination skills).

Apart from the sheer pleasure of reading a good crime novel, the 'added value' in many of the best examples has long been the implicit (or sometimes explicit) element of social criticism freighted in by the more challenging writers. Among popular literary genres, only science fiction has rivalled the crime novel in 'holding the mirror up to nature' (or society). Best-selling modern writers such as Ruth **Rendell**, Minette **Walters** and Ian **Rankin** have kept alive (and developed) the tradition of social commentary, which was always a key element in the genre, although rarely at the expense of sheer storytelling skill, the area in which the crime field virtually demolishes all its rivals. When (in the early twenty-first century) crime fiction became quantifiably the most popular of popular genres (comprehensively seeing off such rivals as romance fiction), it was only the inevitable coda to a process that had been long underway, all the more to be celebrated for this added value of social responsibility.

The crime novels that appeared in Britain between the First World War and the Second World War enjoyed immense success, but the fact that these books constituted a **Golden Age** in British crime fiction was not immediately apparent – something that may seem surprising today, given the iconic status of Ngaio **Marsh**, Dorothy L. **Sayers** and the doyenne of the field, Agatha Christie. Interestingly, all of these writers are still consumed avidly, but their male counterparts (including Freeman Wills **Crofts**, Francis **Iles** (*aka* Anthony Berkeley), Edgar Wallace and honorary Brit John Dickson **Carr**), while still read, have not maintained a grip on the public imagination to the same degree.

But was it a Golden Age? Unquestionably, yes. While the innovations of the day ultimately became clichés (an inevitable process in any field in which subtly varied repetition is a key strategy), the most striking fact about British crime writing in the 1920s and 1930s is the sheer craftsmanship and invention that inform the work of all the best writers. If today the tropes of these writers appear calcified with overuse, such devices as the cloistered setting (for example, the isolated island in Agatha Christie's *And Then There Were None* (1940), also published and filmed as *Ten Little Indians*) were new to readers of the day. Not only do the Golden Age novels afford massive pleasure when read (in the right spirit) even now, their themes and strategies have been highly durable – a fact highlighted by their continuing use by modern writers such as P.D. **James** (although it is debatable whether such riffs on familiar themes will continue in the hands of a generation of writers not brought up on Christie, Sayers and co.).

Interestingly, one of the principal appeals of Golden Age British crime writing – the opportunities afforded to the reader to enjoy the blandishments of sybaritic country-house living – has been hijacked by adaptations in visual media. Audiences perhaps prefer to see big-budget location shooting in a lovingly preserved country pile than rely on the written word. But despite the appeal of adaptations in other media, there is no denying the continuing interest in this remarkable period of British crime writing. Similarly, the fog-shrouded Victorian **London** of Sherlock Holmes may be more familiar to audiences these days from the legion of television and film adaptations (ranging from the out-of-period but exuberant Basil Rathbone Universal series to the exemplary and faithful adaptations featuring the late Jeremy Brett). Sherlock Holmes was the principal *locus classicus* for the Golden Age writers, and the intuitive sleuth became a key figure (notably, of course, in the hands of Agatha Christie). Elements of social criticism were to be found, but these were less important than the construction of a narrative with the precision of the Swiss watch – although writers such as Josephine **Tey**, in *The Franchise Affair* (1948), incorporated more sophisticated material addressing contemporary mores (with their often crippling moral strictures). And while true evil remained almost a metaphysical concept, often divorced from reality (Holmes's arch nemesis, the 'Napoleon of Crime' Professor Moriarty, is undoubtedly one of the great creations of crime literature and possessed no real-life counterpart), writers such as Margery **Allingham** (in *The Tiger in the Smoke* (1952), with its psychopathic protagonist) introduced dark psychopathology into the genteel world of the British crime thriller and transformed it into something far more disturbing (giving the lie, in fact, to Dulwich-educated Raymond **Chandler**'s dismissal of the classic British mystery in *The Simple Art of Murder* as always etiolated and divorced from reality).

The dividing line between crime and **espionage** fiction is often hard to detect, and more strict delineations between genres are a relatively recent phenomenon. Raymond Chandler and Ian **Fleming** maintained a lively correspondence, comparing notes on both their working methods and the careers of their respective protagonists (the fact that one wrote about a private detective and the other about a counter-espionage agent worried neither man). In the Golden Age, there were few worries about whether the exploits of John **Buchan**'s Richard Hannay, in such books as *The Thirty-Nine Steps* (1915), should be classified as espionage or crime; such divisions did not exist, and (in any case) the attentions of the moral guardians of the day were concentrated on the corrupting effects of these 'shockers' (the fact that Buchan and his civilised adventurer-hero now seem the most traditional and comforting of fictions would no doubt inspire bemusement in the author).

Espionage fiction, with its potentially wider canvas than crime novels, has been able to make more pertinent points about the society that produced it than most crime fiction – inevitable, of course, given that the fate of nations is at stake rather than that of individuals caught up in more parochial criminal activities. Similarly, the political stance of the authors has often been far more germane to the fiction they produced than that of crime writers – and the leftwards, anti-establishment drift from the conservative tradition of John Buchan is notable. At the beginning of the twentieth century, novels such as Erskine **Childers**'s classic *The Riddle of the Sands* (1903) located the source of the threat in Germany, and (inevitably) Germany provided British writers with a useful resource to draw upon for many years. However, it was not long before the growling of the Soviet bear became the soundtrack to espionage fiction, and there is an argument for stating that the dispiriting years of the Cold War produced a fine flourishing of the genre, notably in the magnificent early novels of John **le Carré** and Len **Deighton** (the case for Ian Fleming's durable spy James Bond is a more controversial one these days, but Fleming remains an exceptional writer, his energetic narratives and evocations of luxurious living still holding a great appeal, whatever else has dated in the novels).

There is an argument for suggesting that the first great British spy novel is Joseph **Conrad**'s *The Secret Agent* (1907), although his *Under Western Eyes* (1911) bids a fair claim to the title, and this phantasmagorical picture of a nest of anarchists has moved through a variety of perceptions, from shopworn and overfamiliar to all-too-terrifyingly relevant in the twenty-first century (notably the figure of The Professor, who is a walking bomb – the modern terrorist parallels are not difficult to discern). But while early espionage heroes such as Buchan's Hannay defended the Empire (without too much introspection) against sinister foreign threats, it was to be a later generation of writers that infused equivocation and ambiguity into the narratives, shaking forever the certainties of an earlier generation (it should be noted, however, that Buchan was one of the earliest writers to see how thin the veneer of civilisation was, even in the West – a fact not lost on Buchan admirers of a later generation such as Graham **Greene**).

The Ashenden stories of W. Somerset **Maugham** introduced a whole new level of sophistication into the spy story and removed at a stroke the simple antithesis between good and evil that had powered so much of the genre. And apart from the sense of realpolitik that Maugham inaugurated, he also placed far greater stress on multifaceted characterisation – after him, it was nigh on impossible for writers (even those of a populist stamp) to return to the two-dimensional stereotypes of earlier books. Such writers as William **le Queux** and Sapper (creator of the proto-Bond

Bulldog Drummond) lost their lustre – they are read these days mostly as historical curiosities, and this is leaving aside the anti-Semitism to be found in even the best writing from that era.

The next significant development in espionage fiction came in the work of Eric **Ambler** in the 1930s. Building on the innovations of his great predecessor, Ambler destabilised forever comfortable notions of 'us' and 'them', dispensing with the former certainties. But Ambler's most significant innovation was a radical move across the political spectrum from the right-wing ethos of his predecessors towards a more left-leaning orientation in his heroes. Certainly, the antagonists whom the central characters in Ambler's novels came up against could be pretty nasty specimens, but there were several to be found on 'our' side. And the brave causes of earlier generations were now much more murky affairs, with the moral line to be taken by the protagonists far less easy to discern. Ambler (who enjoyed a second career as a highly successful screenwriter) also introduced a new sense of genuine danger into his narratives that made many of his predecessors' narratives look contrived and thin. His most celebrated successors are, of course, Graham Greene and John le Carré, who adapted and developed the tropes found in Ambler's work and produced a stronger case for the espionage thriller to be taken seriously as literature. But the unglamorous approach that had now become the norm did not preclude black and sardonic humour – a key element in such critically acclaimed novels as those of Len **Deighton** – coming to the fore, with a wisecracking protagonist pointing out the absurdity of the espionage game. The end of the Cold War created problems for writers such as le Carré, but by their moving into new areas (such as the untrammelled influence of big business in the Third World), new avenues were forged for the spy novel. And even as the le Carré generation grew older, fresh talents began to appear, such as the highly skilled Charles **Cumming**, whose assiduously detailed novels of espionage – while indebted to his great predecessors – continue to demonstrate that there is much life in the genre.

British crime fiction can (and often does) divide into two distinct (although not mutually exclusive) genres. The first is the undemanding divertissement, wherein the puzzle (and its ingenious solving) is central: in this area, British writers have few equals, notably Christie and the like. But the other stream, that of the dark investigation of psychological states, is quite as strong in the United Kingdom and has been as far back as Conan Doyle. Since the 1940s, this examination of the nether regions of the human psyche (and its inevitable derogation of our behaviour) has been a British speciality, made all the more acute by the carefully preserved decorum of appearance (however turbulent the mental states beneath), which, until recently, was the *sine qua non* of middle-class British society. Such writers as Patrick **Hamilton** have stripped bare this national consciousness with quite as much unsparing rigour as novelists working in more overtly 'literary' fields. And while the sexual arena was *hors de combat* for an earlier generation of writers, modern crime specialists such as Laura **Wilson** have dragged sexual mores into the daylight. If most crime novels hardly suggest sexuality as an ameliorative, life-affirming force, this has more to do with the demand of drama than healing psychoanalytical imperatives.

Addressing the mainstream of crime fiction today (and leaving aside the legacy of the past), it is clear that the field is in ruder health than it has ever been – such is the range of trenchant and galvanic work now that an argument could be made that we are living in a second Golden Age. Take, for instance, the formidable duo of P.D. James and Ruth Rendell. James took the mechanics of the genre as forged by her great predecessors and enriched all the key elements: plotting, setting and (most of all) characterisation – her tenacious protagonist, Commander Adam **Dalgliesh**, is one of the most rounded and plausible series characters in crime fiction, even persuading the reader of the unlikely premise that a copper could also be a respected poet. Ruth Rendell ploughed similar territory in her reliable Inspector **Wexford** novels, but mined a far more disturbing psychological vein in her non-series, standalone crime novels, set in a world of dark criminality and betrayal – quite the equal of the American Patricia Highsmith. Rendell's novels under the pseudonym Barbara Vine have the same queasy concerns, with an even more cold-eyed take on human foibles. The hitherto unquestioned supremacy of the James–Rendell duo is being challenged by such remarkable novelists as Minette Walters and Frances **Fyfield**, who have folded a new social incisiveness into the contemporary British crime novel.

And there are the male writers: the older generation, such as Frederick **Forsyth** and Dick **Francis**, whose productivity has barely faltered over the years; and the younger writers, who have reinvigorated the genre with resolutely non-parochial crime epics as full of exuberance and invention as they are of violence, such as Mark **Billingham**, Michael **Marshall** and Christopher **Brookmyre**. And, of course, there is the male writer who comfortably outsells all his rivals, the formidable Ian Rankin, whose Edinburgh-set novels featuring his doughty copper Jack **Rebus** have propelled him to the upper echelons both in reader numbers and in critical acclaim (the Rebus series has also been distinguished by Rankin's refusal to simply repeat well-loved ideas, as his ex-alcoholic copper takes on new and cogent problems in society).

The remit of this encyclopedia has been as wide as possible: every possible genre that is subsumed under the heading of crime fiction is here, from the novel of detection to the blockbuster thriller to the novel of espionage. The dark worlds of **Noir** and **True Crime** treated, but the more ingratiating fields of Romance and **Humour** are also referenced. And while criminals are central to the text, the police are given their appropriate due. The reader will discover many familiar names, but hopefully the encyclopedia will act as a guide to much unfamiliar terrain.

The experts who wrote this book were chosen on the basis of their boundless enthusiasm for the genre, and (largely speaking) the authors they cover (all entries have individual credits) have their virtues rather than their demerits maximised in the essays. But while there are no hatchet jobs here, many a dispassionate view is given. Generally speaking, though, contributors have been requested to extol the virtues of writers they admire. Working with the brief that the readers will be seeking to extend their knowledge and pleasure in the genre, the assumption was made that positive recommendations would be preferred to adverse criticism – however, anodyne praise has been discouraged, and those elements that have dated badly in certain writers' works are duly noted. And as the contributors include such top British crime writers as Andrew **Taylor**, Natasha **Cooper**, Russell **James**, Carol Anne **Davis**, Philip **Gooden**, Mark **Timlin**, Lauren **Milne-Henderson**, Martin **Edwards**, Carla **Banks**, Nicholas **Royle**, Laura **Wilson** and Michael **Jecks** (along with a variety of key crime reviewers and editors), nonpareil critical writing is the order of the day. The experts here know virtually everything there is to know about the genre – from writers who produced a single long-out-of-print novel in the 1920s to what trends are likely to develop in a healthy, organically expanding genre.

About this Book

Entries are laid out alphabetically. Biographical entries appear under the subjects' surnames (the surname by which they are best-known), and other sorts of entries (on themes, periods, genres, associations, magazines, films, television adaptations and characters) are listed by key word – e.g. **Literature and Crime Fiction** under 'L', **TV Detectives** under 'T', Espionage Fiction under 'E', etc.

When a subject is known by more than one name, dummy entries cover the alternatives (e.g. 'Vine, Barbara see Rendell, Ruth'). When a book is known by different titles in the UK and US, the British title is used in the entry, and the American title given as a variant in the Selected Works section at the entry's end. Dates of publication are usually the dates of first book publication, though the dates of serialisation or magazine publication are given instead when the context demands it. Acronyms (e.g. CWA, MWA, etc.) are spelled out in entries.

One of the pleasures of a good encyclopedia is following lines of enquiry across entries. Here, cross-references to other entries are given in **bold**; in addition, many entries contain, at the end, '*see also*' suggestions. There are also recommendations for further reading after the Selected Works sections at the ends of entries, and, at the end of the encyclopedia, a Select Bibliography which lists key sources of information about British crime fiction in general. Finally, for readers who want to explore a topic in all its aspects, the index provides a detailed listing.

Whether they are seeking general or specific information, a guide to the best (or even the enjoyably meretricious) in crime fiction to add to their shopping list, or looking for a debriefing after enjoying a particular book, I hope they will be comfortably accommodated here.

A

Academe, Death in

Murder in a university setting and murder mysteries written by academics became a flourishing sub-genre of British crime fiction during the period loosely called 'the **Golden Age** of mystery fiction'. Scholars are detectives of thoughts, and as the American Marjorie Nicolson explained in *Atlantic Monthly Magazine* in 1929, their normal habits and interests were continued in their choice of recreational reading. 'The professorial reader, pursuing with eager interest the exploits of Dr Thorndyke or of Colonel Gore, is not in the last analysis escaping from his repressions; is not even consciously returning from a present to the past; but is merely carrying over to another medium the fun of the chase, the ardour of the pursuit, which makes his life a long and eager and active quest, from which he would not willingly accept release.' Or as Michael **Innes** wrote in his autobiography, 'The detective story called for much concentration during effective perusal. The reader was challenged to reach the truth of the matter in hand through a vigilant attention to minutiae much as a scholar is in certain exacting spheres of criticism.'

The appeal of this genre of fiction was to the intellect; in fact, some of the books this notional professorial reader enjoyed, including those featuring the two detectives Professor Nicolson mentioned, were so coldly cerebral as to be the equivalent of a book-length crossword puzzle and are deservedly forgotten. Universities – or at least Oxford and Cambridge – were frequently used as the setting: for example, *Murder at Cambridge* (1933) by Q. Patrick, *Trouble in College* (1936) by F.J. Whaley and *The Oxford Murders* (1929) by Adam Broome (in the last, an undergraduate who is an African prince kills three Oxford dons, sucks out and swallows their brains in order to become as brilliant

1. John Thaw as Inspector Morse in the ITV television series.

as they). Still remembered for the sake of the author's other books is *Darkness at Pemberley* (1932) by T.H. White, set in an easily recognised Queen's College, Cambridge. It has an ingenious locked-room puzzle, an action plot and a preface apologising for the implication that recognisable dons were drug addicted or murderous.

The academic mystery became an identifiable sub-genre in the 1930s when dons themselves began to write as well as read detective fiction. As the former academic Robert **Barnard** remarked, a university setting provides 'a high concentration of eminently murderable and murderous people. Passions, jealousies, pettiness is raised to issues of principle, sexual intrigue of all imaginable kinds, all these flourishing in the hothouse atmosphere.'

Many of these books were expressions of nostalgia by authors who were in permanent or temporary exile from a remembered paradise. When he wrote *Death at the President's Lodgings* (1936), Michael Innes, who had been an Oxford don (and would be again), was on a long sea voyage to a job in Australia. He included a loving description of the city: 'traffic rumbles past and the city's grey and fretted stone, sweeping in its gentle curve from bridge to bridge, shudders and breathes as at the stroke of a great hammer upon the earth'. Another homesick scholar, the archaeologist Glyn Daniel, was stationed in India during the war. He filled in his idle moments reading detective stories; he told an archaeologist colleague (Stuart Piggott) that 'I could do a better one' and came back from leave with the manuscript of *The Cambridge Murders* (first published under the pseudonym Dilwyn Rees in 1945). In it, he remembered Cambridge by each stone, inserting an imaginary college between real ones. 'In the older and more beautiful of the two ancient universities...Fisher College lies between Trinity and St Johns and stretches from Trinity Street down to the Cam.' The book has been in and out of print but is not forgotten, unlike Adam Broome's 1936 book set at Oxford.

The Mummy Case (1933) could be read simply as a celebration of the civilised life led by dons in ancient colleges; its author, Dermot Morrah, had been a Fellow of All Souls (an honour, rather than a job) but never a full-time academic.

Dorothy L. **Sayers** was born in Oxford and returned in 1912 to study French at Somerville College. She had been happy as an undergraduate and half wished she had stayed on in academia, although her Oxford novel gives an angry, chilling denunciation of the university entirely dominated by men; 'I have never read an angrier feminist novel,' remarked the American academic Robin W. Winks. Yet, Sayers's portrait of Oxford in *Gaudy Night* (1935) is also intensely romantic, with the aristocratic detective Lord Peter **Wimsey** proposing to novelist Harriet Vane near the Bridge of Sighs under the window of the Warden of New College. Sayers's portrait of a life of high thinking and low living in a women's college inspired many schoolgirl readers with the ambition to follow her to Oxford or Cambridge.

The critic T.J. **Binyon**, an Oxford don, noted that 'donnish detective fiction revels in the intricacies of academia – its Common Rooms, conventions and floor plans', while the crime novelist and reviewer Edmund **Crispin** (pseudonym of Robert Bruce Montgomery), an Oxford graduate, thought that Oxford was the most likely town in England to be the progenitor of unlikely events and persons. In *The Moving Toyshop* (1946), the protagonist arrives at midnight and in the moonlight sees an underwater city of ghostly towers and spires like the memorials of lost Atlantis. In 1956, Robert Robinson's *Landscape with Dead Dons* (1956), set in Oxford, was the last fling of the facetious style of donnish detection.

By the 1960s, Oxbridge crime novels were moving from facetiousness or fantasy towards quasi-realism. Between 1967 and 1972, V.C. Clinton-Baddeley wrote five novels featuring as detective his contemporary the 'nostalgic septuagenarian' Dr R.V. Davie of 'St Nicholas' College, Cambridge, where his rooms overlook the backs (swathes of lawn) stretching down to the river behind the colleges on Trinity Street and King's Parade. Davie's detection depends on drawing analogies from his own experiences and memories – an academic, masculine version of Miss **Marple**. Roughly contemporary are half a dozen novels by Jocelyn Davey (pseudonym of Chaim Raphael) whose peripatetic detective hero is a sophisticated Oxford don.

In the last decades of the twentieth century, several authors who are not academics have used a university setting. Margaret **Yorke**, who spent some years as librarian of St Hilda's College, Oxford, began her crime-writing career with several books featuring an Oxford don as detective, the handsome and heroic Patrick Grant. In Veronica **Stallwood**'s Oxford series, the amateur detective is a novelist. In Colin **Dexter**'s series featuring **Inspector Morse**, the streets and colleges of Oxford became as corpse strewn as a Shakespearean final act. Joan **Smith**'s take on the university in *Don't Leave Me This Way* (1990) is feminist and politically aware. P.D. **James**'s Cordelia Gray, not a university graduate, sees Cambridge as an outsider (*An Unsuitable Job for a Woman*, 1972). 'How indeed, she thought, could the heart be indifferent to such a city where stone and stained glass, water and green lawns, trees and flowers were arranged in such ordered beauty for the service of learning.'

Readers have contemporary portraits of Cambridge from Jill Paton **Walsh**, who describes academia through the (slightly distanced) perceptive of a college nurse, and by the Canadian-born Michelle **Spring**, whose private investigator works in Cambridge and had been an academic. Ruth Dudley **Edwards** (graduate of Girton College, Cambridge) features in *Matricide at St Marth's* (1994) the comic Baroness Troutbeck, Mistress of 'St Martha's College', holding the balance between Virgins, Dykes and Old Women, who are, in fact, men. Two graduates of Newnham College, Cambridge, set mysteries in invented universities – Janet **Neel** in Gladstone College, Jessica **Mann** in Buriton, Cornwall – while similarly invented is Catherine **Aird**'s University of Calleshire.

A recently developed sub-section of the academic novel is the historical: with six centuries to play with, they are inevitably set in one of the ancient universities. Examples include Ian **Morson**'s thirteenth-century Oxford, Susanna **Gregory**'s (PhD Cantab) fourteenth-century Cambridge and Iain **Pears**'s seventeenth-century Oxford in *An Instance of the Fingerpost*.

Redbrick and plate glass (nineteenth century and modern) universities did appear in crime fiction, although rather less often than in sociological satires such as books by David Lodge and Malcolm Bradbury. However, they pop up in one-off crime novels, by authors such as the former academic Robert Barnard.

But the curious paradox is that the campus crime novel faded away as campuses proliferated. Academia has become too diverse, the spread of universities too wide, and the distinction between institutes of secondary and tertiary education too imprecise. A novel set in one of them may be using a familiar setting but hardly counts as academic crime fiction.

It may be that the heyday of the campus novel was over when detectives ceased to be, as they had been during the Golden Age, infallible. Perversely, the spirit of open-minded inquiry, which ought to be equally conducive to scholarship and to amateur detection, deprives the great detective of the authority that made him (or very occasionally her) so attractive in fiction. The role of **Poirot** or Wimsey was to restore a reassuring order. The crime novel in its more recent form has not dealt with order or with closure but with disorder and uncertainty.

The category's heyday was during the twentieth century. *The Poison Tree* by Tony Strong (1997) could perhaps be regarded as marking the culmination of academic murder in fiction, or perhaps, as its epitaph. In this book, a woman scholar returns to Oxford to resume an abandoned doctorate in detective fiction. The story is punctuated with extracts from her lectures and these extracts add up to a lucid, original analysis of this literary form, and its valediction.

Selected Works
Clinton-Baddeley, V.C. 1967. *Death's Bright Dart*. Macmillan.
Davey, Jocelyn. 1956. *The Undoubted Deed*. Chatto & Windus.
Innes, Michael. 1951. *Operation Pax*. Gollancz.
Stallwood, Veronica. 1998. *Oxford Blue*. Headline.
Strong, Tony. 1997. *The Poison Tree*. Doubleday.

Further Reading
Binyon, T.J. 1989. *Murder Will Out*. Oxford University Press.
Nicholson, Marjorie. 1929. 'The Professor and the Detective'. *Atlantic Monthly*.
Stewart, J.I.M. 1987. *Myself and Michael Innes*. Gollancz.
Winks, Robin W. 1982. *Modus Operandi*. David R. Godine.

Jessica Mann

Ackroyd, Peter (b.1949)

Peter Ackroyd is a multi-talented biographer, historian, critic and literary author as well as a flamboyantly outrageous individualist. His first and foremost love is **London**, of which he is proud to call himself – with typical quirkiness – the 'biographer', although his more conventional biographical topics include Charles **Dickens**, William Shakespeare, William Blake and T.S. Eliot.

His presence in this encyclopaedia is owed to only a few books amongst his prodigious output, especially one of his earliest novels, the magnificent *Hawksmoor* (1985), an intricate, seductive and surreal murder mystery set in the seamy streets of the East End he so obviously adores. The book won the Guardian Fiction Prize, Whitbread Novel Award and Prix Goncourt award, immediately establishing Ackroyd's reputation on the London literary scene. The story switches between the same parts of London in the early eighteenth century and the late twentieth century. In the former, Nicholas Dyer, an architect, is working on completing the churches built in London in the wake of the Great Fire; in the latter, Nicholas Hawksmoor (which was, of course, the true name of the architect) is a detective investigating a bizarre series of murders.

The influence of T.S. Eliot's conflation of the past and present on Ackroyd's work can be seen in the way he melds the two worlds – the powers of darkness with which Dyer secretly imbues his holy architecture and the insanity which threatens the modern detective – as he is drawn into the secrets. Those in search of a classic detective story will be deeply disappointed: what Ackroyd offers instead is a bewitching philosophical novel which just happens to have criminal deeds at its heart.

The House of Doctor Dee (1993) also takes us backwards and forwards in time, between Matthew Palmer, a young man who has just inherited a house in London's ancient Clerkenwell district, and Dr John Dee, a seventeenth-century alchemist. It is full of dark musings and sinister history, which lend what is essentially once again a literary and philosophical novel more than a touch of suspense.

Among Ackroyd's other works, the novel that comes closest to the genres of crime and suspense is *Dan Leno and the Limehouse Golem* (1994). The story opens with Cree's hanging and – just a few pages later – the prison governor dressing up in the smock in which she died, a typical Ackroyd touch of the sexually bizarre. But this is a pastiche horror story as much as a crime **thriller** and a rich evocative depiction of a Victorian music hall; it also includes cameo roles for Karl Marx as well as Charles Babbage, inventor of an analytical machine that was a distant forerunner to the computer.

The Clerkenwell Tales (2003) is a tempestuous romp through medieval London threatened with suicide bomb attacks and religious extremism – in other words, an invitation to rethink our attitudes to today by seeing through the eyes of a different era. It features an apocalyptic sect determined on revolution when the throne itself is under threat from a rebel army. Ackroyd's depiction of the era is rich in mire and mud, fetid and flatulent. It is also, of course, a homage to Chaucer.

The Lambs of London (2004) is a period piece about the Georgian essayist and chronicler Charles Lamb, whom Ackroyd involves with a Shakespearean forgery racket. It is a wonderful, dark, rumbustious literary romp, but hardly in the crime-fiction bracket.

Yet, Ackroyd deserves to be present in any anthology of great British crime writing on the strength of *Hawksmoor* alone. The haunting, powerful and suspense-filled novel may not fit in with the mainstream of the genre, but in its way, it has helped redefine it. *See also* Literature and Crime Fiction.

Selected Works by the Author
Hawksmoor (1985)
Dan Leno and the Limehouse Golem (1994; published in the United States as *The Trial of Elizabeth Cree*)

Peter Millar

Adam, Paul (b.1958)

Appreciated by a growing readership as well as critics, Paul Adam is the master of the seemingly parochial story which then grows into a significant and ambitious **thriller**.

Born in Coventry and brought up in Sheffield, Adam studied law in Nottingham; however, he chose not to practise. Instead, he took up journalism, a job that has guided and informed much of his novel writing, especially when he worked in Italy as a correspondent; however, it is his training in the law which is displayed in his meticulous plotting and careful use of language.

His first three books were not commercially successful, but his fourth, *Unholy Trinity* (1999), for which he moved to a new publisher, established his reputation and career. For the book, Adam took as his starting point the end of the Second World War in Europe and the flight of Mussolini. In Mussolini's convoy of trucks was a vehicle filled with crates of gold. In the present day, Chapman, the Rome correspondent for a London daily newspaper, is intrigued by the curious murder of a left-wing priest, whose papers have been removed from his office by the Vatican a little while before the police arrived. From this subtle beginning, Adam weaves an intricate plot that is genuinely gripping, although lightly written. *Literary Review* described *Unholy Trinity* as a 'tingling political **thriller**...the great Eric **Ambler** would have enjoyed reading this'.

Adam's popularity grew with books such as *Enemy Within* (2005), where he makes good use of his understanding of the laws which constrain us all. Tom Whitehead, a historian at a provincial university, is happily married and has two young children. When he is charged with downloading child pornography to his computer, the shock is palpable. A reviewer in *The Guardian* said of it: 'the "what-if-this-happened-to-me?" factor at times raised the hair on my arms'.

In other books, Adam has returned to Italy. *Sleeper* (2004) is a meticulously researched novel about violins. When Rainaldi, a violin maker, is murdered, his friends suspect that he has discovered the sister violin to the world's most expensive violin, the Messiah, housed at the Ashmolean Museum in Oxford. Although the novel is set in the gentle world of music, Adam has crafted a tale of murder and suspicion with an atmosphere of tension that keeps the reader turning the pages.

Adam is adept at evoking scenes with a brevity other authors envy. His characters are believable and likeable, his plots strong. However, his personal stamp on his work is the plausibility of the tales. As with *Enemy Within*, he frequently picks subject material that challenges the reader to reconsider deeply held prejudices.

Selected Works by the Author
Unholy Trinity (1999)
Sleeper (2004; published in the United States as *The Rainaldi Quartet*, 2006)
Enemy Within (2005)

Michael Jecks

Adams, Jane (b.1960)

Jane Adams's books are characterised by a strong psychological crime element, often blended with an underlying sense of the supernatural.

Jane Ann Adams was born on 4 July 1960 in Leicester, where she was educated at Alderman Newton's School for Girls and Gateway Sixth Form College. She went on to study sociology at the University of Leicester, and in her spare time, she sang for folk rock band The Tellurian Tribe. On leaving university, Adams tried her hand at various jobs, including as darkroom technician and printing-plate maker. When her youngest son started school in 1992, she began writing science fiction and horror stories while formulating what she should do next. In 1995, she came out with her first novel, *The Greenway*.

Based in a real area of East Anglia, *The Greenway* was the first of four books to feature detective Mike Croft. In his first case, he investigates the disappearance of a child in a mysterious area of woodland where, twenty years earlier, another child went missing. The only link between the two cases is Cassie Maltham, whose memory of the first disappearance is still buried deep in her subconscious. The novel combined a spare prose style with a vivid depiction of place and strong characterisation. The novel, which Minette **Walters** described as 'a haunting debut', was nominated for a John **Creasey** award.

In the last Croft book, *Final Frame* (1999), Adams introduced her next series detective, facially disfigured ex-copper Ray Flowers. The three Flowers novels, starting with *The Angel Gateway* (2000), addressed such themes as witchcraft and religious cults, all delivered in the same atmospheric style as her previous series. Like *The Greenway*, *The Angel Gateway* centres around a real place, this time an alleyway near Leicester's marketplace whose name had intrigued the author since childhood.

Adams's third series, written under the name Jane A. Adam, contained what were arguably her most mainstream crime stories, yet (conversely) they featured her most unconventional protagonist: blinded ex-policewoman Naomi Blake. The first, *Mourning the Little Dead* (2002), reworked the themes of *The Greenway* with its central disappearance of a young girl years earlier, but this time the author freighted in a very personal edge to her narrative. In *Heatwave* (2005), Blake is held hostage by a gang of armed bank robbers at the height of summer, and the novel is especially memorable for its realistic rendering of her frustration and stress. The third series is Adams's longest series, and the fifth book, *Legacy of Lies*, was published in 2007.

With *A Reason to Kill* (2007), Adams began a new series featuring former actress Rina Martin, whose retirement proves to be anything but quiet.

The best of her stand-alone novels, *Bird* (1997), was a ghost story based on tales narrated by her grandfather shortly before he died.

Selected Works by the Author

Mike Croft Series
The Greenway (1995)
Cast the First Stone (1996)
Bird (1997)
Fade to Grey (1998)
Final Frame (1999)

Ray Flowers Series
The Angel Gateway (2000)
Like Angels Falling (2001)
Angel Eyes (2002)

Naomi Blake Series
Mourning the Little Dead (2002)
Touching the Dark (2003)
Heatwave (2005)
Killing a Stranger (2006)
Legacy of Lies (2007)

Rina Martin Series
A Reason to Kill (2007)
Fragile Lives (2008)

Non-Series
Dangerous to Know (2004)
A Kiss Goodbye (2005)

Mark Campbell

Adrian, Jack (b.1945)

Adrian is the best-known alias of the British writer, editor and compiler of **anthologies** Christopher Lowder. He has written **thrillers** as Jack Hamilton Teed and other works of fiction under various pseudonyms.

Adrian is almost certainly the world's living expert on old British **magazines**, publishers and writers of mystery, adventure and supernatural fiction. This area of interest has influenced his work both as a writer and as an editor, as his books reflect an interest in the **Golden Age** of storytelling. Sexton **Blake** is one of the areas of his expertise: his first published book was a Sexton Blake adventure, *The Abductors* (1968), written under the alias Desmond Reid. He has also compiled *Sexton Blake Wins* (1986), with a detailed introduction on the history of the Blake stories.

Adrian has written extensively for boys' adventure magazines, comics and books, drawing as much upon his own experiences at boarding school as upon his vast reading of famous boys' books of yesteryear. He began his career as a subeditor at magazines division of IPC Media, penning many scripts and stories for comics and annuals, including episodes of 'Zip Nolan', 'Judge Dredd' and the Sexton Blake alter ego 'Victor Drago'. One of Adrian's scripts for *Action* comic in 1976, 'Kids Rule OK', in which a plague wipes out all adults leaving children to run amok, generated sufficient complaints to have the issue pulped and the magazine relaunched.

Adrian's profound knowledge of popular fiction, acquired from over forty years of research, has led to a number of specialist story collections and anthologies, all noted for their detailed and informative introductions. His interest in crime fiction focuses primarily on the popular writers of the years before 1940, and he owns what is probably the most complete collection of Edgar **Wallace** first editions. He has compiled three volumes of Wallace's uncollected or long out-of-print stories: *The Sooper and Others* (1984), *The Road to London* (1986) and *The Death Room* (1986). He has also compiled *The Best Short Stories of Sapper* (1984) and *The Best of Berry* (1989) by Dornford Yates.

Adrian's fascination for locked-room mysteries and impossible crimes led him to collaborate with Robert Adey on *The Art of the Impossible* (1990), whilst his interest in American pulpsters resulted in *Hard boiled* (1994), with Bill Pronzini. Readers who seek rare and unusual stories will find them in *Detective Stories from the Strand* (1991) and its companion *Strange Tales from the Strand* (1991), *Twelve Tales of Murder* (1998) and *12 Mystery Stories* (1998).

Adrian has also compiled many anthologies of supernatural stories – amongst them a series on **psychic detectives** for Ash-Tree Press, which began with *Aylmer Vance: Ghost-Seer* (1998) by Alice and Claude Askew and includes volumes by Mrs de Crespigny, Dion Fortune, Harold Begbie, Kate and Hesketh Prichard, Margery Lawrence and Ella Scrymsour. Since 1998, Adrian has also edited the Annual Macabre series for Ash-Tree Press, which also includes some weird-mystery stories. *See also The Strand Magazine.*

Selected Works by the Author
Sexton Blake Wins (1986)
The Art of the Impossible (1990; published in the United States as *Murder Impossible*)
Detective Stories from the Strand (1991)
Twelve Tales of Murder (1998)

Mike Ashley

Aiken, Joan (1924–2004)

Although she will probably be best remembered for her children's fiction (such as the outstanding *The Wolves of Willoughby Chase* (1962), which was made into a film in 1988), Aiken was the author of numerous other novels, including several crime **thrillers**.

With her mother an author, her father, Conrad Aiken, an American poet and novelist, and most importantly, her stepfather, Martin Armstrong, an English novelist and fantasist, the whole Aiken family had writing in their blood. At an early age, she invented stories for her younger brother and in her teens began writing short stories. Her children's novels are notable for their literary quality, and her adult novels are equally well written. Her first was a **gothic** romance, one of several in that style. It is not easy to categorise all her other crime novels – some are novels of suspense, others **thrillers**. Most plots are ingenious, incorporating highly imaginative situations. Against convincing, well-described backgrounds, Aiken skilfully creates atmosphere, especially of tension and terror, often with an element of **humour**.

The protagonists of the majority of her books are young women, usually bereft of close relatives, who find themselves in difficult or dangerous situations. Family ties are not always beneficial, as greed and jealousy can threaten danger. Most of her heroines are resourceful in overcoming perils, including pursuits through fog, snow and the ice and raging torrents. In her early books, there is usually a happy ending for these heroines, who, after villains have been vanquished, find love with suitable young men who have come to their rescue. Typical of this plot line is *The Trouble with Product X* (1966). Set mostly in Cornwall, this has a background in the world of advertising. The plot includes a ruthless villain, prepared to kill. A kidnapped baby is saved by the brave heroine, who is pursued more than once, including through thick fog. After escaping the earlier perils, she is almost drowned by the villain, who gets his comeuppance in drowning himself. It all ends, though, with a sharp, humorous twist.

Other plots are bleaker, some with characters manipulated by drugs and psychological pressures, sometimes by close relatives. *The Butterfly Picnic* (1972) not only is more humorous than the other novels but also includes the author's most chilling fantasy. The best description in all of her books appears in this novel – when a valley full of butterflies comes to life.

Aiken was one of the first authors to introduce a murder in a children's novel. Murders, or attempted murders, abound in her adult plots as well. Aiken is fond of arson, using it as a murder method more than once. Deaths by drowning, whether suicide, murder or accident, appear often. *The Ribs of Death* (1967) has possibly the largest body count, with drowning, shooting, falls from a great height and even mauling by an escaped leopard among the causes. Her adult crime novels, like those for children, undoubtedly reflect Aiken's ingenuity and skill as a storyteller.

Selected Works by the Author

The Trouble with Product X (1966; published in the United States as *Beware of the Bouquet*)
Hate Begins at Home (1967; published in the United States and later in the UK as *Dark Interval*)
The Ribs of Death (1967; published in the United States as *The Crystal Crow*) *The Embroidered Sunset* (1970)
The Butterfly Picnic (1972; published in the United States as *A Cluster of Separate Sparks*)
Last Movement (1977)

Christine Simpson

Aird, Catherine (b.1930)

Catherine Aird is the author of the Inspector Sloane police detective series noted for its quirky humour and unusual plots. Aird is the pseudonym of Kinn Hamilton McIntosh. Despite her Scottish ancestry, she was born in Yorkshire and has lived for over sixty years in Kent. Her books, most of which are set in the fictional county Calleshire, are quintessentially English, full of the usual eccentricities of English country life that make the traditional whodunit such a delight. The books are a blend of light-heartedness and ingenious puzzles – what *The Times* called 'delicious concoctions'.

All but one of her books feature the long-suffering Inspector Christopher Dennis Sloan, head of the C.I.D. in Calleshire, and known as 'Seedy' because of his initials. He was the head of the Criminal Investigation Department in Calleshire and also known as 'Seedy' because of his initials. He is assisted by the inept but willing Detective Constable Crosby, who has a passion for driving fast and seems far too impulsive to be a detective. Sloan's boss is similarly irritating, living in a world of bureaucratic fantasy, and he and Crosby make Sloan's working life exasperating. Yet Sloan has the pleasure of encountering and solving some of the strangest crimes in British crime fiction. These include a corpse in a suit of armour in *The Complete Steel* (1969), the discovery of a Second World War murder in *A Late Phoenix* (1971), a body found under a stone statue in an inaccessible room in a church in *His Burial Too* (1973), the theft of an Egyptian mummy which has been replaced by a fresh corpse in *Little Knell* (2000) and a murder in a near impenetrable maze in *Amendment of Life* (2003). To solve all these crimes, Sloan uses his sharp mind and remarkable patience, despite being surrounded by colleagues determined to drive him crazy. In television terms, the series falls somewhere between the eccentricities of *Midsomer Murders* and the **humour** and pathos of Frost.

Though also set in Calleshire, Aird's second novel, *A Most Contagious Game* (1967), falls outside the Sloan series. It is a fascinating puzzle concerning the discovery of a centuries-old body walled up in an old house and the determination by the occupant to discover what happened. His investigations help solve a present-day murder in the village.

Nine of Aird's Sloan novels have been reissued in three omnibus volumes, and there are also two volumes of short stories, *Injury Time* (1997) and *Chapter and Hearse* (2003). *See also* Golden Age Crime Fiction and The Police in Golden Age Crime Fiction.

Selected Works by the Author
The Religious Body (1966)
A Most Contagious Game (1967)
Henrietta Who? (1968)
The Complete Steel (1969; published in the United States as *The Stately Home Murder*, 1970)
A Late Phoenix (1970)
His Burial Too (1973)
Harm's Way (1984)
Injury Time (stories, 1997)
Little Knell (2000)
Chapter and Hearse (stories, 2003)

Further Reading
Friedenthal, Martin H. 1987. 'The Calleshire Chronicles'. *The Armchair Detective* 20.2: 138–145.
Website
www.catherineaird.com

Mike Ashley

Allbeury, Ted (1917–2005)

Ted Allbeury put the ethics of spying at the centre of the genre. He was one of the most productive spy writers of the modern age, at one point producing four books in one year. As the author of forty-one novels and thirteen radio plays, he may be claimed to be one of the most influential of **espionage** writers and consistently delivered a strong, solid story, with pithy insights into the morality of spying freighted into the narrative.

During the Second World War, Allbeury served as an intelligence officer, rising to the rank of lieutenant colonel. His tour of duty included acting as bodyguard to Emperor Haile Selassie and vetting Nazi criminals after the war, and he was one of the first British agents to run undercover networks against the communists. Without any doubt, these experiences contributed to the palpable authenticity of the novels in terms of plot, tradecraft and sense of place. However, many of his best books (notably in *The Lantern Network* (1978)*, The Lonely Margins* (1981), and *Other Side of Treason* (1981)) are about conscience, love and betrayal and the grim transformations war brings about on the survivors. Allbeury presciently portrayed in fictional terms many political trends – principally the increasing use of covert and technological strategies in power politics, which (in his view) occasionally undermined liberal values and liberal democracy.

The early books interpolated political analysis, notably notions concerning the 'red menace' on the point of undermining the British state. However, with the ninth novel, *Consequences of Fear* (1979), he was the first writer to fictionalise the horrific nuclear-waste disaster that occurred during 1957 in the Soviet Union. Allbeury dramatised the fashion in which the Soviet system was endemically careless about the value of human life while exposing the mendacity of the British atomic scientists who insisted that the events never took place. The next novel, *The Alpha List* (1979), centred on the misguided plans for sanctuary during a nuclear attack on Britain; in which the state would protect only the rich and influential. Thereafter, although espousing patriotism, Allbeury became the most articulate critic of the negative and devious practices of the secret state in Britain and the United States.

He effected this critique by cleverly fictionalising real-life political intrigues of the master-spies Philby and Blake in complex contemporary plots, with the portrait of the much-reviled Blake actually quite sympathetic. Subsequently, Allbeury addressed (in three novels) the way in which paranormal techniques of mind control were increasingly being used; and teased out how and why these practices had undermined liberal and democratic values. One such book, *Pay Any Price* (1983), suggested the manner in which the CIA schemed with the mafia to assassinate Kennedy. It is still – in basic terms – the soundest explanation.

Ted Allbeury is celebrated for his astringent character studies of agents compromised by their disdainful handlers. Nearly all his protagonists pay the ultimate sacrifice – demonstrating the author's belief that with issues of the highest importance, conscience comes before pride, duplicity and self-advancement. A writer of substance and conviction, his works repay re-reading and give solace in an unsettling world. *See also* Social Comment in Crime Fiction.

Selected Works by the Author
The Lantern Network (1979)
Consequence of Fear (1979; published in the United States as *Smokescreen*)
The Alpha List (1979)
The Other Side of Silence (1981)
The Lonely Margins (1981) as Patrick Kelly
All Our Tomorrows (1982)
Shadow of Shadows (1982)
Pay Any Price (1983)
Other Kinds of Treason (short stories) (1990)
Show Me a Hero (1992)

Further Reading
Johnson, Michael. *Ted Allbeury: Spy Writer of Conviction* (forthcoming).

Michael Johnson

Allingham, Margery (1904–1966)

Margery Allingham was one of the four 'Queens' who dominated British crime writing in the decades before and after the Second World War – the others being **Christie**, **Sayers** and **Marsh**. Although Margery Allingham wrote historical novels, memoirs, short stories and four excellent novellas, she is best known for her series featuring the gentlemanly sleuth Albert **Campion**. Her novels featuring Campion remain extraordinary and varied. Her novels are characterised by her willingness to experiment, sense of humour, social observation and almost Dickensian appreciation of the quirks of humanity.

2. Margery Allingham at her desk.

Allingham was born on 20 May 1904, the daughter of the writer Herbert Allingham, and educated at the Perse High School for Girls, Cambridge, and the Regent Street Polytechnic in London. In 1921, she began her first published novel, *Blackerchief Dick* (1923), a story of smugglers whose plot emerged to Allingham during a series of thirteen seances. In 1927, she married the artist and editor Philip (Pip) Youngman Carter. They lived in London and Essex, finally settling at D'Arcy House in Tolleshunt D'Arcy. Despite her deteriorating health, she continued writing until her death on 30 June 1966.

Albert Campion arrived with *The Crime at Black Dudley* (1929), a romantic thriller with English country gentry and snarling Teutonic villains. 'Campion' is a pseudonym, adopted to avoid upsetting his aristocratic family. At the start of his career, he was not even a detective but a morally ambiguous adventurer with the mannerisms of a particularly fatuous, bright young thing. As the series progresses, he steadily becomes a quieter and more formidable figure. In the post-war novels, his evolution reaches the point where he is almost a bystander in his own series.

The next book, *Mystery Mile* (1930), introduced two series characters: Stanislaus Oates of Scotland Yard and, more importantly, the lugubrious and joyously plebeian ex-convict Magersfontein Lugg, Campion's manservant and keeper of his conscience. *Police at the Funeral* (1931), set in Cambridge, is an original attempt to reach more intellectual crime readers – those who, such as the poet W.H. Auden, enjoyed pure detective puzzles. *Sweet Danger* (1933), a story of ancient evil, missing heirs and modern villains, has Campion impersonating royalty and introduced another recurring character, his future wife Lady Amanda. As Allingham herself matured, her novels show an increasing willingness to examine social issues. *The Fashion in Shrouds* (1938) is a witty, sometimes savage, dissection of the fashion business and the plight of the working woman.

After a hiatus, due in part to the Second World War, came *Traitor's Purse* (1941). It is a dark **thriller** which turns on a plot to destabilise the country by a method that seemed far-fetched at the time, although Himmler's Schutzstaffel, as it later transpired, had had the same idea. There was another delay before the next Campion novel appeared – *Coroner's Pidgin* (1945), which betrays a sense of weariness, reflecting the mood of the times.

After the war came the four novels that are arguably Allingham's finest: *More Work for the Undertaker* (1949), *The Tiger in the Smoke* (1952), *The Beckoning Lady* (1955) and *Hide My Eyes* (1958). Three of them are set mainly in London, in a version of Bayswater, an area of seedy urban villages full of peeling bomb-damaged buildings and mementoes of former grandeur. *More Work for the Undertaker* (1949) is mercilessly satirical, with intellectual pretentiousness as its main target. It introduces one of Allingham's most engaging series characters – Charlie Luke, a cockney **detective** inspector who bubbles and crackles with vitality. Luke appears in the next Campion story (although Campion himself is almost an incidental figure), *The Tiger in the Smoke* (1952), which many would say is Allingham's masterpiece. Few crime stories are so intimately concerned with the nature of good and evil.

By the 1950s, Allingham's health was deteriorating. Her marriage was going through a difficult period, and she was facing constant demands from the Inland Revenue. Small wonder that in her next novel, *The Beckoning Lady* (1955), she decided to kill off a tax adviser. *Hide My Eyes* (1958), written in the aftermath of a nervous breakdown and four nightmarish doses of electroconvulsive therapy, is an altogether darker book which concerns the unstinting and disinterested love of a parent for a child – even when that child goes hopelessly to the bad and the parental love becomes an unwitting assistant to evil.

The last two complete novels, *The China Governess* (1963) and *The Mind Readers* (1965), are uneven in quality, but yet again they break new ground, dealing (among other things) with the limitations of philanthropy and the potential of telepathy.

Allingham died in 1966. Pip completed *Cargo of Eagles* (1968), her last book, and went on to write two more Campion novels, which were entirely his work. The remaining Campion novels lack the creative intelligence that informs the others.

Margery Allingham wrote crime fiction for nearly forty years, steadily expanding the genre's possibilities. She had no taste for formula writing, however commercially successful. She parted company with her long-term British publisher because an editor asked her to produce mechanical detective puzzles rather than the strange and fascinating crime novels she wanted to write. She thought of the detective story as a box – a convenient receptacle in which she could place anything she pleased. Two constant elements were her humanity and sense of humour, an almost surreal sense of the absurd that spared no one – even herself.

Allingham's books have already stood the test of time. Although she was happy to exploit the trappings of crime fiction and although she never forgot the importance of entertaining her readers, the best of her work pushes the genre into territory generally associated with mainstream literature. *See also* Golden Age Crime Fiction; Humour and Crime Fiction *and* Literature and Crime Fiction.

Selected Works by the Author

Key Campion Novels
The Crime at Black Dudley (1929; published in the United States as *The Black Dudley Murder*)
Mystery Mile (1930)
Police at the Funeral (1931)
Sweet Danger (1933; published in the United States as *Kingdom of Death* and as *The Fear Sign*)
Death of a Ghost (1934)
Dancers in Mourning (1937)
The Fashion in Shrouds (1938)
Traitor's Purse (1941; published in the United States as *The Sabotage Murder Mystery*)
Coroner's Pidgin (1945; published in the United States as *Pearls before Swine*)
More Work for the Undertaker (1949)
The Tiger in the Smoke (1952)
The Beckoning Lady (1955; published in the United States as *The Estate of the Beckoning Lady*)
Hide My Eyes (1958; published in the United States as *Tether's End* and as *Ten Were Missing*)
The Mind Readers (1965)

Further Reading
Martin, Richard. 1988. *Ink in Her Blood: The Life and Crime Fiction of Margery Allingham*. UMI Research Press.
Thorogood, Julia. 1991. *Margery Allingham*. Heinemann.

Website
The Margery Allingham Society, http://www.margeryallingham.org.uk

Andrew Taylor

Ambler, Eric (1909–1998)

An early master of intelligent **espionage** and other mysteries, Ambler was unquestionably one of Britain's top fiction writers, from his debut in the 1930s to the 1970s when his stardom began to wane. Although Ambler never wrote a series, some of his characters occasionally recurred. His grasp of fact and politics was extraordinary, and several of his books were made into films. Eric Ambler won four gold or silver **Crime Writers' Association** (CWA) Dagger Awards – *Passage of Arms* (1959), *The Light of Day* (1962), *Dirty Story* (1967) and *The Levanter* (1972). Each of these – and some of his other books – became book club choices. In 1986, he was awarded the CWA Cartier Diamond Dagger for lifetime achievement. He won an Edgar Award in 1964 from the Mystery Writers of America (MWA) for *The Light of Day* as that year's best novel, and was named Grand Master by the MWA in 1975. From 1944 to 1970, he worked off and on in the **film** business – with Alexander Korda in the United Kingdom and later with other big names in Hollywood. His script for the film *The Cruel Sea* was nominated for an Academy Award. Other notable scripts he either wrote or worked on (in Hollywood it comes to much the same) are *The Magic Box* (1951), *The Card* (1952), *The Purple Plain* (1955), *Yangtse Incident* (1957), *A Night to Remember* (1958), *The Wreck of the Mary Deare* (1960) and *Mutiny on the Bounty* (1962).

Ambler was born in London in 1909, and he died there in 1998. He served in the Second World War, joining the Royal Artillery as a private, earning an American Bronze Star in 1946. In 1981, he was awarded an Order of British Empire. Although his 1985 autobiography was disappointing, he might have been describing his own subject matter in *The Mask of Dimitrios* (1939): the reality of murder, not the kind of neat and tidy 'book murder' which has a corpse and clues and suspects and a hangman, but a murder over which the chief of police has shrugged his shoulders, washed his hands of it and consigned the stinking victim to a coffin. This was not how crime books were meant to be.

At first sight, it seems extraordinary that Ambler became so successful, and so quickly. A critic might say, with some justification, that most of Ambler's books have no engaging leading character and that they rely on too much research dressed up as fiction. Some of his books contain few thrills, too little sex, and too many fascinating but irrelevant diversions. When the unknown Ambler first submitted a manuscript, his prospective publishers could not have been blamed if they had said that they had never seen anything like his books before. But Ambler was original. He was laying out the ground for writers such as **le Carré** and **Deighton** who would come later.

Ambler's competitors in the 1930s were British **Golden Age** puzzle writers and American hard-boiled hacks. Was there a market for this new man's meticulously presented, shockingly informative stories which seemed out of step with current trends? He did not write **police procedurals** or private investigator (PI) tales or arcane, body-in-the-library puzzle stories. Instead, he blandly introduced unusual, yet instantly believable, criminals. They may have been gunrunners, financial fraudsters, small-time con men or jewellery thieves – and soon, given the period in which Ambler wrote, they would learn their craft in the murky shadows of the Second World War – but they would always remain different to and more roundly drawn than other writers' villains. They were also, unusually and sometimes disconcertingly, different and distinct from the characters Ambler himself had used in other tales.

An early success for him was *The Mask of Dimitrios* (1939). The story concerns Charles Latimer, a crime writer who while in Turkey decides, purely for research, to delve more deeply into the past of the vanished Dimitrios, a murderous and powerful real-life criminal in whom the police have ceased to take an interest. Why should they take an interest? Has not his body been found washed up in the Bosphorus? Latimer is fascinated by the villain and decides, understandably, that if he carries out an investigation into the criminal's life and death, it may furnish him with material for future crime books. The investigation will lead Latimer from Turkey through the Balkans into Paris. He is warned off, and he ignores the warnings. Soon he finds that real life is nastier than fiction. In this book, Ambler mocks Charles Latimer as he sets out on his dilettante author research, but he plays with the reader also: nothing turns out to have been as the reader might expect.

A far more capable criminal – Ambler calls him the 'able criminal' – takes the central role in *Send No More Roses* (1977). Here we meet an ascetic extortioner who has a dry accountant's brain, a non-violent but chillingly clinical man to whom human lives are no more than assets or liabilities to be moved from one ledger column to another. Yet by contrast, in *The Light of Day* (1962), Ambler's bumbling hero is a wishful-thinking small-time chancer, Arthur Abdul Simpson, a lifetime victim whose only hope against more capable adversaries lies in his being more at home than they will be in the muddy crevices of failure at the bottom of the swamp. While the 'able criminal' sits above the action and has 'the imagination and business planning skills needed to evolve a new way of investing time and money in order to make a profit', Simpson finds himself forced to become the likely scapegoat in a major gem robbery. The 'able criminal' prepares a foolproof plan to buy up and take over a run-down Pacific island which he can convert into an international tax haven – 'the most remarkable, the most prosperous sovereign state in the entire South Pacific' – while Simpson has, before the book begins, spent several years on a forlorn quest to upgrade his questionable foreign papers to a legitimate British passport. Simpson is no tough-guy hero. He is a frightened man, he tells us himself, and his fear shows: 'The outside of the body can be washed of sweat and grease; but inside there are other substances. Some of these smell. How do you wash away the smells of the inside of the body?' Simpson is a masterly piece of character delineation, gloriously realised on film when Peter Ustinov played him in *Topkapi*.

Simpson, unusually for an Ambler hero, returns in *Dirty Story*. After his Turkish adventure he hides in Greece, still in need of a decent passport and still vulnerable to 'persuasion'. Hoping to make a modest living retailing pornographic books (they are not even good pornographic books), he is cornered and pressurised into taking part in a lethal mercenary engagement in central Africa. Ambler's inside knowledge of the mercenary's trade would make Frederick **Forsyth** blink. Yet the mud and bullet reality of mercenary life in Africa is only part of the plot. The mercenaries themselves are employed only to make the business plan work more smoothly, and the business plan concerns rare minerals. 'Mining used to be so simple,' explains Simpson's new employer, Kinck. 'It is as simple almost as cracking a nutshell to get at the nut.' But things are no longer quite so simple: 'The people I work for still prefer nutcracker methods,' Kinck tells Arthur. He goes on to explain that he needs 'men of experience and resource. Of course, such men are not easy to find, but…where there are great rewards to be had there are always difficulties to overcome. That is the nature of things.'

Kinck is a classic Ambler villain: chillingly polite and, on his own terms, reasonable; a modern businessman. He efficiently briefs the men he is about to send to Africa on the murderous mission, but with equal gravity he sets out their terms and conditions of employment: their advance of salary, which will be paid in local currency. 'You are unlikely to need much ready cash there…. You will not wish to accumulate large sums in the field by receiving your salaries in cash. There are, therefore, two alternative methods of payment from which you may choose.' He gives precise details: the money will be held for them in Europe, and they can choose between direct drafts or pay cheques. 'Some officers may wish to transmit allowances to their wives or other dependants not accompanying them.' The reader realises that it is highly unlikely that any of these payments will ever be made: a dead man draws no salary. But Kinck has already moved on to explain about uniforms, which will be supplied from stores. 'No payment will be involved,' he assures them generously. Like any decent employer, he recommends yellow fever, typhoid and smallpox boosters, because to the company the health of the staff is paramount.

The typical Ambler hero is a man out of his depth and all alone in a dangerous rip tide. Mr Graham in *Journey into Fear* (1940) is an engineer on a business trip to Istanbul (Ambler himself had been an engineer). The company that employs him is in the arms business. Before long Graham has become a quarry so convinced he will not survive that he begins to look forward to his own death. 'Death, he told himself, would not be so bad. A moment of astonishment and it would be over.' One can identify with such a man. He is not a hero: Ambler's characters seldom are. (That is their strength as well as their weakness.) In Ambler's hands, even an accountant can create tension – which is no surprise to anyone who has been interviewed by a taxman. *Send No More Roses* begins thus: 'They stopped the car by the gateway in the wall on the lower coast road. Then, after a moment or two, the three of them climbed out stiffly, their shirts clinging to their backs. It had been a long hot drive. From the end of the terrace I could see them clearly through the binoculars.' As a scene setter, this is splendidly economical. Chapter 2 introduces a typical Ambler conceit, the unreliable narrator: 'Professor Krom's account of the events I am describing differs radically from mine; it does so, I believe, chiefly because his was written while he was still too disturbed by his experiences at the Villa Esmeralda to think clearly. He is, after all, an elderly man unaccustomed to explosions.'

None of the above is to suggest that Ambler cannot handle violence. He does more than that; he exploits the fear of violence. His petty criminals know that they are both insignificant and dispensable – that their very dispensability may be a crucial element in their employer's master plan – while Ambler's masterminds, on the other hand, believe that as sure as man is mortal, they and their kind will remain as inviolable as they have always been. It is to them nature's way.

In some of his books, the master storyteller, wonderfully cynical as Ambler is, sacrifices plot for an overdose of research – but it is arguable whether this detracts or adds to the quality of the books. It is the nature of his work. In *Send No More Roses*, he tells us more than we are entitled to learn about international money laundering in the 1970s, just as after reading his *Passage of Arms* we put down the book with the feeling that we have attended a masterclass in old-fashioned gunrunning. In *Doctor Frigo*, Ambler hits us with such a barrage of political punches that we put down the book feeling weary and punch drunk, but by the time he wrote *Doctor Frigo*, the master storyteller was beginning to show his age.

Ambler's villains were ahead of their time. In the days of his writing, the good guys were generally good – they might be slightly flawed, but they were good at heart – while the bad guys, amusing as they might be, were decidedly bad. But Ambler's villains hardly saw themselves as villains. They were businessmen. If occasional lines had to be crossed, that was business. And the business that they were in was often messy. The key character in *The Levanter* is a terrorist, a Palestinian, someone who back in 1972 was unlikely from any other author to be given the fair, almost indifferent, analysis Ambler gives him. An earlier book, *Passage of Arms* (1959), is about gunrunning, in which, again, the villains hardly see themselves as villains; they are mere wholesalers, service providers. Gunrunning appears in several Ambler books, and in his best-selling *The Mask of Dimitrios*, the gunrunner drums up trade by employing professional terrorists to stage a border incident between volatile states. The state which finds itself fired upon needs more guns – urgently. He supplies them. Is that immoral? No, he would say, it is business strategy.

Ambler is a highly intelligent and informed trickster – on occasions, a witty one, as in *The Mask of Dimitrios*, where when his gaze is not upon international criminals, he pokes fun at the successful but clearly mediocre crime-writer protagonist (from a university, of course), whose books include *No Doornail This* and *A Bloody Shovel*. The plot may climax with an unexpected trick, but by the time Ambler reveals it, he has taken his readers on a labyrinthine journey of deception. One wonders not so much at the trick – one expects tricks in a mystery – but at the mass of criminal knowledge the author seems to have at his command. One is tempted to ask why an author so well versed in the hidden trade routes and techniques of international slave trafficking, drug smuggling, prostitution and gunrunning ever bothered with writing crime novels. Consider *The Light of Day*, in which Ambler explained how to break into and avoid the electronic alarms of one of the world's most tightly protected jewellery museums. The author being Ambler, it is no surprise for us to learn later that he did not invent an imaginary museum and give it an alarm system into which he could conveniently introduce one author-constructed flaw. Instead, he used a real museum and described its actual alarm system. So correct was his analysis that the real-life authorities in the museum quickly updated their real-life alarm system.

This is a clue to Ambler's appeal. By the time Penguin began jacketing books in green and white, the allure of crime stories was on a par with that of crossword puzzles (invented, as we know them, in the 1920s) and the allure of puzzles was at its highest among law-abiding intellectuals and professors. This generation revered Ambler – even if he gently mocked them at times. Here was an author who not only could write and spin a plot but was extraordinarily well informed – and he was prepared to share his knowledge with the reader. Today's readers are less interested in puzzles and subtlety; they prefer to learn new ways of killing people. They want to stand witness at the mortuary slab. Perhaps these areas of specialist knowledge are as interesting as the simpler skills of robbery and fraud, but are they as healthy? Ambler's fans would say that you can keep your reeking formaldehyde; they prefer the open air. The typical Ambler fan would rather transport himself in his imagination to a Maltese backstreet bar or an Armenian cargo boat or to a windy skylight on the roof of an Istanbul museum. Such a reader fancies that he would risk his imaginary hide for a precious jewel; he would love to come home late one night after several unexplainable days away and be greeted by his slightly crumpled but desirable and worried mistress. He would like, in short, to have an adventure. He might be bruised, he might be grimy, but instead of slime beneath his fingernails he would have accrued some decent honest dirt. He would have touched a magic world.

Selected Works by the Author
The Dark Frontier (1936)
Cause for Alarm (1938)
The Mask of Dimitrios (1939, published in the United States as *A Coffin for Dimitrios*)
Journey into Fear (1940)
Judgment on Deltchev (1951)
The Schirmer Inheritance (1953)
The Night Comers (1956, published in the United States as *State of Siege*)
Passage to Arms (1959)
The Light of Day (1962)
Dirty Story (1967)
The Levanter (1972)

Send No More Roses (1977, published in the United States as *The Siege of the Villa Lipp*)
The Care of Time (1981)
Here Lies Eric Ambler (autobiography, 1985)
Waiting for Orders (stories, 1991 in the United States; issued in the UK as *The Story So Far*, 1993, with extra story)

Russell James

Amis, Martin (b.1949)

Martin Amis is a literary *enfant terrible*, whose preoccupation with the postmodern condition has often been the driving force behind his densely written yet vivid novels. Although he has written about crime in several of his stories, *London Fields* (1989) and *Night Train* (1997) are the novels which relate most closely to the crime genre.

The son of British writer and James Bond aficionado Sir Kingsley Amis, Martin Louis Amis was born in Cardiff, South Wales, on 25 August 1949, the second of three children. His education at Swansea Grammar School was interrupted by his family's lengthy sojourns abroad – including America, Mallorca and the West Indies – but he eventually received a First in English at Exeter College, Oxford, in 1971.

The enormous success of Kingsley Amis's debut novel, *Lucky Jim* (1954), marked the cessation of his academic career and the sudden influx of literary figures, such as Robert Graves and Elizabeth Jane Howard (who Kingsley married in 1965), into the young boy's life. Amis's first job was as a reviewer for *The Times Literary Supplement*, and five years later he became a literary editor of the *New Statesman*. His first novel – The *Rachel Papers* (1973), a semi-autobiographical, coming-of-age story set in Oxford – won the Somerset Maugham Award and, in 1989, was made into a film. *Dead Babies* (1975, also published as *Dark Secrets*) and *Success* (1978) followed, while his problematic experience as a screenplay writer – for the execrable *Saturn 3* (1980) – provided much of the inspiration for his fifth novel, the quintessential 1980s satire *Money* (1984), in which the author played a major part in his own narrative.

Amis's increasingly introspective and self-obsessed storylines reached their acme with *London Fields* in 1989. Ostensibly a **science fiction** story set in 1999, the book paints a bleak picture of **London** on the eve of the new millennium. The storyline is sprawling – it is Amis's longest book – detailing the tawdry exploits of three irredeemably repellent characters: Nicola Six (deranged nymphomaniac), Guy Clinch (upper-class weakling) and Keith Talent (working-class scum). As the names suggest, *London Fields* is a Dickensian-style satire that echoes the Victorian author's fondness for long, winding sentences and inventive use of words and narrative. The murder of Nicola Six may be the crux of the plot, but it is the characterisation of West London that is the book's richest asset. However, those seeking a straightforward crime story will probably be disappointed by Amis's postmodern tone and existential angst, especially in the book's climax.

The more obviously fantastical *Time's Arrow* (1991) no doubt had the same effect on science fiction fans with its wildly high-concept plot – a German doctor's life told in reverse – used as an unsubtle tool to examine the complex moralities of the Holocaust perpetrators and their individual responsibility for one of the worst atrocities in human history.

On the surface, *Night Train* (1997) is a clichéd **police procedural**. With Amis adopting the Chandleresque first-person narrative of Mike Hoolihan, a US female detective called in to investigate the suicide of her boss's daughter, it obeys most of the rules of 1930s noir, but as with all Amis, it asked fundamental questions of its readership in regard to what is real and what is fabricated. The glorified novella split the critics in two, and even those who liked it tended to have reservations, especially about its controversial conclusion.

Amis is currently Professor of Creative Writing at the University of Manchester. His autobiography, *Experience*, was published in 2000. *See also* Literature and Crime Fiction.

Selected Works by the Author
Money (1984)
London Fields (1989)
The Information (1995)
Night Train (1997)

Website
www.martinamisweb.com

Mark Campbell

Anderson, James (b.1936)

Although James Anderson's output is small (which includes **thrillers**, black comedies and supernatural stories) he is best known for his affectionate **Golden Age** detective pastiches.

Born in Swindon of Welsh parents, Anderson moved to Cardiff when he was a small boy and has lived near the city all his life, currently residing in the seaside town of Penarth in the Vale of Glamorgan. After taking a degree in History at the University of Reading, he worked as a salesman and advertising copywriter before becoming a freelance journalist, writing for such publications as *The Times*, *The Birmingham Post* and the *South Wales Echo*.

His first novel, *Assassin* (1969), was a political thriller set in an unnamed European country wherein a condemned murderer is offered freedom provided he assassinates the neighbouring country's leader. He is injected with a slow-acting poison that can only be halted if he completes his mission. The *New York Times* praised its 'clean, economical prose and fine plotting'. Anderson followed it up five years later with a futuristic sequel, *The Abolition of Death* (1974). This time the murder is on the side of the angels as he attempts to rescue a scientist who has discovered a drug that makes human life eternal.

The Alpha List (1972) was another thriller, this time set in Britain. In this taut tale of political skulduggery, Scotland Yard Inspector Bob Palmer investigates a blackmail ring and sets off a chain of events that puts his American wife in mortal danger.

But it is a trilogy of cosy 1930s country-house murder mysteries featuring Chief Inspector Wilkins that have proved the author's most enduring legacy.

The Affair of the Blood-Stained Egg Cosy (1975) takes place at a weekend party organised by the Earl of Burford, an event attended by such larger-than-life guests as a Texan millionaire, a jewel thief and a French baroness. When a body is discovered in a lake, and another in a secret passageway, Wilkins is tasked with unmasking the culprit, or culprits, before anyone else is killed.

The Affair of the Mutilated Mink Coat (1981), also published as *The Affair of the Mutilated Mink*, is a more obvious send-up, this time centring on a Hollywood invasion of Burford's stately pile. The final, much belated, episode, *The Affair of the 39 Cufflinks* (2003), revisits the familiar territory, with the guest list made up of the Earl's family attending an elderly relative's funeral.

Other works include the supernatural thriller *Auriol* (1982), the black comedy *Assault and Matrimony* (1980, filmed by the National Broadcasting Company) and three *Murder, She Wrote* novelisations. But it is the Burford novels – as much spoofs of the genre as they are fond homages – that Anderson will be best remembered for.

Selected Works by the Author
Assassin (1969)
The Alpha List (1972)
The Abolition of Death (1974)
Appearance of Evil (1977)
Angel of Death (1978)
The Affair of the Mutilated Mink Coat (1981)
Auriol (1982)
The Affair of the 39 Cufflinks (2003)

Mark Campbell

Anderson, J[ohn] R[ichard] L[ane] (1911–1981)

J.R.L. Anderson was a senior journalist before turning to crime fiction in the last ten years or so of his life. His books are high-class **thrillers**, often with an intriguing **espionage** element.

Many of Anderson's novels feature Major Peter Blair, recruited into military intelligence with cases all over the world: England (*Death in the North Sea*, 1975; *Death in the Thames*, 1975; *Death in the City*, 1977; and *Death in the Greenhouse*, 1978) and abroad (*Death in the Caribbean*, 1977, which begins, startlingly, with an earthquake; and *Death in the Desert*, which finds Blair in the Sahara). Most accomplished of them all, perhaps, is *Death in a High Latitude* (1981), which begins at the Scott Polar Research Institute in Cambridge and ends on the frigid shores of Hudson Bay, where Blair's party have to contend with a plane crash, a polar bear and, for Blair, the effects of a scarcely healed wound – as well as the violent nemeses.

Anderson's other series character is Piet Deventer, a youngish chief constable of Dutch extraction with a talent for painting (a useful 'cover'), whom readers encountered in *A Sprig of Sea Lavender* (1978), set in Suffolk and featuring forgery, hidden gold and hippies. More counterculture figures appear in *Festival* (1979), as the eponymous festival is of the rock variety. In this case, Deventer's infant daughter is kidnapped; the dénouement takes place on the storm-tossed coast of north Cornwall. Deventer does not know whom to trust (surrounded as he is by bent coppers), so he employs the RAF and they do not let him down. A stamp forgery plays a part in the last Deventer (and last Anderson), *Late Delivery* (1982).

A non-series book is *Redundancy Pay* (1976). The protagonist simultaneously loses his job and his wife and decamps to south Devon, where he, in company with a local parson's daughter (the romantic ending is signalled early), finds considerable skulduggery by indulging in much small boat sailing.

It is surprising that Anderson's books, which move quickly and excitingly against varied backgrounds, have not been frequently reprinted. All are worth seeking out.

Selected Works by the Author
Death in the North Sea (1975)
Redundancy Pay (1976; published in the United States as *Death in the Channel*)
Death in the Caribbean (1977)
Death in the Greenhouse (1978)
Festival (1979)
Death in a High Latitude (1981)

Philip Scowcroft

Anthologies

In crime fiction, as in other genres, an anthology is a book that contains short stories or other work by various authors and is usually edited by one or more persons other than the contributors. It is different from a magazine in that anthologies rarely carry editorial features, news or reviews and are seldom on a regular monthly (or weekly) schedule, though they can be annual or half-yearly or, very occasionally, quarterly. Although many anthologies select the best of something, such as the year's best stories or the best detective stories or similar thematic subjects, many are general selections.

The anthology, as a basic form, has an ancient lineage and can claim such famous antecedents as *The Arabian Nights* and the *Gesta Romanorum*, their compilation into written form dating back to the fourteenth century or earlier. The crime fiction anthology, however, as a specific article, is rather less ancient, although it may trace part of its origin, and certainly some of its appeal, to the notorious *Newgate Calendar*, a collection of stories – purportedly factual but over time much embellished – dealing with crimes and criminals and drawn from broadsheets and chapbooks. The first book to bear the title *The Newgate Calendar, or The Malefactor's Bloody Register* appeared in five volumes between 1774 and 1778, although it had its precedence in *The Tyburn Calendar, or Malefactor's Bloody Register* published in 1705. These compilations have been revised and extended over the years and remain in print in various forms. Many writers from Daniel Defoe to Charles **Dickens** used them as source material, and stories from them still appear in anthologies today.

There were also many compilations of **gothic** novels, a mixture of mystery and the supernatural, some of which drew heavily upon folk tales and legends such as *Popular Tales and Romances of the Northern Nations* (1823) and William Hazlitt's four-volume *The Romancist and Novelist's Library* (1839–1840). This form of fiction was still labelled as 'mystery' late into the nineteenth century, as with *Tales of Mystery* (1891), compiled by George Saintsbury.

Anthologies solely of crime and detection, however, remained rare until 1907 when the American editor Julian Hawthorne compiled his seminal, six-volume *Library of the World's Best Mystery and Detective Stories*. Each volume selected stories from different countries or cultures. For example, the volume labelled 'English: Scotch' included three Sherlock **Holmes** stories by Arthur Conan **Doyle** as well as stories by Robert Louis Stevenson, Wilkie **Collins** and Rudyard Kipling. Hawthorne's series, and its successor *The Lock and Key Library* (1909), prompted many multi-volume compilations in the United States, notably those by William Patten, all of which were also available in Britain, but few home-grown crime fiction anthologies appeared until after the First World War.

The popularity of crime fiction in the 1920s saw a profusion of anthologies. Indeed, the decade gave the crime story the seal of academic approval. In 1926, the Canadian Edward Murray Wrong, a Fellow and history tutor at Magdalen College, Oxford, compiled *Crime and Detection* for the Oxford University Press World's Classic series. Besides two stories by Edgar Allan Poe, his selections were entirely British, including works by Arthur Conan Doyle, R. Austin **Freeman**, E.W. **Hornung**, Barry Pain and Arthur Morrison. His thirty-page introduction provided both a disciplined history of the genre and views on its form and nature, defining that detective fiction should not copy real life but present 'deep mystery and conflicting clues'. Wrong's introduction was one of the first on the subject of crime fiction and was subsequently reprinted in Howard Haycraft's *The Art of the Mystery Story* (1946).

The volume was reprinted in 1930 alongside a second selection, compiled anonymously because Wrong had died in 1928 due to heart failure. His work had put crime fiction, as a serious field, on the map. In 1928, Gollancz commissioned Dorothy L. **Sayers** to assemble a huge – running over 1,200 pages – and, to many, definitive selection *Great Short Stories of Detection, Mystery and Horror*. It carried another lengthy, discursive introduction by Sayers on the history and nature of the genre and over sixty stories. About a half were crime and mystery, with selections from as far back as ancient Greece and Rome along with more contemporary items by Conan Doyle, R. Austin Freeman, Victor L. **Whitechurch**, Eden Phillpotts and others, all of them British except Poe. Sayers's volume became an instant classic and set the marker for quality short fiction – its contents almost defining the traditional **Golden Age** detective story. It has remained in print, in one form or another, ever since. Sayers compiled two subsequent volumes under the same title in 1931 and 1934, and the three volumes remain the most important anthologies of the period.

With Wrong and Sayers having established a baseline, it was the turn of Monsignor Ronald **Knox** to take things forward. Knox was well known in crime fiction circles – he had a story in the first of Sayers's volumes – and, together with fellow theologian Henry Hartington, he interested the newly established Faber and Faber in publishing a selection, *Best Detective Stories of the Year 1928* (1929). The selection ranged from the obscure to the better known, including Agatha Christie's first Miss **Marple** story, but what makes the anthology memorable today is Knox's introduction, which set down ten rules to ensure fair play in writing a detective story. The anthologies at this time were as much a guide to the genre as they were a selection of stories. Knox and Hartington compiled only one more year's-best selection, for 1929 before moving on. There was one further anonymous compilation published in 1933, selecting from 1932. There was no further selection of the year's best fiction from a British perspective until Maxim **Jakubowski** began his *Best British Mysteries* series in 2003. However, annual selections would continue to appear in the United States, chiefly from 1946 on, most of which were reprinted in Britain.

Faber, though, did not want to drop the basic idea and, in 1931, started an occasional series where authors selected what they believed were their best stories in a particular theme: *My Best Detective Story* (1931), *My Best Thriller* (1933), *My Best Spy Story* (1938) and *My Best Mystery Story* (1939). Several authors appeared in at least three volumes. Agatha Christie chose 'Philomel Cottage' as her best detective story, 'Accident' as her best **thriller** and 'Dead Man's Mirror' as her best mystery.

Faber also published two other compilations, *Best Crime Stories* (1934) and *Best Murder Stories* (1935), both edited anonymously and both including much contemporary material not previously issued in book form. These were the forerunner of an influential series that Faber began in 1959 with *Best Detective Stories* compiled by Edmund **Crispin**. John Welcome compiled *Best Legal Stories* (1962) and *Best Crime Stories* (1964), each with their follow-up volumes, and there were other similar compilations by Cyril Ray, Roy **Vickers** and Maurice Richardson. Faber's upmarket literary reputation gave these volumes an authority and panache which delineated the image of crime fiction in Britain.

Also in the wake of Sayers's big collection were a number of other big anthologies, sometimes issued as subscription enticements for newspapers. The *Daily Express* started this ball rolling with *A Century of Thrillers from Poe to Arlen*, a bumper 1,087-page volume issued in 1934, followed by a near-900-page second series in 1935. Odhams Press issued similar huge tomes, including *The Mystery Book* (1934) and *The Great Book of Thrillers* (1935), both edited by H. Douglas Thomson, *The Mammoth Book of Thrillers, Ghosts and Mysteries* (1936) by J.M. Parrish and John R. Crossland, *Fifty Masterpieces of Mystery* (1937), edited in-house by Violet Murray and *Fifty Famous Detectives of Fiction* (1938), also anonymous. These books relied heavily on Victorian material but included a scattering of more recent popular material. The one editor who sought to include mostly new material was John Gawsworth, who included stories by his coterie of friends, amongst them M.P. Shiel, Edgar Jepson and E.H. Visiak in *Thrills, Crimes and Mysteries* (1935) and *Crimes, Creeps and Thrills* (1936).

One of the best of the bumper offerings was *A Century of Detective Stories*, published by Hutchinson in 1935 and compiled anonymously by Dorothy M. Tomlinson. This 1,000-page whopper presented predominantly recent material from the post-war years and gave readers an excellent idea of the state of the art in crime fiction. It sold so well that a second volume was published in 1938, edited by E.C. **Bentley**. Meanwhile, Dennis **Wheatley** compiled *A Century of Spy Stories* (1938). The importance of these books was that they provided cheap access to a wide diversity of fiction and were issued in such huge numbers that it was rare for a household not to have access to one or two of them.

These anthologies were to some degree victims of their own success. They provided such a huge selection of top-quality reading matter that readers' appetites were satiated for many years. However, when the Second World War ushered in paper rationing, the day of the mega-volume was over. The last of these mega-volumes was something of a novelty. John Rhode compiled *Detection Medley* in 1939 on behalf of the Detection Club. This club, founded in 1928, had occasionally issued round-robin collaborative novels written by its members, which included G.K. **Chesterton**, Agatha Christie, Dorothy L. Sayers and Ronald Knox. *Detection Medley* was different in that this was a genuine anthology, a showcase of some of the best that the club's members were offering and included some new material.

Although small paperback anthologies continued to appear during the war, usually abridged reprints of pre-war volumes, it took the field some years to rebuild itself. One of the regenerating factors was the **Crime Writers' Association** (CWA), founded in November 1953. The CWA decided to sponsor its own anthology *Butcher's Dozen*, compiled by Josephine **Bell**, Michael **Gilbert** and Julian **Symons** and published by Heinemann in 1956. It provided a representative selection of recent but little-known

stories by CWA members. With the second volume, *Choice of Weapons* (1958), compiled
by Michael Gilbert, Hodder & Stoughton became the regular publisher. Elizabeth
Ferrars compiled *Planned Departures* also in 1958; Roy Vickers, *Some Like Them
Dead* in 1960.

The CWA's anthologies then lapsed for five years because Hodder took on a series
by CWA founder John **Creasey**. *The Mystery Bedside Book* (1960) contained a selection
from the **Creasey Mystery Magazine**. Creasey maintained this series for six volumes
until 1965. Editorship then passed to Herbert **Harris** with a title change to *John
Creasey's Mystery Bedside Book*, which Harris sustained through to 1976. It was then
retitled *John Creasey's Crime Collection* and continued with the new publisher Victor
Gollancz until 1989. All of these volumes by Harris showcased the works of CWA
members. After Harris stepped down in 1990 there have been other CWA anthologies:
Crime Waves (1991) edited by H.R.F. **Keating**; the three *Culprit* volumes compiled by
Liza **Cody** and Michael Z. **Lewin** (and Peter **Lovesey** for the third), which ran almost
all-new stories; and since 1996, several by Martin **Edwards**. These began with *Perfectly
Criminal* and are themed anthologies with specially commissioned stories.

The other series of new crime fiction which began in the 1960s was *Winter's Crimes*,
started by George **Hardinge** in 1969 as part of his role in developing a new crime
list for Macmillan. *Winter's Crimes* consisted of stories specially written for the
anthology, primarily by Macmillan's stable of writers, and Hardinge always went
for strong names. Julian Symons, Michael Gilbert, Edmund Crispin, Ellis **Peters**
and Celia Dale were amongst the ten contributors to the first volume. Eric **Ambler**,
Winston **Graham**, Christianna **Brand** and H.R.F. Keating appeared in the second
volume, whilst for the third Hardinge managed to entice Agatha Christie to add
a final story to her Harley Quin series. Hardinge saw *Winter's Crimes* through
seventeen volumes, alternating editorship with Hilary Watson (later Hilary **Hale**)
from Volume 8. Hale continued the series to Volume 22, and Maria **Rejt** edited
two more before the series bowed out in 1992. The series was always of a consistently
high quality and later volumes presented new material by Ruth **Rendell**, Colin
Dexter, Patricia Highsmith, Geoffrey **Household**, Lionel **Davidson** and Robert
Barnard, amongst many others. When Hilary Hale left Macmillan in 1991, she
began a spiritual successor to the series, *Midwinter Mysteries*, which ran for five
annual volumes.

Whilst the CWA and Macmillan series showcased new and recent fiction, there
have also been, since the 1960s, plenty of anthologies reprinting classic and rare
crime fiction, including the various 'Best' series from Faber, compiled by Edmund
Crispin and John Welcome. In 1960, R.C. Bull compiled *Great Stories of Detection*
(1960) for Arthur Barker, which harked back to the mammoth books of the 1930s
and gave readers over 600 pages of the best of the new and the old. There have since
been plenty of omnibus volumes of old material, sometimes anonymously compiled by
in-house editors, and include *Great Short Tales of Mystery and Terror* (1983), *The Best
Crime Stories* (1984) and two by Mary Danby, *65 Great Detective Stories* and *65 Great
Murder Mysteries* (both 1983).

The more rewarding anthologies, though, are those that both entertain the reader
and widen the reader's experience. Such anthologies are assembled by editors who
go that extra mile to trace little-known but quality stories by both well-known and
lesser-known writers and, in so doing, enhance the reader's awareness of the history
and nature of crime fiction. Hugh Greene achieved this with considerable success
when he compiled *The Rivals of Sherlock Holmes* (1970), which reprinted stories

by Victorian and Edwardian writers who created their own master detectives but where, in some cases, the authors had lapsed into obscurity. The book led to three sequels. Greene also compiled, with his brother Graham **Greene**, a bumper *Victorian Villainies* (1984).

Peter **Haining** was originally more closely associated with gothic and supernatural fiction anthologies but increasingly turned, in the 1980s, to themed crime and mystery compilations. The latter began with *Mysterious Railway Stories* (1984), under the alias William Pattrick, and have continued with *Deadly Odds* (1986), as Richard Peyton, *Murder on the Menu* (1992), *The Television Detectives' Omnibus* (1992) and *Great Irish Detective Stories* (1993) amongst others.

Jack **Adrian**, similarly, had compiled several anthologies of rare but enticing fiction, including *Crime at Christmas* (1988), *The Art of the Impossible* (1990) with Bob Adey, and *Detective Stories from the Strand* (1991). Oxford University Press, which published the last volume, also returned to an interest in crime fiction and since 1990, starting with *The Oxford Book of English Detective Stories* by Patricia Craig, has published several quality anthologies of both classic and rare material, including *Victorian Tales of Mystery & Detection* (1992) by Michael Cox, *Trial and Error* (1998) by Fred R. Shapiro and Jane Garry, *Murder on Deck!* (1998) by Rosemary Herbert and *A New Omnibus of Crime* (2005) by Tony Hillerman and Rosemary Herbert.

Robinson Publishing has brought together both the omnibus and thematic approach with its series of *Mammoth Book* anthologies. These have included various historical crime compilations by Mike **Ashley**, starting with *The Mammoth Book of Historical Whodunnits* (1995) and several volumes by Maxim **Jakubowski**, including *The Mammoth Book of Comic Crime* (2002) and *The Mammoth Book of Future Cops* (2003).

Maxim Jakubowski is perhaps the leading contemporary anthologist of new and reprint fiction. He edited three volumes of mostly original fiction for Robinson, *New Crimes* (1989–1991). With the lack of any regular magazine in Britain catering for short stories and new authors, Jakubowski's series was a welcome addition to *Winter's Crimes* but was all too short-lived. Jakubowski took the series to Constable as *Constable New Crimes* (1992), which ran for only two volumes with Gollancz publishing a third as *Crime Yellow* (1994). Subsequently Jakubowski has edited a short series with Mike **Ripley**, *Fresh Blood* (1996–1999), showcasing new talent and, most recently, has returned to the concept of the annual selection of the year's best new fiction with *Best British Mysteries* (2003).

Publishers have long argued that short-story volumes do not sell as well as novels, and yet anthologies continue to appear and are a vital element that allows new authors to develop and established authors to experiment and test new ideas and characters. They also provide the general reading public with a wide appreciation of the best crime fiction that has been published over the last one hundred years or so and are thus important in establishing the genre's credentials.

Further Reading
Contento, William G., and Martin H. Greenberg. 1990. *Index to Crime and Mystery Anthologies.* G.K. Hall; expanded and revised on CD-ROM by Contento alone as *Mystery Short Fiction Miscellany: an Index* (Locus Press, 2003).

Mike Ashley

Anthony, Evelyn (b.1928)

This prodigally talented author began with immaculately researched historical novels, usually involving romantic entanglements, before moving into the contemporary **thriller** genre in the early 1970s.

Born Evelyn Bridget Patricia Stephens on 3 July 1928 in London, she initially received a convent education before being home-taught during the Second World War. Anthony did not start writing until she met her future husband, a mining-company director, in 1949. After she tasted some success with **magazine** short stories, her first novel, *Imperial Highness*, was published in 1953, under her pseudonym, Evelyn Anthony. The novel was set in eighteenth-century Russia and dramatised the real-life events leading up to the death of Catherine the Great. The book, a vivid mixture of meticulous research and clever extrapolation, won her many admirers.

Several historical novels followed, featuring such famous romantic figures as Anne Boleyn, Queen Victoria and King Charles I. *The Rendezvous* (1967), a wartime romance, paved the way for her first bona fide espionage tale, *The Legend* (1969). Peter Arundsen, a bored City banker, wishes he were back working for the British secret service. His wish is granted when he is asked by his old boss to hunt down a colleague who has defected to East Germany. A dramatic spy thriller, *The Legend* built upon the author's successful track record with historical fiction, blending romance, intrigue and strong characterisation into a complex present-day **espionage** plot.

The Poellenberg Inheritance (1970) maintained the espionage theme, this time centring on the rightful heir of a gold-encrusted Nazi masterpiece called the 'Poellenberg Salt', now in the possession of a German ex-general living in Spain. A chase across Europe leads to an exciting dénouement in Paris.

Anthony's next book is arguably her most well known. *The Tamarind Seed* (1971) was essentially a love story with Cold War trappings, in which holidaymaker Judith Farrow falls in love with handsome Russian communist Feodor Sverdlov in the tropical paradise of Barbados. In order to see her without raising suspicion, Sverdlov tries to recruit her as a Soviet spy; the Home Office is surprisingly accepting of this, hoping she will uncover the identity of another Russian agent. It was made into a film three years later, starring Julie Andrews, Omar Sharif and Anthony Quayle. As director, Blake Edwards (of *Pink Panther* fame) brought the book's complex plot to the big screen in a way that served to counterbalance the increasingly far-fetched James Bond escapades of the period.

Although Evelyn Anthony continues to write well into her seventies, her recent books have not quite achieved the same level of attention as her earliest books. However, more recent titles such as *No Resistance* (2004) and *Mind Games* (2005) still serve to demonstrate her characteristically assured plotting.

Selected Works by the Author
The Legend (1969)
The Assassin (1970)
The Tamarind Seed (1971)
The Occupying Power (1973; published in the United States as *Stranger at the Gates*)
The Silver Falcon (1977)
The Avenue of the Dead (1981; reprinted in the UK as *The Plumed Serpent*)
The Scarlet Thread (1989)

Anthony, Evelyn

The Relic (1991)
The Doll's House (1992)
Mind Games (2005)

Mark Campbell

Appignanesi, Lisa

Lisa Appignanesi is Polish by birth, Canadian by upbringing and British by adoption. She is a novelist, writer and broadcaster with particular passion for the defence of literary freedoms throughout the world. As a novelist, in such books as *The Memory Man* (2004), her examination of human psychology has a forensic intensity, but her most astringent work is to be found in her dark psychological **thrillers**. Such books as *Paris Requiem* (2001), *Sanctuary* (2000), *The Dead of Winter* (1999), *The Things We Do for Love* (1997), *Dreams of Innocence* (1993) and *Memory and Desire* (1991) have redefined the parameters of genre fiction. *Unholy Loves* (2005), for instance, is a powerful and rigorously structured thriller and among her best work. The novel is set in the Loire valley in 1900; the heroine, Marguerite, wife of the Comte de Landois, travels from Paris to the country at the request of her husband, only to enter a dark mélange of death and deceit. Marguerite de Landois is a wonderfully rounded character, both typical of her era and at odds with it,as is Chief Inspector Emile Durand of the Paris branch of the Sûreté, involved in the murder investigation that has Marguerite at its heart. Appignanesi utilises the interaction of her protagonists to examine *belle époque* notions of art and politics while keeping a compelling narrative thread burning brightly.

In *The Dead of Winter* (1999), a savage killer has murdered fourteen girl students in Montréal. The actress Madeleine Blais is consumed by a fear that someone

3. Lisa Appignanesi.

is determined to murder her too. Her old friend and lawyer, Pierre Rousseau, tries to comfort her, but Madeleine is subsequently found hanging in a barn near her grandmother's cottage in the small town of Ste-Anne. Pierre, with a secret life of his own, begins to uncover some disturbing mysteries involving the dead actress. Appignanesi, as ever, maintains an inexorably mounting tension alongside the layered characterisations. Appignanesi's non-fiction includes an important cultural history of madness and mind doctors, *Mad, Bad and Sad* (2008). The acclaimed family memoir, *Losing the Dead* (1999), *Freud's Women* (third edition, 2005) and a life of Simone de Beauvoir. She has edited a collection of writings, *Free Expression Is No Offence* (2005), which arose from the English PEN campaign against the government's religious hatred legislation. The book played a significant part in the House of Common's vote to amend the bill and introduce a protection of Free Expression clause. In 2007, she became president of English PEN.

Selected Works by the Author
Memory and Desire (1981)
Dreams of Innocence (1993)
The Things We Do for Love (1997)
The Dead of Winter (1999)
Paris Requiem (2001)
Unholy Loves (2005)

Barry Forshaw

Archer, Geoffrey (b.1944)

Geoffrey Archer has utilised his experiences as a television journalist – especially during his post as ITN's defence correspondent during the 1980s – to write several well-received, intelligent **espionage thrillers** in the style of his boyhood hero, Nevil Shute.

Not to be confused with his famous near-namesake, the controversial Baron Archer of Weston-super-Mare, Geoffrey Archer was born and brought up in North London, where his main hobby was contributing articles to his school magazine. Keen on acting, at the age of sixteen, in 1960 he had a small role in a National Youth Theatre production of *Hamlet*, a production that also included such future luminaries as Michael York and Simon Ward.

After leaving school, Archer dallied with different career paths, including acting, engineering and the Bar. In 1964, he joined a regional television station in Southampton as a trainee researcher and discovered his vocation. Unfortunately, he was dismissed shortly afterwards for walking into his boss's office and giving him advice on running his company. It was 'a mistake never repeated', Archer later admitted.

He joined London-based ITN in 1969 as a reporter on its flagship daily news bulletin *News at Ten*, and he was often seen reporting from the streets of Belfast during the worst years of the Troubles. In 1976 he covered the brutal civil war in Beirut, and the frustration at the lack of airtime allotted to the conflict spurred him on to write a novel based on the dramatic events he had witnessed. Although not accepted by a publisher, it served as an inspiration for his first published book, *Sky Dancer* (1987). A thriller about a revolutionary British warhead stolen by the Russians, it was set on board the fictional British submarine *HMS Retribution* and based on information gleaned on exclusive visits to a Polaris missile submarine during Archer's stint as ITN's defence correspondent in the 1980s.

Two more books with naval themes followed. In *Shadow Hunter* (1989), an out-of-control captain of a British nuclear submarine steers his ship on a deadly course to the Russian naval base at Murmansk, threatening World War III. In *Eagle Trap* (1993), an Arab gang leader threatens Britain with nuclear warheads stolen from Russia's mouldering stockpile.

Archer's coverage of the 1992 war in Bosnia provided him with a compelling backdrop for *Scorpion Trail* (1995), the story of an aid worker in Bosnia sent on a mission to track down a ruthless killer called 'The Scorpion'.

Archer retired from his television work in 1995 to concentrate full time on writing. *Fire Hawk* (1998) began a three-book series featuring Sam Packer of the British secret service, while his most recent work, *Dark Angel* (2004), showed the author moving into more conventional crime territory with a dark tale of murder in 1948 suburbia.

Selected Works by the Author
Sky Dancer (1987)
Shadow Hunter (1989)
Eagle Trap (1993)
Scorpion Trail (1995)
Java Spider (1997)
The Lucifer Network (2001)
The Burma Legacy (2002)
Dark Angel (2004)

Mark Campbell

Armstrong, David (b.1946)

David Armstrong's five stimulating, idiosyncratic and well-crafted novels stand out from those of his UK contemporaries in the mid- to late 1990s, representing an important strain (realistic, engaged) of British crime writing that has become increasingly neglected as major publishers concentrate on the promotion of more blatantly commercial fiction.

David Armstrong was born in Birmingham, leaving school without qualifications. After working at various casual jobs, he returned to college to study English at the University of Wales in Cardiff. Later, whilst teaching at a College of Further Education in Shropshire, he wrote *Night's Black Agents* (1993).

Night's Black Agents was inspired by an incident in his family and is Armstrong's only period novel to date. In 1933, complicity grows, then fractures, as a canal boatman and a pub landlord plot and carry out the murder of the salesman lover of the landlord's wife. This darkly atmospheric debut proceeds as a series of deftly judged character studies: the murderer and his victim, the erring wife and, as the first clue emerges, the gentle but astute Inspector Hammond, persistently probing the defences of the two conspirators. For Philip Oakes (*Literary Review*), the book evoked Zola; other crime readers might cite Simenon. The book was shortlisted for the **Crime Writers' Association**'s best first novel award, but, in a bizarre decision, no award was given that year.

Although Inspector Hammond is a memorable creation, Armstrong, surprisingly perhaps, returned to the present day for his next few novels. In *Less than Kind* (1994), Birmingham Inspector John Munroe is asked to assist in a case of Welsh cattle rustling. But his observational skills prove invaluable in solving a complex local murder case. In *Until Dawn Tomorrow* (1995), Armstrong introduces Inspector Frank Kavanagh, recently separated from wife Rachael, as he investigates a number of seemingly unconnected deaths. In *Thought for the Day* (1997), Kavanagh, recovering from a breakdown and now based in **London**, must investigate the abduction of a high-flying advertising executive. Detective Constable (DC) Jane Salt proves an invaluable ally. In *Small Vices* (2001), Kavanagh and Salt separately investigate a series of prostitute murders and a number of violent robberies which target garden centres.

With each novel, Armstrong grows in confidence. Because he often draws on his experiences (*Less than Kind*, for instance, reflects his earlier move from town to country), the writing is fresh and immediate, the treatment of the material without cliché. His often complex plots are both pacy and well developed, the characterisation pithy and psychologically acute. Kavanagh, in particular, is an unusually vivid creation, his humanity economically conveyed both in his relationships, notably with Salt, and in his acerbic observations of the society that surrounds him. In *Small Vices*, which is Armstrong's most ambitious book and certainly the best of the series, such skills combine to create a prescient picture of a Britain in the grip of an ever more corrupt reality.

Another Kavanagh-and-Salt novel, *A Kind of Acquaintance*, appeared in 2007. His first four books are available thanks to print-on-demand technology. *See also* Social Comment in Crime Fiction *and* Society and Crime Fiction.

Selected Works by the Author
Night's Black Agents (1993)
Less than Kind (1994)
Until Dawn Tomorrow (1995)
Thought for the Day (1997)
Small Vices (2001)

Website
www.twbooks.co.uk/authors/darmstrong

Bob Cornwell

Arnott, Jake (b.1961)

Jake Arnott's novels are as much about social history as they are about crime. Set in the gangland and gay underworld of **London** from the 1960s to the 1990s, they provide a nostalgia-fest ranging from Kray-style gangsters, strip clubs and Polari in the 1960s, to glam rock and pop svengalis in the 1970s, to Greenham Common and anti-Thatcherism in the 1980s, to raves and 'Cool Britannia' in the 1990s.

The Long Firm (1999) introduces Harry Starks ('I'm homosexual but I'm not gay'), an East End gangster clearly based on Ronnie Kray, fact–fictional characters being one of Arnott's trademarks. Starks's story is told by an ex-boyfriend, a lord, an actress, a fellow gangster and a sociologist who encounters him in prison. The BBC snapped up the television rights before the book was finished, creating a successful series starring Mark Strong as Starks and featuring a different narrator per episode.

Arnott, Jake

He Kills Coppers (2001) follows the stories of Billy Porter (based on the real-life cop killer Harry Roberts), hack tabloid journalist and repressed homosexual Tony Meehan (whose private life is as murderous as that of the criminals he documents) and the morally compromised copper Frank Taylor, who spends much of his life trying to atone for the gunning down of Dave Thomas, his cop partner and light alter-ego. Some characters from *The Long Firm* reappear, notably Harry Starks and bent copper George Mooney. The main action starts in 1966 on the eve of the World Cup and ends in the Thatcher years of poll tax riots and CND protests against cruise missiles, through voyages into worlds as different as those of travellers and fairgrounds, anarchists and squatters, and freemasons.

The novel *truecrime* (2003) is narrated by an older Tony Meehan, who is writing a true-crime biography of old-school villain Eddie Doyle; former skinhead, muscle-for-hire and drug-addict 'Geezer Gaz'; and Julie, actress daughter of 'Big Jock' McCluskey, trying to tempt Harry Starks out of hiding to avenge the murder of her father. The social background dates from the earliest raves to Cool Britannia and New Labour in 1997. There are fictional nods to Barbara Windsor, the Brink's Mat gold bullion robbery, the Ministry of Sound nightclub, lad's mag *Loaded* and other icons of the 1990s. And with the fictional Jez and his movie *Scrapyard Bulldog*, Arnott affectionately pokes fun at the 'geezer chic' typified by Guy Ritchie and the film ***Lock, Stock and Two Smoking Barrels***. In 2005, these three novels were published together in one paperback as the long firm trilogy.

Johnny Come Home (2006) explores 1970s pop and drug culture and the Angry Brigade bombings. David Bowie has described Arnott's novels as 'Pure gangland bliss', and the admiration is mutual. Among several Bowie references is 'Sweet Thing' – a track from Bowie's album *Diamond Dogs* and the moniker of one of the main characters, a rent boy picked up the eponymous Johnny Chrome, a Gary Glitter–style glam rocker.

Fighting Mac (2007) is a historical novel about Hector Macdonald, a famous war hero and soldier of the Afghan War and both Boer Wars, who shot himself after being caught up in a homosexual scandal. *See also* Society and Crime Fiction.

Selected Works by the Author
The Long Firm (1999)
He Kills Coppers (2001)
truecrime (2003)
Johnny Come Home (2006)

Julian Maynard-Smith

Ashley, Mike (b.1948)

Mike Ashley is regarded as one of the most professional – and prolific – anthologists in the United Kingdom, and not just of crime fiction. He is a massively enthusiastic polymath, whose areas of knowledge are truly prodigious (on everything from US crime fiction **pulps** of the 1940s to British history to the history of the **science fiction** magazines – to most major, as well as minor, crime writers). His long-running series of crime-related **anthologies** has been among the most entertaining and wide-ranging contributions to the field in any country. Ashley has said 'my problem is that I'm interested in too many things, and thus divide my time over a variety of books, from history (the Seven Wonders, kings and queens, Arthurian legends, incredible facts and other arcane things), besides compiling all the anthologies, etc'. To keep order in his massive output, he maintains a running checklist of all his writings – a daunting task indeed, as Ashley's output has shown not the slightest sign of slowing down in recent years.

Mike Ashley spent thirty-two years in local government. His father had always encouraged the questioning mind in him, a significant factor (Ashley has said) in driving the fastidiousness of his research, ever needful of filling in gaps in knowledge and never taking anything for granted. His interests are mostly in classic fiction of all sorts ('It's easier to understand dead writers and get their work in perspective – and they don't argue back!' said Ashley). But he is also ever alert for new and original ways of presenting fiction, hence his two anthologies of 'impossible crimes', among his most popular work. Utilising a library of over 40,000 books and magazines, his work has always been a source of scholarship and information, with impeccable research as hallmark. One of his editors, Pete Duncan of Constable Robinson said that Ashley sometimes views his work as an anthologist as more of a hobby, secondary to his primary passion for research. Yet, he added

> He's undoubtedly one of the top anthologists of his generation – and for my money the top anthologist when it comes to: (1) rescuing overlooked classic short stories, and (2) the ability to craft an anthology into a unified whole – I mean where the stories are not simply varied but also somehow complement each other. The best example of the latter is probably *The Mammoth Book of New Sherlock Holmes Adventures* – where each story develops the Sherlock Holmes canon, while doing so in correct chronological sequence. Artistically it's the finest Mammoth anthology.

There are those who would make a similar claim for Ashley's collection of Dickensian Whodunnits, an anthology of some twenty-five stories, which takes either Dickensian characters or episodes from **Dickens**'s life and weave these into a whodunit mystery using all of Dickens's major books. Interlinking the stories is a narrative which brings alive Dickens's own life and characters and shows his historical importance in the early developments of the crime story. As ever, Ashley's marshalling of this material is nonpareil.

Ashley has won various awards for his work, notably The Edgar Award for *The Mammoth Encyclopedia of Modern Crime Fiction*, the Pilgrim Award for Lifetime Contribution to science fiction research and the Stoker Award for his index to weird fiction anthologies, *The Supernatural Index* (with Bill Contento). Ashley has also written a much-acclaimed biography of the writer Algernon Blackwood, *Starlight Man*, and his column, Collecting Crime, for **Crime Time** has long been one of this magazine's most popular features.

Selected Works by the Author
The Mammoth Book of Historical Whodunnits (1993)
The Mammoth Book of Historical Detectives (1995)
Classical Whodunnits (1996)
The Mammoth Book of New Sherlock Holmes Adventures (1997)
Shakespearean Whodunnits (1997)
Shakespearean Detectives (1998)
Royal Whodunnits (1999)
The Mammoth Book of Locked Room Mysteries and Impossible Crimes (2000)

Barry Forshaw

Atkinson, Kate (b.1951)

Kate Atkinson is a literary novelist who has, more recently, turned to crime fiction. Any attempt to pin down her first three novels is likely to fail. Veined with parodies, literary allusions and **humour**, they are – loosely speaking – tragicomic family sagas in which imagination and reality meld. Atkinson favours the term 'comedies of manners' to describe her novels, and her early influences included *Alice in Wonderland* and *The Brothers Grimm*. Nevertheless, there are murder-mystery components to *Human Croquet* (1997) and *Emotionally Weird* (2000), and with two later novels – *Case Histories* (2004) and *One Good Turn* (2006) – she moved more into the realm of crime fiction.

Both *Case Histories* and *One Good Turn* feature private investigator Jackson Brodie, whom Atkinson described in a *Daily Telegraph* interview as, 'a man's man, who's interested in cars.... He may note the makes and models of the vehicles he tails and fancy some of his female clients, and punch his ex-wife's partner, but he still makes time to visit a mad old cat lady and consider the plight of the homeless.'

Case Histories is set in Cambridge and tells an intricate tale built around three of Brodie's cases: a girl child who disappeared from a tent in her back garden; a girl whose throat was slashed by an unidentified man who marched into her office; and a man found dead in his kitchen with an axe in his head and his wife sitting next to him. As Brodie's investigations dig up long-buried secrets, he begins to be followed by an increasingly dangerous stalker. Although death is handled seriously, the novel is leavened with dark humour. Stephen King described it as 'the best mystery of the decade', and it was nominated for the Whitbread Novel Award and Orange Broadband Prize for Fiction.

One Good Turn also received great critical acclaim; it was shortlisted for the British Book Awards Crime **Thriller** of the Year and won the Saltire Book of the Year Award and the Prix Westminster. Ian **Rankin** declared, 'The most fun I've had with a novel this year.' During the Edinburgh Festival, as the story goes, people queuing for a show witness a near-homicidal road-rage incident that changes the lives of everyone involved: the wife of an unscrupulous property developer, a crime writer, a has-been comedian – and Brodie, innocent bystander then murder suspect. 'As the body count mounts', according to the publisher, 'each character's story contains a kernel of the next, like a set of nesting Russian dolls. Everyone in the teeming Dickensian cast is looking for love or money or redemption or escape: but what each actually discovers is their own true self.'

Atkinson's debut novel, *Behind the Scenes at the Museum* (1995), won Whitbread First Novel award and Book of the Year award (given to the best book across all Whitbread categories). In 1996, it won two further awards: *Yorkshire Post* Book Award and Lire Book of the Year (a French award). It is set in Atkinson's birthplace of York, Ruby Lennox narrating, in a whimsical voice full of asides and wry observations, the elaborate history of her family across four generations. Atkinson adapted it for television, and it has also been adapted for radio and theatre.

Her second novel, *Human Croquet* (1997), is another family history, but the realm of the imagination is even more pronounced, with its sixteen-year-old heroine, Isobel Fairfax, 'dropping into random pockets of time then popping out again'. *Emotionally Weird* (2000) is set on an island off the west coast of Scotland and explores the twisting of reality through faulty memories and lies. It contains pastiches of various genres of fiction – including hard-boiled detective fiction – inserted as extracts from novels being written by the characters.

In Atkinson's short-story collection, *Not the End of the World* (2002), the normal and the fantastical again collide: a **London** shopping trip is interrupted by earthquakes, plagues and civil war; *Buffy the Vampire Slayer* references pop up across several stories, as do a number of shared characters; and there are humorous echoes of Greek myths, including a middle-aged mother overtaken on the motorway by Hades's chariot and a nanny who turns into Artemis.

Atkinson obtained a master's degree in English Literature at Dundee University and later studied for a doctorate in American Literature. After leaving university, she had various jobs, from home help to legal secretary and teacher. She briefly lived in Whitby, before moving back to Scotland to teach at Dundee University. It was then that she began writing short stories. She won *Woman's Own* Short Story Competition (1986), was nominated for Bridport Short Story Prize (1990), and won Ian St James Award (1993) for *Karmic Mothers*, which she adapted for BBC2's Tartan Shorts series. She has also won American Academy of Arts and Letters E.M. Forster Award (1997). *See also* Literature and Crime Fiction.

Selected Works by the Author

Jackson Brodie Novels
Case Histories (2004)
One Good Turn (2006)
When Will There Be Good News? (2008)

Other Novels
Behind the Scenes at the Museum (1995)
Human Croquet (1997)
Emotionally Weird (2000)

Julian Maynard-Smith

Aylett, Steve (b.1967)

Steve Aylett's surreal take on the crime genre has resulted in some of the most idiosyncratic books in the field. Although at core a satirist in the Voltairean tradition, the absurdist and joke-filled fittings of his work have made him difficult to categorise: labels have ranged from cyberpunk through irreal and slipstream, to splatterpunk and the Bizarro genre he inadvertently spawned.

Aylett is the son of a cigarette-factory worker. Leaving school at age seventeen after finding it 'anti-learning and anti-creative', he worked in a book warehouse and then in law publishing, at one point working with criminologist and ex-wrestler James Morton.

His first book, *The Crime Studio* (1994), introduced Beerlight, a city where crime is an inventive art form. Seemingly a combination of New York, Chicago and Baltimore, Beerlight would feature in several more Aylett books. The Crime Studio is a series of interlinking stories in which Aylett's casually satirical wordplay hits the ground running: 'it was the fashion to punish crooks severely so as to encourage their assimilation back into the underworld – a process known as "recrimination"'. This was followed by the more futuristic *Slaughtermatic* (1998), the most popular Beerlight novel, which was shortlisted for the Philip K. Dick Award. Guns in

4. Steve Aylett.

Beerlight tend to be sentient and personify philosophical positions so that gunfights represent arguments, often with surprising results. The gunfights are also invariably ultra-kinetic and over the top, influenced by videogames and the John Woo school of movies. By the time of *Atom* (2000) – Aylett's contribution to the ever-growing industry of *Maltese Falcon* parodies – Beerlight has become unliveable: 'What happens when the hitcher and the driver are equally murderous?'

Toxicology (1999), a short-story collection, includes several Beerlight stories and features the all-you-can-eat antics of Henry Blince, the town's lumbering chief of police. Blince is based on Orson Welles's swollen cop in *Touch of Evil* and concerns himself with lateral questions such as 'How many times does a man have to shave before his chin gets the message?'

Aylett's list of titles thus far has combined crime, **humour**, hallucinative surrealism and seriously intended satire to a ratio that has not made categorisation any easier. Some readers find his concentrated density of gags and ideas indigestible, while others find it compelling. His world view is a combination of despair at the human character and glee in creative mischief. Recurring themes are those of power manipulations and 'hypocrisy too extreme to process', as in *Slaughtermatic*: 'There was a time when the extension of illegality to innocent acts could be used to manipulate men. But when guilt is no longer felt over acts of genuine criminality, what hope of instilling guilt in the innocent?' In *LINT* (2005), the story of an author (Jeff Lint) reminiscent of Harry Stephen Keeler, he concludes, 'Reality is the thing that doesn't need to be asserted.' Lint's action comic *The Caterer*, an entire issue of which Aylett re-created, features another 'trickster' archetype pursued by a cop who is barely less strange. Aylett's tendency to be quoted endlessly by fans may have irritated and put off hosts of potential readers.

Selected Works by the Author
The Crime Studio (stories, 1994)
Bigot Hall (1995)

Slaughtermatic (1998)
The Inflatable Volunteer (1999)
Toxicology (stories, 1999)
Atom (2000)
LINT (2005)

Brian Ritterspak

B

Baboneau, Suzanne (b.1958)

Suzanne Baboneau, currently publishing director of the Adult Trade Division
at Simon & Schuster UK, is one of the most inspiring editors in the country.
Her authors, notably the important British crime authors in her portfolio,
are vocally grateful for her subtle and persuasive stewardship of their work.

Baboneau started her career in publishing in 1980, with a degree in French
from Durham University. She worked for three years as secretary to Caroline
Upcher, the fiction editor at Pan Books. She moved to Hamish Hamilton to
work for Managing Director Christopher Sinclair-Stevenson for two years and
left just before the company was taken over by the Penguin Group. A spell at
Pan Macmillan followed, where she worked her way up from being an assistant
fiction editor to become the editorial director (fiction). In mid-2000, she received
an invitation she could not refuse: to join Simon & Schuster UK, under Ian
Chapman's new leadership. She joined as fiction publisher and became publishing
director in 2002.

During her time in publishing, Baboneau has been fortunate enough to work
with some stellar names in crime fiction. These include established authors at
Pan Macmillan such as Clare Francis, who turned to crime writing in the early
1990s, and Lynda La Plante, whose early television success with *Widows* led to
her writing debut, *The Legacy*, in the 1980s. (*Prime Suspect*, La Plante's top-rated
television drama series, came Baboneau's way in the form of tie-in novelisations.)
La Plante is a permanent fixture on the national bestseller lists owing to her series
of novels featuring DI Anna Travis, and Baboneau continues to edit them. Baboneau
has worked on the paperbacks of Dick Francis, mainstay of the Pan list, and edited
Ken Follett and Colin Forbes (who also moved with her to Simon & Schuster UK).
Carl Hiaasen was an exciting find: a Florida-based comic crime writer who found
a solid fan base among readers in the United Kingdom.

At Simon & Schuster UK, Baboneau has been involved in rebuilding and
strengthening the list, with the help of her editorial team. In the non-fiction field,
authors such as Ann Rule and Joe McGinnis have come on board; in fiction,
Mary Higgins Clark and US best-selling author John Sandford have become
mainstays. Natasha Cooper, another prize author of Baboneau's, is getting
considerable recognition for her Trish Maguire series of crime novels. Alongside
these established names, Baboneau has also brought new crime authors into the

fold, and perhaps her most acclaimed acquisition of recent times is *Child 44* by the youthful Tom Rob Smith. Sold for translation in twenty-eight countries, with film rights going to Ridley Scott, *Child 44* is one of the most striking fiction debuts in many years and has been favourably compared with *Gorky Park* and *Fatherland*.

Barry Forshaw

Bagley, Desmond (1923–1983)

This accomplished adventure thriller writer emerged in the early 1960s and quickly established himself as an original – and also as one of the main rivals to Alistair MacLean and Hammond Innes.

Between 1962 and 1983, Desmond Bagley produced fourteen novels – a fertile period that witnessed him scaling the bestseller lists as well as satisfying purists of the thriller genre. And at the apex of his popularity in the early 1970s, Hollywood came knocking: director John Huston filmed a version of *The Freedom Trap* (as *The Mackintosh Man*) starring Paul Newman. Although the film flopped, it did not dent Bagley's sales, and his global popularity resulted in the translation of his works into over twenty languages (he had a particularly large following in Scandinavia). Bagley left behind two unfinished novels, which were completed by his wife, Joan, also a writer: *Night of Error* (1984) and *Juggernaut* (1985).

The son of a Lancashire coal miner, Bagley was born on 29 October 1923 in the Lake District town of Kendal, Cumbria (then Westmoreland). He was educated in local schools, and he developed a speech impediment at an early age, which remained throughout his life. In 1934, Bagley's father retired on medical grounds and relocated the family to Blackpool, where he opened a boarding house. Bagley left school at fourteen sans qualifications and got a job as a printer's apprentice. Dissatisfied, he quit and began working along Blackpool's seafront gambling venues, servicing 'one-arm bandit' fruit machines. When war broke out in 1939, Bagley tried to enlist but was rejected because of his stammer. He then became the foreman of a local factory that had been converted to make parts for Spitfire fighters.

In 1947, Bagley quit England for a new life in South Africa. He travelled overland – across the Sahara and down through North and East Africa, where he caught malaria – finding a variety of mining-related work along the way to fund his journey. It was his adventures travelling in Africa that provided a rich source of background material for his writing. Bagley eventually arrived in South Africa in 1950, and it was there that his interest in journalism was born. In 1951–1952, he penned radio scripts for the South African Broadcasting Corporation, and by the late 1950s, he was a well-respected freelance reporter for the country's top newspapers. Significantly, he published his first short story, 'My Old Man's Trumpet', in 1957 in the British magazine, *Argosy*.

After his marriage in 1960, Bagley and his wife moved to Guernsey, where he wrote his first novel in 1962 at the relatively late age of thirty-nine – legend has it that he used one finger to type up the story (and all subsequent novels). The book, *The Golden Keel*, was published in 1963, and according to the author, it was based on an apocryphal story he heard from a former British soldier in a Johannesburg bar about Mussolini's missing gold. Bagley retooled the tale into a fast-paced yarn about a band of adventurers seeking to locate and smuggle the former Fascist dictator's ill-gotten treasure out of Italy before others can get their hands on it. An exciting, action-packed page-turner, *The Golden Keel* garnered favourable press reviews and quickly ascended the bestseller lists. More importantly, it denoted Bagley as an impressive new exponent of the popular post-war thriller genre that had up to that point been dominated by Alistair MacLean and Hammond Innes.

In 1965, Bagley moved to Totnes, Devon, and produced his second novel, *High Citadel*, another well-wrought slice of adventure fiction which describes a plane hijack in the Andes. An immediate bestseller, *High Citadel* cemented Bagley's burgeoning reputation and earned him an army of admirers that expanded exponentially with each subsequent book.

One of the constants in Bagley's fiction was his heroes – seemingly ordinary yet tough, rugged, men who proved extremely resourceful in tight and tricky situations. There was nothing formulaic about Bagley's *oeuvre*, and like most adventure thriller writers of that particular era, he showed a reluctance to reuse characters and be a slave to series formats (though admittedly the security consultant, Max Stafford, in *Flyaway*, published in 1978, made a return appearance in *Windfall*, in 1982).

All sixteen of Bagley's novels are packed with copious background information, the result of diligent and exhaustive research. Despite this, there is nothing arid or academic in the way factual information is conveyed in Bagley's books – in fact, the way he dispenses knowledge is usually illuminating, certainly in relation to foreign countries, their landscapes and their cultures as well as technical lore relating to machinery and weapons. Undoubtedly, Bagley evinced a craftsman's attention to detail in this aspect of his work and was seamlessly able to marry fact with fiction for the greater good of his storytelling. His intimate knowledge of places – both at home and abroad – created some memorable settings and contributed to the creation of atmosphere as well as establishing authenticity and providing local colour. Bagley also explored natural phenomena in great detail, such as extreme weather conditions (*Wyatt's Hurricane*, 1966) and avalanches (*The Snow Tiger*, 1975).

Though stylistically indebted to his illustrious precursors MacLean and Innes (who were one generation older), Bagley asserted his identity early on and became adept at using first-person narratives in the present tense – this is especially evident in the clever cold war yarn *The Tightrope Men* (1973), where the main protagonist, Giles Denison, wakes up in an unfamiliar hotel to discover that his face has been changed using plastic surgery to look like that of another person. Similarly, in *Landslide* (1967), the first-person narrator, Geoff Boyd, a geologist by trade, suffers from amnesia after an accident, and Bagley shows immense skill in conveying his central character's sense of confusion from memory loss.

Although there has been a marked decline in old school adventure thrillers since Bagley's death from a stroke in 1983, in recent times there has been a palpable resurgence of interest in the Cumbrian author's work. After being out of print for many years, some of Bagley's best titles are back on the shelves, a testament to the consistency and sheer quality of his work. *See also* Thrillers: Novels of Action.

Selected Works by the Author
The Golden Keel (1963)
High Citadel (1965)
Wyatt's Hurricane (1966)
The Vivero Letter (1968)
The Spoilers (1969)

Bagley, Desmond

Running Blind (1970)
The Tightrope Men (1973)
The Snow Tiger (1975)
The Enemy (1977)
Windfall (1982)

Charles Waring

Baker, John (b.1942)

John Baker is a writer of noir, strong on characterisation and issues, though
a vein of melancholy humour runs through all his work. He lives and sets most
of his novels in the city of York, known normally for its history, architecture and
year-round throng of tourists. But Baker's York, predictably, reveals a darker side.
His characters are eerily believable and his plots, if sometimes leisurely, draw the
reader in. The earlier books feature the PI Sam Turner, a very British creation,
a reformed (he hopes) alcoholic burdened with a strong social conscience and
colleagues who can be as much a liability as an aid. Like so many fictional PIs,
Turner champions hopeless causes and old rock music – but he still gets his man.
After six books in the Turner series, Baker switched his sombre gaze to the less
glamorous town of Hull, a grim and neglected fishing port on the east coast, and
to a new hero, Stone Lewis.

Baker's image as a private, rather introverted, man, happy to shut himself away up
north in York, is belied by his membership of a crime writers' travelling performance
group, Murder Squad, and by his occasionally taking up the cudgels against unlikely
targets such as second-hand bookshops, whose sales, in Baker's opinion, generate
nothing for authors and publishers while diverting customers and revenues from
more deserving recipients.

Early Sam Turner books, published by Gollancz, include *King of the Streets* (1998),
Poet in the Gutter (1995) and *Death Minus Zero* (1996), all of which earned critical
praise from top national critics such as Ian Ousby and Philip Oakes. His thoughtful
Walking with Ghosts (1999), having a 'master of disguise' villain, could have taken
a comic book approach but instead explored the difference between what the media
reports as having happened in a case and what actually did. *Shooting in the Dark*
(2001) – perhaps his best book – explores voyeurism, blindness and different ways
of seeing the world, while *The Meanest Flood* (2003), set in York at a time when the
river Ouse has reached its highest level, shares its main crime plot with intelligent
writing about magic and dreams and sleight of hand. All of which suggests that
Baker's interests – like those of his fans – spill out far beyond the mere solving
of everyday mysteries.

His first Hull-based novel, *The Chinese Girl* (2000), introduces an ex-convict
hero Stone Lewis, and although again the plot ranges across a flood of social issues –
racism, drugs, gangs and mental illness – the book is resolutely hard-boiled and
dark, though laced with sardonic humour. Racism continues as a theme in *White
Skin Man* (2004), the second Stone Lewis novel, in which Stone confronts a cast
of skinheads, thugs and violent misfits. Nevertheless, as the series develops, it
may be that Stone's flaws, including his near autism, come to be the strongest
theme of all.

Selected Works by the Author
Poet in the Gutter (1995)
King of the Streets (1998)
The Chinese Girl (2000)
Shooting in the Dark (2001)

Russell James

Balchin, Nigel Marlin (1908–1970)

Artful, intelligent and serious, Nigel Balchin's novels of science, ideas and human relationships may be said to come under the umbrella of general crime fiction, even if the fit is not entirely comfortable.

Born in Potterne, Wiltshire, Balchin was educated at Peterhouse, Cambridge, where he graduated in Natural Science. Afterwards, he became a consultant to Rowntree's Sweets, where he conceived the Aero chocolate bar. He contributed to *Punch* magazine under the pseudonym Mark Spade and wrote satirical books about the world of business. Later, he became a screenwriter, and his credits include the bizarre gay subtext pseudo-Western *The Singer Not the Song* (1961).

Balchin married in 1933, and his first novel, *No Sky* (1934), was written on his honeymoon. His 1936 novel, *Lightbody on Liberty*, is a cynical comedy about a respectable shopkeeper who inadvertently breaks the law and discovers that society is neither as free nor as fair as he had previously thought (a theme explored by several crime writers). *Lightbody on Liberty* was never filmed, which is a shame, as its subject matter – surprisingly hard-headed by the standards of 1930s politics – prefigures later comedies of disenchantment such as the Boulting Brothers' *I'm All Right Jack* (1959).

During the Second World War, Balchin worked as a psychologist in the War Office, before becoming Deputy Scientific Advisor to the Army Council. His pre-war writing had achieved little success, but his fourth novel, *Darkness Falls from the Air* (1942), set during the London Blitz, was a critical and commercial hit.

His best-known book, *The Small Back Room*, was published the following year and filmed by Michael Powell in 1948. Its hero, Sammy Rice, is an embittered, crippled weapons scientist, who battles against personal demons as well as the ineptitude and corruption of his workplace. Rice is a prototype of the reluctant, cynical hero in the Graham Greene mould who has come to dominate modern crime fiction. Multi-layered and intelligent, placing the main character's problems against the background of a scientific puzzle, which, in turn, is presented against the background of the war, *The Small Back Room* is a superb portrait of the time.

A Sort of Traitors, similar in structure to *The Small Back Room* but set against the backdrop of the Cold War, appeared in 1949; and then an event occurred that changed Balchin's life and the way he wrote fiction: his marriage ended. His wife fell in love with artist Michael Ayrton, and the Balchins divorced in 1950. Balchin had first explored the theme of the eternal triangle – usually a married couple and the wife's lover – in *Darkness Falls from the Air*, but his fullest exploration of it came in the 1951 novel *A Way through the Wood* (filmed by Julian Fellowes in 2005 as *Separate Lies*). The theme also appears in *A Sort of Traitors* and *Seen Dimly before Dawn* (1962).

Other themes that characterise Balchin's work include psychiatry and the responsibility of the scientist towards society. They are essentially modern in nature, and *The Small Back Room*, at least, deserves a place in the twentieth-century classical canon.

Selected Works by the Author
Lightbody on Liberty (1936)
Darkness Falls from the Air (1942)
The Small Back Room (1943)
Mine Own Executioner (1945)
The Borgia Testament (1948)
A Sort of Traitors (1949; published in the United States as *Who is my Neighbor?*)
The Anatomy of Villainy (non-fiction, 1950)
A Way through the Wood (1951)
The Fall of the Sparrow (1955)
Seen Dimly before Dawn (1962)
In the Absence of Mrs Petersen (1966)

Laura Wilson

Banks, Carla (b.1949)

Carla Banks began writing as Danuta Reah, under which name she produced four novels, all set in and around Sheffield. In 2005, she inaugurated a separate series of books as Carla Banks. She was Chairman of the Crime Writers' Association (CWA) 2005/06, and in 2005, she won the CWA Short Story Dagger for 'No Flies on Frank'.

The sensitive and atmospheric quality of her writing was evident from her first novel, *Only Darkness* (1999), about an after-hours regular train traveller caught in the web of a Yorkshire serial killer. A woman becomes the target for 'The Strangler' because she caught a glimpse of him on his previous kill. This murder had been his fourth young woman; each victim mutilated and strangled and – until this occasion – no

5. Carla Banks.

crime had left a clue. *Only Darkness* builds into an effective and realistic thriller. The heroine is a wilful and independent young woman who lives alone. For work reasons she has to travel home late, regular as clockwork, every Thursday, by the same empty train from the same station where she saw the killer, who, as the police come to realise, uses trains to carry off his victims.

The lonely woman theme is repeated in Reah's later tales, although she is careful to avoid 'woman in peril' clichés. In *Night Angels* (2001), a stalker targets women in Hull and Sheffield; in *Silent Playgrounds* (2000), a six-year-old child gets lost on a lonely path through a park, and her disappearance leads to the death of a young woman; in *Bleak Water* (2002), two women have been murdered on the canal path running close to a bold new art gallery in Sheffield. Unlike most fictional 'women in peril', the young organiser of the exhibition then demonstrates a caution untypical in the genre. She behaves as a real person would – which increases the suspense. Banks creates fear and suspense from patches of shadow beyond the pool of lamplight, from unexpected sounds in the night. Her villains, when they finally appear, are as warped as those in more sensationalist stories.

The first Carla Banks book was *Forest of Souls* (2005), and the second, *Strangers*, came out in 2007. In *Forest of Souls*, a present-day murder links back to war crimes in Eastern Europe during the Second World War, with fascinating trips to Poland, Belarus and Minsk. *Strangers* tackles a topical theme – that of secrets hidden behind the veil – but is set in Saudi Arabia, among the ex-pat community. In this close-knit community, as distances between people grow smaller, the gulf between them widens. From the claustrophobic Sheffield of the Reah books, Carla Banks has expanded into stimulating territory. *See also* Feminist Readings in British Crime Fiction *and* Women Crime Writers.

Selected Works by the Author
Forest of Souls (2005)
Strangers (2007)

As Danuta Reah
Only Darkness (1999)
Silent Playgrounds (2000)
Night Angels (2001)
Bleak Water (2002)

Russell James

Banks, Iain (b.1954)

One of Scotland's most successful and prolific writers, Iain Banks is known mainly for his non-crime fiction – ranging from mainstream literary novels to cult science fiction – but some of his novels concern crime, and in *Complicity* (1993), he produced an authentic, if unconventional, crime novel.

In fact, Banks makes a point of alternating between writing science fiction (under the name Iain M. Banks) one year and moving back into the 'real' world the next although there are often traces of the surreal in his supposedly more mainstream writing.

A case in point is his first novel *The Wasp Factory* (1984), which made his reputation overnight as Scotland's literary *enfant terrible*. Written with the deliberate intention of shocking, it is the first-person narrative of a sixteen-year-old boy called Frank Cauldhame, who lives with his father outside a remote Scottish village.

But Frank is no ordinary teenager: he has his own religion which revolves around the meticulously planned deaths of the eponymous insects and other routine acts of random violence. Yet Frank is as nothing compared to his brother Eric, who has escaped from a mental hospital and whose imminent reappearance is the brooding presence that haunts this strange, fascinating and disturbing book.

Walking on Glass (1985), no longer as highly regarded as some of Banks's other works (perhaps because of the high expectations that followed *The Wasp Factory*), comes the closest to crossing the line into science fiction, in that one paranoid character believes he is an intergalactic warlord imprisoned in a human body, while another character actually is.

The Crow Road (1992), memorably adapted for the BBC and famed for its opening line 'It was the day my grandmother exploded', rotates around the story of a 'perfect murder', and although it is one of Banks's most enjoyable novels, it comes nearer to a fictional biography than to the crime genre.

Complicity, on the other hand, corresponds to the conventional definition of the genre, although to use the word 'conventional' about any of Banks's books is seriously misleading. It features Cameron Colley, a hard-drinking, drug-using, womanising Edinburgh journalist addicted to computer games who becomes involved in the hunt for a serial killer. This is Banks at his most extreme, with gruesome descriptions of the sadistic killings and nigh-pornographic concentration on Colley's other addiction: rough sex. It is a gripping, clever book, very much of its time and place, and sadly much mauled in a 2000 film adaptation.

Dead Air (2002) provoked a storm on publication simply by being one of the first novels to be set on 11 September 2001, and it features the spectacle of the airplanes colliding with Manhattan's World Trade Centre towers as the backdrop to a London Docklands cocktail party. Although he faced accusations of merely using the tragic events of that day as 'spectacular wallpaper', *Dead Air* is a wry, witty and fast-paced book about the clash between individuals and what passes for society, particularly when his hero – a live radio 'shock jock' – gets mixed up with East End mobsters.

Banks has a unique voice in that he seamlessly blends black humour, extreme violence and graphic sex into books that also have literary aspiration. He is the sort of author readers immediately love or hate. *See also* Literature and Crime Fiction; Male Crime Writers *and* Science Fiction and Crime Fiction.

Selected Works by the Author
The Wasp Factory (1984)
The Crow Road (1992)
Complicity (1993)
The Business (1999)
Dead Air (2002)

Peter Millar

Bannister, Jo (b.1951)

Jo Bannister's intelligently written police procedurals are characterised by her strong and resourceful female investigators.

Born on 31 July 1951 in Rochdale, Lancashire, Bannister attended grammar schools in Birmingham, Nottingham and Bangor in Northern Ireland, whereupon she left school at sixteen to work as an office junior on *The County Down Spectator*; fifteen years later, she was its editor. In 1981, she wrote a science fantasy novel called *The Matrix* (coincidental in name only to the 1999 film) but soon moved into the world of crime fiction. She eventually left her newspaper job in 1988 to concentrate fully on the career of writing.

The author of almost thirty novels, Bannister mainly concentrates on writing for series characters, of which she has many. The earliest pairing – doctor-turned mystery writer Clio Rees and Chief Inspector Harry Marsh – made their debut in 1984s *Striving With Gods* (also known as *An Uncertain Death*). Two books followed in 1989, while a much later addition, *The Fifth Cataract*, appeared in 2005.

American photojournalist Mickey Flynn appeared in just two books – *Shards* (1990, also known as *Critical Angle*) and *Death and Other Lovers* (1991) – as did agony aunt and former pathologist Rosie Holland – in *The Primrose Convention* (1997) and *The Primrose Switchback* (1999). More prolific is lone parent researcher Brodie Farrell, who for a small fee offers to locate objects (and, at a pinch, people). Based ostensibly in the fictitious seaside town of Dimmock, the opening novel in this six-book series, *Echoes of Lies* (2001), sees Farrell team up with torture victim Daniel Hood to discover just why he was attacked so viciously. The intricate plot, so typical of the author, was also arguably her darkest, yet probing beneath the veneer of middle-class respectability to explore some truly frightening psychoses.

Hood became a permanent fixture from the second book, *True Witness* (2002). His complex psychological backstory complemented Brodie's more conventional upbringing, with the relationship between the two forming the backbone of this similarly dark tale. The sixth and latest book, *Requiem for a Dealer* (2006), sees a successful showjumper almost killed with a lethal drug overdose.

The seven novels in the Castlemere series, featuring DCI Frank Shapiro, DI Liz Graham and Sergeant Donovan, began with *A Bleeding of Innocents* (1993), detailing an understaffed provincial police force's attempts to tackle a serial killer. The arrival of ambitious career woman Liz Graham sets the cat among the pigeons, but it is not long before her unconventional methods start bringing in results. In the follow-up, *Charisma* (1994), Graham has barely finished unpacking before she has to lead an investigation into the drowning of a local prostitute in the normally quiet dockside town.

Bannister, whose books have achieved a solid readership, currently lives in County Down, Northern Ireland, and lists archaeology and horse riding as hobbies. *See also* Police Procedurals *and* Women Crime Writers.

Selected Works by the Author
Mosaic (1986)
The Going down of the Sun (1989)
Broken Lines (1998)
The Hireling's Tale (1999)
The Primrose Switchback (1999)
Echoes of Lies (2001)
Reflections (2003)
The Depths of Solitude (2004)
The Tinderbox (2006)

Mark Campbell

Banville, John (also known as Benjamin Black) (b.1945)

Like several other writers who are listed in this encyclopaedia, John Banville is first and foremost a literary author who has from time to time strayed into crime fiction to produce a couple of rare masterpieces of the genre.

Born in Wexford and educated at the Christian Brothers' school, Banville worked for Aer Lingus before moving briefly to the United States in 1968–1969. On his return, he became a subeditor at *The Irish Press* and then the literary editor at *The Irish Times* which he left in 1999.

Steeped in a long Irish literary tradition, some of his best books are fictional historical biographies, notably the superb evocations of the lives of two great luminaries of the Late Middle Ages in *Doctor Copernicus* (1976) and *Kepler* (1981).

But it is *The Book of Evidence* (1989) which stakes his first claim to appear here. Shortlisted for Britain's Booker Prize and winner of the Guinness Peat Aviation Award for Emerging Artists, this is a spine-curdling tale told by amoral narrator Freddie Montgomery, a thirty-eight-year-old scientist who murders a servant girl during the theft of a painting.

Banville has spoken of wanting to give his prose 'the kind of denseness and thickness that poetry has', and the book was compared by *Publishers Weekly* to the style of Dostoyevsky and Camus. This means that he is anything but easy reading: Banville demands attention, and if your interest span is short, he is not going to help you. For example, only some seventy pages into *The Book of Evidence* – written by the narrator to explain his crime – do we find out what it is he has actually done.

His narration demonstrates his character: on the one hand, capable of deep feelings for the portrait he has stolen, but on the other, none at all for the woman he has killed. Montgomery's description of his vomiting after the event is one of the most poetic passages in the book.

Ghosts (1993) is the second volume in what was to become the loosely linked 'Frames' trilogy – Banville archly has called them a 'triptych' – of books featuring Montgomery. It is, however, a much less conventionally structured book. Montgomery is now living on a Mediterranean island, otherwise uninhabited except by a dubious art expert and his strange laid back companion when a party of castaways is washed up with disturbing results. The premise owes a lot to Shakespeare's *The Tempest*.

The final volume, *Athena* (1995), also narrated by Montgomery although he has now assumed another name, is set back in Dublin and has the anti-hero now employed in authenticating fake portraits while falling for a girl who happens to resemble the maid he once murdered. As always, what matters to the narrator is not what happens, but the way it should be remembered; in every case, he is 'framing' the truth.

By contrast to the 'Frames' books with their shifting sands of reliability, *The Untouchable* (1997) is a far more conventionally structured book. This is his finest book with a claim to inclusion in the crime genre, not only rich in the black humour that marks his earlier work but also a lot more accessible to the casual reader.

His protagonist Victor Maskell is loosely based on Anthony Blunt, the one-time curator of the royal art collection who was exposed in 1979 as a former Soviet spy, the so-called 'fourth man' to the Cambridge trio of Kim Philby, Guy Burgess and Donald MacLean. As with Montgomery, Maskell – another art connoisseur criminal – is the essential unreliable narrator, concerned only with burnishing the story of his decline and fall. For Maskell, style is everything, reality nothing. Maskell is literally seduced by his Soviet handler, while there are amusing, clever and easily recognisable versions of each of the Cambridge three, as well as a bitchy personification of Graham Greene.

Banville's other work, most notably *The Sea*, which won the Man Booker Prize in 2005, is firmly in the literary mainstream but will quickly seduce those who fall for his particular heady and beautifully crafted prose style.

There will remain many, however, for whom his early historical 'biographical' novels are most accessible and who will find the twisting vagaries of his uniquely unreliable narrators too much like hard work.

Benjamin Black, Banville's alter ego as crime writer, has allowed him to produce several well-turned novels written in a less allusive style. *Christine Falls* (2006) introduced his gloomy pathologist Quirke in a dark, Dublin-set mystery. This book did not immediately win readers over to Banville's new literary identity, but *The Silver Swan* (2007) and *The Lemur* (2008) began to consolidate the achievement of the first Benjamin Black outing. *See also* Literature and Crime Fiction.

Selected Works by the Author
Doctor Copernicus (1976)
The Book of Evidence (1989)
The Untouchable (1997)

As Benjamin Black
Christine Falls (2006)
The Silver Swan (2007)
The Lemur (2008)

Peter Millar

Barnard, Robert (b.1936)

Although never quite having enjoyed the level of recognition that is his due, Robert Barnard is the author of a number of witty, highly enjoyable and quintessentially English detective stories. In 2003, he received the CWA Cartier Diamond Dagger.

Barnard was born on 23 November 1936 in Burnham-on-Crouch, Essex, and educated at Colchester's Royal Grammar School, before graduating from Balliol College, Oxford, with a Bachelor's degree in 1959. A distinguished academic career followed, and it was during his stint as professor of English at Norway's University of Tromsø, the world's northernmost seat of learning, that he wrote his first novel, *Death of an Old Goat* (1974). Concerning the brutal murder of a doddery university lecturer, the book's mixture of black humour and carefully observed details would define much of the author's output.

More humorously slanted detective novels followed, usually featuring academic or upper-class victims, such as *Death on the High C's* (1977) and *Unruly Son* (1978, published in the United States as *Death of a Mystery Writer*). A devotee of Agatha Christie, Barnard's predilection for cosy English country house and village murder mysteries should come as no surprise. *A Little Local Murder* (1976) had a radio documentary spark a grisly murder in the East Anglian village of Twytching, while *The Skeleton in the Grass* (1987) told of a 1930s murder at a country estate finally resolved during the Blitz.

Barnard has created three major series characters. The first was Scotland Yard superintendent Perry Trethowan, whose first case, *Sheer Torture* (1981, also known as *Death by Sheer Torture*), saw him investigate the murder of his father. *The Missing Brontë* (1983) reflected the writer's fascination with Emily Brontë – a subject he returned to in 2000 with a handsomely illustrated biography.

His second protagonist ventured into darker territory. Sharing his name with the infamous Victorian murderer, detective Charlie Peace (together with his boss Mike Oddie) featured in a series of eight provincial murder stories, beginning with *Death and the Chaste Apprentice* in 1989. Over the course of the series, which documented Peace's domestic and professional crises, the character was eventually promoted to a detective inspector.

Writing as Bernard Bastable, the author's third series detective was none other than composer Wolfgang Amadeus Mozart, who in his twilight years had turned an amateur sleuth in a series of three amusing alternative history novels starting with *Dead, Mr Mozart* (1995).

The CWA Cartier Diamond Dagger was awarded in recognition of the versatility of his writing. A former chair of the Brontë Society, Barnard currently lives in Leeds, Yorkshire, where he continues to write. His 1980 Agatha Christie appreciation, *A Talent to Deceive*, is still considered one of the best books on the author who inspired him.

Selected Works by the Author
Death of an Old Goat (1974)
Death on the High C's (1977)
Death in a Cold Climate (1980)
Sheer Torture (1981; published in the United States as *Death by Sheer Torture*)
The Missing Brontë (1983; published in the United States as *The Case of the Missing Brontë*)
Scandal in Belgravia (1991)
No Place of Safety (1997)
Unholy Dying (2000)
A Fall from Grace (2007)

Mark Campbell

Barnes, Julian (b.1946)

Julian Barnes is a highly regarded literary author (three of his novels have been shortlisted for the Booker Prize), who has made a brief but memorable contribution to the crime genre with the Duffy series, written in the 1980s under the pseudonym 'Dan Kavanagh'.

Born in Leicester on 19 January 1946, Barnes was privately educated at the City of London School, before graduating from Magdalen College, Oxford, with a Modern Languages degree in 1968. He worked as a lexicographer for the *Oxford English Dictionary* supplements for three years, after which he became a reviewer and television critic for *New Statesman* and *The Observer*.

His first novel, *Metroland*, was published in March 1980. A coming-of-age drama set in the suburbs of London in the 1960s, it won him much critical acclaim, as well as the prestigious Somerset Maugham Award (a prize he shared that year with Clive Sinclair and A.N. Wilson).

Hot on its heels came a second book, one that Barnes had deliberately written as light relief alongside the arduous process of getting *Metroland* off the ground. *Duffy* (1980) was a tongue-in-cheek detective story about a sexually confused, bisexual ex-policeman whose search for a violent blackmailer takes him into the seedy underworld of London's Soho district. Unlike the author's elegantly written literary works, the Duffy books were characterised by a rough, raw narrative style awash with sex and sleaze, often with a distinctly humorous edge.

Barnes's pseudonym was taken from his partner's surname, literary agent Pat Kavanagh. According to his website, the fictitious author is described as follows:

> Dan Kavanagh was born in County Sligo in 1946. Having devoted his adolescence to truancy, venery and petty theft, he left home at seventeen and signed on as a deckhand on a Liberian tanker. After jumping ship at Montevideo, he roamed across the Americas taking a variety of jobs: he was a steer-wrestler, a waiter-on-roller-skates at a drive-in eatery in Tucson, and a bouncer in a gay bar in San Francisco. He is currently working in London at jobs he declines to specify, and lives in North Islington.

Duffy's next outing was *Fiddle City* in 1981. Set in the customs area of Heathrow Airport, it had Duffy investigating the shadier side of immigration control, revealing many scams that were still in evidence two decades later in Tony Saint's 2004 novel *Refusal Shoes*. *Putting the Boot In* (1985), which tackled the twin 1980s obsessions of football hooliganism and the threat of AIDS, followed Barnes's breakthrough mainstream novel, the Booker-nominated *Flaubert's Parrot* (1984).

Going to the Dogs (1987) was the final Duffy offering, prior to Barnes gaining literary superstar status with his quirky bestseller *A History of the World in 10½ Chapters* (1989). An English country-house murder mystery, the author gleefully twisted the conventions of this most familiar of sub-genres to produce what is probably the funniest and most memorable story in the series.

The four Duffy stories were collected into an omnibus in 1991. *See also* Literature and Crime Fiction.

Selected Works by the Author

As Dan Kavanagh
Duffy (1980)
Fiddle City (1981)
Putting the Boot In (1985)
Going to the Dogs (1987)

Website
www.julianbarnes.com

Mark Campbell

Beat Girl (film, 1960)

(Edmond T. Gréville, director)

'Straight from the fridge' purrs beatnik Tony (Peter McEnery) in approval of the guitar-playing of pack-leader Dave (Adam Faith). This British attempt at a coffee-house

Rebel without a Cause is strong on vintage hipster slang, courtesy of a snappy script from Dail Ambler (a reliable purveyor of **pulp** crime fiction), but is as often hilarious as it is to-the-point, offering a middle-aged take on troubled youth ('go on, get out of it, you jiving, drivelling scum', snarls an irate father) and a delightfully lurid-cosy depiction of the coffee bars and vice dens of Soho. Pouting wild child arts student Jennifer Linden (Gillian Hills, later one of the groupies in *Blowup*) sneaks out at night because her divorced architect father Paul (David Farrar) has brought home a French wife, Nichole (Noelle Adam). Paul is obsessed with building the concrete high-rise city of the future, which Jennifer perceptively thinks would be hideous to live in. Her near-sociopathic rebel streak is really set off by the innocent overtures of her 'French poodle' stepmother, who is exposed as a former prostitute. Jennifer hangs out at the Off Beat Café, with disreputable types like a manic Plaid Shirt (Oliver Reed) and tight-trousered Dodo (Shirley Anne Field), but traipses across the street to Les Girls, a joint run by jailbait-chasing Kenny (Christopher Lee, also a Soho strip-club sharpie in *Too Much to Handle*). It is suggested that the problems of post-war tearaways are due to their emotionally or physically deprived upbringings: upper-crust Tony and working-class Dave compare blitz boyhoods and everyone shrugs at the possible nuclear destruction of the world, but blonde, heavy-eyed Jennifer (Hills was actually *younger* than her screen character) turns out to be a malicious little monster. Simultaneously frigid and an exhibitionist, she nearly gets molested by the Dracula-hands of the club owner – before he ends up being stabbed to death by somebody else (it is possible Jennifer did it, and lets another woman take the blame). A down-to-earth copper sums up the heroine's destructive juvenile angst with 'if it weren't for my pension, I'd wallop her', but she is led off sobbing by just-reconciled Paul and Nichole – with no sense that things will get much better. In a bizarre punchline which recalls the star-in-the-dust finish of *High Noon*, wise voice-of-a-generation Dave – having been abused by some passing Teddy boys – throws his broken guitar into a dustbin and remarks that this is where they are all going. Besides endlessly quotable dialogue ('love, huh? That's just the gimmick that makes sex respectable') and wonderful casting (Nigel Green does a lot with the tiny role of a strip-club choreographer who constantly nags the girls with 'remember, *tease*'), the film offers an outstanding score by the John Barry Seven. Field is awkwardly dubbed for 'It's Legal', her solo number, but her own voice is heard in a superior take on the best-selling soundtrack LP. *Beat Girl* is at once a prurient peek into the lives of chicken-playing, drag-racing, jazz-loving troublemakers and a disenchanted look at the mostly worthless adult world that has let them go to hell. *See also* Film and Crime: Page to Screen *and* Social Comment in Crime Fiction.

Kim Newman

Beaton, M.C. (b.1936)

One of the many pseudonyms of romantic fiction writer Marion Chesney, M.C. Beaton is the author of the mystery series featuring PC Hamish Macbeth (subject of a 1990s television series starring Robert Carlyle) and culinary sleuth Agatha Raisin.

Born Marion McChesney in Glasgow, the author worked as a fiction buyer for a local bookshop before moving into journalism. It was while living as a farmer's wife on a solitary sheep farm in the wilds of Scotland that she turned to fiction writing as a much-needed diversion. Her first book, *Henrietta* (1979), was swiftly followed by a long-running series of Regency romances, which, despite their lurid covers, are highly regarded for their historical accuracy.

In 1985, she wrote her first detective story featuring laid-back bobby PC Hamish Macbeth. Set in the sleepy Scottish Highlands village of Lochdubh, *Death of a Gossip* was a standard whodunit concerning the drowning of a sharp-tongued gossip columnist who left behind a veritable crowd of suspects. Twenty-three books on, the series shows no signs of running out of steam; *Death of a Gentle Lady*, the latest, was published in 2008. A popular BBC Scotland television series of twenty episodes ran from 1995 to 1997, with Robert Carlyle in the title role.

Also as 'M.C. Beaton', Chesney has written a series of comic tales featuring elderly cook Agatha Raisin, a thinly disguised spoof of Christie's Miss Marple. The title of her first case – *Agatha Raisin and the Quiche of Death* (1992) – set the tone for the rest of the series. It has adapted well to radio, starting in 2004, with Penelope Keith in the title role.

A planned Edwardian mystery series, featuring debutant Rose Summer and aristocrat Harry Cathcart, and written under the Marion Chesney by-line, opened with *Snobbery with Violence* in 2003, but was discontinued after four books, with *Our Lady of Pain*, in favour of the author's perennially popular Macbeth and Raisin series. See also Humour and Crime Fiction *and* Scottish Crime Fiction.

Selected Works by the Author
Death of a Gossip (1985)
Death of a Prankster (1992)
Death of a Scriptwriter (1998)
Our Lady of Pain (2006)

Mark Campbell

Beckett, Simon (b.1960)

In a relatively short time, Simon Beckett has established himself as a reliable purveyor of tautly orchestrated, grisly novels that transmute his fascination with violent death into Hitchcockian exercises in suspense. The eight-year hiatus in Sheffield-born Beckett's writing career marked a notable change in direction. His first four novels, published in the 1990s, may be described as dark psychological thrillers. The first two, *Fine Lines* (1994) and *Animals* (1995), are narrated from the point of view of the killer – in both cases a damaged (rather than evil) personality. While the third and fourth, *Where There's Smoke* (1997) and *Owning Jacob* (1998), were arguably more mainstream – his work at this stage was still not easily categorised.

The change came when Beckett, a freelance journalist, was commissioned by *The Daily Telegraph Magazine* to visit the Body Farm in Tennessee, the unique forensic research facility that uses real human cadavers to study decomposition. Struck by the work carried out there, Beckett wanted to incorporate it into a UK setting with a British protagonist. The result was *The Chemistry of Death* (2006), in which one-time forensic anthropologist Dr David Hunter, who is now a rural GP after the death of his

6. Simon Beckett.

wife and daughter, is forced back into his old profession by a series of brutal killings. Drawing on influences as wide-ranging as *Straw Dogs* and *The Silence of the Lambs*, *The Chemistry of Death* – utterly unsparing in its treatment of violence – became an international bestseller, in which the psychological themes of Beckett's earlier work combined with hard-edged forensic detail. But the book's main strength lay in David Hunter, a sympathetic character who – for all his knowledge of the physical realities of death – remains haunted by its essential mystery. The sequel *Written in Bone* (2007) sees Hunter now fully returned to his old profession and called on to investigate an inexplicable fire death on a remote Scottish island. A third novel in the series has a 2009 publication date. *The Chemistry of Death* was shortlisted for the CWA Dagger Awards. It may not have won the award, but Beckett is probably consoled by the fact that the book has been translated into twenty-two languages and has sold over a million copies worldwide.

Selected Works by the Author
Fine Lines (1994)
Animals (1995)
Where There's Smoke (1997)
Owning Jacob (1998)
The Chemistry of Death (2006)
Written in Bone (2007)

Barry Forshaw

Bell, Josephine (1897–1987)

Today, Josephine Bell is primarily remembered for her medical mysteries from the Golden Age of British crime fiction.

Born Doris Bell Collier, she came from a medical family and married a doctor, Norman Ball, in 1923. They ran a general practice in South London until his death in 1936, and though she continued with a new practice in Guildford until 1954, she turned to writing. With her background, it is no surprise that her first book was a medical mystery, *Murder in Hospital* (1937), which introduced two of her regular characters. Dr David Wintringham is a young doctor who often becomes suspicious about deaths and calls in Scotland Yard DI Steven Mitchell. It is Mitchell who always solves the crimes in a methodical manner but usually from clues provided by Wintringham. The two appeared in some fifteen novels, though occasionally Wintringham or Mitchell went it alone. Bell was good at developing characters and situations and sometimes good at developing plots, but not always together. When she got them all right, the books worked exceedingly well, such as *Fall over Cliff* (1938), where beneficiaries of a will meet a series of apparent accidental deaths, and *Death at the Medical Board* (1944), which includes several ways of administering nicotine as a poison. Perhaps the best of the solo Mitchell novels is *The Port of London Murders* (1938), which deals with drug smuggling, an uncommon theme at that time, and contains a fascinating portrayal of the London docks, already then in decline.

Mitchell also appeared in three novels with barrister Claude Warrington-Reeve. These were better plotted though the characters were less attractive. Nevertheless, *Easy Prey* (1959), in which an old lady is accused of murdering a baby, is especially powerful. One of Bell's strengths was in her portrayal of elderly people, especially as she grew older. After Bell retired from her surgery, she penned *Death in Retirement* (1956). An elderly couple retire in *The Upfold Witch* (1964) to a village full of dark secrets. Most poignant is one of her last books, *A Swan-Song Betrayed* (1978), in which a former best-selling novelist returns to write one last book with tragic consequences.

Bell continued to produce occasional medical mysteries throughout her long career, though dropped any series characters. Among her last works were *The Trouble in Hunter Ward* (1976) and *Such a Nice Client* (1977). She wrote a number of non-crime books, among them several historical novels, and though not specifically historical mysteries, crimes do abound, especially in *Jacobean Adventure* (1969), which deals with the Gunpowder Plot.

Bell wrote many crime short stories, mostly for newspapers, several featuring Wintringham and Mitchell, and though a few have appeared in anthologies, none has been collected in book form.

Selected Works by the Author
The Port of London Murders (1938)
Death at Half-Term (1939)
Trouble at Wrekin Farm (1942)
Death at the Medical Board (1944)
Bones in the Barrow (1953)
Easy Prey (1959)

Mike Ashley

Bell, Pauline (b.1938)

Pauline Bell is primarily known for her series of well-turned Yorkshire-based police procedurals featuring DC Benny Mitchell.

Born in Sheffield, she was educated at a county grammar school before taking a degree in English at the University of London in the late 1950s. She married a Lancastrian schoolteacher, had three children and spent the next thirty years in a full-time teaching career working in various schools in Yorkshire. Always an enthusiastic amateur writer, it was not until the late 1980s that she put pen to paper with a professional goal in mind.

That goal she achieved in 1990 owing to the publication of her first novel, *The Dead Do Not Praise*, at the age of fifty-two. Steeped in a world of which Bell had close knowledge, the book was set in a comprehensive school in the fictional town of Cloughton (loosely based on Halifax) and dealt with the fatal bludgeoning of the establishment's unloved harridan of a headmistress, Sarah Bland. Introducing DCI Thomas Browne, Sergeant Jerry Hunter and DC Benny Mitchell, it was the latter character – an ex-pupil of the school who felt obliged to impress his former tutors – who took the lion's share of the action, culminating in a romantic proposal to his boss's daughter Virginia in the closing moments.

Mitchell's domestic life continued in *Feast into Mourning* (1991), in which the discovery of a charred body in the woods disturbs the tranquillity of a church cricket match on the village green. During the course of Mitchell's investigations, he becomes engaged to Virginia, but by the next book he has sought solace in another while Virginia is away studying at Oxford. However, by the time of *Downhill to Death* (1994), Mitchell and Virginia have patched up their differences and are married and have already speedily provided Browne with a grandchild.

To date, Bell has written fourteen novels featuring Mitchell. *Swansong* (2002) is one of her most recent and dramatic work: a famous soprano is found with her throat cut backstage during an amateur production of *Carmen*, in a case that would make Inspector Morse envious (were he alive to see it).

Bell has also written an excellent stand-alone novel about former police officer Zoe Morgan, a Relate marriage counsellor who becomes suspicious of the death of a client's husband in *A Multitude of Sins* (1997). Her intuitive skills coupled with her police training make for a believably rounded character whose investigative skills are inextricably linked to her empathic personality.

Selected Works by the Author
The Dead Do Not Praise (1990)
The Way of a Serpent (1993)
Blood Ties (1998)
Stalker (2000)
A Multitude of Sins (2003)

Mark Campbell

Bentley, E[dmund] C[lerihew] (1875–1956)

E.C. Bentley's reputation in crime writing largely rests on a single novel, *Trent's Last Case* (1913), although it was eventually followed by *Trent's Own Case* (1936), written jointly with H. Warner Allen; a book of collected short stories, *Trent Intervenes* (1938); and a few trifles. This slender output sufficed, however, to give him the presidency of the Detection Club in succession to G.K. Chesterton.

Bentley was a newspaperman, associated particularly with the *Daily News*, then the *Daily Telegraph*. He explained in his autobiography that *Trent's Last Case* was written as an 'exposure', or at least as a parody, of detective stories, in that Trent's carefully reasoned and seemingly absolutely correct reconstruction of the killing of leading financier Sigsbee Manderson is eventually shown to be completely wrong. (Yet, it is possible to see Trent's version as more convincing.) Much to Bentley's surprise, the book was hailed as a classic, and it proved to be influential for several generations after its appearance, primarily for its title character, who spawned a progeny of 'gentlemen detectives', among them Dorothy L. Sayers's Lord Peter Wimsey, Margery Allingham's Albert Campion, Philip Macdonald's Colonel Gethryn (*The Rasp*, published in 1924, remarkably resembles *Trent's Last Case*) and the Scotland Yard detectives Ngaio Marsh's Roderick Alleyn and Josephine Tey's Alan Grant.

Philip Trent may be a gentleman detective, though strictly not an amateur, as he is paid for his journalistic despatches. Being an investigative pressman is not his 'day job', as he is a painter of distinction. He is interested in other arts, notably literature, drama and opera. He gets a wife out of his 'last case' as he marries Manderson's widow; Dorothy Sayers felt that Bentley handled this love interest less perfunctorily than most other crime writers. Yet he does not feel the case reflects much credit on him, and, at the end, having been told the 'truth' by two different characters, he vows it will be his last, hence the title *Trent's Last Case*. It is not, of course, as not only *Trent's Own Case* but at least nine of the twelve cases in *Trent Intervenes* post-date *Trent's Last Case*. *Trent's Own Case* is his 'own' as so many personal friends are significant characters, and an attempt is made, by faked fingerprints, to blame Trent himself for the murder. It is not clear exactly what part co-author H. Warner Allen played in writing the book: Allen wrote detective fiction on his own account and was an expert on wine, which figures briefly in *Trent's Own Case*, which is a well-constructed novel, and some have even preferred it to its predecessor.

And that was it, very nearly, for Bentley's crime fiction. There is the late 1950, rather quirky, *Elephant's Work*, in which an amnesiac is the detective, and a few uncollected short stories of little consequence. (His son Nicolas produced a number of readable thrillers in the post-1945 era, notably *The Floating Dutchman*.)

It may be that few people read *Trent's Last Case* today (it was, incidentally, filmed three times, most recently in the early 1950s), but in its day, it was influential, playing a considerable part in the emerging Golden Age, not only in the personality of its principal detective but in signalling a shift to a situation where the novel, rather than – as had been the case for a generation – the short story, became the dominant form of the detective story.

Selected Works by the Author
Trent's Last Case (1913; published in the United States as *The Woman in Black*)
Trent's Own Case (1936)
The Ministering Angel (1938)
Trent Intervenes (stories, 1938)
Those Days (autobiography, 1940)
Elephant's Work (1950; published in the United States as *The Chill*)

Further Reading
Scowcroft, P.L. 1988. 'Some Thoughts on Trent's Last Case'. *CADS* 9.

Philip Scowcroft

Berkeley, Anthony

See Iles, Francis

The Bill (television series, 1984–)

A police procedural television series devised by writer Geoff McQueen, *The Bill* is one of the longest-running police drama television series in the world, second to *Taggart* in duration, but with considerably more episodes. There are usually two episodes per week, and to date, over 2,300 episodes have been broadcast. The series began on 16 October 1984, developed from a one-off episode called 'Woodentop' in the *Storyboard* series, broadcast on 16 August 1983. After three individual seasons, it has run continually since 19 July 1988.

The series is set at Sun Hill police station in London and follows the day-to-day lives of both the uniformed police officers and the CID. One of the guiding rules of the series, which has only rarely been broken, is that a police officer must be in every scene so that the viewer knows no more than they know. It follows their investigations from beginning to end. Initially each episode was one hour long, but it shrank to a half-hour from 1988 to 1998. The half-hour episodes tended to concentrate on one case or incident, resolved in that episode, but since it has returned to one hour, it has developed multiple storylines running through several episodes, with some story arcs running up to a year. In this respect, *The Bill* has been equated with other television 'soap' series, a charge which became more accurate when Paul Marquess took over as executive producer in 2002. He had previously produced the soap series *Brookside* and his first act on *The Bill* was to wipe out many of the old guard characters in a massive explosion that destroyed part of the station. During his tenure, which ceased in 2005, *The Bill* became more soap orientated, concentrating on the characters' personal lives rather than the cases and this lost *The Bill* some of its following. Recently, the series has returned to focus on strong crime storylines with less emphasis on personal lives.

Although there is a huge turnover in characters with an unnaturally high quota being killed, mostly in the line of duty and some by other police officers, there have also been many long-serving characters. The roles of PC Jim Carver and WPC June Ackland featured in the original 'Woodentop' episode, which focused on Carver's first day at Sun Hill, and continued through to March 2007, and included storylines such as Carver's battles with alcoholism and gambling and Ackland giving her illegitimate child up for adoption and this coming back to haunt her in the shape of psychotic Gabriel Kent who pretends to be her son.

Other characters have proved to be extremely popular including DI Frank Burnside, who had also been in the first episode (as Sergeant Tom Burnside) but who came into his own from 1988 to 1993. Burnside had previously been shown as a corrupt officer, but this was subsequently explained as being due to undercover operations, though his character continued to operate on the shady side of the law and became increasingly violent. His relationship with DS Ted Roach, who had a drink problem, was often explosive. Roach resigned in 1993 and thereafter the Burnside character faded from the series though returned briefly in 1998–2000 and also starred in a short spin-off series, *Burnside* (2000). A similar dark character was the corrupt detective-sergeant Don Beech, who appeared between 1995 and 2000 and who was in the pay of local criminals. When he was rumbled, he killed a fellow officer in a struggle and was thereafter on the run. This resulted in two special *Bill* sub-series, *Beech on the Run* (2000) and *Beech Is Back* (2001), plus a final appearance in 2004 when he escaped from prison.

One other spin-off series was *M.I.T.: Murder Investigation Team* (2003–2005), which included occasional crossover characters. *The Bill* has also undertaken the challenge of broadcasting two-hour-long episodes live. It has often attempted to push boundaries and explore difficult issues, including child abuse, incest and racial issues, even though it is broadcast before the 9 p.m. watershed.

Despite occasional lapses, the series is known for its high-level authenticity and accuracy in reflecting day-to-day police work. During its long run, it has depicted the change in the nature of crimes, the growth in drug-related crimes, the impact of the Internet and the problems of the police in trying to stay the right side of the law when criminals gain the upper hand. It is frequently nominated for awards and won the National Television Award for Most Popular Drama in 2004. *See also* TV Detectives: Small-Screen Adaptations.

Further Reading
Silver, Rachel. 1999. *The Bill: The Inside Story*. HarperCollins.
Tibballs, Geoff. 2004. *The Bill: The Official History of Sun Hill*. Carlton.

Website
www.thebill.com

Mike Ashley

Billingham, Mark (b.1961)

Mark Billingham's Tom Thorne novels have been the most commercially successful police procedurals since John Harvey's Resnick and Ian Rankin's Rebus. They synthesise a number of popular ingredients into pacy narratives whose North London settings are sharply defined, and the breadth of his characters may reflect a sensibility developed in his earlier career as a stand-up comic and actor. Influenced by Michael Connelly's Harry Bosch and Lawrence Block's Matt Scudder, Billingham's Thorne is edgier than most of his British counterparts, with Bosch's gloomy introspection mixed with Scudder's awareness of his shortcomings. The early Thorne novels, especially in their nursery rhyme titles, showed the gothic overtones of John Connolly's Charlie Parker series, lending darker depths to Thorne's investigations. The crimes Thorne investigates are both horrific and often ingenious, appealing to fans of the often gory forensic series, which seem to be the domain of female writers from Patricia Cornwell to Mo Hayder.

In Billingham's hands, none of this seems calculated; rather he has a performer's instinct for delivering the story in the most entertaining way. In fact performing led to his career as a writer. His most notable acting credit was as a regular in the series *Maid Marian and Her Merry Men*, although he was also the first non-puppet to appear in an episode of *Spitting Image*. But he acted in two episodes, which he also wrote, of the television series *Knight School* and then co-wrote a novelisation from the series.

Three years later, the first Thorne novel, *Sleepy Head* (2001), appeared, with Thorne pursuing a serial killer who stages heart attacks in his victims. *Scaredy Cat* (2002) deals with dual killers, while *Lazybones* (2003) finds rapists being murdered after release from prison. *The Burning Girl* (2004) reopened a twenty-year-old case and signalled a move by Thorne into more active conflict with his department, a theme intensified in *Lifeless* (2005), where Thorne goes undercover among the homeless, with Billingham making much of the thin line between their lives and Thorne's. *Buried* (2006) again put Thorne at odds with the force, as he investigates

7. Mark Billingham.

the disappearance of a colleague's son. *Death Message* (2007) opens with Thorne receiving images of a killing on his mobile and pits him again an old adversary and its protégé. The Thorne books have won Billingham the Sherlock and Theakston's awards and have been nominated for five CWA Daggers. His first stand-alone novel, *In the Dark*, appeared in 2008. Built around the topical theme of youth gangs, it deals with the effects of one terrible random act of violence on the lives of three people.

Selected Works by the Author

Tom Thorne Novels
Sleepy Head (2001)
Scaredy Cat (2002)
Lazybones (2003)
The Burning Girl (2004)
Lifeless (2005)
Buried (2006)
Death Message (2007)

Michael Carlson

Bingham, John (also known as Lord Clanmorris) (1908–1988)

In the 1950s and 1960s, John Bingham was regarded as one of the finest authors of spy novels of the period. Combining authenticity with elegant style, his books show a writer of intelligence and wit.

John Michael Ward Bingham was born in York and educated at Cheltenham College. He went to France and Germany to learn the languages before taking up his first job as a reporter on *The Hull Daily Mail* and then moved to London to work as reporter and picture editor for *The Sunday Dispatch*. In 1939, he joined the army but was soon transferred to the intelligence service. He inherited the title 'Seventh Baron Clanmorris' in 1960, by which time he had published several books under the name John Bingham. His work was praised for its psychological insight and the authenticity of its portrayal of police and intelligence procedures, but it was not until later that it became known that he had for many years been a member of MI5. The secrecy prevailing at the time meant that his precise duties there were unknown, but it is now apparent that between 1945 and 1950 he was head of F Division, running deep-cover penetration agents in the communist party.

Bingham made his publishing debut in 1952 with *My Name Is Michael Sibley*, a disquieting psychological suspense novel whose eponymous narrator is a reporter wrongly accused of murder. It was followed a year later by *Five Roundabouts to Heaven*, which H.R.F. Keating in *Crime & Mystery: The 100 Best Books* described as 'lit by flashes of dark humour, a little shocking yet invigoratingly delightful'. The spies in Bingham's books are not glamorous, just ordinary people doing an important, if sometimes routine job. In a foreword to *The Double Agent* (1966), a story about a fairly minor British spy, Bingham asserted that all the characters and events in the book were fictitious. He went on, 'But are they? How can I be sure? How can anyone say for certain what has, or has not, happened in the world of secret agents? I will merely add that if the characters exist, then several of them have my profound sympathy.'

The security services have long provided a training ground for British novelists, among them was the young Bingham's staff, David Cornwell. Bingham encouraged him to write his first novel, *Call for the Dead*, which was eventually published under the name John le Carré. After the considerable success of his novel, le Carré later revealed that Bingham was one of two men who had inspired his character, George Smiley.

Bingham's books are classics of the Cold War period and they stand the test of time. A writer of such quality deserves better than to be remembered principally for inspiring another author's character. *See also* Espionage Fiction *and* Police Procedurals.

Selected Works by the Author
My Name Is Michael Sibley (1952)
Five Roundabouts to Heaven (1953; published in the United States as *The Tender Poisoner*)
Murder Plan Six (1958)
A Fragment of Fear (1965)
The Double Agent (1966)
The Hunting Down of Peter Manuel (non-fiction, 1973) with William Muncie

Susanna Yager

Binyon, T[imothy] J[ohn] (1936–2004)

T.J. Binyon was primarily an academic, producing near the end of his life a prize-winning biography of the Russian poet Pushkin. But he had an abiding passion for crime fiction, and his enthusiasm (and encyclopaedic knowledge) made him a connoisseur of the genre. He was influential too, both as a newspaper reviewer and as an academic. Binyon produced an authoritative overview of detective fiction in *Murder Will Out* (1989) and he helped to set up the Fulbright/Raymond Chandler Visiting Fellowships, which brought established crime writers from the United States to Oxford during the 1990s.

Binyon was born in Leeds. He was educated at a grammar school in Skipton and Exeter College, Oxford, where he read Russian and German. Before that Binyon's interest in Russian had been stimulated when, as part of his National Service, he had been posted to the Joint Services School of Linguists at Bodmin, where he became friends with other embryonic writers such as Michael Frayn and Alan Bennett and where weekly tests ensured that they could reel off the names of tank and submarine parts in the language of the Cold War adversary. Binyon went on to teach Russian at Leeds University before returning to Oxford and held a fellowship at Wadham College from 1968 until his retirement in 2003. At the time of his unexpected death in 2004, Binyon was working on a biography of Lermontov.

Binyon produced two thrillers, which reflect not only his allegiance to the mystery/thriller format but also his linguistic and academic pursuits. The first was *Swan Song* (1982). The novel recreates the old, pre-Gorbachev Soviet Union and undoubtedly has its origins in the period in 1958 which Binyon spent at Moscow University perfecting his Russian. (It may be significant that he apparently never returned to the country.) Among the thrillers of the era, *Swan Song* is distinctive in being set entirely in Russia – or, rather, the USSR – and being told from the non-Western point of view of Vanya Morozov, a Moscow lecturer in English literature. Vanya is pressured by an old friend, now a rising star in the KGB, to investigate the involvement of a mutual girl friend with a religious revival movement and a dangerously charismatic Rasputin-like figure. The Moscow and Leningrad settings were unusual territory for a Cold War thriller as were the first-person, insider's perspective as well as the lightly worn knowledge of the Soviet system and Russian culture (a key part of the novel relates to an opera by Mussorgsky). There are only a couple of Western characters in *Swan Song*, both secret agents, and the book has an attitude towards the Communist world which is slightly reminiscent of Len Deighton's early books, both cynical and accepting.

Binyon's other thriller also exploited a neglected corner of the East–West struggle in exploring a lost episode from Balkan history. At the beginning of *Greek Gifts* (1988), Sir Henry Pewsey, soldier, historian and head of an Oxford college, commits suicide. At first, it seems he feared exposure as a Blunt-type spy or the scandal surrounding rumours that he might have stolen gold intended for Greek partisans during the Second World War. Pewsey's son-in-law, David Burnsall, is caught up in the search for the real motive for the suicide, which turns on the *pedomazoma* (or 'gathering-up of the children'), an authentic historical tragedy of the late 1940s when the communists forcibly removed Greek children to Yugoslavia and other socialist states. *Greek Gifts* is populated with renegade and sinister Greeks and Albanians, but perhaps the most plausible villain is a glib, unscrupulous Oxford historian on the lookout for scandal and revisionist readings of history. Among the sometimes Buchanesque goings-on and the references to *Treasure Island*, this character is a reminder of Binyon's dry, satirical touch.

Both *Swan Song* and *Greek Gifts* are Cold War offshoots, focusing on generally overlooked locales and scenarios. Binyon showed some prescience in each novel. *Swan Song* referred to the growing power of the Muslim minorities in the Soviet territories and more generally illustrated the continuing influence of religious belief in Russia, while *Greek Gifts* showed foresight about the separatist Albanian movement in Kosovo and the fragile ties which held Yugoslavia together. Yet for all their historical/political realism, the two thrillers provide a healthy dollop of action and a touch of sex.

Binyon's most substantial contribution to crime writing came in the form of his study *Murder Will Out: The Detective in Fiction*. This is a straightforward account of the development of the detective in all his and her shapes and sizes. Binyon has no particular line to push, and the book is, fortunately, not weighed down with cultural theorising or sociology. Rather, it works as a catalogue history organised under chapter headings such as 'The Professional Amateur' and 'The Police'. But it is in the subsections that the breadth of Binyon's reading is really evident. What other crime reference book subdivides its coverage of police detectives into 'younger', 'more cultured' and 'peripheral', among others? Similarly, when you require a run-down blind detectives in fiction or accountants as investigators, then *Murder Will Out* provides the information. If the range is striking (several hundred authors and many more titles are listed in the index), Binyon's judgements are crisp and sensible whether he is commenting on individual authors or on trends in fiction. As an example, he says of the distinction between the amateur detective and the amateur policeman (the kind, perhaps, who writes poetry in his spare time): 'But whereas it is the situation of the amateur detective which fails to convince, with the amateur policeman it is the implausibility of his character' (*Murder Will Out*, p.91).

Binyon does not make overblown claims for the crime genre, identifying Edgar Allan Poe as the only 'literary genius' to have produced detective stories, but there is evidence in *Murder Will Out*, as in his sadly small fictional output, of an infectious enjoyment and an almost daunting knowledge of the field.

Selected Works by the Author
Swan Song (1982)
Greek Gifts (1988)
Murder Will Out (1989)

Philip Gooden

Blake, Nicholas (1904–1972)

Nicholas Blake was the pseudonym of Cecil Day-Lewis, who was Poet Laureate from 1968 until his death in 1972, aged sixty-eight. He had an illustrious career both as an academic and as a literary figure, producing many collections of poetry, critical works, translations and novels under his own name. Meanwhile, he wrote mysteries, and as a crime writer, he published twenty-one novels, sixteen of which featured his hero Nigel Strangeways.

Though clearly a literary writer, Blake took care not to burden his crime stories with too many literary or poetic devices. So successful was he in achieving this objective that in the 1930s he was for a while considered Britain's leading male crime writer.

Blake was born (as Lewis) at Ballintubbert, Queen's County (now County Laois), Ireland, to a Protestant clergyman. After his mother's death, his father brought him up in London. He went to Oxford (Wadham College) in 1927, where he became part of the Marxist circle that revolved around W.H. Auden. Soon recognised as a promising poet, Lewis's first collection of poems, *Beechen Virgil*, appeared in 1925, and two years later, he helped Auden edit *Oxford Poetry*. But poetry seldom pays. So in 1935, he decided to supplement his income by writing a detective novel, the first Strangeways novel, *A Question of Proof*. It was almost an immediate success.

Blake produced a crime novel every year until 1940, when the restrictions of wartime publishing enforced a pause. His crime books resumed in 1947 with *Minute for Murder* and continued with a book roughly every two years until 1966, when he produced the final in the series, *The Morning after Death*. One other (non-Strangeways) title came out during the war: *The Case of the Abominable Snowman* (also known as *The Corpse in the Snowman*) which was published in 1941.

Blake's crime novels are rooted in the Golden Age before the war, and his attractive amateur detective Strangeways tackles the kind of baffling mysteries which delighted many readers who turn to mysteries for their puzzle element above all. But Blake took care not to aim his books specifically at Oxford dons who liked nothing more than to tax their brains with a good mystery; instead he adhered to the unwritten rules of successful crime stories (nothing crass, nothing overly intellectual). Nevertheless, his books, especially the early titles, are scattered with literary references to amuse educated readers. Indeed, his second book, *Thou Shell of Death* (1936), is a twentieth-century reworking of the Jacobean tragedy by Cyril Tourneur, *The Revenger's Tragedy*, though one does not need to know the play to enjoy the book.

Strangeways, too, is a product of the Golden Age. A gifted amateur, he, like his creator, is an Oxford graduate and a left-wing poet and is tall, good-looking and very well connected. His face, wrote Blake, 'gave him a resemblance to an overgrown prep schoolboy'. He had blue eyes. 'His gestures were nervous and a little uncouth; a lock of sandy coloured hair dropping over his forehead.' (Both quotes are from *Thou Shell of Death*.) Conveniently for the tales, he had contacts with the top investigators of Scotland Yard and the Secret Service, and he was not a gung-ho boys' story adventurer. These were puzzle stories, and his high-level contacts existed either to supply otherwise unobtainable snippets of information or to deliver the retribution that was beyond the scope of a well-behaved amateur detective. He existed in a real-time world, dominated by the Second World War. He married a dashing young explorer, Georgia Cavendish, whom, to the horror of many fans, Nicholas Blake allowed to die, but this meant that Strangeways could continue after the war as an attractive and perhaps available widower. He aged with the times he lived in and became less impulsive and idealistic as he grew older.

Blake's stories came from the real world. In one of his earliest novels, *The Beast Must Die* (1938), a distraught father (who, interestingly, is a crime writer) seeks revenge on the hit-and-run driver who killed his young son. Outside the Strangeways series, in *A Tangled Web*, a cat burglar and his girlfriend find themselves 'tangled' in an investigation into a murdered Brighton policeman. One of Blake's finest books,

The Private Wound (1968), while it becomes a mystery, begins as a drama of love and deception and goes on to deliver a penetrating study of the long-running problems of a divided Ireland. (It is set in 1939.)

Given the success he achieved as a crime writer, it is remarkable that in parallel he was a poet of such quality that he became Poet Laureate. But he was a practising and equally successful poet all his life. Indeed, it is as a poet that he saw himself principally. During the war, he worked at the Ministry of Information as an editor in the publication department, and when war ended, he joined the firm Chatto & Windus as a director and senior editor. Under his name, he also wrote two children's books, of which *The Otterbury Incident* (1948) is the best known (not only for its Edward Ardizzone illustrations). He was professor of poetry at Oxford in 1951–1956 and a lecturer in the 1950s and 1960s at several universities. He was chairman of the Arts Council Literature Panel, vice-president of the Royal Society of Literature, honorary member of the American Academy and member of the Irish Academy of Letters. In 1951, he married the actress Jill Balcon, with whom he lived in Greenwich. He had four children, one of whom is the actor Daniel Day-Lewis. *See also* Literature and Crime Fiction.

Selected Works by the Author

Nigel Strangeways Series
A Question of Proof (1935)
Thou Shell of Death (1936; published in the United States as *Shell of Death*)
The Beast Must Die (1938)
End of Chapter (1957)
The Worm of Death (1961)

Other Titles
The Case of the Abominable Snowman (1941; published in the United States as *The Corpse in the Snowman*)
A Tangled Web (1956; published in the United States as *Death and Daisy Bland*)
The Private Wound (1968)

Russell James

Blake, Sexton

To many, he was 'the office boy's Sherlock Holmes' or 'the *other* Baker Street detective', but a saga of over 3,800 individual cases and 150 million words cannot be so easily summarised in five simple words. Dorothy L. Sayers was rather more eloquent when, in her introduction to *The Omnibus of Crime*, she claimed that Sexton Blake's stories 'present the nearest modern approach to a national folk-lore'.

'Sexton Blake belonged to the new order of detectives,' revealed Harry Blyth in the opening paragraphs of 'The Missing Millionaire' (*Halfpenny Marvel 6*, 13 December 1893), which marked Blake's debut in print, and from that early remark, it can be seen that Blake was intended to be a modern, up-to-date crime-fighter. 'He possessed a highly-cultivated mind which helped to support his active courage. His refined, clean-shaven face readily lent itself to any disguise, and his mobile features assisted to clinch any facial illusion he desired to produce.'

The 'new order of detectives' was then a recent creation, although the model for the ingenious detective, C. Auguste Dupin, was over fifty years old, dating back to 1841 when Edgar Allan Poe had laid down the fundamentals of the detective story in 'The Murders in the Rue Morgue'.

While Poe is rightly recognised as the father of the detective story, it was Arthur Conan Doyle who proved the greater influence by far. A direct line can be drawn from Sherlock Holmes to most detective fiction whether it was an effort to emulate Doyle's creation or somehow invert it. Holmes's appearance in *The Strand* truly launched the detective into fiction, although it was his *disappearance* from that magazine in December 1893 – released in the last week of November – that gave the impetus for a great many rivals to appear.

8. Cover of *The Sexton Blake Library.*

Blake debuted only two weeks after Holmes plunged to his apparent death in the fearful torrent of the Reichenbach Falls, and there is a certain satisfaction in linking two of the most famous detectives the world has seen. His first recorded case is 'The Missing Millionaire'. He is already a successful detective with a staffed office – albeit a grimy one with an unfashionable address at the Inns of Chancery.

It is clear that Blake's author set out deliberately to create a character who was emphatically not a copy of Sherlock Holmes. Indeed, the similarities between the two were, at first, only fleeting and sharing a talent for disguise. It was only his later chroniclers who added more Holmesian characteristics and, in 1904, set Blake up with a practice in Baker Street.

The story of Blake's creation has been the subject of some confusion in the past as for many years it was believed that his first appearance was in 'Sexton Blake, Detective', in the second issue of *Union Jack* (4 May 1894); the fact that this was actually Blake's fourth appearance only became widely known to fans of the saga in the 1940s and the error was still being perpetuated outside fan circles as late as 1968.

Blake's creator was a forty-year-old Scotsman named Harry Blyth. For seven years he had published a penny paper called *Chiel* ('The Chick'), subtitled the 'Scottish Punch', but this folded in January 1890 when the financial backer dropped out.

Always on the brink of financial trouble, Blyth, his wife and young son, nicknamed 'wee Harry', moved to Peckham Rye, a suburb of London south of the Thames popular with visitors thanks to the common.

Joseph Hatton, playwright, novelist and former editor of *The Gentleman's Magazine*, was for twenty years the author of a regular column for *The People* entitled 'Cigarette Papers', which was syndicated to many journals. Hatton dropped out or was otherwise indisposed, and *The People* commissioned Blyth to fill that column each Sunday; his subject was the undiscovered crime of London.

Somers J. Summers, the youthful editor of Harmsworth's new paper *The Halfpenny Marvel*, launched in November 1893, knew precisely what his young readers wanted, and the early numbers featured stories of high adventure with titles such as 'Dead Man's Land', 'The Gold Fiend', 'The Slave King' and 'The Black Pirate'. 'If you see your children reading "penny dreadfuls" take them away and give them the *Halfpenny Marvel*,' Summers wrote – but to many parents, the *Marvel* and the companion papers which soon joined it, *Union Jack* and *Pluck*, were precisely the kind of 'blood and thunders' they wanted their children to avoid whether they claimed to run 'only pure, healthy stories' or not.

The *Marvel* was quickly established and the *Union Jack* was launched within a few months. By the summer of 1894, both papers were selling around 150,000 copies a week and Blake can claim to have had a big part in that success. Under the pen-name Hal Meredith, Blyth's first Blake yarn had appeared in issue 6 of *Marvel*, followed a week later by 'A Christmas Crime: The Mystery of "the Black Grange" ' in issue 7 (20 December 1893) and then 'The Golden Ghost' in issue 11 (17 January 1894). By then, plans for *Union Jack* were probably well advanced and it may have been felt that this new detective character would help the paper off to a good start: Blake made his *Union Jack* debut in issue 2 with 'Sexton Blake – Detective: The Story of a Great Mystery' (4 May 1894).

But after this racing start, Blyth penned only two more Blake stories ('Sexton Blake's Peril', *Halfpenny Marvel 33*, 30 June 1894, and 'Sexton Blake's Triumph!', *Union Jack 15*, 4 August 1894), before bowing out.

Why he should do this is not known, although an educated guess would be the low rates that Harmsworth was paying. 'Harmsworth's price for the copyright of those tales about 25,000 or 30,000 words, was somewhere about 7 or 8 guineas,' recalled 'wee Harry' many years later. Records showed that the first Blake story for *Halfpenny Marvel* had earned its author the princely sum of 9 guineas – 10 shillings per thousand words – for all rights.

At the end of each story, the villain – always recognisable from the moment he takes the stage – is killed: dropped 40 feet into a turbulent stream in a gig and drowned, gored to death by a loose bull or by mistaking a blackened skylight for firm slates while making a rooftop escape. While coincidence plays a major role in Blyth's stories, they are reasonably well told and have occasional touches of humour. ('It is surmised that she is either in England or America,' Blake is told of someone he is trying to trace. 'A very wide address,' he responds with a smile.)

Although Blake was Blyth's creation, his portrayal of Blake was nothing special and brought nothing new to the art of detection. What the Blake stories did have was plenty of action; they were long stories which allowed Blyth to move his characters through a number of different locations as the story progressed towards its climax. At the same time, the story was complete in itself which meant not only a satisfying lengthy read but a beginning, middle and end.

Blake, Sexton

One seeming innovation of Blyth's was the pairing up of two detectives – Blake and Gervaise – who were in partnership, occasionally working solo and occasionally as a team. The Blake/Gervaise team may predate the appearance of four stories featuring Kala Persad, an elderly Indian detective, and his young British partner Mark Poignand. These stories by Headon Hill were published in book form as *The Divinations of Kala Persad* in 1895; it is likely that the stories had a prior magazine appearance but where and when is unknown.

The other, and more important, aspect of Blyth's creation of the character was in his naming. It is well known that Arthur Conan Doyle had earlier toyed with other names – Sherrinford Holmes, Sheridan Hope, and so on – before settling on Sherlock Holmes. One wonders what inspired Blyth to construct such a name. Blake was a common surname, but its use with the uncommon Sexton created an unusual, eye-catching combination, albeit not a unique one as a number of Sexton Blake's have existed in real life, including one at the time of the detective's debut, an official by that name working for the Inland Revenue in Holborn.

According to Harry Blyth Jr, 'He had two titles for the hero of this series, [Sexton Blake] and Gideon Barr. When asked which I liked the better, I hesitated, and my father got impatient – he'd a touch of gout at the time – and I blurted out "Sexton Blake", and so it was.' (Gideon Barr subsequently appeared in a later Blyth story in 1895.)

Whether this is the definitive answer to how Blake came to be named has been argued down the years. Blake expert Bill Lofts once quoted William H. Maas as saying that 'the original intention was to call the detective Frank Blake, but somehow the first name did not seem "lurid" enough, and so either Somers J. Summers or even possibly Alfred J. Harmsworth changed this to "Sexton" Blake, which sounded so much better.'

Both stories have a ring of myth about them; although in Blyth's favour, it would be odd to have two characters with the same name appearing within a line (the opening of 'The Missing Millionaire' would have been ' "Mr Frank Ellaby wishes to see you, sir". "Good!" exclaimed Mr Frank Blake'), and there are many other examples of Blyth's abilities to dream up evocative names: 'The Missing Millionaire' features Calder Dulk, Dr Tuppy, Madame Vulpino, Leon Polti, Nizza Polti; 'Sexton Blake, Detective' included Fenton Joyce and his daughter Ninian, Joe Tax, Gaspard Sellars; 'Sexton Blake's Triumph!' was over the evil lawyer Jabez Forge.

Whatever the truth, most critics believe Blake was well named. But well named or not, Blyth's Blake lasted for only six stories. Given that the lead-in time for a magazine was around six weeks and Harmsworth was notorious for giving his editors almost impossible deadlines when it came to launching a new title, it seems unlikely that Blyth was interviewed any earlier than September 1893, so Sexton Blake could easily have been conceived, lived out his brief but exciting life and had the door closed on his career all within twelve months.

Thankfully, that was not to be, although his creator was never to see Blake at his peak. Blyth died of typhoid fever in February 1898, aged only forty-six, leaving his wife and teenage son penniless.

The tales of Blake had been chronicled in the *Union Jack* since 1894, appearing on a weekly basis since 1905, but the appetite for his adventures were such that, in 1915, William H. Back, the senior editor at Amalgamated Press for story-papers and comics, decided to introduce *The Sexton Blake Library* which provided one long novel of 40,000–50,000 words each month. He used the same team of writers, who now had more space to create ever more bizarre and novel crimes, villains and escapades for the indefatigable and seemingly indestructible Blake. The *Library* proved so popular that it soon shifted to two issues a month and subsequently three. By 1927, it was appearing weekly and effectively superseded the stories in *Union Jack* which, by 1933, had been refurbished as the more general crime magazine *Detective Weekly*.

Back saw the *Library* through its early issues and then left the guiding hand to William Home-Gall, assisted by Leonard Pratt. Pratt assumed full editorship in 1921 and remained there until 1955. The *Library* went through a number of 'series', each change meaning its numbering reverted to no.1, though the changes were usually only in the format or cover price. There was no break in continuity from the first issue in September 1915 until June 1963 when the fourth series issue no.526 brought the run to a close after 1,652 numbers.

During the peak of Blake's popularity in the mid-1920s to mid-1930s, there were over a hundred novellas and novels appearing each year. This required a regular team of writers which could include ten or more all working at any one time. The leading authors included G.H. Teed, Andrew Murray, Edwy Searles Brooks and William Murray Graydon at the outset, plus R. Coutts Armour, Robert Murray Graydon, Anthony Skene, Gwyn Evans, John Hunter and Rex Hardinge in the 1920s and 1930s. A few surprising names appear among the roll of honour including John Creasey, Barry Perowne and Edgar Wallace's son, Brian.

The *Library* continued unabated during the war, paper rationing not even denting the series, but eventually in July 1947, it slimmed from ninety-six to sixty-four pages and seemed to be on a downward spiral with none of the old super villains to tax Blake's mind and body. Leonard Pratt retired in 1955, aged sixty-five, and after a brief period under acting editor David Roberts, the series was taken over by W. Howard Baker. He breathed new energy into it, moving Blake out of Baker Street into plush new offices in Berkeley Square and acquiring a female secretary. The storylines and artwork became sexier and the tone closer to American gangster novels than traditional British derring-do. In effect, *The Sexton Blake Library* was restyled for adults rather than for juveniles. Several of the old guard writers continued, for a while, but new writers were drafted in including Jack Trevor Story, George Mann (Arthur MacLean), Wilfred McNeilly, V.J. Hanson, Stephen Frances and Michael Moorcock. In this guise, the *Library* continued for another eight years. To all intents, it was set to rest in June 1963 with the novella 'The Last Tiger' (in recognition of the first issue's title, 'The Yellow Tiger'), written by Baker. However, Baker revived the series one last time in February 1965, and now it is published by Mayflower Books as a standard paperback edition. It ran for a further forty-five books until October 1968, and with its final novel, *Down Among the Ad Men* by W.A. Ballinger (McNeilly), the Blake saga concluded.

Further Reading

Adrian, Jack. 1986. *Sexton Blake Wins*. Dent.
Hodder, Mark. 2006. 'The Sexton Blake Bibliography'. http://www.sextonblake.co.uk/blakebibliography.html.
Holland, Steve. 1994. 'The Case of the Perplexing Pen-Names' (an index to the 3rd and 5th series of the Sexton Blake Library and a Guide to their Authors). *CADS* Supplement 3.
Packman, Leonard. 1965. *Sexton Blake Catalogue*. Sexton Blake Circle.

Steve Holland and Mike Ashley

Blake, Victoria (b.1963)

The author of an Oxford-based crime series featuring the likeable PI Sam Falconer, Victoria Blake originally trained as a solicitor before settling on a career in bookselling.

9. Victoria Blake.

Blake was born in Oxford on 18 November 1963. Her mother was a huge crime fan, so Blake grew up on writers such as Agatha Christie, Dorothy Sayers and Alistair MacLean. She studied history at Lady Margaret Hall on the river Cherwell (alumni including Antonia Fraser and Lindsey Davis) and then law at Lancaster Gate's College of Law. She qualified as a solicitor after working in the property department of a law firm but found that a career at the Bar did not interest her, so instead took a warehouse job at an independent literary publisher Gerald Duckworth. After several years packing books, she was promoted to the sales department, but on the death of her mother, she left the company and decided to make a career of writing.

Sharing with a cameraman, a Tai Chi instructor, an actress and a feral cat, Blake moved into a housing association property and tried to write that difficult first book. But having failed to find an agent or a publisher, she returned to the book trade and took up a part-time job at the Silver Moon Women's Bookshop on Charing Cross Road. Eight years after she first started writing, her debut novel, *Bloodless Shadow*, finally saw the light of day in 2003.

The novel introduced four times world judo champion Samantha Falconer, now running Gentle Way Investigations in Putney. When she is asked to return to her old stamping ground of Oxford in search of a missing woman, she finds herself facing old ghosts among the dreaming spires – this quiet world of academia was the place she discovered the body of a four-year-old girl, her first big case, and the memory of it still haunts her. As she reluctantly investigates the disappearance, her private life becomes intractably linked to the trail of clues – culminating in a letter claiming to be written by her long-dead father.

Bloodless Shadows made for a promising debut, with the tough, yet unapologetically feminine, Sam Falconer reflecting the author's love of sport and the works of Dashiell Hammett (the name is a jokey reference to Sam Spade and *The Maltese Falcon*). Blake's second novel, *Cutting Blades* (2005), is set in the outwardly sedate world of university rowing; an unlikely backdrop for a brutal murder, but perfect for the author's purposes, brought to life in vivid detail. Investigating the disappearance of a gifted Oxford University rower during a cold, wintry January, Sam finds the sport is every bit as competitive as any other – in this case, fatally so.

With four books under her belt so far, the author shows no sign of penning stand-alone novels, although at the time of writing she is working on biographies of true-life killers Florence Maybrick and Ruth Ellis. *See also* Academe, Death in.

Selected Works by the Author
Bloodless Shadow (2003)
Cutting Blades (2005)
Skin and Blister (2006)
Jumping the Cracks (2007)

Mark Campbell

Blincoe, Nicholas (b.1965)

Generally regarded as being in the vanguard of British 'New Wave' crime writers, this Lancashire-born author made a name for himself in the late 1990s with a series of original, well-wrought novels steeped in popular culture and the idioms of street slang. A native of Rochdale, Nicholas Blincoe went to Middlesex Polytechnic to study art before a career in hip-hop music diverted his attention. He then recorded for the now-defunct Manchester-based Factory Records in 1987 but later returned to an academic life when he attended Warwick University, where he graduated in contemporary European philosophy (in 1993, he successfully acquired a doctorate in the same subject). His acquaintance with the seedier aspect of the music business and Manchester's drug-fuelled club culture provided the background to his debut novel, *Acid Casuals* (1995), which garnered rave reviews for its bizarre story of a transsexual called Estela intent on murdering her money-laundering low-life boss. An outrageous mélange of tenebrous comedy with lashings of gangland violence, backstreet sleaze and lubricious sex thrown in, it established Blincoe as a vital new voice in British crime fiction.

Two years later, Blincoe's second book, *Jello Salad*, raised the ante even further. Featuring a motley assortment of larger-than-life characters, a slew of illegal substances and peppered with an unremittingly dark humour, it is an oddball tale set in Soho about a gangster's wife who finances a restaurant with money she filched from her husband. With *Manchester Slingback* (1998), Blincoe switched his attention back to the north-west and produced a crackerjack crime caper that portrayed a sleazy, morally suffocating world of dope, sex, violence and petty crime. Layer by layer, this gripping tale of redemption and payback unravelled a sordid, often harrowing narrative that revolved around the thorny subject of ritual sexual

10. Nicholas Blincoe.

abuse. The book resulted in Blincoe being awarded a Crime Writers' Association Silver Dagger.

Dope Priest, a turbo-charged yarn about drug smugglers in the Middle East, followed in 1999, while *White Mice* (2002) focused on the decadence and intrigue lying beneath the glamorous facade of the *haute couture* fashion world. Blincoe's *Burning Paris* (2004) represented a marked departure in terms of subject matter – it is, in fact, a nineteenth-century historical novel that focuses on a romantic entanglement between the two main protagonists against the backcloth of the siege and fall of the Paris Commune in 1870. Besides being a novelist, Blincoe has also been a journalist, screenwriter and broadcaster. In the early 1990s, he was a critic for the short-lived magazine *Modern Review*, working alongside its editors Julie Burchill and Toby Young. For several years, he was also a columnist at the *Daily Telegraph* and wrote episodes of the television series *Gold Plated* for Channel Four and the BBC crime thriller, *Waking the Dead*. In addition, Blincoe co-edited *All Hail the New Puritans*, a prose anthology showcasing the key writers of the New Puritan literary movement, which he co-founded.

Boasting a high-octane prose style and armed with a hyper-vivid imagination and mordant sense of irony, Blincoe is undoubtedly one of the most memorable young British crime writers to have emerged in recent years. *See also* Humour and Crime Fiction.

Selected Works by the Author
Acid Casuals (1995)
Jello Salad (1997)
Manchester Slingback (1998)
The Dope Priest (1999)
White Mice (2002)
Burning Paris (2004)

Charles Waring

Bond, James

See Fleming, Ian

Bonfiglioli, Kyril (1928–1985)

Crime fiction, like other branches of literature, has its maverick writers, and Kyril Bonfiglioli was an outstanding example of the category. It was not so much the subject matter of his books or the profession of his hero-narrator which caught the attention since art scams and general skulduggery have always been popular, for example in Jonathan Gash's Lovejoy series. No one else, however, has provided quite the stylised exuberance and absurd tone of Bonfiglioli's novels featuring Charlie Mortdecai.

Bonfiglioli was born in 1928, the son of an Italo-Slovene immigrant who was an antiquarian book-dealer. After service in the army (where he was a sabre champion), he read English as a mature student at Balliol College, Oxford. Later he started dealing in art, as well as editing the magazine *Science Fantasy* and its successor *Impulse*. Having made a killing in the art field, he was able to retire and start a new life as a crime novelist, although Bonfiglioli's somewhat rackety life did not really allow anything so structured as a career. In the years between *Don't Point That Thing at Me* (1972), which won the John Creasey Memorial Dagger for the best first crime novel, and his death from cirrhosis in 1985, Bonfiglioli produced almost four further novels, although his final decade was dogged by poverty and alcoholism.

Mortdecai is described by his creator as 'portly, dissolute, immoral', with a liking for 'art and money and dirty jokes and drink'. If not an idealised version of Bonfiglioli, he is certainly a projection of his creator. At the beginning of *Don't Point*, Mortdecai is burning the frame of a Goya painting which has been stolen to order. (In a more orthodox novel, the theft would have come later.) A totally implausible web of events then ensnares Mortdecai with the Texan tycoon who has commissioned the theft; various murderous secret agencies of the British and US governments; the tycoon's sexy wife Johanna, already a widow by the time Mortdecai arrives on the scene; and Jock, a thuggish sort of anti-Jeeves to Mortdecai's louche Wooster.

Chronologically, the next Mortdecai novel is *After You with the Pistol* (1979), takes up where *Don't Point* leaves off – although the bleak, resigned ending suggested that Bonfiglioli had not initially planned a sequel. Mortdecai is married to Johanna and gets caught up in a drug-running plot. Also thrown into the mix are an assassination attempt on the queen, suspicions of white-slaving, a Bond-style training college which tutors women in violence and subversion, and so on. The third novel in the sequence, *Something Nasty in the Woodshed* (1976), is set in Jersey, where Bonfiglioli lived for a time, and seems to be loosely based on the real-life case of the Beast of Jersey. This time Mortdecai is involved in tracking down a rapist. There are overtones of Satanism – a defrocked priest dies during an attempted black mass – and the rapist turns out to be Mortdecai's friend and neighbour. For all its jaunty grimness, *Something Nasty* has a sourer edge than Bonfiglioli's other novels. The fourth novel, *The Great Mortdecai Moustache Mystery* (1999), was one chapter short at the time of Bonfiglioli's death and was finished by the parodist and satirist Craig Brown. Characteristically, Bonfiglioli did not provide the chapter which would resolve the mystery, insofar as it could be resolved. But then he never did care much about plotting.

So no one would read Bonfiglioli for his plotting or for the traditional pleasures of suspense and mystery. Rather, his attraction lies in the highly distinctive tone adopted by Mortdecai – a snobbish tone which is discursive – and often being Wodehousian in phrasing: gamey and rich.

Selected Works by the Author
Don't Point That Thing at Me (1972; published in the United States as *Mortdecai's Endgame*)
Something Nasty in the Woodshed (1976)
After You with the Pistol (1979)

Philip Gooden

Bonner, Hilary (b.1949)

Hilary Bonner bounced on to the British crime-writing scene in the mid-1990s with a best-selling first novel in which murder, sex and a bid for political power at the highest level combined in a potent and controversial debut.

Almost all her books are inspired by real-life events, either drawing on her past as a leading journalist or relying on in-depth research, often into major current issues (as in her *No Reason to Die*, published in 2005, which focuses on the series of unexplained deaths at Deepcut Barracks and elsewhere within the British army).

Bonner, who has the journalist's inbuilt antipathy towards anything remotely resembling a cover-up, worked together with the families of several of the dead soldiers to produce a complex conspiracy theory which, while presented as fiction, may actually have come close to the truth and led *The Times* to describe her as 'keeping on the public agenda the stories our masters would prefer buried'.

Another of her novels, *When the Dead Cry Out* (2003), draws on her experiences of living next door to a murderer. It is inspired by the real-life case of John Allen, her friend and neighbour during the 1980s, who in 2003 was found guilty of the murder of his wife and two children twenty-seven years earlier.

Both these books attracted widespread media attention and provoked considerable controversy – but Bonner is no stranger to either of these; she is a writer with a past. In her life in Fleet Street, she variously reported on the troubles in Northern Ireland (on one occasion leaving the last remaining hotel in Londonderry hours before it was destroyed by a bomb); chased about one hundred runaway vicars; pursued the then bachelor Prince Charles through assorted romances, the Sierra Nevada, the South of France, and all manner of other places by motorcar, airplane, helicopter and once (precariously) on skis; and in 1980, Bonner was one of the first British journalists to travel extensively in China.

Besides her novels, Bonner, a past chair of the Crime Writers' Association, has written five non-fiction books – two ghosted autobiographies, one biography and two companions to television programmes – and a number of short stories.

Selected Works by the Author
The Cruelty of Morning (1995)
A Fancy to Kill For (1997)
A Passion So Deadly (1998)
For Death Comes Softly (1999)

A Deep Deceit (2000)
A Kind of Wild Justice (2001)
A Moment of Madness (2002)
When the Dead Cry Out (2003)
No Reason to Die (2005)

Brian Ritterspak

Booth, Stephen (b.1952)

Stephen Booth's multi-award winning series of police procedurals set in the Peak District creates a dramatic sense of place. Unusually, his two central characters are junior officers, not the conventional pairing of inspector or chief inspector and sergeant.

11. Stephen Booth.

Booth, who was born in Burnley and grew up in Blackpool, spent twenty-five years as a journalist. In 1999, he won the Lichfield Prize for a mystery novel, *The Only Dead Thing*, but decided against publication of the book at that time, preferring to concentrate on his planned series of police procedurals. DC Ben Cooper and DS Diane Fry made their debut in *Black Dog* (2000), the only title by a British writer included in the London *Evening Standard*'s six best crime novels of the year. It also won the Barry Award for Best British Crime Novel and was nominated for an Anthony Award for Best First Mystery. As a result of the success of this and of the following book, *Dancing with the Virgins* (2001), which was shortlisted for the CWA Macallan Gold Dagger, Booth gave up his journalistic work to write fiction full time. The relationship between Cooper and Fry is central to the stories. From the start, when Fry joins Cooper's small country squad from a city division, it is clear that there is going to be friction between the two. Fry is fiercely ambitious and does not relate well to her colleagues. The problems which shaped her personality are partly explained in the first book and developed in later volumes. Cooper comes from a local farming family, with whom he has strong ties, and has lived in the area all his life. A gentle, perceptive young man and an intuitive detective, he is burdened by trying to live up to the reputation of his father, the widely respected village policeman who was killed in the course of duty.

Booth's atmospheric depiction of the Peak District's dramatic scenery plays an important part in every book. In *Blood on the Tongue* (2002), a snow-covered hill is the site of several deaths, recent and past. *Blind to the Bones* (2003) is set in a village on the desolate moors of the forbidding Dark Peak, and the climax of *One Last Breath* (2004) takes place in the vast labyrinth of caverns, passages and subterranean rivers for which the district is famous. Recognising the increased interest in the area which the series has inspired, its official guide has included some of the locations featured in the books. The series won praise from police for its authenticity, and its popularity was confirmed in 2003, when Booth won the CWA Dagger in the Library, presented to him whose books have given readers most pleasure.

Selected Works by the Author
Black Dog (2000)
Dancing with the Virgins (2001)
Blood on the Tongue (2002)
Blind to the Bones (2003)
One Last Breath (2004)
The Dead Place (2005)
Scared to Live (2006)

Susanna Yager

Bowers, Dorothy (1904–1948)

Many Golden Age detective writers less celebrated than, for instance, Christie, Sayers and Allingham have largely disappeared without trace. Yet, several had marked ability as writers or as plot constructors and had often demonstrated an agreeable freshness of approach. A notable example is Dorothy Violet Bowers.

Born in Leominster, Herefordshire, and later a Hereford resident, she was educated in Monmouth and at Oxford University. She worked as schoolteacher and assistant librarian and, during the Second World War, for the BBC European Service. She compiled crosswords and was interested in criminology and psychical research; from these interests, it was only a step to writing detective novels, of which she produced five intelligently written examples (she published nothing else) between 1938 and 1947.

The careful plotting and elegant writing of these books (starting with *Postscript to Poison* in 1938) earned Bowers admission to the Detection Club, and her works were published in America (all five titles) and France (two of the books). The most accomplished of them is generally considered to be *A Deed without a Name* (1940), set in London in October 1939 in the early days of the Phoney War. The murderer is admittedly not too difficult to spot, even if the main clue to his guilt is a touch *outré*, but the portrayal of Chelsea, slightly shabby in the blackout, is evocative, and the characterisation is of a high order – careful, detailed and not at all precious.

As in her other novels, the lead sleuth is a policeman: the amiable, shrewd DI Pardoe of the Metropolitan Police. (The amateur detective is, sadly, the second victim.)

Bowers is now largely overlooked except by more adventurous crime devotees, but any connoisseur would find pleasure in any of her work they might track down.

Selected Works by the Author
Postscript to Poison (1938)
Shadows Before (1939)
A Deed without a Name (1940)
Fear for Miss Betony (1941)
The Bells at Old Bailey (1947)

Philip Scowcroft

Brahms, Caryl (1901–1982)

Co-authored with S.J. Simon, Caryl Brahms's DI Quill novels are charming examples of the humorous Golden Age crime stories.

The daughter of a jewellery wholesaler, she was born Doris Caroline Abrahams in Croydon, Surrey, in 1901. She studied at the Royal Academy of Music during the 1920s, where she met Manchurian-born S.J. Simon (Simon Jasha Skidelsky), who later found fame as a championship bridge player and joint inventor of the Acol bidding system.

Abrahams became a ballet correspondent for the *London Evening Standard*, where she first joined forces with Simon to provide humorous captions for political cartoons by satirist David Low. Later, while deputising for her colleague Arnold Haskell at *The Daily Telegraph*, a chance encounter with Simon prompted the creation of a tongue-in-cheek detective plot, initially with Haskell as the victim, which, co-authored by Abrahams (writing as 'Caryl Brahms') and Simon, appeared as *A Bullet in the Ballet* in 1937.

Penned in a deliberately light-hearted style, the novel opens with the shooting of ballet dancer Anton Palook while performing Stravinsky's *Petrushka*. Called in to investigate is DI Adam Quill and his assistant, Sergeant Banner. Quill is a fair-haired Adonis-like individual, living in digs at Earls Court. But unlike his erstwhile colleagues – such as his favourite fictional detective, Freeman Wills Crofts's Inspector French – his success in the field of detection is sorely lacking. He has rarely arrested the right victim (a previous suspect sued for wrongful arrest) and his only successes in the field have been due to serendipity rather than intelligence. Banner, whose interest lies in womanising rather than crime solving, is not much better.

Quill resurfaced a year later in a direct sequel, *Casino for Sale*. Impresario Vladimir Stroganoff, from *A Bullet in the Ballet*, has decamped to the Riviera to put on a show at the seedy 'Casino-by-the-Sea', where he is in direct competition with a rival impresario. Full of larger-than-life characters, and showcasing Quill's inept attempts to uncover the murderer of vitriolic ballet critic Pavlo Citrolo, the book led to a third and final outing, *Envoy on Excursion*, in 1940. Here, the arch theatricality of the previous works was replaced by an unsubtle wartime satire in which an ambassador from the principality of insomnia is found dead in Whitehall's Ministry of Elimination.

The pair also wrote a non-crime prequel to the Stroganoff chronicles, entitled *6 Curtains for Stroganova* (1945), as well as several historical lampoons, such as

Don't, Mr Disraeli (1940) and *No Bed for Bacon* (1941). After Simon's death in 1948, Abrahams collaborated with satirist Ned Sherrin on several projects, including television series *That Was the Week That Was* (1962) and *BBC3* (1965). Her last book, an irreverent biography of Gilbert and Sullivan, appeared in 1975. She died on 5 December 1982, and her memoirs, *Too Dirty for the Windmill*, appeared four years later. *See also* Humour and Crime Fiction.

Selected Works by the Author

With S.J. Simon
A Bullet in the Ballet (1937)
Casino for Sale (1938; published in the United States as *Murder à la Stroganoff*)
Envoy on Excursion (1940)

Mark Campbell

Brand, Christianna (1907–1988)

Christianna Brand possessed a remarkable ability to bring style and wit to the crime genre, while never losing the sense of excitement that was her hallmark. Her other principal attribute was her nonpareil skill at creating intriguing puzzles. Brand was born in what were then the Federated Malay Straits in 1907 – or, if you believe her own account, in 1905. In this, as in so much, she reversed the usual comic stereotype – that of the woman who knocks years off her age. In her Asian years, she was looked after by a nursery-maid who figured at the top of the list of demons in her life. When, still a young child, she returned to England to attend a Catholic school run by nuns, and she found absolute, childish happiness for the first time. After trying out, seemingly, every single job open to a woman at that time, she settled into a very happy marriage with Roland Lewis, a surgeon, and into a career as a writer. For the question 'Why writing?', it is perhaps more relevant to cite the fact that she wrote as naturally and as gracefully as a swan swims, rather than the attempts of her father to write fiction. ('My father', she wrote, casting aside rose-tinted spectacles [if she ever had any], 'a very talented but silly and conceited amateur writer, wrote a short story imitating S(omerset) M(augham) to a "t" – not sending him up, I don't mean: he thought that was the way to write.') She says she rewrote this story and earned her first money as a writer when a women's magazine accepted it. I would bet there was very little left of her father in it by that stage.

Though Brand wrote from the late 1930s onwards and was engaged on a comedy crime novel when she died (with a duchess as detective and a barmaid called Topless), her heyday was in the 1940s and 1950s, with a late second flowering in 1979 with *The Rose of Darkness*. In those years, she wrote (mainly, but not only) crime novels, which were always her first love. She used for them characters from real life, including those for whom she had feelings of bitterness – they tended to end up as corpses or murderers. Though there is a flavour of cyanide in several of these portraits, they are saved by the gusto of their delineation; both the loveable and the unlovely share in the comic vigour of Brand's world view – she only really hated the dreary and, consequently, almost never used them.

She unveiled the strength of her talent with *Death in High Heels* (1941). She shared with Allingham (who at that date had already more than ten years of book-writing experience behind her) the distinction of being a real writer, who could produce feelings of joy and intense satisfaction merely from her way of shaping a sentence or playing with the possibilities of a word. This is a contrast with many of the other Golden Age practitioners, who were at best workaday wordsmiths and at worst pretentious and heavy. Read the first page of *High Heels* with its bravura description of the glamorous cloth showroom that is the setting of the novel, where sheen and surface hide a reality of tawdriness and the downright unwholesome: 'Upstairs in the great gleaming showroom, with its golden carpet and shimmering curtains, its crystal light and flattering mirrors, the silver glittered and the parquet shone…but in the basement, where the gilded staircase gave way abruptly to an unwholesome chocolate brown, a flick and a promise would do: a flick and a promise was all Mrs "Arris vouchsafed".' By the time she began her career in that bravura manner, Brand already had many times the experience of most well brought-up young middle-class girls. The war gave her still more, and it was as a chronicler of the Home Front that she made her first big impact on the reading public. *Green for Danger* (1945) depicted a nation at war with none of the usual gallant-little-nation assumptions, but instead a sense of rush, overwork, jangled nerves and unconquerable tiredness. It feels, in fact, closer to the real thing than many more ambitious war novels. It has other attributes that account for its great success: Inspector Cockerill, Brand's disreputable, cigarette-smoking detective (grandfather of Frost), here reaches his apogee, at least until *Tour de France* (1955); the plot hinges on a sleight of hand, as in the best of Christie; and all the usual repertoire of Brand characteristics are here used with flair and confidence.

One figure who tends to crop up in Brand's fiction in various guises is the young girl – gay, brave, full of effrontery and insouciance. It is surely her take on the young, poor Christianna, though in conversation she tended to dwell on how cold and hungry she was in those years. These characters never let circumstances or other people grind them down: they stand up courageously to any blow and, above all, never lose the ability to view life through the glass of wit and satire. The world of her books and the world she saw around her are one. In her letters, she loved repeating good stories or sharp observations of people; she tells of the relatives who come to stay with her: 'All communists, belly-buttons enlarged by the banners they had carried'. Come Wimbledon and she explodes at 'the dreadful little German, eighteen years old, inevitable winner – all chubby bottom and fat pink thighs. I shall never eat pork again, I said to Roland'. And there are in those letters copious crime writers, such as Anthony Berkeley: 'I must have told you of the time I asked him to pick up on the way to my house for a drink a bottle of gin and six tonics, and he plonked them down on the dining room table and said, "Look Christianna, I've drunk oceans of gin in your house, you must let me pay for…" and he plonked down the price of the tonics.'

With Christie, we are conscious of another person, jealously guarded from our gaze, who is more educated, better read, even more liberal-minded than she ever allows to be freighted into her fiction. With Brand, the books show us the whole person, her prejudices, her innate generosity and, above all, her humorous and wise world view. She is one crime writer who will last.

Selected Works by the Author
Death in High Heels (1941)
Heads You Lose (1941)
Green for Danger (1945)
Suddenly at His Residence (1947; published in the United States as *The Crooked Wreath*)

Death of Jezebel (1949)
Cat and Mouse (1950)
London Particular (1952; published in the United States as *Fog of Doubt*)
Tour de Force (1955)
What Dread Hand? (1968)
The Honey Harlot (1978)
The Rose in Darkness (1979)

Robert Barnard

Brenchley, Chaz (b.1959)

Inspired to become a fantasy writer after meeting J.R.R. Tolkien at the age of twelve, Chaz Brenchley is equally adept at writing books that blend the crime and horror genres in a contemporary setting.

Born in Oxford, he briefly attended St. Andrews University before leaving in 1977 to become a full-time writer. After contributing (usually anonymously) hundreds of stories to teenage romance and women's magazines, he published his first novel (a pseudonymous romance) in 1983.

12. Chaz Brenchley.

His first accredited book was the crime novel *The Samaritan* (1988), about an ex-alcoholic writer who becomes involved in a series of horrifying 'Butcher' killings terrorising Newcastle. The protagonist makes the mistake of confiding in a senior worker at the Samaritans, who has secrets of his own to hide. It was followed by the dark psychological thrillers *The Refuge* (1989), *The Garden* (1990) and *Mall Time* (1991). As Daniel Fox, he contributed three stories to the *Dark Voices: The Pan Book of Horror* anthology series (volumes 4–6, 1992–1994).

The author was then unexpectedly offered the position of crime writer-in-residence on the St. Peter's Riverside Sculpture Project in Sunderland, where he worked with various sculptors, finding ways of incorporating text into their work. He also visited schools, gave lectures, organised workshops and judged competitions. He later described it as 'the strangest job in the known universe'. He published a collection of ten stories, *Blood Waters* (1995), inspired by the area and its history, as well as the sculptures.

Although contracted by his publisher for a horror novel, *Dead of Light* (1995) turned out to be an unusual hybrid involving murder and magic, which the author described as being more 'a rites-of-passage story about power and the perception of power'. *Dispossession* (1996) was about an amnesia victim who awakened from a coma only to discover he had acquired an entirely new life. The British Fantasy Award–winning *Light Errant* (1997) was a sequel to *Dead of Light* and involved that book's protagonist being forced into using his unique talents again, while *Shelter* (1999) was about a university student under suspicion for the sadistic murder of a friend. With his gritty urban settings and invariably flawed protagonists, Brenchley's beautifully crafted work reveals a moral conscience often found lacking in most mainstream crime and horror fiction. He also has the ability to diffuse the most gruesome circumstances with a sly sense of humour. *Dead of Light* and *Shelter* have been optioned for film and television, respectively.

Brenchley has also served as writer-in-residence at the University of Northumbria. He is also a member of Murder Squad and the Write Fantastic group of fantasy writers. His two stories 'Scouting for Boys' and 'The Day I Gave Up Smoking' were shortlisted for the CWA Macallan Short Story Dagger. In 2000, he won the Northern Writer of the Year Award.

Selected Works by the Author
The Samaritan (1988)
The Refuge (1989)
The Garden (1990)
Mall Time (1991)
Blood Waters (stories, 1995)
Shelter (1999)

Stephen Jones

Brett, Simon (b.1945)

It is ironic that such a prolific and talented writer of humorous crime fiction as Simon Brett should be best known for his works with the BBC (especially as the producer of the first episode of Douglas Adams's *Hitchhiker's Guide to the Galaxy*).

He was born in Worcester Park, Surrey, and educated at Oxford University. His first job was 'a father Christmas', he told *The Independent* (7 December 2006). After university, he joined the BBC but left to join London Weekend Television in 1977. His first published work was a crime novel, *Cast, in Order of Disappearance* (1975). In 1979, he turned to writing full time.

Brett's first crime fiction novel featured the easily distracted actor, Charles Paris. Paris is regularly resting between jobs, and his wry, light-hearted view of the world is coloured by his continuing interest in the bottle. The stories are hilarious, largely because of the 'murderous clashes of egos centre-stage' (Julian Earwaker and Kathleen Becker, *Scene of the Crime*, Aurum Press, 2002), which Paris witnesses from his corner. Brett's affection for the acting profession is evident in all these stories.

The next series to which he turned his mind was the Pargeter series. In this, Brett manages to turn the Miss Marple concept of an elderly spinster investigator on its head. Mrs Pargeter is an elderly widow, but her husband was not a pillar of the community. He was involved in 'business'. Mrs Pargeter is glad of the help of his contacts on occasion but would prefer not to know what their relationship was with her dead husband.

These stories are demonstrably written with enormous enthusiasm by Brett, and he gives full rein to his delight in puns:

'I had, like, a convergence.'
'Did you?'
'Yes. Just like St Paul on the road to Domestos.' (*Mrs Pargeter's Plot*, 1996)

More recently, Brett has created another series, set in a fictional village, Fethering in Sussex, and inspired by the village he has made his home. In the first of this series, Carole Seddon and her friend Jude discover a body, but it has disappeared by the time the police arrive.

All the books in this series are easily categorised as cosies: light-hearted and gentle tales. However, Brett has displayed a different side to his writing character with two other stories. The first, *A Shock to the System* (1985), which was made into a film starring Michael Caine, features an arrogant businessman who thinks he can literally get away with murder, while *Singled Out* (1995) is a tale of child abuse and serial murder.

Although prolific as a novelist and crime writer, Brett has also written radio and television dramas such as *No Commitments* and *After Henry*, respectively. He was the author of the best-selling *How to Be a Little Sod* books and has written several collections of short stories, as well as editing *The Detection Collection* (2005), an anthology of short stories by members of The Detection Club. He was the Chairman of the Crime Writers' Association (1986–1987) and has been the president of the Detection Club since 2001.

He is best known for his broadcasting career, but for such an accomplished humorist and deft plot-smith, his enduring legacy will surely be his gentle crime-fiction works. *See also* Humour and Crime Fiction.

Selected Works by the Author

Charles Paris Series
Cast, in Order of Disappearance (1975)
An Amateur Corpse (1978)
A Comedian Dies (1979)
Not Dead, Only Resting (1984)

Mrs Pargeter Series
A Nice Class of Corpse (1986)
Mrs Pargeter's Pound of Flesh (1992)
Mrs Pargeter's Plot (1996)

Fethering Series
The Body on the Beach (2000)
Death on the Downs (2001)
The Torso in the Town (2002)
Death under the Dryer (2007)

Michael Jecks

Brighton Rock (film, 1947)

(John Boulting, director)

This celebrated 1947 movie, adapted by Graham Greene and Terence Rattigan from Greene's 1938 novel, opens with happy holidaymakers thronging Brighton beach and a caption which tries to persuade the audience that razor-wielding racetrack thugs are things of the past and that the police have efficiently put an end to all the crookedness rampant in the town between the wars. The film proper begins with a nervous newspaperman wandering along the front on a Lobby Lud–style circulation-building stunt; he is nervous because extortionist Pinky Brown (Richard Attenborough) blames him for the death of his best friend and is pursuing him into the end-of-the-pier ghost train with murder in mind. A body is soon washing up under the pier, but hard-drinking entertainer Ida Arnold (Hermione Baddeley) realises who is to blame and sets about prodding the police to bring Pinky to justice. Meanwhile, the seventeen-year-old Catholic psycho embarks on an extremely reluctant courtship of naive waitress Rose Brown (Carol Marsh) who has seen too much, less from affection than from his understanding that a wife cannot testify against her husband. Though best remembered as a gangster film (retitled *Young Scarface* in America) and though the young Attenborough pulls out all the ice-eyed creep stops as Pinky, *Brighton Rock* is at heart a tender cruel story of bizarre young love, with a hideously ironic punchline involving a stuttering record that preserves Pinkie's sham declaration of devotion ('what you want me to say is "I love you"') but cuts off his bitter outpouring of hate against the innocent heroine ('But I don't, I hate you, you little slut'). Decades on, with the star's ascension to the position of avuncular British showbiz legend, there is a frisson in seeing young Dickie cast as a murdering bastard in a sharp suit, not to mention William Hartnell, the original 'Doctor Who', as his ablest lieutenant,

13. Actors William Hartnell, Richard Attenborough and Harry Ross in *Bringhton Rock* (1947).

though Greene and Rattigan seem almost more interested in such pathetic flotsam as Baddeley's end-of-the-pier pierrot or a dandruff-plagued, Shakespearean-crooked lawyer (Harcourt Williams). Once the opening stalk-and-strangle sequence has been played out, the plot winds down as Pinky's gang is broken up by more ambitious mobsters, livening up only in the rainswept under-the-pier finale which affords Pinky a desperate death scene worthy of ranking alongside the best of Cagney's gangster demises. The film has gained some interest by embalming the seaside seediness of its era and Attenborough's performance has classic stature, but *Brighton Rock* could have done with a stronger, more interesting director than John Boulting who delivered a superior suspense item in *Seven Days to Noon*, his follow-up film, before settling into grumpily conservative comedies such as *I'm All Right Jack* and *Heavens Above*. Greene manages to slip a little philosophy into the crime drama, with Ida insisting that people do not change ('It's like those sticks of rock. Bite one all the way down, you'll still read Brighton. That's human nature.') And a nun expressing the apt but extremely unhelpful thought that 'You or I cannot fathom the appalling strangeness of God'. *See also* Film and Crime: Page to Screen.

Kim Newman

Broadbent, Tony (b.1948)

In Jethro, a cat burglar in austere, black-market-riddled post-Second World War London, Tony Broadbent created a character with the best qualities of the great action adventure heroes such as Raffles, the Saint, Richard Hannay and James Bond.

Broadbent was born in Windsor, England. He was an art student in London, then a copywriter and creative director at advertising agencies in London, New York and San Francisco. Based in the San Francisco Bay Area, he now is a consulting brand strategist and a crime novelist. His 'creeping narratives' – 'creeper' is Cockney slang for cat burglar and 'the Smoke' for London – are entertaining, fast-paced and informative, providing wonderfully evocative descriptions of both time and place, with London in many ways as much a story character as the main protagonist. Readers first meet Jethro in *The Smoke* (2002) as he burgles the Bulgarian embassy in London in 1947. Besides some items of jewellery, he also 'lifts' what turn out to be code books. Jethro's patriotic fence, Ray Karmin (also known as 'Buggy' Billy, London's Bug Powder King) returns the items to the British authorities, bringing both himself and Jethro to the attention of a Colonel Walsingham (an allusion to Elizabeth I's famed spymaster) of MI5. Walsingham blackmails Jethro into burgling the embassy again, this time 'in Defence of the Realm' and to assist in the defection of a beautiful cipher clerk. In the sequel, *Spectres in the Smoke* (2005), set in 1948, fearing that MI5 has been penetrated by spies, Walsingham again calls on Jethro's 'creeping' skills; this time to help foil an extreme right-wing plot to bring down Clement Attlee's Labour Government. It also touches on a Royal cover-up of the Duke of Windsor's alleged dealings with Adolf Hitler during the war, and the government's attempts to root out Fascist sympathisers and Communist moles from the corridors of power in Whitehall. In the process, Jethro has to pass for 'a gentleman' among the English upper classes, and for help, Walsingham turns to his old friends David Niven and Ian Fleming. Once he is suitably polished, Jethro is then ready to tackle 'the enemy within'. The creator of James Bond is just one of the many 'real' people who populate the novels, including contemporary policemen, gangsters – Jack Spot and Billy Hill – newspaper columnists and entertainers of radio, stage and screen. Scattered throughout *Spectres in the Smoke* are tributes and references to John Buchan's hero Richard Hannay and to the Bond novels and films. *See also* Thrillers: Novels of Action.

Selected Works by the Author
The Smoke (2002)
Spectres in the Smoke (2005)

Adrian Muller

Brookmyre, Christopher (b.1968)

Former film critic and journalist, Scottish writer Christopher Brookmyre brought his distinctive voice to the world of crime books when he introduced unsuspecting readers to his sarcastic anti-hero and investigative journalist, Jack Parlabane in *Quite Ugly One Morning* (1996). His subsequent books became part of the sub-genre labelled 'Tartan Noir'. Brookmyre is sometimes referred to as the 'British Carl Hiaasen', but he admits that he owes more to Canadian author Robertson Davies.

14. Christopher Brookmyre.

Brookmyre grew up and was educated in Glasgow but states that he never set out to write about Scotland for Scottish readers, although his novels contain heavy Scots argot. He has worked for the film magazine *Screen International* and as subeditor for *The Scotsman* and the *Edinburgh Evening News*. Drawing on his journalistic background, Brookmyre's main series character Jack Parlabane is energetically characterised as a man with a strong sense of justice but not one sticking to the rules to get results. In *Quite Ugly One Morning*, he investigates the death of a medic and along the way Brookmyre takes a swipe at the Thatcherite NHS reforms of the late 1990s. It won the Critics' First Blood Award for Best First Crime Novel of the Year. Its follow-up, *Country of the Blind* (1997) – about the murder of a media mogul allegedly by a gang of housebreakers – has Parlabane taking on the assignment and finding himself in the murky world of corruption. While fully prepared to aim vitriolic attacks against the Tories in earlier works when 'New Labour' appeared, Brookmyre sensed the change in the political landscape when he wrote the third Parlabane novel *Boiling a Frog* (2000), which, set against the backdrop of post-devolution Scotland, sees some corrupt politicians come to a very sticky end and also a change for his hero who ends up behind bars.

Not the End of the World (1998) moves away from Scotland to California with another main lead: Steff Kennedy, a 6-foot 7-inch (200.66 centimetres) Motherwell-supporting photographer. He is set loose among the lights of Los Angeles and delights of the porn industry and a fundamental religious movement and a maniac who wants to destroy the world. There is no denying that the book was heavily influenced by the millennial hysteria sweeping the world before 2000. In Brookmyre's fourth novel, *One Fine Day in the Middle of the Night* (1999), he returns to Scotland in a story about a school reunion party on a converted oil rig which is gate-crashed by terrorist. The characters are easily recognisable from the *Die Hard* movies.

His book titles can be as uncompromising as his stories: *Be My Enemy or, Fuck This for a Game of Soldiers* (2004), or as simple as the children's nonsense rhyme 'Two Dead Boys', *One Fine Day in the Middle of the Night* (1999). Whether he is exploring terrorism as in *A Big Boy Did It and Ran Away* (2001) or unravelling the mystery of a double murder in *A Tale Etched in Blood and Hard Black Pencil* (2006), Brookmyre's highly developed sense of social justice shines through. His books contain hard-edged language, black comedy and a mix of politics and satire which all help to raise his books above the comic thriller genre. *See also* Humour and Crime Fiction *and* Social Comment in Crime Fiction.

Selected Works by the Author
Quite Ugly One Morning (1996)
Not the End of the World (1998)
One Fine Day in the Middle of the Night (1999)
A Big Boy Did It and Ran Away (2001)
A Tale Etched in Blood and Hard Black Pencil (2006)
Attack of the Unsinkable Rubber Ducks (2007)

Mike Stotter

Brother Cadfael (television series, 1994–1998)

This television series, based on the *Brother Cadfael* books by Ellis Peters (Edith Pargeter), ran for thirteen episodes over four seasons – May 1994 to December 1998. Cadfael was played throughout by Sir Derek Jacobi. Among the other principal characters, Prior Robert was played by Michael Culver and Brother Jerome by Julian Firth. Hugh Beringar was portrayed by Sean Pertwee in the first series, Eoin McCarthy in the next two series and Anthony Green in the final series, an unfortunate recasting for a major character that affected continuity. The first series was directed by Graham Theakston but subsequent episodes were directed by various hands. Between them, writers Russell Lewis and Christopher Russell adapted ten of the novels. The series was filmed on location, using a special set constructed near Budapest in Hungary, with the location itself having been selected as best reflecting the Welsh Marches around Shrewsbury in the twelfth century.

The series concerns Cadfael, a former soldier who has turned his back on secular life and turned to God, becoming a brother at the abbey in Shrewsbury. The stories are set during the time of the civil war in Britain between the claimants to the English throne, Stephen and Matilda. Loyalties to parties within the conflict provide both background and motive to many of the crimes that emerge in and around Shrewsbury and with which Cadfael becomes involved, usually with the reluctant blessing of the Abbot. In the first episode, *One Corpse Too Many*, Cadfael has to solve a murder where the corpse is found among the bodies of people killed during the siege of Shrewsbury. This episode introduces all of the primary characters, including Hugh Beringar, who, at this time, is not known locally and of whom Cadfael is suspicious. However, Beringar subsequently becomes Cadfael's trusted friend and confidant; in due course, he becomes the town's sheriff and consults Cadfael when incidents arise.

The books were not adapted and broadcast in sequence, so that the tight continuity of time and characters, and Cadfael's own personal reflection and development, were not captured. The series did, though, start with the most suitable volume, *One Corpse Too Many*, which is the first book where his character comes to the fore. The first book in the series, *A Morbid Taste for Bones*, was originally written as a one-off, and neither Cadfael nor Shrewsbury is central to the story. This was eventually adapted to end the second series once the characters were developed; however, the storyline needed to be revised. Generally the adaptations remained faithful to the plot, though the cast of characters was sometimes reduced and a few locations dropped for budgetary reasons and to keep them simple for the small screen. Only *The Pilgrim of Hate*, which in the book version has considerable introspection and diversity of locale, was significantly revised for filming.

Jacobi, whose casting had to be approved by Edith Pargeter, brought considerable sensitivity and piety to the part, but also the inner strength required by the character. Though physically he did not fit the author's description of Cadfael, he captured Cadfael's spirituality and, above all, his concern for others. The series relied heavily on relationships, both within the Abbey, and between the Abbey and the outer world, and Jacobi's portrayal captured this. He was the rock in a world of chaos.

The series ended because of budgetary constraints, leaving seven books and three short stories unadapted. *See also* Historical Crime.

Further Reading
Whiteman, Robin. 1991. *The Cadfael Companion*. Macdonald.

Website
http://www.tv.com/cadfael/show/7244/summary.html

Mike Ashley

Buchan, John (1875–1940)

John Buchan is remembered as the creator of an exuberant *Boy's Own* kind of yarn, full of brave men having wild adventures and besting every breed of villain, with barely a woman in sight. But there is far more to him, both as a writer and as a man, than this stereotype suggests, and his contemporary admirers included not only Kipling but also Ezra Pound and Rose Macaulay and, later, Graham Greene. Buchan sometimes played up to the image himself, dedicating one novel to 'A Young Gentleman of Eton College', who had been given one of his serious works of non-fiction and wrote, 'complaining I had "let you down", and summoning me, as I valued your respect, to "pull myself together". In particular you demanded to hear more of the doings of Richard Hannay, a gentleman for whom you professed a liking....'

Born in 1875, Buchan was the son of a minister of the Free Church of Scotland. At the age of five, he suffered an accident in which his skull fractured. This led to a year in bed, when he was forbidden to read or walk, an experience that must have marked him emotionally as well as physically.

Recovered, he was educated at the local school in Kirkcaldy, grammar school in Glasgow, Glasgow University and Brasenose College, Oxford, where he took a first. By then, he was already writing and had astonishingly achieved an entry in *Who's Who*. He had had articles published while he was at Glasgow, and there were five books in print before he left Oxford, having become, as he put it in his memoirs, *Memory Hold-the-Door* (1940), rather rich for an undergraduate. He also won the Newdigate poetry prize.

After graduation, he read for the Bar, while simultaneously working as a journalist. He spent two years as private secretary to Lord Milner in South Africa (1901–1903), before resuming his legal career. During the First World War, despite increasingly poor health, he worked for the War Office, the Foreign Office and GHQ France. In 1927, he became a member of parliament, and his public life culminated in 1935, when he was created the first Baron Tweedsmuir and appointed the governor-general of Canada. He died there, after a cerebral thrombosis, in 1940.

In the meantime, he had published a series of successful novels, using his professional experience to give them credible backgrounds. The first was *Prester John* (1910), which deals with the adventures of David Crawford, a young Scot with his way to make in the world. Sent to South Africa to learn about running a business in Blaauwildebeestefontein, David becomes embroiled in desperate feats of physical endurance and intellectual exploration. He not only wins wars and finds treasure but also works for the resettlement of the local tribesmen and restitution of the wrongs they have suffered. He is typical of Buchan's heroes. Like the rest, he does not consider himself heroic, but he never gives in to any misery, emotional or physical, however many tears of relief he may shed when it is all over.

The fiction can be divided into four groups. One consists of historical novels, which do not concern us here. Then there is the Richard Hannay series, written during and after the First World War and usually dealing with conspiracies that threaten not only the security of the British Empire but also civilisation. At a time of unparalleled slaughter, with real doubt about the war's outcome, to have Hannay and his friends saving the world time and again on a mixture of wits and grit had to be a source of comfort.

This series is narrated in the first person by Hannay, who is said to have been based on General 'Tiny' Ironside, and it opens with *The Thirty-Nine Steps* (1915). Newly arrived in London from South Africa and bored, Hannay becomes enmeshed in a conspiracy to assassinate one Karolides. Chasing and chased all over England and Scotland, Hannay survives to identify the conspirators in time to save the day.

Pulled away from the Western Front, he is sent to the Middle East to prevent a world-shattering uprising of Islamic fanatics in the prescient *Greenmantle* (1916), which also introduces Sandy Arbuthnot. Later the Master of Clanroyden, Sandy is modelled on the real scholar and adventurer Aubrey Herbert. Herbert's wife wrote, 'I must confess I prefer my Aubrey to his Sandy but I daresay it's like him' (FitzHerbert 1983, 1). Herbert seems not to have objected to being used in this way, commenting only: 'he brings in my nerves all right doesn't he?' Sandy plays a part in many of the novels, bringing brilliance and wit to Hannay's more stolid qualities.

In *Mr Standfast* (1919), Hannay meets Mary Lamington, and together they unmask the conspirators, who are – once again – threatening the survival of Britain and its empire. Hannay does well in the war, becoming a general and being knighted for his pains. Peace sees him married to Mary, owner of Fosse Manor in the Cotswolds, and father of two-year-old Peter John. But no one of his spirit and talents could remain with hayseed in his hair for ever, and in *The Three Hostages* (1924), he is sucked back into the world of conspiracy. Although he crops up in cameo roles in some of the other novels and introduces *The Courts of the Morning* (1929), which belongs to Sandy, his last full appearance is in *The Island of Sheep* (1936).

Linked to Hannay by a series of minor characters, the next series is more theatrical, dealing with plots concerning exiled royalty pursued by a variety of enemies. The first novel is *Huntingtower* (1922), which introduces retired grocer Dickson McCunn, a Scottish businessman of unprepossessing physical appearance but of romantic bent, undaunted common sense and huge generosity. He joins the rescue of an incarcerated Russian princess, meeting on the way the Gorbals Die-hards.

These are a poverty-stricken group of slum children, who have formed themselves into a Boy Scout-like band with marching songs and rules and raggle-taggle uniforms. They are among the perkiest of Buchan's creations and allow some of his humour to emerge. Wee Jaikie, the most bedraggled of all, passes on a song he learned at a Socialist Sunday School, 'Class-conscious we are, and class-conscious will be Till our fit's on the neck o'the Boorjoyzee'. When McCunn asks what the 'Boorjoyzee' might be, Jaikie told that he does not know but assumes it is 'some kind of a draigon'. (Another example of Buchan's humour comes in *The Three Hostages* with Sandy's description of some light-hearted electioneering in Scotland.)

Adopted by the generous McCunn, the Die-hards move into the wider world and acquire an education, reappearing with McCunn in *Castle Gay* (1930) and *The House of the Four Winds* (1935), which deals with Prince John of Evallonia and his fight to regain his throne. Although the characters have great charm, the novels in which they figure have survived less well than the rest.

Jaikie, graduated from Cambridge, and travelling around Europe under his more dignified name John Galt, he encapsulates a reserved masculinity that is typical of Buchan's characters. In *The House of the Four Winds*, he confesses that he knows nothing of women and has barely met any. He is, however, deeply attached to Alison Westwater, an aristocratic Scottish lover of the outdoor life. Brave, no-nonsense, pretty, with bright hair, but without any obvious – or dangerous – sexuality, she is typical of Buchan's good women characters. There are, however, some of the other kind, who exude sexuality and behave like Morgan le Fay, threatening to overtake strong men with their wily seductiveness and weaken them for ever. Hilda von Einem in *Greenmantle* is the prime example.

For the first part of *The Dancing Floor* (1926), which is set in London and Greece and deals with the expiation of ancestral sins and the release of an isolated community from group hysteria, Kore Arabin appears to be another of the type but is ultimately revealed as pure and heroic and as stainless as Alison Westwater.

Hannay's Mary is the most virtuous of all. She, too, has bright hair and is both intensely brave and deeply modest. Hannay is told by John Scantlebury Blenkiron, an American philanthropist, that Mary can never be tainted by anything she does or anyone she meets. *The Three Hostages* sees her overcoming the villain, but not before she has had to degrade herself to dress and behave like a chorus girl. In the interests of saving the hostages, she is happy enough to do this, but the idea that her husband should see her plastered with make-up and vulgarly dressed fills her with horror.

The hero of the third series never risks himself in marriage, although he does have women friends whom he admires. Sir Edward Leithen shares his creator's twin professions, barrister and politician, and eventually becomes attorney general. He features in *John Macnab* (1925), *The Dancing Floor* (1926), *The Gap in the Curtain* (1932) and *Sick Heart River* (1941) as well as in a novella, *The Power House* (1919), where he is shown to be at the heart of wild and great events even though he never stirs from London.

The Gap in the Curtain is an intriguing novel, arising from Buchan's interest in the paranormal, which he explored extensively in his short fiction but which, in his novels, usually reveals itself only in his characters' dreams and presentiments. The first part takes place during a country-house weekend, when a Scandinavian professor persuades his hostess that with training and a careful diet the subjects of an experiment can learn to see into the future. The rest of the novel is narrated by Leithen and describes the activities of each member of the experiment during the year that elapses before the events of which they read can come to pass. Two read of their deaths, another of his embarkation on a most unlikely expedition to Yucatán and the fourth of an even more unlikely stock market surge in a particular commodity.

Leithen takes a more active role in *John Macnab*, which is probably Buchan's greatest novel. Leithen and three friends are suffering from accidie, which the Catholic church counts a mortal sin. It clearly troubled Buchan, who describes it as a kind of lassitude and depression. In *John Macnab*, Charles Lamancha (glamorous and brilliant politician), Sir Archibald Roylance (wounded flying ace and member of parliament), John Palliser-Yeates (international banker) and Leithen are advised by their doctor that the only cure for their malaise is to put themselves in danger. Lamancha (whose name comes from that of a Scottish village and has nothing to do with Don Quixote) suggests that they should risk their reputations, and therefore careers, by repairing to Archie Roylance's shooting lodge in Scotland and turning poacher. Under the name John Macnab, they inform the neighbouring landowners that within a certain time they will poach a stag or salmon and escape unseen, returning the kill to the relevant estate's owner.

Love of the natural world crops up in nearly all the novels and is the source of some surprisingly lyrical description amidst the mainly plain prose, but it is in *John Macnab* that Buchan realises it most fully. The action is fast and compelling, unsullied by the kind of not-quite-believable coincidence that is a feature of many of the other novels, in particular *The Three Hostages*. And the four heroes' return to full humour and good health provides an equivalent of the comfort generated by Hannay's demolition of world-threatening conspiracy.

There is, however, an interesting coda to *John Macnab*, when one of the owners points out that the challenge was never genuine. No one in his position would ever have betrayed any of the four to the press. Their reputations and careers were not at risk after all. This puncturing of high drama is typical of the Leithen novels and would not fit in any of the Hannays.

Leithen is a dry, realistic, clever character, and despite touches of the fantastic in *The Dancing Floor* and *Gap in the Curtain*, he usually operates in a wholly credible world. His last appearance in *Sick Heart River* is the most moving of any in Buchan's entire output. Leithen is suffering from tuberculosis and is summoned by Blenkiron to travel to Canada to search for and, if possible, bring back an errant French-Canadian financier named Francis Galliard.

Despite having no interest in Galliard, Leithen accepts the challenge. He has no surviving family and detests the idea of eking out his last days in the soft impersonal care of a nursing home. He wants to die standing, according to Vespasian's ideal of a Roman emperor's stoicism. And so he travels first to New York to meet Galliard's wife and then in the company of a half-Scottish, half-Cree guide and two members of the Hare tribe, he goes on into the Arctic Circle to find Galliard. In the clean ferociously cold air of the Arctic, eating half-raw Caribou steaks, Leithen feels the start of a miraculous recovery. But he sacrifices his chance of survival to rescue from accidie the rest of the Hare tribe, who are half-starved, ill and living in the greatest squalor, despite all the efforts of their local French Catholic priest.

Leithen and the priest succeed in bringing the tribe back to full vigour. The effort does cost him his life, but it has its own compensation. In the words of the priest, 'he had been frozen by hard stoicism which sprang partly from his upbringing and partly from temperament.... I witnessed the thawing of the ice.'

This novel was published in the year after Buchan's death. Besides showing a man finding a way to die that he can consider honourable, it deals with two of the great themes in his fiction: the retrieval of someone lost and the fight within one man between the drive for worldly success and a desire to return to a simpler, more natural existence in a beautiful wild country, where your only food comes from what you kill.

The figure of the lost one crops up again and again, most obviously in *The Three Hostages*. The hostages are lost in two ways: they have been kidnapped and imprisoned, but they have also been stripped of their self-knowledge and identity by hypnosis, so that Hannay has to find not only them but also the means to bring them back to themselves.

Other characters in other novels are physically removed from their normal sphere of existence and must be rescued, but the sense of lost identity also recurs. Galliard has gone to the far North to make peace with his ancestral ghosts and becomes a prisoner of his fear. Charles Pitt-Heron has a similar journey to make in *The Power House*. One of the characters from *The Gap in the Curtain* dies, Buchan suggests, of fear generated by the foretelling of his death. And Vernon Milburne of *The Dancing Floor* suffered acutely as a child with nightmares and an inability to settle to his life. In the novel, he has to rescue Kore Arabin and bring her out of terrible danger, so releasing himself from his panics. Along with accidie and fear, a failed sense of self must have felt very real to Buchan. Indeed, Janet Adam-Smith in her biography writes that 'Buchan as a child had been haunted like a nightmare by Alice in Wonderland's loss of identity'.

The other important theme of the split between a desire for worldly success and the pull of the wilder world is made explicit in *Sick Heart River*, but it forms the background to many of the other novels. Hannay feels it each time he is dragged away from his happy country life and cannot resist. The four heroes of *John Macnab* find their healing in a return to the primaeval way of life.

They are all grandees and many commentators have criticised Buchan for his snobbery. The novels are certainly full of swells, aristocrats and great fortunes, and the villain of *The Three Hostages* is described as 'the best shot in England after His Majesty'. There is little doubt that Buchan enjoyed moving in the highest circles and wrote about the kind of people he admired.

His characters also show considerable prejudice against 'kaffirs', Jews and women. A brave, beautiful (and terrifying) Evallonian heroine from the McCunn series is described approvingly as an anti-feminist, and at times, it seems that the greatest compliment anyone could make of a woman is to say that she is like an untainted boy. The racism is more obviously shocking. Hannay, in particular, frequently uses language that is unrepeatable now but would have been natural to a white South African mining engineer whose life straddled the late nineteenth and early twentieth centuries.

Again in *The Three Hostages*, he is describing the richest man in England, Julius Victor: 'Blenkiron, who had no love for the race, once called him "the whitest Jew since the Apostle Paul".' A more offensive remark is hard to imagine, but Buchan adapted it from the reported comment of Raymond Robins, a real American millionaire philanthropist, who referred to Trotsky as 'a four kind son of a bitch, but the greatest Jew since Christ'.

Read with the historical background in mind, Buchan's novels are engrossing and illuminating. And in the Leithen series, they offer a lightly sketched but moving psychological portrait of a thoughtful, quietly brave, withdrawn, distinguished man, whose greatest battles were within his mind and who died far too soon. *See also* Godfathers of British Crime Fiction *and* Literature and Crime Fiction.

Selected Works by the Author
The Thirty-Nine Steps (1915)
Greenmantle (1916)
The Power House (1916)
Mr Standfast (1919)
Huntingtower (1922)
The Three Hostages (1924)
John Macnab (1925)
The Dancing Floor (1926)
The Courts of the Morning (1929)
The Island of Sheep (1936)
Sick Heart River (1941; published in the United States as *Mountain Meadow*)

Further Reading
FitzHerbert, Margaret. 1983. *The Man Who Was Greenmantle*. John Murray.

Website
The John Buchan Society, http://www.johnbuchansociety.co.uk/

Natasha Cooper

Bulldog Jack (film, 1935)

(Walter Forde, director)

Light-hearted but always interesting, *Bulldog Jack* is one of the best films adapted from the novels by 'Sapper' featuring 'Bulldog Drummond', one of the most imperishable heroes of British crime/thriller writing – and one that encapsulates the pleasures and limitations of its source material – 'I shall be very disappointed if we don't find somebody gagged and bound!'

Captain Hugh 'Bulldog' Drummond first appeared in *Bulldog Drummond*, a 1920 novel by 'Sapper' (Herman Cyril McNeile). McNeile produced follow-up books and – in collaboration with Gerard Fairlie – plays; on his death, Fairlie continued the series. Carlyle Blackwell was the first movie Drummond in *Bulldog Drummond* (1922), but Jack Buchanan (*Bulldog Drummond's Third Round*, 1925) and Ronald Colman (*Bulldog Drummond*, 1929) modified the hero's screen image: Blackwell was a two-fisted upper-class bruiser like the (fairly unpleasant) book character, but the silent Buchanan and the talkie Colman made him a suave, slick gentleman sleuth, forging the template followed by most subsequent movie Drummonds (who include Kenneth MacKenna, Ray Milland, John Lodge, John Howard, Tom Conway, Walter Pidgeon and Richard Johnson). Sapper's novels are offensive tosh, shot through with racist attitudes which would seem to make Drummond an ideal Mosleyite fascist, but the character had an enormous currency, and the screen adaptations tended to downplay the nastiness.

Oddly, *Bulldog Jack* is among the best films in the series – though it is a light send-up of their conventions. A vehicle for the big-chinned comedian Jack Hulbert, it has a surprising canonicity – with both McNeile and Fairlie involved in the script, along with Hulbert and Sidney Gilliat – and a decent cameo from the unfortunately named Atholl Fleming as the adventurer. It opens with Drummond en route to a meeting with a mystery woman (Fay Wray) who has sought his help in a time of rare peril, and because of some typical sneaky conspirators sabotaging his car, he crashes into Jack Pennington (Hulbert), a cricketer who dreams of adventure, and breaks his arm. With Drummond laid up, Jack takes over and teams up with the hero's usual supporting cast – butler Denny (Gibb McLaughlin) and silly Algy Longworth (Claude Hulbert) – to tackle a good mystery, with Ralph Richardson (who had played the hero in *The Return of Bulldog Drummond*, 1934) having an Einstein-look criminal mastermind and a cracking finale involving a chase through a disused London underground tunnel which has afforded the villains access to the British Museum so that they can loot a valuable art object.

Some of the comedy is surprisingly subtle – like the stream of visitors to Drummond's flat who disappoint Jack as he eagerly awaits the beautiful damsel in dire peril – and the jovial, stupidly intrepid Jack is an amusing caricature of the books' and the films' daring but often ridiculous hero. Algy, usually the comic relief in Drummond stories, interestingly becomes an exasperated straight man when partnered with a hero who is *not* cleverer, luckier or more dignified than he is. The script has some pulp verve (the villain is after The Goddess With a Hundred Hands) and director Walter Forde stages good action and mysterioso sequences; in America, some of the backchat was trimmed and the film was released as *Alias Bulldog Drummond*, a more-or-less serious adventure. In 1983, long after everyone had forgotten Drummond, Dick Clement directed *Bullshot*, a sadly weak 'ripping yarn'-style satire of the character. *See also* Film and Crime: Page to Screen.

Kim Newman

Burke, John F. (b.1922)

John Burke is the prolific (and highly adroit) author of around 150 books in all genres under a variety of pseudonyms, with a very individual approach to the crime novel being a specialty. Burke was born in Rye, Sussex (where his daughter runs a quirky hotel in which he is a notable 'presence'), and grew up in Liverpool, where his father was a chief inspector of police. He won an Atlantic Award in Literature for his skilfully written first novel, *Swift Summer* (1949), and worked in publishing and the oil business before joining 20th Century Fox Productions in 1963 as European story editor.

During the 1950s Burke concentrated primarily on science fiction, though he also wrote the Sexton **Blake** episode *Corpse to Copenhagen* (1957). In the 1960s he branched out into a variety of fields, writing mostly as Jonathan Burke. These included a number of **thrillers** which looked at crime and intrigue in all corners of society from the boardroom in *Only the Ruthless Can Play* (1965) to the music scene in *Deadly Downbeat* (1962). Perhaps his tensest novel of this period was *The Twisted Tongues* (1964) about the old hatreds stirred up when a wartime traitor is released.

Burke developed a substantial sideline in producing novelisations for television shows and films, with Britain's Hammer Films being a celebrated account. He wrote six volumes based on scripts of early episodes of ***The Bill*** (1985–1992). He is also the author of the highly individual Dr Caspian trilogy, about Victorian psychic detective Dr Alexander Caspian and his assistant Bronwen Powys. The series comprises *The Devil's Footsteps* (1976), *The Black Charade* (1977) and *Ladygrove* (1978). Rich, well-wrought atmosphere is the defining element of these books.

Burke has also edited the anthology series *Tales of Unease* (1966), *More Tales of Unease* (1969) and *New Tales of Unease* (1976). These much-collected anthologies contain both new and reprint work.

Selected Works by the Author
The Devil's Footsteps (1976)
The Black Charade (1977)
Ladygrove (1978)

Stephen Jones

Burke, Richard (b.1963)

Richard Burke is both a writer (of psychological thrillers) and an award-winning documentary film-maker, producing and directing science-based films for television, which include *Tomorrow's World* and *Space* for the BBC, *Electric Skies* for Channel 4 and *Raging Planet* for the Discovery Channel. He was born in London but grew up in Oxfordshire and now resides with his family in Somerset. He started his writing career as part of the *Orion New Blood* series with *Frozen* in January 2003. The tale, like many debut novels, follows the tradition of the (potentially) unreliable narrator. *Frozen* (written in the first person) follows the haunted protagonist Harry, who discovers that his childhood friend and secret love Verity has attempted suicide by throwing herself off the cliffs at Beachy Head. Harry's life is plunged into turmoil as he struggles to understand why such a positive personality he knew years ago would wish to end her life so dramatically. As Verity lies in a coma, Harry consults with her friend Adam and her business partner Sam to try to piece together what led her to Beachy Head. In his journey (which includes examining his past), where Verity rejected his love, he discovers a variety of sinister secrets, and his journey throws up more questions than answers (see interview with Mike Stotter, **Shots**, January 2004). As a story of unrequited love, the book is resonant, but by adding the psychological thriller dimension, Burke gives it an edge that makes it a mature and thought-provoking read. Peter Guttridge in *The Observer* described it as 'An intriguing mystery with a beguiling narrator' ('Driven to Suicide by Emily Dickinson', 29 February 2004).

Burke's second novel, *Redemption*, was published in 2006 and is the story of Matthew Daniels, a prison governor, and the difficult choices he has to make. Daniels's wife Charlotte is kidnapped, and he finds the only way he can attempt to get her back is to cross the boundaries of what is legally acceptable and morally right. His plan requires him to acquaint himself with some of the prisoners who used to be in his care. He is obliged to enter the criminal world to reclaim his wife and everything he holds dear. Burke stated in *The Independent* that it was no coincidence that there is a miscarriage at the heart of his novel *Redemption* (the two central characters Mathew and Charlotte Daniels have suffered one) – Burke only realised after he had finished writing it that the genesis of the tale was his wife's miscarriage, which played a major role in the creative process.

Selected Works by the Author
Frozen (2003)
Redemption (2006)

Website
http://www.richardburke.co.uk/

Ali Karim

Burley, W[illiam] J[ohn] (1914–2002)

W.J. Burley, born in Falmouth and educated, like many other twentieth-century crime writers, at Balliol College, Oxford. He pursued careers as engineer and teacher, both in the south-west, before coming, late, to writing crime fiction in the mid-1960s. Of his first three novels, two (*A Taste of Power*, published in 1966, and *Death in Willow Pattern*, in 1970) featured Henry Pym, zoology professor and keen criminologist; the other, *Three-Toed Pussy* (1968), introduced Burley's principal series detective, Superintendent Charles Wycliffe, a good family man whose profile has in more recent times been raised by television and who is described by Burley as 'diligent but compassionate, earnest but with a wry sense of humour and sufficiently idiosyncratic to be interesting'. In some ways, he seems rather like an English Maigret, but more proactive in a detective sense than Simenon's sleuth. The Wycliffe books have a setting in Cornwall, where Burley made his home, or (less frequently) Devon; the two counties share a police force in real life as well as in Burley's fiction. They are mostly concerned with tensions which arise between people in small groups, families, partners in a family business, and so on. Both plotting and writing are highly competent. Burley is one of several latter-day crime writers with a keen sense of place, usually from the same area. His books give a very enjoyable impression of Cornwall, in particular, as the background to crime: *Wycliffe and the Winsor Blue* (1987) is set in Falmouth with an artistic background; *Wycliffe and the Tangled Web* (1988) in Mevagissey; *Wycliffe and the Quiet Virgin* (1986) near St Ives at a stormy Christmas; *Wycliffe and the Four Jacks* (1985) in Roseland (an archaeological setting); and *Death in a Salubrious Place* (1973) in the Scillies. *See also* The Shires: Rural England and Regional Crime Fiction.

Selected Works by the Author
A Taste of Power (1966)
Three-Toed Pussy (1968)
Death in Willow Pattern (1969)
Death in a Salubrious Place (1973)
Wycliffe and the Schoolgirls (1976)
Wycliffe and the Scapegoat (1978)
Wycliffe in Paul's Court (1980)
Wycliffe's Wild Goose Chase (1982)
Wycliffe and the Four Jacks (1985)
Wycliffe and the Quiet Virgin (1986)
Wycliffe and the Winsor Blue (1987)
Wycliffe and the Tangled Web (1988)
Wycliffe and the Dead Flautist (1991)
Wycliffe and the Last Rites (1992)
Wycliffe and the Guild of Nine (2000)

Website
http://www.wjburley.com

Philip Scowcroft

Burn, Gordon (b.1948)

A literary novelist and sports writer, Gordon Burn has also produced immaculately researched true crime books about serial killers Peter Sutcliffe (also known as The Yorkshire Ripper) and Rose and Fred West.

Burn was born in Newcastle, but later moved to London and became a special writer on the *Sunday Times Magazine*. In the early 1980s, intrigued by Peter Sutcliffe's crimes, he moved to the killer's hometown Bingley where he spent almost two years researching his subject, extensively interviewing Sutcliffe's father, brothers and sisters and briefly talking to Sutcliffe's wife. Burn studied the locale at length, and uncovered a misogynistic and macho society, a society which Sutcliffe, a sensitive and introverted child, had loathed and feared. Bullied and beaten, Sutcliffe had at last acquiesced to the dominant culture, taking up weightlifting and visiting prostitutes. He attacked one such girl who cheated him, but it was only when family pressures reached their zenith that he began to kill. Burn's book on the case, *Somebody's Husband, Somebody's Son*, was published in 1984 and favourably compared to Truman Capote's classic *In Cold Blood* (1965).

He gained similar acclaim with *Alma Cogan* (1991), a novel which speculates about what would have happened if singer Cogan had not died in the 1960s and which makes passing reference to infamous killers such as the Manson family, Dennis Nilsen, Dr Crippen and Reginald Christie. The Moors murderers are also mentioned, and the ending of the novel references the infamous tape the killers made of victim Lesley

Ann Downey. *Alma Cogan* won the Whitbread Best First Novel Award in 1991. That same year, Burn also won a Magazine Publishing Award for his sports column in *Esquire*. Four years later, he produced *Fullalove* (1995), an intense exploration of the life of a tabloid hack.

Burn then returned to true crime, interviewing many of Rose West's family members and one of her surviving victims for *Happy Like Murderers* (1998), a book which shows the complex and changing relationship of Fred and Rose West. It was followed by a novel, *North of England Home Service* (2002), which captures the atmosphere of post-war London and examines fame and growing old.

In 2006, he published a book about football, *Best and Edwards*, exploring the career of rising Manchester United star Duncan Edwards, tragically killed in an air crash at age twenty-one, and George Best who died after liver replacement due to his alcoholism.

Burn is a regular contributor to *The Guardian*, often on the subject of contemporary art. (He wrote *On the Way to Work* with artist Damien Hirst in 2001, Hirst having previously provided the cover graphic for Burn's *Happy Like Murderers*.)

Whether he is exploring the lives of serial killers, singers or footballers, Burn excels in highlighting the difference between fame and celebrity.

Selected Works by the Author
Somebody's Husband, Somebody's Son (true crime, 1984)
Alma Cogan (1991)
Fullalove (1995)
Happy Like Murderers (true crime, 1998)
North of England Home Service (2002)

Carol Anne Davis

Burns, Alan (b.1929)

Alan Burns is an experimental novelist, whose contribution to crime fiction is *The Angry Brigade* (1973), which concerns both crime and political activism.

The Angry Brigade was Burns's sixth novel. His earlier books had employed certain experimental techniques. *Europe After the Rain* (1965) took not only its title but also its mood and tone from a painting by Max Ernst. Burns continued to use Surrealist methods in *Celebrations* (1967) and *Babel* (1969), while *Dreamerika!* (1972) reads like Ballard's *The Atrocity Exhibition* (1970) cut up by Burroughs. *The Angry Brigade* tells the story of the leftist urban guerrilla group of the same name that was active in Britain in the early 1970s, but tells it in an oblique, unconventional way. The self-styled documentary novel purports to be based on interviews with members of two direct-action groups penetrated by the author. In a preface, he informs the reader that although names have been changed, his method is one of 'collective autobiography'. The entire novel is presented in the voices of those group members interviewed, namely Dave, Barry, Jean, Ivor, Suzanne and Mehta. The development of the group's ideology is pieced together from interspersed fragments of transcripts. Class conflicts within the group are dramatised as members disagree as much over day-to-day methods as political aims. Different group members having been radicalised in various distinct ways, the collective struggle is constantly in danger of falling apart. Dave, who was beaten up by the police at the age of fourteen, is motivated by a dislike for authority: 'The Angry Brigade began like the IRA and the Panthers, as a defence organisation, to keep out the police and others who are coming into our neighbour-hood, trying to break up the group and smash it.' Others are more intellectually motivated and talk of relishing a fight, but then recoil from physical violence. A confrontation inevitably comes, however, in which a police officer receives injuries serious enough to keep him out of the force.

In an interview with David Madden published in the *Review of Contemporary Fiction* in 1997, Burns revealed his disappointment with the way *The Angry Brigade* was perceived, as an attack on the real Angry Brigade. 'The darned thing is that I wrote the novel in protest against, and with the intention of off-setting, the demonising of the members of the Angry Brigade in the press and other media. However, the book was pretty widely reviewed and generally seen as an attack on the "real" Brigade, satirising them, depicting their petty squabbles, their male chauvinism, and so on.' Burns paid the novelist's price for drawing realistic, warts-and-all portraits of his protagonists. 'Finally I think I regret the novel's title. I now think I should have removed it more clearly from seeming-reportage.' *The Angry Brigade* remains a fascinating fictionalised glimpse of a time when crime and political activism converged in a way that may come to be viewed with a certain nostalgia.

Selected Works by the Author
Buster (1961)
Europe after the Rain (1965)
Celebrations (1967)
Babel (1969)
Dreamerika! (1972)
The Angry Brigade (1973)
The Day Daddy Died (1981)
Revolutions of the Night (1986)

Nicholas Royle

Butler, Gwendoline (b.1922)

Along with such luminaries as Agatha Christie and Margery Allingham, Gwendoline Butler was among the most talented – if not the most widely read – female crime writers of her generation.

She was born in Blackheath, south-east London, one of twins, although her sister died soon after birth. She was educated at the prestigious Haberdashers' Aske's Girls' School in nearby Hatcham and went on to study modern history at Lady Margaret Hall, Oxford (whose later incumbents included fellow crime writers Antonia Fraser and Lindsey Davis). She continued in Oxford for eight years as a lecturer on modern history before marrying Dr Lionel Butler, Professor of Medieval History at the University of St Andrews, Fife, in 1949.

Having read voraciously since the age of eight, and with such authors as Jane Austen and Sir Arthur Conan Doyle being favourites, Butler tried her hand at a detective novel while her husband was away in Malta for three months. The result was *Receipt for Murder*, published in 1956, featuring Inspector Winter. Three more Winter novels followed quickly, but it was her fifth novel, *The Interloper* (1959), that marked her most important creation – Inspector John Coffin.

Although Coffin had made a fleeting appearance in *The Dull Dead* (1958), his first proper outing was in *The Interloper*, an edgy tale of an American student in London whose researching of the Great Plague of 1665 appears to bring about visitations from the past. Part ghost story, part mystery, the book showcases the author's love of history and the supernatural. Its delightfully atmospheric descriptions of London won many fans, and Coffin himself – Chief Commissioner of the so-called 'Second City of London' – went on to feature in many further books. From 1963, with *A Coffin for Baby*, his name would always feature in the title. Most of these mysteries were set in and around Greenwich, Deptford and Blackheath in south-east London, but after a twelve-year interregnum (in which only three non-Coffin books appeared), Coffin emerged on the other side of the river in 1986 with *Coffin on the Water*. These later books never quite managed to recapture the atmosphere of Butler's earlier works, although there were still many compelling cases.

Butler also uses the pseudonym 'Jennie Melville'; as Melville, she created the female sleuth Charmian Daniels, a character who virtually kick-started the woman's police procedural. The first in the series was *Come Home and Be Killed* in 1962; this was followed by eighteen more books. Under this name, Butler also writes stand-alone crime books as well as romance and historical fiction.

Selected Works by the Author

As Gwendoline Butler
Receipt for Murder (1956)
The Interloper (1959)
A Coffin for Baby (1963)
Coffin Waiting (1964)
Coffin's Dark Number (1969)
A Coffin from the Past (1970)
A Coffin for the Canary (1974; published in the United States as *Sarsen Place*)
Coffin in the Black Museum (1989; published in the United States as *Coffin in the Museum of Crime*)

As Jennie Melville
A New Kind of Killer, an Old Kind of Death (1970)
Windsor Red (1988)
The Woman Who Was Not There (1996)

Mark Campbell

C

CADS Magazine

CADS (Crime and Detective Stories) is unique among UK **magazines** devoted to crime fiction. Like the American fanzines (Allen Hubin's *The Armchair Detective*, Guy Townsend's *The Mystery Fancier* and Jeff Meyerson's *Poisoned Pen*) that inspired it, *CADS* was always intended to be driven entirely by the enthusiasm of its readers and contributors. Sub-titled 'an irregular magazine of comment and criticism about crime and detective stories', it was first published in July 1985 by editor Geoff Bradley. In

2006, it celebrated its fiftieth issue, in its twenty-first year. It is the United Kingdom's longest running publication devoted to the study of crime fiction.

Geoff Bradley was a teacher of mathematics and a connoisseur of crime literature. In the early 1980s, he occasionally issued catalogues of books. It was in the March 1984 catalogue that the idea for a magazine was mooted. 'Letters, articles, reviews of books new or old' was the first specification for magazine material. The list of prohibitions was lengthier: 'no true crime (too grizzly [*sic*] for me)...nothing supernatural...no fiction'. A later catalogue (February 1985) is more specific: 'if you are highly knowledgeable about one aspect of the **detective** story, say, detective stories set in Wigan...then I would be delighted if you would share your erudition with us'.

CADS 1, now a collector's item in its own right, is worth looking at in some detail. It was produced largely by Bradley himself (which continued to be the case throughout the magazine's history) and has fifty-six typewritten pages with occasional hand-written amendments. The cover is printed on green paper (a perhaps unfortunate choice that persists to this day) and features an ingenious reworking of a Frank Wiles drawing of Sherlock **Holmes**. Holmes is examining the new magazine – which features the drawing of Sherlock Holmes examining the new magazine, ad infinitum. The editorial hand is quickly evident: two pages of editorial comment, two other short pieces and Bradley's appeals for information on other magazines in the field. Most of all, he institutes the editorial habit of commenting thus '*** *Plot details revealed* ***GHB' as issues are raised or suggested by the text. Readers would come to expect and enjoy these interjections – always authoritative, often delightfully dry-humoured and sometimes a shade tetchy.

The remaining pages are taken up by an intriguing range of material. Philip T. Asdell's article concerning author errors occupies the pole position (as it was the first submission received). The article on ways of reconciling the conventions of the **Golden Age** with more modern forms of crime fiction by H.R.F. **Keating** is significant. It was the first indication that *CADS* would receive support from established writers. They would later include David **Williams**, Catherine Aird, Andrew **Taylor** and Mike **Ripley**, along with Martin **Edwards**, who contributed many an article.

Another such contribution came from Bill Pronzini and Marcia Muller, who allowed *CADS* a preview of their forthcoming book *1001 Midnights*. Doug Greene, later a distinguished biographer of John Dickson **Carr**, contributed an authoritative essay on round robin detective novels. Peter Tyas penned an article on the Hodder & Stoughton 'Signature' editions of the 1920s. Ethel Lindsay welcomed the early Joan Hickson/Miss Marple television adaptations (P.A. Watt, nineteen pages later, had reservations). Underrated authors and favourite novelists – *CADS* perennials – were first covered by Donald Rudd and Mrs N. Hooker, respectively. Shorter contributions covered *Jazz and the Mystery Story*, the Sherlock Holmes Collection in Marylebone Library, Robert Eustace and *Cricket and Crime*.

The article by John Boyles, a regular contributor until his death in 2001, on Jack **Higgins**'s *A Prayer for the Dying* – along with the reviews (by Bob Adey and Donald Yates, among others) of books by Robert B. Parker, John Bowen, P.M. Hubbard and a thriller from Edgar-winner W.J. Weatherby – should also help to destroy the myth that *CADS* was solely concerned with Golden Age fiction.

Book reviews were always a regular feature of the magazine, which relied not on review copies but only on the enthusiasms of its readers. Reviews were therefore soon divided into 'new' and 'older' books. The former category has always 'covered' contemporary fiction. The editor's expertise in private eye fiction was supplemented in the early days by Steven Caine's reviews, later by Bob Cornwell's reviews and (from *CADS* 5) by Angela Morgan's pithy and wide-ranging reviews (later Youngman). 'Older' book reviewers included Bob Adey, Martin Edwards and Bill Deeck. In one area, however, *CADS* can be considered indispensable. The section entitled 'Books about the Books' features reviews, often by Geoff Bradley, of many key English-language reference books on the genre.

The letters page is also vital – 'the life-blood of any magazine' – as Bradley stated in *CADS* 2. By *CADS* 23, the letters pages totalled nineteen, a record for the publication. (For that issue, a letter arrived from Julian **Symons**, another of Bradley's early inspirations. Symons briefly mentioned *CADS* in the final paperback edition of *Bloody Murder*.) Most major articles draw forth a barrage of comments, corrections and observations, many leading to more correspondence. Particularly vigorous contributions have come from the erudite Barry Pike, John Jeffries, John Cooper, Agatha **Christie**, expert John Curran and even Allen Hubin himself. *CADS* 8 is notable for the arrival in the letters column of New Yorker Charles Shibuk, *CADS*'s resident fact-checker. Subsequent issues were rigorously checked for errors – a valuable service indeed, but one that would usually guarantee a rash of editorial comments, some with just a hint of rancour. The geographic range of correspondents is also impressive, covering the United Kingdom, the United States and Australia by way of Europe, Japan and even Greenland.

Early on, the *CADS* page count moved to eighty and the production vehicle from a typewriter to an Amstrad and finally to a personal computer with *CADS* 19. New desktop publishing software was a major factor in Bob Cornwell's offer to design the *CADS* covers (which he did from *CADS* 9) and in the institution of The *CADS* Questionnaire from *CADS* 16, in which many prominent (and not-so-prominent) UK authors have featured.

In June 1989, the first *CADS* Supplement became available. It was a comprehensive index covering *CADS* 1 to 10, compiled by Bill Deeck, a contributor from *CADS* 3. Deeck became well-known for his hilarious work cataloguing the oeuvre of James Corbett, but it is for his several indices covering much of the life of the magazine that he is most valued. Later, the supplements accommodated those substantial articles which were too long for the magazine itself. There are now eleven, including a survey of *Railways in British Crime Fiction* from the prolific Philip Scowcroft, a contributor from *CADS* 2 to date, as well as *Private Passions, Guilty Pleasures* compiled to celebrate *CADS* 50, with contributions from eighty-seven authors, critics and *CADS* alumni.

Whatever importance *CADS* has acquired surely rests upon its writers. Philip Scowcroft and Peter Tyas (in every issue until his death in 1996), for instance, have been responsible for a wide range of material: Tyas's series on Ellery Queen, for example, and Scowcroft's regional crime surveys of the United Kingdom (and beyond). Tony Medawar's series *Serendip's Detections* has pulled off several *CADS* coups, including the discovery of an unknown work by Agatha Christie and a previously unknown pseudonym for the prolific John Rhode. Ian Godden wrote perceptively on writers as varied as James Crumley and Compton Mackenzie, while highlighting more obscure talent in his series *Digging up the Unknown*. Nick Kimber's many contributions include *Cornerstones*, a fresh look at selected titles from the 1951 Haycraft/Queen book on classic crime. William Sarjeant's series *Crime Novelists* as *Writers of Children's Fiction* is both eye-opening and enlightening. Ethel Lindsay contributed to the recording of earlier reference books with her series *Here Be Mystery and Murder*. André Michielsen is best known for his series on writers of *Paperback Originals*. And among the varied contributions from ex-*Armchair Detective* veteran Marvin Lachman was his obituary column, *Death of a Mystery Writer*, from *CADS* 20. Now covering nine or so pages of each issue, this column has become an indispensable source of information on English-language mystery and mystery-related deaths.

Outstanding individual contributions have come from writers like Christine Simpson and Dick Stewart. Simpson has contributed excellent work on, for instance, Edmund **Crispin** and Colin Watson. Dick Stewart's scholarly and dry-humoured contributions on Wilkie **Collins**, George Bellairs and his less than straightforward publisher, or Die-agrams (detective stories with plans!) are other highlights. Also notable are the personal memories of Donald Yates about the last days of Cornell Woolrich and John Dirckx's masterly construction (from thirty-nine Sherlock **Holmes** stories) of Holmes on *The Art of Detection*. Even later would come Pierre Bondil's superb last-ever interview with George V. Higgins and Josef Hoffmann's salutary article on Ludwig Wittgenstein's fondness for **pulp** novelist Norbert Davis.

Finally, perhaps *CADS*'s true 'importance' lies in the way that its contributors have consistently championed the neglected and under-appreciated writers of the genre. Too many to mention, but *CADS*'s 4,000-odd pages (and counting) should, at the very least, provide future students of the genre with much to ponder – and enjoy.

Further Reading
Deeck, William F. 1997. 'CADS – An Index to Issues 1-30'. *CADS* Supplement 6.
Deeck, William F., and Christine R. Simpson. 2007. 'CADS: An Index to Issues 31-50'. *CADS* Supplement 11.

Bob Cornwell

Cain, Tom (b.1959)

The publication of Tom Cain's debut **thriller** *The Accident Man* (2007) provoked press speculation about the author – supposedly an investigative journalist – said by his publishers and agents to be hiding behind this pseudonym. One Sunday newspaper even quoted the aristocratic television celebrity and convicted fraudster Lord Charles Brocket who claimed that he was the author. The actual Cain was, and is, David Thomas, born on 17 January 1959. His eclectic writing career involved investigative reportage, notably for his non-fiction book *Foul Play* (2003), an in-depth account of a football corruption case, eight years in the writing, that was shortlisted for the William Hill award for sports book of the year. But Thomas's serious, observational work and celebrity interviews ran alongside a parallel career as a humorist, which saw him appear as a television panellist on *Have I Got News for You* and serve as the youngest editor in the 150-year history of *Punch* magazine.

Jokes are in short supply in a Tom Cain book (as critics maintained they were in *Punch*). His protagonist, Samuel Carver, is a Royal Marine–turned paid assassin. As a cold-blooded killer, who finds time between terminations to seduce a beautiful Russian blonde, Carver is clearly in the tradition of James Bond, Jason Bourne and Jack Bauer. But, in keeping with a more cynical, sceptical age, he has neither Bond's suave self-assurance nor the moral certainty that comes from working on Her Majesty's service. On the contrary, Carver is fatally compromised, almost beyond redemption. Within the first fifty pages of *The Accident Man*, he has stood at one end of the Alma Tunnel in Paris and taken out a black Mercedes, whose occupant – never named in the book – is quite clearly Princess Diana.

15. Tom Cain.

The notion of depicting the most famous car-smash of the twentieth century as murder and then making the killer the hero of a thriller risked obvious accusations of tastelessness and exploitation. Yet, its audacity and narrative pace won admirers, including the novelist Wilbur Smith, who described *The Accident Man* as, 'The finest first thriller I have read since *Day of the Jackal*'. Hollywood also saw the commercial potential: months before its UK publication, film rights had already been optioned by Paramount.

Cain, however, was left with the problem of finding other, equally significant targets for Samuel Carver's deadly skills. A second book, with the working title *The House of War* (2008), was inspired by a number of global events that occurred in the months after Diana's death. Beneath the façade of classic, high-octane thriller writing, Cain seems to be using Carver to provide a sly commentary on our times. *The Accident Man* possesses a strong streak of acerbic observation on media-obsessed politicians, amoral intelligence officers, hysterical mourners and gangster-like Russian oligarchs. *The House of War* takes on Islamic and Christian extremism alike. Carver's involvements in 9/11 and Iraq cannot be many books away.

Selected Works by the Author
The Accident Man (2007)
The House of War (2008)

Brian Ritterspak

Campbell, Ramsey (b.1946)

Although Ramsey Campbell is best known for his highly accomplished horror writing (according to the *Oxford Companion to English Literature*, he is 'Britain's most respected living horror writer'), most of his non-horror novels can be classed as crime fiction. *The Face That Must Die* (1979) is a study of paranoia and is the first anti-homophobic crime novel. John Horridge, a homophobic loner, becomes wrongly convinced that he has identified the subject of an identikit portrait and eventually kills the man in mistaken self-defence. The killing leads to further crimes as Horridge attempts to cover up his involvement and find refuge. Campbell based many of his observations on his mother's schizophrenia.

The Count of Eleven (1991) adroitly parodies the serial-killer genre. Jack Orchard, a family man who runs a small business, becomes unhinged by a run of bad luck and attempts to use a lucky chain letter to change it. When this fails, he is convinced that some of the recipients have broken the chain, and his meetings with them lead to murder. Despite the violence of some of these scenes, this is essentially a comic novel. Campbell's criminals are typically driven by their own inadequacies, often linked to extreme introversion and an exaggerated sense of self-worth – characters far removed from the serial killers who became the iconic monsters of turn-of-the-century fiction. Orchard is more sympathetically pathetic, a quality that – along with the social pratfalls he suffers – may recall the silent comedians he admires. Like the murder in *Lolita*, his crimes are horrifying partly because they are comic.

16. Ramsey Campbell.

At the beginning of *The One Safe Place* (1995), an American professor antagonises a Manchester motorist and attracts the wrath of his criminal family. As the hostility escalates, the professor's young son Marshall is given LSD and lured away by Darren, the criminal's young son. The book is concerned with the omnipresent violence that the American family seeks to escape by moving abroad and with the process by which Darren becomes criminal. Abduction often figures in Campbell's crime fiction. In *The Last Voice They Hear* (1998), having left clues from their shared childhood for his journalist brother Geoff to decipher and relive, the murderous Ben Davenport kidnaps the brother's young son to compel Geoff to track him down. In an irony typical of Campbell, Ben goes unnoticed in public by behaving badly towards the child – 'something else parents were supposed to do'. In *Silent Children* (2000), Hector Woollie kidnaps and kills children because, having watched a sibling die of spina bifida, he cannot bear to see them suffer. Despite this motivation, he is among the most monstrous of Campbell's grotesques.

Secret Stories (2005) deals with Dudley Smith, a civil servant who writes clandestine tales based on murders he has committed. When his mother submits one of his stories to a literary competition on his behalf without telling him, the unwanted fame forces him to seek new inspiration. Like *The Count of Eleven*, this book foregrounds the dark comedy evident in much of Campbell's work. It also displays the acute psychological enquiry and social comment that is central to his horror fiction.

Selected Works by the Author
The Face That Must Die (1979)
The Count of Eleven (1991)
The One Safe Place (1995)
The Last Voice They Hear (1998)
Silent Children (2000)
Secret Stories (2005; also published in the United States as *Secret Story*)

Barry Forshaw

Campion, Albert

A character created by Margery **Allingham** (1904–1966) as a none-too-subtle dig at Dorothy **Sayers**'s upper-class detective Lord Peter **Wimsey**, Albert Campion swiftly carved out his own niche in the pantheon of **Golden Age** sleuths.

He first appeared as a minor character, and indeed a suspect, in Allingham's fourth novel, *The Crime at Black Dudley* (1929). At a dinner party held at the remote Black Dudley manor house, the masked owner, Colonel Coombe, is killed following a sinister ritual involving a supposedly cursed dagger. But while pathologist George Abershaw is clearly Allingham's mooted hero, it is the vapid-eyed gatecrasher Albert Campion who ends up as the most intriguing character. Thin, blond and bespectacled, his seemingly innocuous manner hides a brooding intelligence coupled with a freewheeling desire for risk and adventure.

As revealed in his second appearance, in *Mystery Mile* (1930), 'Albert Campion' is a pseudonym for something grander: his real first name is Rudolph and his surname begins with K. Nothing more is ever ventured on this subject, but there are occasional hints that he hails from aristocratic stock. Rare guest appearances of relatives include his sister Valentine Ferris (*The Fashion in Shrouds*, 1938) and his uncle Canon Avril, a pragmatic clergyman who first appears in the smog-bound chase adventure, *The Tiger in the Smoke* (1952). Campion meets his future wife, Amanda Fitton, in *Sweet Danger* (1933; also published in the United States as *Kingdom of Death* and as *The Fear Sign*). She later appears in *The Fashion in Shrouds*, now an aircraft engineer, before the couple finally wed at the end of *Traitor's Purse* (1941; also published in the United States as *The Sabotage Murder Mystery*), producing a son named Rudolph who would feature heavily in *The Beckoning Lady* (1955; also published in the United States as *The Estate of the Beckoning Lady*).

From *Mystery Mile* onwards, Campion is accompanied by a manservant named Magersfontein Lugg. A former burglar, the uncouth Lugg acts as Campion's right-hand man when the going gets tough, in much the same way that Bunny had protected Raffles in E.W. **Hornung**'s Edwardian escapades. And like **Holmes**, Campion utilises a network of criminal allies to stay one step ahead of the stuffy Scotland Yard inspector Stanislaus Oates (cf. Lestrade).

The perfect example of a journey being more important than its destination, the appeal of the Campion stories relies not so much on their 'whodunit' aspect – which is usually somewhat arbitrary – but on characters and locations in which said tales take place. Never has the English countryside appeared so idyllic, its country houses so cosy and its inhabitants so richly eccentric.

Surprisingly, there have not been many attempts to adapt the stories for film or television. A short-lived BBC series starring Peter Davison as Campion and Brian Glover as Lugg was transmitted between 1988 and 1990, compromising eight extremely well-made adventures, but since then Allingham's most famous creation has lain dormant.

Selected Works
The Crime at Black Dudley (1929; published in the United States as *The Black Dudley Murder*)
Mystery Mile (1930)
Police at the Funeral (1931)
Dancers in Mourning (1935)
More Work for the Undertaker (1948)

Mark Campbell

Canning, Victor (1911–1986)

The prolific **thriller** writer Victor Canning represents a brand of solid, unpretentious professionalism rare today in the crime/thriller field. Canning was born on 16 June 1911 in Plymouth, the eldest son of a coach builder. He quit education early to become a clerk as his family could not afford to educate him beyond sixteen. Three years later, he was publishing stories in juvenile magazines to supplement his meagre salary. He published his first novel *Mr Finchley Discovers His England* in 1934 with publishers Hodder and Stoughton. When the book sold well, he gave up his job and started writing full-time, producing thirteen more novels in the next six years under the names Victor Canning, Julian Forest and Alan Gould. Canning then started writing for the *Daily Mail*, and a number of his pieces were collected in a book (with illustrations by Lesley Stead) entitled *Everyman's England* in 1936. He also continued to write short stories between novels.

Canning enlisted in the army in 1940, where he trained alongside his friend and fellow thriller writer Eric **Ambler**. Ambler wrote about Canning in his autobiography, *Here Lies Eric Ambler*. Canning served overseas in 1943 in North Africa and took part in the invasion of Sicily and the Italian campaigns. After the war, Canning was assigned to an Anglo-American unit doing classified experimental work with radar, though Canning never discouraged the assumption of publishers and reviewers that his espionage stories were partly based on this experience (which had little to do with espionage). He was discharged in 1946 at the rank of major and then went back to writing.

Canning published (to great acclaim) a novel about a Nazi collaborator hiding out in an isolated village: *The Chasm* (1947). Canning's next book, *Panther's Moon* (1948), was filmed a year later as *Spy Hunt* by Director George Sherman. From 1950, Canning was established as someone who could publish a successful thriller a year on both sides of the Atlantic (and in the new mass-market paperback format). His material was well suited for the emerging film and television audiences hooked on suspense and thrillers. He spent time in Hollywood working on scripts for movies of his books and for television shows. One of his big hits was Ronald Neame's film version of *The Golden Salamander* (1950), which starred Trevor Howard. The proceeds allowed Canning to buy property in Kent, where he lived for the next twenty years. Apart from a plethora of film adaptations which he wrote (based on his novels), he also wrote for many popular US and UK television shows such as *Alfred Hitchcock Presents, Mannix, Man in a Suitcase* and others. He appeared in a 1967 episode of *Dixon of Dock Green* in a rare acting role.

After the 1950s, his books became more formulaic, blending exotic locations and robust action sequences with less well-defined characters, as Canning seemed to be concentrating on his film and television work. However, he also published short stories for the fiction **magazines**, *Argosy, Suspense, Ellery Queen's Mystery Magazine, John Bull, Saturday Evening Post, This Week* and others. In 1965, he began a series of four books featuring a private detective called Rex Carver, and these were among his most successful in terms of sales (*The Whip Hand*, published in 1965; *Doubled in Diamonds*, in 1966; *The Melting Man*, in 1968; and *The Python Project*, in 1967). The five and a half years from 1975 was a very productive time for Canning's fiction output, containing arguably his best work, including the first five of his *Birdcage* novels, a trilogy of books for children (*Smiler* series) starting with *The Runaways*, and a trilogy retelling the legends of King Arthur, starting with *The Crimson Chalice*. Canning died on 21 February 1986, in Cirencester. His last book, *Table Number Seven*, was completed by his wife Adria and his sister Jean.

In assessing Canning's contribution to the genre, one must not forget that he is probably best remembered for *The Rainbird Pattern* (1972) which was awarded the **Crime Writers' Association** (CWA) Silver Dagger and nominated for the Edgar award. It was also filmed by Alfred Hitchcock as *Family Plot* (1976). His later works were all far darker and more realistic than any of his thrillers of the 1950s and 1960s. These novels were bleaker stories of people trapped in the sinister machinations of dark government. Canning is often compared with contemporary thriller writers of the golden-age period such as Eric Ambler, Ian **Fleming**, Hammond **Innes**, Alistair **MacLean** and Desmond **Bagley**, but his contributions to film and television are often overlooked (as the majority were pre-colour). Canning did change style in the 1970s when the thriller turned a more cynical eye towards the security services with Len **Deighton** and John **le Carré** leading the pack, both of whom probably influenced Canning's later work but had greater literary ability and insight, deploying a far more cynical and literary eye on the changing world. However, Canning's contribution to the golden age of crime and thrillers should not be underestimated. *See also* Espionage Fiction.

Selected Works by the Author
Fly Away Paul (1936)
Fountain Inn (1939)
Green Battlefield (1943)
The Golden Salamander (1949)
The Hidden Face (1956; also published in the United States as *Burden of Proof*)
The Manasco Road (1957; also published in the United States as *The Forbidden Road*)
The Limbo Line (1963)
Doubled in Diamonds (1966)
The Python Project (1967)
Great Affair (1970)
Firecrest (1971)
The Rainbird Pattern (1972; also published in the United States as *Family Plot*)
The Kingsford Mark (1975)
The Doomsday Carrier (1976)
The Satan Sampler (1979)
Fall from Grace (1980)

Smiler Series
The Runaways (1972)
Flight of the Grey Goose (1973)
The Painted Tent (1974)

Crimson Chalice Series
The Crimson Chalice (1976)
The Circle of the Gods (1977)
The Immortal Wound (1978)

Further Reading
Ambler, Eric. 1985. *Here Lies Eric Ambler*. Weidenfeld and Nicholson.
Higgins, John. 2007. 'Life of Victor Canning'. http://myweb.tiscali.co.uk/wordscape/canning/biography.html.
Thomas, David A. 1986. 'Victor Canning: Popular and Now Very Collectable Author of Thrillers, Comic Novels, and Mysteries'. *Book and Magazine Collector* No. 32.

Ali Karim

Carr, John Dickson (1906–1977)

John Dickson Carr, noted for his 'impossible crime' stories, was American, not British, but he spent many years in Britain and contemplated becoming a British citizen.

He was born in Uniontown, Pennsylvania, where his father was a lawyer, but he followed in the footsteps of his grandfather, who was part-owner of a local newspaper. Carr wrote occasional articles on court proceedings as a teenager and soon had his own column. At Haverford College, he became editor of its literary magazine, *The Haverfordian*, which published several of his early stories.

His very first story, 'As Drink the Dead...' (1926) is an impossible murder, using the ploy of a man poisoned when he drinks from a cup that others have drunk from without ill effect. The story introduced Carr's detective, Henri Bencolin, the prefect of police in Paris. Carr, who studied at the Sorbonne in 1927, became fascinated by Paris, and much of Europe, delighting in the historical atmosphere. Some of that is apparent in his first novel, *It Walks by Night* (1930; reworked from 'Grand Guignol', serialised in *The Haverfordian* in 1929). Bencolin is a more matter-of-fact, no-nonsense individual than Carr's better-known detectives. He undertakes his investigations methodically and purposefully and is not prone to grandiloquence, though he enjoys the final staged revelation. There are three other Bencolin novels, *The Lost Gallows* (1931), *Castle Skull* (1931) and *The Corpse in the Waxworks* (1932), all in the same atmospheric vein.

Carr's fascination for history led him to write *Devil Kinsmere* (1934, under the alias Roger Fairbairn), where the protagonist is transported (literally) from the present-day to the time of Charles II. Carr clearly liked that device as he used it again in *Fear Is the Same* (1956, under the alias Carter Dickson) and *Fire! Burn!* (1957). Generally, Carr's **historical crime** novels are less satisfying than his contemporary ones, though he clearly enjoyed writing them, as shown by their pace and bravado. *The Murder of Sir Edmund Godfrey* (1936) is of particular interest because Carr researched an unsolved seventeenth-century murder and set forth his solution in a novel. He did not return to the historical novel until the 1950s and then they became something of a self-indulgence. They include *The Bride of Newgate* (1950) and *Captain Cut-throat* (1955), both set during the Napoleonic era; *Scandal at High Chimneys* (1965) set in nineteenth-century England; *The Witch of the Low-Tide* (1961) set in 1907; and *The Demoniacs* (1962) set at the time of the Bow Street Runners.

Carr's most famous detective is Dr Gideon Fell, modelled to a large extent on G.K. **Chesterton**: overweight, pompous, opinionated but brilliant. Carr was heavily influenced by Chesterton's writings, especially his Father Brown stories. The first Fell novel, *Hag's Nook* (1933), carries over some of the grotesqueries of the Bencolin novels, but the murder itself, of a man found dead of a broken neck in a building under watch, is well handled and ingeniously resolved. We meet Fell in all his blusterous glory, though we also see his childlike innocence, which allows him to see through fabrication to the heart of a crime.

Fell, however, did enjoy pontificating on the puzzles he encountered, and in *The Three Coffins* (1935), Carr allows Fell to step outside the novel in one chapter and give the reader a lecture on the nature of the impossible crime, 'The Locked-Room Lecture', which has remained standard reading ever since. There are twenty-three Fell novels in all. None match the ingenuity or audacity of *The Three Coffins*, but most are worth reading, especially *The Arabian Nights Murder* (1936), *To Wake the Dead* (1937), *The Problem of the Green Capsule* (1939; also known as *The Black Spectacles*) and *The Case of the Constant Suicides* (1941). There was also the scarce collection *Dr Fell, Detective and Other Stories* (1947) and the more recent *Fell and Foul Play* (1991).

Carr concocted the alias Carter Dickson for the books featuring Sir Henry Merrivale, who was head of Military Intelligence, though he seems to do precious little work. Unlike Fell, Merrivale is stubborn, even bloody-minded, and his humour is more irritating than funny, verging on self-parody. Yet his cases are often among the best that Carr wrote. Merrivale was apparently based, to some extent, on Carr's father, but over time took on some of the characteristics of Winston Churchill. There are twenty-two Merrivale novels, starting with *The Plague Court Murders* (1934) and including the equal of, some say even superior to, *The Three Coffins* – *The Judas Window* (1938), also published as *The Crossbow Murder* (1964). Bob Adey, the doyen of the impossible crime, has called it 'Probably, the best locked-room mystery ever written'. It concerns how a man is killed by an arrow in a completely sealed locked-room. According to Carr's biographer, Douglas Greene, Carr experimented many times to be sure it could be achieved. Carr acted out his impossible-murder methods to prove that all were feasible. Of the other Merrivale novels, of particular interest is *He Wouldn't Kill Patience* (1944), which arose following a challenge from Clayton Rawson who claimed he had contrived a murder in a room completely sealed with gummed tape.

Carr lived in England from 1933 to 1948, including the War years. During this time he contributed stories to *The Strand*, including most of the bizarre crime stories collected as *The Department of Queer Complaints* (1940, as Dickson); wrote dozens of scripts for the BBC radio series *Mystery Playhouse* and *Appointment with Fear*, as well as many propaganda talks; and wrote *The Life of Sir Arthur Conan Doyle* (1949). He also collaborated with Adrian Conan Doyle on several new Sherlock Holmes stories, published as *The Exploits of Sherlock Holmes* (1954). Carr returned to America in 1948, disenchanted with the post-war Labour government, but returned to England in 1953 and remained until 1965, when he left for tax reasons. In his final decade, his health failed considerably and few of his later books compare with his best work. His final novel is another historical, *The Hungry Goblin* (1972), which includes Wilkie Collins as the sleuth, but it is a minor work.

At his best – and this extended through more books and stories than might normally be expected – Carr was an ingenious and courageous writer, as every bit as bold and as daring as a magician seeking to baffle and outwit his audience. He invented many of the solutions for impossible crimes that have been used by writers since, all too few of whom have bettered him. That he is not given the same accord as Agatha **Christie** or Dorothy L. **Sayers** may be because much of his work may appear as gimmicks – good fun but not serious – and yet his work endures and will no doubt still be enjoyed by generations to come. *See also* Golden Age Crime Fiction.

Selected Works by the Author
The Three Coffins (1935; also published in the United States as *The Hollow Man*)
The Bride of Newgate (1950)
Fell and Foul Play (stories, 1991)
Merrivale, March and Murder (stories, 1991)

As Carter Dickson
The Judas Window (1938; also published in the United States as *The Crossbow Murder*)
He Wouldn't Kill Patience (1944)
The Department of Queer Complaints (stories, 1940)

Further Reading
Greene, Douglas G. 1995. *John Dickson Carr: The Man Who Explained Miracles*. Otto Penzler.
Joshi, S.T. 1990. *John Dickson Carr: A Critical Study*. Popular Press.
Kierans, James E. 1996. 'Poison and Poisoners in the Mysteries of John Dickson Carr'. *CADS* Supplement 5.

Mike Ashley

Carver, Caroline (b.1959)

Caroline Carver's exciting **thrillers**, set in exotic locales, mirror her own adventurous lifestyle. She was born in Britain in 1959 to antipodean parents with decidedly glamorous backgrounds; her mother Mary Morton had set an Australian land speed record two years earlier, while her father was a jet fighter pilot for the

Australian Fleet Air Arm. Carver grew up on a dairy farm and was educated at Westonbirt School in Gloucestershire. She left home at eighteen and worked in **London** before living in Australia for ten years, where she worked for several Sydney publishing houses. After backpacking around Southeast Asia, New Zealand and Nepal, she finally returned to her birthplace to enter the 1992 London-to-Saigon car rally: a gruelling sixty-three-day, 12,500-mile trek across Russia, Hungry and the Takiamakan Desert.

An article on the rally for *Autocar Magazine* led to further travelogues, but when these proved less lucrative than she had hoped, she decided to write a novel instead. Persevering despite a stream of rejection slips, her fourth attempt, *Blood Junction*, finally saw print in 2001.

Inspired by the 'stolen generation' of aborigine children forcibly removed from their families during the 1950s, Carver's story took place in a dusty sheep station deep in the Australian outback, a location she had personal experience of. Her heroine, India Kane, is a Sydney reporter whose car breaks down in the remote village of Cooinda. When her best friend Laura is killed, the townspeople accuse her of the murder, forcing her to seek out some life-or-death answers before she is lynched by the mob.

Strong on atmosphere and featuring a gutsy and independent female protagonist, the book's first chapter and synopsis (submitted under the name Caroline Seed) had already won the 1999 **Crime Writers' Association** (CWA) Debut Dagger.

Her next novel, *Dead Heat* (2003), although still set in Australia, could not have had a more different backdrop. After a plane crash – which she suspects is sabotage – Georgia Parish finds herself struggling to survive in the bug-filled, sultry rainforest of Nulgarra in northern Queensland. But the crocodiles are not the only danger; a killer is on the loose and Georgia must brave the savage elements to stop him. A key scene involving an angry bull crocodile was experienced firsthand by the author, while on a boat trip researching for the book.

India Kane returned in *Black Tide* (2004), highlighting the author's interest in the activities of environmental group Greenpeace, with a far-fetched plot revolving around a 'ghost ship' and a desolate Australian coastal resort. With *Beneath the Snow* (2005), Carver came back to earth with a tale of sabotage and skulduggery, big-business style, in the frozen wastes of Alaska. The discovery of a revolutionary new energy source is the MacGuffin that kick starts a high-tech thriller packed with incident.

Among recent novels, *Killer's Cargo* (2007) deals with the emotive issue of people trafficking; Carver is clearly determined to continue marrying her social concerns with well-honed thriller narratives. *See also* Social Comment in Crime Fiction.

Selected Works by the Author
Blood Junction (2001)
Dead Heat (2003)
Black Tide (2004)
Beneath the Snow (2005)
Killer's Cargo (2007)

Website
www.carolinecarver.com

Mark Campbell

Caudwell, Sarah (1939–2000)

Sarah Caudwell Cockburn was a barrister who wrote four witty crime novels about a group of young lawyers at Lincoln's Inn and their mentor, an androgynous Oxford law professor.

Caudwell was born on 27 May 1939, the daughter of the journalist Claud Cockburn and his wife Jean Ross (the model for Isherwood's Sally Bowles). Formidably well educated, with degrees from Aberdeen, Oxford and Nancy, she was called to the bar. In 1974, she joined the Trust Division of Lloyds Bank. Her novels draw both on her legal background and her knowledge of the classics. They are frivolous murder mysteries, populated with dashing young lawyers with Oxbridge educations and an awesome capacity for alcohol. Caudwell, who was a pipe-smoker and rarely without a glass of wine at her elbow, died on 28 January 2000.

The first (and perhaps best) of her novels, *Thus Was Adonis Murdered* (1981), introduced her cast of recurring characters. Their spiritual home is the Corkscrew, a wine bar in High Holborn. Professor Hilary Tamar, the main narrator, is a distinguished scholar of medieval law whose gender is never revealed and who rarely pays for a drink or indeed anything else. Younger colleagues include Serena Jardine, who resembles a Persian cat (claws included); the impossibly beautiful but lamentably high-minded Desmond Ragwort; Michael Cantrip who (as his friends frequently remind him) labours under the misfortune of having gone to Cambridge; and the curvaceous Julia Larwood – the sort of woman who has only to open her handbag for its contents to fall on the floor.

Adonis, which involves the murder of Julia's bisexual lover in Venice, established the narrative format which Caudwell was to use, with variations, in all the books. The preferred methods of exposition are the letter and the symposium – often in combination. Scholarship (Hilary always gives the word a capital 'S') and eavesdropping are vital aids to detection.

The Shortest Way to Hades (1984) and *The Sirens Sang of Murder* (1989) revolve around multi-million pound trust funds. Caudwell's last novel, *The Sybil in Her Grave* (2000), was published posthumously. Its climax involves a remarkably disgusting episode with a vulture and a corpse in a black drawing room.

The four novels are uneven in quality – the first two books have stronger narratives than the later two and have a more carefree atmosphere. The law of diminishing returns begins to apply as the series progresses. But the books still deserve to be read partly because they are funny – good comic crime fiction is very rare indeed – and partly because they affirm the pleasures of congenial company and a shared sense of humour. The writing is consistently good, capable of the subtlest nuances. Finally, Caudwell's novels are tolerant as well as literate; they reveal humanity as well as wit. *See also* Humour and Crime Fiction.

Selected Works by the Author
Thus Was Adonis Murdered (1981)
The Shortest Way to Hades (1984)
The Sirens Sang of Murder (1989)
The Sybil in Her Grave (2000)

Andrew Taylor

Chandler, Raymond: The British Connection

In his memoir *Front and Center* (1979), producer John Houseman suggested that
Raymond Chandler persisted – under trying, alcohol-fuelled circumstances – with
work on the script of *The Blue Dahlia* (1946) because Chandler felt an instinctive
loyalty to the Clifton-educated producer as 'a fellow public school man'. Though
Chandler was a great American classic, he was also, in a number of ways, the product
of Britain and Britishness.

Chandler (1888–1959) was born in Chicago but brought to England when he was
eight (after his parents' divorce). He attended Dulwich College, where he just missed
sharing the classroom and cricket field with P.G. Wodehouse or Dennis Wheatley. In
1907, he became a naturalised British citizen, passed the Civil Service exam and took
a position as a clerk in the Admiralty. After six months, he abandoned the promising
career (the first of many times he shut a door behind him) to become a 'man of letters'.
For three years, he worked sporadically. He made his first professional sale – a poem
('The Unknown Love') – to *Chambers' Journal* in 1908; he was a junior reporter for the
Daily Express and he contributed poetry, essays, translations and brief notices to the
Westminster Gazette and *The Academy*. Trawling through these bits and pieces reveals
little about the writer he would become – they are about as indicative of his future
talents as the twee poems Wilfred Owen published before the First World War. At
twenty-five, Chandler emigrated to America – only to enlist in the Canadian army in
1917. He served in the trenches for three months. Towards the end of the war, he was
attached to the Royal Air Force and trained as a pilot, though he never saw action
in the air. Surprisingly, little of his varied wartime-experience seeped through into
his novels, and he did not make use of his flying stint to turn out stories for the many
air ace-themed **pulps** when he turned to **magazine** fiction.

After the war, he moved to Los Angeles, married the much older Cissy Pascal
(married to someone else when they met) a month after the death of his mother (with
whom he had been living) and toiled as a bookkeeper in the oil industry. He rose to
the position of vice-president of the Dabney Oil Syndicate before being dismissed for
alcoholism, absenteeism and erratic behaviour. Only then, as a washed-up forty-five-
year-old drunk, did Chandler start writing hard-boiled mysteries in the Dashiell
Hammett style for the pulps, selling 'Blackmailers Don't Shoot' to *Black Mask*
magazine in 1933. Throughout his life, Chandler was ambiguous about his
nationality and national identity. He claimed that he returned to America with
'an English accent you could cut with a baseball bat' and several folks who worked
with him in Hollywood were under the impression that he was British. By 1958, and
as was evident in a bizarre radio conversation with Ian **Fleming** recorded for the
BBC (who did not transmit it for some years), the accent had mutated to the point
when few listeners (especially given Fleming's cut-glass Etonian tones for contrast)
would have taken him for anything other than a Yank.

In 1939, just as he was perfecting his own vernacular but epigrammatic narrative
voice, Chandler scribbled an essay 'Notes (very brief, please) on English and
American style' in which he muses 'it's fairly obvious that American education is
a cultural flop' and that 'American style has no cadence'. The implication, of course,
is that Chandler would give American English its cadence. Though his novels (at first,
fix-ups cannibalised from pre-existing short stories – then made up from whole cloth)
were popular in America, especially when they started to sell to the movies (landing

Chandler, Raymond: The British Connection

Chandler a lucrative if frustrating sideline as a screenwriter), Chandler felt that they were better understood and certainly better reviewed in Britain. In the 1950s, he made several long visits to the old country and was lionised by literary admirers; whereas in America, he was a mere mystery writer and not to be taken seriously. The question of how British (or American) Philip Marlowe is remains open. Hammett's private eyes have no such confusion (Nick Charles is American enough to have shortened his Greek surname), and more than any other writer, Chandler aspired to Hammett's achievements. The writers only met once, at a lunch organised by *Black Mask*, and the haunted alcoholics can be seen warily eyeing each other amid a crowd of grinning hacks in the photograph that recorded the occasion.

Chandler's 1930s short stories feature narrators called Mallory, John Dalmas and Carmady, who are all on their way to becoming Philip Marlowe, who first appears in the novel *The Big Sleep* (1939). The publisher Alfred Knopf's blurb indicates the author's (and the publisher's) ambition – 'not since Dashiell Hammett first appeared has there been a murder mystery story with the power, pace, and terrifying atmosphere of this one. And like Hammett's this is more than a "murder mystery"; it is a novel of crime and character, written with uncommon skill and in a tight, tense style which is irresistible.' Marlowe returned in *Farewell, My Lovely* (1940), *The High Window* (1942), *The Lady in the Lake* (1943), *The Little Sister* (1949), *The Long Good-Bye* (1953) and *Playback* (1958). Though Chandler commended Hammett for taking murder 'out of the library' and giving it back to 'the people who commit it', Chandler was concerned from the first with more than making his protagonist and his milieu 'realistic'. When we first meet Marlowe, he is visiting General Sternwood in his orchid-house – precisely the sort of household frequented by Hercule **Poirot** or Philo Vance (their weekend-party country houses tended to feature fewer nymphomaniac drug addict daughters, though). Over the entrance doorway of the Sternwood place is 'a broad stained-glass panel showing a knight in dark armour rescuing a lady who was tied to a tree and didn't have any clothes on but some very long and convenient hair'. Of the knight, Marlowe muses, 'if I lived in the house, I would sooner or later have to climb up there and help him'.

Named for Christopher Marlowe (rather than Conrad's narrator Marlow), with an echo of Thomas Malory (more directly evoked in Mallory), Marlowe does not much sound like an American. Philip is a rather fussy, British first name (he is rarely called 'Phil'), and the extra 'e' that softens the surname almost seems an affectation. Compare 'Sam Spade', which could hardly be a more functional, earthy name. There is always an irreverence in Marlowe's narration, but he seems to be sneering at the phoniness of that stained-glass window, rather than the tradition it represents. A detective who relaxes with chess problems, Marlowe is explicitly a knight, and courtly behaviour is expected of him. He is chaste enough to spurn the blatant advances of the poisonous Carmen Sternwood, savagely ripping apart and remaking his single bed after he has kicked her out of it, and persistent on his various quests in the service of usually unworthy patrons. Arthurian references recur throughout the series – from character names (Vivian Sternwood, a *Big Sleep* gunman named Lanny, Orfamay Quest) to titles (*The Lady in the Lake*). Marlowe is a chivalrous character, but constantly let down by women – indeed, the misogyny grows so thick that the books tend not to work as whodunits (the strongest female character is always guilty). Even in this, Chandler might have been pursuing the Matter of Britain, where adulterous Guinevere and sundry witchy seductresses, schemers and murderesses are as responsible for the fall of Camelot as Carmen, Velma/Helen,

Mildred/Muriel, Mrs Murdick, Dolores and Eileen are for the ruin of great and small men alike in the Chandler canon.

Though rooted in 'mean streets' – an expression Chandler may have taken from Arthur Morrison – the world of the Marlowe books reaches up to the mansions in the Hollywood hills, especially in later books after the author had time to work up some venom about the movie business, and is always highly fantastical. Chandler's closed universe – we never stray far from the sprawl of Los Angeles – is as self-contained and artificial as that of his fellow Dulwich College man, Wodehouse. It is a world where every walk-on cop, clerk, bartender, thug, witness or corpse has distinctive, picturesque traits, and we see them filtered through the sensibilities of a detective who has an epigram for every occasion, most of which have the feel of the endless polishing and honing Chandler applied to his prose (he was famously a slow writer).

The movies first hit on Chandler for his plots, buying up *Farewell My Lovely* and *The High Window*, to be turned into B series adventures for other sleuths: Tom Conway's *The Falcon* (*The Falcon Takes Over*, 1942) and Lloyd Nolan's *Mike Shayne* (*Time to Kill*, 1942). After Chandler had scored an Academy Award nomination for co-writing the screenplay of *Double Indemnity* (1944) with Billy Wilder, more faithful adaptations appeared and Hollywood tough guys competed to make an impression as Marlowe (like everyone from Leslie Charteris to Ian Fleming, Chandler would have preferred Cary Grant as his hero). Edward Dmytryk's *Murder, My Sweet* (1944), with Dick Powell, reverted in Britain to *Farewell, My Lovely*, reflecting the higher regard Chandler was held in as a novelist; John Brahm's *The Brasher Doubloon* (1947), with George Montgomery, and Paul Bogart's *Marlowe* (1969), with James Garner, went the same route, released in Britain as *The High Window* and *The Little Sister*.

In adapting the novels, Hollywood got cute. Howard Hawks's *The Big Sleep* (1946), with Humphrey Bogart, was originally a tough **thriller** that made sense, but it was re-cut and re-shot as a dazzling romantic entertainment which surrendered to incoherence (partly out of pique because the censors would not allow Chandler's ending – though Hawks arguably sneaked it in anyway). Robert Montgomery's *Lady in the Lake* (1947), in which the director takes the lead, is built around the unsuccessful gimmick of using a first-person camera and putting the audience in Marlowe's position. Robert Altman's *The Long Goodbye* (1973), with Elliott Gould, has fun with the idea of Marlowe as a man out of his time, though the sunny, amoral 1970s now seem as apt for the character as the retro-noir look of Dick Richards's *Farewell, My Lovely* (1975), with Robert Mitchum. Michael Winner's *The Big Sleep* (1978), also with Mitchum, takes the British connection to its logical extreme and relocates the entire plot to England, with a few left-over Yanks (James Stewart) amid coppers, crooks and scheming skirts played by the likes of John Mills, Edward Fox, Oliver Reed, Harry Andrews and Joan Collins.

The films seize on Chandler's dialogue scenes, and all the movie Marlowes relish the insolent talk – when Vivian (Lauren Bacall) tells Marlowe (Bogart) she does not like his manners, the star delivers a virtuoso snarl: 'I don't mind if you don't like my manners, I don't like them myself. They are pretty bad. I grieve over them on long winter evenings.' But tough talk is only a small part of the Chandler package, and many adaptations (and his own screen work) find excuses for voice-over narration: *Double Indemnity* is a long, dictaphone confession by the dying Walter Neff (Fred MacMurray) and the first *Farewell, My Lovely* is narrated during a police interrogation by the temporarily blinded Marlowe. ('Okay Marlowe', I said to myself. 'You're a tough guy. You've been sapped twice, choked, beaten silly with a gun, shot in the arm until you're crazy as a couple of waltzing mice. Now let's see you do something really tough – like putting your pants on.')

The best, and most ambitious, of the novels is the elegiac, elegant *Long Good-Bye*, in which Marlowe is involved with a drunken writer of historical novels who seems to be the author's tragic self-portrait. Roger Wade ends up dead but Marlowe traipses on into the hastily rewritten screen treatment *Playback and The Poodle Springs Mystery* (an unfinished case Robert B. Parker eventually wrapped up as Poodle Springs).

Chandler was, of course, not a British writer – though there have been attempts at cockney Marlowes (P.B. **Yuill**'s Hazell, Mark **Timlin**'s Nick Sharman). A figure of enormous importance in the evolution of the mystery as an art and entertainment form, he retained to the last ambiguous British roots.

Kim Newman

Charles, Kate (b.1950)

Though firmly contemporary, Kate Charles writes both series and stand-alone **clerical** mysteries firmly in the 'cosy' or **golden age** tradition. However, her works concentrate on characters and the 'unruly passions' (in fact, the title of a standalone) stirred up by love, sex and religion, rather than complex clue-puzzles. Charles is interested in the small groups of priests and helpers in the Church of England and how doctrinal division combines with personality to tip those supposedly dedicated to God and peace into murderous rage. There is always a mystery to be unravelled in the identity of the assailant. Solving it enables the series sleuths, solicitor, David Middleton-Brown and artist Lucy Kingsley, or the baffled police and well-meaning curates of the stand alone novels, to uncover more of the hidden corruptions of spirit. Recurring topics that breed killers are the painful issues of women priests in the church and homosexuality in the congregation and the clergy.

Charles herself has compared her work to Barbara Pym for her interest in church settings and people such as the 'good' spinsters and to P.D. **James** for her pursuit of character-led plots. Indeed, her stories are usually seen from the point of view of a mature yet vulnerable person who is both 'inside' and 'outside' the peculiar rituals of the church establishment. David Middleton-Brown opens the series as a middle-aged bachelor recently bereaved of his dominating mother. He carries a deep wound from his past in the desertion of his lover, Father Gabriel Neville, for marriage. Yet David is also an expert in old church buildings and their silver, providing excellent cover for Gabriel to send for him when terrified by blackmailing anonymous letters.

David's expertise in the past is symptomatic of Charles's concerns. For despite the depiction of a comforting community of friends and believers, Charles's works are metonymic of a Christian history of 2,000 years of dispute, conflict, schism, blood and death. Her narratives centre on those who can reconcile a ritualised past with a loving future. So her 'heroic' church people are those like David, Lucy and the ebullient West Indian priest, Leo Jackson in *Evil Intent* (2005), lovers of tradition in ritual and art, yet inclusive and welcoming to women and gay church clergy (like

Leo himself). These figures hold the line against the Church being torn apart between traditionalists who hate modernity and see women clergy and homosexuality as its representatives, and, evangelicals who equally reject women in authority and gay men while eager to strip away all ritual and art from worship. Too often, the 'golden age' format is accused of simple conservatism, of maintaining the status quo. In a world of ideological struggle, such as the established church, Charles's fictions are a plea for kindly revolutions! She re-shapes the form into a myth of reconciliation of past, present and future: a solved murder is the violence of the past that the Church, and modern England too, must learn to put away.

Selected Works by the Author
A Drink of Deadly Wine (1991)
The Snares of Death (1992)
A Dead Man Out of Mind (1994)
Evil Intent (2005)

Website
www.twbooks.co.uk/authors/katecharles.html
www.katecharles.com

Susan Rowland

Charteris, Leslie (1907–1993)

Leslie Charteris was a prolific **thriller** writer who modernised British crime writing in the 1930s with the adventures of his hugely popular protagonist Simon Templar. Templar, in the guise of the Saint, was the twentieth-century crime fiction answer to Robin Hood. With over 160 Saint stories to his name in a career that spanned almost fifty years, Charteris created a remarkably long-lived gentleman hero and succeeded in igniting the popular imagination for seven decades. While seemingly adhering to potboiler convention, the Saint books actually subverted the orthodoxies of adventure fiction. Such was the popularity of Simon Templar's escapades that he quickly became a brand name, moving from print onto celluloid film, then radio, comic strips and in the 1960s and 1970s to television. In 1992, Charteris received the prestigious Diamond Dagger of the Crime Writers' Association.

The son of an affluent Chinese physician and English mother, Charteris was born Leslie Charles Bowyer Lin in Singapore on 12 May 1907. His first short story was published when he was seventeen, and three years later – as a Cambridge undergraduate – he published his first novel, *X Esquire*. By this time, he changed his name by deed poll to Leslie Charteris. Quitting university for a life of adventure, Charteris travelled around the globe and undertook a variety of jobs to support his writing endeavours – these ranged from bus driver and bartender to more exotic occupations such as pearl diver and gold prospector. A second novel, *The White Rider*, was published in 1928, closely followed the same year by what was to be the first Saint book, *Meet – The Tiger*. Although Charteris later dismissed the novel, it turned out to be significant in introducing Simon Templar, an urbane English adventurer whose wit was as sharp as the knife he usually concealed up his sleeve.

Charteris had no intentions to create a long-running series detailing the Saint's action-packed exploits, but he brought Templar back with *Enter the Saint* (1930).

Though, Charteris began gaining popularity only after *The Saint Closes the Case* (1930). From then on, through a raft of novels, novelettes and short stories, Charteris would write almost exclusively about his swashbuckling modern-day pirate with the fixed moral compass.

Templar was, in essence, a voracious thrill seeker who sought to outwit his adversaries by stealth and guile. Often donning disguises, he took it upon himself to rid the world of blackmailers, thieves and nefarious underworld types (while appropriating their plunder). His early adventures saw the Saint in a variety of dubious guises: as a gunrunner, card sharp, whisky smuggler and even mercenary for hire. His accomplices included his romantic sidekick, Patricia Holm, plus Roger Conway, Peter Quentin, Monty Hayward and Hoppy Uniatz.

Significantly, although Charteris described Templar as a modern-day Robin Hood, the Saint possessed few altruistic motives – rather, the spoils he acquired helped finance an opulent lifestyle (he had a swish pad in Upper Berkeley Mews, drove an expensive Hirondel car and never seemed to be wanting for any material comforts). Templar's visiting card was a drawing of a matchstick man with a halo, which he left behind at crime scenes to distinguish himself from imitators.

An uneasy moral ambivalence lay at the heart of Charteris's fictional creation. Although Templar perceived himself as an arbiter of moral justice, he took great pleasure in frustrating the forces of law and order with his intrepid feats. In particular, he was the bane of Chief Inspector Claude Eustace Teal, a gum-chewing policeman who was usually made to look as if he is a fool.

After a trip to the United States in 1932, Charteris fell under the spell of American gangster movies – he briefly worked as a scriptwriter in Hollywood – and his books took on a transatlantic tone, peppered with US colloquialisms (this is exemplified by *The Man from St. Louis* (1933), in which a notorious Stateside gang boss tries to set up business in London).

The first of the Saint's US adventures began with *The Saint in New York* (1934). By 1938, Simon Templar's popularity in America was so great that Radio-Keith-Orpheum (RKO) Pictures adapted it for a movie, with Louis Hayward playing Templar. He was later succeeded by the suave George Sanders. At the same time, the Saint was finding his way onto radio and into comic books and newspaper strips. Such was the fictional character's ubiquity that it became an early example of a brand name.

With the advent of the Second World War, there was a notable change of emphasis in the Saint books – for the first time, Templar relinquished his devil-may-care autonomy and allied himself with the US government in *The Saint Steps In* (1942), which focused on the evils of fascism. Books from this period also found Templar voicing his concerns about politics and the changing world order – romance, too, was toned down, and the books usually had a sober, downbeat ending.

In the 1950s, Charteris largely abandoned Saint novels, concentrating instead on short stories. **The Saint Detective Magazine** was launched in America at the end of 1952, feeding the public's insatiable hunger for new or lesser known adventures. A television series in the United Kingdom starring Roger Moore as Simon Templar in the early 1960s stimulated new interest in the Saint. Charteris continued to write in the 1960s and 1970s, although often with the help of collaborators (including Fleming Lee, Graham Weaver, Peter Bloxsum and John Kruse). Another television series, *Return of the Saint* injected new life into the Saint brand in 1978, with the final novel, *Salvage for the Saint*, following in 1983. The franchise was briefly revived in 1997 with the Hollywood film *The Saint*.

Although the Saint's stock has diminished in recent years, the importance of Charteris's fictional phenomenon should not be undervalued: Simon Templar's adventures brought the visceral excitement of US **pulp** fiction to UK audiences and by so doing dragged the British crime novel into the modern age. A consummate storyteller, Charteris's blend of stylish prose, quicksilver wit and adrenalin-inducing action scenes set a benchmark for other crime writers to aspire to in the mid-twentieth century. *See also The Saint* on Television.

Selected Works by the Author
Meet – The Tiger! (1928)
Daredevil (1929)
Enter the Saint (1930)
The Saint and Mr Teal (1933)
The Saint in New York (1935)
Prelude for War (1938)
The Saint in Miami (1940)
The Saint Steps In (1942)
Saint Errant (1948)
The Saint in Europe (1953)
The Saint around the World (1956)
The Saint to the Rescue (1958)
The Saint in the Sun (1963)

Further Reading
Adley, Derek, and W.O.G. Lofts. 1970. *The Saint and Leslie Charteris*. Howard Baker.
Barer, Burl. 1993. *The Saint – A Complete History in Print, Radio, Film and Television of Leslie Charteris' Robin Hood of Modern Crime, Simon Templar, 1928–1992*. McFarland & Company, Inc.

Charles Waring

Chase, James Hadley (1906–1985)

Best known for his controversial 1939 debut novel, ***No Orchids for Miss Blandish***, James Hadley Chase carved a successful career from penning almost one hundred sensationalist gangster novels characterised by a vivid prose style and garishly lurid covers.

Chase was the pseudonym of René Brabazon Raymond, born in London on Christmas Eve 1906. Educated at King's School in Rochester, Raymond left school at eighteen and worked as a bookseller, a door-to-door children's encyclopaedia salesman and a book wholesaler before finding that his talents lay in writing books, not selling them.

An admirer of James M. Cain's novel *The Postman Always Rings Twice* (1933), Raymond decided to emulate Cain's aggressive mix of sex and violence, along with plot elements from William Faulkner's *Sanctuary* (1931). Armed with a dictionary of American slang and some maps, he wrote the eminently marketable hard-boiled crime novel *No Orchids for Miss Blandish* over six weekends in the summer of 1938. The furore about *No Orchids for Miss Blandish* (including an attack by George Orwell) resulted in its huge sales of half a million copies. Arguably, Raymond never equalled its heady concoction of criminality and masochism, although he spent over forty years trying.

In the Second World War, he joined the Administrative and Special Duties Branch of the Royal Air Force, eventually rising to squadron leader. He continued to write, not only as Chase, but also as James L. Docherty (*He Won't Need It Now*, 1939), Raymond Marshall (over twenty novels, beginning with *Lady – Here's Your Wreath* in 1940) and Ambrose Grant (*More Deadly than the Male*, 1946).

Returning characters included Vic 'Brick Top' Corrigan (in three books, starting with *You're Lonely When You're Dead*, 1949), private-eye Frank Terrell (in five books, starting with *The Soft Centre*, 1964) and rich desperate housewife Helga Rolfe (in three books, starting with *An Ace Up My Sleeve*, 1971).

Later books tended to retread plots from earlier efforts, and Raymond was not adverse to charges of plagiarism, notably from Raymond Chandler, who claimed that Raymond had lifted material from him in his *Blonde's Requiem* (1946); Raymond was forced to print an apology in *The Bookseller* magazine.

The author's predilection for straightforward gangster stories told in a direct, 'American' style and involving the promise (if not the delivery) of copious amounts of sex, kept him in the bestseller lists for several decades. As times changed, so did the levels of violence in his books, although his pre-1950s view of organised crime always remained a constant factor. Married since 1933 to Sylvia Ray, he moved to Corseaux-Sur-Vevey in Switzerland in 1961, where he died peacefully on 6 February 1985.

Selected Works by the Author
No Orchids for Miss Blandish (1939)
Eve (1945)
I'll Get You for This (1946)
Lay Her among the Lilies (1950, also published as *Too Dangerous to Be Free*)
The Things Men Do (1953)
I'll Bury My Dead (1953)
The Sucker Punch (1954)
Ruthless (1955)
Never Trust a Woman (1957)
This Is for Real (1965)
An Ace up My Sleeve (1971)

Mark Campbell

Chesterton, G[ilbert] K[eith] (1874–1936)

If any writer could be described as prolific, it would be Gilbert Keith Chesterton. Even though he turned out literally hundreds of books and essays, he is primarily remembered for the six volumes of stories featuring Father Brown, the gentle, apparently insignificant priest, one of crime fiction's shrewdest sleuths.

Chesterton was born to a wealthy family and studied art and literature at University College, London. His passions include literature, politics (he advocated distributism – fair shares for all – rather than socialism) and religion. He converted to Catholicism early in his life and was extremely devout.

Chesterton wrote several pieces about detective fiction, and in one of these essays, 'A Defence of Detective Stories', published in *The Speaker* in 1901, he expounded his views on the essential nature of the genre. He stated that the detective story was the popular realisation of the poetry concealed in city life. The detective crosses **London** in which 'the casual omnibus assumes the primal covers of a fairy ship' and in which the lights of the city are the guardians of a secret known to the writer but not to the reader: 'Every twist of the road is like a finger pointing to it; every fantastic skyline of chimney pots seem wildly and derisively signalling the meaning of the mystery.' Chesterton lamented that the detective story was, with the exception of the work of Robert Louis Stevenson, the only modern literature which explored the fascinating but sinister aspects of the modern city.

In Chesterton's view, the detective-story writer should be regarded as the dark poet of the city. We can see how this definition applies not only to himself and indeed **Doyle**, whose deft descriptions of London created a rich backdrop for the investigations of Sherlock **Holmes**, but also to many writers who came later. Consider the poetry of Margery **Allingham**'s presentation of London in her **Campion** stories, especially *Tiger in the Smoke* (1952); Raymond **Chandler**'s Marlowe and his 'mean streets'; Colin **Dexter** and Morse's sunlit but blood-soaked Oxford; and Ian **Rankin**'s Edinburgh, the black nest of Inspector **Rebus**.

If the writer was the poet, Chesterton maintained that the detective was the romantic hero, the protector of civilisation:

> It is the agent of justice who is the original and poetic figure, while burglars and footpads are merely placid old cosmic conservatives, happy in the immemorial respectability of apes and wolves. The romance of the police force is thus the whole romance of man.... It reminds us that the whole noiseless and unnoticeable police management by which we are ruled and protected is only a successful knight-errantry.

While these words were written before the genesis of his priest sleuth, we can see that Chesterton applied that mixture of poetry and chivalry, which he saw as being imbued in detective fiction, to the Father Brown stories. Because these tales conceal a purpose more than to entertain by presenting a mystery and then solving it: the stories reveal themselves as parables, in which moral theology is presented as detection. That is not to say that the moral content forces itself upon the reader – Chesterton is much too good a writer for such obvious and invasive preaching. In fact, Chesterton's skill with a narrative manifests itself precisely in the same manner that the moral aspects are hidden.

Regardless of his versatility and profligacy of his writings – for the last twelve years of his life he ran his own magazine, *G.K.'s Weekly* – Chesterton's finest works are his mystery and detective tales. Although he had a love of the genre, he regarded it principally as a potboiler; he indulged in what he considered were his more important writings concerning politics and religion. The success of the Father Brown stories was a surprise to Chesterton, but it delighted him as it allowed him to carry out two of his passions, writing fiction and the church.

Late in 1903, Chesterton set out across the moors that separate Keighley from Ilkley in the company of a Roman Catholic curate, a guest of the household where Chesterton was staying. In the course of their conversation, Chesterton mentioned that he intended to support in print a certain proposal concerning some rather sordid questions of vice and crime. He recorded the curate's response in his *Autobiography* (1936):

> As a necessary duty and to prevent me from falling into the mare's nest, (the curate) told me certain facts he knew about perverted practices...it was a curious experience to find that this quiet and pleasant celibate had plumbed those abysses far deeper than I.... I had not imagined that the world could hold such horrors.

When we returned to the house, we fell into conversation with two hearty and healthy Cambridge undergraduates, one of whom, when the priest had left the room, burst out: 'I don't believe his sort of life is the right one. It's all very well to like religious music and so on when you don't really know anything about the evil in the world.' To me, still almost shivering with the appalling practical facts of which the priest had warned me, this comment came as a colossal and crushing irony. And there sprang up in my mind the vague idea of making some artistic use of this comic yet tragic cross purpose; and constructing a comedy in which a priest should appear to know nothing and in fact know more about crime than the criminals...I permitted myself the liberty of taking my friend, punching his intelligent countenance into a condition of pudding faced fatuity, and generally disguising Father O'Connor as Father Brown.

The transformation was not immediate, for the first Father Brown detective story, 'The Blue Cross', did not appear until 1910 with its first British appearance in *The Story-teller*. The intriguing paradox of knowledgeable innocence was a masterstroke.

Father Brown, the East Anglican Roman Catholic priest and sleuth, was generally regarded as the second most successful detective creation after Sherlock Holmes. But Brown, unlike Holmes, is not an idiosyncratic superior individual who, after a period of quiet cogitation, will leap from his chair with a cry of 'The game's afoot'. Father Brown's personality is almost the opposite of Holmes's: self-effacing to the point of invisibility and with no apparent charisma. He is always the supporting player in his stories. But it is Father Brown's engaging insignificance that is part of the enigma surrounding his character and his appeal. In *The Crime and Mystery Book* (Thames and Hudson, 1997), Ian Ousby observed that 'with his meek manner, his umbrella and his brown-paper parcels, he is one of the few early detectives, if not the only one, to escape successfully the long shadow cast by Sherlock Holmes'.

Father Brown relies on intuitive detection, psychological insight and an extraordinary knowledge of philosophy and moral teaching. His 'goodness' allows him to see into the hearts of people and identify the sinner. Certainly the stories are not exercises in deduction, for rarely does Chesterton provide the reader with a set of clues and logical problems to work through. The veteran crime writer and Chesterton enthusiast H.R.F. **Keating** observed, 'The Father Brown stories are games of masks – it is rare that an unmasking of some kind does not occur. The denouement tends less to be a summation of misdirected clues, than a revelation of who, in the story one has read, was really who' (*100 Great Detectives*, edited by Maxim Jakubowski, Xanada, 1991). This approach draws the readers into the story entirely and does not distract them in trying to fit various clues to several theories.

While Chesterton's quiet little cleric is to all appearances unremarkable, he does solve some of the most bizarre crimes ever recorded: a killer who apparently cannot be seen ('The Invisible Man'), a man's head crushed by one blow of a small hammer ('The Hammer of God') and a famous man who commits 'a fearful sin' by figuratively growing a forest to hide a leaf ('The Sign of the Broken Sword').

Brown is not a clues man but approaches the crime from the psychological angle. The character explains his approach thus:

I try to get inside the man. I am inside the man, moving his arms and legs, but I wait until I know I'm inside a murderer, thinking his thoughts, wrestling with his passions; till I have bent myself into the posture of his hunched and peering hatred; till I see the world with his bloodshot squinting eyes, looking between the blinkers of his half-witted concentration...[t]ill I really am the murderer. And when I feel like the murderer, of course, I know who he is.

Being a man of God, Father Brown is as much concerned about the possible redemption of the culprit and saving his soul, as he is with solving the crime. His greatest success in this pursuit is with one of his early antagonists, the dashing French jewel thief, Flambeau, a colossus of crime, a man of incredible strength and blazing intelligence. In 'The Blue Cross', from *The Innocence of Father Brown*, Chesterton's hero prevents Flambeau from stealing a rare jewelled cross; after several encounters, under the influence and guidance of the gentle priest, the thief reforms and becomes a private investigator in London. Flambeau's constant nemesis during his criminal days was Aristide Valetin, chief of the Paris police, an eccentric person whose success relied on 'plodding logic' rather than brilliant detective work. Flambeau and Valetin are larger-than-life creatures, but they remain satellites of the retiring star of the stories, which is another Chesterton paradox.

Father Brown found instant success with readers, and within a few years of his first appearance there were two collections, *The Innocence of Father Brown* (1911) and *The Wisdom of Father Brown* (1914), each containing twelve tales. After the second collection, Chesterton, rather like Doyle, grew a little tired of his detective hero. He suffered a bout of illness around this time and then later was preoccupied with the editorial chair of the radical magazine *The New Witness*; the time had come to abandon Father Brown. However, over ten years later, the increasing financial burdens brought about by the launching of *G.K.'s Weekly*, a mouthpiece for his political theories and beliefs, forced the author to whisk Father Brown away from his parish duties to investigate further crimes. Told by his wife that the bank balance was rather low, he would sigh and say, 'That means Father Brown again.' In this respect, the parallels with Doyle are uncanny. In his later life, Doyle turned to writing Sherlock Holmes stories only when he needed money to fund his work with spiritualism. Unlike Doyle, Chesterton did not push his character into a raging waterfall or kill him off in any other way. His ten-year hiatus was explained in the first story of the new series, *The Resurrection of Father Brown*, in which we are told that our hero had been sent out to South America 'to officiate, as something between a missionary and a parish priest'.

Chesterton produced a further three volumes of stories: *The Incredulity of Father Brown* (1926), *The Secret of Father Brown* (1927) and *The Scandal of Father Brown* (1935). The later stories, however, are not as ingenious as the earlier ones, and Chesterton imbued them with more religious and moral teaching than was perhaps good for them. However, Julian **Symons** observed in *Bloody Murder* (Faber, 1972) that 'the best of these tales are among the finest short crime stories ever written'.

Chesterton created other detectives, including Horne Fisher, a gentleman sleuth who is adept at ferreting out the secrets of little-publicised crime but is always prevented by higher considerations from bringing them to justice. His unusual exploits are collected in *The Man Who Knew Too Much* (1922). Another of Chesterton's crime solvers was Mr Pond, described as 'the quietest man in the world to be a man of the world'. He is a mild-mannered civil servant – shades of Edgar Wallace's J.G. Reeder – who has a fondness for paradoxes and is a paradox himself. He appeared in the short story collection *The Paradoxes of Mr Pond* (1936).

Another work of interest to the crime fiction enthusiast is *The Club of Queer Trades* (1905), a collection of puzzle stories, all centred around a club that allows membership only if one has created a new profession. One member, for example, provides a suitable romance for lonely souls.

Chesterton's only novel in the genre – and it only touches lightly on it – is *The Man Who Was Thursday* (1908). In essence, it is an allegorical novel disguised as a detective story which involves the poet Gabriel Syme, a member of a newly formed police force called Philosophical Policemen, who infiltrates a secret society of anarchists known as the Supreme Council of Seven, each member of which is named after a day in the week. This novel, as with all Chesterton's work is a blend of the cunning, the whimsical, the philosophical, the paradoxical and the entertaining. A large man with an avuncular manner, G.K. Chesterton was not only one of the pioneers of crime fiction but also, in his typical paradoxical fashion, one of the most original and individual practitioners of the art. *See also* Clerical Crime.

Selected Works by the Author
The Club of Queer Trades (stories, 1905)
The Man Who Was Thursday (1908)
The Innocence of Father Brown (stories, 1911)
The Wisdom of Father Brown (stories, 1914)
The Man Who Knew Too Much (stories, 1922)
The Incredulity of Father Brown (stories, 1926)
The Secret of Father Brown (stories, 1927)
The Scandal of Father Brown (stories, 1935)

David Stuart Davies

Cheyney, Peter (1896–1951)

Although his career as a novelist lasted only fifteen years, Peter Cheyney managed to produce thirty-five novels and numerous short stories, breaking effortlessly into the million-seller belt and remaining there till he died. His own life reads like fiction (some people have claimed that parts of it are fiction) and among his claims was that he had his own criminal investigation department.

Certainly, his knowledge of criminals and the underworld was prodigious. A droll and snappy exponent of tough-guy fiction, Cheyney had several series characters, the most famous of which (and a cult figure in France) was Lemmy Caution.

Cheyney had a hero's First World War, joining at the outbreak, at seventeen, and being (he said) badly injured at the Somme. (Actually, he lost an earlobe.) Between the First World War and the publication of his first novel in 1936, Cheyney worked in the theatre, briefly in films, and his successful journalistic career culminated in his becoming news editor on the *Sunday Graphic*. He was a big man (6 feet 2 inches) who went bald early, and he was an expert pistol shot and sword fencer. He could handle himself in a scrap, and after flirting with British fascism in the early thirties, he made use of connections he had made there, taking care to disguise his own humble origins by sporting a gold monocle, a red carnation and ornate cloak. But his first novel brought him fame, and from that time on he concentrated on fiction. Prolific seems an inadequate word for Cheyney; in a single year he would produce two full-length novels along with a stream of short stories, scripts and even poems.

Despite being born in Whitechapel and having Irish ancestry, Cheyney was most at home with his American hero, Lemmy Caution. Caution tricked his way to fame in *This Man Is Dangerous* (1936), seeming for the first part of the book to be a hoodlum visiting Britain on a crime jaunt but turning out to be an undercover FBI agent, or G Man. (Those were the days when an FBI agent could be a hero.) Caution, the trench-coated, fedora-wearing G Man, was a hit before the Second World War, but in the war he flourished, his special-agent status enabling him to freely roam wartime Britain in pursuit of criminals and spies, ostensibly on behalf of American Intelligence, although this thin excuse for his presence in Britain faded as he was assimilated by the British masters and took on tasks for them. Caution seemed to be one of the few men at the time capable of laying his hands on a fast car – and fuel – when he wanted it. He laid hands on a number of compliant 'dames' as well. He was unashamed about this: 'Either I got an overdeveloped eye for beauty or I'm just one of them guys who is never happy unless he is tryin' out somethin' new. Or maybe I like learnin'. I wouldn't know.' In the heated wartime atmosphere, slipping out of **London** to drive at 60 miles an hour through dark English lanes, anything could happen and anyone could be other than they seemed: 'It is as dark as hell. The moon has scrammed an' a fine rain is fallin'. It is one of them nights when you oughta be discussin' the war with something' in a pink negligee an' a nice frame of mind.'

Caution was equally at home at Scotland Yard, the American Embassy, in low-life nightclubs and on romantically dangerous private boats moored a few miles offshore. In those drab and troubled 1940s, his two-fisted direct approach had everything his readers could wish for. War was dreary. Life was careful. But with Caution it could be fun.

Next to Caution in popularity was Cheyney's British private eye Slim Callaghan, appearing two years after Caution in 1938 in *The Urgent Hangman* and then at yearly intervals with *Dangerous Curves*, *You Can't Keep The Change*, *It Couldn't Matter Less* and others until *Uneasy Terms* in 1946. Both Callaghan and Caution appeared in many, often lurid, short stories. They were also popular in France, in translations and on screen. In the 1950s, several film noir dramas were made starring Eddie Constantine as Lemmy Caution. First came *La Mome Vert Des Gris* based on *Poison Ivy*, and this was followed by *Cet Homme Est Dangerous* and five other Caution movies before the extraordinary Jean-Luc Goddard borrowed the character for his science-fiction film *Alphaville*. Slim Callaghan meanwhile lit up the screen in *A Toi De Jouer Callaghan*, *Plus De Whiskey Pour Callaghan* and *Callaghan Remet Ça* and two British movies, *Uneasy Terms* and *Meet Mr Callaghan*. In 1940, the BBC made a popular radio series *Lemmy Caution Calling* in which Caution was played by Ben Wright.

The concerns of wartime led Cheyney into creating the 'Dark' series, more loosely organised than those for Caution and Callaghan in that the books had several central characters, but the 'Dark' stories shared plots about British and Nazi agents, dirty dealings and, inevitably, gorgeous but wicked women. Of the repeating characters in these tales, the most haunting was Johnny Vallon, ex–Military Intelligence who carried an unhealed stomach wound from the war. The stories sold well, although not as sensationally as the Caution and Callaghan books; yet their amoral darkness might make them the most profitable Cheyney books to read today – for it cannot be denied that, rooted as most of them are in wartime attitudes, Cheyney's books are dated. They retain their humour and are refreshingly fast and vigorous, but they tell of a vanished world. That, equally, is their virtue.

Selected Works by the Author

Lemmy Caution
This Man Is Dangerous (1936)

Cheyney, Peter

Poison Ivy (1937)
Don't Get Me Wrong (1939)
I'll Say She Does! (1945)

Slim Callaghan
The Urgent Hangman (1938)
Dangerous Curves (1939)
Uneasy terms (1946)

Caution and Callaghan Combined
Mr Caution – Mr Callaghan (stories, 1941)

Russell James

Child, Lee (b.1954)

In tough guy Jack Reacher, Lee Child created an icon of the **thriller** genre – a gutsy, hulking, hard-loving, tough-talking, no-nonsense hero with an incurable wanderlust that leaves him riding off into the sunset at the end of each adventure and pulling into a new town just in time for the next. Put simply, Reacher is a cliché that works. To the legions of fans that have made Lee Child rich, he is an uncomplicated role model: an action-hero with bags of sex appeal – beefcake with brains. He is also, of course, unquestionably and undilutedly all-American. Child's decision to uproot himself and his family and move to New York paved the way for Reacher's creation and gave Child the base to explore the vast continental landscape that is his footloose hero's constant yet ever-shifting arena.

Child (real name Jim Grant) was born in Coventry in 1954 but moved at an early age to the Handsworth area of Birmingham where his parents believed he and his brothers would obtain a better education. He proved them right by winning a scholarship to King Edward's School, coincidentally that which was once attended by J.R.R. Tolkien.

He subsequently studied law at Sheffield but was drawn more to the glamour of acting, and after part-time work in the theatre, he joined Granada Television in Manchester. He worked eighteen years for them as a presentation director only to be fired in 1995 – during a bout of corporate restructuring – at the awkward age of forty.

According to his own, self-crafted legend, he spent 'six dollars' on paper and pencils and sat down to write. What was important was his move to New York and an instant absorption of enough US cultural references to create a tough-guy hero who really could not credibly belong to any other nationality.

Killing Floor, the first Reacher novel which was published by Putnam in 1997, won a couple of minor awards for crime/mystery novels and set Child up straight away in his new career.

Unlike most of the succeeding novels, *Killing Floor* is written in the first person. The novel begins, as Reacher would in other novels, with him stepping off a Greyhound bus, which in itself is an iconic symbol of rootless America, in the fictional town of Margrave, Georgia. Like his creator, Reacher is the victim of early redundancy, in this case dismissed as a result of the US military's post–Cold War 'peace dividend'.

It is clear that this is a colossal, barrel-chested, giant of a man, an ex-Military Policeman, 6 feet 5 inches tall with a 50-inch chest on which he never displays the

rows of military medals to which he is entitled. He also has a sophisticated taste
in cool jazz which is why he has come to find the traces of a long-dead black musician
called Blind Blake, once mentioned by his brother.

Instead, he finds himself arrested by mistake for murder – the sort of thing that will
happen to Reacher more than once – and during the few days he spends in jail before
establishing his innocence, Margrave is swept by a murder spree. Reacher meanwhile
sets another career precedent by bedding a sassy local police officer. When he
discovers the man for whose murder he was mistakenly arrested was actually his
brother, he sets about solving the mystery with a wry mix of subtle intuition and
clunking fisted violence.

Child got into the rhythm of turning out a Reacher novel annually. In *Die Trying*
(1998) Reacher turns up in Chicago, stops to help a limping young woman and ends
up chained to her – feeding many a female reader's fantasy – and kidnapped. The
vulnerable young woman – few of Reacher's women are anything less than ruthlessly
self-reliant – claims to be an FBI agent, but the truth is just a little more complex
than that. Her identity and the kidnappers' aims are closely linked, while the gore-
fest at the end establishes Reacher's ruthlessness beyond doubt.

Tripwire (1999) has Reacher in the Florida Keys short on money and working in a
strip club but soon gets involved – through the death of a private investigator sent to
seek him out on behalf of his old army mentor – in a world of corruption and US army
bureaucracy. This is the first of a gradual series of glimpses into Reacher's past which
comes to a head in *The Enemy* (2005) which, along with *Persuader* (2003), is again
written in the first person. *The Enemy* is the first Reacher retrospective taking us
back to his days in the army, as duty military police officer on a South Carolina base
investigating the killing of a two-star general who should have been in Europe where
the Berlin Wall had just come down.

In the meantime, Reacher hitchhiked his way into Texas and the troubled world of
Mexican illegal immigration (*Echo Burning*, 2001); he got hired to try to penetrate the
vice president's security schedule (*Without Fail*, 2002) and to solve a shopping-mall
massacre in rural Indiana (*One Shot*, 2005) and the murders of two high-flying women
soldiers found separately in baths of army-issued camouflage paint (*The Visitor*, 2000;
published in the United States as *Running Blind*).

The author says his hero's name originated when Child was asked to reach
something down for an old lady in a supermarket and his wife told him that if the
book did not work out he could always have a career as a 'reacher'.

The 'Reacher' section of Child's own website treats his hero as most of his readers
want: like a real person, giving biographical details, including parentage, date of birth,
height, weight, military rank, medals and known lovers – thirteen and counting – not
to mention chest measurements (50 inches) and 'pants' inseam': an impressive inside
leg measurement quixotically quoted in centimetres (95).

Child's contractual obligation to provide one Reacher book a year ran out in 2006
but is hard to imagine Child writing about another character or indeed slowing his
production rate. So far his almost superhuman hero has provided him with homes
in Manhattan and the south of France and a supercharged Jaguar. It is a partnership
set to last as long as there are sunsets for Reacher to keep riding off into.

Selected Works by the Author
Killing Floor (1997)
Die Trying (1998)
Tripwire (1999)

Child, Lee

Echo Burning (2001)
Without Fail (2002)
Persuader (2003)
The Enemy (2004)
One Shot (2005)
The Hard Way (2006)
Bad Luck and Trouble (2007)

Website
www.leechild.com

Peter Millar

Childers, Erskine (1870–1922)

Erskine Childers's only work of fiction was so highly regarded at the time of its publication – and remains so to this day – that his reputation as father of the modern spy novel remains unassailable.

The second of five children, Robert Erskine Childers was born in **London** on 25 June 1870. His father was Robert Caesar Childers, a noted oriental scholar. Orphaned at the age of thirteen, Robert was sent to Ireland, where he was brought up by his uncle and aunt, Charles and Agnes Barton, at their home in Annamoe, County Wicklow. Educated in Haileybury College, Hertfordshire, and Trinity College, Cambridge, he took a job as committee clerk in the House of Commons in 1895.

After the outbreak of the second Boer War in 1899, Childers joined the British Army and served for tenth months as an officer. Wounded and sent back to England, he immediately collated his diary entries as a memoir, *In the Ranks of the C.I.V.* (City Imperial Volunteers), published in 1900. A second volume followed in 1903.

His third book, *The Riddle of the Sands: A Record of Secret Service*, a prescient work of spy fiction, also appeared in 1903. A bestseller, it captured the public's fear of invasion by an enemy nation, a very real threat in the turbulent years before the First World War (although France, not Germany, was the perceived aggressor).

Childers was a skilled yachtsman, with an 1897 cruise around the Baltic in his converted lifeboat *Vixen* clearly inspiring both the location and events of the novel. Carruthers, a young Foreign Office official, is invited by a college friend, Davies, to go duck hunting off the East Frisian Islands. There they uncover a fiendish plot by Germany to launch a surprise attack on Britain. Part travelogue, part 'Boy's-Own' adventure story, the novel's documentary-style narrative and sharp attention to detail made it an instant classic.

Rudyard Kipling's 1901 espionage tale *Kim* may have predated it by two years, but owing to its getting rid of old-fashioned exoticism and its stunning attention to detail, *The Riddle of the Sands* is arguably the superior work. Certainly it provided the basic formulae for all future spy novelists, from John **Buchan** to Eric **Ambler** and John **le Carré**.

Childers married Bostonian Mary Ellen Osgood in 1904 and resigned his parliamentary job in 1910. An advocate of Home Rule, Childers later smuggled arms to Irish Volunteers, which were used during the Easter Uprising of 1916. During the First World War, he received Distinguished Service Order (DSO) for his role as an intelligence officer in the Royal Navy, but following the end of hostilities he moved to

Dublin and joined Sinn Féin, later becoming secretary general of the Irish delegation that negotiated the infamous Anglo-Irish Treaty of 1921. Opposed to the final draft agreement, he was captured by Irish Army soldiers and executed by firing squad on 24 November 1922, during the opening months of the Irish Civil War. *See also* Espionage Fiction.

Selected Works by the Author
The Riddle of the Sands (1903)

Mark Campbell

Christie, Agatha (1890–1976)

Rightly called the 'Queen of Crime', Agatha Christie's extraordinarily prolific and versatile output – whodunits, **thrillers**, romances, ghost stories, short stories, poems, plays, memoirs and children's books – has made her the world's bestselling author, outsold only by the Bible and the works of William Shakespeare.

HOUNDS SEARCH FOR NOVELIST

Beagles were used yesterday in the renewed hunt around Newlands Corner for Mrs. Agatha Christie, the vanished novelist, the latest portrait of whom appears above. On the right is Rosalind, her seven-year-old daughter, photographed in the grounds of her home at Sunningdale.

17. A newspaper of 1 January 1926 reports Christie's mysterious disappearance.

Key to her enduring popularity was her ability to construct fiendishly complicated murder stories populated by intriguing casts of likely suspects, each of whom could have been the murderer. Although rarely dealing in anything other than broad stereotypes, the transparency of her prose and the fashion in which she could weave a puzzle from the most unlikely of situations – the murder victim usually being killed in 'impossible' circumstances – has cemented her populist appeal. Critics have sometimes made disparaging assessments of her plots, likening them to arid crossword puzzles, but there is no doubting that many of her books, specifically those written during the 1930s and 1940s, display a keen intelligence and sharp wit that makes them amount to far more than merely the sum of their parts.

Agatha Mary Clarissa Miller was born in Tor Mohun, a district of the seaside town of Torquay in Devon, on 15 September 1890. She was the last of Frederick and Clarissa ('Clara') Miller's three children: Margaret was born in 1879, and Louis arrived a year later. Her father was a wealthy American businessman, and her mother was an Anglo-Irish aristocrat. Educated at home, she largely taught herself to read and write at an early age; her first published work was a poem about electric trams, printed in an Ealing newspaper when she was eleven – the same year that her father died of pneumonia. In 1910, after Agatha's return from a Parisian finishing school, she and her mother spent the winter months in Egypt, an experience that would stay with her for the rest of her life.

Back in England, she had some of her poetry published in *The Poetry Review*, the magazine of the *Poetry Society*, and won some prizes. But her attempts at prose were less successful: writing under the pen names of 'Mac Miller' and 'Nathaniel Miller' they were all rejected. Her mother suggested that local Devon author Eden Phillpotts (whose 1924 play *The Farmer's Wife* would be made into a silent film by Alfred Hitchcock) might be permitted to give her some advice. He proved very encouraging, complimenting her on her grasp of structure and dialogue and recommending that she persevere with her writing.

In 1912, Agatha became engaged to Major Reginald Lucy, but while he was serving in Hong Kong she fell in love with Lt Archibald Christie of the Royal Field Artillery. They married eighteen months later on Christmas Eve in 1914, with Archie now a captain in the Royal Flying Corps. He went to war two days later, and Christie began working as a nurse in Torbay Hospital, later moving to the dispensary where she acquired an extensive knowledge of poisons, something that would be central to the plot of her 1920 debut novel, *The Mysterious Affair at Styles*.

This is the book that introduced readers to the dapper Belgian detective Hercule **Poirot**, a protagonist designed to be as different as possible from that other literary sleuth, Sherlock **Holmes**, while channelling elements of the latter (Christie was an avid reader of Conan **Doyle**). Short, well dressed, with a military-looking moustache and a head resembling an egg, Poirot's slightly comic appearance disguises a razor-sharp brain and a tireless sense of moral rectitude. Christie's inspiration for the character came from memories of a colony of Belgian war refugees in Torquay, and she wondered what would happen if one of them was a retired police officer.

Christie worked on the book during quiet periods at the dispensary, spurred on by her sister Margaret's assertion that she was incapable of writing a detective story. With the final draft typed on Margaret's old typewriter, she sent it to various publishers – but it would be almost two years before she got a reply. In 1919, John Lane, managing director of The Bodley Head, told her that if she altered the courtroom denouement, he would publish it. She did as requested and signed a six-book deal with them, on patently unfair terms: subsidiary rights would be shared fifty-fifty between author and publisher and she would get no royalties until 2,000 copies were sold. She earned more money from its serialisation in *The Weekly Times* than she did on the book itself. While at The Bodley Head, she acquired Edmund Cork (of Hughes Massie) as a literary agent, remaining with the firm until her death fifty years later.

Archie, now a colonel, was posted to the London Air Ministry in 1918. The couple then moved into two rooms on the second floor of 5 Northwick Terrace (now demolished) in St John's Wood, **London**. After the birth of her only child Rosalind Margaret Clarissa on 5 August 1919, they realised they needed a larger flat and so moved into first 25 and then 96 Addison Mansions, an apartment block behind Olympia in Earls Court.

In 1922, the Christies travelled round the world with Archie's friend, the rather unfortunately named Major Belcher, organiser of the British Empire Exhibition Mission. They visited South Africa, Australia, New Zealand, stopped off for a brief holiday in Honolulu and finally ended up in Canada. On their return in December, Archie got a job at the city firm of Austral Trust Ltd and they moved into a house called Scotswood in Sunningdale, about 30 miles from central London. In 1924, they moved to a larger house in the same area which they christened Styles, in honour of Christie's first book.

Christie's mother died of bronchitis in 1926, the year that her most audacious whodunit, *The Murder of Roger Ackroyd*, was published. The book received divided opinion, with the *Daily Sketch* calling it 'the best thriller yet' and the *News Chronicle* deriding it as 'a tasteless and unfortunate let-down by a writer we had grown to admire'. Nowadays it is regarded by many as a groundbreaking piece of detective fiction and one of the true classics of the genre.

Shortly after Christie's mother's death, Archie revealed that he had fallen in love with another woman – Nancy Neele, a joint acquaintance – and wanted a divorce. On 3 December, after a quarrel, Archie left Styles to spend the weekend with Nancy in Godalming, Surrey. That evening Christie fled the house, leaving her daughter asleep upstairs, with a note for her secretary saying that she was going to Yorkshire. She posted another to the Deputy Chief Constable for Surrey saying she feared for her life.

Next day her car was found by a gypsy, abandoned by the side of the road at Newlands Corner, near Guildford in Surrey. But Christie was nowhere to be found. The *Daily News* offered £100 for information leading to her whereabouts, a pool near the car was dredged and police from Surrey, Essex, Berkshire and Kent were drafted in to look for her. Archie Christie was the chief suspect. A week after her disappearance, 15,000 volunteers searched the Merrow Downs where her car had been found, but discovered nothing. Thriller writer Edgar Wallace postulated in the *Daily Mail* that Christie had faked her disappearance to spite her husband and that she was probably alive and well in London.

Wallace was partially right. A banjo player at the Hydropathic Hotel in Harrogate, North Yorkshire – now the Old Swan Hotel – had been thinking for a few days that one of the guests could have been the missing novelist. He told the Harrogate police, and shortly afterwards, the news was leaked to the press. *The Daily Mail* sent a special train filled with reporters and photographers, and reporter Ritchie Calder accosted the author directly. Finally the game was up – Christie admitted who she was, and on Tuesday, 14 December, the *London Evening Standard* reported that the hunt was over.

Archie came up to the Hydro on the fourteenth and identified her, and two doctors issued a statement claiming she had suffered a loss of memory. In fact, Christie had booked into the hotel on 4 December as 'Mrs Theresa Neele' from Cape Town. She had spent the time there like any other guest, taking tea in a local teashop, going on walks and playing billiards; she had even posted an announcement in *The Times* asking for friends and relatives to contact 'Neele' at a particular box number.

Unsurprisingly, the so-called Eleven Missing Days have thrown up a variety of wild and fanciful theories about her disappearance, leading to books, documentaries and even films on the subject. The Oscar-nominated *Agatha* (1979), starring Vanessa Redgrave, Timothy Dalton and Dustin Hoffman, postulated a rather unlikely love affair between a suicidal Christie and a hotshot American reporter, while the 2008 television series of *Doctor Who* featured the author as a character, with a bizarre fantasy solution for the mystery. The truth (not that we will ever know it) is undoubtedly less interesting. Some claim she had planned the whole thing, others that it was a publicity stunt to sell her latest book – but from then on, one thing became clear: she spent the rest of her life actively shunning the limelight.

A divorce was granted in April 1928 and Archie then married Nancy Neele, who died of cancer in 1958, Archie dying four years later. In 1929, Christie bought a mews house, 22 Creswell Place, in Chelsea, London. The following year, she met the archaeologist Max Mallowan while he was conducting a dig at Arpachiyah in Iraq (then called Ur); they fell in love and married in Scotland on 11 September, shortly after the publication of her first romantic novel, *Giant's Bread* (1930), written under the pseudonym of Mary Westmacott.

The year 1927 saw the first appearance of her indomitable elderly sleuth Miss Jane **Marple** in the series 'The Tuesday Night Club' in *The Royal Magazine*, though the stories were not collected in book form until *The Thirteen Problems* in 1932. By then, her first novel-length adventure, *The Murder at the Vicarage* (1930) had appeared. Based partially on the character of Caroline Sheppard from *The Murder of Roger Ackroyd*, Miss Marple was a white-haired spinster who lives in the tranquil village of St Mary Mead. A keen gardener (facilitating spying on neighbours), her expertise at crime solving had hitherto been relegated to such mundane cases as the disappearance of some pickled shrimps. But like Hercule Poirot before her, Miss Marple's outward appearance conceals an intellect bordering on genius. Miss Marple is also a shrewd judge of character, a talent that often helps her unmask miscreants, despite a dearth of evidence.

From 1930, Christie and Max Mallowan divided their time between England and the Middle East. Further houses were purchased: 48 Sheffield Terrace in Kensington, London, and Winterbrook House in Wallingford, Oxfordshire. They even built their own home at Chagar Bazar in Syria where Christie began a diary that would form the basis of her 1946 memoir *Come, Tell Me How You Live*. In autumn 1936, Mallowan's expedition dug up seventy cuneiform tablets which linked Chagar Bazar with the Royal House of Assyria – a significant historical find.

In 1938, the Christies bought another property, a large Georgian house overlooking the river Dart near Dittisham in Devon, a few miles upriver from Dartmouth. This was Greenway House, and they would live there, on and off, for the rest of their lives. During the Second World War, the building became a nursery for London child-evacuees and later, accommodation for United States Navy personnel. For a while, Christie returned to her job at the Torbay Hospital dispensary before joining Max in London, where he had a job at the Air Ministry. They lived in a succession of flats; in Half Moon Street, Park Place and then Sheffield Terrace. When this last place was bombed, they moved to a modern block of flats at 22 Lawn Road, Hampstead. Christie worked as a dispenser at University College Hospital, while Max was seconded to North Africa, where he became an adviser on Arab affairs.

Away from Max, she spent much of her free time writing. Many of her most famous books were composed during this time, including *Death on the Nile* (1937), *Ten Little Niggers* (1939, also known as *And Then There Were None*) and *Evil Under the Sun* (1941). In 1943, Christie's daughter Rosalind married Hubert Prichard, a soldier in the Royal Welch Fusiliers, and on 21 September she gave birth to Mathew. Tragically, Hubert was killed in action a year later, and Rosalind married again in 1949, to barrister and oriental scholar Anthony Hicks. In the same year, Christie accompanied Mallowan (by air, in what she called a 'dull routine') for the most important archaeological dig of his career – to Nimrud, the ancient military capital of Assyria. They would return there every year for almost a decade.

In 1954, Christie's secondary career as a playwright reached its acme, with three shows running concurrently in London: *The Mousetrap*, *Witness for the Prosecution* and *Spider's Web*. The first was based on her short story *Three Blind Mice*, which itself is a prose version of a 1947 BBC radio play commemorating the eightieth birthday of Queen Mary (1867–1953) broadcast on the Light Programme (now Radio 2). Originally entitled *Three Blind Mice*, it was soon changed to *The Mousetrap* (after Hamlet's 'play within a play') to avoid clashing with a similarly titled play written by Emile Littler several years earlier. Christie did not want the story published in Britain as long as *The Mousetrap* was still running. The story was collected in the United States in *Three Blind Mice* (1950), but was not published in Britain. An 'Acting edition' of the play has been available since 1952, but it was not commercially published in Britain until 1993, in *The Mousetrap and Other Plays*.

Premiering on 6 October 1952, theatrical entrepreneur Peter Saunders oversaw *The Mousetrap's* initial run at the Ambassadors Theatre, London, before moving it to the slightly larger St Martins Theatre next door in 1974. After eight years, a system was introduced of changing the cast and director annually, and by 1958, it had broken box-office records for the longest running play in London. By the end of 2008, it will be fifty-six years old and still shows no sign of closing.

In 1950, Christie was made a Fellow of the Royal Society of Literature, and on 1 January 1956, she became a Commander of the British Empire. Max received the same honour four years later. Crippling taxation forced the author to set up a private company, Agatha Christie Ltd, and in 1968, Bookers Books, a subsidiary of agricultural and industrial conglomerate Booker McConnell, bought a 51 percent stake, increasing later to 64 percent; the remainder being held by Christie's daughter and grandson. In June 1998, Booker sold their shares to Chorion plc, an entertainment and leisure company that also owns and manages the works of George Simenon and Raymond Chandler, among others.

A 1959, UNESCO report claimed that Christie had been translated into 103 languages – with sales of around 400 million copies to date, she came third after the Bible and Shakespeare. Her husband was knighted in 1968, and three years later, aged eighty-one, she was made Dame Commander of the British Empire. Sadly, on 16 June that year she broke her leg in a fall at her home in Wallingford and this led to a decline in her health. For the rest of her life she walked with a stick and made even fewer public appearances. In March 1972, she was measured for Madame Tussaud's Wax Museum, and shortly afterwards, her life-size figure appeared in the conservatory, seated below film director Alfred Hitchcock.

A banquet at Claridge's Hotel after the London gala premiere of *Murder On The Orient Express* in November 1974 was the last public event Christie attended. Interviewed by Lord Snowdon for the *Toronto Star* of 14 December 1974, she was asked what she would like to be remembered for. 'I would like it to be said that I was a good writer of detective and thriller stories,' she replied. *Curtain: Poirot's Last Case*, written during the Second World War, was published in 1975 when it was clear that the author would not be able to produce a new book that year.

A few days into 1976, just after luncheon on 12 January, Christie died at Winterbrook after a short cold. She was buried four days later following a private service in St Mary's Church in the nearby village of Cholsey. Later that year, the last Miss Marple adventure, *Sleeping Murder* (like *Curtain*, written during the 1940s) finally saw the light of day.

There have been innumerable film and television adaptations of her stories, specifically those that involve Poirot or Miss Marple. On film, Peter Ustinov played a portly version of the former, while David Suchet provided the definitive television portrayal in a long-running London Weekend Television/Granada series from 1989 to the present day. Meanwhile Margaret Rutherford, Joan Hickson and Geraldine McEwan – to name but three – have donned knitted shawls to play Miss Marple over the years, while James Warwick and Francesca Annis took on Tommy and Tuppence Beresford for a 1983 series made by London Weekend Television.

Christie's pre-eminence as the doyenne of British crime writers continues to this day. Reading one of her books guarantees a polished and meticulously plotted mystery with a solution that is almost always impossible to guess. Her characterisations may be broad and her later books less effective than her earlier ones, but the sheer number of brilliantly constructed whodunits she has authored, and their continued existence in all forms of media (including, now, comic books) vindicates her appeal to both mainstream readers and crime aficionados alike. *See also* Golden Age Crime Fiction.

Selected Works by the Author

Hercule Poirot
The Mysterious Affair at Styles (1920)
The Murder of Roger Ackroyd (1926)
Murder on the Orient Express (1934)
The ABC Murders (1936)
Death on the Nile (1937)
Evil Under the Sun (1941)
Curtain: Poirot's Last Case (1975)

Miss Marple
The Murder at the Vicarage (1930)
4.50 from Paddington (1957; also published in the United States as *What Mrs McGillicuddy Saw*)
At Bertram's Hotel (1965)

Others
Why Didn't They Ask Evans? (1934; also published in the United States as *The Boomerang Clue*)
Ten Little Niggers (1939; also published in the United States as *And Then There Were None;* title later revised to *Ten Little Indians*)
The Pale Horse (1961)
An Autobiography (autobiography, 1977)

Further Reading
Barnard, Robert. 1980. *A Talent to Deceive*. Collins.
Bunson, Matthew. 2000. *The Complete Christie*. Pocket Books.
Cared, Jade. 1998. *Agatha Christie and the Eleven Missing Days*. Peter Owen.
Gill, Gillian. 1990. *Agatha Christie: The Woman and Her Mysteries*. Free Press.
Morgan, Janet. 1984. *Agatha Christie: A Biography*. Collins.
Osborne, Charles. 1982. *The Life and Crimes of Agatha Christie*. Collins.

Website
www.agathachristie.com
www.deliciousdeath.com

Mark Campbell

Clarke, Anna (1919–2004)

A prolific author throughout the 1970s and 1980s, Anna Clarke wrote psychological crime mysteries that are characterised by ingenious plotting and a richly detailed prose style.

Anna Emilia Clarke was born in Cape Town, South Africa, on 28 April 1919, daughter of the noted educationalist Fred Clarke. She was brought up in Cape Town and Canada and studied economics in London in 1945. She abandoned a promising career in mathematics after suffering debilitating bouts of agoraphobia brought on by extreme travel sickness as a child. Later, overcoming severe panic attacks, she managed to complete a master's degree in nineteenth-century literature at the University of Sussex.

Clarke married German-Jewish refugee David Hackel in 1947, but the marriage was later dissolved. In 1964, she moved to Brighton, where, due to her phobia, she remained for long periods inside her home. She professed to feel secure only in her office, which also doubled as her bedroom and living area. She avoided enclosed spaces, such as lifts and underground trains, and rarely travelled alone. Refusing to fly, if visits to her New York publisher proved unavoidable, she always insisted on making the journey by ship, usually the *Queen Elizabeth II*.

Clarke used her illness as the basis for her first novel, *The Darkened Room* (1968), which highlighted the crippling fear experienced by a fellow sufferer subjected to intense psychological stresses. After a gap of three years, twelve novels appeared in quick succession during the next decade in Britain, the majority of them appearing shortly afterwards in United States, where the author also enjoyed great popularity.

The subjects are varied, but they all demonstrated Clarke's gift for strong characterisation and vivid description. *My Search for Ruth* (1975) was an intense character study about a young girl separated from her mother shortly after the First World War and raised by the well-meaning headmistress of a girls' school. The book described her struggle to unravel her violent past. In *The Deathless and the Dead* (1976), a literary scholar unearthed a deep-seated hatred in an Oxford couple's fifty-year marriage, not only for each other but also, fatally, for him. *The Poisoned Web* (1979), also set in Oxford, had an embittered wheelchair-bound widow whose malicious murder accusations against her daughter may well prove justified.

In the 1980s, a nine-book series featuring scholars-turned-sleuths Paula Glenning and James Goff appeared, beginning with *Last Judgement* (1985) and ending with the last book Clarke wrote, *The Case of the Anxious Aunt* (1996). While more loosely plotted than earlier works, the series was nonetheless an enjoyable entry in the cosy English crime genre, with an eccentric ensemble of characters guaranteed to appeal to both British and American readers alike.

Selected Works by the Author
The Darkened Room (1968)
Plot Counter-Plot (1974)

Clarke, Anna

My Search for Ruth (1975)
Legacy of Evil (1976)
The Deathless and the Dead (1976; also published in the United States as *This Downhill Path*)
The Poisoned Web (1979)
Poison Parsley (1979)
Soon She Must Die (1983)
Last Judgement (1985)
Cabin 3033 (1986)
Murder in Writing (1988)
The Case of the Paranoid Patient (1991)

Mark Campbell

Cleeves, Ann (b.1954)

An award-winning crime novelist who sets most of her books around Northumberland, Ann Cleeves's first series featured bird-watching amateur **detectives**, the second, the solid Inspector Ramsay and, her most recent, the vivid Inspector Vera Stanhope. Her nineteenth novel, *Raven Black*, won the 2006 Duncan Lawrie Gold Dagger.

Daughter of a teacher in a North Devon village, Cleeves worked as a childcare officer, Women's Refuge worker, and then as a cook for a Bird Observatory on Fair Isle where she met her husband, an ornithologist. In 1987, they moved to the North East, an area which provides the background for her novels.

A Bird in the Hand was set in the world of bird watchers and introduced the Palmer-Joneses. Molly is a retired social worker and George has retired from the Home Office, where he wrote an acclaimed police manual on interviewing techniques. This link allows him to be accepted by the police when he and his wife help with crimes, all set in remote areas. In *Come Death and High Water* (1987), the murder happens on the privately owned island of Gillibry; *Murder in Paradise* (1988) moves to the northerly isle of Kinness; and *A Prey for Murder* sets the greed of men who plunder the nests of birds of prey against the noble savagery of the sport of falconry (though it is Molly rather than her ornithologist husband who gets to the heart of the mystery). *Sea Fever* (1991) returns to bird-watchers, this time off the Cornish coast, and behind *Another Man's Poison* lies the illegal use of poison by gamekeepers. Though there were to be two more titles in this series, Cleeves had by then begun a parallel series character, Inspector Ramsay.

In *A Lesson in Dying* (1990), Ramsay investigates the death of a headmaster, and in the even-better second book, *Murder in My Back Yard*, he exposes graft and corruption in small-town politics. In the third, *A Day in the Death of Dorothea Cassidy* (1992), a small town is preparing for its summer carnival when the vicar's wife is found strangled. These summaries make the series sound 'cosier' than it is, but the tales are efficiently written, modern in tone and veer at times towards the bleak. Ramsay is a loner, unpopular with colleagues, but methodical enough to outdo those colleagues.

With Vera Stanhope, Cleeves introduced her most interesting detective. Vera is plain, overweight, single and lonely. Too tough and forthright to put up with sexism from her colleagues, at home she wishes there was a man in her life. But knowing there would not be one, she consoles herself with junk food and beer, which perversely helps her empathise with the ordinary people she meets on her cases – though the crimes themselves are far from ordinary.

Selected Works by the Author

Palmer-Jones
A Bird in the Hand (1986)
A Prey to Murder (1989)
Another Man's Poison (1992)

Inspector Ramsay
Murder in My Back Yard (1991)
The Baby Snatcher (1997)

Vera Stanhope
The Crow Trap (1999)
Hidden Depths (2007)

Russell James

Clerical Crime

The extra dimension of evil added to a crime committed by religious people, or on religious premises, has, over a long period, drawn authors to the genre of 'clerical crime'. One of the earliest, and most distinguished, among them is Charles **Dickens**, whose unfinished *The Mystery of Edwin Drood* (1870) is largely set in a cathedral city. In the early twentieth century, a number of writers on this theme were themselves clergymen: Victor L. **Whitechurch**, C.A. Alington and Austin Lee among them. Whitechurch alleged that many clergymen were readers of detective stories and amateur students of criminology. Monsignor Ronald **Knox** was certainly among them. An active member of the Detection Club, he was so dedicated to detective fiction that he composed 'ten commandments' for writers of the genre.

Church buildings not only provide backgrounds for crime but sometimes contribute to deaths. *The Nine Tailors* (1934) by Dorothy L. **Sayers** is a striking example of the use of a church in this way. Many ecclesiastical buildings offer the opportunity for persons or projectiles to fall from great heights, causing death or destruction. G.K. **Chesterton** made effective use of this in 'The Hammer of God' (*The Innocence of Father Brown*, 1911). The body count in Colin **Dexter**'s *Service of All the Dead* (1979) is high and includes some pushed off the tower of an Oxford church. Monuments and tombs may become murder weapons, as in Catherine **Aird**'s *His Burial Too* (1973) and Edmund **Crispin**'s mixture of farce, espionage, black magic and drugs in *Holy Disorders* (1946). Sacred buildings are defiled by murdered bodies. In *A Taste for Death* (1986), P.D. **James** has two strangely incompatible people slaughtered in the vestry of a London church, which is central to the plot. Similar desecration occurs in *The Case of the Headless Jesuit* (1950) by George Bellairs and W.J. **Burley**'s *Wycliffe and the Last Rites* (1992). Bellairs describes a dying man staggering into a church service, while Burley theatrically disposes a corpse on the chancel steps of a village church.

Following the example of *Edwin Drood*, some authors have chosen cathedrals as settings. H.C. Bailey's Reggie Fortune uses his knowledge of Dante to solve *The Bishop's Crime* (1940). A female detective is chosen by Austin Lee to investigate the puzzle of a dean found dead in the cathedral library (*Miss Hogg and the Dead Dean*, 1958). Two of Michael **Gilbert**'s detective novels are set in the precincts of Melchester Cathedral: his first, *Close Quarters* (1947), and, nearly forty years later, *The Black*

Seraphim (1983). As its title suggests, E.C.R. Lorac's *Policemen in the Precinct* (1949) has a similar background. Much more brutal is S.T. Haymon's *Ritual Murder* (1982). In this, the horribly mutilated body of a choirboy is discovered in a Norfolk cathedral. Almost as gruesome is Robert **Richardson**'s *The Latimer Mercy* (1985), in which severed hands are delivered to residents of a cathedral close. With her usual humorous disregard for political correctness, Ruth Dudley **Edwards** has chosen this setting for her satirical *Murder in a Cathedral* (1996).

Many misdeeds have been concealed within the enclosed premises of religious groups and communities. Such institutions lend themselves to the 'closed community' school of detective fiction. Of her prolific output, Gladys **Mitchell** set two books in convents. The earlier one, *St Peter's Finger* (1938), has a wide field of suspects, as a school, an orphanage and a guest house are attached to the convent. *Convent on Styx* (1975) provides a much later test of Dame Beatrice Bradley's investigative skills. Catherine Aird (*The Religious Body*, 1966) and Antonia **Fraser** (*Quiet As A Nun*, 1977) used nunneries as backgrounds, although Fraser's plot is more a gothic horror story than traditional detection. Robert **Barnard** places a group within a group in *Blood Brotherhood* (1977). A religious conference is taking place in a Yorkshire Anglican monastery, which gives Barnard scope for some biting satire. The scene of several crimes in *Death in Holy Orders* (2001) by P.D. James is not a monastery but an Anglican theological college, which has much of the atmosphere of a monastery. Nevertheless, Adam **Dalgliesh** encounters one of his most horrific cases. By contrast, Tim **Healds**'s *Unbecoming Habits* (1973) is a jolly romp.

Church politics and disputes among clergy and laymen are used as motives. These are handled with humour by Robert Barnard in *The Disposal of the Living* (1985) and David **Williams** in *Holy Treasure!* (1989). In the latter, Williams portrays with his usual wit the dissension among cathedral staff at the proposed sale of a copy of Magna Carta. Kate Charles has written a series of 'clerical mysteries' dealing with such issues, whose outcome is murder. Beginning with *A Drink of Deadly Wine* (1991), these mysteries are mostly investigated by an amateur sleuth who is a solicitor and student of church architecture. The settings are usually churches, but a cathedral is not spared. The most unusual crime scene is the shrine at Little Walsingham in Norfolk, where a body is discovered on the day of the annual pilgrimage there. P.D. James and Kate Charles consider moral issues in their novels, to a greater extent than other authors. The dilemma of the secrets of the confessional is sometimes an issue. A priest in Elizabeth George's *A Great Deliverance* (1989) agonises over this, and the question is raised in Colin Dexter's *A Way through the Woods* (1992), although neither of these is actually a clerical mystery.

Clerics appear as stock characters, especially in older detective fiction. Often they are described as bookish and scholarly. They have appeared as victims, perpetrators or investigators of crime. One of the most rounded clerical characters is that of the Revd Theodore Venables in *The Nine Tailors*, who helps Lord Peter **Wimsey** to decipher a coded letter. Margery Allingham's Swithin Cush (*Mystery Mile*, 1930) commits suicide, increasing Albert Campion's investigations. Unusually, the vicar in *Overture to Death* (1939) by Ngaio **Marsh** is a possible motive for the murder of one of two spinster rivals for his attention. Agatha **Christie**'s nearest approach to clerical crime is *Murder at the Vicarage* (1930), in which the vicar is the narrator. Among clerical murder victims is Father Baddeley, friend of Adam Dalgliesh in P.D. James's *The Black Tower* (1975). In *The Snares of Death* (1992), Kate Charles disposes of two clerics. Deans are not spared from slaughter – one is killed in procession to his own cathedral in *The Dean It Was That Died* (1991) by Barbara Whitehead. Investigation is a popular sideline for clerical characters, as a study of theology is considered conducive to the necessary logical mind. G.K. **Chesterton**'s Father Brown, an unassuming priest, is a very clever detective, but he cares more for saving the soul of a criminal than bringing him to justice. In mediaeval detection, Ellis **Peters**'s Brother Cadfael succeeds in a whole series of novels. A contemporary series character is a female sleuth – Dean Theodora Braithwaite – who appears in a number of 'ecclesiastical whodunits' written by D.M. Greenwood. Victor L. Whitechurch raises an interesting point in *Murder at the Pageant* (1930). His vicar dismisses all lesser mortals as investigators – asserting that only the Pope could be the perfect detective, as he is infallible.

Selected Works

Kate Charles: *The Snares of Death* (1992); *Evil Intent* (2005)
Edmund Crispin: *Holy Disorders* (1946)
Colin Dexter: *Service Of All The Dead* (1979)
Michael Gilbert: *Close Quarters* (1947)
P.D. James: *A Taste For Death* (1986); *Death In Holy Orders* (2001)
Dorothy L. Sayers: *The Nine Tailors* (1934)
David Williams: *Holy Treasure!* (1989)

Further Reading

Spencer, William David. 1989. *Mysterium and Mystery: The Clerical Crime Novel.* UMI Research.

Christine Simpson

Cleverly, Barbara

A former teacher, Barbara Cleverly has rapidly risen to be among the front-rank **historical** mystery writers. Her novels are strong in setting and plot, with a wide range of intriguing characters.

Set in colonial India in the early 1920s, her first series featured Scotland Yard **detective** Joe Sandilands. The first book, *The Last Kashmiri Rose* (2001), won the **Crime Writers' Association** Debut Dagger and was listed by *The New York Times* as one of the best books of the year. Commander Sandilands has been seconded to a tour of duty with the police force in India. He is about to return home when he becomes involved in a reported suicide, which he discovers is the latest in a connected series of murders at a local army regiment. Cleverly brings the India of the Raj alive, not only depicting the British in India, especially the women, but also identifying the inequalities between the British and the Indians and between the different levels of Indian culture. The book's success allowed Cleverly to develop the characters and the local atmosphere into a series, continuing with *Ragtime in Simla* (2003), *The Damascened Blade* (2004) – which won the CWA Ellis Peters Historical Dagger – and *The Palace Tiger* (2004). With her fifth book, *The Bee's Kiss* (2005), Cleverly brought Sandilands back to England at the time of the General Strike, whilst both *Tug of War* (2006) and *Folly du Jour* (2007) saw him in France. *Tug of War* is an especially powerful novel involving the identity of a shell-shocked soldier and is reminiscent of the works of Rennie Airth and Charles Todd.

Cleverly, Barbara

The Tomb of Zeus (2007) is the first of a new series featuring precocious young archaeologist Laetitia Talbot, who encounters murder during excavations in Crete. Cleverly's interest in archaeology was already evident from an earlier supernatural time-slip novel, *An Old Magic* (2003), in which an archaeologist, seeking to record the details of an Old Manor and a long-lost Roman villa before it is destroyed by a new motorway, opens a window on the days of Boudicca and the British revolt.

Selected Works by the Author
The Last Kashmiri Rose (2001)
The Damascened Blade (2004)
Tug of War (2006)
The Tomb of Zeus (2007)

Mike Ashley

Clifford, Francis (1917–1975)

Although neglected today, Francis Clifford was one of the most accomplished of British novelists working within the parameters of the adventure/**espionage** field; his métier was creating situations of extreme danger for his protagonists and freighting in a *crise de conscience* that pushes them to the furthest limits of human resilience.

Clifford was born Arthur Leonard Bell Thompson in Bristol in 1917 and initially pursued a career in the rice industry in China before the Second World War. As a soldier, he undertook a gruelling odyssey of 1,000 miles through Burma (occupied at the time by the Japanese army); this experience appeared in his book *Desperate Journey* in 1979. He worked in the Special Operations Executive and (like many other writers) was to utilise this experience in his writing (which he undertook to encapsulate for himself his wartime experiences). Clifford was soon producing novels which showed an adroit mastery of plotting allied to a skill in the creation and manipulation of suspense worthy of Alfred Hitchcock. His greatest literary attribute was his characterisation, notably of his beleaguered heroes, always (at some point in the narrative) pushed to the extremes of endurance. Clifford's careful building of sympathy for his heroes inevitably involves the reader to a degree almost unprecedented in adventure/crime fiction. His first masterwork in the genre was *Act of Mercy* in 1959, which justifiably won the **Crime Writers' Association** Dagger Award for that year. All of the author's considerable virtues are present here: his hero, Tom Jordan, is a successful businessman in a volatile South American country. His wife has just told him she is pregnant when the country erupts into murderous revolution, and the old regime is brutally exterminated in a totalitarian coup. All except Camara, the deposed president, who stumbles, bloody and weakened, into Jordan's garden. Almost as a reflex action, Tom finds himself trying to spirit Camara out of the country – on foot, with Tom's pregnant wife in tow and with brutal soldiers on their trail. And when Jordan is forced to kill to protect his charges, he is forced to ask himself (as his wife has continually done) why he has thrown away everything he owns and risked their lives to protect a man he barely knows. It is hard to know what to praise first in *Act of Mercy*: the characterisation (the conflicted Jordan, the sympathetic, injured ex-president who sets the narrative in train, and even Jordan's wife Susan, a fully developed protagonist), the orchestration of tension (which has a laser-sharp proficiency) or the sultry evocation of locale and landscape. *Act of Mercy* was filmed, in efficient (if workaday) fashion as *Guns of Darkness* (1962, director, Anthony Asquith).

Subsequent books by Clifford consolidated this success, such as the espionage novel *All Men Are Lonely Now* (1967) and, notably, *The Naked Runner* (1966). These books utilised espionage motifs: a businessman is forced to act as an agent of the West and ends up acting as ruthlessly as his opponents (the film rights were purchased by Frank Sinatra, who made a solid adaptation in 1967 under the direction of Sidney J. Furie). *The Blind Side* (1971) extended Clifford's achievement with a portrait of two brothers with very different backgrounds (one is in Naval intelligence, and one is a priest in Biafra) forced into life-threatening (and life-changing) situations.

As with his contemporary Alan **Williams** (who wrote in a not-dissimilar vein) Francis Clifford's star has waned, and many far-less talented writers have enjoyed greater success. In an ideal world, all of his highly accomplished novels would remain permanently in print.

Selected Works by the Author
Act of Mercy (1959; also published in the United States of *Guns of Darkness*)
The Naked Runner (1966)
All Men Are Lonely Now (1967)
The Blind Side (1971)
Amigo, Amigo (1973)
The Grosvenor Square Goodbye (1974; also published in the United States as *Good-Bye and Amen*)

Barry Forshaw

Cody, Liza (also known as Liza Nassim) (b.1944)

Liza Cody achieved immediate success with her first book, *Dupe* (1980), which began the Anna Lee series. It won the **Crime Writers' Association** (CWA) John Creasey award for best first-time crime novel, and the resulting series went on to be televised (with Imogen Stubbs playing Anna). However, Cody was dissatisfied with the adaptations. She switched to a different series based around a dysfunctional female wrestler, Eva Wylie, with whom she won a second CWA award, the Silver Dagger, given in 1992 for *Bucket Nut*, the first in the series.

Cody's earlier career was as an artist. She trained at the Royal Academy School of Art and worked for a while as an artist, designer and photographer. Nowadays, despite the **London** settings of most of her books and short stories, she lives in Somerset.

When Cody's Anna Lee first appeared, she seemed unlike previous British female PIs, and Cody can make a fair claim to have set the mould for the gutsy, independent-minded female investigator. Some later female **detectives** may seem tougher and less restricted by gender, but they owe their genesis to Anna Lee. As a sleuth she was credible: a detective officer in the police who left the force and joined a detective agency, the Brierly Detective Agency. But she was no superwoman or Modesty Blaise. Dogged as she could be on investigations, she was sensible enough to call for male help when things got too physical. (It helped that she had a wrestler friend Selwyn Price.) Compared to the wretched home life frequently given to male detectives, Anna Lee had a reasonably domesticated – if romantically bohemian – existence living on a houseboat moored on the Thames. She had a love life, without angst, but her life was in her work.

When working she made no concessions to her femininity, insisting she be given the same tasks as might be handed to a man: in *Bad Company* (1982) she was kidnapped, while in *Under Contract* (1986) her task was to provide physical protection to a rock star.

Eva Wylie, Cody's next lead character, was as different from Anna as could be: a one-time female wrestler (now barred from fighting), thickly built and not too agile mentally, struggling in an all-too-clever world, Eva was employed by Anna as a security guard. (But these remain Eva's stories, not Anna's.) It is Eva who really needs protection: wayward and floundering in a world that bewilders her; unattractive, she feels, and unemployable; vulnerable to temptation. Though this series gained a loyal following, her creator turned away from her after three books to edit anthologies and write a different non-series novel. That book, *Gimme More* (2000), told of a once-successful rock singer, now reduced to con tricks and her memories. *See also* Women Crime Writers.

Selected Works by the Author

Anna Lee
Dupe (1980)
Bad Company (1982)
Stalker (1984)
Under Contract (1986)
Backhand (1991)
Gimme More (2000)

Eva Wylie
Monkey Wrench (1994)
Musclebound (1997)

Other titles
Rift (1988)

Russell James

Cole, Martina (b.1959)

Martina Cole is a homespun phenomenon of what might best be called 'anti-girlie' fiction: a female-oriented genre dominated by tough, down-to-earth, put-upon women living in a world of violent men.

Cole's fictional world is the one she grew up in. Her heroines – she is almost invariably on the side of the female protagonist – are able to give almost as good as they get, matriarchs of wayward criminal families or daughters fighting to get respect in a culture of abuse, drugs, alcohol and prostitution.

What primarily distinguishes her books is her instinctive and unerring use of street language; another factor is the atmospheric evocation of down-at-heel milieu of her novels. Cole grew up in Essex – the English county which became an overflow zone for the more affluent, and occasionally criminal elements, of **London**'s East End. With her platinum-blonde hair, razor wit and tough in-your-face attitude, she has grown her image as an intelligent, aggressive example of the 'Essex girl' cliché of so many bad jokes.

Cole was the youngest of five children, brought up in an immigrant Irish Catholic family. She was sent to a convent school but was expelled at the age of fifteen. She was pregnant with her first child by the age of seventeen, when she was working as a waitress in a local restaurant. When she was heavily pregnant, she moved into the kitchen and worked right until the last moment when the owners called a taxi to take her to hospital in labour.

Her family's view was that it was up to her to get on with her life, and she was left to live in, as she puts it, 'a carpetless hostel in Tilbury surviving on £11.10 social security a week'. When her young son was given money for his birthday, she confessed to pinching it to get by.

A hard fate for a woman whose girlhood idol had been **pulp**-fiction writer Jackie Collins, until she decided that the only solution was to emulate her. She had seen a television programme on Collins with a walk-in wardrobe and drawers full of diamonds and had dreamed that one day she too would have her name on book covers.

In her teens, she had experimented writing 'mini Mills and Boon' romantic novellas for her friends and neighbours. By age twenty-one, she had already completed *Dangerous Lady* (1992), the novel that would make her famous, but she was so doubtful that she would be taken seriously – her colleagues in the wine bar laughed at her ambition – that it was nine years before she approached a literary agent. The agent, Darley Anderson, was astonished that a woman could write such a dangerous book and told her that she would have a notable career, a prognosis proved correct when the novel immediately fetched an advance of £150,000.

Dangerous Lady was about a tough London family of Irish extraction, called the Ryans, in which the little sister Maura takes on the hard men to become a feared crime boss of a world of thieves, robbers, pimps and bent coppers. It is a violent, rags-to-ill-gotten-riches tale in which the characters are largely one-dimensional and shallow, but its pace, violence and language carry the momentum. Its timescale, from the 1960s to the 1990s, gave it the reputation of a downmarket (in every sense) *Forsyte Saga* for post-war Britain. The book was made into a widely respected television mini-series in 1995. The lead character, retired but as dangerous as ever, returned ten years later in *Maura's Game* (2002).

Her second novel, *The Ladykiller* (1993), shifted the ground slightly to put a female policewoman to the fore in a brutal sexual murder of a gang boss's daughter, which throws the protagonists of organised crime and law and order into an uncomfortable collaboration.

Here is a theme that is to be seen in all Cole's books: loyalty to family versus loyalty to society. It might be summed up in the apocryphal East End comment about the notorious Kray mobster twins: 'They was bad boys but they was good to their mum' as well as in the still-current local oath when something serious has to be adjured: 'Upon my life, upon my daughter's life.'

It is certainly a message that has found a global market, with worldwide sales of her seventh novel, *The Know* (2003), being over three million. *The Know*, in which the heroine is a prostitute devoted to her wayward teenage children, found a place on *The Sunday Times* bestseller list for seven consecutive weeks.

In the years since *Dangerous Lady*, Cole has turned out a further dozen novels that could all be termed variations on a theme, albeit a highly successful theme that her childhood heroine Collins would certainly recognise: sex, violence and money are what make the world go round, whether it be among the stars or in the gutters. *See also* Women Crime Writers.

Selected Works by the Author
Dangerous Lady (1992)
The Ladykiller (1993)

Cole, Martina

Goodnight Lady (1994)
The Jump (1995)
The Runaway (1997)
Two Women (1999)
Broken (2000)
Faceless (2001)
Maura's Game (2002)
The Know (2003)
The Graft (2004)
The Take (2005)
Close (2006)

Website
www.martinacole.co.uk

Peter Millar

Collins, (William) Wilkie (1824–1889)

One of the giants of Victorian literature, Wilkie Collins specialised in stories of sensation and mystery and, in *The Moonstone* (1868), wrote the first full-length English **detective** novel.

He was born in **London** in 1824, the son of a successful and popular painter. Collins demonstrated some artistic talent in his youth and had a painting hung in the Royal Academy Summer Exhibition in 1849, but his real passion was for writing. He read law as a student at Lincoln's Inn but his writing career was already flowering. His first novel, *Antonia*, was published in 1850. In 1851, the same year he was called to the bar, he began his lifelong friendship with Charles Dickens.

As a character, Wilkie Collins was an odd mix of the practical and the bohemian, the prudent and the daring. When he first left home, at the ripe old age of thirty-two, it was to set up house with his mistress, Caroline Graves, a girl in her early twenties who already had a daughter, and apparently also a husband somewhere. Although this bold move shocked his family, friends and society, he was not bothered by their censure. He cared for Caroline – that was all that mattered to him. However, although he had been contemplating this action for some time, he did not make a move until he was sure that he was financially capable of supporting his new ménage. This contrasting mixture of romanticism and a sense of realism were the hallmarks of Collins's fiction, too. In the preface to his second novel, *Basil* (1852), the author stressed the difference between the 'Ideal' and the 'Actual', observing that 'the more of the Actual I could garner up as a text to speak from, the more certain I might feel of the genuineness of the Ideal which was sure to spring out of it'. This clever use of realism, the Actual to use his phrase, especially with characterisation, helps to give a sense of believability to the sensational, highly melodramatic elements – the Ideal – in his plots.

It is this combination of the exciting and at times fanciful story peopled by wholly credible and engaging characters that makes *The Woman in White*, Collins's first great success, such a superb mystery novel.

It was Wilkie Collins's friend and mentor Charles **Dickens** who commissioned him to write *The Woman in White* (1860) for his new magazine, *All the Year Round*. It is to Collins's great credit that the manacles of instalment writing – the need

18. William Wilkie Collins, photographed c.1870.

to reach a kind of cliffhanger situation at regular intervals to bring the readers back the following week – did not lead him to create a formulaic plot. The intricacies of the storyline and the multi-voiced narration help to blur any sense of segmentation and homogenise the flow of the story. When reading the book today, the reader is seldom conscious of the episodic nature of its original presentation. Another reason for this is that Collins planned the novel meticulously and he knew exactly how situations would develop and how characters would behave. Five years after the publication of the novel, he wrote in a letter to a friend:

> Neither 'The Woman in White', nor any of my serial stories were completed in manuscript form before their periodical publication. I was consequently *obliged* to know every step of the way from beginning to end, before I started on my journey.... When I sat down to write the seventh weekly part of 'The Woman in White', the first weekly part was being published in 'All The Year Round' and in 'Harpers Weekly'. No afterthoughts...were possible under these circumstances.... Months before a line of it was written for the press, I was accumulating...a mass of 'notes' which contained a complete outline of the story and characters. I knew what Sir Percival Glyde was going to do with the marriage register, and how Count Fosco's night at the opera was to be spoiled by the appearance of Professor Pesca, before a line of the book was in the printer's hands.

The use of multiple narratives draws on Collins's legal training, and as he points out in his preamble, 'The story here presented will be told by more than one pen, as the story of an offence against the laws is told in Court by more than one witness.'

Some of the basic details of the plot were borrowed from a collection of French criminal records bought by Collins in Paris while on a visit there with Dickens. Among these papers was a case involving the Marquise de Douhault who was drugged on a journey by her brother's agents and imprisoned under a false name. Thus she was presumed dead and her scheming brother inherited her estate. After two years of incarceration, the girl managed to smuggle a letter out to a close friend explaining her plight. The plot was uncovered and she was released. This account was the inspiration, the starting point, for *The Woman in White*, but the brilliance of the novel comes from Collins's development of this simple scenario into a dark and labyrinthine plot with wonderfully dramatic moments and effective characterisations.

There is an interesting account, apocryphal in nature, if not in fact, concerning another influence on the writing of the novel which concerns Collins's first encounter with his lover Caroline Graves. The story was told by the painter Millais to his son and appears in *The Life and Letters of Sir John Everett Millais* by J.G. Millais (1899). Apparently, during the early 1850s, Millais had dined with the Collins family in Hanover Terrace and at the end of the evening walked home to his studio in Gower Street accompanied by Wilkie Collins and his brother Charles. On their way, in the dark they heard a piercing scream which came from the garden of a nearby villa:

> The iron gate to the garden was dashed open and from it came the figure of a young and very beautiful woman dressed in flowing white robes that shone in the moonlight. She seemed to float rather than run in their direction and on coming up to the three young men, she paused for a moment in an attitude of supplication of terror. Then, seeming to recollect herself, she suddenly moved on and vanished in the shadows cast upon the road.

While Millais and Charles stood there mesmerised by this sight, Wilkie chased after the girl and he too disappeared. The next day, when the three men met up again, the author was somewhat reticent to talk about his adventures of the previous night. However, he explained that he had managed to catch up with the lady who had told him that 'She was a young lady of good birth and position, who had accidentally fallen into the hands of a man living in the villa in Regent's Park. There for many months he had kept her a prisoner under threats and mesmeric influence of so alarming a character that she dared not escape, until in sheer desperation, she fled from the brute, who, with poker in hand, threatened to dash her brains out.'

This dramatic incident, most probably embroidered and exaggerated in the re-telling, not only brought Collins into contact with Caroline, the strange and beautiful woman who lived with him from about 1858 until his death in 1889 (apart from a two year interlude from 1868), but also provided the raw material, a sparking point, for one of the most vivid images of the novel. The encounter with this strange woman dressed in white was no doubt instrumental in firing his imagination and is replicated to a large extent in the scene in the novel where Walter Hartright first meets Anne Catherick on the lonely road to Hampstead: '...there, as if it had that moment sprung out of the earth or dropped from heaven – stood the figure of a solitary Woman, dressed from head to foot in white garments; her face bent in grave enquiry on mine, her hand pointing to the dark cloud over London, as I faced her'.

One of the most original aspects of the novel is the detective work carried out by Marian Halcombe and, in particular, the conventional hero, Walter Hartright, who employs many of the sleuthing techniques of later fictional private investigators. In true detective hero fashion, Hartright jumps in a cab to lose his pursuers, and later in the story, before setting out to confront Count Fosco, he leaves a letter to be opened if he fails to return at a certain time. All very Sherlock **Holmes**.

Collins refined this detection element in his later work, *The Moonstone*, in which his character Sergeant Cuff, the rose-growing detective sergeant, sees right to the heart of the mystery of the missing jewel. T.S. Eliot called *The Moonstone* 'the first and greatest of English detective novels'. This comment may be a little fulsome and not necessarily absolutely accurate, but it does alert us to the importance of the book as a ground-breaking work of fiction. What is unique about *The Moonstone* is that it was the first novel to shift the emphasis from the crime itself – which in the end is comparatively insignificant – to its investigation. It is the process by which the mystery, baffling to the readers as well as the players in the drama, is solved and the villain is exposed that fascinates and engrosses the reader. As Collins states in his preface, in writing the novel he was attempting 'to trace the influence of character on circumstances' and in this way *The Moonstone* is unlike his earlier books, which trace 'the influence of circumstance upon character'.

Much has been made of the role of Sergeant Cuff in the drama. He is often regarded as one of the first detectives in British fiction. Nevertheless, one must note that the able but thwarted Cuff is actually dismissed from the case after wrongly accusing the heroine and he fades from the picture until the closing moments. The investigative baton is picked up by Ezra Jennings, a doctor's assistant whose detective credentials are limited to his personal knowledge of the effects of opium. However, Cuff does make an impression, and in his behaviour and proclamations we can see the genesis of numerous sleuths who were to appear in the future. His remark that 'the pieces of the puzzle are not all put together yet' is now the mantra of many a detective from Sherlock Holmes to Hercules **Poirot** and on to the more modern crime solvers like Morse and even *Midsommer Murders'* own Inspector Barnaby. Similarly, there is Cuff's observation that, 'In all my experience along the dirtiest ways of this dirty little world, I have never met with such a thing as a trifle yet', which combines in one sentence the essence of Doyle's Sherlock Holmes and **Chandler**'s Phillip Marlowe. What is all the more intriguing about Cuff is that he was based on a real policeman, a certain Inspector Whicher, who had achieved a degree of notoriety by having a number of his cases written about in *Household Words* where he was thinly disguised as 'Sergeant Whichem'. This serves as an example of Collins's constant recourse, throughout his career, to authentic criminal records for ideas, plots and, indeed, characters.

However, *The Moonstone* is far more than just a detective story. In its basic form, the whodunit mystery is formulaic: all the players must be seen as possible culprits and this, of course, restricts character development and depth. However, this is not the case with *The Moonstone*. Like the precious gem of the title, this novel has many facets. It is a narrative of richness and depth and was originally subtitled 'A Romance' rather than 'A Mystery'. Much of it was written while Collins was taking large quantities of opium to alleviate the agonies of gout. And indeed, the dreamlike qualities which are found in certain sections of the book were no doubt influenced by Collins's self medication.

The author's own experiences are reflected in the character of Ezra Jennings, the incurably ill addict who takes opium to achieve some relief from his suffering. It could be Collins himself speaking when Jennings endures, 'the vengeance of yesterday's opium pursuing me through a series of frightful dreams'.

The story of *The Moonstone* is told in the form of multiple narratives. Collins saw this as an essential format in which to the present the mystery. In this novel, he was experimenting with form to create a multi-faceted vision of the events leading up to the theft of the diamond and then to the discovery of the culprit and solution of the crime.

Just before he began writing the novel, Collins attended a criminal trial in London, and he was struck by how a chain of evidence and an overall picture of incidents concerning the crime was created from a series of testimonies given by various witnesses as they presented their views from the witness box.

It came to me then that a series of events in a novel would lend themselves well to an exposition like this. Certainly by the same means employed here, I thought, one could impart to the reader that acceptance, that sense of belief, which I saw produced here by a succession of testimonies, so varied in form and nevertheless so strictly unified by their march toward the same goal. The more I thought about it, the more an effort of this kind struck me as bound to succeed. Consequently, when the case was over, I went home determined to make the attempt.

The result was *The Moonstone*. The process of this form of narrative is best explained by the chief exponent, Gabriel Betteridge, the likeable, pipe-smoking eccentric and faithful old house-steward of Lady Verinder, who guides his life by constant reference to Daniel Defoe's *Robinson Crusoe*, a work of self-record which he seems bent on emulating. It is Betteridge who, in setting out the rules, asserts: 'I am forbidden to tell more in this narrative than I knew myself at the time. Or, to put it plainer, I am to keep strictly within the limits of my own experience.'

Indeed, it is as though he is in the witness box with his hand on the Bible. The reader is assured that there will be no sleight of hand to fool them. They will get 'the truth, the whole truth and nothing but the truth'. It is a stance taken up by all the other narrators in the novel. This approach also lends the narrative a veracity and sense of realism which was new and refreshing to the Victorian audience. Collins does not spring the solution on us but instead provides a reconstruction of the crime and in doing so foreshadows the exposure scenes that became a standard feature so beloved of crime writers in the pre–Second World War Golden Age of detective novels, epitomised by the work of Agatha **Christie**. Collins presents all the answers and explanations with all the suspects present.

It is strange and disappointing that Wilkie Collins never used this approach to mystery writing again. It is true that he used multiple narrative voices in other works, but here it was a means of propelling the plot along rather than providing a set of interlocking jigsaw pieces to create the overall picture of events. His use of several narrators to tell the story was a real development of a popular formula used by several other writers. Samuel Richardson, for example, had employed it on a large scale in combination with his epistolary convention in *Clarissa* (1748). But no one had manipulated the form in quite the way that Collins did in *The Moonstone* to tell his story slowly, to uncover the facts tantalisingly.

One suggested explanation for Collins not using this original approach in dealing with a mystery story again is that he was not fully aware of what he had done – that he had in fact created a new genre of story-telling: 'detective fiction'. It is difficult to accept this theory, and it is most likely that he had a greater interest in the other ideas and themes that he wished to express and develop within the novel. It may well be that in his estimation these may have been more important than the explanation of how a precious stone came to be stolen.

While the basic premise and theme of the novel lend themselves to dramatisation, the complex structure proves a problem. It was filmed twice, but on both occasions as a lack-lustre old dark-house mystery, based more on Collins's own inferior stage version than the novel. In the silent 1915 version, Sergeant Cuff is eliminated from the plot altogether, and a 1934 version produced by Monogram was a poverty-row production of little merit. It would seem that television with its luxury of time could cope much better with the convoluted narrative. In 1972, the BBC went perhaps a little too far in producing a five-hour serial of the novel. It was terribly wordy and slow, but the plot, characters and tone of the novel were intact. A much better version was produced by the BBC in 1996. It was dramatic, atmospheric and had a splendid portrayal of Cuff by Anthony Sher.

A late flowering gem in Collins's career was *The Haunted Hotel* (1878), where once again he mixes the bizarre and the gothic with detective elements. These elements are not merely shoe-horned into the narrative for gratuitous purposes to spice up the story. They are there to add that suggestion of danger and confusion which spill out into life when the moral rules are broken and when evil is committed.

There is an emphasis on physical horrors quite unlike his avoidance of such elements in his more famous novels. The visible and olfactory presences are described in grisly detail. It was as though Collins was trying to show in this novella that he could throw off the shackles of subtlety and restraint if necessary to shock and frighten. It was his last great work and there are echoes within the text of *The Woman in White* – the substitution plot in particular – but nevertheless it is an individual piece, effectively and excitingly handled.

The Haunted Hotel appears to be loosely based on a case from the annals of French crime, as was *The Woman in White* – a case of reality touched with imagination converted into engrossing fiction.

The Haunted Hotel was serialised in *Belgravia* magazine in six monthly parts, from June to November 1878. Though the story was very popular, Collins was only paid £50 for each part, which reflects to some extent how the author was observed rather short-sightedly by the publishing world at this time. It was generally regarded that he had passed his prime. Sadly, *The Haunted Hotel* was the last significant work of this great author before ill health and opium drained his powers. He died in 1889. *See also* Literature and Crime Fiction.

Selected Works by the Author
The Woman in White (1860)
No Name (1862)
Armadale (1866)
The Moonstone (1868)

David Stuart Davies

Connolly, John (b.1968)

John Connolly's work does not fit comfortably into any particular category of crime fiction. His unconventional **thrillers** are written in lyrical prose, which weaves elements of the supernatural into otherwise wholly contemporary stories.

Although often thought of as an American writer, Connolly is an Irishman from Dublin, who has chosen to set all his thrillers in the United States. He has lived and worked in America, which he has described as the most suitable medium through which to explore the themes that interest him: compassion, morality, reparation and salvation. In his view, British crime fiction lacks compassion for the victims, and he states that his use of the 'sometimes horrifyingly explicit' violence in his books is to ensure that readers understand the victims' sufferings. This is evident in his first novel, *Every Dead Thing* (1999), which introduced Charlie 'Bird' Parker (the name is a nod to the alto saxophonist), a former policeman who is searching for the man who killed his wife and daughter. In all the stories in which he features, Parker is haunted by their deaths, gradually changing from a violent, self-absorbed man into one hardly less volatile, but driven by an awareness of the suffering of others. *Every Dead Thing* was the first book by a non-American to win the Private Eye Writers of America Shamus Award, and it heralded the arrival of a major new talent.

Every Dead Thing was followed by *Dark Hollow* (2000), a subtler and more complex book, in which Parker has developed into a more sympathetic personality. In *The Killing Kind* (2001), while investigating the death of a young woman, Parker is confronted by one of Connolly's most chilling villains, Mr Pudd. The recurring characters Angel and Louis, who seem to be Parker's only friends, are prominent in *The White Road* (2002), in which the supernatural element is more explicit. Parker can only be glimpsed in *Bad Men* (2003), an atmospheric, stand-alone novel set on an island. *Nocturnes* (2004), an intriguing collection of supernatural novellas and stories, includes a substantial tale featuring Parker, who returns to his central role in the next novel, *The Black Angel* (2005). *The Book of Lost Things* (2006) is a departure from Connolly's crime fiction, a fascinating book which displays his inventiveness. The story begins during the Second World War and develops into a fantasy which follows the adventures of a little boy who encounters many of the characters from children's fairy tales. *The Unquiet* (2007) is a gentler, more thoughtful mystery, in which Parker, while investigating an old crime, attempts to come to terms with his own past.

Connolly's technically brilliant, disquieting thrillers are notable in particular for the powerful, poetic quality of his writing and the breadth of his imagination, a distinctive voice in the twenty-first-century crime fiction.

Selected Works by the Author
Every Dead Thing (1999)
Dark Hollow (2000)
The Killing Kind (2001)
The White Road (2002)
Bad Men (2003)
The Black Angel (2005)
The Book of Lost Things (2006)
The Unquiet (2007)

Susanna Yager

Connor, John (b.1963)

John Connor debuted as part of Orion's *New Blood* series in December 2003 with *Phoenix*, the first in what would become a very dark police procedural series featuring troubled former undercover security services agent Karen Sharpe. John Connor is a pseudonym used by a former barrister who spent fifteen years working for the Crown Prosecution Service (from 1988) in London and West Yorkshire. He was involved in over fifty homicide and drug-related prosecutions and provided advice to the police in numerous long-term undercover operations. Connor was born in Carlisle but now lives with his wife and two children in Belgium, writing fulltime.

With *Phoenix*, Connor had inaugurated a very promising crime-writing career. The protagonist Karen Sharpe is haunted by the memories of her undercover past in Northern Ireland. She is working on a drug investigation (Operation Anvil) with colleague D.S. Phil Leach, and his attractive informer Fiona Mitchell Leach takes Sharpe home, disgusted at her drunkenness. In the morning, the bodies of Leach and Mitchell are discovered in what seems like a professional hit. Sharpe may well have been the last person they saw before the killer came for them. In Connor's follow-up, *The Playroom* (2004), Sharpe's obsessive nature finds her in pursuit of a paedophile group responsible for a child abduction which results in a violent climax. Third in the series, *A Child's Game* (2006) features an identity crisis for the troubled Sharpe as she appears to be involved in an undercover sting operation with a criminal cartel involved in property development, drugs smuggling and money-laundering. The fourth book, *Falling* (2007), is again a dark and moody thriller which sees Sharpe fall in love only to find that life has a cruel shock in store. This time, Connor tackles topical race-hate issues in Yorkshire and the murder of a heavily pregnant woman, all with the beleaguered Sharpe at the centre.

The most interesting aspect of Connor's work is his series character – he has explained:

> Originally, I started writing about Karen Sharpe because I was fascinated by the idea of what happens to people in deep undercover roles. This interest arose out of meeting police officers who had actually been in roles which had required so great a personality shift that they had clearly suffered psychological consequences when the time came to quit the role, to get out. Karen's entire history is like this. She is a woman who seriously struggles with the idea of who she is. She tries desperately to be a good mother and fulfil her duties at work (as a detective), but at bottom the tragedy is that she is only good for one thing – pretending not to be herself.

Selected Works by the Author
Phoenix (2003)
The Playroom (2004)
A Childs Game (2006)
Falling (2007)

Ali Karim

Conrad, Joseph (1857–1924)

Although Joseph Conrad wrote only three novels with crime themes, they have proved influential on literature and the cinema and are more than a little prophetic. *The Secret Agent* (1907) is the first serious novel to feature a double agent and is rumoured to have inspired the anti-left anarchist known as 'The Unabomber' who waged a campaign of terror against American universities and airlines from the late 1970s to the early 1990s. *The Nature of a Crime*, co-written two years later with the English novelist Ford Madox Ford, is a perceptive indictment of later twentieth century financial malfeasance; *Under Western Eyes* (1911), the compelling portrait of a young student drawn into the world of espionage, has been compared to the real-life activities of the British spies Guy Burgess, Donald Maclean and Sir Anthony Blunt. Conrad's narrative style and anti-heroic characters can also be seen reflected in the work of later writers such as Graham **Greene**, Ernest Hemingway and Joseph Heller.

Conrad, Joseph

One of Alfred Hitchcock's early triumphs was his version of *The Secret Agent* – re-titled *Sabotage* (1936) – and Francis Ford Coppola's brutal Vietnam movie *Apocalypse Now* (1979) owes its inspiration to one of Conrad's finest novellas, *Heart of Darkness* (1899).

Born Teodor Jozef Konrad Nalecz-Korzeniowski in the Polish town of Berdyczow, Conrad's father was a revolutionary with literary gifts who translated Victor Hugo's *Les Travailleurs de la Mer* and wrote a number of patriotic tragedies that revealed his dislike of the Tsarist Russian authorities. After becoming involved in an uprising in 1863, he and his family were exiled to Vologda, a town of biting cold and hardship 300 miles north of Moscow, where the young Joseph first experienced the cost of revolutionary fervour. To avoid being conscripted into the Russian Army, he fled to France and became a merchant seaman. The following years at sea were full of adventure – gunrunning, political conspiracy and a narrow escape from death when his ship caught fire, and he was adrift in a lifeboat for twelve hours. These exploits were to inspire several of his great novels. In 1886, after gaining his Master Mariner's certificate, he became a British citizen and changed his name to Joseph Conrad. Later voyages to the Far East filled his imagination with ideas for stories, and the atrocities he witnessed while serving as the captain of a Congo steamboat formed the core of *Heart of Darkness*.

The Secret Agent tells the story of an anarchist plot to commit an act of violence in the heart of **London** and is clearly based on a similar incident in the city a few years earlier. Agent provocateur Verloc, an idle and unscrupulous man who is ostensibly a small businessman, has been assigned by his masters to spy on London anarchists and organise a bombing of the Greenwich Observatory. Although he believes the plot is bound to cause an anti-anarchist campaign by the London police, Verloc makes his plans – including using his wife's simpleton brother, Stevie, to plant the bomb. When she discovers her husband's plan, Winnie Verloc kills him with a carving knife. She is, however, unable to prevent her brother from killing himself when the bomb accidentally explodes. It is then left to the methodical Chief Inspector Heat to discover the real cause of the tragedy and its implications for London. The Hitchcock version of the novel – which was re-titled *The Woman Alone in America* – was made into a movie starring Sylvia Sidney, Oscar Homolka and Desmond Tester and was remade in 1996 as *The Secret Agent*, directed by Christopher Hampton, starring Bob Hoskins, Patricia Arquette and Gerard Depardieu. The book itself is said to have been a source of inspiration to Dr Theodore Kaczynski, the Chicago-born mathematics professor, who wrote in his *Industrial Society and Its Future* that his campaign of mailing bombs that killed three people and injured twenty-three was necessary to draw public attention to the dangers of modern technology. His soubriquet was developed from his FBI codename, 'Unabom' for university and airline bomber. In 1995, Kaczynski wrote to the *New York Times* promising to 'desist from terrorism' and agreed to plead guilty to avoid the death penalty. He is still serving life imprisonment.

The Nature of the Crime first appeared in the April and May 1909 issues of *The English Review* under the curious by-line 'Baron Ignatz von Aschendorf' and has been described by Conrad scholars as 'a freakish collaboration' between Conrad and Ford Madox Ford (1873–1939), an English novelist, poet and editor who wrote more than sixty books but is today often remembered more for his literary associations than his own work. Conrad was among those writers he befriended, and apart from their collaborations published him in *The English Review* alongside Thomas Hardy,

H.G. Wells, T.S. Eliot and others. Both men were apparently very interested in financial malfeasance and 'wrote and read aloud one to the other'. How much of the writing of this story of fraud in city banks and financial institutions can be attributed to Conrad is hard to say, as he confessed to having 'soon got tired of *The Nature of Crime*' and did not include it in his list of titles for the collected editions of his work. A single edition carrying both authors' names was published by Ford in 1924.

In 1906, Conrad wrote his only short story of crime, 'The Informer', which recounts the exploits of a **detective** described as 'X'. (It can be found in *A Set of Six* published in 1908.) His final novel of criminality, *Under Western Eyes* (1911), returned again to the theme of a double agent. Razumov is a keen student unwittingly drawn into the assassination of a politician by a fellow student, Victor Haladin, who needs Razumov to help him escape. Misunderstanding what he is to do, Razumov reports the murder to the police and as a result of his encounter with the revolutionaries is asked to become a double agent and go to Geneva to investigate a community of Russian exiles. But there he meets Haladin's mother and sister and confesses to them and the other revolutionaries his part in the exposure of his fellow student. He is brutally punished and ends his last days as a cripple and a pariah. *See also* The Godfathers of British Crime Fiction *and* Literature and Crime Fiction.

Selected Works by the Author
Heart of Darkness (1899)
Lord Jim (1900)
Nostromo (1904)
The Secret Agent (1907)
The Nature of a Crime (1909)
Under Western Eyes (1911)

Peter Haining

Conventions

Over the years, the United Kingdom has had its share of significant crime fiction conventions, ambitious events that allow fans and authors to meet and share their enthusiasm for the genre.

Britain's first major convention was the World Mystery Convention: the Bouchercon. Named after the American writer, critic and editor Anthony Boucher (one of the first reviewers to credit crime fiction with literary merit), the structure consists of multiple strands of readings, panels and interviews. Registered authors are offered an opportunity to participate. This format is followed by most other conventions. The Bouchercon has been held in North America since 1970, but in 1990, readers and authors from around the world gathered in London for a rare non-US outing.

The following year, Nottingham's Broadway Media Centre put on the first annual Shots in the Dark, a week-long celebration of crime and suspense in cinema. Complementing it was a literary strand called Shots on the Page, with author panels that focused on crime and suspense in fiction.

While the Nottingham events were growing in popularity, another, more intimate conference had started up in Oxford. In 1994, St. Hilda's College held its first Mystery & Crime Weekend. Initially organised to reunite former students, it has become popular among a small group of crime fiction aficionados. Appropriate to its scholastic setting, the weekend conference sees a mix of authors and readers give papers on topics related to that year's theme. Speakers appear by invitation only.

By 1995, the annual Shots events had become the highlight of the British crime-fiction calendar and had also given birth to a magazine, *A Shot in the Dark*, which later became *Shots*. The event organisers made a successful bid to host that year's Bouchercon in Nottingham. Once again an international mix of readers and authors gathered together to celebrate the genre. Due to the assimilation of that year's Shots in the Dark, the World Mystery Convention also included a cinematic strand. Shots in the Dark proceeded as usual in 1996, but the literary strand took a one-year break. When Shots on the Page returned in 1997 it was announced that cuts in funding would necessitate it being the final one.

At the last Shots on the Page event, members of the **Crime Writers' Association** (CWA) lobbied their committee to establish a replacement. The CWA put together a working party and decided to go with a proposal from the Deansgate branch of Waterstone's Booksellers in Manchester. With the Manchester Waterstone's organising Dead on Deansgate – the first was held in 1998 – the CWA supported the event by lending the expertise of individual members on various fronts, including the programming. Towards the end of the convention's successful five-year run, Waterstone's commercial necessities increasingly conflicted with the CWA policy of not offering preferential treatment to some members over others. Following the 2002 convention, the Manchester Deansgate branch continued Dead on Deansgate as a scaled-down in-store event.

In the meantime, the organisers of the Shots events revived their convention in 2000 at the National Film Theatre (NFT) under the name Crime Scene. The first of five annual conventions included a literary strand but, befitting its location, Crime Scene was dominated by its film programme.

In 2002, the longstanding Harrogate Festival set up the annual Crime Writing Festival under the umbrella of its events. Authors appear by invitation only, and with only one panel on at any time (other conventions typically offer two or three simultaneously), the Harrogate Crime Writing Festival has a high reader-to-author ratio. Though this results in fewer authors participating, the sponsorship of publishers ensures the attendance of popular and international crime writers.

A more recent crime fiction convention to celebrate the genre was Left Coast Crime. Like the Bouchercon, Left Coast Crime is an American convention, but in 2006 it was organised on the left coast of England, in Bristol. Its organisers recognised that travel expenses might be high for international delegates, so to make their visit worthwhile, additional day trips to British locations with strong links to crime fiction were offered in the days immediately before the convention. For the delegates participating in the excursions, Left Coast Crime became a weeklong event.

Adrian Muller

Cook, Judith (1933–2004)

A passionate anti-nuclear campaigner from the 1960s onwards, Judith Cook spent her eventful life fighting against injustices. The author of many highly regarded non-fiction books, she also found time, late in life, to pen a number of well-researched crime stories.

Judith Anne Cushing was born in Manchester on 9 July 1933, brought up in a village near the historical Bosworth Field and educated at Stretford Girls' Grammar School in Manchester. She became secretary to Sir John Barbarolli, conductor of Liverpool's Hallé Orchestra, where she met her first husband, Douglas Cook; they married in 1952 and had four children.

During the 1960s, she founded the anti-nuclear organisation Voice of Women, following a series of articles she wrote for *The Guardian* in the wake of the Cuban Missile Crisis. Cook took part in protests in Washington DC and Moscow, and from her base in the eccentrically named Ding Dong Cottage in Penzance, Cornwall, she and her husband spearheaded the group as it grew in size and influence.

The marriage was dissolved in the early 1970s, and she returned to journalism to work for *The Guardian* and *The Birmingham Post*. A promising career at Anglia Television was curtailed when Cook sustained injuries from a car crash. In 1979, she moved back to Cornwall, to the fishing village of Newlyn, with her new partner Martin Green.

From the 1980s, she began channelling her energies into writing non-fiction books. Some of these proved highly contentious to the government, especially her investigation into the mysterious death of a prominent anti-nuclear campaigner, *Who Killed Hilda Murrell?* (1985). *Red Alert* (1986) looked at the dangers of nuclear power, and *An Accident Waiting to Happen* (1989) highlighted prominent gaps in disaster prevention.

In the 1990s, she ventured into historical fiction, inspired by her love of Elizabethan and Jacobean history – a subject she taught part-time at Exeter University. *Death of a Lady's Maid* (1997) introduced charismatic Elizabethan physician and astrologer Dr Simon Forman, who found himself investigating a series of perplexing murders in the sixteenth-century London. *Murder at the Rose* (1998), set in Southwark's Rose Theatre, showcased the author's love of Elizabethan theatre, a subject she would return to several times in her non-fiction books of this period, alongside biographies of J.B. Priestley and Daphne du Maurier.

A second series, set in the present day and featuring crusading environmental activist John Latymer, began in 2003 with *Dead Ringer* but was brought to an abrupt end by the author's sudden death following a stroke, on 12 May 2004, merely days after her marriage to Martin Green. *Keeper's Gold* (2004) was published posthumously.

Selected Works by the Author
The Slicing Edge of Death (1993)
Death of a Lady's Maid (1997)
Murder at the Rose (1998)
Blood on the Borders (1999)
Kill the Witch (1999)
School of the Night (2000)
Dead Ringer (2003)
Worm in the Bud (2003)
Keeper's Gold (2004)

Mark Campbell

Cooper, Natasha

Natasha Cooper is one of the foremost exponents of crime fiction as a vehicle for the exploration of social issues. Her work is characterised by meticulous plotting, detailed research, emotional literacy and strong female protagonists who work in fields – the civil service and the law – that, until very recently, have been entirely dominated by men.

19. Natasha Cooper.

Born Daphne Wright in London, the granddaughter of novelist Catherine Wright (Cooper describes her grandmother's work as 'psychological relationship novels, some with a crime element') Cooper was educated at St Mary's, Wantage, and worked in publishing for a number of years before becoming a full-time writer. After writing several novels of historical romance, she published her first crime novel, the frivolous *Festering Lilies*, featuring amateur detective (and romantic novelist) Willow King, in 1990. Six further Willow King novels followed, and in 1998, Cooper introduced a new series character, barrister Trish Maguire, in *Creeping Ivy*. To date, there are eight Trish Maguire novels, and Cooper has also written two stand-alone psychological thrillers under the name Clare Layton.

Through her protagonist Trish Maguire, an astute and often sceptical lawyer with a background in family law and a crusading spirit, Cooper has tackled a range of subjects from libel (*Gagged & Bound*), wrongful imprisonment (*Prey to All*) and the duties of parents and those in loco parentis (*A Greater Evil*), to corruption in the city (*Out of the Dark*) and the food industry (*Keep Me Alive*). Supporting characters – such as Maguire's partner, high-flying solicitor George Henton, and her friend, police officer Caro Lyalt, with whom she sometimes finds herself at odds – ensure that the books take in the full breadth and complexity of Britain's legal machine. Although, as with many crime novels, the quest for truth is at the heart of each book, Cooper's perception of justice as an ambiguous notion that is frequently at odds with the strict letter of the law means that it is the gap between the two that fuels both the tension and the pathos in her work.

Essentially, Maguire, at home with the intellectual jousting of the social elite of her elegant Temple chambers but painfully aware of the struggles of the underprivileged, excludes people with whom she frequently deals, is a cerebral heroine and uses a combination of brains, instinct and empathy to solve cases. Her past – a charming, feckless father who abandoned his family when she was a baby and the later discovery of a young and vulnerable half-brother – makes her feel a strong kinship to others with fractured family backgrounds.

Cooper does not shy away from scenes of graphic violence, but she is keenly aware that it is psychological cruelty that often causes the worst damage to those on the receiving end. Her often harrowing accounts of both, and her thoughtful analysis of the state of modern Britain, are lightened by lavish and entertaining descriptions of food, friendship and bonhomie. *See also* Social Comment in Crime Fiction *and* Women Crime Writers.

Selected Works by the Author
Creeping Ivy (1998)
Fault Lines (1999)
Prey to All (2000)
A Place of Safety (2003)
Keep Me Alive (2004)
Gagged & Bound (2005)
A Greater Evil (2007)

Writing as Clare Layton
A Clutch of Phantoms (2000)
Those Whom the Gods Love (2001)

Website
www.natashacooper.co.uk

Laura Wilson

Copper, Basil (b.1924)

Although best known as a specialist in horror short stories and novels, Basil Copper is also the author of two popular **detective** series, set almost half-a-century and two totally different genres apart.

Born in **London**, Copper served in the Royal Navy for four years during the Second World War before taking up a career in journalism. He made his debut as a fiction writer with 'The Spider' in *The Fifth Book of Pan Horror Stories* (1964). Around the same time, Copper began writing his first novel while working in a newspaper office. He set out to write a tongue-in-cheek crime story in the Dashiell Hammett/Raymond **Chandler** mode entitled *The Dark Mirror*. When it was completed, he sent it to thirty-two publishers, who all turned it down because it was too long. After four attempts at cutting it down, Robert Hale eventually published the novel in 1966.

The Dark Mirror launched a series of hard-boiled thrillers featuring Los Angeles private investigator Mike Faraday, an obvious and acknowledged homage to Chandler's Philip Marlowe. Although critics admired the author's authentic descriptions of the City of Angels, Copper had in fact never been to California.

All his knowledge was gleaned from watching old movies and referring to maps. The first book was popular enough to spawn a series, and, over the next twenty-two years, Copper produced fifty-two volumes, often at the rate of two or more books a year, until the series ended in 1988. Faraday's charm as a tough protagonist and poetry-quoting narrator, ably supported by his faithful secretary Stella, proved popular among readers in other countries as well, and the books were translated into numerous foreign-language editions.

American author August Derleth had begun writing his series of stories about consulting detective Solar Pons (whose name in Latin literally means 'Bridge of Light') in the late 1920s after he received a letter from Sir Arthur Conan **Doyle** stating that there would be no further tales of Sherlock **Holmes**. Derleth's Pons was closely modelled on Doyle's character – he lived at 7B Praed Street, not far from Paddington Station; his own Watson was Dr Lyndon Parker, and Mrs Johnson was their long-suffering landlady. Eight volumes of these Holmes pastiches were published between 1945 and 1973 under Derleth's specialist Mycroft & Moran imprint.

Unfortunately, Derleth's research left much to be desired, and upon the author's death in 1973, Copper was asked to revise and edit the entire series of seventy short stories and one novel. The task took almost eighteen months, and Mycroft & Moran published the result in 1982 as *The Solar Pons Omnibus*. Copper was eventually invited to continue the Pontine canon, and he produced seven collections of novellas and the novel *Solar Pons versus the Devil's Claw* (2004). Copper's Pons stories have been collected by various publishers, although the author has disowned some editions after unauthorised rewriting by in-house editors.

Basil Copper has been a member of the Crime Writers' Association for more than thirty years and served as its chairman during 1981–1982.

Selected Works by the Author
The Exploits of Solar Pons (stories, 1993)
The Recollections of Solar Pons (stories, 1995)
Solar Pons: The Final Cases (stories, 2005)

Stephen Jones

Coulter, Stephen (also known as James Mayo) (b.1914)

Like his contemporary James Mitchell (who along with his novels under his own name wrote a series of Bond-style novels as James Munro), the versatile and inventive Stephen Coulter supplemented his income from adroit **thrillers** in a variety of styles by penning a series of 007-ish *jeu d'esprits* as James Mayo. The latter were more parodic but perfectly serviceable in a brash and outrageous fashion. Regrettably, Coulter's novels under either name are now remembered more by cognoscenti than from actually being read, but remain well worth seeking out.

Born in Britain but educated in Paris, Coulter – like many other thriller writers before and after – worked as a journalist (notably travelling for Reuters). He served on Eisenhower's staff at supreme Headquarters during the war and wrote fiction (before becoming a published author) during his two decades or so as a journalist. Ironically, Coulter advised Ian **Fleming** on the casino sequences in the first 007 novel, *Casino Royale* – so perhaps his own endeavours in the fiction field later were not surprising.

The Loved Enemy (1962) instantly established Coulter as a writer of considerable professional expertise, and both *Threshold* (1964) and *Offshore!* (1965) demonstrated a refinement of these skills; the latter two books were particularly well-turned adventure novels. *A Stranger Called the Blues* (1968) is a vivid and involving saga of smuggling and danger set in India, with an attention to the details of locale that suggested the nonpareil skills in this area of Graham **Greene**. *Embassy* (1969) is more redolent of Arthur Hailey than Graham Greene and pleased Coulter's growing list of admirers somewhat less. At the height of Bondmania in the 1960s, several publishers commissioned ersatz 007-style novels, many of indifferent quality. But Coulter's series as James Mayo (featuring Charles Hood, his own equivalent of Fleming's human blunt instrument) were unquestionably among the more accomplished entries in this publishing phenomenon. Charles Hood has all the requisite characteristics of the urbane secret agent: well travelled, knowledgeable in *haute cuisine* etc., but Coulter/Mayo decided to make his protagonist a dealer in fine art who moonlights as an agent for British intelligence. The Hood books (beginning with *Hammerhead* in 1964) were Fleming with the volume turned up: all the elements that characterised the templates for the Hood novels were ratcheted up an almost operatic level – notably, the grotesque villains, who made even Ian Fleming's monstrous psychopaths seem quotidian. *Let Sleeping Girls Lie* (1965) maintained the frantic pace and jaw-dropping plot developments of its predecessor, while *Once in a Lifetime* (1968) continued to add pungent ingredients to the mix of high living, full-blooded violence and expertise in antiques. While the time for Coulter's novels (under either name) may have passed, the fact that one of the books, *Shamelady* (1966), was filmed as recently as 2007 – albeit on a very restricted budget – suggests that the books may someday be rescued from their status as historical artefacts. *See also* Espionage Fiction.

Selected Works by the Author

As Stephen Coulter
The Loved Enemy (1962)
Threshold (1964)
Offshore! (1965)
A Stranger Called the Blues (1968; also published in the United States as *Players in a Dark Game*, and reprinted in UK as *Death in the Sun*)

As James Mayo
Hammerhead (1964)
Let Sleeping Girls Lie (1965)
Once in a Lifetime (1968; also published in the United States as *Sergeant Death*)
Shamelady (1966)

Barry Forshaw

Coward, Mat (b.1960)

A self-confessed jobbing writer, Mat Coward has written for a great many publications on a great many subjects. His novels and short stories, however, have tended towards **science fiction**, fantasy and crime.

Coward contributes regular columns to a variety of independently produced periodicals. These include *Fortean Times*, in which he debunks well-known but groundless beliefs; *Mystery Scene*, in which he puts recent short stories under the microscope; and the socialist newspaper *Morning Star*, in which he writes about gardening and crime fiction (although not usually in the same column). His longest running contribution is the sardonic 'Down the Garden Path' for *Organic Gardening*, which he began in 1988.

Coward's love of organic gardening provided the background for his first crime novel, *Up and Down* (2004). A humorous **police procedural** featuring Detective Constable Frank Mitchell and the manic-depressive Detective Inspector Don Packham, the plot revolves around the death of Arthur 'Beans' Jones, found stabbed to death using a pitchfork on his own allotment. The murderer appears to be one of the other eccentric gardeners (appropriately called 'plotters') who worked alongside him. In a review allegedly *not* written by Coward, *Organic Gardening* praised it as 'ingenious and very funny – especially for the gardening-literate reader'.

Having hit upon a memorable double act (and title format), Coward came out with his next book, *In and Out* (2001), taking the readers into the murky world of money, sex and power that is pub darts. Yvonne 'Chalky' Wood is found clubbed to death in the ladies' lavatories of the Hollow Head public house, and it is up to the two detectives to sort through the long line of suspects. Based on the author's many years of playing darts as a youth, the book was praised for its sharp observational humour and well-crafted whodunit element.

His third novel in the series, *Over and Under* (2004), lifted the lid on another typically British pastime – cricket. Bruce Lester's murder in the local cricket pavilion is bad enough – and to do it with a baseball bat is just too much for the villagers to bear. Even funnier than in his first two books, the prose and dialogue zings along with an enviable dry wit that never feels forced. Reviewing *Over and Under*, Jon L. Breen of *Ellery Queen's Mystery Magazine* called Coward 'one of the funniest writers in the history of crime fiction'. A more recent offering, *Open and Closed* (2005), dealt with the lending-library closures and was once again received with delight by his growing fan base.

His short stories encompass many genres and have been included in several anthologies, while two collections – *Do the World a Favour and Other Stories* (2003) and *So Far, So Near* (2007) – are devoted to his uniquely skewed tales. *See also* Humour and Crime Fiction.

Selected Works by the Author
Up and Down (2000)
In and Out (2001)
Do the World a Favour and Other Stories (stories, 2003)
Over and Under (2004)
Open and Closed (2006)
So Far, So Near (stories, 2007)

Mark Campbell

Cracker (television series, 1993–2006)

Cracker was a Granada television series which enjoyed a high profile in the mid-1990s, rounded off by two feature-length sequels in 1996 and 2006. Most *Cracker* stories ran in arcs of two or three fifty-minute-long episodes, with three stories per series, often hinging on cliffhanger endings. Its creator and main writer was Jimmy McGovern (b.1949), and Paul Abbott (b.1960), its producer, was responsible for much of the series' later development. The original series led to tie-in novels from Virgin Books and an unsuccessful US remake for ABC television. More unusually, the series title entered common parlance in Britain: for tabloid newspapers, psychological profiling in criminal investigations meant that 'the real *Cracker*' was involved.

The award-winning drama combined strong casting and strong writing. The original line-up was led by Robbie Coltrane as Dr Eddie 'Fitz' Fitzgerald, Geraldine Somerville as Detective Sergeant (DS) Jane Penhaligon and Christopher Eccleston as Detective Chief Inspector (DCI) David Bilborough. Barbara Flynn played Judith Fitzgerald and Lorcan Cranitch was DS Jimmy Beck. Later episodes saw Bilborough replaced by DCI Charlie Wise (Ricky Tomlinson). The main series made the most of its Manchester location, turning industrial decline and urban renewal alike into effective and thematic settings. Strong casting of and performances by the real or alleged perpetrators – including Robert Carlyle, Adrian Dunbar and Andy Tiernan – reinforced the dramatic impact.

Fitz was a deeply flawed human being; his gambling addiction, alcoholism, chain-smoking and brutal sarcasm meant that he was played as an anti-hero throughout. His amorous pursuit of DS 'Panhandle' Penhaligon looked equally unsavoury, not least since it coincided with his shabby treatment of long-suffering wife Judith, even with a new baby imminent during the third series.

The writing eschewed the conventional whodunit format. It first depicted a crime being committed, before exploring the motives of the perpetrator. As audiences were granted a partial exposure to the criminal's psyche, this exposition was paralleled by Fitz developing a psychological profile, usually in the face of police scepticism. Prior to an untidy resolution – often with consequences for a later episode – some confrontations between Fitz and his antagonist(s) would tease out the underlying explanations for a murder or sex crime. Over time, these uniformly grim cases started to impact upon the lives of the recurring characters.

Part of *Cracker*'s reputation rested on its topical character. A left-inclined political sensibility characterised the opening episodes, critical of trends in British life in the aftermath of the Thatcher years. Typical 1990s-themed subplots involved tabloid journalism, televised celebrity and notoriety, and male responses to changing gender relations. Some stories suggested real crimes through the specific details of the offences committed, although concrete links between storylines and actual events were rare.

A turning point for *Cracker* was 'To Be a Somebody', which took the Hillsborough disaster as the starting point for a murder spree, claiming the life of DCI Bilborough. In turn, Bilborough's murder was the catalyst for a more introspective presentation of the lives of various police characters, turning the psychological scrutiny inwards and seeing how the individuals themselves responded to the terrible scenes they had witnessed. (In 1996, McGovern and Eccleston collaborated on a 1996 television dramatisation of the Hillsborough Inquiry.)

Several storylines attracted viewer complaints because of the violence and cruelty involved. This was probably compounded by a majority of the scripts refusing to adopt neat and morally virtuous endings. Often, the intervention of the authorities was shown as making matters worse. An early episode sees an innocent man imprisoned as a child murderer, after Fitz advises police using an inaccurate profile and thereby initiates a nihilistic battle of wits with the main suspect. On one occasion, Fitz goads a serial rapist into becoming a murderer; on another, his public interventions during a case invite direct retribution against the Fitzgerald family. Few characters were spared the emotional consequences of the investigations Fitz became involved in.

After 'The Big Crunch', scripted by Ted Whitehead and guest-starring Samantha Morton, it was claimed that McGovern was tired of writing the series; creative responsibility began shifting to Paul Abbott. Broadly coinciding with this was Coltrane's decision to leave, leading to the closure of the show. Coltrane made a cameo appearance as a villain in the US adaptation of *Cracker* (renamed *Fitz* for distribution in overseas markets), which starred Robert Pastorelli in the title role.

The subsequent feature-length revivals took Fitz and Wise to Hong Kong ('White Ghost', 1996) and, through Australia, to a Britain overshadowed by the second Iraq war ('Nine Eleven', 2006). Like the main series, allusions to current affairs (the handover of Hong Kong to China, international conflicts) remained an important aspect of the storylines, although modern Manchester receded into the background. The uneven critical reception accorded to the one-off specials suggested *Cracker*'s time had passed.

The Virgin novelisations used established writers of television tie-ins, such as Jim Mortimore (*Doctor Who*) and Liz Holliday (*Soldier, Soldier*). Aligned closely to the screenplays and written with access to preview tapes, each novel fleshed out character motivation through interior monologue, aiming for a worldview consistent with the show's characters and a reading experience not dissimilar to watching an episode. Each novelisation corresponds to an original series episode; books based on the later, feature-length specials have yet to appear.

It is uncertain whether *Cracker* will return to our screens in future. The release of the complete series as a DVD boxed set (1993–2006) suggests some finality, but the drama's impact on the television crime genre – and popular culture more broadly – should not be underestimated. *See also* TV Detectives: Small-Screen Adaptations.

Selected Works

Novelisations by Jim Mortimore
The Mad Woman in the Attic (1994)
Men Should Weep (1995)
Brotherly Love (1996)

By Molly Brown
To Say I Love You (1994)

By Liz Holliday
One Day A Lemming Will Fly (1994)
The Big Crunch (1995)
True Romance (1996)

By Gareth Roberts
To Be a Somebody (1995)
Best Boys (1996)

By Tom McGregor
White Ghost (1996)

Website
www.crackertv.co.uk

Graham Barnfield

Creasey, John (1908–1973)

Although few publishers keep John Creasey's titles in print anymore, it would be wrong to underestimate his importance to the crime genre. Thanks to his incredibly prolific writing career (the jury is still out as to exactly how many novels he wrote) – and his exhaustive enthusiasm for the genre that made him a household name, Creasey's contribution to the subject is immeasurable.

Born in Southfields, Surrey, on 17 September 1908 to Ruth and Joseph Creasey, the seventh of nine children, he suffered polio as a young child and did not walk properly until the age of six. He was educated at Fulham Elementary School and Sloan School in Kensington, where he was encouraged to write by the headmaster. Leaving at fourteen, Creasey worked in a variety of jobs while trying, somewhat precociously, to become an author. But it was not until the age of twenty-three, following a staggering 743 rejection letters, that his debut novel, *Seven Times Seven*, finally appeared.

Published in January 1932, *Seven Times Seven* was a well-formed exercise in breathless prose concerning the kidnapping of a film starlet by a gang of international hoodlums. Reviews were favourable (every one of which, for every title, Creasey carefully preserved in scrapbooks), although he continued in menial clerical jobs until 1935 and the publication of *Death Round the Corner*, the fourth in a highly successful series featuring the exploits of the secretive Department Z under the auspices of Gordon Craigie. It was then that he began writing full-time.

The Department Z series opened with *The Death Miser* in 1932 and continued for a further twenty-seven titles, until 1958's *The Black Spiders* saw the series finally end. Part of the reason for its demise was its similarity in style to the author's concurrent spy series featuring Dr Palfrey's Z5 organisation, although the latter series had more overtly science fiction overtones. Beginning in 1942, with *Traitor's Doom*, the adventures of Dr Palfrey entertained a generation of impressionable young readers with their lurid tales of international espionage and even more lurid titles. The series eventually stretched to thirty-four books.

Written alongside Department Z, Creasey's third, and longest running, series featured the exploits of his most famous creation: 'The Toff'. The Honourable Richard Rollison was a cricket-loving aristocratic private eye aided by his dour manservant Jolly. He first appeared in *Introducing the Toff* in 1938, and the stories that followed were characterised by a mixture of cosy English crime and action-packed adventure. Bearing a passing resemblance to Leslie **Charteris**'s *The Saint* (even down to the characters' iconic line-drawn silhouette), 'Rolly', as he was affectionately known, battled London's criminal underworld for an amazing fifty-eight books, the last few published posthumously. In 1952, film adaptations were made of *Salute the Toff* (1941) and *Hammer the Toff* (1947), both starring John Bentley as the eponymous **detective**.

Besides writing these action-orientated tales, Creasey was also a fine exponent of the straightforward police procedural. Evolving from the character of Bill Grice, the police detective from the Toff series, Inspector Roger West of Scotland Yard first appeared in the 1942 book, *Inspector West Takes Charge*. A more realistic figure than Craigie or Rollison, West was an independent crime fighter who solved his various murders, thefts and kidnapping cases intellectually– backed up, of course, by fisticuffs where necessary. The series of forty-three titles is generally considered to feature some of Creasey's best writing.

His other main police procedural series starred Inspector George Gideon; modelled on a police friend, he was a deliberate antidote to West's somewhat idealised portrayal. Gideon is a hard-working family man, whose introduction in *Gideon's Day* (1955; also published in the United States as *Gideon of Scotland Yard*) was over-shadowed by the recent loss of the detective's child. More likely to win through by luck than skill, Gideon's day-to-day activities at the Yard showed him working on several cases at once, most of them of a more realistic nature than seen in previous series. In all, Creasey wrote twenty-two Gideon books, with Jack Hawkins playing the role of Gideon in a 1958 film version of *Gideon's Day*, and John Gregson in a 1964 television series entitled *Gideon's Way*. The series was written under the pen-name of J.J. Marric.

From an early stage, Creasey understood the importance of creating a portfolio of *noms de plume*. A quick, albeit meticulous, writer, he always had many manuscripts going at the same time (sometimes up to sixteen) and would deliver them to his publishers in 'bulk'. But his readers could be expected to buy only one or two books of a particular series per year, and so by splitting his aliases across many series and standalone novels, he could guarantee a greater income from his enormous creative output, as well as enjoying success in a wide variety of genres.

His alter egos were many and varied. As Michael Halliday, he wrote *Three for Adventure* (1937), the author's favourite novel, as well as the *Fane Brothers* and the Dr Emmanuel Cellini series. (Confusingly, in America, Halliday became Jeremy York.) As Anthony Morton, he wrote the famous Baron series, opening with *Meet the Baron* (1937), concerning the not-unfamiliar exploits of an upper-class contemporary Robin Hood figure who robbed the rich to give to the poor. Other pen-names included Robert Caine Frazer, Brian Hope, Richard Martin and Tex Riley (the latter solely for Westerns).

Creasey's enormous output – he purportedly wrote 6,000 words a day and is credited with 562 books – should not militate against the sheer quality of his prose, which is always sharp and well written. Besides being a founding member of the **Crime Writers' Association**, he won innumerable awards including the Mystery Writers' of America's highest accolade, the Grand Master Award, in 1969. Four times married, he died on 9 June 1973 in Bodenham, Salisbury. The following year, the Crime Writers' Association (CWA) honoured him with the John Creasey Memorial Award (later know as the New Blood Dagger) for best new author. *See also Creasey Mystery Magazine.*

Selected Works by the Author
Seven Times Seven (1932)
The Mark of the Crescent (1935)
Meet the Baron as Anthony Morton (1937; also published in the United States as *The Man in the Blue Mask*)
Three for Adventure as Michael Halliday (1937)
Inspector West Takes Charge (1942)
Vote for Murder as Richard Martin (1948)
A Knife for the Toff (1951)
Gideon's Fire as J.J. Marric (1962)

Website
www.johncreasey.co.uk

Mark Campbell

Creasey Mystery Magazine

One of the least common among Britain's post-war mystery **magazines**, *Creasey* ran for eighty-nine issues, mostly monthly, from August 1956 to April 1965.

In the 1950s, John **Creasey** was one of Britain's most prolific and most popular writers. Surprisingly, however, no major magazine publisher took up his proposal for a mystery magazine. Instead, it was published by Dalrow Publications based in Bolton, Lancashire, run by Leslie Syddall, who served as an editor and who was developing two other magazines, *Combat* and *Phantom*. At the outset, Creasey had to rely primarily on reprints, using material by Agatha **Christie**, Dennis **Wheatley**, Dorothy L. **Sayers** and Julian **Symons** besides that by Dashiell Hammett, Ellery Queen and Stuart Palmer from the United States. There were a few new stories by Nigel **Morland**, Victor **Canning** and Michael **Underwood**, and Creasey also ran at least one of his own stories each issue, initially adventures related to Richard Rollison, 'the Toff', which were later reworked into books in series. The overall feel of the magazine was of good-quality, if generally familiar, material of traditional crime fiction but framed in a rather lacklustre format.

20. Cover of *Creasey* Mystery Magazine for July 1958.

Although the magazine would last for nine years, it was a constant struggle for Creasey to finance and to find suitable printers. He parted company with Syddall after the August 1957 issue and thereafter published the magazine under his own imprint. For a period, he resorted to having it published in the Netherlands, but reverted to a British printer after a printing dispute in July 1959 disrupted the publication for a few issues. Throughout its life, the magazine's size varied considerably with various permutations of digest and pocketbook. Its title was variously *Creasey* or *John Creasey Mystery Magazine*, and its price doubled. These and other changes cannot have helped the magazine, and it is a credit to Creasey's persistence that the magazine survived as long as it did.

Under his control, the magazine ran a high quota of non-fiction – 'Real Life stories' as Creasey called them – and with these, the reprints and book reviews, there was little space for much new fiction. It cannot claim to have discovered any major new writer, although it did publish some of the earliest mystery fiction by Terry Harknett. There were occasional new pieces by Josephine **Bell**, Peter Godfrey and Anthony Gilbert. Creasey drew upon the contents, both new and reprint, for his anthology series *Mystery Bedside Book*, which began in 1960, and this promotion may have helped sustain the magazine; however, it slipped to a quarterly schedule in 1963, recovered briefly in 1964, and then stopped abruptly with its April 1965 issue, although another was announced.

Like the *Edgar Wallace Mystery Magazine*, with which it has much in common, *Creasey* provided a reasonable mixed fare of fact and fiction but never produced anything of significance.

Further Reading
Cook, Michael L. 1982. *Monthly Murders*. Greenwood Press.

Website
www.johncreasey.co.uk

Mike Ashley

Creed, John (also known as Eoin McNamee) (b.1961)

'John Creed' is the Anglo-friendly pseudonym of Eoin McNamee. Under his real name, he writes complex political **thrillers** set against the background of the Troubles, while as 'Creed', he pens fast-moving spy thrillers in the style of Alistair MacLean.

Born in 1961 in Kilkeel, Northern Ireland, Eoin McNamee attended Trinity College, Dublin, before embarking on a career as a novelist and screenplay writer, mainly concentrating on the then-ongoing conflict in Northern Ireland. He was awarded the Macauley Fellowship for Irish Literature in 1990.

McNamee's first book, a novella entitled *The Last of Deeds* (1989), concerned a Catholic boy in a small Northern Irish fishing village who falls in love with a Protestant girl; it was shortlisted for the Irish Times Aer Lingus Award for Irish Literature. His second novella, *Love in History* (later published with *The Last of Deeds* in 1995) focused on an American air-force base in the Second World War.

The thrillers published under his own name tend to be based on real people and events. *Resurrection Man* (1994), probably the author's best-known work, tells the story of the notorious 'Shankill Butchers'. It does not flinch from the graphic nature of the gang's crimes, elements that were also brought to the fore in the 1998 film adaptation directed by Marc Evans. However, despite McNamee penning the screenplay, the film is generally considered inferior to its source material.

His next book, *The Blue Tango* (2001), long-listed for the Booker Prize, was a retelling of the murder of Patricia Curran, the nineteen-year-old daughter of an

Irish judge in the small village of Whiteabbey in 1952. Iain Gordon, an Englishman stationed at a nearby RAF base, was arrested and tried on circumstantial evidence, but later released.

The Ultras (2004), based on Robert Nairac's undercover operations in South Armagh during the 1970s, drew praise for its well-researched retelling of controversial **historical** events.

Under the name 'John Creed', McNamee has penned three alert and fast-moving thrillers featuring special agent Jack Valentine. In *The Sirius Crossing* (2002), Valentine is forced to undertake a hazardous journey to the Shetland Islands, while in *The Day of the Dead* (2003) he travels to New York and Mexico in search of a drug baron who has abducted the woman he loves. In his most recent outing, *Black Cat Black Dog* (2006), Valentine has fallen out with his mysterious paymasters who seek their revenge by ensnaring him in a dangerous covert operation.

McNamee wrote the screenplay for *I Want You*, Michael Winterbottom's critically acclaimed 1998 film about obsessive love played out against the bleak backdrop of an English coastal town. He has also written two children's stories: *The Navigator* (2006) and *City of Light* (2007) and a collection of poetry, *The Language of Birds* (1995). He lives in Sligo on the west coast of Ireland. *See also* Espionage Fiction.

Selected Works by the Author

As Eoin McNamee
Resurrection Man (1994)
The Last of Deeds & Love in History (1995)
The Blue Tango (2001)
The Ultras (2004)

As John Creed
Sirius Crossing (2002)
The Day of The Dead (2003)
Black Cat Black Dog (2006)

Mark Campbell

Cribb (television series, 1980–1981)

The bowler-hatted Victorian detective, Sergeant Cribb, first appeared in a 1979 Granada adaptation by Pauline Macauley of Waxwork, directed by June Wyndham-Davies. This was the pilot for more adaptations of Peter **Lovesey**'s novels in 1980 and 1981. Alan Dobie, who played Cribb, was nominated for an Emmy as best actor in 1981, and William Simons, as Constable Thackeray, was nominated as best supporting actor. Transmitted in prime time on Sunday evenings, *Cribb* regularly drew audiences of around twelve million and, in 1979, grossed the highest takings of any Granada programme, ahead of *Coronation Street* and *World in Action*. The appeal of the Sergeant Cribb stories is that they were based on Victorian entertainments or enthusiasms that were visually attractive: spiritualism, the music hall, photography, bare-knuckle boxing, ultra-running, the seaside, boating on the Thames, the zoo, Madame Tussaud's and even the royal court at Windsor. Cribb was a realistic policeman working without scientific help or Holmesian powers of deduction. Shrewd observation and penetrating questions were his strengths, a dry sense of humour his style.

Highlights included Alan Plater's adaptation of *Wobble to Death*, Bill MacIlwraith's *Mad Hatter's Holiday* and Arden Winch's *A Case of Spirits*. Lovesey cut his teeth as a television writer by doing a script for his own book *The Detective Wore Silk Drawers* and later teamed up with his wife Jacqueline to write a further six original episodes including the memorable *The Last Trumpet* based on P.T. Barnum's purchase of the famous elephant Jumbo from the London Zoo. Actors in the series included Judy Cornwell, Rosalie Crutchley, Michael Elphick, Fenella Fielding, Patsy Rowlands, Carol Royle, Elizabeth Spriggs, Clive Swift and David Waller. *Cribb* was chosen to launch the long-running *Mystery!* series on PBS in America and sold to thirty-five countries worldwide. It was produced by June Wyndham-Davies, who later created the long-running *Sherlock Holmes* series for Granada. In 2004, Cribb was reissued in the DVD medium. *See also* TV Detectives: Small-Screen Adaptations.

Brian Ritterspak

Crime Time Magazine

Crime Time **magazine** – which initially published its issues in an A4 magazine format but switched to 'B' paperback format – has, throughout its history, attempted to cover crime fiction and film in every genre and from every country in the world. The current editor, Barry Forshaw, is pleased by the fact that readers who only vaguely know of the magazine have alternately said to him '*Crime Time* – doesn't that specialise in American hard-boiled crime?' or '*Crime Time* – that's all English cosies, isn't it?' This uncertainty, Forshaw feels, proves that the magazine is on the right track. Long-time readers (who include many top professionals as well as a solid cadre of aspirant writers) are all well aware that the magazine shows no predilection for any one genre but casts its spotlight very far afield.

Crime Time was originally published in 1995 by Peter Dillon-Parkin and Paul Duncan, with an early involvement (from issue number 3) for Ion Mills, managing director of the highly enterprising publisher No Exit Press (NEP), and Mills is still the publisher in the twenty-first century. Mills's NEP had made a name for itself by publishing some of the most quirky and cutting-edge crime fiction, as well as once again making available some shamefully neglected masters of the past. With such a profile, it was important that any magazine associated with this publisher would similarly adopt an unorthodox approach – an approach effortlessly achieved by the formidable team of Dillon-Parkin and Duncan. Dillon-Parkin had long harboured a desire to create a crime fiction magazine and knew that his computer expertise would be an asset in any such enterprise. He had met Paul Duncan several years earlier (Duncan is now a commissioning editor for the publisher Taschen and generally acknowledged as the leading expert on the cult writer Gerald Kersh), when the latter had published a comics magazine which had impressed Dillon-Parkin, and asked him if he would be the editor of *Crime Time*. The initial concept involved making information on current and forthcoming crime fiction available to readers, as well as communicating the duo's particular passion for the Noir form in both fiction and cinema. After hammering out the first issue, the team persuaded the publisher Little, Brown (who had a significant crime list) to pay for the cover, and the

21. Cover of *Crime Time*, issue 52, 2007.

magazine was up and running. Struggles with recalcitrant printers and contributors who supplied handwritten copies (which Duncan dutifully re-keyed, often working into the early hours of the morning) did not dampen the enthusiasm of the pair, and before long, an extremely lively and information-packed magazine had become established, developing a considerable following. A key factor in the magazine's success (apart from Duncan's adroit editorial skills) was Dillon-Parkin's quirky skills as a designer: each of the early issues of *Crime Time* has a markedly individual look and identity; Dillon-Parkin and Duncan were never content to simply repeat themselves and came up with strikingly different design concepts for each issue.

Initially, the two major British book chains, Waterstone's and Dillon's, were content to take the magazine for free, but despite the exposure this gave *Crime Time*, it was obviously not cost-effective, and new solutions had to be found to ensure the magazine's survival. When Ion Mills assumed responsibility for publishing the magazine, he initiated a distribution deal with British news-stands, using the idea of a free book being given away with each issue as a promotional tool.

The second (and current) editor of *Crime Time* is Barry Forshaw, who took over the magazine with issue 2.2 in 1998. Forshaw (author of *The Rough Guide to Crime Fiction*) had reviewed crime for such broadsheets as *The Times*, *The Independent*, the *Daily Express* and the *Times Literary Supplement*. He had written a book on Italian cinema for publisher Ion Mills and had long been a major contributor to *Crime Time*. Accepting the role somewhat reluctantly (fully aware of the prodigious amount of work involved), Forshaw requested that the magazine be changed to a paperback style format, complete with spine, considering this to be more collectable, and believing that most readers of *Crime Time* were ardent collectors. He also changed the 'volume' system of numbering, considering that most readers of the magazine had no idea how many individual numbers there were in a given volume. The latter change began with issue 21.

Forshaw built up the established team of contributors, who now included crime specialists Michael Carson (who became the authoritative **film** editor) and the immensely well-read Mark Campbell, along with television reviewer Charles Waring. Top British crime writers were drafted in to write opinionated columns, including Mark **Timlin**, Natasha **Cooper** and Russell **James** (the latter two are still on board, contributing pugnacious and informed columns on current genre fiction). The leading British crime anthologist Mike **Ashley** was persuaded to write a regular column on collecting crime fiction (an extremely popular feature with readers); another of the United Kingdom's most respected anthologists (and novelists), Maxim **Jakubowski**, came on board, to complement this already-impressive roster of talent. Forshaw persuaded two more excellent British novelists and critics, Kim **Newman** and Paul **McAuley**, to join him in reviewing DVDs, which had now become the principal medium through which *Crime Time* readers kept in touch with current crime cinema.

Forshaw maintains the concept of themes for each issue, even though (by now) most concepts have been touched on. However, some of the most popular issues of the magazine were to be based around specific themes. In 2001, issue 23 was devoted to Women in Crime, with most major female novelists in the United Kingdom and the United States talking about the craft (this particular issue was to become one of the most quoted over the years). Issue 25, devoted to the subject of sex in crime fiction, enjoyed the distinction of upsetting the great Swedish crime-writer Henning Mankel: he publicly tore off the cover at a launch for one of his books (despite it showing nothing more than a half-open pair of female lips).

By now, Judith Gray had come on board as associate editor and contributed some sterling proofreading services. Peter Dillon-Parkin had moved on to other areas, and the new designer was Paul Brazier. More popular themed issues followed: a Sherlock **Holmes** issue (issue 26, 2002), crime movies in issue 27 (with film editor Michael Carson particularly flourishing in this issue) and a more controversially received violence issue (issue 32, 2003). A sign of changing perceptions in the crime field was reflected in the immense success of issue 37 in 2004, which was devoted to foreign crime in translation – the impact that the magazine made (as great, for instance, as the more obviously commercial sex issue) showed that crime in translation had moved from the sidelines to being a key area of interest for British crime readers. Forshaw always strove to cast the spotlight of coverage as far afield as possible; there was a Batman issue and one on historical crime fiction, while the celebratory fiftieth issue in 2006 had forty top crime novelists and editors picking their favourite novels in a feature called 'Crime fiction to die for'.

In the twenty-first century, the magazine has moved to a quarterly format, and a great deal more attention is given to its website (always an important adjunct) under the stewardship of Webmaster Jem Cook. *Crime Time* continues to be a beacon of coverage in the field. The magazine could certainly quote impressive encomiums from top crime writers, such as '*Crime Time* is easily the wittiest, most intelligent crime magazine I have ever read' (Jason Starr), 'This is what the rest of the magazines want to be when they grow up' (James Sallis) and even James Ellroy, no less, with '*Crime Time* rules! Others drool!'

Website
www.crimetime.co.uk

Brian Ritterspak

Crime Writers' Association, The

The year 2007 was the centenary of the birth of the founder, John **Creasey**, and the fifty-fifth year of the Crime Writers' Association (CWA). Creasey's aim in launching the association was to support professional writers and promote the genre, and that still holds good today. The CWA continues to raise the profile of crime writing by providing a forum for all writers and others connected with it, but particularly for those who do not reach the heights of the best-seller lists.

The annual Dagger Awards acknowledge the best in crime writing and include fiction, non-fiction, thrillers, psychological and historical mysteries, first novels, short stories and authors whose work has proven most popular with libraries and readers groups. Aspiring writers can enter their opening chapters and the synopsis of a proposed crime novel into the Debut Dagger. To be shortlisted does not guarantee publication, but it does mean their work will be seen by agents and editors who since the CWA's inception have signed up over a dozen winners as well as shortlisted entrants.

Membership of the CWA is open to anyone who has had one crime novel (or work of scholarship) produced by a bona fide publisher. The association also supports writing and readers groups, workshops, festivals, conferences and other literary events. Authors are always prepared to talk about their craft either singly or in groups.

At a luncheon ceremony a special award was presented to celebrate the CWA's fiftieth anniversary. The recipient was the association's founder, John Creasey. This was nothing short of a miracle because Creasey died in 1973, which might explain why he looked remarkably like Peter **Lovesey** (who stood in for his illustrious predecessor).

With Britain's rich tradition in crime fiction, it is surprising that this organisation was only just celebrating its fiftieth year. Its American counterpart, the Mystery Writers of America (MWA), banded together in March 1945, taking their inspiration from the British Detection Club. The latter was founded in 1928, but limited its membership to only a chosen few. The MWA, from the very start, allowed all writers of mystery fiction to join.

It was not until eight years later, on 5 November – Guy Fawkes Night in England – that John Creasey convened a meeting at the National Liberal Club to form an organisation along the lines of its American equal. According to the minutes of that day 'those present, all authors of crime stories and met at the invitation of John Creasey, were: Josephine **Bell**, John Bude, John Creasey, Ernest **Dudley**, Elizabeth Ferrars, Andrew **Garve**, Bruce **Graeme**, Leonard Gribble, T.C.H. Jacobs, Nigel **Morland**, Colin Robertson and Julian **Symons**'.

The notes go on to say that 'it was unanimously agreed that those present should found forthwith an association of crime writers, the specific purpose of which should be to raise the prestige and fortunes of mystery, detective story and crime writing and writers generally'. And so the Crime Writers' Association came to be.

Chairing the association through its first three years was John Creasey who, to this day, is the only person to have presided over both the CWA and the MWA – the latter presenting the author with a Grand Master Award in 1969. (That Creasey had time for anything other than writing is impressive: the *St. James Guide to Crime & Mystery Writers* credits him with twenty-four pseudonyms and eight pages of book entries!)

Over the years, the association has opened up its membership to non-British authors published in the United Kingdom, agents, editors and other professionals in the field. Most people of note have become members of the CWA; however, Agatha **Christie**, arguably the best known British crime-writer, never joined. When asked if she would like to become a member she replied that she was at a time in her life where she felt happier resigning from things rather than joining them. She also said that, 'what you want in your association are the up-and-comings, not those sliding happily down to the grave'. (It should be noted that the Christie Estate has been a generous benefactor of the CWA in the past.)

Soon after its founding, a newsletter came into being. Initially called *CWA News*, it was later renamed *Red Herrings*, though it is only available to CWA members.

One project that the association sponsors for the general public are **anthologies**. The first was called *Butcher's Dozen* (1956), and a recent instalment, *Mysterious Pleasures*, appeared – in time to celebrate the anniversary. It was edited by Martin **Edwards** (author of the crime novels featuring Liverpool lawyer Harry Devlin), and the contributors include Robert **Barnard**, John Creasey, Lindsey **Davis**, Colin **Dexter**, Dick **Francis**, Val **McDermid**, Peter Lovesey, Ian **Rankin** and Ellis **Peters**. Each story is by a member who has won the Diamond or Gold Dagger Award or served as Chairman of the CWA. (Some have done all three.)

The CWA Dagger Awards were first presented in 1955 (Winston Graham won with *The Little Walls*). Initially there was only one award, that for Best Crime Novel. Since then other awards have been added, including the Diamond Dagger for lifetime contribution to crime writing. A full list of the CWA's awards is maintained at the Association's website listed at the end of this entry.

Besides John Creasey, other luminaries such as H.R.F. **Keating**, Dick Francis, Peter Lovesey, Ian Rankin and Lindsey Davis have chaired the CWA.

Since 1998, the Debut Dagger has launched the careers of many writers. Open to unpublished writers, the CWA Debut Dagger is judged on the first 3,000 words, plus synopsis, of a crime novel. The competition's aims are to raise the profile of the CWA and encourage new writers. CWA members are known to be welcoming, but is it wise to add to the already fierce competition?

'A thriving genre is good for everyone', believes Andrew **Taylor**, who ran the inaugural competition under the slightly less-snappy title of the 'Crime Writing Competition for New Writers'. Taylor had insider knowledge of the difficulties faced by unpublished writers. 'I'd worked for many years as a publisher's reader', he says, 'so I knew how hard it can be for a new writer, however good, to claw his or her way out of the slushpile.'

Joolz Denby won the first competition, and has since been shortlisted for the Orange Prize. In the first two years alone, shortlisted authors included Stephen **Booth** and Barbara **Cleverly**. The Debut Dagger is good at spotting talent.

The competition was given a boost by free advertisements in the *Sunday Times* with the tagline 'Are you the next Ian Rankin?' Edward Wright happened to be on holiday in Dublin when he saw the ad. 'Hey, that's me', he recalls saying to his wife. 'The next Ian Rankin?' Mrs Wright looked doubtful. 'No,' he said, 'a new writer'. He was not sure if he was eligible – he is an American. 'On the other hand, the ad said nothing about Yanks being unwelcome'. Wright won with *Clea's Moon* (2003), and with subsequent novels he has been honoured with both the Shamus Award and the CWA Ellis Peters Historical Crime Award.

Caroline Carver, whose entry, *Blood Junction* (2001), won the second Debut Dagger, assesses the benefits as a veteran of the award. 'It affirms we have talent, even when we think we don't, and encourages us to keep going and not to give up.'

Having seen the competition from both sides, Edwin Thomas (Debut Dagger Chair 2005–2006) was keen that his supportive and communicative approach competitors should continue when Margaret **Murphy** took over. So, as chair of the competition, she produced a bi-weekly newsletter to keep potential competitors informed of deadlines and to provide tips on writing technique. Communication is key, and in a departure that may be unique in literary competitions, one of the duties of the chair is to put together a detailed critique of each of the shortlisted works, culled from written comments submitted by the panel of four editors and an agent. This has proved very popular with entrants and is another important factor in the success of the Award.

Canadian author Louise Penny had tried to get publishers interested in her first book, without luck. 'Until the shortlisting. Suddenly it seemed everyone wanted it!' she exclaims. She was so impressed that she approached Crime Writers of Canada with an idea for a new award based on the CWA Debut Dagger. It even includes advice and writing tips borrowed from the CWA. Ms Penny has just completed a hat-trick in the awards stakes after winning the CWA New Blood Dagger, the Arthur Ellis Award and the Dilys Award for her debut novel *Still Life* (2005). She says, 'It all leads back to the CWA, who are generous enough to give a boost to unknowns'.

Like most competitions, the shortlist is judged blind by the panel of judges. Only the title of each novel is revealed. For three consecutive years, between 2003 and 2005, Otis Twelve was shortlisted. 'In 2006 I had switched from laconic-gonzo-noir to gothic-transgressive-noir. The judges, worn down at last, gave me the Debut Dagger in abject surrender,' he observes with typically dry humour.

When the name of the winner was revealed to the judges, they burst into spontaneous applause. 'The Debut has been a real door opener,' Twelve continues. 'I've met the best kinds of people in the industry, and learned a great deal along the way. All a writer like me wants is a chance to be read; the Debut has given me that opportunity and more.'

So what makes a 'good' competition entry? Edwin **Thomas** was runner-up for the award in 2001 with *The Blighted Cliffs* (2003). He emphasises the mandate that it is the quality of the writing that matters, and beyond this, the award should encourage the full range of writing within the genre: 'The competition has always encouraged a broad interpretation of crime writing', he says, 'and this is usually reflected in the variety of the shortlist.'

One beneficiary of this approach is self-styled 'runner-up winner', US author Susan Runholt. Her young-adult novel, *The Mystery of the Third Lucretia* (2008), reached the shortlist in 2005. 'The Brits seemed to be landing contracts right and left,' she remembers. She, however, heard nothing. 'Edwin Thomas explained that the mystery world represented by CWA is predominantly British and almost exclusively adult. With characteristic generosity of spirit, he spoke to a Dagger judge, an agent at the London office of ICM.' A couple of phone calls later, Runholt had a New York agent, a 'mini-bidding war' followed and she now has a 'satisfying' two-book contract with Viking Children's Books.

Ten years ago, the crime fiction section in most bookshops was limited to a couple of shelves. Industry figures for the value of the crime market in 2006 stood at £126 million and entire walls of shelving are given over to a genre that ranges from the cosy classics of Agatha Christie and Dorothy L. **Sayers** to the urban grit of Ian Rankin, Val McDermid and John **Harvey**. A number of factors are responsible – the Debut Dagger being one of them. With entries coming in from all over the United Kingdom as well as from Europe, the United States, South Africa and Australia, the profile of the CWA has never been higher.

Website
www.thecwa.co.uk

Adrian Muller, Lesley Horton and Margaret Murphy

Crimewave Magazine

Crimewave has established itself as the most innovative crime fiction magazine of the new generation. It is an occasional publication, produced when publisher and editor Andy Cox of TTA Press, based in Ely, has sufficient quality stories. Since its first issue in 1999, it has appeared on average only once per year. The emphasis is on literary crime fiction with a dark edge. The magazine does not publish conventional detective stories, but rather stories that pursue the crime, its perpetrator and the aftermath. The stories may be classified as noir or dark suspense or horror – and some have been reprinted in horror anthologies – but regardless of category, they all evoke reflections of the dark side of the soul and the true nature of crime.

Crimewave publishes work by authors from all over the English-speaking world. Among the British contributors whose work best exemplifies the magazine's direction are Jerry Sykes, Chaz **Brenchley**, Simon Avery, Christopher **Fowler**, Antony Mann and Marion Arnott. The stories published in *Crimewave* are frequently shortlisted for awards, and two have won the **Crime Writers' Association** MacAllan Short Story Dagger: 'Taking Care of Frank' (Volume 2, 1999) by Antony Mann, in which an ageing celebrity is worth more dead than alive; and 'Prussian Snowdrops' (Volume 4, 2000) by Marion Arnott, a powerful story about the realisation of 'truth' in Fascist Germany in the 1930s. Both these stories demonstrate the new approach *Crimewave* has taken to crime fiction, looking realistically at the dark side of humans who commit crime.

Apart from the first volume, which was comparatively slim and edited by Mat Coward, who helped Andy Cox in developing and compiling the first three issues, each issue has been a substantial size, more like a regular large-format paperback anthology, and has borne a subtitle. The subtitles do not necessarily relate specifically to that issue's content but rather convey a mood that the fiction evokes. Volume 2 was *Deepest Red*, Volume 3 *Burning Down the House*, Volume 4 *Mood Indigo*, Volume 5 *Dark before Dawn*, Volume 6 *Breaking Point*, Volume 7 *The Last Sunset*, Volume 8 *Cold Harbours*, and Volume 9 *Transgressions* – all titles that evoke despair, angst and hopelessness. Few of the stories in *Crimewave* have happy endings, if endings at all, as they remind the readers that we all have to live with the consequences of our actions.

Website
http://ttapress.com/category/crimewave/

Mike Ashley

Criminal, The (film, 1960)

(Joseph Losey, director)

Although it has a robbery sequence mid-way through and a bleak finish as desperate men scrabble for stolen money buried in a snowy field, Joseph Losey's *The Criminal* (also known as *The Concrete Jungle*) is essentially a prison movie, a very rare genre in Britain (other examples include *The Pot-Carriers*, *Scum* and *Scrubbers*).

Johnny Bannion (Stanley Baker, playing Welsh-Irish) is a top dog inside, secure of his place in a brutal pecking order, which takes in the slightly fey chief warder (Patrick Magee, calling everyone 'mister' and doing wonderful nasty little smiles), who dispenses punishment beatings, and the remote warden (Noel Willman) as well as a whole array of differing convicts. His sentence up, Bannion gets out with a plan devised by the hyperactive Snipe (John Molloy, an unforgettable Spike Milligan lookalike who made too few films) for a big raid, has enjoyed much at a welcome-home party – as in the earlier **The Frightened City**, the lead crook neglects his British steady bird to chase after a foreign bit, here Jill Bennett and Margit Saad – then gets promptly nabbed after burying the loot and finds himself back on the block. The bigger criminal fish (headed by 'our friend in Highgate', whom we never meet) works hard to force him to reveal where the money is, fomenting a riot whose sole purpose is to get Johnny framed as a traitor to the convicts and busted out in a raid that is as much a kidnap as a jailbreak.

Most British gangster films of the 1960s depict a post-war/post-rationing gangland, where brutal thugs and mostly genial petty crooks are ordered about by semi-untouchable higher-ups; however, *The Criminal*, made by a director on the run from Joe McCarthy back home and scripted by *A Hard Day's Night's* Alun Owen (with uncredited work from Hammer horror specialist Jimmy Sangster – a novel was issued), extends this rottenness to the whole of society. Even Bannion – who rises above the mobs as the maverick copper in **Hell Is a City** or as the uncompromising lorry driver in **Hell Drivers** – is ultimately trapped in the system, and prison authorities are as much a part of the big, corrupt picture as the gang bosses on the outside. It is a sensationalist picture – considering the fuss made about Hammer horror, it is odd that few British critics carped at the far more explicit violence and even flashes of nudity in the crime movies – as well as a melancholy one, with Cleo Laine's prison ballad accompanying images of men shuffling around bleak grounds and even the desperate gaiety of the coming-out party ending in Bannion's realisation that the only home he really has is prison.

A newcomer to Britain, Losey casts fellow, blacklisted Sam Wanamaker as an almost effete criminal middleman and relishes the faces and accents of an astonishing range of UK acting talent: Kenneth Warren as a bald, jolly Australian named 'Clobber', Nigel Green, Rupert Davies, Laurence Naismith, Grigoire Aslan, Derek Francis, Kenneth Cope (a doomed squealer), Patrick Wymark, Murray Melvin (as 'Antlers'), Neil McCarthy, Edward Judd, Tom Bell, John Van Eyssen, Jerold Wells and Roy Dotrice. *See also* Film and Crime: Page to Screen.

Kim Newman

Crispin, Edmund (1921–1978)

Edmund Crispin was the pseudonym of the composer Bruce Montgomery. He is best known for his nine comic crime novels – traditional **detective** stories featuring Oxford Professor Gervase Fen – and in particular for *The Moving Toyshop* (1946). The best of his witty work has a lasting place among the comic classics of the genre.

Montgomery was born on 2 October 1921 and educated at Merchant Taylors' School and St John's College, Oxford, where his friends included Kingsley Amis and Philip Larkin. The first of the Fen novels, *The Case of the Gilded Fly* (1944), was written in fourteen days while he was still an undergraduate. Montgomery was principally a composer, with a useful talent for turning out film scores. He worked with Amis on several collaborations, among them a projected grand opera. His other works ranged from *An Oxford Requiem* to *An Opera for Children*. He also edited science-fiction anthologies and for many years reviewed crime fiction in *The Sunday Times*. Later in his life, he was dogged by alcoholism and osteoporosis. He died on 15 September 1978. It is ironic, if unsurprising, that he is now remembered for his detective novels rather than his music. Julian **Symons** called him 'the last and most charming of the Farceurs' (Symons, *Bloody Murder*).

John Dickson **Carr** and Michael **Innes** influenced Crispin's detective stories. According to Roda M. Morrison, in her entry on Crispin in *Twentieth Century Crime and Mystery Writers* (St James Press, 1991), Crispin believed that 'detective stories…should be essentially imaginative and artificial in order to make their best effect' (Morrison, 269). His plots are intricate puzzles, untangled in an atmosphere of literate frivolity and leading to often implausible solutions. His series hero – the erratic and combative Gervase Fen, who is rarely seen without a cigarette and a glass of whisky – is Professor of English Language and Literature at Oxford and combines his academic career with lordly excursions as a detective.

Crispin's first two novels, *The Case of the Gilded Fly* and *Holy Disorders* (1945), are little more than jejune intellectual slapstick. Then came *The Moving Toyshop* (1946), dedicated to Philip Larkin, with its title taken from Alexander Pope's *The Rape of the Lock*: Pope's toyshop is metaphorical; Crispin's, entirely literal. The story opens with an eminent poet (and closet song lyricist) fleeing from impending middle age to search for adventure in Oxford. In the early hours, he idly tries the door of a shop, finds it opens and stumbles into a darkened toyshop. In the flat upstairs, he just has time to find the garrotted corpse of an elderly woman before someone knocks him out. Hours later, he struggles back to consciousness and fetches the police. But the corpse has gone. So has the toyshop. In its place is a grocer's. And the flat upstairs is entirely different.

Swan Song (1947) also had an Oxford setting – and in this case a musical background. Weakness of the motive perhaps undermines the story, but it still reads well. *Love Lies Bleeding* (1948) signalled a return to form. Fen is invited to give away the prizes at a public school's speech day. A local schoolgirl – crisply described by her headmistress as 'rather a fast little baggage' – disappears, and soon afterwards the English master is murdered. A psychotic bloodhound liable to trimestral homicidal fits is a distinguished addition to Crispin's already varied menagerie of bizarre animals.

Buried for Pleasure (1948) is less well known than *Toyshop*, but in some ways a better book. In need of recreation, Fen arrives at Sanford Angelorum, a village where he prepares to contest an approaching by-election as an independent. The cast of characters ranges from an unprepossessing animal known as the non-doing pig and an early example of DIY Man to a poltergeist in the Rectory and a butler with an advanced grasp of economic theory. The murder mystery is resolved with a deft sleight of hand reminiscent of **Christie** at her best. But this takes second place to the business of canvassing and the build-up to the election. Crispin had a talent for comic set-pieces, and this book contains several of his finest.

Frequent Hearses (1950) is a darker book, although the wit is as fresh as ever. It brings Fen – hired to purvey expert information about the life and works of Pope – in collision with the ailing British film industry. Crispin made the most of a background he knew well. It is also one of the few books of this period – and certainly of this type – to portray a battered husband. The next novel, *The Long Divorce* (1951), is set in a painfully picturesque village which has become a cross between a museum and a ghetto largely inhabited by 'the cultured upper-middle classes' and the tradesmen who serve them. Increasingly, the comedy was tempered not only with satire but with compassion.

Crispin's readers had to wait twenty-six years until the next novel. In the meantime, there were short stories, most of which were published in book form in *Beware of the Trains* (1953) and *Fen Country* (1979). *The Glimpses of the Moon* finally appeared in 1977. It is longer than the other novels and more laboured. The world had changed, and so had Fen's creator.

Crispin himself would have been the last person to make inflated claims for his work. His best books are first-class comfort fiction, the literary equivalent of chocolate gateau. *Toyshop* is in a class of its own and may well remain a classic of the genre, but some of the later books were arguably even better for in parts the comedy is leavened with intelligent satire.

Selected Works by the Author
The Case of the Gilded Fly (1944)
Holy Disorders (1945)
The Moving Toyshop (1946)
Swan Song (1947)
Love Lies Bleeding (1948)
Buried for Pleasure (1948)
Frequent Hearses (1950)
The Long Divorce (1951)
The Glimpses of the Moon (1977)

Andrew Taylor

Crofts, Freeman Wills (1879–1957)

Freeman Wills Crofts became the most celebrated British exponent of the crime novel in the 1920s. The steady, hard-working police **detective** in his novels would apply his mind over and over again to a painstakingly constructed crime until the solution becomes clear.

Crofts was born in Dublin in 1879 and brought up in Northern Ireland by his mother and step-father. He became a railway engineer. It was while convalescing after a long illness that he started to write. His first novel, *The Cask* (1920), became a classic of the genre. Inspector Burnley of Scotland Yard investigates the appearance of a cask containing the body of a young woman in London. The story switches between London and Paris before Burnley, cooperating with M. Lefarge of the Sûreté, eventually tracks down all the movements of the cask. However, it is not until Georges La Touche, a private investigator, takes up the case that the manufactured alibi of the perpetrator is unravelled.

This established a pattern for later Crofts books: a meticulously planned crime, usually involving a contrived alibi, is eventually unravelled by the hard work of an investigator. In his second and third books the investigators are Scotland Yard inspectors Tanner and Willis respectively, while for the fourth, the excellent *The Groote Park Murder* (1923), Inspector Ross from Edinburgh takes charge.

Although the eponymous Inspector Joseph French appears only in his fifth book, *Inspector French's Greatest Case* (1924), Crofts was to use Inspector French in all his subsequent novels. French is a kind but relentless man whose reliance on good manners leads to his nickname of Soapy Joe. The clerk of a Hatton Gardens diamond merchant is murdered and jewels stolen. French's investigation takes him to Amsterdam, Chamonix and Barcelona before he confronts the criminals on a Brazilian-bound liner. After French has worked hard and to great effect to unravel the case, he is surprised by the identity of the criminal. This is to happen several times, especially in the earlier books.

Crofts was a great admirer of Austin **Freeman**'s 'inverted' stories in which the reader follows the crime as it is perpetrated and then the detective as it is solved. Later, Crofts wrote several short stories in this fashion, first as radio plays and then as stories in his collection *Murderers Make Mistakes* (1947). He also wrote novels in this style, the best of which is perhaps *The 12.30 From Croydon* (1934). Andrew Crowther plans to murder his elderly uncle for the money to keep his business afloat. Unusually for Crofts, he makes his murderer sympathetic, and it is almost a disappointment for the reader when French arrests Crowther and explains how he has constructed his case.

Golden Ashes (1940) is a partly inverted story in that we know all along who the killers are, but it is difficult to work out how they have managed to do the deed. French uncovers their arson midway through the book, but the alibis they have established for the killing are particularly clever.

French is a wonderfully rounded character, and in the course of the thirty novels featuring him, he is promoted to chief inspector, then superintendent and, in the final book, chief superintendent. Poet W.H. Auden opines in his essay 'The Guilty Vicarage' that he knows of only three completely satisfactory detectives: Sherlock **Holmes**, Father Brown and Inspector French. According to him, French is driven not by a sense of duty but by a fear of failure and the criticisms that would arise from the Yard.

Crofts deliberately ensured that French is an ordinary kind of man. French's method is to get hold of the facts and then to try to formulate a theory that would account for them all. If this theory fails, then he will sit down and go through all the facts again until he can find a convincing theory, an almost mathematical procedure that fits in well with Crofts's engineering background. Crofts uses this background in other ways. The plots often involve journeys on railways or boats that lead to checking of times and alibis. The criminals may use devices to ensure that at the supposed time of the crime they have an alibi. These devices are always fully explained, often with the aid of a diagram, and Crofts himself would have manufactured such devices to make sure that they would work.

Crofts is not without his faults. Raymond **Chandler** described him as 'the soundest builder of them all when he doesn't get too fancy', but occasionally Crofts does fall into the latter trap. His plots can rely on the criminal disguising himself as the victim, and although this often seems reasonable, at times it stretches credibility. Also, Crofts sometimes has shopkeepers or taxi drivers remembering (in unlikely fashion) the faces of customers they have briefly seen a few weeks before. Latterly, the author also slipped into telegraphing his villains by their description: a weak look around the eyes or thin lips would indicate that someone was not to be trusted.

For all that, Crofts is unrivalled for the construction of his plots. In his juvenile novel, *Young Robin Brand Detective* (1947), in which French plays a part, Crofts has a character explain how a detective-writer friend goes about his craft: 'I begin with the important adventures or happenings, and then I plan the necessary characters and situations and locations to enable these adventures to take place' (p.68). *See also* Golden Age Crime Fiction.

Selected Works by the Author
The Cask (1920)
The Groote Park Murder (1923)
Inspector French's Greatest Case (1924)
The 12.30 from Croydon (1934; also published in the United States as *Wilful and Premediated*)
Golden Ashes (1940)
Death of a Train (1946)
Murderers Make Mistakes (stories, 1947)

Further Reading
Keating, H.R.F. 1986. 'Freeman Wills Crofts'. *CADS* 3.
Shibuk, Charles. 1996. 'Freeman Wills Crofts (1879–1957)'. *CADS* 28.

Geoff Bradley

Cross, Neil (b.1969)

Neil Cross made his literary debut with the novel *Mr In-between* (1998). This followed an unsuccessful stint in music, fronting a band called the Atrocity Exhibition, and a low-key role in London publishing. His early years were documented in the autobiographical volume *Heartland* (2005): a troubled relationship with a cruel stepfather-turned Mormon bishop, which fuelled an interest in the relationship between domination and religious faith and the existential consequences of this relationship.

The narrative of *Mr In-Between* is organised around a familiar cinematic trope – the hit man with a crisis of conscience. Jon Bennet works for the sinister Tattooed Man, a mentor whose tastes in cruelty coincide with Bennet's own abilities as a torturer and enforcer. When the assassin meets two ex-pupils from his former school, now a married couple, he is paralysed with self-doubt, torn between his grim occupation and a vision of domesticity. In turn, his boss and spiritual guru exacts unavoidable retribution. (Cross's first novel was subsequently adapted into the directorial debut of cinematographer Paul Sarossy in 2001, with several plot changes and brief cameos from Cross himself, to greater critical than commercial success.)

Cross's sophomore effort returned to the themes of belief and authoritarianism, pitting smuggler and mercenary Malachi Thorndyke against an expansionary, post-apocalyptic Christian fundamentalist state called New Jerusalem. Thorndyke's profession also demands a thorough working knowledge of criminal activity, coupled with an ability to improvise, in order to free him up of responsibility and concentrate on his drinking. Such opportunities are rare and rarely enjoyable. Ahead of its time, *Christendom* (1999) anticipates themes that would prove popular both in Dan Brown's *The Da Vinci Code* (2003) and in critiques of the second Bush presidency. Combining the **thriller** with **science fiction** and theology, *Christendom* demonstrates Cross's long-term refusal to be pigeonholed by genre.

Holloway Falls (2003) revives William Holloway, a detective from *Mr In-Between*, who could not catch Jon Benet. His subsequent descent into depression and domestic violence triggers a complex conspiratorial tale in which faces from the past menace its police protagonist. Dream **detectives**, religious gurus and meticulously detailed landscapes – Leeds, Bristol, North London and more – all give the work a sense of eerie menace. A suicide-faking swindler botches Holloway's biggest responsibility, causing a trail of mayhem and introspection on the part of the protagonists.

During the gestation of *Holloway Falls* (which Cross admits was difficult), Cross relocated his young family to New Zealand and worked on a novel depicting the lengths to which a father would go in order to protect his son. 'Tabloid justice' grumbled *The Guardian*, although (intriguingly) the nature of the bullying that opens this tale of stewing paranoia and disproportionate force is never disclosed. Attempts to deal with a heavyweight local family are strictly amateurish until a former in-law is persuaded to call in a criminal acquaintance. In an age of anti-social behaviour orders and generalised 'bullying', *Always the Sun* (2004) touches on suburban life in a very recognisable Britain.

Natural History (2007) is a murder mystery set in 'Monkeyland' animal sanctuary, with far-reaching existential implications for all involved. It follows the tradition Neil Cross has established: delivering for readers a violent and disturbing – yet strangely spiritual – experience.

Selected Works by the Author
Mr In-between (1998)
Christendom (1999)
Holloway Falls (2003)
Always the Sun (2004)
Heartland (non-fiction, 2005)
Natural History (2007)

Graham Barnfield

Cullingford, Guy (1907–2000)

Guy Cullingford was the pseudonym of Constance Lindsay Taylor (nee Dowdy). She published twelve striking works of fiction, of which eleven were published under the name of Cullingford. Her books were written over a long period of time from the early fifties to the early nineties.

Constance Dowdy was born in Essex in 1907. She married in 1930 and it was her married name that she utilised for her first novel, *Murder with Relish*, which was published under the name of C. Lindsay Taylor in 1948. It was not until 1952 that the author began to use Guy Cullingford as her nom de plume, as it was perceived wisdom of the day that readers bought crime novels by male writers. Several female writers concealed their identities behind a male façade (Anthony Gilbert is most probably the most famous male pseudonym to be adopted by a female writer).

Cullingford's first foray into the crime scene was *If Wishes Were Hearses* (1952). Shortly after came her most celebrated title, *Post Mortem* (1953). This is a classic tale of its time and emblematic of the golden age of crime fiction. *Conjurer's Coffin* (1954) is a curious piece about a middle-aged receptionist who becomes involved with guests staying in the hotel where she works. These include a trio from a conjuring act; one of whom disappears while another is found murdered. *Framed for Hanging* (1956) and *The Whipping Boys* (1958) are among Cullingford's best-known books, evidence that her most accomplished novels came from this early period.

The sixties saw a healthy rate of production with *A Touch of Drama* (1960), *Third Party Risk* (1962), *Brink of Disaster* (1964) and *The Stylist* (1968). A decade later came the quirky *The Bread and Butter Miss* (1979) and, finally, *Bother at the Barbican* (1991), nearly forty years after Cullingford's first literary appearance.

Unfortunately, although Cullingford was well regarded for the fine writing on display, at times the narratives were over-suffused with a wealth of character detail. But Cullingford did publish some very winning novels, notably *Post Mortem* and *Conjurer's Coffin*, which reward reading today.

Selected Works by the Author

As C. Lindsay Taylor
Murder with Relish (1948)

As Guy Cullingford
If Wishes Were Hearses (1952)
Post Mortem (1953)
Conjurer's Coffin (1954)
Framed for Hanging (1956)
The Whipping Boys (1958)
Third Party Risk (1962)

Chris Simmons

Cumming, Charles (b.1971)

One of Britain's most celebrated contemporary **espionage**-fiction writers, Charles Cumming has produced a number of novels noted for their authenticity. Indeed, at the age of twenty-four, he was approached for recruitment by the United Kingdom's Secret Intelligence Service (MI6), and his first novel, *A Spy by Nature* (2001), was partly based on his experiences in the secret world. Narrated in the first person, the novel introduces us to Alec Milius, an ambitious, morally flawed loner in his early twenties who is recruited by MI5 to sell doctored research data on oil exploration in the Caspian Sea to the Central Intelligence Agency (CIA). Robert Harris described the book as 'a wonderfully assured first novel. From the first page to the last it has the ring of absolute authenticity. Tautly written, cleverly plotted and with a real sense of moral anger at the cruelties and duplicities of modern espionage.'

Cumming's second novel, *The Hidden Man* (2003), is a contemporary spy thriller about the story of two brothers, Mark and Benjamin Keen, whose father abandoned them as small children in order to take up a position with MI6 in Moscow. Many years later, he reappears, only to be murdered by an unidentified assailant. The brothers set about trying to find his killer, a journey which takes them back to the Soviet invasion of Afghanistan and into the brutal world of Russian-organised crime in contemporary London. Once again, Cumming balanced verisimilitude with solid novelistic virtues.

22. Charles Cumming.

The Spanish Game, a sequel to *A Spy by Nature*, was published in 2006. Alec Milius has been living in self-imposed exile in Madrid, where he becomes involved in a plot by Euskadi Ta Askatasuna, or ETA, to bring down the Spanish government. As before with Cumming, plausible plotting was married to strong characterisation. Cumming followed *The Spanish Game* with *Run* (2008). In Hong Kong in 1997, on the eve of the transfer of sovereignty to the Chinese, Joe Lennox interrogates Wang Kai Xuan, a Han academic who has risked his life to tell the British government about human-rights abuses in Xinjiang province. Eight years later, Lennox is sent to Shanghai to investigate the death of a former MI6 officer whose body has been dragged out of the Huangpu River. Lennox's presence in Shanghai brings him back into contact with Wang as well as with his former girlfriend, Isabella Aubert, and the ruthless CIA officer who stole her from him. This novel (and 2008's *Typhoon*) is further proof that the modern spy novel is in rude health in Cummings's capable hands.

Selected Works by the Author
A Spy by Nature (2001)
The Hidden Man (2003)
The Spanish Game (2006)
Typhoon (2008)

Brian Ritterspak

Curtis, James (1907–1977)

Nowadays largely overlooked, the pseudonymous James Curtis should be considered alongside his more famous contemporaries – such as Gerald **Kersh** and Patrick **Hamilton** – as an exemplary chronicler of the 1930s low-life **London** noir.

Born in the rural Kentish village of Sturry in 1907, Geoffrey Basil Maiden attended King's School in nearby Canterbury before embarking on a career as a novelist under the pen name 'James Curtis'. Among the handful of novels he wrote under this moniker, *The Gilt Kid* (1936) is easily the most representative of his style.

Based on his experiences of working-class London (Curtis wore his left-wing politics on his sleeve, rebelling against his upper middle class lifestyle from an early age), the novel's bleak, unsparing prose describes the life of a burglar and Communist sympathiser freshly released from jail and keen on retracing his old haunts. 'The world to which he belongs is that segment of Soho where in their dirty little cafes parasites of all the human species abound,' commented the publisher's blurb of 1946.

Like **Dickens** a century before, Curtis was keen to make none-too-subtle judgements on the role that society played in producing dysfunctional citizens; his villains were usually products of broken homes rather than self-consciously evil. His novels *They Drove by Night* (1938) and *There Ain't No Justice* (1939) were made into popular British films, but following the war, he only produced one more title: the forgettable *Look Long upon a Monkey* (1956).

Selected Works by the Author
The Gilt Kid (1936)
What Immortal Hand (1939)
They Drove By Night (1939)

Mark Campbell

Curzon, Clare (b.1922)

The author of a great many novels, written under several pseudonyms, Clare Curzon's chief contribution to crime fiction consists of her twenty-book series featuring dogged Superintendent Mike Yeadings.

Born Eileen-Marie Duell Buchanan in 1922 at St Leonards-on-Sea in Sussex, she studied French and Psychology at King's College, London, before beginning her literary career in 1963 with *Death in Deakins Wood*. Written under the pseudonym of Rhona Petrie, this marked the first in a short series featuring Inspector Marcus Maclurg of Scotland Yard, and was followed by four more titles, concluding with *Maclurg Goes West* (1968). Under the same name, two further books appeared with science professor-turned-amateur sleuth Dr Nassim Pride: *Foreign Bodies* (1967) and *Despatch of a Dove* (1969).

As Petrie, a collection of eleven crime, horror, ghost and spy stories, *Come Hell and High Water*, appeared in 1970, while a standalone novel, *Thorne in the Flesh* (1971), described in vivid detail the experiences of a mild-mannered schoolteacher drawn into the Soho underworld.

The publication of *Greenshards* in 1972 marked a new phase for the author. Written under her real name of Marie Buchanan, *Greenshards* was a gripping psychological mystery that ventured into the murky waters of the paranormal. The title referred to a country house that had been taken over by the charismatic Giles Blanchard, his medium wife Fenella, and their servants. At an impromptu séance, their next-door neighbour, Olive Minton, relives the suicide of her father there years earlier, and soon falls under Giles's sinister spell. Buchanan's cleverness here is in suggesting occult forces at work without ever explicitly confirming it; the story could work equally well if the antagonists employed psychological mind-tricks, as one character claims.

Four **historical** novels followed, all with fantasy/supernatural overtones, but it was not until 1979, and with a further change of name to Clare Curzon, that the author returned to mainstream, mainly contemporary, crime novels. The first, *A Leaven of Malice* (1979), echoed the London of *Thorne in the Flesh* with its depiction of a bleak Fulham bedsit and its disparate occupants. Her third book as Curzon, *I Give You Five Days* (1983), introduced Mike Yeadings, a Scotland Yard detective who proved extremely popular with readers and has subsequently dominated the author's output until the present day. A solid example of the British police procedural, Yeadings's investigations are gentle, slow-moving affairs with the emphasis on strong characters and believable crimes.

Still writing in her eighties, Buchanan's latest creation is Lucy Sedgwick, an Edwardian detective who made her debut with *Guilty Knowledge* in 1999.

Selected Works by the Author

As Rhona Petrie
Death in Deakins Wood (1963)
Murder by Precedent (1964)
Running Deep (1965)
Thorne in the Flesh (1971)

As Marie Buchanan
Greenshards (1972; also published in the United States as *Anima*; later re-issued in UK as *Flawed Light* by Curzon)

As Clare Curzon
A Leaven of Malice (1979)
Masks and Faces (1984)
The Trojan Hearse (1985)
Trail of Fire (1989)
The Blue-Eyed Boy (1990)
Cat's Cradle (1991)
Close Quarters (1996)
Guilty Knowledge (1999)
The Glass Wall (2005)

Mark Campbell

Cutler, Judith (b.1946)

Following an early career in education, Judith Cutler turned to crime writing in the 1980s. She has written several series of crime novels, mainly set around the Midlands, based on the separate heroines Sophie Rivers, Kate Power, Josie Welford and Fran Harman. Cutler was for some years secretary to the Crime Writers' Association and is married to fellow crime writer Keith Miles.

The Sophie Rivers series, which began with *Dying Fall* (1995), tells of a Birmingham-based college lecturer and expert cook who is, as her creator once was, an English lecturer at an inner-city college of further education. As the series begins, Sophie ranges further afield as a professional caterer but gains a new interest when, after being drawn into an investigation, she befriends the man in charge of the case, Detective Superintendent Chris Groom. Sophie gets as much of a buzz from sleuthing as from cooking, and she and Chris have several subsequent adventures. In the second series, based around a CID team in central Birmingham, Kate Power is, when we first meet her in *Power on Her Own* (1998), a Detective Sergeant in her thirties, although in later books she is promoted to Inspector. Her cases are also set in Birmingham and the West Midlands.

The third series, which began with *The Food Detective* (2005), returns to the format of the investigator's female friend: in this instance the friend, Josie Welford, is a restaurateur, and the series becomes a menu of culinary cases. Josie is an Exmoor-based gastro-publican and her contact, Nick Thomas, no longer in the force, is a Detective Inspector, retired. If this sounds too convenient, Cutler throws in two wildcards: Josie the restaurateur is a successful Weightwatcher and, from a previous life, is widow to one of the United Kingdom's most-wanted criminals. Blessed or cursed with a strong sense of justice, she now operates on the right side of the law – when it suits her (according to Josie).

In parallel with this series runs another, again away from the Midlands but again with a cop at its core: Fran Harman, who first appears in *Life Sentence* (2005), is an experienced Detective Chief Superintendent who tackles her cases in the company of Assistant Chief Constable Mark Turner. Fran is based at Kent Police Headquarters in Maidstone, and although she appears tough and impregnable she is battling with a trio of personal problems: middle age, a fast-changing job and senile parents. Against this she can set her romantic relationship with her colleague, though even that will bring problems.

Cutler has written two non-series novels about innocent people caught up in a crime: *Scar Tissue* (2004) revolves around Caffy Tyler, a painter and decorator, and *Drawing the Line* (also 2004) concerns Lena Townend, antiques restorer. In 2007, Cutler published her first historical crime novel, *The Keeper of Secrets*, featuring the Reverend Tobias Campion, an early-nineteenth-century parson.

Selected Works by the Author

Sophie Rivers
Dying Fall (1995)
Dying to Score (1999)
Dying to Deceive (2003)

Kate Power
Power on Her Own (1998)
Power Shift (2003)
The Chinese Takeout (2006)
Life Sentence (2005)
Running Deep (2008)

Russell James

D

Dalgliesh, Adam

P.D. **James**'s detective of choice, Commander Adam Dalgliesh of the Metropolitan Police Service (he has appeared in over a dozen of her novels) is a remarkably fleshed-out and complex individual whose cool, authoritative exterior masks an intensely private man with a deep streak of melancholia.

Taking his name from an old English teacher of hers, James featured Dalgliesh in her debut novel, *Cover Her Face* (1962), in which he is called in from New Scotland Yard to investigate the strangulation of a young maid, Sally Jupp, during an aristocratic house party. Emerging fully formed from a cast of equally well-drawn characters, it is no exaggeration to say that Dalgliesh was one of the most memorable British detectives to have appeared in post-war crime fiction (a fact no doubt helped by James's lucid prose).

A dedicated and efficient policeman, Dalgliesh's sensitive side is highlighted by his propensity for writing poetry (he has had several volumes published), although he is reluctant to display any emotion when it comes to traumatic incidents in his personal life – especially concerning the death of his wife in childbirth many years earlier. He is reluctant to embark on another serious relationship, often burying himself in his work to avoid painful reminders of his short-lived marriage, coupled with a nagging feeling of guilt over her untimely death.

We first find Dalgliesh living in a flat above the Thames at Queenhithe, London. One of his few extravagancies is a red vintage Jaguar, which he drives with characteristic sobriety around the streets of the city. His father was the rector of a Norfolk country parish, although he has no Christian beliefs. (Ironically, James is well-known for dealing with religious issues in many of her works, most notably her dystopian science fiction parable, *The Children of Men*, published in 1992).

Later, the death of his aunt Jane allows him to move out of the capital and move into a converted windmill on a remote Norfolk headland in the spookily atmospheric *Devices and Desires* (1989).

Dalgliesh's solitary nature is softened by a succession of more approachable sidekicks, such as DS Martin (*Cover Her Face*), DS Masterson (*Shroud for a Nightingale*, 1971) and, more recently, DI Kate Miskin, formerly of the Special Investigations Squad, who comes into her own in *The Lighthouse* when Dalgliesh is laid low with SARS.

A romantic interlude beckons with Deborah Riscoe in *Cover Her Face*, but due to Dalgliesh's commitment issues, by *Unnatural Causes* (1967) they have split up, never to reconcile. A more promising liaison occurs much later with university lecturer Emma Lavenham in *Death in Holy Orders* (2001). And by *The Lighthouse* (2005), Dalgliesh has agreed to marry Emma – although it remains to be seen whether this will actually happen.

At the beginning of *The Black Tower* (1975), Dalgliesh receives a get-well card from James's other series detective Cordelia Gray, while he crops up in a minor role in both *An Unsuitable Job for a Woman* (1972) and *The Skull Beneath the Skin* (1982).

Roy Marsden successfully captured the innate loneliness of the character in ten well-made adaptations for Anglia TV from 1983 to 1998. Despite changes being made because of the seemingly random choice of transmission order (*Cover Her Face* being third in the run, for instance), the stories were generally faithful to their source material and showcased some of Britain's most talented actors and actresses. When the BBC obtained the rights to the character in 2003, Martin Shaw took on the role in two further adaptations: *Death in Holy Orders* and *The Murder Room*. It remains to be seen, however, whether his interpretation will have a long-lasting appeal as that of Marsden, who still remains synonymous with the role. *See also* The Detective in British Fiction *and* TV Detectives: Small-Screen Adaptations.

Selected Works by the Author
Cover Her Face (1962)
The Black Tower (1975)
Devices and Desires (1989)
The Murder Room (2003)

Mark Campbell

Dalton, John (b.1949)

John Dalton is the author of two Birmingham-based crime novels that combine authentic settings with strong psychological noir elements. He is an example of the kind of crime writer who, starting in middle age, brings a wealth of experience and literary influence to bear on his work. Dalton has lived in Birmingham (UK) for some decades and has worked in adult education. His two novels, *The City Trap* and *The Concrete Sea*, have been published by the Birmingham-based Tindal Street Press and were enthusiastically received nationally, with crime critic Maxim **Jakubowski** commending 'the tidal wave of noir that engulfs the plot' of his first novel and calling his second 'British dirty realism at its strongest'.

The City Trap transposes familiar aspects of American noir – an alcoholic private investigator (PI), a sexual psychopath and a chain of corruption leading back to a powerful businessman – to the low-key and ethnically diverse culture of the West Midlands. The result may remind some readers of the 1970s film and television series *Gangsters*, though Dalton's approach is more subtle. A recurrent motif is the lure of 'the big wallow' inside every bottle. We know from the outset who the killer is: what remains to be unravelled is the complicity of others in a bitter chain of events. As one character comments, 'No blame, but also totally to blame. That's what experience is.'

The Concrete Sea is a more stylish and literary noir novel than its predecessor, but shows no signs of lightening up. It is set in an unnamed city (apparently Birmingham), and the sense of urban claustrophobia is powerful throughout. Harsh nocturnal lights, rain-soaked streets and ruined buildings are recurrent images. PI Don teams up with another PI, Jackie, to investigate the murder of a teenage girl. Don has psychotic tendencies, including paranoia and hearing voices in his head. While the resolution of the core mystery is grim and disturbing, the novel's real strength lies in its blending of real and psychological landscapes.

Dalton's short story 'The Mentality' contrasts imagination and reality within a terse, cynical narrative about a dead man who had kept his creativity a secret.

The power of conformity (and especially of money) is starkly conveyed here; and as ever, Dalton transposes key elements of the American noir tradition to a West Midlands setting in which quiet rage and sardonic passivity are the norm.

In half a decade, Dalton has produced two novels that embody the radical spirit of noir fiction while remaining true to the understated realism of Birmingham's culture. Much can be expected of him in the future. While Dalton's world is corrosively downbeat, his faith in human endurance and the value of truth suggests that he will continue to find potent narrative material in the psychological and social conflicts that his work portrays.

Selected Works by the Author
The City Trap (2002)
'The Mentality' in *Birmingham Noir* edited by Joel Lane and Steve Bishop (2002)
The Concrete Sea (2005)

Joel Lane

Dalziel & Pascoe (television series, 1996–)

The television productions based on the characters invented by Reginald **Hill** show a complex connection between page and screen. Beginning as full-blooded dramatisations of novels, the core partnership of gross but intuitive Chief Inspector Andy Dalziel and his more conventionally educated, modern-mannered, Sergeant Peter Pascoe, has outlived the scriptwriter's taste for adaptation. The novels and television series parted company. While Hill went on to write teasingly hard-to-film literary puzzle narratives such as *Death's Jest Book* (2003), television productions focused on developing *Dalziel & Pascoe* into one of the post-***Inspector Morse*** dual detective series, such as *Heartbeat* (1992–), *Wycliffe* (1997–1998), *A Touch of Frost* (1992–), *Midsomer Murders* (1997–) and *Hetty Wainthrop* (1996–1998). All these television series feature an old school detective uneasily bound to a younger colleague who is familiar with new technology and/or political correctness.

Unsurprisingly, 'television Dalziel' has developed dissimilarities to his novel counterpart. 'Novel Dalziel' was a divine trickster only loosely constrained by police conventions. Credited with supernatural powers by some, Dalziel terrified his bosses, and his fearsome intuition had little respect for the proper boundaries of investigation. Perhaps his greatest power was that everyone else believed in it too, including the reader. Television Dalziel retains as much of this semi-divine monster as is possible to embody in a recurring series. That is, he is physically less vast, so not endangering the health of actor, Warren Clarke. He is less intimidating and more vulnerable. While he remains superbly intuitive and confident of past police methods, he is also a friend to Pascoe.

As Pascoe, Colin Buchanan began with the tricky task of making his character awed yet not colourless when compared with Dalziel's ability to challenge those around him. Fortunately, the scriptwriters increased Pascoe's ironic wit. In fact, Pascoe on screen is not too different from Pascoe on the page. One of the biggest shifts between page and screen is the elimination or paring down of the lively ancillary characters of the novels. Television Ellie leaves Pascoe who becomes a divorced father. Sergeant Wield, an important character for Hill and not just because he is gay, is written out. What in the novels is a complex interlocking web of work and social relationships is rendered sparely on screen as two lonely professional men. Dalziel is lonely because he alienates people and needs Pascoe because he has the intelligence to appreciate him. Pascoe is lonely because his job has cost him his wife and daughter. He needs Dalziel because only this colleague has the depth to extend the working relationship into that of a paternal friend. These narrative destinations are foreshadowed in the filming of the first three novels, *A Clubbable Woman*, *An Advancement of Learning* and *An April Shroud* (filmed as *An Autumn Shroud*), all broadcast, in the first season of the series, in 1996. Later programmes, tuned less to Hill's novels than to the perceived tastes of the television audiences, are not so highly regarded.

When Dalziel and Pascoe first appear together, their exchange is emblematic. Dalziel remarks that Pascoe is the first recruit to pronounce his name properly, thus educating the audience and establishing Pascoe's cleverness. He then quashes Pascoe's complacency by saying that such an achievement is 'unforgivable', so establishing Dalziel's idiosyncratic concept of justice and man management. The question of whether Pascoe's university education equips him with the right kind of cleverness for police work runs through the series. Also, Dalziel's apparent uncouth disdain for learning becomes more and more like grim humour. In *A Clubbable Woman*, he quotes Shakespeare's *The Tempest* on the fading of dramatic spectacle as the murder of a rugby club wife unravels rituals of friendship and masculinity. Typically, he is willing to combine his social knowledge with his intuition to get behind middle-class pretences. Pascoe, on the other hand, is given to making charts and adopting a police persona of rational separation. By the end, Dalziel's command of the territory is comically undercut by needing Pascoe to open a plastic packet of sandwiches. Ellie has flitted in and out with her new book against the police. It first signifies as a displacement of Pascoe's rebelliousness and second shows his growing adherence to Dalziel as he berates her for it. Her exit from the series is foreshadowed.

An Advancement of Learning shifts to Ellie's territory and significantly that of Pascoe's *past*, a university. When a dead body found under a statue turns out to be the former woman principal, Dalziel takes his scepticism about higher education along with Pascoe. It is suggestive that Dalziel and Pascoe seem to investigate separately. Pascoe woos Ellie, paving the way for their marriage at the opening of *An Autumn Shroud*, while Dalziel sees off a student protest. *An Autumn Shroud* is Dalziel's case and teases the viewer by placing the large detective in both a social and a generic setting foreign to him. Dalziel arrives in rain-sodden Norfolk and the Tennysonian setting of funereal barges and black-veiled women. Quoting 'The Lady of Shalott', who died from the touch of reality, Dalziel becomes involved with the mourning Fieldings, whose bereavement proves to be due to murder. Dalziel's intuitive absorption into this country-house mystery is shown both by romancing the widow and by his dressing up as Henry VIII at a medieval banquet. He later refuses the temptation to compromise justice and even for the possibility of ameliorating his loneliness. *An Autumn Shroud* validates Dalziel as a detective who upholds the law even by personal sacrifices. In this, Dalziel and Pascoe join the legion of cops and cowboys whose masculinity rests upon a willingness to sacrifice the feminine and Eros in a quest for an ideal of justice. *See also* TV Detectives: Small-Screen Adaptations.

Further Reading
Moody, Nickianne. 2003. 'Crime in Film and on TV'. Pp.227–244 in *The Cambridge Companion to Crime Fiction*. Edited by Martin Priestman. Cambridge University Press.
Priestman, Martin. 1998. *Crime Fiction from Poe to the Present*. Northcote House.
Sparks, Richard. 1992. *Television and the Drama of Crime*. Open University Press.

Susan Rowland

Danks, Denise (b.1953)

Given that computers have directly impacted on our lives since the mid-1980s, it is strange that so few crime novels, particularly on this side of the Atlantic, have exploited either the technology or the milieu. In fact until 1989, when Denise Danks published her first novel, there were none. The six books featuring computer journalist Georgina Powers are not only the leading examples of the sub-genre, but Danks's heroine is a major addition to the roster of female sleuths in UK crime.

Born in England to a Greek mother and an English (RAF) father, Denise Danks had a nomadic childhood. Briefly a teacher, she switched to journalism, later covering the computer industry. Then she founded both the world's first daily computer newsletter and its first technology news agency. During a period as a freelance journalist, she wrote her first Powers novel, *The Pizza House Crash* (1989). In 1994, she became the first female writer to win the Chandler-Fulbright Award for the most promising writer of crime. One consequence was the six-month attachment to the prestigious film school of the University of California, Los Angeles (UCLA), which resulted in the screenplay of *Torso*, a calling card for Danks's current career as a screenwriter.

From the very first pages of *Crash*, it is evident that a considerable talent has arrived. Broad-minded, tough, intelligent Powers was conceived as a contemporary equivalent to George, the most free-spirited member of Enid Blyton's The Famous Five. Powers is also attracted to the more devious (and deadly) of the male species. In the first book, Powers uncovers a piece of 'killer' software that has many applications, mostly criminal. Remarkably assured for a first novel, it is also a most entertaining way in which to understand the impact of computers on the world of City finance.

In *Better Off Dead* (1991), Danks and Powers swap the financial setting for the popular music field, while the author exhibits her expertise in the newly rampant world of East End crime. In *Frame Grabber* (1993), perhaps the best of the series so far, Powers meets Dr David Jones, the most dangerous of her lovers. It is a chilling but erotic tale with morbid sexual fantasies moving from virtual reality into the real world. *Wink a Hopeful Eye* (1994) is equally good. A taut, complex **thriller**, it is set against a background of an actual international shortage in (for the time) high-capacity computer chips.

Back from America, Danks completed the process, begun with *Better Off Dead*, of paring down her style to one unique in the United Kingdom, certainly among female writers. In *Phreak* (1998), she returns to the world of East End crime with another fast-moving thriller, this time featuring the illicit use of mobiles. In *Baby Love* (2001), Danks presciently combines computer games, a bomb plot and religious fundamentalism. Both *Phreak* and *Baby Love* were shortlisted for the **Crime Writers' Association**'s Gold Dagger Award.

In between the two books (1999), she wrote a novel version of her screenplay *Torso*. Set in southern California, it is a twisted 'love' triangle with murder at its heart, her only non-series novel to date. It recalls Charles Williams in its style and Patricia Highsmith in its psychological depth.

But though technology is a key theme for Danks, it is her many strengths as a writer that pulls the reader through to the end. Always up to the minute, her absence from today's publishing lists is sorely felt. *See also* Sexuality in British Crime Fiction *and* Women Crime Writers.

Selected Works by the Author
The Pizza House Crash (1989; also published in the United States as *User Friendly*)
Better Off Dead (1991)
Frame Grabber (1993)
Wink a Hopeful Eye (1994)
Phreak (1998)
Torso (1999)
Baby Love (2001)

Bob Cornwell

Davidson, Lionel (b.1922)

As one of the most lauded (with three **Crime Writers' Association** Gold Dagger awards) and most popular authors of the 1960s and 1970s, Lionel Davidson was a major force in bringing the action/adventure tale up to date.

His books are difficult to categorise, crossing and weaving sub-genres, and even subverting type with elegance and style. He wrote comedy with action, an anti-puzzle mystery, adventure in foreign lands with exotic and fantastic twists, and action **thrillers** for young people and children. Underpinning, his cross-genre trek was a sincere interest in people and places in the trouble spots of the world. His work is multi-dimensional containing both entertainment and a serious outlook.

Davidson was born the son of a Lithuanian mother and Polish father. He held a junior post with *The Spectator* and became a well-known investigative journalist. He was the literary editor of *John Bull* (he commissioned authors as diverse as **Christie**, Brian **Masters** and Doris Lessing), and his interest in writing/producing drama nearly led to a career as a media tycoon in the late 1950s (he was involved with a television company). Exasperated and facing near ruin, he turned his talent to writing fiction. The immediate result was *Night of Wenceslas* (1960), a sardonically funny send-up of the spy novel and a favourite of Kingsley Amis. It was one of several novels where Davidson purposely wrote against the prevailing fashion – in this case, the James Bond-style secret agent. The strong appeal of the story is that it satirises both **Fleming** and the darker aspects of espionage while celebrating the adventure tradition of **Buchan**. Davidson wrote his own screenplay for a Hollywood adaptation, but a casting problem with the stars meant it was sold to the Arthur Rank Studios, whose uninspiring adaptation emphasised the novel's comic rather than darker aspirations, becoming a light-hearted romp, *Hot Enough for June* (1963). Nevertheless, other film projects beckoned including a draft of Len **Deighton**'s *The Ipcress File* (1962).

The ingenious adventure story *Rose of Tibet* (1962) demonstrated Davidson's ability to anchor a fantastic tale in contemporary reality and is often cited by many readers as a particular favourite. It harks back to Rider Haggard's classic tale of legends, strange lands and true love, *She*. The book was rightly credited with resurrecting the adventure story proper from hibernation or more correctly from its entire sublimation into other genres (e.g. war, **espionage** and **science fiction**).

Davidson then negotiated a different direction with the archaeological mystery, *A Long Way to Shiloh* (1965). It was his first novel in which he unequivocally expressed his inner self and his love for Israel. It combines action, adventure, mystery and some delicious **humour**. It was an influential book with writers such as Anthony **Price** for its clever dovetailing of an historical puzzle with the thriller form.

Davidson regarded the popular attempts to make commercial product of the Holocaust as 'repellent'. He decided to research the subject of restitution and *Making Good Again* (1968) was the result. It captured the pain and anguish of the survivors yet was balanced by a fresh look at German society – asking pointed questions about how the swindle of the victims could continue. A suspense thriller with emotive power and prose that echoes the best works of Primo Levi, it gets under the reader's skin and makes us relate to the issues ourselves. It is still one of the most moving and thoughtful books on the subject and can be compared to **Conrad** in its climatic building of ever-higher levels of intensity.

In the mid-1960s, Davidson resided in Tel Aviv and was involved with the Israeli film industry as writer and producer. This experience broadened his horizons, and several important novels flowed from it. *Smith's Gazelle* (1971) was four-squarely in the tradition of Stevenson and Kipling; a story where young Arab and Jewish boys, by force of imagination find concord in an undiscovered ravine, surrounded by the reality of a blazing battlefield. *Gazelle* became a cult novel on the campus and kibbutz. Another work of romantic imaginative skill was *The Sun Chemist* (1976), a suspense thriller about the suppression of Dr Weizmann's alternative to oil. Surprisingly, *The Chelsea Murders* (1978), a tour de force parody of the whodunit set in the trendy London district, was written in Israel. This is his most playful adult book and the only one that is a 'pure' murder mystery.

When Davidson returned to the United Kingdom, he found that the publishing industry would no longer countenance authors who were difficult to categorise, and therefore to market. Several works in progress were abandoned, but his last (and perhaps best) book, *Kolmysky Heights* (1994), showed what an outstanding talent he remained. The task of Dr Johnny Porter, a Canadian Indian, is to disguise himself as an Asiatic worker and get himself into a secret Siberian laboratory and escape undetected with a scientific discovery. Full of criss-crossing sub-genre touches, it adroitly synthesised adventure and espionage, referencing its over-arching predecessors with spins on devices and escapades not dissimilar from those faced by Prof Challenger, Alan Quatermain and Richard Hannay. A sensitively handled love interest is integral to the plot, but the proper development of humanity, the balance of modernity and romanticism is also shown to be betrayed by an inhumane system and misguided scientific endeavour. It is also a clever, provocative and prescient novel of continuing relevance.

Davidson has published just seven novels for adults, one novel for young people and four adventure tales for teenagers. His credits include the Authors' Club award for best first novel (*Night of Wenceslas*), three Gold Daggers (*Night of Wenceslas*, *A Long Way to Shiloh* and *The Chelsea Murders*), a Diamond Dagger for lifetime achievement and a BAFTA for best children's work based on his novel (*Soldier and Me*). His work straddles entertainment and serious literature and is an important link to precursors such as Haggard and Buchan on the one side and Conrad, Somerset **Maugham** and **Greene** on the other. Friends and colleagues such as Len Deighton and Anthony Price rate his work highly. Despite winning a record number of Gold Daggers, it can be argued that his other adult novels are as least as good – if not better – than those that bagged these trophies.

Selected Works by the Author
Night of Wenceslas (1960)
The Rose of Tibet (1962)
A Long Way to Shiloh (1965; also published in the United States as *The Menorah Men*)
Making Good Again (1968)
The Chelsea Murders (1978; also published in the United States as *Murder Games*)
Kolmysky Heights (1994)

Further Reading
Johnson, M., ed. 2006. *Masters of Crime: Lionel Davidson & Dick Francis – Essays, Interviews & Annotated Bibliographies*. Scorpion Press.

Michael Johnson

Davies, David Stuart

David Stuart Davies is regarded as one of the world's leading experts on Sherlock **Holmes**. It was his fascination with this iconic character that first led Davies into print. While studying at university in the 1970s, he wanted to write his final dissertation on Arthur Conan **Doyle** but was told that this author was not important enough for such a project (an attitude echoed in recent UK Government pronouncements). As an antidote to this literary snobbery, Davies began writing an article on the films of Sherlock Holmes for his pleasure. The article grew into a book

23. David Stuart Davies.

Holmes of the Movies (1976). It was over ten years before the second book appeared: the demands of the teaching profession robbed him the time and energy for writing.

In 1988, he co-founded the Northern Musgraves Sherlock Holmes Society with Kathryn White, who later became his wife. The renewed interest in Holmes prompted Davies to try his hand at Sherlockian pastiche. Over the next ten years, four Holmes novels, including the well-regarded *The Tangled Skein* (1992), followed. Davies states that in writing these pastiches, he attempts to add new elements to Doyle's formula rather than slavishly following the style of the originals. 'If Doyle were alive today, he certainly would be adding new ingredients to the mix,' Davies maintains. This approach is evident in Davies's most recent Holmes novel to date: the ingenious and entertaining *The Veiled Detective* (2004), in which he presents us with an alternative version of the events of Holmes and Watson's career up to the supposedly fatal Reichenbach incident.

Davies left teaching in 1996 on being offered the editorship of *Sherlock* magazine and began to pursue a full-time writing career. Since that time, he has broadened his output, including creating his sleuth Johnny One Eye, a young private detective operating in London during the Second World War. Johnny first appeared in *Forests of the Night* (2005), and since then, there have been two further novels in the series: *Comes the Dark* (2006) and *Without Conscience* (2008). The novels effectively capture the wartime and attitudes and are full of character and wry humour.

However, Holmes still (inevitably) hovers in the background. In 2001, the publisher Titan brought out Davies's *Starring Sherlock Holmes* (updated in 2007), a definitive survey of the screen career of the man from Baker Street. And the one-man play *Sherlock Holmes – The Last Act*, which premiered at Salisbury Playhouse in 1999, is still touring. Davies was commissioned to create another Holmes play in 2007 and *The Death and Life of Sherlock Holmes* premiered at the Yvonne Arnaud Theatre in Guilford in March 2008 before going on tour.

In 2008, Davies was appointed general editor of Wordsworth's Mystery and Supernatural series, which brought out attractive paperback editions of his *The Tangled Skein* and *Sherlock Holmes and the Hentzau Affair*. Davies is on the national committee of the **Crime Writers' Association** of Great Britain and is editor of their monthly newsletter *Red Herrings*.

Selected Works by the Author
The Tangled Skein (1992)
Bending the Willow: Jeremy Brett as Sherlock Holmes (1996)
The Veiled Detective (2004)
Forests of the Night (2005)
Starring Sherlock Holmes (2007)
Without Conscience (2008)

Barry Forshaw

Davis, Carol Anne (b.1961)

Contemporary **Scottish** crime writer Carol Anne Davis, who has written both fiction and **true crime**, has rapidly won a reputation for her engagement with the criminal mind, exploring primal fears and authentic murders in her crime novels and charting the formative experiences of killers in her true crime books.

Born into an abusive, working-class family in Dundee, she left school at fifteen but later graduated from the universities of Dundee and Edinburgh. Her first three novels are set in the Scottish capital where she lived for many years. *Shrouded* explores a repressed mortuary worker's descent into necrophilia and sexually motivated murder, while *Safe As Houses* looks at life through the eyes of a sadistic sociopath. In stark contrast, *Noise Abatement* charts the journey of a law-abiding man who, as a last resort, elects to kill the neighbours from hell.

24. Carol Anne Davis.

Moving to Salisbury in Wiltshire, Davis produced the true crime *Women Who Kill: Profiles of Female Serial Killers* which included a rare interview with the minister who Myra Hindley confessed to. Salisbury was also the setting for her fourth novel, *Kiss It Away*, a harrowing look at male on male rape and at society's response to this under-reported crime.

It was followed by *Children Who Kill: Profiles of Preteen & Teenage Killers*, an insightful exploration of damaged childhoods, which includes unique information from the detective responsible for catching Peter Dinsdale, Britain's youngest serial killer. Regarded as a damning indictment of hard-hitting parents, the book was reprinted three times in 2006. For its successor, *Couples Who Kill: Profiles of Deviant Duos*, she corresponded with a convicted serial killer and met with one of Rose and Fred West's surviving victims.

The year 2007 saw the publication of *Sob Story*, a novel set in her birthplace of Dundee in which a naïve teenage girl corresponds with a prisoner serving time in HMP Maidstone, unaware that he's a psychopathic killer who is due for release. Davis drew on her own alienated teenage years to create the portrait of an isolated student and interviewed a life prisoner at length to get the prison detail right. Its publication coincided with her true crime *Sadistic Killers: Profiles of Pathological Predators*, which incorporated information from a leading psychiatrist who treated some of Britain's most violent men. Noting that recreational sadists are often unfairly compared to criminal sadists, the book includes a chapter on consensual sadomasochism, with detailed input from a well-known practitioner.

By exploring each killer's seminal experiences in her true crime books, Davis shows that they are made rather than born, yet, as adults, they still have to take responsibility for their murderous actions. By avoiding the use of a detective or private eye in her fiction, she concentrates on the innermost thoughts of the killer and his or her intended victims, charting the fatal journey where the two collide. *See also* Sexuality in British Crime Fiction *and* Society and Crime Fiction.

Selected Works by the Author
Shrouded (1997)
Safe As Houses (1999)
Noise Abatement (2000)
Women Who Kill (2001)
Kiss It Away (2003)
Children Who Kill (2003)
Couples Who Kill (2005)
Sob Story (2007)
Sadistic Killers (2007)

Website
www.carolannedavis.co.uk

Eve Tan Gee

Davis, Lindsey (b.1949)

Lindsey Davis is the best-selling and award-winning writer of the **historical** crime series set in ancient Rome featuring Marcus Didius Falco.

Born and raised in Birmingham, Davis studied at Oxford University, gaining a BA in English language and literature. She entered the civil service where she remained until 1985. Davis had long wanted to write and was planning the definitive English Civil War novel, but instead she sold romantic stories and serials to *Woman's Realm*. She became attracted to the true love story between the Roman Emperor Vespasian and his mistress Antonia, resulting in *The Course of Honour* (1998), though it was over ten years before it saw print. During her research, she became fascinated with first-century Rome and the ideas developed for her Falco series. While these are well steeped in the classical tradition of crime fiction, they are also romance novels – or rather, they explore relationships. There would be no Falco stories without his partner Helena.

Falco and Helena meet in the first book in the series, *The Silver Pigs* (1989), which is set in AD 70, when Falco is twenty-nine. Falco saves a girl from would-be kidnappers but she is later murdered. The girl's family employs Falco to get to the truth of the matter, and the trail takes Falco to Britain, where he meets the dead girl's cousin, Helena. At the outset, they are far from friends, but he and Helena become allies after his mistreatment in the lead mines. He had gone to work there, undercover, to investigate an illegal trade in lead blocks with traces of silver, but he uncovers a plot against the Emperor Vespasian.

We learn a little about Falco during the novel. We know that he had a stint, somewhat ignominious, in the military service, some of which had been spent in Britain, before he was invalided out of the army. Falco's brother had been killed on active service in Germany and Falco has still to come to terms with this. Falco is a commoner, from the plebeian rank, while Helena is a senator's daughter of patrician descent. Normally the two should not be associated, and Falco has a deep-held dislike

25. Lindsey Davis.

of the upper class. Nevertheless, their adventures bring them close together, a bond formed as much by their similarities – both are headstrong, impetuous and single-minded – as their differences. Falco's discovery of the plot against Vespasian, which continues into the second book, *Shadows in Bronze* (1990), earns him the emperor's patronage, and through him, Falco has an opportunity to improve his status, if he can afford it – a factor which remains a driving force in Falco's choice of work. Falco and Helena become lovers, an arrangement accepted by her father but despised by her mother. They have to live in a less salubrious part of Rome, and, over time, they raise two children. She proves to be a crucial element in Falco's role as informer and imperial agent, as her connections and knowledge of upper-class society occasionally allow her to help resolve the mystery.

Though most of Falco's investigations are set in Rome, there are occasions when they take him further afield. He has to travel to Germany on an imperial mission in *The Iron Hand of Mars* (1992), to Syria in *Last Act in Palmyra* (1994) (which also reveals Falco's playwriting skills), to Spain in *A Dying Light in Corduba* (1996) and to Carthage in *Two for the Lions* (1998), while *A Body in the Bath House* (2001) and *The Jupiter Myth* (2002) see him back in Britain.

The series has many strengths and does not rely solely on the fascination for solving the mystery: indeed, not all mysteries are resolved, as Falco openly admits in *Two for the Lions*. Falco is a well-developed character who encourages reader sympathy. Although he is streetwise and sharp-witted and tries to give the impression that he is tough and capable, he is actually a romantic and emotionally vulnerable. He cares deeply for those he loves and is wracked with guilt about those he believes he has let down. In *One Virgin Too Many* (1999), Falco becomes distraught because he did not take seriously the request by a young girl that he protect her, and when she is later found dead, Falco will not rest until he has done her justice. Falco, though, is not naïve and is suspicious of many of those about him. At the head of this list is Anacrites, Vespasian's head spy, who sees Falco as a rival, and in *Last Act in Palmyra*, he tries to engineer Falco's death. However, over time, Falco and Anacrites form a kind of unholy alliance, each uncertain of the other but prepared to work with the other as occasion demands for mutual benefit. This highlights another of the series' strengths: the cast of fascinating characters. There are few who have simply a walk-on role. All of the characters have a purpose and a past and, if they are fortunate, a future. Many appear in several novels, especially Falco's own far-flung and far from helpful family, and Falco's circle of friends and confidantes, a few of whom, such as Petronius, the Vigile Watch Captain, prove to be saviours in times of peril.

It is through the characters and Falco's own dry, witty observations that the Roman world comes to life. Falco reveals what goes on behind closed doors, at all levels of society, enabling the reader to see everyday Roman life, not just the high and mighty. Davis's research unearths considerable details, revealing not only the lives of building contractors, tax collectors, journalists, gladiators, the production of olive oil, the law of property and much else, but also the fraudulent and underhand practices that often accompany them. Falco is a man of the people. Even when he is up to his neck in trying to solve a crime, he is also worrying about the day-to-day problems of raising his family, sorting out his building problems and agonising over what to buy his wife for her birthday. Falco talks in the vernacular, and while he may not speak or act like his genuine Roman counterpart, he is close enough to be believable while also being accessible to modern-day perceptions. Davis thus allows us to understand the idiosyncrasies of the ancient world, where attitudes – especially towards life, death and religion – are at variance with most of the present day, but where otherwise little else changes in the daily struggle of getting on with life.

The novels form an almost continuous narrative, events often following closely on from previous books, with three or four novels set within a single year. Currently, Falco's investigations have taken place between AD 70 and 76, and there is scope for many more before Vespasian dies in AD 79. Fortunately, Falco is also favoured by Vespasian's eldest son, Titus (who succeeds Vespasian), but his brother, Domitian, dislikes Falco immensely, and readers wonder what fate awaits Falco when Domitian comes to power in AD 81.

The popularity of the novels is evident not just from their sales, but from their critical success. *The Silver Pigs* won the Authors' Club Best First Novel award, while *Two for the Lions* won the inaugural **Crime Writers' Association** (CWA) Ellis Peters Historical Dagger award. Davis also won the CWA Dagger in the Library in 1995 as the author whose work has given the most pleasure, and the Herodotus Award in 2001 for Lifetime Achievement, and Falco won the Sherlock Award in 2000 as best comic detective. Davis was honorary president of the Classical Association (1997–1998) and served as Chairman of the Crime Writers' Association in 2002–2003.

Although Davis has written a handful of short stories, none of these feature Falco, and she does not regard herself as a short-story writer.

Davis has sustained the character of Falco and an inventiveness of plots through eighteen novels as of 2007, a series that has become organic as it has grown, melding Falco and his contemporaries into a realistic and believable world.

Selected Works by the Author
The Silver Pigs (1989)
Shadows in Bronze (1990)
A Dying Light in Corduba (1996)
Three Hands in the Fountain (1997)

Two for the Lions (1998)
One Virgin too Many (1999)

Website
www.falcophiles.co.uk/
www.lindseydavis.co.uk/

Mike Ashley

Day-Lewis, C.

See Blake, Nicholas

Dead Man's Shoes (film, 2004)

Shane Meadows, director

A coolly lethal, if slyly humorous avenger takes apart the small-town crooks who caused his simple-minded brother's death. Shane Meadows's film (with a screenplay the equal of many a crime novel in adroitness) obviously owes a debt to the film of Ted Lewis's *Get Carter*, the touchstone of laddishness, but also feels like a gloss on the drive-in vigilante classic *Walking Tall*. The improvisational realism of its low-rent villains is constrained by the Jacobean schematics of the revenge plot, and the film is shot through with melancholy Midlands pastoralism about a lost, imaginary idyll. Richard (Paddy Considine), neatly bearded and wry, is a deceptively gentle apparition, briefly exploding with terrifying force when one of the thugs asks him what he is looking at, then cornering him to apologise with apparent sincerity for losing control. The point is that Richard intends to observe niceties and carry out his vengeance according to a code of etiquette which requires him to act dispassionately but which he finds it hard to stick to. Another precursor is *The Bride Wore Black*, a plot which Cornell Woolrich reworked several times, as a series of variously culpable culprits is stalked and killed by an avenger – this has the same range of sympathies and characters among the victims. The most obnoxious and bullying thug, broken-faced handsome goon Sonny (Gary Stretch) is killed at mid-point, leaving only stragglers, and the final confrontation is with the one man (Paul Hurstfield) who was so shocked by the brother's death that he shaped up and got a real, non-layabout family life. Richard begs his putative victim to kill him, to prevent him from becoming a total monster. Meadows and Considine, who co-wrote the script, give the avenger many layers – Richard feels worse about incidentals such as lying to a victim than he does about the killing and he is also driven by guilt in that his warm relationship with the dead Anthony (Toby Kebbell) is only retrospective wish-fulfilment (he was actually horribly embarrassed by his 'spastic' brother's antics). The milieu is unusual for British crime films – a small, mostly ugly town amid green, desolate but lovely countryside (a ruined abbey is a gothic touch for the climax). The crooks are sadder than fearsome, spending most of their time lounging around messy flats rabbiting at each other (reading aloud from porn magazines, doing drug jokes, etc.) and culpable in the original sin not because of real evil (except in Sonny's case) but because they just go along with things. Considine and Stretch are direct, forceful and potent presences, and their confrontations are outstanding (note Considine's spasm of mock and mocking terror). It has almost slasher-style scary-humorous moments, as Richard lurks in a long-snouted gas mask (one of his victims thinks he is an elephant) and torments victims-to-be by sneaking into their homes at night and painting them like clowns or dumps all their stolen drugs into the kettle they use to make a nice cup of tea. With their mismatched crockery, messy flats and boring routine, these are the least cool, most convincing contemporary gangsters in British films. *See also* Film and Crime: Page to Screen *and* Humour and Crime Fiction.

Kim Newman

Deighton, Len (b.1929)

Len Deighton is a major figure whose appearances in the bestseller lists have spanned three decades. It is always a precarious enterprise to try to categorise an author's work, yet Deighton's includes tales of adventure, comic satire, suspense, detective stories and – notably – **espionage**; and that is just the genre material that 'fits' into the heading 'crime, mystery and suspense'. He is also a social novelist, military historian and a man of strong opinions about the world we live in and how it was formed in the recent past. An appraisal of Deighton's significance is best achieved by viewing his work as a whole, where it becomes apparent that the creator of exciting fictional worlds is also informed and influenced by his non-fiction interests; the questions he asks about authority, freedom, class and national purpose are explored with different layers of depth.

Britain's national security was impaired in the late 1950s and early 1960s by a flurry of spy scandals that rocked the Establishment; the defections of Burgess, Maclean and Philby (after he had been exonerated by the foreign secretary) all created an atmosphere of unreality about the secret affairs of state. The Official Secrets Act and the D-Notice system prevented any details being published in Britain, although the foreign press did cover the stories, and the government would resort to 'planting' its version in the press. Officially, the British intelligence services did not exist. The public appetite to know more had been whetted. The publication of Deighton's *The Ipcress File* in November 1962 was an immediate critical and popular success.

During his early working life, Deighton had been something of a restless spirit. He attended the Royal College of Art and found work as an illustrator. He learned continental cooking, had a spell as an air steward for BOAC, ventured to New York into the world of advertising and generally looked for an outlet for his talents. Deighton developed a wide cortege of acquaintances who attended weekly dinners at his London basement flat. Just how officials from the American and Soviet embassies came to be present is a mystery. As a trained illustrator, Deighton had represented his subjects in a highly individual manner; as he developed into a professional writer, he demonstrated that he had internalised his varied experiences of people and places. But he also viewed them, as an artist would, from different angles and perspectives – something that developed into a fascinating approach to the dense and complicated subjects of his later work.

In the five successive spy novels of the 1960s, the main angle or viewpoint that Deighton revealed to his readers was that of a professional field agent battling to succeed as much against the rivalry of the higher echelons as the designated targets of foreign enemies. The novels show for the first time that 'the service' is not a uniform whole and that it combined, in fact, a group of rival intelligence agencies that represented different competing interests – some working for the military, others for commercial interests, security, foreign affairs and so on. Because the various organisations are intertwined by gentlemen's clubs, secret intelligence committees, City directors' meetings and senior civil servants who went to the 'right school', the system was able to function smoothly – provided personal vendettas and rivalries did not break out. In Deighton's world (and, by extension, the real world), the norm is often that the individuals involved did not know what was going on. And politicians not involved in the plotting were left out in the cold.

The genius of Deighton's early **thrillers** is that they are uncanny representations of a rapidly changing Britain and also an appealing parody of the old order. **London** is starting to 'swing', women are more independent socially and a new affluence is seen in the style of clothes, chic eating-out places and so on – all of which the author relishes (cf. *London Dossier*, 1967) and contrasts with a dowdier style of the unnamed secret agent and other civil servants working for a low-wage living. The contrast of social change at one level with a still-ossified top layer is marked: a dimension that is accentuated further as the narrative moves to continental locations, and further afield. Yet the unnamed secret agent is twice removed from his masters, he has no independent income or a 'classical education'. The Official Secrets Act and a strong sense of duty tie him to them, but he remains an archetypal loner, living on his wits. This figure is conduit for the reader to perceive the antiquated nature of how Britain was really governed, behind the smoke and mirrors. His boss, Dawlish, resides in an office akin to a junk shop, and the office talk in *Funeral in Berlin* (1964) is that the latter's hobby is to grow weeds. Dawlish is a generalist in the broadest sense, and his main preoccupation is to ensure the longevity of his department (and guaranteeing his pension).

Deighton also began writing when an unprecedented sense of a dangerous reality (post-Cuba) made the public uneasy about the Russians, nuclear war and unrestrained science. The confrontations of his protagonist are made all the more palatable by a wry sense of humour characterising many of the tricky situations. For instance, the meeting between the British agent with the Russian Colonel Stok and the extrovert 'Americanised' German Vulkan in *Funeral in Berlin* artfully compares chess pieces to the key power brokers of the capitalist world. The message of these confrontations is usually that the agents on both sides are more worried by the machinations of interlopers such as Vulkan and about pressures from prejudiced factions/interests on their side than from that of each other. Allied to the humour is the effective and disarming use of dialogue. Deighton's smooth use of authentic, contemporary dialogue of quite different classes and outlooks – whether British, German or American – is extraordinary. It brings depth to situations and appeal to characters. The breezy style, sense of place, ironic humour and convoluted plots that became clear later in the narrative provided the pure entertainment, while the harder-edged social and political commentary was again underscored by another innovation – the liberal use of footnotes giving authentic details of the technicalities of espionage. The idea was furthered by appendices and, in *An Expensive Place to Die* (1967), even reproductions of utterly persuasive 'secret documents' from the office of the British Prime Minister and the President of the United States of America.

The 1970s was a turbulent time for a spy writer. Britain's economic decline led to social tensions, militancy and extra-parliamentary action together with 'the Terror' in Northern Ireland pointed the genre in the direction of a search for 'enemies within'. During this period, Deighton did pen some more spy thrillers, again with the unnamed agent, his boss and Colonel Stok, but they were holding works as different narrative styles were essayed. His main response was to examine the Second World War in greater depth in both fiction and non-fiction. The results were provocative, invigorated his writing and, significantly, broadened his readership.

Deighton's first wartime-set novel, *Bomber* (1970), was a literary tour de force (and recognised as such in Anthony Burgess's *Best 99 Novels*). It grew from his skill at observation of social milieu, combined with a sympathy for 'ordinary' heroes, a flair for conveying technical details, stirring action sequences – all encompassed in a broader landscape than most writers of any genre attempt. The narrative takes the reader on a journey with an aircrew, based at Bomber Command aerodrome Warley Fen, through the hazards of night flying on a Lancaster raid over Nazi Germany. *Bomber* is both a splendid action story and a critical, but factual view of how the air war was prosecuted that raises issues about man and machines.

It is beyond the scope of this overview to discuss Deighton's studies of the progress of World War II, *Fighter* (1977), *Blitzkrieg* (1979) and the weighty *Blood, Tears and Folly* (1993), except to make a few general points. One of his most penetrating approaches is to examine leadership, strategy, military strength and so on in the round, showing that everything is connected back to the economy, industry, educational system and upbringing. He had long demonstrated considerable skill at balancing his critique of warfare and leadership with detailed analysis of the German position, and this synoptic approach drew him to consider his Bernard Samson trilogies, with the first volume set in Berlin.

The trilogies – including *Berlin Game* (1983), *Mexico Set* (1984), *London Match* (1985), *Spy Hook* (1988), *Spy Line* (1989) and *Spy Sinker* (1990) – marked the 1980s comeback of Deighton's espionage novels with greater realism and depth. The cynicism and reasons for it are still present, but the narrative is concerned with notions concerning the human cost of espionage. Bernard's wife Fiona is a top agent in her own right, and more than holds her own (as one would expect) with her Oxford PPE, Russian language and yachtswoman expertise. Her betrayal is one of the key moments of the series, yet Bernard has to rely, as with his earlier counterpart in the 1960s, on his inner instincts of self-preservation against a wider number of enemies, indifferent schemers and dolts – many of them from the 'Old Boy Network'. The sense of place and the iconography of espionage are developed further with greater historical dimensions. *Violent Ward* (1993), one other important novel, was a satire of Californian 'pressure cooker' life. It is a beautifully written crime novel with universal themes.

Over the years, Deighton has been identified as an 'Angry Young Man' and a 'Class Warrior'. The former is true, but the latter is way off the mark. His books show that he sees through the foolishness of the extreme ideologies of left and right, but he is no centrist either. His target is statism, the enlarged restricting state, run by penny civil servants and protected by secrecy. He has said, 'I believe the writer is best employed when challenging established authority each and every time that authority tries to restrict the freedom of its citizens.' He is against the idea of a Britain run by planners, bureaucrats and schemers behind layers of humbug and hypocrisy.

The early books are obviously full of artifice, but the document wallets and insights about the real world of espionage inform the reader that the subtext was a kind of docu-drama, something like it may have happened. Indeed, intelligence experts read his books, for it is now known from material published in the last decade that Deighton was close to exposing the 'hidden hand' of the secret intelligence world. In outlook and zeal for the subject matter of espionage, he was particularly close to Ted **Allbeury**. Both writers immersed themselves in the exegesis of the Second World War and foraged for sensitive material to the extent of talking to real-life spies such as CIA agents and the master-spies such as Philby and Blake. In range and power, Deighton is the equal of **Ambler** and **Greene**. If in the twenty-first century his books are not read as assiduously as those of his colleague John **le Carré**, Deighton's reputation and achievement could not be higher. *See also* Social Comment in Crime Fiction.

Selected Works by the Author
The Ipcress File (1962)
Funeral in Berlin (1964)
An Expensive Place to Die (1967)
Bomber (1970)
Berlin Game (1983)
Mexico Set (1984)
London Match (1985)
Spy Hook (1988)
Spy Line (1989)
Spy Sinker (1990)

Michael Johnson

Denby, Joolz (b.1955)

Denby is primarily one of Britain's most popular performance poets, appearing regularly on radio and television, and a familiar face (and voice) at various music, art and literary festivals but, since her first novel, *Stone Baby* (2000), received Debut Dagger from **Crime Writers' Association** (CWA), she has also made a reputation as a writer of suspense-filled crime fiction.

Born on 8 April 1955, Denby married an outlaw biker at the age of nineteen, and under the name Joolz carved a niche for herself as a punk performance poet during the 1970s, one of only a handful of women to achieve this distinction. From 1980, she became heavily involved with singer-guitarist Justin Sullivan of the rock band New Model Army. Often credited as consultant or muse, she has designed and illustrated the band's many album covers since its inception. An acclaimed touring exhibition of her work for the group, 'One Family One Tribe', opened in Denby's hometown of Bradford in 2005, subsequently appearing in Hamm, Germany – Bradford's twin town – and Salford in Manchester.

Since 1983 Denby has released audio recordings of her poetry, sometimes in association with New Model Army or Jah Wobble of punk band Public Image Ltd. She has had poems commissioned from a variety of organisations and regularly tours as a 'spoken word artist' (her preferred title), performing in such disparate venues as the Royal Albert Hall, the House of Commons, university student unions, rock clubs, libraries and pubs. Overseas, she has conducted readings and seminars in Germany, Austria and South Africa.

The author of several volumes of poetry, she wrote her first novel, based on her experiences on the touring circuit. The novel describes the iterant life of a Bradford-based alternative comedian, Jamie Gee, and her desperate quest for a man to treat her properly. Her friend and manager, Lily Carlson, provides a refuge for her in her home, but it is not long before homophobic thug Sean Powers, a psychopath with the body of Adonis, threatens to destroy all that they have built up together. Denby's narrative begins at the climactic ending before backtracking and describing in dark and vivid detail what lead to such an explosive dénouement. As well as winning a CWA Debut Dagger, she was also shortlisted for a John Creasey award and won an American audio book award for her unabridged reading of the novel.

Her next book, *Corazon* (2001), explored the murky world of religious cults, while the heavily autobiographical *Billie Morgan* (2004) was a murder story set in the biker-gang subculture of 1970s Bradford. *Corazon* was shortlisted for the 2005 Orange Prize and the CWA Dagger in the Library award, the latter chosen by reading groups around the United Kingdom.

In *Borrowed Light* (2006), the author expanded her horizons with an emotional tale of romance and revenge, set Daphne du Maurier–style on the windswept Cornish coastline. Awash with haunting descriptions of the locale, Denby's natural gift for storytelling perfectly suited the dramatic storyline.

Selected Works by the Author
Stone Baby (2000)
Corazon (2001)
Billie Morgan (2004)
Borrowed Light (2006)

Website
www.joolz-denby.co.uk

Mark Campbell

The Detective in British Fiction

Detectives who feature in long-running series have long been a staple of the genre. Fictional detectives fall into three broad categories: amateurs, private investigators and the professional police. Categories overlap: many amateurs are lawyers, journalists or have other business connections that bring them into regular contact with crime. In the **Golden Age** between the two world wars, amateur sleuths reigned supreme; today, the professionals are ascendant. Originally, detectives tended to be memorable for their eccentricities; now the emphasis is on in-depth characterisation. The field has become crowded, with detectives of many different kinds, operating in a wide variety of places and periods.

Real-life policemen inspired the first major detectives in British fiction. Charles **Dickens** based Inspector Bucket of *Bleak House* (1853) upon Inspector Field, while his friend Wilkie **Collins** modelled Sergeant Cuff, who investigates in *The Moonstone* (1868), on Sergeant Whicher, who was famous for his work on the 'Road Murder' of 1860. Neither character is the main protagonist of the book in which he features, nor did Bucket or Cuff return for further adventures. Dickens and Collins did not regard themselves as detective novelists; crime and mystery were incidental to their wider concerns. Not until Sherlock **Holmes** made his debut in *A Study in Scarlet* (1887) did the professional private investigator come into his own.

Holmes, like Edgar Allan Poe's Chevalier Auguste Dupin, was a supreme reasoning machine, and Arthur Conan **Doyle** equipped him with characteristics that, although sometimes bizarre, transcended gimmickry and ensured his ranking as the most famous of all characters in British crime fiction. He is introduced as a strange, anti-social depressive, given to moody silences and taking cocaine when he is not playing the violin or firing shots into his landlady's wall. As the years passed, the portrayal softened and Holmes's drug habit was explained as a reaction against monotony. Throughout he remained a genius among detectives, alert to 'the importance of sleeves, the suggestiveness of thumb-nails, or the great issues that may hang from a bootlace'. He outshone Lestrade and other policemen often, while Dr Watson proved a doughty and devoted (yet not uncritical) friend as well as an ideal foil.

Conan Doyle's imitators dutifully copied the pairing of detective and admiring sidekick narrator, without capturing the unique flavour of the Holmes–Watson relationship. R. Austin **Freeman**'s Dr John Thorndyke was aided by Christopher Jervis and Ernest Bramah's blind Max Carrados by enquiry agent Louis Carlyle. In an intriguing variation, Conan Doyle's brother-in-law E.W. **Hornung** created the amateur cracksman A.J. Raffles whose exploits were recorded by the adoring Bunny, who had fagged for him at school. Hercule **Poirot**'s early cases saw him partnered by Captain Arthur Hastings until Agatha **Christie** retired Hastings to the Argentine; he reappeared in the last book in the series, *Curtain* (1975). Like Holmes, the Belgian Poirot was an outsider, unmoved by sentimentality when investigating a crime and, above all, capable of thinking the unthinkable – recognising in one of his most celebrated cases that murder might have been committed not just by one or two of the suspects, but by all of them. Such daring touches helped cement his legendary reputation, second only to Holmes.

G.K. **Chesterton**'s Father Brown (modelled on a cleric from Bradford) was unusual not merely in his calling but also in drawing morals from the cases he investigated. For the first thirty years of the twentieth century, however, the prevailing fashion was for ingenious mysteries to be solved by upper-class detectives of independent means. The trend was initiated by E.C. **Bentley**'s Philip Trent and by Antony Gillingham, created by A.A. Milne, whose fame today rests on books about Winnie-the-Pooh.

Some detectives of the Roaring Twenties boasted a proud military record. Colonel Lysander Gore appears in novels by Lynn Brock, such as *The Kink* (1925), characterised by puzzles so elaborate that the explanations were exhausting. The reputation of Philip **Macdonald**, creator of Colonel Anthony Gethryn, has survived better than Brock's, because he wrote with panache. Gethryn first appeared in *The Rasp* (1924) and made his final bow as late as 1959 in *The List of Adrian Messenger*, a novel which in style and spirit belongs to the Golden Age. Anthony Berkeley's vain, erratic yet irrepressible writer sleuth Roger Sheringham, Nicholas **Blake**'s Nigel Strangeways and Edmund **Crispin**'s breezy don Gervase Fen are notable for the ingenuity which they bring to solving a string of elaborately contrived murders.

In Dorothy L. **Sayers**'s first novel, *Whose Body?* (1923), Lord Peter **Wimsey** might have escaped from the pages of a P.G. Wodehouse comedy. But soon Sayers became frustrated by the superficiality and constraints of the classic form. Previously, detectives' characters had scarcely been developed during a series – with a few largely unsatisfactory exceptions, such as Raffles's late metamorphosis into a hero during the Boer War – but once Wimsey met the love of his life, Harriet Vane, he embarked on a journey towards becoming that Golden Age rarity, a three-dimensional character. Unfortunately, his detective work suffered in the process; *Gaudy Night* (1935) and *Busman's Honeymoon* (1937) are, despite their prolixity, much admired by Sayers fans, but when judged as mysteries must be counted as inferior. A critical cliché is that Sayers made the mistake of 'falling in love with her detective'. It is more accurate, and less patronising, to conclude that the transformation in the portrayal of Wimsey is simply too ambitious. If Sayers could have conceived a fresh hero, she might not have become so disenchanted that she abandoned the genre.

Margery **Allingham** went a step further in the snobbery stakes by hinting that her detective Albert **Campion** might be an heir to the throne. Like Wimsey, Campion grew more serious as the years passed, but he tends to be more of an observer than Lord Peter, less central to the novels in which he appears. In common with many amateur sleuths, he enjoyed excellent connections with the official police. Wimsey's brother-in-law was a chief inspector; Campion was on close terms with the Cockney Scotland Yard man Charlie Luke.

Female detectives appeared from the 1860s onwards, but few showed staying power until Christie introduced Miss Jane **Marple**. Christie's master stroke was to focus on the universal nature of human frailties and to have Marple draw endless parallels between misdemeanours in a small village and the events in the murder mysteries she began to encounter with startling regularity in her twilight years. Yet for all her self-deprecation, Marple benefited from a first-class network. Her nephew Raymond is a novelist rich enough to send his aunt on holiday trips which inevitably resulted in close encounters with murder, while her insight is much admired by Sir Henry Clithering of Scotland Yard. Gladys **Mitchell**'s Mrs Bradley, consultant psychiatrist to the Home Office, is a lively but improbable character who first appears in *Speedy Death* (1929), only to commit murder and be duly tried. Acquitted, she confesses her guilt to the defence counsel, who happens to be her son. Compared in appearance to a pterodactyl, she pursued her investigations for a further fifty-five years, before becoming transformed by the magic of television into glamorous Diana Rigg – like Mrs Bradley, a Dame of the British Empire.

One of the first policemen to take centre stage, rather than playing second fiddle to a talented amateur, was Inspector Joseph French. The title of his debut, *Inspector French's Greatest Case* (1925), suggests that Freeman Wills **Crofts** failed to anticipate the eventual length of his career. But French's methodical style suited the meticulously constructed narratives, and he continued to eat heartily (this was almost the limit of Crofts's attempts at characterising his hero) and dismantle seemingly unbreakable alibis until the late 1950s. Raymond **Chandler** damned Crofts with faint praise for his mastery of 'plodding detail', and Julian **Symons** rated him as foremost of the 'Humdrum' school of writers, whose members included John Rhode, creator of the humourless mathematics professor Dr Lancelot Priestley, and the eminent Fabians G.D.H. Cole and Margaret Cole, whose Superintendent Henry Wilson is a contender for the dubious accolade of dullest series detective.

Sir Basil Thomson drew on experience as head of the CID at Scotland Yard to write about the cases of Richardson, a Scot who advanced with amazing speed from the rank of police constable to chief constable. However, Thomson lacked the literary skills of the under-rated Henry **Wade**, whose sound understanding of police work (he was a Justice of the Peace) was allied with a flair for plotting and characterisation. Many of his finest books featured the Oxford graduate Inspector John Poole; *Lonely Magdalen* (1940) offers an impressive blend of detailed (but never tedious) police procedure, moving characterisation of a murdered prostitute and a sophisticated narrative structure.

Ngaio **Marsh**'s Roderick Alleyn and Michael **Innes**'s John Appleby were well-bred senior police officers who owed much in conception to the tradition of the Golden Age sleuth. More believable is Cyril **Hare**'s stolid Inspector Mallett, who initially worked solo, but grew in stature after developing a mutually respectful relationship with the unlucky barrister Francis Pettigrew. The pair's first encounter is in *Tragedy at Law* (1942), a masterpiece of legal mystification. The collaboration of professional and amateur is much more credible than in, say, the cases of Rupert Penny's Inspector Beale, whose stock-broker friend Tony acts his Watson. Penny's enjoyable books, written in a quick burst between 1936 and 1941, represent the last gasp of the Golden Age. Hare pointed the way ahead.

After the Second World War, the '**police procedural**' novel was developed in the United Kingdom by writers with personal experience of routine police work, such as Maurice Procter, whose DCI Harry Martineau's cases included the excellent *Hell Is a City* (1954), and John **Wainwright**. John **Creasey**'s books about George Gideon of Scotland Yard are among the best of hundreds of novels produced in an extraordinarily busy life. The most successful police series have, however, featured detectives as memorable as, if rather more realistic than, their illustrious fictional forebears. P.D. **James**'s Adam **Dalgliesh**, who rises to the rank of Commander in the Metropolitan Police, beguiles his leisure hours by establishing a considerable reputation as a poet. *Devices and Desires* (1989) is among the most finely wrought of all novels in the tradition of the conventional detective story. Ruth **Rendell**'s Reginald **Wexford** is a devoted if sometimes irascible family man, whose wife and daughters play an important part in the stories. The early Wexfords are relatively orthodox, although praiseworthy for plotting that is as incisive as Rendell's prose. Later books address contemporary social issues such as racism within the whodunit framework in a way that Innes and Crispin never contemplated. Yet utilising a series detective imposes constraints on a writer, and many of Rendell's finest novels, under her own name and as Barbara Vine, dispense altogether with an investigating police officer.

Reginald **Hill**'s duo Dalziel and Pascoe relish their sparky relationship; the contrast between the coarse superintendent and the intellectual sidekick is as cleverly depicted as their concealed but deeply felt mutual respect. The well-realised Yorkshire setting adds depth to the books; rich humour and literary fireworks enable books such as *Dialogues of the Dead* (2001) to succeed on several levels. The development of Colin **Dexter**'s Oxford pairing, Chief Inspector Morse and Sergeant Lewis, was influenced by the success of the television series which made them household names; again, the grudging regard that exists between the gifted, if often fallible sleuth and his loyal second in command, is skilfully conveyed. John **Harvey**'s Charlie Resnick (Nottingham) and Peter **Robinson**'s Alan Banks (Yorkshire) are appealing examples of that increasingly common figure, the regional cop; no longer do local forces faced with complex murder enquiries routinely call in Scotland Yard, let alone a gifted and idiosyncratic amateur. Ian **Rankin**'s bestsellers about Edinburgh-based DI John **Rebus** have achieved even greater heights with their blend of taut prose, sharp characterisation and an in-depth depiction of a society in the throes of change.

The private eye sub-genre has always enjoyed more popularity with American writers than with British writers, and such beguiling home-grown gumshoes as James's Cordelia Gray and Liza **Cody**'s Anna Lee flourished for relatively short periods. So did Duffy, who appeared in four books written by the celebrated novelist Julian **Barnes** under the pseudonym Dan Kavanagh, and James Hazell, created by P.B. **Yuill**, a name concealing the identities of Gordon Williams and the former England football manager Terry Venables. Reginald Hill's black shamus Joe Sixsmith cannot match Dalziel and Pascoe for popularity. The definitive British private eye has yet to emerge.

Oddly, the amateur detective has continued to flourish. In the 1950s, Beverley Nichols introduced Horatio Green, whose exceptional 'olfactory sense' was an aid to his detective work. The twin Shaffer brothers, Peter and Anthony, both better known as playwrights, created Mr Verity (also, confusingly, called Mr Fantom in one book), who investigated three ingeniously contrived mysteries. V.C. Clinton-Baddeley's elderly academic, Dr Davie, meddled with five recorded cases in the 1960s and 1970s, while the actor Charles Paris nearly drank himself to death in the course of solving crimes entertainingly concocted by Simon **Brett**. Ann **Cleeves** began with books featuring an elderly pair of ornithologists with a penchant for stumbling across mysteries in rural Britain, before concentrating on a variety of police detectives: Stephen Ramsay, Vera Stanhope and Shetland's Jimmy Perez. Series characters with professional links – albeit sometimes rather tenuous – to murder investigation have continued to proliferate. Among the lawyers with a taste for crime are Michael **Underwood**'s Rosa Epton, Martin **Edwards**'s Liverpool-based Harry Devlin and Frances **Fyfield**'s Helen West. Journalist sleuths include Lesley **Grant-Adamson**'s Rain Morgan, Jim **Kelly**'s Philip Dryden and Mike **Phillips**'s Sam Dean. Dean is one of the few notable ethnic minority detectives so far created by a British crime novelist, but his appearances are infrequent. Merchant bankers Mark Treasure and Tim Simpson encounter mysteries in novels by David **Williams** and John Malcolm, respectively, while the lecherous antique dealer Lovejoy, created by Jonathan **Gash**, developed an appreciative audience, initially among the reading public and later through television adaptations. During the past decade, forensic psychiatrists and pathologists have become more prominent and Val **McDermid**'s profiler Tony Hill has also made the transition from page to screen.

Julian Symons noted that the law of diminishing returns applies to comedy crime series. The same applies to detectives in those series. Among the most entertainingly drawn are Tim **Heald**'s Board of Trade investigator Simon Bognor and Peter **Guttridge**'s journalist Nick Madrid. Humorous series about professional cops include Joyce **Porter**'s featuring fat and lazy Chief Inspector Dover and Colin **Watson**'s DI Purbright.

Historical detective stories were written from time to time before the 1970s, but only after Peter **Lovesey** created the Victorian policeman Sergeant Cribb, and Ellis **Peters** the medieval herbalist Brother Cadfael, was the potential of the past for crime fiction fully recognised. An advantage of history mysteries is that authors are not fettered by the complications, and intermittent tedium, of modern police routine and investigative techniques. Another is that, especially in the days before professional police forces, the amateur detective can operate more plausibly than in the present day. The enormous success of the Cadfael books opened the floodgates;

almost all historical periods have now seen a good deal of fictional sleuthing – frequently by characters created, either under his own name or under a pseudonym, by the astonishingly industrious Paul **Doherty**. Leading detectives of bygone days include Rome's Marcus Didius Falco, the fourteenth-century Cambridge physician Matthew Bartholomew and Tudor London's hunchback lawyer Matthew Shardlake, created by Lindsey **Davis**, Susanna **Gregory** and C.J. **Sansom**, respectively. Two different series, by Bruce Alexander and Deryn **Lake**, centre on the same real-life historical figure, the blind magistrate John Fielding, while both Keith Miles and Andrew **Martin** have followed the example of Victor L. **Whitechurch** a century earlier by writing about specialist 'railway detectives'. A recent trend has been the setting of books in the relatively recent past. Andrew **Taylor**, whose first series detective was the amoral William Dougal, has more recently focused on stand-alones and the Lydmouth series, which derives as much strength from its evocation of austere post-war Britain as from its setting in a small town on the Welsh borders and the complex relationship between DI Richard Thornhill and journalist Jill Francis.

H.R.F. **Keating** with India's Inspector Ghote, James **Melville** with Japan's Superintendent Otani and Michael **Dibdin** with the Italian Aurelio Zen led the way in setting detective series overseas. But there is a never-ending tide of UK-based police detectives. Lovesey has switched successfully from Cribb, and three books in which the future King Edward VIII detects murder mysteries, to contemporary crime with Bath-based Detective Superintendent Peter Diamond. Mark **Billingham**'s DI Tom Thorne is one of the most popular of the relative newcomers, but many worthy names could be added to the list.

Inevitably, readers would be tired of detectives with personalities drawn from formula or cliché – such as the maverick loner with a drink problem who carries on investigating even when his unsympathetic boss throws him off the case. In the 1990s, the novel of psychological suspense gained in popularity. Like Rendell when writing as Barbara Vine, Minette **Walters** proved that it was possible to match critical acclaim with high sales by writing well-plotted and sophisticated stand-alone novels; several writers of high calibre have followed this lead. Nevertheless, the attractions of series to both readers and writers remain strong and crime novelists will undoubtedly continue to conjure up fresh and intriguing mystery-solvers. The detective is a character with enduring appeal. *See also* The Great Detectives: Sherlock Holmes, Hercule Poirot, Lord Peter Wimsey; Male Crime Writers; Origins of British Crime Fiction; The Police in Golden Age Crime Fiction; Psychic Detectives; TV Detectives: Small-Screen Adaptations *and* Women Crime Writers.

Selected Works
Wilkie Collins, *The Moonstone* (1868)
Arthur Conan Doyle, *A Study in Scarlet* (1887)
Agatha Christie, *The Mysterious Affair at Styles* (1920)
Dorothy L. Sayers, *The Nine Tailors* (1934)
Cyril Hare, *Tragedy at Law* (1942)
Ruth Rendell, *Shake Hands Forever* (1975)
Ellis Peters, *A Morbid Taste for Bones* (1977)
Peter Lovesey, *Waxwork* (1978)
James, P.D. *Devices and Desires* (1989)
Reginald Hill, *Bones and Silence* (1995)
Ian Rankin, *Black and Blue* (1997)
Val McDermid, *The Wire in the Blood* (1997)

Further Reading
Binyon, T.J. 1989. *Murder Will Out: The Detective in Fiction*. Oxford University Press.
Keating, H.R.F. 1982. *Whodunit?* Windward.
Symons, Julian. 1992. *Bloody Murder: From Detective Story to Crime Novel*, 3rd edn. Viking.

Martin Edwards

Detective Magazine

Britain's first specialist crime fiction magazine was published fortnightly by Amalgamated Press and edited by George Dilnot. It ran for sixty-five issues from 24 November 1922 to 8 May 1925.

The **magazine** was published in the standard quarto size, running to 100 pages, and was a mixture of pulp paper and semi-coated stock to allow reproduction of illustrations and photographs. Dilnot was a student of detection as well as a writer. He invited many former superintendents and chief inspectors at Scotland Yard to write about their greatest cases and also secured articles from pathologists and early forensic scientists.

The first issue led with a serial by Edgar Wallace, 'Flat 2', and after the third episode readers were asked to predict the solution. Many of the short stories were reprints from leading American magazines, including works by Octavus Roy Cohen, Arthur B. Reeve, R.T. Maitland Scott and Clarence B. Kelland. Other stories were by the publisher's own stable of writers, most notably Gwyn Evans, although Valentine Williams contributed a new serial, 'The Orange Divan' (30 March–20 July 1923), Oliver Madox Hueffer presented several stories about his clever villain Monsieur Letruc, starting with 'The Day of the Envelopes' (6 June 1924), and there was an early mystery by Georgette **Heyer**, 'Linckes' Great Case' (2 March 1923).

Although it was well illustrated and ran some good quality fiction, the magazine never seemed to catch on. It may be due to the lack of any central, regular series character and too great a preponderance on non-fiction, and the magazine was merged with its companion, *The Premier Magazine*, in May 1925, the title continuing in the magazine for just two further issues.

Further Reading
Indexed by Steve Holland at 'The FictionMags Index' Website http://www.philsp.com/homeville/ FMI/0start.htm.

Mike Ashley

Dexter, Colin (b.1930)

Colin Dexter would claim a place in British crime-writing history along with Arthur Conan **Doyle** and Agatha **Christie** for the simple feat of having given us an iconic detective hero Morse, whom some would argue is worthy to rank alongside **Holmes**, **Marple** and **Poirot**.

Educated at Stamford School, Dexter did National Service in the Royal Corps of Signals before going on to read Classics at Christ's College, Cambridge, and going into teaching, a career he was forced out of early, to the immense benefit of the world of popular fiction, by deafness in 1966.

Dexter made a fateful move with his family from Northampton to Oxford, and while on a holiday, he was inspired by a bad detective story he read to try to do better. He spent three years struggling with this first effort, and the result, *Last Bus to Woodstock*, a crime mystery set indelibly in his new local environment, was published in 1975, introducing Morse to an unsuspecting world.

It was not yet – not wholly – the Morse we have all come to know and love, though many of the traits are established here. Morse is bright (ferociously so) and loves good real ale, crosswords, classical music and a lively literary discussion; he is incisive, instinctive but tends to leave most of the **police procedural** to his sidekick Detective Sergeant Lewis.

Dexter is a keen crossword fan and claims to have taken his hero's surname from the crossword solver champion Sir Jeremy Morse. Morse's first name, as we shall see, is another matter.

What surprises most latter-day Morse aficionados on encountering this inaugural book for the first time is that initially the roles of the protagonists were slightly reversed: with Morse the younger man and Lewis his dependable elder factotum.

The story line, firmly anchored in the Oxford landscape but with a delicious overlap between town and gown, begins with the discovery of a young woman's body in a pub car park. The only clues to her death are a coded letter to a friend and a hand-delivered envelope which looks as though it might have contained a lot of money.

The plot which unfolds concerns illicit sex, academic jealousy and the hypocritical morals of a prestigious university town, all the elements which came to be quintessential to the Morse series, particularly as the detective evolved.

In *Last Seen Wearing* (1977), the case of a schoolgirl gone missing on her way home is reopened after unexpected evidence turns up two years later. Morse's traits here become increasingly fleshed out: his academic sensibilities as well as his tetchiness and the fallibility that occasionally accompanies his flights of brilliance are more marked.

As the character evolves, the reader is given more and more clues to his make-up: a passion for classic cars, a promising academic background including scholarship to Oxford that ended in unexplained circumstances with him being 'sent down' (forced to leave) and a spell in the army before joining the police with a consequent chip on his shoulder about academic pomposity.

The one thing we are definitely *not* given at this stage is his first name. Consistently he acts as if he does not have one and tells those who ask him that they can call him 'Inspector' if they do not like 'Morse'. There is another chip on his shoulder: an embarrassing first name.

There were to be thirteen Morse novels plus several short stories. But it was not until Dexter had published the first seven that Morse mania really took off, fired by a supremely well filmed and acted ITV television series, starring John Thaw as Morse and Kevin Whately as (the by-now-younger) Lewis.

The first three episodes shown in 1987 were based on novels *The Dead of Jericho* (1981), *The Silent World of Nicholas Quinn* (1977) and *Service of All the Dead* (1979) and were phenomenal successes, watched by eighteen million people.

While the overwhelming success of the television series ensured huge sales of the Morse books, at this stage it also risked taking over Dexter's character as the demand for further episodes outstripped Dexter's output.

While ITV were commissioning scriptwriters to turn out more and increasingly adventurous Morse episodes, Dexter was still working on *The Wench Is Dead* (1989), a quasi-historical mystery investigated by Morse partly at long range with Lewis's assistance from a hospital bed.

Highly reminiscent of Josephine Tey's *The Daughter of Time* (1951), a fictional reinvestigation of the deaths of the 'princes in the Tower' under the reign of Richard III, *The Wench Is Dead* was based on a real Victorian murder which Morse convincingly reinterprets. It was, however, a wild departure from the previous books and by its very nature – with Morse confined to hospital – less immediately telegenic than the others. By now, in fact, the success of the ITV series was already self-perpetuating as series after series scripts were commissioned from other writers.

The second series had exhausted all the previous Morse books – in all there were to be thirty-three two-hour episodes of the television series, twenty more than the total number of books.

Dexter consulted on the series, providing all the plot lines in the early days and regularly appearing – à la Alfred Hitchcock – in cameo scenes: as an attendee at a funeral, drinker in a bar, man in college porter's lodge, etc.

By this stage, the television series and books had effectively fused and cross-fertilised. As John **le Carré** would admit that Alec Guinness's portrayal of George Smiley in the televised version of *Tinker, Tailor, Soldier, Spy* (1979) had transformed his mental image of his hero, so John Thaw had become Morse for Dexter as much as for the millions of viewers.

This had visible effects: not only had the originally older character of Lewis long since rejuvenated to fit the younger actor, but also the classic car that Morse so ostentatiously treasures in the early books morphs without mention from a Lancia into the red classic Jaguar Mark 2 that the television producers had preferred.

The one thing that Dexter could not do, however, was keep up with the voracious appetite of the television studios and by now global audiences. From the beginning, he had been providing plot lines and supervising the scriptwriters, but as Morse on the box moved into the sixth and seventh series, Dexter was obliged to take a back seat.

Although the television version continued to garner acclaim, one or two of the episodes, noticeably a trip to Australia, veered worryingly away from the original character, while the death count in Oxford soared alarmingly (a fact much mocked by Dexter).

However, Dexter never lost control of (or became out of touch with) his character. It was the books that were his prime concern. 'The Wolvercote Tongue' was an original Dexter story line which appeared on television as the first episode in the second series broadcast in 1988 and it did not appear as a Morse book until 1991, when it was published as *The Wolvercote Tongue*.

Throughout the 1990s, as Morse on television became a national institution, Dexter continued to pursue his hero's exploits on the printed page, with each new book now guaranteed automatic instant bestseller status.

As the books appeared, now they were immediately put into television production. In *The Way through the Woods*, the conviction of a four-times murderer posed Morse with a problem when a fifth woman's body is found in the woods. The book appeared in 1992 and it was broadcast as a television 'special' in 1995.

The Daughters of Cain (1994), a story of multiple sexual obsession within a college ending in murder, got the same treatment, its broadcast treated as almost a national event. *Death Is Now My Neighbour*, another story of academic skullduggery leading to murder, was published in 1996 and rushed into production to meet Morse fever for 1997.

Such was the demand for Dexter's work, rather than that of the hired-in series scriptwriters whose attempts, it was by now widely felt, had begun to stretch the context too far, that even the long-neglected *The Wench Is Dead* was successfully adapted for the screen.

Dexter's long-term fans, however, were by now beginning to feel that the cross-fertilisation had perhaps gone too far and that the books, which had become noticeably shorter, too often felt like television scripts.

There were clear signs too that Dexter was eventually, reluctantly tiring of the lovably irascible monster he had created. He decided to do the indecent thing: he killed him off.

'He started out in his early forties and he must be at least seventy now. Very few police officers are over their mid-fifties. Right from the word go he was drinking too much and not looking after himself very well, not spending enough time sleeping or exercising.'

It was perhaps a rather dispiritingly realistic way to end the existence of a major character in British fiction, but almost certainly inevitable: Agatha Christie had long yearned to kill off Poirot whom she had come to find 'insufferable'.

At least Dexter was not about to make the Conan Doyle mistake, after he at long last achieved his ambition of sending Sherlock Holmes to his death, of bringing him back from the grave.

Rune readers would have seen the sign of Morse's impending demise in the ending of *Death Is Now My Neighbour*, not so much in the title (though it was a broad hint) but in the fact that Morse finally revealed his first name.

The dread name was, he confessed with no little embarrassment, Endeavour, a curse bestowed on him by the fact that his parents were Quakers who believed in naming children after virtues, and the fact that his father had been a huge admirer of Captain Cook and saw no difficulty naming his son after a ship.

The revelation put to an end a speculation which had swept the British nation, prompting major coverage even in the national newspapers. No surprise, therefore, that it seemed almost a millennial event when the detective died on the page in 1999 and on screen in 2000.

Unfortunately – if inevitably – it was not the best book and the title, *The Remorseful Day*, was by far the worst thing about it. Although actually, and fittingly, a quotation from a poem by A.E. Housman, it came across as too much of a cheap pun. Thaw, however, managed to put so much emotion into the television death that a nation was virtually weeping into its pints of ale, just as the Chief Inspector would have expected.

The Morse phenomenon was a perhaps unique late-twentieth-century synthesis of page and screen, taking a character from a popular novel and making him a contemporary national icon in a way unmatched except for **Fleming**'s James Bond whose on-screen incarnation soon parted company from the original in a way Morse thankfully never did.

Dexter has listed his unfulfilled ambitions as batting in a test cricket match for England and crossing swords with Margaret Thatcher in parliamentary debate during her time as prime minister. Those he has little chance of achieving, but in Morse he has given the nation a legacy that his legions of fans would rate as much more valuable.

ITV has since played with reinventing Inspector Lewis in a series entitled simply *Lewis*. Dexter has wisely stayed well clear. *See also* Academe, Death in; *Inspector Morse* (television series, 1987-2000) *and* TV Detectives: Small-Screen Adaptations.

Selected Works by the Author
Last Bus to Woodstock (1975)
Last Seen Wearing (1977)
The Riddle of the Third Mile (1983)
Daughters of Cain (1994)
Death Is Now My Neighbour (1996)
The Remorseful Day (1999)

Peter Millar

Dibdin, Michael (1947–2007)

'This anthology is dedicated to the proposition that good crime writing is good writing' is the opening sentence of Michael Dibdin's introduction to his anthology *The Picador Book of Crime Writing* (1993). It was an assertion that Dibdin exemplified in his work, which challenged generally with good humour, sometimes with impatience – the constraints and parameters of crime fiction. Dibdin was not a conventional producer in the genre, and there is moodiness to his books, often reflected in the shifting emotional states of his principal creation, Aurelio Zen, which not only causes their quality to vary but also guarantees that they are far removed from the conveyor-belt smoothness of some other writers in the field. When you open one, you are never quite sure what you are going to get. Nevertheless, in Aurelio Zen, Dibdin created one of the most memorable and popular detectives of recent years as well as producing several distinctive stand-alone novels.

Dibdin was born in Wolverhampton. His father was an academic physicist (who then became a collector of folk songs), and the family moved several times in his early life, a pattern he was to replicate in adulthood. He was educated in Lisburn, County Antrim, and afterwards took degrees in English Literature at Sussex University and the University of Alberta in Edmonton. He did various jobs in Canada, returned as a married man to England and then went on alone to Italy, where he taught English at Perugia University in the early 1980s, before taking up a full-time writing career following the success of the Zen novels. He married the American mystery writer K.K. Beck in 1997 and for several years lived in Seattle, where he died.

Dibdin's first crime novel, *The Last Sherlock Holmes Story* (1978), was produced at a time when revisions and pastiches of the **Holmes** saga were even more in fashion than usual. His take on the canon was characteristically mordant and individual, even if the set-up was hardly new. The book, masquerading as a manuscript written by Dr Watson and discovered years after his death, pits Holmes against Jack the Ripper. This collision between two of the most iconic figures in late Victorian England had been done before (and will probably be done again), but Dibdin's 'solution' was both satisfying and likely to offend the purists. Several years were to pass before the appearance of the next book, *A Rich Full Death* (1986), again a knowing and enjoyable literary recreation like the Holmes/Ripper story, but this time poet Robert Browning turns detective in mid-nineteenth-century Florence.

If there was a sense in which Dibdin had merely seemed to be playing with the form in his first two books, he found his voice in *Ratking* (1988), the first of the Zen novels and the winner of the **Crime Writers' Association** Gold Dagger for best crime novel of the year. The narrative, in which Zen is sent to investigate a kidnapping in Perugia, at once introduced us to Dibdin's favourite themes of corruption, Kafkaesque bureaucracy and family secrecy. These subjects were revealed, in the sequence of novels which followed *Ratking*, to be an inescapable part of the Italian – if not the human – condition. Zen was at first a curiously unfocused figure, lacking in background, partly because Dibdin had not begun by contemplating a series and partly because, as he explained in an interview with *January* magazine in 1999, he was not particularly interested in him at the outset. 'He's really just a facilitator who comes in and makes it possible for other things to happen. My main interest was in the other people. The potential suspects and accomplices and so on.' In a later description which he provided of Aurelio Zen, Dibdin might have been harking back to Sherlock Holmes, the subject of his earliest novel, since he refers to his hero as being 'tall and rather gaunt, with a pale grave face dominated by an angular nose' (*Dead Lagoon*, 1994). Like Holmes, Zen is a loner. He has colleagues rather than friends, although some characters recur in the novels and offer support at crucial moments or are there for the exchange of banter. Unlike Holmes, though, Zen is of the world rather than above it. He enjoys a tangled love and sex life, as well as having a mother to be cared for and placated, while in *A Long Finish* (1998), he encounters a putative illegitimate daughter Carla, who also appears in *Blood Rain* (1999).

Ratking was followed by the Sardinian-set *Vendetta* (1990), a variant on the locked-room mystery (the murders being caught on video tape), and ten other Zen novels, one of them – titled, with ironic aptness, *End Games* (2007) – appearing posthumously. Aurelio Zen's position in the Criminalpol department at the Ministry of the Interior gave him a roving brief to investigate cases all over mainland Italy, as well as in Sicily and Sardinia, and provided Dibdin with the opportunity to show off his profound familiarity with a country which inspired equal measures of affection, exasperation and cynicism. Each book draws some of its flavour from the milieu in which it is set. Taken together, the Zen novels offer a panorama of Italian culture at the end of the second millennium, a panorama which prompted some critics to claim that Dibdin was a more insightful commentator than many journalists or academics. Italy is revealed not so much as a country but as a land of jostling regions and provinces, uneasily linked to a Roman centre which will regularly fail to hold.

The labyrinthine and self-serving bureaucracy of Italian life, the country's constant shifts of government and the national taste for conspiracy and paranoid speculation serve as a backdrop to the tales and provide fertile material for detective fiction. In *Cabal* (1992), Zen is called on to investigate the death plunge of a minor aristocrat from the dome of the basilica of St Peter's in Rome. The setting in the Vatican, conventionally seen as an archetypal centre of conspiracy and back-stabbing, allows Dibdin to play with our expectations. The 'cabal' is apparently a shadowy organisation dedicated to restoring the prestige of the Catholic Church by subterfuge or force. In fact, the organisation is non-existent, although belief in it fuels much of the plot of the book (the last paradoxical words of which are 'it turned out to be real'). Zen's cynical acceptance of his country's traditions is shown by his willingness to go along with whatever story the Vatican wants to spin and his (failed) intention to extract money from the villain at the end.

In *Dead Lagoon*, Zen returns to his birthplace Venice, and the spectral quality of that place, with its phantasmagoric changes of light, informs a story which is preoccupied with the ghosts of the past. The immediate context is a drug-smuggling plot and the machinations of a political party based on the real-life Northern League, but the shadows of the break-up of former Yugoslavia and, beyond that, the deportation of Jews from Venice under Fascism give a regressive feel as one layer of historical 'truth' is unpeeled to provide a glimpse of the next. Zen's world is customarily the middle-class state, church and police bureaucracy – whose functionaries the detective struggles to keep at arm's length while always being conscious that he depends on their favour – but in his next book, *A Long Finish*, set among the truffle-hunters and wine-growers of Piedmont in the north of Italy, his creator showed that he was equally at home with the contadino or peasant class. Their cynical savvy and ruthlessness outdoes, if anything, that of the cardinals and the politicians.

No author can examine Italy with the intensity that Dibdin did and ignore the Mafia, and so in *Blood Rain*, he sent Zen to the heartland, Sicily. The book begins with the discovery of a decomposing corpse in a railway goods wagon, and the narrative switches between Zen's investigations and the complicated and competing factions of the Mafiosi families. At the end of *Blood Rain*, Dibdin again played a Holmes-style card when it seemed as though he might have killed off Zen after the policeman's car was blown up in an apparent Mafia ambush. The successor novel, *And Then You Die* (2002), opens with the teasing sentence 'Aurelio Zen was dead to the world'. He is, of course, still with us but living under an assumed identity on the Ligurian coast as he prepares to be flown to the United States to give evidence in a crucial anti-Mafia trial. The book – best read as a coda to the previous one since it clears up the mystery of exactly who targeted Zen in Sicily – has a disorientating feel, perhaps reflecting the hero's fragile physical and mental state. A surreal and faintly pointless excursion to Iceland, where the detective's US flight is grounded because the plane's toilets are blocked, is characteristic of this least successful of the Zen novels. Fortunately, Dibdin and Zen were back on form for what is the best of the later books, *Medusa* (2003), at the beginning of which human remains are discovered in a military tunnel in the Dolomites. As in *Cabal*, the subject is the Italian love–hate relationship with the idea of secret societies and hidden events. Drawing an analogy with the underground tunnels, the author says in a characteristic aside that the country's public history remains 'riddled with the secret network of events collectively dubbed the *misteri d'Italia*' (*Medusa*, ch.V). In this case, the conspiracy dates from the 1970s when a quasi-Fascist group set up to undermine that the left is, in fact, used as the cover for a murder instigated by a military man who has been cuckolded. As often, the reverberations of a crime echo through the following decades.

Apart from the Zen books, which were commercially and critically his most successful work, Dibdin produced a number of distinct novels in which the focus was more on psychology and interior suspense than the traditions of the whodunit mystery. 'The Tryst' (1989) is a brooding story concerned with drop-outs and the dispossessed, whose place in the glitzy, materialistic world of 1980s Britain was increasingly of interest to novelists at the time. A more mischievous look at the same period is to be found in *Dirty Tricks* (1991), which races along in fine satirical style and is the most purely entertaining of Dibdin's non-series stories.

Dibdin's longest and most ambitious novel outside the Zen sequence is *Dark Spectre* (1995). Written soon after his move to Seattle, the book is in part a reflection of his thoughts and feelings about the United States, a land which is daunting in its size, its dizzying opportunities and the constant potential for idealism to turn murderous. Dibdin was always interested in playing off established forms and *Dark Spectre* also takes a fresh look at the quintessentially American sub-genre: hunt the serial killer. The novel is intentionally disorientating in its structure. A suburban beginning in Seattle introduces a mother and children whose lightly sketched-in characters suggest that they are not going to last beyond the opening pages. They are abruptly slaughtered by unseen killers. Other deaths take place at apparently random and anonymous locations around the States, in a Chicago suburb, Atlanta, Kansas. Kristine Kjarstadt, a female detective back in Seattle, starts to join up the dots between the murders, but it is characteristic of the book that the leads peter out and that her involvement in the resolution of the story comes about largely by chance. Interwoven with the third-person accounts of the killings and the police investigations is the first-person narrative of a college teacher who, following the apparent disappearance of his son and the suicide of his wife, becomes caught up in a cult responsible for the deaths, a religiose organisation whose teachings are based on warped interpretations of William Blake. The sections of *Dark Spectre* devoted to the cult and its charismatic but demented messiah figure, and the somewhat perfunctory shoot-out which forms a climax, are arguably the less successful parts of the novel, given their inevitable overtones of Jonestown and Waco. But the theory behind the killings, a combination of logic and craziness, is authentically disturbing. At one point, the narrator makes an observation about 'the essential trinity of American life: democracy, idealism, violence', and *Dark Spectre*, Dibdin's most substantial book, offers a semi-outsider's perspective on his adoptive land and on the forces which continue to shape it. Dibdin was something of a one-off figure in British crime writing. A not-quite Englishman and a sort of adoptive American, he wrote at greater length and with more feeling about Italy than he did about anything or anywhere else. When asked, in the *January* magazine article already cited, whether he objected to being regarded as a crime writer, he said, 'The answer is no, I don't, on the whole.' The qualification at the end of the sentence is more revealing than the rest of it. Part of him did want to be taken seriously as a novelist, satirist, commentator, whether on Britain, the United States or Italy – and he was, on the whole, taken seriously by the critics even if most of his public read him 'just' for entertainment.

Dibdin's books are full of acute digressions on architecture, food, politics, regional niceties and cultural attitudes to sex, race, etc. He regularly introduced episodes which are faintly surreal or near-absurd and which have a tangential relation to the plot. The detective element often took second place, and he occasionally showed weariness with the genre to which he had devoted himself. But, at his best, Dibdin was one of the most notable practitioners of crime fiction of the last half century. *See also* Literature and Crime Fiction.

Selected Works by the Author
The Last Sherlock Holmes Story (1978)
A Rich Full Death (1986)
Ratking (1988)
Dirty Tricks (1991)
Cabal (1992)
The Dying of the Light (1993)
Blood Rain (1999)
End Games (2007)

Philip Gooden

Dickens, Charles (1812–1870)

Considered by many to be the greatest British novelist of the Victorian age, Charles Dickens captured the popular imagination as no other writer of fiction had done. Held in high esteem during his lifetime, his work has continued to attract much academic attention, and his general popularity, bolstered by constant film and television adaptations, remains high. Several of his novels concern crime, notably *Oliver Twist* (1841), and, in *Bleak House* (1853), he created the first significant police detective in English fiction, Sergeant Bucket.

Born near Portsmouth, Hampshire, Dickens's childhood was impoverished. The family moved to London in 1815 and then to Chatham, Kent, before returning to London in 1822. His father, a clerk in the Naval Pay Office, was imprisoned for debt in the Marshalsea, and, at the age of twelve, Dickens was sent to work in a blacking factory. Later, he became a shorthand reporter for the law courts and a reporter of debates in the House of Commons. He began contributing articles to periodicals in 1833. *The Posthumous Papers of the Pickwick Club*, published in twenty monthly numbers from April 1836, achieved immense popularity and was published the following year in volume form. Throughout his life, his output, both as novelist and journalist, was prodigious, and he launched two weekly magazines, *Master Humphrey's Clock* (1840), which he wrote single-handedly, and *Household Words* (1850), for which he wrote a series of articles about the 'Detective Office'. *Household Words* was superseded by *All the Year Round* in 1859, which he continued to edit it until his death eleven years later at the early age of fifty-eight. His last novel, *The Mystery of Edwin Drood*, was unfinished at the time of his death, and although there have been attempts to complete it, the extant fragments of material are not sufficient to indicate the solution intended by the author.

There had been various attempts to create detectives in fiction prior to the work of Charles Dickens, and indeed Dickens created one of the first private investigators with Mr Nadgett in *Martin Chuzzlewit* (1843), but it was in *Bleak House* (1853) that the first realistic portrayal of an English police detective emerged. As Julian **Symons** points out (in *Bloody Murder*), 'Bucket engages in no spectacular feats of detection, but he is shown as a shrewd and sympathetic man. In a general way he serves as a model for many later professional detectives.'

The complicated plot of *Bleak House* contains, in the murder of Mr Tulkinghorn, the closest Dickens comes to a 'whodunit' element, but crime, as a motivating force, is central to many of his novels, as are the associated themes of guilt and repentance. Dickens's plots, which are complex (and sometimes far-fetched), are frequently characterised by webs of mystery, and he explores many subjects commonly found in crime fiction, from how poverty can lead to crime (*Oliver Twist*) and to drug addiction (*The Mystery of Edwin Drood*). Obsessive love is tackled in, among others, *Our Mutual Friend* (Bradley Headstone attempts to murder Eugene Wrayburn, his rival for Lizzie Hexam); fraud in *Martin Chuzzlewit*; and greed in *David Copperfield* (where it is accompanied by forgery and theft), *Oliver Twist* and *The Old Curiosity Shop*. Revenge is treated in *Great Expectations* (Miss Haversham enjoying vicarious revenge on men through the heartless Estella). Dickens's work encompasses human weakness in its various forms (gambling, alcoholism, profligacy and the 'ruin' of women) and demonstrates how the secrets of the past can ruin lives. It also abounds in instances of psychological cruelty, from bullying schoolmasters and parents who (wittingly or unwittingly) torment their children to the cruel treatment of wives by husbands.

While Dickens did not fictionalise the lives of real criminals in the manner of the Newgate novels of the highly successful Edward Bulwer-Lytton (1803–1873), he was thorough in his researches and greatly interested by the workings of the **London** police. Much of his material was obtained from men such as Inspector Charles Field of Scotland Yard's Detective Department, who is widely thought to be the model for Inspector Bucket.

Guided by police officers, Dickens took a number of walks through the poorer areas of London (principally, the East End), which he sometimes referred to as 'Babylon', or 'the Great Oven'. There he visited the penny lodging houses, pubs and opium dens that he was to describe so vividly in his novels.

Besides the policeman, Inspector Bucket, amateur investigators make frequent appearances in Dickens's work. Their motives range from the desire for gain to pure altruism. Pancks, in *Little Dorrit*, makes it his business to find those who are missing heirs, and he is thus able to release the Dorrit family from prison. Guppy, in *Bleak House*, discovers Lady Deadlock's secret, although it does not have the desired effect of winning him Esther Summerson's hand in marriage. Tulkinghorn also discovers the secret, but is killed before he can make use of it. In *Martin Chuzzlewit*, the hero's grandfather exposes Pecksniff's treachery and hypocrisy; Micawber discovers the crimes of Uriah Heep in *David Copperfield*; and in *Nicholas Nickleby*, the plots of the wicked Ralph Nickleby are thwarted with the help of his clerk, Newman Noggs.

There is plenty of evidence to suggest that, although the idea of crime writing as a genre did not exist in the nineteenth century, many of Dickens's novels were castigated for reasons that would not be unfamiliar to modern writers of mystery fiction. Victorian commentators criticised Dickens for glamorising violence in his second novel, *Oliver Twist*, and there was much carping about his portrayal of such 'low-life' characters as Bill Sikes the housebreaker, and Nancy, his mistress (presumably a prostitute, although this is not explicitly stated). Contemporary dramatic versions of the book were banned by the Lord Chamberlain on the grounds that the murder of Nancy by Sikes was too violent and degrading a spectacle to put before the public. Dickens (who in later years made this particular scene the highlight of his public readings), defended his book on the grounds that it was a moral tale illustrating how crime did not pay. While this is superficially true, the book's importance lies in the way in which Dickens, for the first time, used the subject of crime as a vehicle for the exposure of social inequities (here, the Poor Law and the exploitation of children by those supposed to be concerned with their welfare) in a manner that must surely be familiar to any reader of twenty-first-century crime fiction. As a journalist, Dickens campaigned for – among other things – more humane measures for reforming juvenile delinquents and against public hanging, because of its degrading effect on the spectators, and these concerns are reflected in *Oliver Twist*. As George Orwell pointed out in his famous essay ('Charles Dickens' in *Decline of the English Murder and other essays*), Dickens 'attacked English institutions with a ferocity that has never since been approached' in his other novels, too (*Hard Times*, *Bleak House* and *Little Dorrit* for example).

Dickens's name is often evoked as a shorthand for the Victorian jollies of the plum-duff-and-party-piece variety. While his work certainly does contain elements of this, it is important to remember that the London he inhabited, bisected by the stinking open sewer that was the river Thames, was a place of degradation and squalor unimaginable to those who have grown up with the safety-net of the Welfare state (not to mention modern plumbing). *Oliver Twist*, to name but one of his works, contains elements which will strike a chord with any reader of twentieth-century noir fiction. This is, perhaps, not surprising – the grim desperation of life during the Great Depression in 1930s America was not, after all, so different from the unremitting harshness of life for the Victorian underclass. The world portrayed in *Oliver Twist* is both literally and metaphorically filthy (in the sense of being corrupt and amoral), and the central character is caught in a Kafkaesque nightmare whereby he can never (until the end) escape from the net in which he is caught. It is interesting to note that Dickens, although concerned that 'the good', in the person of Oliver himself, along with Mr Brownlow and Rose Maylie, 'end happily' as Oscar Wilde has it, the end meted out to Fagin is cruelly and unusually harsh. As Professor John Sutherland has pointed out (in *Can Jane Eyre Be Happy?*), Fagin is hanged, but Pip, in *Great Expectations*, who has assisted in defrauding the Exchequer out of a considerable sum of money, is not even prosecuted. Perhaps Dickens considered that Pip, much sadder and much wiser by the end of the book, had suffered enough. Or perhaps, as Sutherland puts it, the reason is that 'one is a dirty old man and the other is a nice young gent.'

The reader feels sympathy for the devilish Fagin, because, although he is a corrupter of youth (though any pederasty implied in later film or television makeovers of the book is nowhere present in the original), he is, like the wily Artful Dodger, more vividly drawn than any of the 'good' characters, including the hero. Both have a certain music hall quality (greatly exaggerated in Lionel Bart's 1960 chirpy Cockney musical) and seem to delight in sticking two fingers up at the establishment – the latter, of course, being something that the modern crime reader has come to appreciate.

Besides the condemned cell of Fagin, there are many images of prisons in Dickens's work, from the shadow of the hulks from which the convict Magwitch escapes in *Great Expectations* and the long incarcerations of Mr Dorrit in the Marshalsea and Dr Manette in the Bastille (*Little Dorrit* and *A Tale of Two Cities*, respectively) to the more humorous treatment of Mr Pickwick in the Fleet and the satire of Uriah Heap as a model prisoner in a model prison (*The Pickwick Papers* and *David Copperfield*, respectively). Imprisonment, in Dickens's writing, is not always something imposed by a higher authority. This can take the form of parents or guardians, as well as the law courts – the terrible Dotheboys Hall *in Nicholas Nickleby* ('no vacations') with its maltreated, starving pupils, is nothing less than a prison, and Dr Blimber's school (*Dombey and Son*), with its 'forcing system' and strenuous discipline, is not much better. Dickens's work is also full of characters who have chosen to imprison themselves either literally (Miss Haversham in *Great Expectations*) or psychologically, through the straightjackets of adherence to dogma (Mr Gradgrind in *Hard Times*), the demands of fashionable society (Mr and Mrs Merdle in *Little Dorrit*) or emotional repression (Mr Dombey in *Dombey and Son*).

Dickens has been described by some critics as a novelist who created characters who are 'types' that represent a single trait and who are, in the words of Orwell, 'already finished and perfect' as opposed to 'growing'. Although, as Ruskin had it, Dickens, who loved acting, 'chose to work in a circle of stage fire' (everything heightened and melodramatic) and he is never particularly subtle; his grasp of psychology should not be underestimated. In terms of crime writing, this is the whydunit, as opposed to the whodunit – the challenge of establishing the influences and motivation that drive an individual to commit crime, whether it be murder or a lesser transgression – and in this, Dickens excels.

Pre-Freud, he understood clearly that what happens to the child informs the adult (for example, in *David Copperfield* and *Great Expectations*) and was fascinated by the idea of a secret or double life. This dual-identity or self-division is a necessity in a world that depends, largely, upon appearance and the veneer – if nothing else – of respectability. The theme can be seen in its most basic form in characters such as Wemmick, in *Great Expectations*, who, in his working life, plots legal deception in the office of the lawyer Jaggers, yet is gentle and kindly at home. Josiah Bounderby, in *Hard Times*, has fabricated a deprived childhood for himself to make his success seem more impressive, and Mr Boffin, in *Our Mutual Friend*, pretends to have been transformed by his wealth into a hardhearted miser to make Bella Wilfer understand that a loving heart is more important than a fat wallet. In this novel, the dual-identity theme is also presented as a search for wholeness in the character of John Harmon, who is forced to live under assumed names. Esther Summerson, in *Bleak House*, does not know her parentage, and Oliver Twist, named by the guardians of the workhouse, has no idea of his true identity until it is revealed at the end of the book. The quest for truth – a theme that runs through all of fiction, and particularly crime fiction – is paramount in Dickens's work.

He is superb at creating atmosphere, whether it is the semi-criminal waterside milieu in *Our Mutual Friend*, the endless grinding dryness of the court of Chancery in *Bleak House* or the gloomy, claustrophobic household of Mrs Clennam in *Little Dorrit*. His attention to detail is unique, and his strong theatrical instinct, derided by some critics, ensured that his work not only displays a masterful handling of tension but also has an unparalleled visual impact. His fascination with convoluted plots, startling denouements, crime and punishment has ensured that Dickens, like his contemporary Wilkie Collins, played an important part in the development of British crime fiction. *See also* The Detective in British Fiction; Godfathers of British Crime Fiction; Origins of British Crime Fiction *and* Social Comment in Crime Fiction.

Selected Works by the Author
Oliver Twist (1838)
Nicholas Nickleby (1839)
The Old Curiosity Shop (1841)
Barnaby Rudge (1841)
American Notes (non-fiction, 1842)
Martin Chuzzlewit (1844)
Dombey and Son (1848)
David Copperfield (1850)
Bleak House (1853)
Hard Times (1854)
Little Dorrit (1857)
A Tale of Two Cities (1859)
Great Expectations (1861)
Our Mutual Friend (1865)
The Mystery of Edwin Drood (unfinished, 1870)

Further Reading
Ackroyd, Peter. 1990. *Dickens*. Sinclair Stevenson.
Carey, John. 1973. *The Violent Effigy*. Faber.
Collins, Philip. 1962. *Cambridge Studies in Criminology: Dickens and Crime*. Macmillan.

Forster, John. 1874. *The Life of Charles Dickens*. Chapman & Hall.
Leavis, F.R., and Q.D. Leavis. 1970. *Dickens the Novelist*. Chatto & Windus.

Website
http://charlesdickenspage.com/dickens_web.html

Laura Wilson

Dickinson, David (b.1946)

David Dickinson has established his reputation as one of the most elegant practitioners of the **historical** crime novel; his books are civilised, smoothly plotted and crammed with pleasing incidental detail about various branches of the arts (the author's own enthusiasms clearly shine through). If Dickinson has not quite achieved the success that is demonstrably his due, it may be because of the unfortunate confusion of his name with that of a permatanned, bouffanted television personality who is a populist antiques expert. The literary David Dickinson utilises antiques in his excellent novels, but when they are newly minted some centuries ago.

The very English Dickinson was actually born in Dublin. After acquiring a first-class honours degree in classics at Cambridge, he made his mark at the BBC as editor of *Newsnight* and *Panorama*. Another notable success in this field for him was his work as series editor on *Monarchy*, a penetrating examination of the British Royal family. But it was in his subsequent career as a novelist that he found his true métier. His series protagonist is Lord Francis Powerscourt, a patrician art expert called upon to crack baffling mysteries that arise within his own field. A choice example of Dickinson's work is *Death of an Old Master* (2007), in which Powerscourt is called in to investigate the death of one of Britain's leading art experts, only to find that every book, scrap of paper and notepad has mysteriously vanished from the scene of the crime. The dead man had recently produced an article claiming that a number of old Masters were the result of a single hand, and the narrative that follows takes the reader from Corsica to an isolated corner of the English countryside. Like all of Dickinson's novels, it is constructed with subtle skill and couched in alluringly literary prose. The more recent *Death on the Holy Mountain* (2008) demonstrates that Dickinson is continuing to burnish his skills.

Selected Works by the Author
Goodnight, Sweet Prince (2002)
Death and the Jubilee (2002)
Death of an Old Master (2004)
Death Called to the Bar (2006)
Death on the Holy Mountain (2008)

Barry Forshaw

Dickinson, Peter (b.1927)

Poet, novelist and intellectual, Peter Dickinson has written for adults and children in many genres – including crime, fantasy and adventure – and in each, he has set a new benchmark for quality.

He was born Peter Malcolm de Brissac Dickinson on 16 December 1927 in Livingstone, Northern Rhodesia (now Zambia). His family moved to England in 1935 so that he and his three brothers could study at English schools. He was educated at Eton, and after serving in the signal corps during the Second World War, went on to receive a Bachelor of Arts at King's College, Cambridge in 1951. He then became assistant editor and book reviewer of *Punch* magazine for seventeen years, under the aegis of Malcolm Muggeridge among others.

Two-thirds of the way through writing his first detective novel in the late 1960s, Dickinson experienced severe writer's block. To get rid of it, he hurriedly wrote a children's novel, *The Weathermonger* (1969), based on a particularly vivid nightmare he had had, in which the populace of Britain turn against machinery due to an ancient force unearthed from a Welsh hillside. Two further novels expanded on this apocalyptic scenario, *Heartsease* (1969) and *The Devil's Children* (1970), together forming a trilogy that was adapted, in reverse order, into a stunning, ten-part BBC television series in 1975.

After writing *The Weathermonger*, in 1968, Dickinson was finally able to finish his first novel, originally published in the United Kingdom as *Skin Deep* (1968) and in the United States under the author's preferred title of *The Glass-Sided Ants' Nest* (a title it then reverted to in the United Kingdom). Featuring the first appearance of New Scotland Yard detective James Pibble, called on to investigate the death of a New Guinea tribesman in a West London townhouse, the book's eerie blend of surreal fantasy and cosy murder mystery was rewarded with a **Crime Writers' Association**'s Gold Dagger for Fiction. The same accolade was bestowed on the author's second Pibble novel, a baroque spoof about an English stately home run as a theme park, *A Pride of Heroes* (1969, also known as *The Old English Peep-Show*). Four more Pibble titles followed – the final entry, *One Foot in the Grave* (1979), had an old and enfeebled Pibble unmasking a murderer's identity from his nursing-home sickbed.

Dickinson's output is hard to categorise. He is an instinctive writer – plotting is anathema to him – and his books emerge as organic creations that often disobey genre 'rules' in order to tell good stories. *The Green Gene* (1973), for example, was a freewheeling racial satire about a race of green-skinned Irishmen; *The Poison Oracle* (1974), an Arabian murder story with a philological backdrop, while *Walking Dead* (1977), a horror story blending voodoo and vivisection.

His last adult crime book to date was *Some Deaths before Dying* (1999).

Selected Works by the Author
Skin Deep (1968; also published in the United States and later in the UK as *The Glass-Sided Ants' Nest*)
The Seals (1970; also published in the United States as *The Sinful Stones*)
Mandog (1972, with Lois Lamplugh)
The Poison Oracle (1974)
The Lively Dead (1975)
Walking Dead (1977)
One Foot in the Grave (1979)
Hindsight (1983)
Perfect Gallows (1988)

Website
www.peterdickinson.com

Mark Campbell

Doherty, Paul (b.1946)

A British schoolmaster (currently headmaster of a Catholic comprehensive school in Essex), Paul Doherty is also a prolific writer of **historical** mysteries.

Doherty originally studied for the Catholic priesthood but, after three years, switched to History at Liverpool University, where he gained a first-class honours degree. His doctorate was on King Edward II, whose fate he explored in *Isabella and the Strange Death of Edward II* (2003). Doherty puts forward the theory that the king was not murdered but was instead spirited away to the continent. Doherty had originally explored Edward's death in his first novel, *The Death of a King* (1982). He likewise considered what became of the Princes in the Tower in *The Fate of Princes* (1991) and the identity of the Man in the Iron Mask in *The Masked Man* (1991). While he has written several one-off books, the majority of his work falls into a number of series.

The earliest and longest-running series features Sir Hugh Corbett, a clerk in chancery, who, in *Satan in St. Mary's* (1985), is employed by Robert Burnell, the Lord Chancellor, to look into the apparent suicide of a known murderer which the king, Edward I, believes is connected to a movement seeking to depose him. Corbett's success allows him to rise in status, becoming the king's personal spy by the fifth book, *The Prince of Darkness* (1992), and thereafter Keeper of the Secret Seal. The background to each book is firmly rooted in history, using genuine incidents (many of them unsolved mysteries) as the basis for his investigations, although Doherty allows himself licence in developing his idea on the identity of Robin Hood in *The Assassin in the Greenwood* (1993). Doherty revealed that Corbett is based on the historical character of John de Droxford (or Drokensford), who was Keeper of the King's Wardrobe and later became Bishop of Bath and Wells. Doherty also wrote two novels under the alias Vanessa Alexander, of which *The Love Knot* (1999) parallels the Hugh Corbett books, although it features a different clerk-investigator, Henry Trokelowe.

Another series features Matthew Jankyn, a self-confessed liar and thief, who looks back over a long life when he is first employed, in *The Whyte Harte* (1988), to investigate the death of Richard II. Several of Doherty's books emulate the style of John Dickson **Carr**, and this series is the most overt, with ingenious locked-room mysteries and melodramatic intrigue. Also in the style of Carr are Doherty's time-slip novels written as Anne Dukthas, starting with *A Time for the Death of a King* (1994), in which Nicholas Segalla finds himself in various historical periods. This series was short-lived, however, as Doherty experimented with a number of settings and periods, several written under pseudonyms. The best of these experiments is that featuring Sir Roger Shallot, written under the alias Michael Clynes, starting with *The White Rose Murders* (1991) and set in the early years of the reign of Henry VIII.

The Brother Athelstan series, which began with *The Nightingale Gallery* (1991), is set in the late fourteenth century, during the reign of Edward III, and was originally written under the pen-name Paul Harding. It is perhaps the closest Doherty comes to evoking Ellis **Peters**'s Brother Cadfael stories, although Athelstan is no monastic detective, but a penitent who has been assigned to work in the slums of Southwark and assists the coroner, Sir John Cranston. Doherty's other series set in the Middle Ages are the Canterbury Tales sequence narrated by Chaucer's pilgrims, starting with *An Ancient Evil* (1994) and the Kathryn Swinbrooke series, written as C.L. Grace and set in Canterbury in the 1470s.

Doherty has also written several novels set in the ancient world. Under the alias Anna Apostolou, he penned two books, *A Murder in Macedon* (1997) and *A Murder in Thebes* (1998), set during the reign of Alexander the Great, in which two Jewish clerks, Miriam and Simeon Bartimaeus, investigate crimes on his behalf. However, this series was stifled, and with *The House of Death* (2001), Doherty began a new series featuring Telamon, a physician who travels with Alexander on his conquests, resolving any number of violent murders that arise. *The Mask of Ra* (1998) introduced Lord Amerotke, chief judge to the Pharaoh Tuthmosis II in Egypt in 1479 BC. With the second novel, *The Horus Killings* (1999), set after Tuthmosis's death, Amerotke continues as judge and adviser to the pharaoh's widow and successor, Hatusu (or Hatshepsut), and this pairing works well, balancing Hatusu's astuteness and determination against Amerotke's shrewdness and understanding. *Murder Imperial* (2003) began another series, this time set in Rome at the time of Constantine the Great, in which his wife Helena employs female agent Claudia to investigate various intrigues.

At times Doherty's books can be superficial and repetitive, despite a loyal attention to detail. His plots have a tendency to favour the dark and frequently melodramatic aspects of history, with a fascination for the grotesque, but at his best, especially in the Corbett, Shallot and Amerotke series, he succeeds in creating fascinating crimes in authentic and realistic period settings.

Selected Works by the Author
The Death of a King (1985)
The Angel of Death (1989)
The White Rose Murders (as Michael Clynes, 1991)
The House of the Red Slayer (as Paul Harding, 1992)
A Tapestry of Murders (1994)
The Eye of God (as C.L. Grace, 1994)
A Murder in Macedon (as Anna Apostolou, 1997)
The Horus Killings (1999)
The House of Death (2001)

Website
http://www.paulcdoherty.com/index.html

Mike Ashley

Doyle, Arthur Conan (1859–1930)

Arthur Conan Doyle needs less introduction than most crime writers. Quite simply, he is the writer who, more than any other, established the detective-fiction genre as we know it and created the world's most famous fictional detective, Sherlock **Holmes**.

Doyle became a key public figure in Late Victorian and Edwardian Britain and was involved in many different fields of activity – medicine (he trained and practised as an oculist), sports (he founded and played in goal for Portsmouth FC), politics (he was knighted for his public support of the Boer War) and, later in life, spiritualism (he became convinced of a spirit life after death). But it is for his writing that he is mainly remembered. Sherlock Holmes and his commonplace comrade Dr Watson made their literary debut in *A Study in Scarlet* (1887) and their final appearance

The Adventure of the Missing Three Quarter.

We were fairly accustomed to receive weird telegrams at Baker Street but I have a particular recollection of one which reached us on a gloomy February morning some seven or eight years ago and gave Mr. Sherlock Holmes a puzzled quarter of an hour. It was addressed to him and ran thus

"Please await me; Terrible misfortune; Right wing three quarter missing, indispensable tomorrow. Overton"

"Strand post mark and dispatched 9.36" said Holmes, reading it over and over " Mr. Overton was evidently considerably excited when he sent it and somewhat incoherent in consequence. Well, well, he will be here by the time I have looked through the Times and then we shall know all about it. Even the most insignificant problem would be welcome in these stagnant times."

Things had indeed been very slow with us, and I had learned to dread such periods of inaction for I knew by experience that my companion's brain was so abnormally active that it was dangerous to leave it without material upon which to work. For years I had gradually weaned him from that drug mania which had threatened once to check his remarkable career nature. Now I knew that under ordinary conditions he no longer craved for this artificial stimulus but I was well aware that the fiend was not dead but sleeping, and I have known that the sleep was a light one and the waking near when in periods of idleness I have seen the drawn look upon Holmes' ascetic face, and the brooding of his deep set and inscrutable eyes. Therefore I blessed this Mr. Overton, whoever he might be, since he had come with his enigmatic message to break that dangerous calm which brought more peril to my friend than all the storms of his tempestuous life.

26. Autograph fair copy of 'The Adventure of the Missing Three Quarter'. The story was first published in *The Strand Magazine* in August 1904.

in the stories of *The Case-Book of Sherlock Holmes* (1927) and, in all, star in four novels and fifty-six short stories, forming Doyle's most enduring achievement, although he wrote numerous other novels, including the Professor Challenger series, a variety of historical tales and a number of high-profile non-fiction books, including *The Great Boer War* (1900) and *A History of Spiritualism* (1924).

Arthur Ignatius Conan Doyle was born in 1859 in Edinburgh and attended the Jesuit school Stonyhurst before studying medicine at Edinburgh University (1876–1881). After graduating, he served as a doctor in a ship on a voyage to the West African coast, then in 1882 set up a medical practice in Plymouth. The practice was unsuccessful. In his autobiography, *Memories and Adventures* (1924), he revealed that it was while waiting for patients that he began to write stories. His first published story, 'The Mystery of Sasassa Valley', had appeared in the Edinburgh periodical *Chambers's Journal* (6 September 1879), while he was still a student; now, especially after moving his practice to Southsea, he began to take his writing more seriously and started to plan a novel – the only way to 'assert your individuality', he wrote in his autobiography.

In the longueurs between his infrequent patient visits, Doyle considered writing a long detective story, one in which the sleuth would reach his conclusions by deductive reasoning and not by accident or the carelessness of the criminal. It was during these musings that he began to pull together various threads from past influences. Edgar Allan Poe's Dupin, the detective in 'The Murders in the Rue Morgue' (1841), had been one of Doyle's heroes. He also admired 'the neat dovetailing' of the plots in Gaboriau's crime novels. And then there was Joseph Bell, one of Doyle's tutors at Edinburgh University. Bell had had the most remarkable powers of observation, priding himself on his ability to deduce not only a patient's disease from their appearance but very often also their occupation and place of residence. As these influences swirled around in Doyle's brain, Bell's influences were uppermost. After a false start with the name (Sherrinford Holmes), Doyle's famous detective was conceived. The creative process was not yet complete, however. Doyle felt that the detective could not recount his own exploits – he would need, 'a commonplace comrade as a foil – an educated man of action who could both join in the exploits and narrate them'. Doctor John H. Watson was created to fill this role. Now that he had his characters, he began work on his first detective novel, *A Study in Scarlet*.

In *A Study in Scarlet*, Doyle created all the elements of the Sherlockian world that still live today. Apart from the protagonists Holmes and Watson, we are introduced to their cosy sitting room at 221b Baker Street; their landlady, Mrs Hudson; and the unimaginative police officers, Lestrade and Gregson. More brilliant still is the richly detailed world of Victorian London with its gas-lit chambers, cobbled streets, thick fogs and hansom cabs: so expertly drawn is this milieu that readers were, and are still, easily drawn into the vivid reality of it. But the key to the book's originality is Holmes himself, the brilliant, enigmatic crusader against crime and criminals. It is in *A Study in Scarlet* that Doyle presents us with the fundamental elements that make up this magical character; although Doyle later added various other characteristics, here you have the essential Sherlock Holmes.

A Study in Scarlet is as much a work of drama and romance as a mystery. The second half of the novel, which provides the background to the intrigue and murderous goings-on investigated by Holmes and Watson, is given an exotic setting among the Mormon community in America. (Doyle seems to have been fascinated by notions of revenge arising from the activities of American sects and secret societies: he would return to this theme in his last Holmes novel, *The Valley of Fear*.) *A Study in Scarlet* is an unevenly constructed novel. In essence, the search for the murderer and the real detective work has been completed half way through the book, and Holmes only appears briefly after this, at the end of part two, to tie the loose ends. (This uneven construction plagued Doyle in two of his other Holmes novels, *The Valley of Fear* and *The Sign of Four*). It is as though two plots have been dovetailed together, with Sherlock Holmes acting as a kind of literary catalyst. While both parts are enjoyable, the American section is far more conventional than the groundbreaking first part; the dark early scenes, when a corpse is discovered in a derelict house in the Brixton Road where the dead man has scrawled the word *RACHE* on the wall in his own blood, have rarely, if ever, been bettered in crime-fiction writing. For all its groundbreaking qualities, *A Study in Scarlet* caused barely a ripple of interest with the reading public. This revolutionary new detective, it seemed, had not yet caught the collective imagination.

Doyle considered the book his best work so far, but he was obliged to send it to several publishers before it was accepted, for the unexceptional sum of £25 ('Even I, poor as I was, hesitated to accept it,' said Doyle). His personal life at this time was growing happier, with his first child, Mary, born in 1889.

By the time of *The Sign of Four* (1890), Doyle developed as a writer of greater flair and confidence, capable of handling the dramatic construction of plots. What triggered his second novel is not recorded: perhaps he had already had some sketchy ideas about a revenge story involving Indian treasure and a one-legged man, and with a reasonably successful reprint of *A Study in Scarlet* earlier that year, the two elements came together in his imagination. By making Holmes a drug user (which the detective justifies as an escape from boredom: 'my mind rebels against stagnation'), Doyle played up the detective's Bohemianism, appealing to the Victorian middle-class reader, who loved to flirt secretly with such vices. It may have been Doyle's meeting with the outré figure of Oscar Wilde that inspired him to add this colourful facet to Holmes's makeup (interestingly there are echoes of Wilde in the character of Thaddeus Sholto, whose house is 'an oasis of art in the howling desert of South London' and who, in typical Wildean fashion, observes that 'there is nothing more unaesthetic than a policeman').

Watson, too, develops as a character in *The Sign of Four*. No longer the stiff and awkward character of the first novel, whose only display of anger is relegated to momentary outrage at an article in *The Book of Life* and throwing down his egg spoon, he is more outspoken and emotional, daring to rail at Holmes over his drug addiction and displaying an endearing passion for the novel's heroine, Mary Morstan, a romance that turns the novel into a love story as well as one of criminal detection.

Structurally, the novel also marked an advance. Like *A Study in Scarlet*, *The Sign of Four* contains a flashback section, filling in Holmes's original involvement with the mystery, but it is considerably shorter – allowing Holmes to stay centre stage for longer – and handled with greater skill. The main plot, which deals with treachery and revenge over the fabulous Agra treasure, is cleverly combined with Watson and Morstan's romantic subplot. Famously, *The Sign of Four* contains some now-celebrated anomalies. In *A Study in Scarlet*, Watson revealed that he had no relatives, but in the opening chapter of the new novel he is miraculously in possession of his brother's watch (used, for those readers unfamiliar with Holmes, to demonstrate the detective's remarkable deductive powers). Similarly, his war wound has travelled from his shoulder to his leg. These minor blunders were typical of Doyle who was loathe to look back at his previous writings to check details. In the end, these slips of the pen do not detract one iota from the pleasure of reading these two novels.

By the beginning of the 1890s, Holmes and Watson had been established, but their popularity received a boost with the short stories in *The Strand Magazine*. The first issue of *The Strand* appeared in January 1891, and very shortly afterwards, the editor, H. Greenhough Smith, received two Sherlock Holmes short stories, 'A Scandal in Bohemia' and 'The Red-Headed League'. He read them with growing excitement and 'at once realised that here was the greatest short story writer since Edgar Allan Poe'. The first Sherlock Holmes short story appeared in July 1891 issue, attracting immediate attention. The die was cast, and with the appearance of 'The Copper Beeches', in June 1892, the twelfth and final story in the first series (to be published in October 1892 in book form as *The Adventures of Sherlock Holmes*), the Holmes stories had become the mainstay of the magazine, and Doyle's detective had scaled the heights of popularity. A legend had been created.

In *Adventures*, 'The Speckled Band' remains one of the best-loved tales. It is the ultimate locked-room mystery, graced with rich characterisation of the villain – a Doyle trademark. 'The Blue Carbuncle' shares this trait, adding a layer of ingenious plotting that not even Poe had attempted.

However, even before the ink was dry on the manuscript of 'The Copper Beeches', its author was already weary of Sherlock Holmes. In fact, by the end of 1891, he had written to his mother, one of Sherlock's greatest admirers, to say that he was thinking of 'slaying Holmes. He takes my mind from better things.' Doyle's disenchantment only grew when he was approached by the editor of *The Strand* for a further twelve stories. In order to put him off, he asked for what he regarded as the ridiculously high fee of £50 a story. The magazine accepted his request without question. Aware of the hawk-nosed sleuth's incredible popularity, the publishers knew how important Holmes was to the young magazine's fortunes.

The second series of stories, which became known as *The Memoirs of Sherlock Holmes* (1894), began in December 1892 issue with 'Silver Blaze'. But the weary task of continued composition convinced Doyle that he had to rid himself of this literary shackle, and despite ardent pleas from his mother, in the last episode of the series, 'The Final Problem', he did just that. Realising that the end of Sherlock Holmes had to be brought about by someone who was the detective's intellectual equal, he created a mastermind as brilliant at carrying out crimes as Holmes was at solving them. Here enters Professor Moriarty, 'the Napoleon of Crime', whom Holmes described as 'the organiser of half that is evil and of nearly all that is undetected in this great city. He is a genius, a philosopher, an abstract thinker.' He was, in essence, Holmes's dark alter ego. The location for their final struggle was at the Reichenbach Falls in Switzerland, where the two giants faced each other for the last time on a narrow pathway overlooking the tremendous torrent of water. Grappling, they fell together and disappeared into the swirling foam at the base of the falls. Watson was beside himself with grief. So were the readers of *The Strand*: the offices of the magazine were besieged with messages of grief, condolences and, most of all, anger – anger at both the publication and the author for allowing the terrible incident to occur. George Newnes, addressing his shareholders, referred to Holmes's death as a 'dreadful event'. One irate lady wrote to Doyle describing him as a 'brute', and men in the city wore black arm bands out of respect for the deceased detective. Doyle's own reaction was somewhat different. Maybe still having the letter of abuse from the irate lady in mind, he expressed grim satisfaction – 'Thank God, I've killed the brute' – explaining later, during a speech to the Author's Club in 1896, 'I hold that it was not murder, but justifiable homicide in self-defence, since, if I had not killed him, he would certainly have killed me.'

For years, Doyle disregarded all pleas to resurrect Holmes, but in 1901, listening to a friend's account of some legends of Dartmoor, he conceived a mystery story about a family supposedly haunted by a spectral hound. Doyle realised that the story required a detective and saw that there was little point in creating a new character. So, one suspects with some reluctance, Conan Doyle converted his ghostly dog saga into a Holmes adventure, the most famous of them all – *The Hound of the Baskervilles* (1902). He was adamant that this story did not herald a permanent return of Holmes (the story is set prior to the Reichenbach Falls incident), but there must have been the sound of champagne corks popping in the offices of *The Strand*. The publishers and their readers were ecstatic that Sherlock Holmes was back. The novel was a tremendous success.

Arthur Conan Doyle was knighted in 1902 and it was felt by some that this accolade was as much due to the reappearance of Holmes in *The Hound of the Baskervilles* as to the author's public service. Now that Sherlock Holmes had appeared in print once more, readers and publishers alike hoped that the author could be persuaded to relent and drag the fellow up from his watery grave for more adventures. A more relaxed and confident man, Doyle no longer found the idea of writing further detective stories so abhorrent, and when, in 1903, the New York publisher of *Collier's* magazine offered him $4,000 per story, he relented. The first tale in the new collection (published in 1904 as *The Return of Sherlock Holmes*) was 'The Empty House', which incidentally gave rather unconvincing details relating how Holmes had escaped death. But readers were not concerned with the credibility of The Great Detective's explanation – they were just delighted that he was back again. The canon of Holmes stories continued, although more sporadically than before. After *The Return*, there were two further collections, *His Last Bow* (1917) and *The Casebook of Sherlock Holmes* (1927), and a final novel, *The Valley of Fear* (1914). The last Holmes story appeared in *The Strand* in July 1927.

Sherlock Holmes remains a fascinating enigma, which perhaps accounts for his widespread and enduring appeal. He is a cerebral animal – 'I cannot live without brainwork, what else is there to live for?' – and his cognitive pursuits cover many areas: 'He spoke on a quick succession of subjects – on miracle plays, on mediaeval pottery, on Stradivarius violins, on the Buddhism of Ceylon and on the warships of the future – handling each as though he had made a special study of it.' Recognising the need for Holmes to be a man immune from ordinary human weaknesses and feelings, Doyle allows him to reject passion or, indeed, any strong emotion towards women. He does admire the adventuress Irene Adler, who features in the story 'A Scandal in Bohemia' (referring to her as 'the woman'), but only, we are assured, because she proved his equal in quickness of wit and decisiveness of action. But Holmes is not merely a thinker. He is also a man of action, and it is through this aspect of him that the potency of the stories reaches full power: the call in the night, the hansom cab ride through the gas-lit streets into danger. Watson, the reliable, sensible, stockier figure behind the lean silhouette of the Great Detective, is also Holmes's chronicler, and, as such, as necessary to the Holmes legend as Holmes himself. While Holmes, from time to time, criticises Watson for overdramatising the investigations ('looking at everything from the point of view of a story instead of as a scientific exercise'), we know that we are being presented with a finely crafted version – the definitive version – of the career of the greatest consulting detective.

The success of Holmes overshadowed most of Doyle's other mystery fiction, though some of his historical novels, such as the *Brigadier Gerard* series, and his Professor Challenger stories, starting with *The Lost World* (1910), have retained a readership. Some of his early novels, such as the melodramatic *The Mystery of Cloomber* (1889), and the story of financial chicanery, *The Firm of Girdlestone* (1890), incorporate elements of crime and mystery. He wrote many supernatural stories and a few other mysteries, two of which, 'The Man with the Watches' and 'The Lost Special' (both 1898), are regarded as quasi-Holmes stories, just lacking the named detective. The best of these tales were collected in *Round the Fire Stories* (1908).

Doyle also established a reputation for his public causes and campaigns. He interested himself in true crime and sought to redress what he saw as miscarriages of justice, notably in the cases of Oscar Slater and George Edalji. It was partly thanks to Doyle's involvement in the Edalji case that the Court of Criminal Appeal was created in 1907. Doyle may have sullied his personal reputation in later years with his belief in the Cottingley Fairies and his involvement in spiritualism – something that the rational Holmes would not have condoned – but his literary reputation has never diminished, and continues to grow with each passing decade. *See also* The Detective in British Fiction; The Great Detectives: Sherlock Holmes, Hercule Poirot, Lord Peter Wimsey; Holmes on Television; Holmes's Rivals *and* Origins of British Crime Fiction.

Selected Works by the Author

Sherlock Holmes
A Study in Scarlet (1887)
The Sign of Four (1890)
The Adventures of Sherlock Holmes (stories, 1892)
The Memoirs of Sherlock Holmes (stories, 1894)
The Hound of the Baskervilles (1902)
The Return of Sherlock Holmes (stories, 1905)
The Valley of Fear (1915)
His Last Bow (stories, 1917)
The Casebook of Sherlock Holmes (stories, 1927)

Other Works
Mysteries and Adventures (stories, 1889; also published in the United States with additional stories as *My Friend the Murderer*)
Round the Fire Stories (stories, 1908)
Memories and Adventures (autobiography, 1924)
The Unknown Conan Doyle (1982; also published in the United States as *Uncollected Stories*)

Further Reading
ACD: The Journal of the Arthur Conan Doyle Society (published annually).
Booth, Martin, 2000. *The Doctor and the Detective: A Biography of Sir Arthur Conan Doyle*. Hodder and Stoughton.
Carr, John Dickson. 1949. *Life of Sir Arthur Conan Doyle*. John Murray.
Green, Richard Lancelyn, and John Michael Gibson. 1983. *A Bibliography of A. Conan Doyle*. Clarendon Press.
Harrison, Michael. 1972. *The London Sherlock Holmes*. David and Charles.
Symons, Julian. 1979. *Portrait of an Artist: Conan Doyle*. Mysterious Press.

Website
Official website of the Sir Arthur Conan Doyle Literary Estate, http://www.sherlockholmesonline.org

David Stuart Davies

Dudley, Ernest (1908–2006)

Ernest Dudley, the pseudonym of writer and actor Vivian Ernest Coltman-Allen, was the creator of the popular BBC radio hero, eminent psychiatrist and criminologist Dr Morelle. He was also the man behind the radio/television series, *The Armchair Detective*.

Dudley began his career as a theatre actor but soon made the move into journalism, working as a society reporter, music critic and boxing correspondent. He began writing plays for BBC Radio in the 1930s and got his big break during the Second World War when he was asked to create his detective series. His hero, Dr Morelle, whom Dudley – a dab hand at self-publicity – dubbed 'The Man You Love to Hate' because of his patronising and cruel manner, was a great success. This led to his popular radio series *The Armchair Detective*, work on television and to a career writing novels and plays.

Dudley worked regularly for BBC Light Entertainment throughout the 1930s. Notable credits during this period included *Calling X2, SOS Sally, Mr Walker Wants to Know* and *Enter Sexton Blake*. At the outbreak of the Second World War, Dudley was deemed 'not fit for active service' and worked for the BBC from a studio in Bristol, sending out coded messages for Allied forces and agents during broadcasts. While there, Dudley was asked to write a comedy mystery series that avoided making the hero a Scotland Yard detective. The hero he developed was a psychoanalyst whose powers of detection were dazzling, but whose manner was deliberately offensive: a man seemingly oblivious to other people's feelings. Dudley has stated in numerous interviews that Dr Morelle, dreamed up while taking refuge in a coal cellar during a bombing attack, was based on the tyrannical silent film star and director Erich von Stroheim (from whom Dudley stole the description 'The Man You Love to Hate'). Although Dr Morelle's rude personality is taken to an extreme, it could be argued that he was no more than an amalgamation of other forbidding detectives, most notably Sherlock **Holmes**. Dudley created a foil for his overbearing hero in the shape of 'feather-brained' secretary Miss Frayle, and the sleuthing team made their first appearance in the anthology programme *Monday Night at Eight* in July 1942. The voice of Dr Morelle was provided by Dennis Arundall and Dudley's wife Jane Graham played his secretary. The series that followed soon boasted millions of listeners who were perhaps tuning in to listen to the cruel and vindictive Dr Morelle as much as following the mystery. Dudley, who in 1939 had already written a novelisation of the radio show *Mr Walker Wants to Know*, published two collections of short stories – *Meet Dr Morelle* (1943) and *Meet Dr Morelle Again* (1944) – featuring his creation before the radio series returned in April 1946. The first full-length novel based on his character, *Menace for Dr Morelle*, appeared a year later, and the series continued for eleven more novels concluding with *Nightmare for Dr Morelle* (1960). The Dr Morelle of the printed page is described as being tall, sombre looking with dark hair greying at the sides. Residing at 221B (where else?) Harley Street, Dr Morelle is a world-renowned psychiatrist. An expert on the criminal mind – as well as any other subject you could name – he regularly assists the police in the shape of pipe-smoking Inspector Hood from New Scotland Yard. Arguably, the most enjoyable aspect of these stories can be found in the relationship between Dr Morelle and his long-suffering secretary. Although the bespectacled Miss Frayle often exasperates her employer, he would clearly be at a loss without her. The Dr Morelle mysteries proved popular enough to attract interest from the British film industry, and in 1949 the movie, *The Case of the Missing Heiress,* was produced by Hammer Studios with Valentine Dyall as Dr Morelle and Julia Lang as Miss Frayle. Dudley thought that the best thing about this rather pedestrian film was his having been paid £500 for staying well away. Dudley also co-wrote (with Arthur Watkyn) a play about his beloved character. Simply called *Dr Morelle*, it scored a modest success in the early 1950s. In 1957, Dr Morelle was revived again for radio in a series of thirteen half-hour adventures entitled *A Case for Doctor Morelle* with Cecil Parker and Sheila Sim. Dudley's other big radio hit, *The Armchair Detective*, which began back in 1942, was an anthology programme in which Dudley reviewed mystery novels and dramatised a chapter from each as well as chatting about real-life crime and crime writers. The show, which had over ten million listeners at its peak, made the transformation to television in the 1950s. A film spin-off was also produced in 1952 with Sally Newton as a radio singer suspected of murdering her hateful boss. This film also featured Dudley as both narrating the story and observing the action from the sidelines. In the same decade, Dudley presented an early example of a viewer participation show, *Judge for Yourself*, in which viewers were invited to send in their verdicts – guilty or not guilty – after watching a fictionalised trial. For the next few decades, Dudley continued to work in radio, notably adapting Dick **Francis**'s racing thriller *Proof* in 1987 for Nigel Havers. He continued to write novels among which were historical works and animal books. He also penned the autobiographical *Run for Your Life* (1985) about his passion for marathon running, which he claimed helped him cope with depression. Until recently, Dudley's work had been all but forgotten, when US publishers such as Wildside Press began reprinting the Dr Morelle novels in 2003. Dudley had begun planning a new novel, *Dr Morelle and the Lap Dancer*, but died before this was realised.

While Dudley's work may not be as enduring as some of his contemporaries, his creation, Dr Morelle, is nevertheless important in the history of the radio sleuth.

Selected Works by the Author
Meet Dr Morelle (stories, 1943)
Menace for Dr Morelle (1947)
Dr Morelle and the Drummer Girl (1950)
Callers for Dr Morelle (1957)
Dr Morelle Takes a Bow (1957)
Dr Morelle and Destiny (1958)
The Mind of Dr Morelle (1958)
Alibi and Dr Morelle (1959)
Confess to Dr Morelle (1959)
Dr Morelle at Midnight (1959)
Dr Morelle and the Doll (1960)
Nightmare for Dr Morelle (1960)

Terry Fountain

Duffy, Stella (b.1963)

Born in England but brought up in New Zealand, Stella Duffy – an actress, radio playwright and author of both crime and non-crime novels – has always been upfront about being lesbian. The usual hero of her crime books, private investigator Saz

27. Stella Duffy.

Martin, is gay, and her sexuality is a part of the stories – and the stories gain from this. Duffy does not preach, thump the barrel or deliver lectures on sexuality; she uses it instead to add humour and warmth to her dark but lively tales.

Duffy's personal vivacity bubbles over into her books. The first, *Calendar Girl* (1994), explored a world Duffy knew from the inside, that of the stand-up comic in pubs and clubs, and a world she presumably knew less well, that of gambling, drug smuggling and high-class prostitution. 'A lot of lesbian lore and sex', commented the *Times*, but 'a fast, witty and clever crime story, with cracking dialogue and exuberant characters'. *Wavewalker* (1996), perhaps her best crime novel, came next; it had Saz employed by a mysterious woman – the Wavewalker – who walks at the tide's edge where waves cover footprints and who leads Saz into a case that begins with an alternative lifestyle guru from 1970s San Francisco and spurts forwards into Saz's hectic private and professional life in 1990s **London**. Duffy's third crime novel, *Beneath the Blonde* (1997), placed her 'very near the top of the new generation of modern crime writers', according to Marcel Berlins in the *Times* again, and had Saz investigate a stalker and potential murderer pursuing the female lead singer of the group Beneath the Blonde. In her fourth, *Fresh Flesh* (1999), Saz and her partner Molly are having a baby and Saz in consequence has vowed to take on no more dangerous cases. That vow, unsurprisingly, lasts a lot less than do her vows to Molly. *Parallel Lies* (2005) is almost a cross-over novel between Duffy's crime and non-genre stories, telling the tale of a Russian-born Hollywood legend (lesbian, of course) desperate to know who is sending her threatening and intimately well-informed poison-pen letters. Duffy has also written the very personal and at times painful book *State of Happiness* (2004), as well as *Singling Out The Couples* (1998), *Eating Cake* (1999) and *Immaculate Conceit* (which she adapted as a stage version for the National Youth Theatre). She has published more than thirty short stories and was co-editor of the crime short-story anthology *Tart Noir* (2002). She has also written for the radio and the stage.

Duffy is one of the few overtly gay crime writers to make her books not only accessible but attractive to both gay and non-gay readers. Her gay women are as exuberant in their sexuality as are the heterosexual heroines and *femmes fatales* of straight fiction. The gay relationships in her books are never dragged in or attached to conventional crime plots but are central, indeed pivotal, to the action. *See also* Gay and Lesbian Crime Fiction *and* Sexuality in British Crime Fiction.

Selected Works by the Author
Calendar Girl (1994)
Wavewalker (1996)
Beneath the Blonde (1997)
State of Happiness (2004)
Parallel Lies (2005)

Russell James

Dunant, Sarah (b.1950)

Although she began in radio in 1974 and for a time presented *Woman's Hour*, Sarah Dunant really came to public prominence when she headed the intellectual television programme *The Late Show*, after which she went on to combine television and writing. She wrote both sharp crime and non-crime novels, as well as intelligent journalism. After publishing two books co-written with her husband, she continued on her own with two stand-alone thrillers and a short series starring the investigator Hannah Woolfe. Despite her success with these, she moved away from crime fiction into writing books with broader appeal. She won the **Crime Writers' Association** (CWA) Silver Dagger, and for many years divided her time between homes in London and Florence. She has two children.

Almost a decade before the Hannah Woolfe novels, Dunant (with her husband Peter Busby, under the shared name Peter Dunant) had co-written two political thrillers featuring Marla Masterson (*Exterminating Angels* and *Intensive Care*) but these did not achieve great success. *Snow Storms in a Hot Climate*, her first stand-alone novel, about drug smuggling, came out in 1988. Then *Birth Marks*, the first Hannah Woolfe story, written again by Dunant alone, was published in 1991 to be followed by two more: *Fatlands* in 1993 (the most successful of the series and winner of the CWA Silver Dagger) and *Under My Skin* in 1995. In parallel with these books she wrote a work of non-fiction, *The War of the Words: The Political Correctness Debate* (1994), and despite the excellent reviews for her Woolfe novels she became increasingly drawn to non-crime subjects. In 1996, she co-wrote *Age of Anxiety* with Roy Porter, and in 1998, with Tibor Fischer, edited *Arc Short Stories: An Anthology of Contemporary Writing: Vol 9*. After 1995, Dunant gave up the Woolfe stories to produce two straight thrillers, *Transgressions* in 1997 (a tense and exciting stalker novel) and *Mapping the Edge* in 1999, which combined two parallel versions of events in an attempt to explain (or perhaps to leave it to the reader to explain) the mysterious disappearance of an apparently ordinary young mother. Did she disappear or was it all a sexual fantasy? Dunant then moved further from the crime field to write *The Birth of Venus* (2003) and *In the Company of the Courtesan* (2006). She continued with journalism and was a long-running presenter of Radio 3's flagship arts show *Night Waves*.

Crime fans will regret Dunant's turning away from Hannah Woolfe, who was an attractive hero, out of the mould of most of today's female investigators. Far from being an all-action tough girl, Hannah avoided violence and assumed that in any face-to-face fight with a man she would come off worse. (This did not stop her occasionally rigging the odds in her favour.) She had her creator's wit and intellectual breadth and found herself involved in credible modern cases – even if in the end it came down to the same old PI work, tracking missing persons and exposing dodgy businesses. *See also* Women Crime Writers.

Selected Works by the Author
Birth Marks (1991)
Fatlands (1993)

Russell James

E

Eccles, Marjorie (b.1927)

The work of Marjorie Eccles represents a valuable tradition in British crime fiction: well-written and reliably entertaining mysteries set in recognisable British towns and villages and featuring credible characters.

Eccles was born in Yorkshire and has lived in Northumbria and Hertfordshire. Her knowledge and understanding of the English countryside and towns is evident both in the crime novels she has written under her name and in her romantic fiction written under the names of Judith Bordill and Jennifer Hyde.

Although she has written several stand-alone mysteries, she is best known for a series of **police procedurals** featuring Superintendent Gil Mayo. Set in the Black Country, the series is notable for its neat plots and the well-drawn characters of the police officers who are regularly involved in Mayo's cases. Detective Inspector Mayo, as he was then, made his debut in *Cast a Cold Eye* (1988) and since then made a more or less annual appearance until the most recent *Untimely Graves* (2001). The stories are constructed in the conventional style of the genre, following the details of the investigation by Mayo and his team. The relationships between the police officers, especially Mayo and his closest colleagues, play an important role in all the books. Despite the sometimes stereotypical characters – the ambitious career woman and the absent-minded academic – Eccles gives them personalities which bring them to life. The series was adapted for television and screened in eight instalments in the spring of 2006, with Alistair McGowan playing Mayo.

In 2004, Eccles's *The Shape of Sand*, set in post-Second World War Britain, was shortlisted for the **Crime Writers' Association** (CWA) Ellis Peters Historical Dagger. This book, written after producing several entertaining but not particularly original mysteries, shows her at her best once again. It follows the fortunes of a once wealthy English family, whose remaining members are struggling to come to terms with the devastating changes resulting from the two world wars. It is a fine example of Eccles's skill at getting into the minds of her characters while creating a clever, suspense-filled mystery.

Eccles's novels best display her talents when she is dealing with her characters than her plots, which are absorbing but have not always been demandingly complex. A sharp eye for detail, an understanding of human relationships and the quality of her writing have placed her among a select group of mainly female writers who have over many years provided fans of traditional British crime fiction with enjoyable, skilfully composed puzzles. *See also* TV Detectives: Small-Screen Adaptations.

Selected Works by the Author
Cast a Cold Eye (1988)
Death of a Good Woman (1989)
An Accidental Shroud (1994)
Killing Me Softly (1998)
The Superintendent's Daughter (1999)
The Shape of Sand (2004)
Shadows and Lies (2005)

Susanna Yager

Edgar Wallace Mystery Magazine

Edgar Wallace Mystery Magazine was a 128-page, pocketbook-size, monthly magazine published initially by Micron Publications, Mitcham, Surrey, in 1964, under licence to Edgar Wallace Limited. Although Edgar **Wallace** died in 1932, his name still meant something in British mystery circles and was topical because the television series *Edgar Wallace Mystery Theatre* had been running since 1960. The series was in its fourth season when the **magazine**'s first issue appeared in August 1964. A scene from different episodes was reproduced on the back cover of the issues.

28. Cover of the second issue of the *Edgar Wallace Mystery Magazine*, September 1964.

The first six issues were edited by Keith Chapman, who was also editing a series of 'picture library' comic-books for Micron, such as *Western Adventure Library* and *Combat Picture Library*. He had previously worked at Amalgamated Press, assisting on the *Sexton Blake Library*, and was able to attract several of those authors. The first few issues, therefore, were filled with stories – often long – by Arthur Kent (1925–1998), Rex Dolphin (1915–1990) and Thomas Martin (1913–1985). Each issue led with an Edgar Wallace story reprinted from an uncommon source, chiefly the *Reader's Library* series of the late 1920s. The covers, by Chacopini, gave the impression of American gangster stories, although few of the stories reflected it. Nigel **Morland** contributed several stories featuring Mrs Pym, and Arthur Kent began a short series about the police surgeon Rex Diamond, of which 'Killed with a Loving Kiss' (issue 4, November 1964) is a complete short novel.

Micron were in financial difficulties, and Edgar Wallace Limited stepped in to act as publisher. Dissatisfied with the magazine, the new publisher instigated changes. Morland, a close friend of Wallace in his youth, was installed as editor. The front cover did not carry illustrations anymore and simply listed highlights of the contents. The magazine continued to run predominantly new stories, although in addition to the regular Edgar Wallace reprint, Morland instigated a 'Period Piece' feature, which reprinted little-known Victorian stories, and occasionally selected other uncommon stories. Morland also ran a series on true-crime cases, with several contributors. The magazine saw considerable discussion about the case of James Hanratty hanged for murder but whose guilt was contested. It would remain a *cause célèbre* for over thirty years.

Morland relied on a few regular contributors, including Bill Knox (1928–1999), John Boland (1913–1976), John Salt, Paul Tabori (1908–1974), Jeffrey Scott (b.1937) and Morland himself – what one reader dubbed the 'backbone' writers – but he also acquired material from top-line authors. The May 1965 issue saw the first appearance of Margery **Allingham**'s 'It's All Part of the Service'. (Although the other Allingham stories used had seen prior newspaper publication, none had yet appeared in book form.) Michael **Gilbert** contributed several new stories, including the Young Petrella story, 'The Conspirators' (issue 25, August 1966). Victor **Canning**'s golfing murder story, 'The Handicap' (issue 13, August 1965), was presented as new, although it had seen a prior US publication. While most of Sax **Rohmer**'s stories were reprints – including 'Escape to Peril' (issue 14, September 1965), which was presented as new – 'The Night of the Jackal' (issue 28, November 1966) was a previously unpublished story written during, and set in, the Second World War. Also of interest were several previously unpublished stories by Wallace himself, two featuring Robin Hood–style Michael Hex – 'Blackmail, with Roses' (issue 26, September 1966) and 'Ricochet in Pearls' (issue 31, February 1967) – plus 'The Light in E Flat' (issue 35, June 1967).

The magazine relied heavily on British contributors, with the emphasis on traditional detection, but it can lay claim to publishing one of the earliest African crime stories, 'The Kamalu Men' (issue 35, June 1967) by Nigerian writer Akpan Eyen Efik.

Despite the popularity of the magazine, it suddenly ceased publication with the June 1967 issue, although a further issue was announced. No explanation was given. Two years later, some of the contents of the unpublished issue appeared from Canova Press, edited by Leonard Holdsworth, and included a new Mrs Pym story by Nigel Morland and a new story by Anthony Gilbert. Unaccountably, that issue was number 31 instead of 36, and a few months later issue 32 appeared, undated apart from '© 1970'. This issue consisted entirely of a full-length black-magic mystery novel, 'The Witch-Killers' by a pseudonymous John Jacey. However, Canova Press was not ideally suited for a mystery magazine as its usual line was publishing fetish books, and its distribution was geared to a different readership. The revived series also ended abruptly.

Under Morland, *Edgar Wallace Mystery Magazine* was a fine magazine of good quality traditional fiction, although perhaps a little dated for the swinging sixties.

Further Reading
Cook, Michael L. 1982. *Monthly Murders*. Greenwood Press.

Mike Ashley

Edric, Robert (b.1956)

Gary Edric Armitage, who switched to the pen name Robert Edric after his first two books, is known primarily for his mainstream literary novels. The first under his Edric alias, *Winter Garden* (1985), won the James Tait Black Award, while the second, *A New Ice Age*, was runner-up for the Guardian Fiction Prize. Three of his novels, published between 2003 and 2005, constitute a trilogy of contemporary noir, or since they are set in and around Hull, Humberside Noir. There had been little in Edric's *curriculum vitae* to suggest that he would suddenly publish a hard-boiled crime novel, *Cradle Song*, in 2003. He pared his prose down to the bone in *Cradle Song*, in which James Bishop, the father of one of several missing girls, hires private investigator Leo Rivers, when time-serving paedophile and child murderer Martin Roper appeals against his conviction. Roper had confessed to the murder of Nicola Bishop, but no evidence was found to back up his confession and, as Rivers finds when he starts digging, numerous corners had been cut in the original police investigation. Sullivan, the former plod whose securing of Roper's conviction had allowed him to retire in a blaze of glory, now inhabits a widower's bungalow within spitting distance of the caravan park where Roper's mother had kept a temporary home.

In 469 pages, there are probably fewer than 469 words of geographical description, yet Edric brings Hull to life. We believe that we are right there in the streets and police stations and second-hand car lots and that we could instinctively find our way from the detective's Humber Street office, itself located above a murder site, to the 'spartan beauty' of Spurn Head, with its mudflats and lonely bird calls. We learn very little of the history of Leo Rivers, but his reactions to traumatic events illuminate his character. The way he narrates his account, using a mixture of naturalistic dialogue and minutely observed details of the behaviour of other characters – from corrupt cops and bent screws to decent officers as hardworking as they are hardbitten – is extraordinarily compelling.

The second book in the series, *Siren Song* (2005), opens: 'The phone rang just as I was about to leave the office.' It could be Philip Marlowe talking. Rivers even has frosted glass in his door. The interview between Rivers and his prospective client, Alison Brooks, the mother of a young woman missing, presumed drowned, is straight out of **Chandler**. The most striking differences are the Humberside setting and the particular focus on the river and the North Sea. 'With a falling tide, the water, cold and silt-laden, would be moving in excess of 20 miles an hour.' The fluidity extends to motivation and morality, and the narrative builds as powerfully and inexorably as the rising tide.

Book three, *Swan Song* (2005), finds Rivers hired by the mother of the chief suspect in a series of murders of young women. Once again, the river is at everyone's backs. The truth may be as fluid and unpredictable as the sea, different versions of it drifting in and out on the tide.

The trilogy complete, Edric wrote a novella, *The Mermaids* (2007), where he flirted with the supernatural and then returned to general literary fiction. *Gathering the Water* (2006) was longlisted for the Man Booker Prize.

Selected Works by the Author
The Sword Cabinet (1999)
Peacetime (2002)
Cradle Song (2003)
Siren Song (2004)
Swan Song (2005)
The Kingdom of Ashes (2007)

Nicholas Royle

Edwards, Martin (b.1955)

Both as a crime writer and as a keen exponent of the genre, Martin Edwards has long been sought out by his peers and is now becoming recognised as a contemporary crime author at the top of his form.

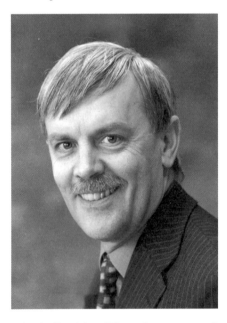

29. Martin Edwards.

Born in Knutsford, Cheshire, Edwards went to school in Northwich before taking a first-class honours degree in law at Balliol College, Oxford. He went on to join a law firm and is now a highly respected lawyer specialising in employment law. He is the author of Tottel's *Equal Opportunities Handbook*, fourth edition, 2007.

Early in his career, Edwards began writing professional articles and completed his first book at twenty-seven, covering the purchase of business computers. His non-fiction work continues with over 600 articles in newspapers and magazines and seven books dedicated to the law (two of which were co-authored).

His life of crime writing began with the Harry Devlin series, set in Liverpool. The first of the series, *All the Lonely People* (1991), was shortlisted for the **Crime Writers' Association** (CWA) John Creasey Memorial Dagger. With the advent of his second novel, Edwards was becoming recognised as a writer of imagination and flair. This and subsequent books also referenced song titles from his youth.

The Harry Devlin series demonstrates a great sympathy for Liverpool, past and present, with gritty, realistic stories. 'Liverpool is a city with a tremendous resilience of spirit and character,' he says in *Scene of the Crime* (2002). Although his protagonist is a self-effacing Scouser with a dry wit, Edwards is not a writer for the faint-hearted. 'His gifts are of the more classical variety – there are points in his novels when I think I'm reading Graham **Greene**,' wrote Ed Gorman, while *Crime Time* magazine said, 'The novels successfully combine the style of the traditional English detective story with a darker noir sensibility.'

More recently, Edwards has moved into the Lake District with mystery stories featuring a historian, Daniel Kind, and Detective Chief Inspector Hannah Scarlett. The first of these stories, *The Coffin Trail* (2004), was shortlisted for the Theakston's Old Peculier Crime Novel of the year 2006. In this book, Edwards has made good use of his legal knowledge. Scarlett is in charge of a cold-case review unit, attempting to solve old crimes, and when Kind moves into a new house, seeking a fresh start in the idyllic setting of the Lake District, they are drawn together by the murder of a young woman. The killer, who died before he could be convicted, used to live in Kind's new cottage. Not only does Edwards manage to demonstrate a detailed knowledge of the law (which he is careful never to force upon the reader), but with the Lake District mysteries he has managed to bring the locations to vivid life. He has a rare skill for acute description.

More recently, Edwards has published *Take My Breath Away* (2004), a stand-alone psychological suspense novel, which, as Martin Edwards himself described, offers a satiric portrait of an upmarket London law firm 'eerily reminiscent of Tony Blair's New Labour government'.

Using his legal experience, he has written articles about actual crimes. *Catching Killers* (2003) is an illustrated book describing how police officers work on a homicide case all the way from the crime scene to presenting evidence in court.

When the writer Bill Knox died, Edwards was asked by Knox's publisher to help complete his final manuscript. Knox's method of writing was to hone each separate section of his books before moving on to the next, so Martin was left with the main thrust of the story, together with some jotted notes and newspaper clippings. From these, he managed to complete *The Lazarus Widow* (1999) in an odd departure for him.

More conventionally, Edwards is a prolific writer of short stories. He has published the collection *Where Do You Find Your Ideas?* (2001) which offers Harry Devlin tales mingled with historical and psychological short stories. His *Test Drive* was shortlisted for the CWA Short Story Dagger.

Edwards edits the regular CWA anthologies of short stories. These works have included *Green for Danger* (2003) and *I.D. Crimes of Identity* (2006). In 2003, he also edited the CWA's *Mysterious Pleasures* anthology, which was a collection of the Golden Dagger winners' short stories to celebrate the CWA's Golden Jubilee.

A founder member of the performance and writing group Murder Squad, Edwards has found the time to edit their eponymous book. When not writing and editing,

Edwards is an enthusiastic reader and collector of crime fiction. He reviews for magazines, books and websites, and his essays have appeared in many collections. He is the chairman of the CWA's nominations subcommittee for the Cartier Diamond Dagger Award.

Edwards is one of those rare creatures, a crime writer's crime writer. His plotting is as subtle as any, his writing deft and fluid, his characterisation precise, and his descriptions of the locations give the reader the impression that they could almost walk along the land blindfolded. He brings them all to life.

Selected Works by the Author

Harry Devlin Series
All the Lonely People (1991)
Suspicious Minds (1992)
I Remember You (1993)
Yesterday's Papers (1994)
Eve of Destruction (1996)
The Devil in Disguise (1998)
First Cut Is the Deepest (1999)
Waterloo Sunset (2008)

Lake District Mysteries
The Coffin Trail (2004)
The Cipher Garden (2005)
The Arsenic Labyrinth (2007)

Website
www.martinedwardsbooks.com

Michael Jecks

Edwards, Ruth Dudley (b.1944)

Ruth Dudley Edwards's method of combining elements of the **Golden Age** crime novel with savagely intelligent satire is unique amongst contemporary writers. Her literary abattoir contains the gutted corpses of many of the British Establishment's sacred cows, ranging from gentlemen's clubs and the literati to the Civil Service and the House of Lords. An exuberant iconoclast, Dudley Edwards hurls brickbats at everything from the hunting debate and the Northern Ireland peace process (targeting both sides with equal accuracy and gusto) to religious fanatics, management jargon and processed foodstuffs.

Born in Ireland, Dudley Edwards was educated at University College, Dublin, and Cambridge. Having worked as an academic, a marketing executive and a civil servant, she has been a freelance journalist since 1979. Now living in London, she writes prizewinning history books and biographies as well as mysteries.

Although her novels take place in traditional 'closed-world' settings, such as colleges, offices and cathedrals, and although there are similarities in form and style to writers such as **Christie** and **Sayers** and **Crispin**, which she cites as formative influences, there is little active detection in Dudley Edwards's work, and plot, as puzzle, tends to take second place to **humour**. This tends to be of an observational or linguistic nature, rather than physical comedy of the farcical type that characterises the work of satirical novelists such as Tom Sharpe, although she does exploit the

30. Ruth Dudley Edwards.

comic potential of the two creatures that feature in the novels, an aggressive cat and a foul-mouthed parrot.

Dudley Edwards's earlier protagonist, Robert Amiss, is an intelligent but often bewildered individual who finds himself in a variety of establishments (the church, the civil service, a ring-wing political magazine and so on) where crimes occur. Frequently, he plays the role of go-between as he makes unofficial investigations and reports back to his policeman friends Jim Milton and Ellis Pooley. Dudley Edwards's fifth novel, *Matricide at St Martha's* (1994), introduces another amateur detective, the engagingly eccentric Ida 'Jack' Troutbeck. She acts as a mouthpiece for an exaggerated version of her creator's libertarian views, champions academic rigour, is unapologetically partisan and is an unremitting scourge of political correctness in all its forms. Jack Troutbeck is ebullient, ribald and promiscuously bisexual, and her initial impact is so vivid that nothing that comes afterwards can efface it; a literary descendant of Dickens's 'monster' characters, she provides a perfect foil to Amiss's liberal, middle-class equivocation and desire not to offend.

As with Golden Age crime fiction, some of Dudley Edwards's chosen methods of murder tend towards the outlandish and ingenious (drowning in punch bowls, scooting out of a high window on a doctored library ladder, jamming pacemakers at long range), but all the violence happens off the page.

Dudley Edwards's work is characterised by a talent for pastiche and includes many references to classic crime fiction, both cosy and hardboiled. Her sense of humour, which allows her to mix the sophisticated with the unashamedly bawdy, is also the vehicle for penetrating observations on the preoccupations and absurdities of modern life. *See also* Academe, Death in *and* Clerical Crime.

Selected Works by the Author
Corridors of Death (1981)
The School of English Murder (1990; also published in the United States as *The English School of Murder*)
Clubbed to Death (1992)
Matricide at St Martha's (1994)
Murder in a Cathedral (1996)

Edwards, Ruth Dudley

Publish and Be Murdered (1998)
Carnage on the Committee (2004)
Murdering Americans (2007)

Website
www.ruthdudleyedwards.com

Laura Wilson

Egleton, Clive (1927–2006)

Often mentioned alongside such authors as Len **Deighton** and John **le Carré**, Clive Egleton spent years in the fields of intelligence and counter-espionage. This experience enabled Egleton to bring a wealth of realism to his many highly regarded **thrillers**.

Born in Middlesex in 1927 and educated at Haberdashers' Aske's Hampstead School, Clive Frederick Egleton enlisted – underage – in the Royal Armoured Corps in 1945 where he trained as a tank driver. He soon joined the South Staffordshire Regiment and served in India, Hong Kong, Germany, Egypt, Cyprus, the Persian Gulf and East Africa before retiring in 1975 as lieutenant colonel.

His first books formed a gripping trilogy about an imminent Soviet invasion of Britain. *A Piece of Resistance* (1970; reissued in 2004 as *Never Surrender*), *Last Post for a Partisan* (1971; reissued in 2005 as *The Sleeper*) and *The Judas Mandate* (1972; reissued in 2005 as *The Last Refuge*) featured intelligence agent David Garnett's ongoing mission to aid Britain's resistance movement in its struggles against the Russian nemesis.

His next book, *Seven Days to a Killing* (1973; reissued in 2003 as *A Spy's Ransom*), is nowadays more famous for the screen version, *The Black Windmill* (1974). Adapted by Leigh Vance, directed by Don Siegel and starring a more-than-usually-taciturn Michael Caine, it told the violent story of the British secret agent John Tarrant's one-man mission to rescue his son, held for ransom by Russian arms dealers.

As Patrick Blake, Egleton also novelised Edward Anhalt's screenplay of wartime prison break drama *Escape to Athena* (1979). He wrote twelve **espionage**/crime novels featuring Peter Ashton of the Special Intelligence Service, beginning with *Hostile Intent* in 1993. This long-running series took Ashton all over the world, fighting an assortment of terrorists, foreign powers and secret organisations. Notable entries include *Warning Shot* (1996), *Dead Reckoning* (1999) and, his last, *The Renegades* (2005).

The Winter Touch (1981), reissued posthumously as *The Presidential Affair* (2006), concerns the blackmailing of Dwight Eisenhower in 1956 by a former lover on the eve of war in the Middle East – a story packed with many modern-day parallels.

Selected Works by the Author
A Piece of Resistance (1970; reissued in 2004 as *Never Surrender*)
The Winter Touch (1981; also published in the United States as *The Eisenhower Deception* and reissued in the UK as *The Presidential Affair*)
Gone Missing (1988; also published in the United States as *Missing from the Record*)
Death of a Sahib (1989)
Last Act (1991)

Mark Campbell

Ellis, Kate (b.1953)

Kate Ellis-Bullock, writing under the name Kate Ellis, is best known for her atmospheric, Wesley Peterson archaeological mysteries. Born in Liverpool, Ellis studied drama before working in teaching, marketing and accountancy. In 1990, she won a competition for North-West Playwrights, which encouraged her to write further, and a holiday in Devon provided the inspiration for her novels.

The first of her books, *The Merchant's House* (1998), introduced readers to black Detective Sergeant Wesley Peterson on the first day of his new posting in South Devon, based at Tradmouth. The locations are transparent versions of real places in South Devon – Tradmouth is Dartmouth, Neston is Totnes, Morbay is Torbay – with Ellis using her author's licence to develop the towns. Peterson is married – although later novels chart problems – and he is soon identified as an empathic, caring detective, whilst his superior, the Liverpudlian Inspector Gerry Heffernan is more direct and blunt. Key to each book is Peterson's archaeological friend Neil Watson. The novels explore parallels between Watson's archaeological digs, which usually start with the discovery of an ancient skeleton, and Peterson's latest case. For example, in *The Merchant's House* (1998), a young woman is murdered and a child goes missing, whilst Watson's research has unearthed the bodies of a woman who had been strangled and a newborn baby. Similarly, *The Armada Boy* (1999) connects relics of the Spanish Armada with the murder of a veteran of the D-Day landings. The historical investigations do not intrude on the primary story but rather are integrated through chapter headings and brief references, but these help develop surprising links between the past and the present, showing that crime and human motivation have changed little over the centuries.

Ellis has also written *The Devil's Priest*, set in the small port of Liverpool in the sixteenth century, during the time of Henry VIII's dissolution of the monasteries. The abbess of a local convent finds herself investigating the murder of a young nun. Ellis vividly brings to life an almost unrecognisable Liverpool during the turbulence of the Middle Ages.

A new series, set in Eborby (a thinly disguised York) and featuring Detective Inspector Joe Plantagenet begins with *Seeking the Dead* (2008).

Selected Works by the Author
The Merchant's House (1998)
The Bone Garden (2001)
A Painted Doom (2002)
The Plague Maiden (2004)
The Marriage Hearse (2006)

Website
www.kateellis.co.uk/

Mike Ashley

Ellory, R[oger] J[ohn] (b.1965)

Although all of his published works are set in the United States, Ellory is, in fact, English. Still resident in Birmingham, he believes that his chosen subjects would

31. R.J. Ellory.

not comfortably sit within a British context. His utterly individual voice has forged a body of work quite unlike that of any of his contemporaries – and his prose has a richness rarely found in the genre.

Ellory's first novel, *Candlemoth* (2003), is a Death Row **thriller** set in North Carolina and Florida, and it was with this book that he created interest within the British and European crime fiction arena, securing immediate translation into Dutch, German and Italian and a shortlisting for the **Crime Writers' Association** (CWA) Ian Fleming Steel Dagger for Best Thriller for 2003. His subsequent novels established Ellory as a crime author of singularity and distinction: *Ghostheart* (2004) is a mystery with two interweaving narratives which took the reader from the liberation of Auschwitz to the violent underworld gangs of New York in the 1960s and 1970s; and *A Quiet Vendetta* (2005) is an epic journey across two countries (Cuba and the United States), spanning ten cities and covering the history of the Mafia, narrated by a Cuban hit man employed by organised crime. In particular, *A Quiet Vendetta* continues to be recognised as a benchmark in modern fiction dealing with the subject of organised crime.

Ellory's fourth novel, *City of Lies* (2006), again defied easy categorisation, moving away from the epic nature of *A Quiet Vendetta* and delivering a fast-paced and multi-layered thriller set in modern day New York, spanning twelve days, and culminating in four violent bank heists perpetrated in Manhattan on Christmas Eve. Once again, Ellory secured a place on the CWA Ian Fleming Steel Dagger Shortlist for the Best Thriller of 2006. His fifth novel, *A Quiet Belief in Angels* (2007), has perhaps become more widely known than all its predecessors, as it enjoyed much attention on British TV, subsequently selling in excess of 70,000 copies in little more than a month. *A Quiet Belief in Angels* evoked the prose styles of Hemingway and Steinbeck (with a soupçon of Harper Lee) and is a serial killer novel beginning in rural Georgia in the late 1930s and following the protagonist as he spends much of his life identifying and bringing to justice the perpetrator of a series of child murders. Subsequent work is demonstrating that Ellory's upwards trajectory shows no sign of abating.

Selected Works by the Author
Candlemoth (2003)
Ghostheart (2004)
A Quiet Vendetta (2005)
City of Lies (2006)
A Quiet Belief in Angels (2007)

Website
www.rogerjonellory.com

Barry Forshaw

Espionage Fiction

British espionage fiction belongs to three distinct periods: (1) the early novels published at the turn of the twentieth century, often with war between nations as a central theme, (2) the so-called **Golden Age**, which drew on the Cold War, and (3) contemporary work using fundamentalism, fanaticism and the 'War on Terror' as plot engines. Pertinently, as a backdrop throughout the writings that populate this genre, we see the British Empire in recession, but with lone protagonists still acting as mavericks, proving that Britain remains a significant force – a trope perhaps best exemplified by Ian Fleming's urbane spy James Bond. Moreover, this genre is significant in the fashion in which it illustrates the gradual erosion of the class system within British society, mirrored by the inexorable loss of Empire. This motif is explored in stunning detail by Geoffrey **Household** in his highly influential *Rogue Male* (1939), with a lone British gunman out to assassinate a thinly disguised Adolf Hitler: the key nemesis of the British Empire.

A striking dichotomy in the British espionage novel may be discerned in the glamorous and adventurous escapist tales forged by Ian **Fleming**, set against the more realistic and cynical view represented by Graham **Greene**, Len **Deighton**, John **le Carré** and Adam Hall (Elleston **Trevor**). Inevitably, there are texts such as Eric **Ambler**'s *A Coffin for Dimitrios* (published in the United States as *Mask of Dimitrios*) and John **Buchan**'s *The Thirty Nine Steps* that feature a provocative synthesis of escapism and cynicism.

The Early Novels

The first British espionage novels are from writers considered British but who also had roots (and allegiances) elsewhere than the mainland. Received opinion generally identifies the father of the British espionage novel as Erskine **Childers**, born in London of Anglo-Irish stock, author of *The Riddle of the Sands: A Record of the*

Secret Service (1903). Childers's novel is as intriguing as his own life, which is well documented in his allegiances to the Irish Republican movement (an allegiance which resulted in his facing the firing squad in 1922). The novel indicated how intertwined the political world is with the looking-glass world of espionage. It is nominally a tale of a sailing adventure off the British coast, incorporating a plot to invade the mainland by German forces. The sailing aspect is authentic (Childers's love of yachting doing him a service here), and the novel was hugely influential for the next generation of espionage writers. Politically, *The Riddle of the Sands* was also significant as Winston Churchill credited Childers's novel with influencing the establishing of naval bases at Invergordon, Scapa Flow and others to protect the mainland from precisely the type of enemy attack detailed in the novel. Ironically, on hearing of Childers's capture during the Irish insurrection (in which Childers's fought on the side of the Irish), Winston Churchill stated, 'No man has done more harm or done more genuine malice or endeavoured to bring a greater curse upon the common people of Ireland than this strange being, actuated by a deadly and malignant hatred for the land of his birth.'

But is Childers the onlie begetter of British Espionage fiction? A dissenting view comes from the aficionados of the work of Rudyard Kipling (1865–1936). Their assertion is that Kipling's novel *Kim* (1901) should be identified as the first British espionage novel. And if publication dates are the sole mechanism to establish this distinction (as opposed to theme and content), then Kipling's followers are correct. *Kim* was serialised in *Mclure's Magazine* (in the United States) from 1900 to 1901 (and a month later in *Cassell's Magazine* in Britain) before being published as a novel, two years before Childers's *The Riddle of the Sands* was published. The backdrop for *Kim* is what was contemporaneously termed 'The Great Game' – the struggle between the British Empire and the Russian states for supremacy in Central Asia. Less of a distinct espionage narrative and more a colonial adventure tale with an espionage theme, *Kim* details the journey the orphan Kimball (Kim) O'Hara must make in order to take a message to a British outpost in Northern India. Kim and his mentor (a Tibetan lama) become embroiled with Russian intelligence agents. (Harold Adrian Russell 'Kim' Philby, 1946–1965 – the notorious British double agent – took his nickname, from Kipling's novel.)

Besides the pro-Irish Childers and the Indian-born Kipling, the Polish-born Teodor Józef Konrad Korzeniowski, better known as Joseph **Conrad**, proved a literary significance in terms of espionage fiction. Conrad penned two espionage novels that are absolutely pivotal to this genre – *The Secret Agent: A Simple Tale* (1907) and lesser-known (but equally remarkable) *Under Western Eyes* (1911). *The Secret Agent* is a dark and often blackly comic tale of a motley group of anarchists, terrorists and spies plotting and counterplotting (in the clandestine backstreets of London) a significant outrage. It is also the first espionage novel to feature terrorism in an overt fashion, with a narrative concerning the bombing of Greenwich Observatory. *Under Western Skies* is often considered as a response to Fyodor Dostoyevsky's *Crime and Punishment*. Alternating between Russia and Switzerland, Conrad's tale of political assassination and subterfuge is a cogently and complex masterwork that anatomises the relationship between oppression and revolution, with the individuals trapped in the struggle working as agents for opposing sides. Conrad here invests notions of duplicity and betrayal with a universal resonance.

The most popular British espionage novelist to follow was the prolific (and now largely neglected) William Tufnell **Le Queux** (1865–1927), a former journalist and diplomat who at one time was Britain's best-selling author. Following Le Queux in terms of popular espionage fiction was Edward Phillips **Oppenheim** (1866–1946). Both these writers were prolific, but their work is now considered dated and formulaic and is dismissed by most genre scholars. The status quo is never questioned. However, they nevertheless require consideration – if only as footnotes.

Espionage fiction received a boost in terms of both literary merit and commercial success with Baron Tweedsmuir (1875–1940) – more commonly known as John Buchan – with his exhilarating *The Thirty Nine Steps* (1915). While it is apparent that this tale of gentleman adventurer Richard Hannay was influenced by Childers's *The Riddle of the Sands*, it is still considered as one of the most significant British espionage thrillers, with its brilliantly realised picaresque narrative. The novel is set against the backdrop of First World War Britain. Buchan's clubland protagonist has to prevent a German spy ring carrying out a political assassination that would destabilise Europe. Part gonzo-chase thriller and part political espionage adventure, this little novel remains essential reading even in a more politically sophisticated era.

The two World Wars brought former intelligence men into the genre. The most prolific and influential is perhaps Somerset **Maugham**, whose *Ashenden: The British Agent* (1928) was reputed to have influenced Ian Fleming. Playwright John Ashenden is enlisted into the British secret service to manipulate a German agent into a trap. The book (a series of linked stories) was based on Maugham's own experiences as a British agent working undercover. Even though Maugham's contribution to espionage fiction is minimal when compared to the myriad plays, novels and short stories he wrote, his influence and significance is so great that his literary progeny could be said to include Greene, Fleming, Ambler and le Carré.

Mention must be made of the underrated Scottish writer Helen (Clark) MacInnes (1907–1985) who is often referred to as 'The Queen of Spy Writers'. MacInnes wrote dramatic and character-driven novels grounded in a plausible reality. Her debut was *Above Suspicion* (1939), a tale of subterfuge set in pre-war Nazi Germany and Austria. MacInnes featured on bestseller lists throughout her career and was more a commercial success than a critical one; however, her work is intelligent and subtle, and she has always been considered a professional. MacInnes's books explore ordinary people caught in the labyrinthine world of spies, although some find her work lacking perspective, with a simplistic and Manichean structure. After the Second World War (with the Nazis vanquished), her espionage tales shifted to the battle against communism, with her later work mining gunrunning and terrorism as resilient themes.

In the same era, the much-admired Eric **Ambler** mined the theme of the articulate amateur who finds himself embroiled with career criminals and cynical spies. Ambler's debut was *The Dark Frontier* (1936), set against a Balkan backdrop – Balkan features in much of Ambler's work – and in which the author predicts a weapon of mass destruction akin to a nuclear device. A variety of agents try to seek control of the manual to produce the super-weapon. On the side of the angels (relatively speaking) are physics professor Henry Barstow and the virtually superhuman Conway

Carruthers. The novel is notionally a parody of the genre and distinct from Ambler's later work. His most revered novel is *The Mask of Dimitrios* (1939), a complex, self-reflexive work that became paradigmatic for a future generation of writers. Charles Latimer, a former-academic-turned detective novelist, is on holiday in pre–Second World War Turkey. Latimer meets Colonel Haki, a Turkish police official (and a fan of detective fiction) who wants the Englishman to use a plot Haki has constructed for his next book. Latimer tries to decline gracefully, but when Haki tells him about the discovery of the body of underworld enforcer, master criminal and spy, the Greek Dimitrios Makropolous, Latimer's curiosity is piqued. Dimitrios was an international gangster, murderer, pimp/woman trafficker, spy and assassin who hid behind different names and identities, operating for a shadowy banking group (the Eurasian Credit Trust). Latimer investigates the hidden life of the man who lies dead on Colonel Haki's morgue slab, after being dragged out of the Bosporus, and decides to trace Dimitrios's life.

Dimitrios is a master criminal who has faked his death. Latimer comes to realise that Dimitrios is really the personification of the crisis that Europe was facing with the malign influence of big businesses forging the foreign policy of nations. The power of Ambler's novel makes it one of the most important existential thrillers of the twentieth century. Ambler's other major novels include *Journey into Fear* (1940), which also features Colonel Haki, and is a precursor to the chase sections of Ian Fleming's *From Russia with Love*, where the protagonists flee Istanbul for sanctuary in the West.

Another writer who, like Ambler, acted as a catalyst for the espionage genre is, of course, Graham **Greene**. Although he wrote widely (including plays and short stories as well as many film and book reviews for *The Spectator*), it is perhaps his *soi-disant* 'entertainments', crime thrillers and insightful espionage novels that are more enjoyed today than his searing novels of catholic guilt (however impeccably written the latter are). Associated with the British Secret Service (SIS) and reporting to double-agent Kim Philby, Greene travelled widely, bringing a grounded reality to the world of spies and political machinations. *The Quiet American* (1955) is a bitter critique of US actions in Indo-China that demonstrated the writer's left-wing stance (and prefigured the corrosive dislike of US politics to be found in such later British writers as Harold Pinter). Many consider Greene to be one of the few left-wing espionage writers in a field that generally attracted those of a right-wing stamp. *Our Man in Havana* (1958), sardonically used Greene's own experience of Cuba, while *The Comedians* (1966) sharply anatomised the chaos that was Haiti under Papa Doc Duvalier. *The Honorary Consul* (1973) brought the iniquities in South America into focus. Greene's most commercially successful work was *The Human Factor* (1978), which was a *New York Times* bestseller for over six months. As per Greene's standard predilection, for *The Human Factor* he chose another exotic location – South Africa – for a narrative involving a secret agent who falls in love with a black woman while on an assassination mission. Greene's immaculately written, brilliantly characterised novels remain a major influence on spy novelists today.

Special mention must be made of the prolific Geoffrey **Household** and the book that is considered one of the pinnacles of the British espionage genre *Rogue Male* (1939). Household held many jobs and travelled extensively throughout America, Africa, Europe and the Middle East, but it was his service with British

Intelligence during the Second World War that would enable him to write his gritty thrillers. *Rogue Male* is a precursor of such major contemporary pieces as Richard Condon's *The Manchurian Candidate* (1959), Frederick **Forsyth**'s *The Day of the Jackal* (1971) and Ken **Follett**'s *Eye of the Needle* (1978). The anonymous protagonist in Household's novel states, 'Like most Englishmen, I am not accustomed to inquire very deeply into motives.... I remember asking myself when I packed the telescopic sight what the devil I wanted it for; but I just felt that it might come in handy.' An unnamed big-game hunter enters an unnamed European state to assassinate an unnamed tyrannical dictator – a thinly veiled Adolf Hitler. *Rogue Male* is a gonzo-chase thriller, with the hero being captured, then escaping back to England, only to be pursued on the bleak Dorset moors. Household's novel *A Rough Shoot* (1951) was filmed as *Shoot First*, with Eric Ambler penning the screenplay.

The Cold War and Contemporary Espionage Novel

After the end of the Second World War, the espionage novel was an established popular entertainment, with the Nazis continuing to supply the requisite nemesis, but this would slowly change as a new enemy emerged from the communist states that formed the Soviet Russia, Cuba and China.

Several post-war writers would mine the genre to great effect, including Scotsman Alistair **MacLean**, who became one of Britain's best-selling writers during the 1960s and 1970s. Although MacLean was primarily a writer of action thrillers, many of his plots used international intrigue as well, featuring the apparatus of spies and surveillance (without, however, the political sophistication of Eric Ambler and Graham Greene). Today, Maclean's work is sometimes dismissed as formulaic, but his impressive narrative skills influenced many contemporary writers such as Lee **Child**, Dennis Lehane and Robert Crais. His later novels suffered as alcohol sapped his skills and ever-increasing film commitments hijacked his talent. Key works that featured an espionage backdrop include *The Guns of Navarone* (1957), *The Last Frontier* (1959), *Night without End* (1960), *Fear Is the Key* (1961), *Ice Station Zebra* (1963), *When Eight Bells Toll* (1966), *Where Eagles Dare* (1967) and his hugely underrated novel set against a Cold-War backdrop, *Circus* (1975).

An emphasis on the escapist tropes of espionage fiction rather than its socio-political elements may be found in a contemporary of Maclean's, perhaps (in this area at least) the most significant writer in the genre whose iconic creation – the sybaritic British Secret Agent 007, James Bond – is a key paradigm of popular culture: Ian **Fleming**.

Fleming, scion of an aristocratic family, drifted after his education at Sandhurst. He worked in Naval Intelligence during the Second World War. After the war he made a mark in upmarket journalism. But it was after his marriage and relocation to the house he would call Goldeneye in the West Indies that he started to write his James Bond novels and short stories beginning with *Casino Royale* (1953) and ending with *Octopussy and the Living Daylights* (1966). The Bond novels all juggle elements of a carefully controlled formulae (actually synthesising classical heroic motifs), which (in essence) consist of Bond travelling to an exotic location where he meets a beautiful woman who harbours secrets from her past. Bond is captured and tortured by a super-villain with power mania. Bond overcomes the villain and saves the day (and in most cases the world), and his prize is the woman. All of this delivered in stylish, vigorous prose that is totally at the service of irresistible narrative drive. One of the Bond novels, however, fractures the formulae. Fleming's tenth Bond novel, *The Spy Who Loved Me* (1962), is delivered in a first-person narrative by the heroine, Vivienne Michel. It is the shortest and most sexually explicit of the series, with Bond only making a late appearance in the narrative; it was also the Bond novel that Fleming was least satisfied with.

Following Fleming's death in 1964, Gildrose Publications (which would later become Ian Fleming Publications) employed a series of writers to continue writing the James Bond novels, beginning with Bond aficionado Kingsley Amis, who wrote *Colonel Sun* (1968) under the penname Robert Markham. The novels then continued under the pen of British thriller writer John **Gardner**. In his obituary in *The Independent* (August 2007), Gardner was reported as having said: 'What I wanted to do was take the character and bring Fleming's Bond into the Eighties as the same man but with all he would have learned had he lived through the Sixties and Seventies.' Gardner penned fourteen original James Bond novels and two film novelisations – *Licence to Kill* (1989) and *GoldenEye* (1995). 'The first new Bond was *Licence Renewed* (1981) in which M reminds Bond that the Double zero section has been abolished; however, M retains Bond as a troubleshooter, telling him "You'll always be 007 to me".' Other titles included *Nobody Lives Forever* (1986), *Win, Lose, or Die* (1989) and, the one Gardner considered his best, *The Man from Barbarossa* (1991).

Gardner was ambivalent about Bond, regarding the character as 'one-dimensional', and was at first reluctant to write about a character he had not devised himself. He said, 'I'm used to putting a lot more flesh on my characters. And of course with Bond I can't. It wouldn't be in keeping with the way Fleming depicted him.' However, he refused to 'dumb down' Bond. 'What the Americans wanted', he said, 'was: "Bond goes to see M, flirts with Moneypenny, goes off, Bond loses the baddy, baddy gets Bond" and then "Bond triumphs". And I thought, "erm, no".' But he enjoyed the trappings, including a Bentley (his second) and a silver Saab 900 Turbo, which his version of Bond switched to later.

A series of Juvenile Bond novels were released by comedy writer and performer Charlie Higson – *Silverfin* (2005), *Blood Fever* (2006), *Double or Die* (2007) and *Hurricane Gold* (2008). These have become very successful, joining the trend started by Anthony Horowitz's Alex Ryder novels.

Samantha Weinberg, under the pseudonym Kate Westbrook, was the first woman to write official James Bond fiction, *The Moneypenny Diaries*, depicting the life of M's secretary. She has published *Guardian Angel* (2005), *Secret Servant* (2006) and *Final Fling* (2008).

Following intense speculation and rumour for several years, *Devil May Care* (2008) by Sebastian Faulks revived the Bond franchise. It was released on the hundredth birthday of the late Ian Fleming. As with the character, the Bond novels seem to be indestructible, as are the film adaptations with Daniel Craig's celluloid interpretation in *Casino Royale* (2006) reinvigorating interest in this icon of British espionage fiction.

The world of espionage fiction took a cynical turn into realism when Len Deighton arrived on the scene with the novels *The Ipcress File* (1962), *Horse under Water* (1963),

Funeral in Berlin (1964), *Billion Dollar Brain* (1966), *An Expensive Place to Die* (1967), *Spy Story* (1974) and *Twinkle, Twinkle, Little Spy* (1976). Interestingly, as they all feature first-person narration, the protagonist is never named and, in fact, in the last two novels, Deighton stated that the central character (Patrick Armstrong) is a different individual. It was the film versions that gave the anti-hero his name. For many readers, however, Harry Palmer would be the antithesis of Ian Fleming's James Bond, especially when one compares the actors who played James Bond (such as Sean Connery) with Michael Caine, who played Harry Palmer. Intriguingly, Bond producer Harry Saltzman was also involved with the Harry Palmer films. The protagonist in these novels is a not-so-clandestine class warrior up against Public School types and deeply cynical about the world he sees around him. The Deighton books are required reading for anyone with an interest in British espionage fiction.

Deighton also wrote a series of critically and commercially successful thrillers featuring a central character named from the Biblical *Book of Judges* – Bernard Samson. The first of them, *Berlin Game* (1983), became part of a trilogy with *Mexico Set* (1984) and *London Match* (1985) – which became denoted as *Game, Set and Match*. Samson works for British Intelligence hunting a KGB agent hidden within the service, alternating between London and East and West Berlin in a game of rivalry and treachery, as British Intelligence and the KGB find that their staff has conflicting loyalties. Such was the popularity of the series that a second trilogy appeared – *Spy Hook* (1988), *Spy Line* (1989) and *Spy Sinker* (1990) – The *Hook, Line and Sinker* series, as it became known. It details Samson's getting on with his life after his wife, Fiona, has defected to the KGB, but there is a problem within his department, the matter of a missing half and a million dollars. This leads him to Berlin accused as a traitor, while Fiona is coping with the Berlin wall coming down. Deighton continued his series with yet another trilogy – *Faith* (1994), *Hope* (1995) and *Charity* (1996) – which continue the Samson family saga in a post–Cold War world, but even with the Wall down, there are still shadows surrounding Samson. Following the end of the Cold War, Deighton's espionage output ceased, but his reputation lives on.

In 2005, David Cornwell, better known as John le Carré, was awarded the **Crime Writers' Association** (CWA) Dagger of Daggers for his highly acclaimed third published novel, *The Spy Who Came in from the Cold* (1963), which also received the Mystery Writers of America (MWA) Edgar Award. Alec Leamas is a British spy who gets involved in a complex and tortuous plot to kill an East German master spy Mundt; Leamas goes undercover in the guise of a double agent. Complex, multi-layered and eloquent of the queasy moral universe of espionage, the novel deserved the recognition it received from both the CWA and the MWA. However, it is perhaps George Smiley of the British Foreign Service that le Carré is now best known for. Smiley was first introduced in le Carré's debut novel, *Call for the Dead* (1961), which he dismissed (with great injustice) as 'not very good'; his second novel, *A Murder of Quality* (1962), was a detective mystery set in a boys' school, featuring Smiley. However, it would be many years before Smiley achieved acclaim as a series character. Le Carré now admits that he worked for both the British Foreign Office as well as MI5 and MI6, and that his intelligence background gives his fiction a distinctive authenticity. *Tinker, Tailor, Soldier, Spy* (1974) reintroduces spymaster Smiley, who tries to discover a mole amongst moles in this tale of identity and loyalty. Other important works include a probing look at the Israeli–Palestinian conflict in *Little Drummer Girl* (1983), and a stream of complex, character-driven spy tales – *A Perfect Spy* (1986), *The Russia House* (1989), *The Night Manager* (1993), *Our Game* (1995), *The Tailor of Panama* (1996) and *Single and Single* (1999). With the Cold War at an end, le Carré began to focus on the duplicitous world of multinational pharmaceuticals with a caustic novel set in Africa – *The Constant Gardener* (2000). Le Carré took a controversial stance on the War on Terror and the British–American attack on Iraq in several angry articles highly critical of the US President George Bush and British Prime Minister Tony Blair. He produced two angry and bitter novels – *Absolute Friends* (2003) and *The Mission Song* (2006) – which focussed on a troubled African Continent. Le Carré's work serves as a salutary reminder that people involved in espionage are as duplicitous as the leaders that position them on the world stage.

There are a series of other British espionage novels that perhaps occupy the middle ground between the glamorous excesses of Ian Fleming's James Bond and that of the cynical and corrupt world depicted by le Carré – and it is the world of Quiller. The Quiller novels were written by Adam Hall, a pseudonym of British novelist Trevor Dudley Smith, also known as Elleston **Trevor**, who had a string of other pen names and wrote in many genres. Hall's debut Quiller novel won Edgar Award (published in the United States as *The Quiller Memorandum*). The second Quiller novel, *The 9th Directive* (1966), was rated by the influential critic Anthony Boucher in *The New York Times* as 'a grand exercise in ambivalence and intricacy, tense and suspenseful at every moment, with fascinating complex characters, unusual plausibility in detailing the professional mechanics of espionage, and a genuine uncompromising tough-mindedness comparable to le Carré's'.

There were nineteen novels featuring Quiller, which are now mostly forgotten. They are trenchantly written pieces, but very much of their day with their lingua franca of the Cold War. Quiller is portrayed as a self-reliant British agent who works alone for a outwardly non-existent wing of British Intelligence – and therefore expendable.

There are several other key writers (who perhaps focus more on British adventure fiction than spy fiction) that deserve mention: Ken Follett, the best-selling author whose pivotal works include *The Eye of the Needle* (1978) and *The Key to Rebecca* (1980); Frederick **Forsyth** with his remarkable debut novel, *The Day of the Jackal* (1971), and *The Odessa File* (1972) and whose later works such as *The Afghan* (2006) focussed on the War on Terror; and the prolific ex-spymaster and former SOE agent Ted **Allbeury**, who came to novel writing late in his life (at the age of fifty-six) and wrote over forty novels under his name as well as utilising the pen names Richard Butler and Patrick Kelly.

There are other British writers of adventure tales who also dabbled in the dark world of British espionage fiction.

Jack **Higgins** wrote over forty novels (also deploying pen-names Harry Patterson, James Graham and Hugh Marlowe). He is famous for *The Eagle Has Landed* (1974) as well as many other taut tales of espionage.

Colin Forbes (Raymond Harold Sawkins; 1923–2006) wrote prolifically as Jay Bernard, Harold English, Richard Raine, Raymond Sawkins, penning several adventure yarns which feature espionage backdrops. The most interesting is the first in his Tweed and Co. series – *Double Jeopardy* (1982) with the British SIS fighting various threats.

Craig Thomas (b.1942) is best remembered for *Firefox* (1977), which like most of his work, is a technothriller set against an MI6 backdrop. Thomas is often referred to as the British Tom Clancy.

Geoffrey **Archer** is a former ITN journalist, who pens military thrillers with an espionage flavour; *The Lucifer Network* (2001) is particularly rewarding, featuring MI6 agent Sam Packer discovering a terrorist network operating out of Africa.

Gerald **Seymour** is another former ITN journalist, most renowned for his IRA espionage thrillers. His debut, *Harry's Game* (1975), is his most celebrated novel. Other themes that Seymour explores include the Gulf War, The Institute for Intelligence and Special Operations (MOSSAD) and the Arab–Israeli conflict.

Stephen **Leather**, an action writer in the vein of Jack Higgins, employs an espionage backdrop with works such as *The Chinaman* (1992) and *The Bombmaker* (1999), both featuring Northern Ireland Terrorism as a motif. Later work from Leather, such as *Cold Kill* (2006) and *Hot Blood* (2007), feature SAS operative Dan Shepherd and focus on the War on Terror.

The film director and actor Bryan Forbes (John Theobald Clarke; b.1929) wrote three novels featuring discredited MI6 officer Alec Hillsden, starting with *The Endless Game* (1986), which he subsequently directed as a film in 1989.

Andy **McNab** and Chris **Ryan** are both former SAS-operatives-turned best-selling novelists. Their books are more action-orientated but do feature espionage within their plotting.

Other contemporary writers with a more literary orientation include Henry **Porter**, with *A Spy's Life* (2001), *Empire State* (2003) and *Brandenburg* (2005), which are well worth exploring; Robert **Harris**, whose *Enigma* (1995) and *Archangel* (1998) are classic espionage tales that have literary merit. Both Porter and Harris are journalists. An up-and-coming British SIS-operative-turned novelist – Charles **Cumming**, often referred to as a young le Carré – is well worth reading, notably his *A Spy by Nature* (2001), *The Hidden Man* (2003), *The Spanish Game* (2006) and the highly accomplished *Typhoon* (2008).

Further Reading
Ambler, Eric. 1985. *Here Lies Eric Ambler*. Weidenfeld & Nicolson.
Atkins, John. 1984. *The British Spy Novel*. Calder.
Denning, Michael. 1987. *Cover Stories: Narrative and Ideology in the British Spy Thriller*. Routledge.
Lycett, Andrew. 1995. *Ian Fleming*. Weidenfeld and Nicholson.
McCormick, Donald. 1977. *Who's Who in Spy Fiction*. Elm Tree Press.
Merry, Bruce. 1977. *Anatomy of the Spy Thriller*. Gill & Macmillan.
Milward-Oliver, Edward. 1987. *The Len Deighton Companion*. Grafton Books.
Panek, LeRoy L. 1981. *The Special Branch: The British Spy Novel, 1890–1980*. Bowling Green Popular Press.
Pearson, John. 1966. *The Life of Ian Fleming*. London: Jonathan Cape.
Sherry, Norman. 1989, 1994, 2004. *The Life of Graham Greene*, 3 volumes. Jonathan Cape.
Webster, Jack. 1991. *Alistair MacLean*. Chapmans.

Ali Karim

F

Feminist Readings in British Crime Fiction

Killers and Victims

In 1997, a portrait of the notorious British child killer, Myra Hindley, was displayed at the Royal Academy in London. Within days, it was defaced by people protesting about its presence, as if the representation of Hindley was, in fact, the woman herself and the destruction of an image could be equated with the destruction of this notorious killer.

Western society has always had an uneasy relationship with women in the criminal world, both as perpetrators and as victims. Even today, acceptable roles for women are circumscribed by the expectations of society. Women in the world of crime, particularly women who kill, are seen as stepping beyond the boundaries they are permitted to occupy – a fact reflected in crime fiction.

It is rare for men who kill – no matter how heinously – to be viewed with the same abhorrence or ambivalence as women who take life. The monsters abound: moors murderer Myra Hindley, rather than her partner Ian Brady (who was the prime mover in these crimes), became the primary target of hate for the tabloid newspapers; similarly Maxine Carr, the girlfriend of another vilified child killer Ian Huntley who lied to police to support her lover's alibi, was treated with almost the same outrage as Huntley himself, even though there was no suggestion that she was implicated in his crime; Rose West, the wife of serial killer Fred West (whose house – now demolished – became famous as a site of horror and mass murder), was deemed guilty by association before the courts ever decided her guilt (a verdict that is still viewed with some doubt by people who observed the case).

Women as victims, particularly victims of sex crimes, are seen through the same distorting lens. The police investigating the so-called Yorkshire Ripper killings were quite open in their division of his victims into the 'innocent' and the 'deserving'. More recent murders suggest that attitudes have not changed much. In 1989, Jason Swift, a fourteen-year-old boy was gang-raped and killed. His killers were charged with manslaughter because there was concern about attitudes in the jury towards the young victim who had been a rent boy. More recently still, women murdered in East Anglia were identified by their work as prostitutes.

Women who are professionally involved with the law are also viewed through the distorting mirror of their gender. The woman who was prison governor of Wayland Prison when Jeffrey Archer was an inmate was described in the *Sun* newspaper in terms of her looks, her clothes, her figure and her presumed resemblance to Archer's wife, Mary. The first woman to achieve the rank of Assistant Chief Constable in the United Kingdom, Alison Halford, was suspended from her job not on grounds of incompetence but because she, dressed only in her underwear, allegedly shared a jacuzzi with a male police officer. Even in the twenty-first century, the mores and expectations surrounding women are very different from those applied to men. All of this informs much current crime writing.

Fact into Fiction

Popular fiction holds a mirror up to society. How do writers of crime fiction treat women in their pages: women who kill, women who are killed and women who hunt killers? Across this vast market, it is impossible to identify every example, but it is possible to distinguish patterns.

Women's **sexuality** has frequently been seen as threatening within Western society (and further afield, of course, notably in middle-Eastern counties). Many customs, restrictions and taboos exist to rein in and control this powerful and dangerous force. The Christian Church, whose voice and mores underlie large swathes of western art and thinking, has at its centre that ultimate contradiction: the virgin mother, a concept that allows a woman to move from one acceptable role, that of virgin and innocent, to another, that of mother, without having to undergo the necessity of defiling the first status in the course of achieving the second.

The ways in which women as sexual beings are depicted in fiction (crime and other genres) demonstrates the threat they can represent. The woman who uses sex to destroy men is a staple of myth, folklore and fiction. Clytemnestra (in the *Orestia*), Medea, no end of wicked stepmothers, Chaucer's Wife of Bath: all have given the sexual woman a bad press. Lady Macbeth is an archetype that is still with us, and even in the twenty-first century, we are saddled with the opposing images of the virgin and the slut. Crime fiction is not immune. Overt sexuality in a woman often marks either evil or victimhood – frequently deserving victimhood.

Turning to notions of women as killers, it is notable that British crime fiction is strongly influenced by the American model in this regard: Dashiell Hammett's Sam Spade, arguably the model for all hard-boiled detectives that follow, makes his appearance in *The Maltese Falcon* (1930), in which the innocent-seeming Brigid O'Shaughnessy uses sex to manipulate the men she encounters and also kills. Phyllis Dietrichson in James M. Cain's *Double Indemnity* (1943) seduces Walter Huff into murder and destroys him. (The original novel was based on a real-life case which demonstrates the fascination that our culture has with the woman who kills: Ruth Snyder plotted with her lover to murder her husband for the insurance. Snyder is usually seen as the prime mover in this case. Her moment of execution was photographed clandestinely by a reporter and published to great controversy in *The New York Daily News*.)

The sexual woman-as-villain runs through noir and the hard-boiled sub-genre of crime fiction both in the United States and Britain. Raymond **Chandler** uses this image repeatedly. Carmen in *The Big Sleep*, Velma in *Farewell, My Lovely* and Eileen Wade in *The Long Goodbye* are all depicted in terms of their sexuality, and they all kill.

But it is not only these sub-genres in which this image appears. The woman as sexual predator and killer also stalks the pages of the so-called cosy novels of the British **Golden Age**. The 'queen of crime' Agatha **Christie** was not averse to using a woman's sexuality in this way. In *Five Little Pigs* (1943), Elsa Greer, the lover of the artist Amyas Crayle, is revealed as the women who feeds her lover slow poison and watches him die as he paints her – an image as far from cosy as it is possible to find. In *A Murder is Announced* (1950), the motive for the murder is tied up in the complexities of a lesbian relationship, which becomes a symbol for social isolation and secrecy.

Christie also uses the audience's own stereotypes to mislead, in which the apparently predatory woman becomes the victim. In both *Death on the Nile* (1937) and

Evil under the Sun (1941), the overtly predatory woman is murdered by her apparent rival, who becomes a sexual predator in her own right, aided by the man who is the object of passion of both women.

The Seducers and the Seduced

Dorothy L. **Sayers**'s *Gaudy Night* is a fascinating exploration of attitudes to woman's sexuality. Set in a women's college in Oxford, issues around the conflict between professional success and the personal fulfilments of marriage and motherhood are openly explored. Harriet Vane, as non-virgin professional and object of the passion of Lord Peter **Wimsey**, occupies a pivotal place in this debate.

A certain element of wish fulfilment and (probably unintentional) humour appears (in *Gaudy Night*) in the image of Harriet Vane parading the sexually desirable but unavailable Lord Peter around the senior common room in a passage redolent of repressed sexuality:

> [H]e has made a complete conquest of Miss Hillyard...
> 'And Miss de Vine is making a complete conquest of him.'
> 'It's mutual I fancy. At any rate, her back hair is coming down which is a sure sign of pleasure and excitement.'

Lord Peter 'seduces', he masks his intentions behind an 'innocent profile' and he retrieves a woman's scarf as it 'slips from her shoulders'. Though Lord Peter is there to gain information from these women, the sexual undertones of the scene are unmistakeable. The whole book is imbued with sexual threat: set in a women's college in which a malicious, anonymous campaign is being waged in overtly sexual terms:

> It was not in any way an agreeable drawing – not at all the kind of thing that one would expect to find in a college quadrangle. It was ugly and sadistic. It depicted a naked figure of exaggeratedly feminine outlines, inflicting savage and humiliating outrage upon some person of indeterminate gender clad in a cap and gown.

The book carries a true sense of menace, and the denouement once again places the sexual woman in the role of villain, in this case, the woman who values her role as a wife more than she values academic integrity.

The sexual woman as villain and killer is a widely found image. More disturbing is the sexual woman as deserving victim. P.D. **James**, in *Cover Her Face* (1962), presents the image of a woman who has insinuated herself into a family via a home for unmarried mothers and is apparently in the process of seducing the son of the house to fall in love with her. The killer of this woman is another woman who has acted to defend her family honour, and James's detective, Adam **Dalgliesh**, is apparently sympathetic towards this motive and perceives the dead woman as someone who has brought her fate upon herself:

> 'Poor Sally. What an exhibitionist! She had to have drama if it killed her.'
> 'In a way it did', said Dalgliesh. 'If she hadn't played with people, Sally would be alive today.'

Sexual Extremes

In another field, Alex Forrest in the Adrian Lyne film *Fatal Attraction* (1987) – a model for several characters in British crime fiction – is a prime example of the threat incarnated in the sexual woman. Rejected, she becomes the hunter, using first the 'women's' weapons, manipulative weakness, and later the threat of violence. Her own subsequent brutal murder is depicted as something that she has brought upon herself, and the implication is that it will carry no consequences. By a blood sacrifice of the sexual woman who has led him astray, the adulterous man has redeemed himself.

Frannie, the narrator of Susanna Moore's *In the Cut* (1995), becomes sexually involved with a man she believes may be a serial killer who murders and mutilates his victims. Her sexual availability to this man makes her a clear and obvious target for his violence. When she becomes the victim of the real killer – her misinterpretation of her lover, Malloy, leads her directly into his path – she brings the extremes of violence on herself by resisting so that Malloy will see that she did not acquiesce in her own death, he will 'know how hard I fought'. This death of the sexual woman is subverted at the end of the book. Frannie wants to turn her own body into something her lover can read to locate her killer. The victim becomes hunter.

The pages of crime fiction are filled with images of the sexual woman as victim, from raped and murdered prostitutes to the singer in Ed McBain's *The Frumious Bandersnatch* (2004), who has devised and performed a rape scenario to accompany her song and who is ultimately raped and murdered herself.

The message is clear: the sexual woman is dangerous and must be controlled or destroyed.

Hunters and Detectives

But in crime fiction, women are not just killers and victims. They are also hunters – and detectives. The image of the damaged, conflicted male detective that has become a cliché of the genre is generally seen as originating in the noir novels of Dashiell Hammett. Even earlier, there is Sherlock **Holmes**, solitary, drug-using and obsessed (it is beyond the scope of this piece to speculate about Holmes's sexuality, but the question does arise), and Charles **Dickens**'s Inspector Bucket in *Bleak House*, who is as ruthless as any twenty-first century detective in his search for answers, his investigation costing the life of Jo, the young crossing sweeper. The first female private investigator to appear in the wake of Sherlock Holmes was Loveday Brooke in the stories by Catherine L. Pirkis collected as *The Experiences of Loveday Brooke, Lady Detective* (1894). Brooke is depicted as a determined, unmarried woman who knows her own mind and is determined to overcome the prejudices of the day.

The depiction of women in crime fiction has moved on over the years from Hammett's and Chandler's cigarette-smoking blonde, seductive and dangerous, to the unnerving automata of Dr Sam Ryan in the TV series *Silent Witness* or Patricia Cornwell's Kay Scarpetta. But do these women present any more a realistic picture of women that the earlier depictions? In Patricia Cornwell's first novel, *Postmortem* (1990) – a book that spawned many imitations in the United Kingdom – Kay Scarpetta presents a figure of rounded humanity: she has a home life, she has to deal with the professional challenges of being a successful woman in a field dominated by men and she makes mistakes in her relationship choices, but as the series develops, the humanity of the character retreats.

Despite the dark and sometimes graphic themes of these novels, Cornwell's work reflects a tradition that has a lot in common with Agatha Christie and the Golden Age writers. In Scarpetta, Cornwell is recreating a concept that first appeared in the earliest work that is recognisably crime fiction: the detective as superhero. Auguste

Dupin is possibly the earliest detective and probably the inspiration for Conan **Doyle** to create Sherlock Holmes. The detectives of the so-called Golden Age were equally incredible: Hercule **Poirot**, Miss **Marple** and Lord Peter Wimsey are all lacking in many of the attributes of humanity, and all solve crimes and catch the villain by methods that are little short of miraculous.

The sub-genre within crime fiction of the 'hard-boiled' noir narrative was the domain of male writers until women such as Sarah Paretsky, Sue Grafton and Val **McDermid** began writing books in which women were the lead investigators, either as private detectives or as police officers. The female detective may be a more recent development, but she is as conflicted, damaged and involved in a struggle to survive in a hostile world as the heroes of Raymond Chandler and Dashiell Hammett.

Her sexuality is frequently part of the conflict she faces. Lynda **La Plante**'s DCI Jane Tennison, in the *Prime Suspect* series, places her sexuality below her career ambition. Though she is faced with hostility because she is a woman, she rejects or neglects her personal relationships to succeed as a detective. She barters her personal life for success, in a similar way that the academic women in Dorothy L. Sayers's *Gaudy Night* are seen as having to make a choice. Paretsky's V.I. Warshawski constantly comes up against the conflict between the demands of her work and the demands of a relationship. When these two come into conflict, it is the demands of work that take priority.

Val McDermid presents different interpretations of the woman as hunter. Her earlier characters, the journalist Lindsay Gordon and the PI Kate Brannigan are very much of the hard-boiled genre. Her *Wire in the Blood* series presents almost a Janus-faced persona in the form of Carol Jordan and Tony Hill. Carol Jordan, a police officer, has to deal with the expected conflict of a woman succeeding in a largely male environment, but the conflicted and damaged character is the psychologist Tony Hill. Both characters pay the penalty of extreme sexual violence for mistakes they make in the course of their investigations.

But a different kind of woman as hunter emerges in the pages of *A Place of Execution* (1999), in which the matriarchal power and the strength of the apparent victim, a female child, combine to turn the perpetrator of the crimes into a victim himself. He is convicted and executed for a crime he did not commit.

Agatha Christie's Miss Marple presents yet another image of the woman as investigator. She is an elderly unmarried woman who has lived all her life in an archetypal English village and acts as an amateur detective using her knowledge of human nature, usually derived by extrapolating from behaviour within the village to the outside world, to solve crimes. She is the archetype of the virgin spinster (despite recent attempts by television adaptations to give her a more raunchy past).

Christie presents two images of Miss Marple. One is a stereotype of the elderly single woman as both weak and redundant. In the novels, she is described as *foolish, fluffy, soft, vague, twittering*. However, it is important to note that these descriptions never come from Christie herself as narrator – they are always mediated through the eyes of another character. The other image of Miss Marple is presented via another range of adjectives: *shrewd, implacable, relentless, wise*. Again, it is not the voice of the author that gives us these views; it is the voice of observing characters.

Christie's writing is the art of secrecy, and the way in which she depicts Miss Marple, firstly as the world might expect her to be and then as she is in her role as nemesis, reflects this aspect of the novels. Miss Marple belongs to a tradition of female power that is far older than that of Jane Tennison or V.I. Warshawski. It is a concept that is almost medieval – that of the wise woman and the witch. The apparently weak exterior conceals something that is implacable and dangerous.

New Trends

Towards the end of the twentieth century, crime fiction took a turn towards extreme and graphic violence and bizarre murder. One of the earliest books in this genre (a massive influence on UK fiction), Thomas Harris's *The Silence of the Lambs* (1988) presented the reader with a killer who murdered women for their skins, pursued by a young trainee FBI agent, Clarice Starling. Following on from this book came the extremes of sexual torture in several accomplished novels: *Prime Suspect* (1991) by Lynda La Plante, *Birdman* (2000) by Mo **Hayder** *Blindsighted* (2001) by Karin Slaughter and *The Torment of Others* (2004) by Val McDermid.

All of these books present women as victims, and their rapes, bondages, tortures and deaths are graphically described. The fact that they are written by women can make them uncomfortable reading.

For a long time, the role that women could play in the system of justice was restricted. They could be victims, they could be killers and they could face the full weight of the law. They had no say in the formation of laws, and they had no rights to any role in the legal system other than those outlined above. Many of the women writers of the Golden Age wrote their first books in the days before women had any significant rights under the law. They created a fictional legal world in which women had that major role that the real world denied them. Within this world, women could be not only victims or perpetrators, but a force to be reckoned with within the legal world itself.

The emergence of the historical mystery has also added a new dimension to recasting women. Marilyn Todd's vixen Claudia, in the Roman mystery series that began with *I, Claudia* (1995), knows how to use her femininity to work the system. Most striking is the character of Sister Fidelma in the series by Peter Tremayne set in seventh century Ireland, that began with *Absolution by Murder* (1994). Fidelma is an advocate of the Brehon Law Court which grants her absolute authority in the investigations she undertakes, even when questioning kings. The roles of women in crime fiction have expanded to reflect the expanding roles of women in society. Recent trends in fiction, particularly in the United Kingdom, have led crime fiction down a darker path, and the woman as victim of extreme sexual violence once again haunts the pages of crime fiction. *See also* Gay and Lesbian Crime Fiction.

Further Reading
Barnett, Colleen A. 1998. *Mystery Women, An Encyclopedia of Leading Women Characters in Mystery Fiction.* Ravenstone Books.
Birch, Helen, ed., 1993. *Moving Targets: Women, Murder and Representation.* Virago
Gamman, Lorraine, and Margaret Marshment, eds. 1988. *The Female Gaze: Women as Viewers of Popular Culture.* The Women's Press.
Gray, Frances. 2003. *Women, Crime and Language.* Palgrave Macmillan.
Heising, Willetta L. 2000. *Detecting Women.* Purple Moon Press, 3rd edition.
Masters, Brian. 1997. *She Must Have Known: The Trial of Rosemary West.* Corgi.
Munt, Sally R. 1994. *Murder by the Book? Feminism and the Crime Novel.* Routledge.
Nichols, Victoria and Thompson, Susan. 1998. *Silk Stalkings.* Scarecrow Press.
Swanson, Jean and James, Dean, eds. 1996. *By a Woman's Hand, A Guide to Mystery Fiction by Women.* Berkley Books, 2nd edition.

Carla Banks

Fforde, Jasper (b.1961)

Embracing the same absurdist universe as Douglas Adams and Terry Pratchett, infused with a smidgeon of *Monty Python's Flying Circus*, Jasper Fforde's broad literary pastiches, although ostensibly crime-related, are equally at home in the fantasy/**science fiction** genre.

The son of a former RAF pilot and chief cashier of the Bank of England, Fforde was born in London on 11 January 1961 and educated at Dartington Hall School, Devon, a progressive boarding school in which he was encouraged to make super-8 cine films. Inspired by a Milk Marketing Board commercial showing behind-the-scenes footage of Roger Moore on the set of *Live and Let Die* (1973), Fforde knew by the age of ten that he wanted to be a film director.

Leaving Dartington at sixteen, Fforde worked as an odd-job man for several years until a decorating assignment at a producer's house led him to his first job in the British film industry – as a runner on *The Pirates of Penzance* (1983). Graduating to a focus puller on blockbusters such as *Golden Eye* (1995) and *The Saint* (1997), he submitted a tongue-in-cheek **police procedural** entitled *Who Killed Humpty Dumpty?*, written in his spare time, to various agents. It was universally rejected. Other doomed projects included *The Fourth Bear* (a Goldilocks mystery) and *The Solution of Edwin Drood*. His sixth attempt, *The Eyre Affair*, was accepted for publication in 2001.

The Eyre Affair introduces the eccentric Thursday Next, a literary detective (or LiteraTec) working in department twenty-seven of Swindon's SpecOps force in a surreal, alternative late 1980s in which the Crimean War never ended and Wales is a Leninist republic. Together with her cloned pet dodo, Pickwick, Next's job is to police important works of fiction, ensuring that villains like Acheron Hades do not get away with their dastardly plans to hold minor **Dickens** characters to ransom or abduct the heroine of *Jane Eyre*. Fforde blurs fact, fiction and plain silliness into an audacious mélange of bookish in-jokes and groan-worthy puns that, although not appealing to every taste, is often strangely beguiling.

Having married Crimean War soldier and novelist Landon Parke-Laine in Fforde's debut, Next returned in its direct sequel, *Lost in a Good Book* (2002), only to find her husband wiped from history by a temporal hit man. While taking a holiday in an unpublished detective novel in *The Well of Lost Plots* (2003), Next accompanies Miss Havisham to fight a new kind of book that threatens the fabric of literature itself. The convoluted storyline continued in two further instalments.

Fforde's other series, subtitled 'Nursery Crimes', postulates a *Shrek*-like alternative reading in which nursery rhyme and fairy tale characters are real. The first in the series, *The Big over Easy* (2005) was a reworking of his first attempted novel.

In his spare time, Fforde flies a 1937 de Havilland Tiger Moth over Wales. *See also* Humour and Crime Fiction.

Selected Works by the Author
The Eyre Affair (2001)
Lost in a Good Book (2002)
The Well of Lost Plots (2003)
Something Rotten (2004)
The Big Over Easy (2005)
The Fourth Bear (2006)
First among Sequels (2007)

Website
www.jasperfforde.com

Mark Campbell

Film and Crime: Page to Screen

British crime fiction has long provided textual fodder for the film industry. At the same time, film has greatly influenced British crime fiction. Yet, less than 15 percent of the more than 1,000 British crime movies from the late 1930s to the present have been based on British crime novels. However, back in the silent era, British crime fiction was a prime source of material. For instance, Hitchcock's 1926 silent film, *The Lodger* was the director's first real film, based on the novel by Marie Lowndes (1868–1947) about a landlady who suspects her lodger is Jack the Ripper, while, before that, there were films like *A Study in Scarlet* in 1913, adapted from Conan **Doyle**'s novel, and *The Ringer* in 1925, based on Edgar **Wallace** novel *The Gaunt Stranger*.

32. Director Alfred Hitchcock contemplates Robert Donat and Lucie Mannheim on the set of *The 39 Steps* (1935).

The early talkies were, if anything, more receptive to adapting crime fiction. If Edgar Wallace was one of the most adapted of twentieth century crime writers, Hitchcock set the standard for modern suspense adaptations. After silent films based on the work of Lowndes, Cosmo Hamilton (1870–1942) and Noel Coward (1899–1973), he adapted novels by Ethel White (1876–1944) (*The Lady Vanishes*, 1938), Daphne du Maurier (1907–1989) (*Jamaica Inn*, 1939; *Rebecca*, 1940; and *The Birds*, 1963), Francis **Iles** (*Suspicion*, 1941), John **Buchan** (*The 39 Steps*, 1935), Joseph **Conrad** (*Sabotage*, 1936) and Jack Trevor Story (1917–1991) (*The Trouble with Harry*, 1955).

Wallace was a popular source of suspense movies for some five decades, with well in excess of a hundred films made from his books, beginning with *Nurse and Martyr* in 1915. Most Wallace adaptations came from Britain and Germany, though some were made in the United States. In the 1930s, Walter Forde's remake of *The Gaunt Stranger* (1938) and William Howard's *The Squeaker* (1937) compared favourably with Hitchcock's early output. Only slightly less influenced by Hitchcock was Arthur Woods's 1938 *They Drive by Night*, about lorry drivers helping an ex-con solve a murder in which he has been implicated. Adapted from a novel by the pseudonymous James **Curtis**, the film caught the eye of Graham **Greene**, who considered it on a level with the French cinema. Curtis would also write *There Ain't No Justice*, adapted by Penrose Tennyson in 1939, about boxing and racketeering, which, in turn, would influence post-war crime films.

Aside from Wallace, there were others whose work was frequently adapted. Not least of which was Conan Doyle whose Sherlock **Holmes** stories have lent themselves to countless movies, beginning in 1909 with a Danish film *Baskervilles/ Da graa dame/The Grey Dame*, and, in Britain, *The Speckled Band* in 1912. Another frequently adapted novelist was James Hadley **Chase**, whose ***No Orchids for Miss Blandish*** appeared in 1948 – remade in 1971 by Robert Aldrich, re-titled *The Grissom Gang*. Chase was particularly popular in France where his novels led to films like *The Sucker Punch* (1957), *Miss Callahan Comes to Grief* (1957), *The Things Men Do* (1958) and Joseph Losey's *Eva* (1962).

But it was Graham Greene who created the template for the modern British crime novel and its cinematic counterpart. Not as prolific as Wallace, Greene was the acceptable face of British crime fiction. British readers and middlebrow critics might have been divided over the merits of Spillane, Chase or Peter **Cheyney**, but few objected to Greene's *entertainments* or their subsequent adaptations.

Greene's visual sense was second-to-none: 'When I describe a scene, I capture it with the moving eye of the cine-camera rather than with the photographer's eye – which leaves it frozen. In this precise domain I think that the cinema has influenced me...I work with the camera, following my characters and their movements' (*The Other Man: Conversations with Graham Greene*, Bodley Head, 1981).

He also possessed an inordinate understanding of how to move from the page to the screen. Or vice versa, as in his novelisation of *The Third Man*, which began as a story and was adapted as a movie, before Greene finally turned it into a novel.

A former *Spectator* film critic, Greene's fiction would be utilised by directors like Reed, Alberto Cavalcanti, Fritz Lang, John Boulting, Joseph Mankiewicz, John Ford and Phillip Noyce. Adaptations of his work would include *Orient Express* (1934), *This Gun for Hire* (1942), *Went the Day Well?* (1942), *The Ministry of Fear* (1944), *The Confidential Agent* (1945), *The Man Within* (1947), *The Fallen Idol* (1948), *The Third Man* (1949), *The Heart of the Matter* (1953), *Short Cut to Hell* (1957), *Our Man in Havana* (1959) and *The Quiet American* (1958).

Greene's ***Brighton Rock*** (1947), directed by Boulting, ranks among the most influential British crime movies ever made. Like *The Third Man*, it portrays the criminal as subversive, even if, unlike the latter, it takes place in seedy pre-war Britain rather than post-war Vienna. Interestingly, the original US title was *Young Scarface*, a clear attempt to place Greene's protagonist in the same cauldron as the Cagney character in Hawks's 1932 movie and, in doing so, exploit the idea of the criminal as hero. However, the subtexts of British crime movies invariably relate to class, and so offer a different view regarding criminal protagonists than their

American counterparts. Pinky can barely be compared to Scarface or even to Alan Ladd in Frank Tuttle's adaptation of Greene's *This Gun for Hire*, in which the personal and political defects of the novel's protagonist are curtailed for the benefits of an American audience. Moreover, British crime movies derive from social realism, rather than the dream world manufactured by Hollywood. Consequently, British films would not portray anti-authoritarian tough-guys until late 1940s films like **Hell Drivers** and **Hell Is a City**.

Despite, or because of, the austerity of the post-war years, cheap British crime adaptations during the late 1940s came fast and furious, many depicting a post-war *spiv* culture. Among the key crime movies adapted from novels during the 1940s were *They Made Me a Fugitive* (1949) from Jackson Budd's *A Convict Has Escaped*, **It Always Rains on Sundays** (1947) from the novel by Arthur La Bern (1909–1990) and Roy Baker's *The October Man* (1947), produced and written by Eric **Ambler** from his novel. That same year saw Anthony Kimmins's *Mine Own Executioner*, based on a psychological **thriller** by the respected Nigel Balchin, who also wrote the screenplay. Two years later, Powell and Pressburger adapted Balchin's *The Small Back Room*. Meanwhile, in the United States, *Kiss the Blood off My Hands* appeared in 1948, directed by Norman Foster, from the noir novel by Gerald Butler (1907–1988), as did two films based on Eric Ambler's thrillers: *Journey into Fear* (1943), directed by Orson Welles, and Jean Negulesco's *Mask of Dimitrios* (1944).

The film that most unsettled critics during that decade was *No Orchids for Miss Blandish*. Directed by St. John Clowes in 1948 from Chase's novel, the film, like the novel, was unashamedly influenced by American hard-boiled fiction ('hardly a wasted word or jarring note anywhere', said George Orwell). Even before its release, *No Orchids'* violence and the relationship between the middle-class Blandish and the gangster caused problems with the censors. Middlebrow critics despised the movie. 'The most sickening exhibition of brutality, perversion, sex and sadism ever to be shown on the screen', said *Monthly Film Bulletin*, while future Prime Minister Harold Wilson, in the year Clowes's film was released, condemned 'gangster, sadistic and psychological films' and called for 'more films which genuinely show our way of life' (Barr 1986).

One critic to speak-up for British crime movies and fiction was Julian Maclaren-Ross. In his essay, 'A Mirror of Darkness' (*New World Writing*, 1945), he makes a case for their importance, citing a variety of novels and two films in particular: the aforementioned *They Drive by Night* and David Macdonald's 1938 *Dead Men Tell No Tales*. The latter is based on *The Norwich Victims* (1935) by Francis Beeding, about a murder of a matron in a boys' school after she wins the lottery. But Maclaren-Ross maintained that, rather than imitating American films, British crime movies should follow the model of inexpensive continental classics like Fellini's *I Vitelloni* and Marcel Carné's *Quai des Brumes*.

That did not happen, even when there was no shortage of British crime movies made by small studios during the 1950s. More crime movies were released in that decade than in any previous one, many with American actors and some in conjunction with American studios. Due to the economic upswing of the 1950s, a declining crime rate and the reintegration of former underworld figures, *spiv* films had run their course, replaced by full-scale crime movies, many of which were still about readjusting to post-war life. The decade's most noteworthy films include *Soho Incident* (1956), directed by Vernon Sewell, about gambling and racketeering, from *Wide Boys Never Work* (1937) by Robert Westerby (1909–1968); the excellent **Tiger in** *the Smoke* (1956) directed by Roy Baker, from a novel by Marjorie **Allingham**; J. Lee Thompson's *Yield to the Night* (1956), from a novel by Joan Henry (1914–2000), based on Ruth Ellis's case; Cy Enfield's *Hell Drivers* (1957) from a John Kruse (b.1919) story; Jack Clayton's *Room at the Top* (1958) from the novel by John Braine (1922–1986); *Sleeping Tiger* (1954), a robbery film based on the novel by Maurice Moisiewitsch (1914–1972), directed by Losey; and *Blind Date* (1959), also by Losey, from a novel by Leigh Howard (1914–1979). While in the United States, Nicholas Ray adapted Butler's *Mad with Much Heart*, re-titling it *On Dangerous Ground* (1952).

A memorable (if not entirely successful) film of the period was Alfred Hitchcock's adaptation of Frederick Knott's *Dial M for Murder* (1953) which had started life as a radio and stage play in 1952 before being adapted as a novel and then filmed in 1954. The film, about a man who plans to murder his wife, was rated amongst the top ten mystery films by the American Film Institute in 2008.

One of the best-known crime movies of the era also came from America: Twentieth Century Fox's 1950 *Night and the City*, directed by Jules Dassin, from Gerald **Kersh**'s low-life novel. Owing more to the romanticism of film noir – Dassin had made noir classics *Brute Force*, *Naked City* and *Thieves Highway* – than the tradition of British crime movies, it manages, thanks to Max Greene's cinematography, to capture the sleazy world of Kersh's novel. It's a flawed film with a disjointed, tourist-oriented view of London, yet considerably better than Irwin Winkler's 1992 US remake. Like *No Orchids*, Dassin's film was met with hostility, viewed as another Hollywood incursion into British cultural life.

British crime films hit their apogee between 1959 and 1963, as the country was caught between the repressiveness and assurances they had never had it so good, and the 'swinging sixties'. Consequently, early 1960s films depicted a society in transition. Policing and attitudes to crime were changing – partly due to the effect of the Street Offences Act of 1959 and the Betting and Gaming Act of 1960, relating to prostitution and gambling. Nevertheless, it remained an era of rampant police corruption and gangland crime, exemplified by scandals within the Metropolitan police and the emergence of the Kray Brothers. Many of the era's crime movies imitated American films, though some offered a more realistic portrayal of the criminal end of the culture. This was a time of anxiety regarding Britain's place in the world, as well as how society should be organised, and how it coped with moral deviation. Among the notable adaptations were Val Guest's excellent *Hell Is a City* (1960), adapted from the robbery and gambling novel by Maurice Procter (1906–1973); Dearden's classic readjustment to society film, ***The League of Gentlemen*** (1960), from the bank robbery novel by John Boland (1913–1976); Dearden's robbery movie *A Place to Go* (1963) from the novel by Michael Fisher (b.1933) *Bethnal Green* (1961); Montgomery Tully's prison-break movie *Clash By Night* (1963) adapted from a novel by Rupert Croft-Cooke (1903–1979); and, in the same year, Ken Annakin's *The Informers* from the novel *Death of a Snout* (1961) by Douglas Warner; Preminger's *Bunny Lake is Missing* (1965), a London-set American film from the novel by Evelyn Piper (1908–1994); and David Greene's *The Strange Affair* (1968), based on the novel by Bernard Toms (b.1931).

Unfortunately, the growing popularity of television meant the death of double features and the closure of small studios that had produced British movies. By the end of the decade, fewer crime films than ever were being made. With the cold war at its peak and the Vietnam war in full swing, it was not surprising that the decade should see three films based on novels by spy writer John **le Carré**, all financed by American money: *The Spy Who Came in from the Cold* (1965), directed by Martin Ritt for Paramount/Salem (UK); *The Deadly Affair* from le Carré's novel *Call For the Dead* (1966), directed by Sidney Lumet for Columbia (UK); and *The Looking Glass War* (1969), directed by Frank Pierson for Columbia/Frankovich (UK).

The 1970s saw even fewer crime movies based on books. With the three-day week and energy shortages, the decade provided the backdrop for a landmark adaptation. ***Get Carter***, directed by Mike Hodges from Ted **Lewis**'s racketeering novel, would come to rank alongside classic American films of the era like *Point Blank*, *The Friends of Eddie Coyle* and *Dirty Harry*. Released in 1970, *Get Carter*, with its violence, despair and dark humour, depicts clashing criminal cultures and echoes the kitchen-sink realism of movies and novels like *This Sporting Life* and *Saturday Night and Sunday Morning*. Though Lewis's novel is set in Scunthorpe, Hodges switches the action to Newcastle, notorious at the time for political corruption. Like *No Orchids* two decades earlier, *Get Carter* would have problems with the censors and was met with critical disdain. Hodges's movie was too bleak to be all that popular. In fact, so unrecognised was the film that a year after its release it would be remade in America by George Armitage with a black cast, re-titled *Hit Man*.

The 1970s saw some other interesting adaptations. Besides Aldrich's aforementioned *The Grissom Gang*, there was Michael Tuchner's *Villain* that appeared in 1971, loosely based on the Krays. Derived from *The Burden of Proof* (1968) by James Barlow (1921–1973), Tuchner's film was a holdover from the early 1960s in how it used the genre to raise social issues. In 1972, Tony Richardson's *Dead Cert*, from Dick Francis's horse-racing novel, appeared, and, in 1973, Nicolas Roeg's follow up to ***Performance*** was the frightening *Don't Look Now*, from a story by Daphne du Maurier. However, the quirkiest crime film of the decade was Stephen Frears's 1971 ***Gumshoe***, adapted from the novel by Neville Smith (b.1940) about a Liverpool bingo caller who dreams of becoming a Bogart-Marlowe private detective. If nothing else, Frears's directorial debut was a declaration that hard-boiled literature was now acceptable, so fair game for parody.

In the 1980s, as Thatcherism dominated the political landscape, the era of classic British crime adaptations was truly over. Original screenplays – ***Long Good Friday***, ***Mona Lisa***, *Stormy Monday* – written in response to the politics of the moment, were favoured by studios and the film-going public. The decade, however, did begin with two adaptations derived from memoirs that read like novels: Tom Clegg's 1980 *McVicar,* based on the book by John McVicar (b.1940), and John MacKenzie's 1981 *A Sense of Freedom*, based on the memoirs of the criminal Jimmy Boyle (b.1944). More genre-oriented was *Bellman and True* (1985), directed by Richard Loncraine from the novel by Desmond Lowden (b.1937) about a computer programmer hired by thieves to steal confidential information from his former employer. In the United States, John le Carré's *The Little Drummer Girl* was adapted by George Roy Hill. Of greater significance were two French films adapted from the work of one of Britain's best crime writers, Derek **Raymond**. *He Died with His Eyes Open* was adapted by Jacques Deray in 1985. *On ne meurt que deux fois* concerned a police inspector who seeks to put himself in the place of the victim, an unsuccessful pianist, only to become involved with the victim's mistress. Two years later, Laurent Heynemann adapted Raymond's *The Devil's Home on Leave*, starring Jean-Pierre Marielle, re-titled *Les mois d'avril sont meurtriers*, about a cop who investigates a murder, confiding in his dead daughter, who has been killed by her deranged mother.

Though the 1990s saw the publication of numerous British crime novels, few adaptations were forthcoming. Besides the previously mentioned remake of *Night and the City*, there was *The Big Man*, made in 1990, directed by David Leland, based on William **McIlvanney**'s racketeering and illegal prize-fighting novel, and Suri Krishnamma's *The Turnaround* (1994) based on Mark **Timlin**'s London-based novel. While in the United States, le Carré's *The Russia House* (1990) was adapted by Fred Schpesi. However, most crime films still derived from original screenplays, either under the influence of Tarantino, like *Shopping* (1994) or *Shallow Grave* (1995), or harking back to earlier eras, like *Let Him Have It* (1991) or *Dance with a Stranger* (1985).

During the first decade of the new millennium, British crime fiction would, to some extent, be rediscovered, even if there were still relatively few adaptations made. Among the most successful were *Layer Cake* (2004), directed by Matthew Vaughan from J.J. Connolly's novel; *Young Adam* (2003), directed by David Mackenzie from the cult novel by Alexander Trocchi (1925–1984); *Divorcing Jack* (1998) from Christopher **Brookmyre's** hilarious novel, directed by David Caffrey; *The Tailor of Panama* (2001) directed by John Boorman from le Carré's novel; *The Quiet American* (2002), remade by Noyce; *The Constant Gardener* (2005), also adapted from a le Carré novel, directed by Fernando Meirelles; and Alfonso Cuaron's *Children of Men* (2006) from P.D. **James**'s novel.

Clearly this is a subject that awaits closer examination. Of course, there will never be another period such as that between 1938 and 1960, when adaptations of British crime fiction were plentiful, even if many of the films (and the novels from which they derived), have been forgotten. In a buyer's market, adapting novels depends not only on the quality of the work but its relevancy to someone's idea about what will make an interesting and profitable movie. It is often cheaper and easier to opt for original material, if only because it is more malleable and arrives without preconceived notions. These days, adaptations by writers like Timlin, John **Harvey**, Jake **Arnott**, Ian **Rankin**, Ruth **Rendell**, R.D. **Wingfield** and Val **McDermid** are more likely to appear on television than in cinema. The golden age may be over, but British crime novels, as long as they remain true to the genre and the society from which they derive, will continue to find their way onto the screen in one form or another. *See also Beat Girl; Bulldog Jack; Criminal, The; Dead Man's Shoes; Frenzy; Gangster No. 1; Lock, Stock and Two Smoking Barrels*; London in Crime Fiction; *Murder on the Orient Express; Night and the City and Villain*.

Further Reading

Barr, Charles. 1986. 'Introduction: Amnesia and Schizophrenia'. *All Our Yesterdays: 90 Years of British Cinema*. Edited by C. Barr. BFI.
Chibnall, Steve, and Robert Murphy, eds. 1999. *British Crime Cinema*. Routledge.
Hardy, Phil, ed. 1998. *The BFI Companion to Crime*. Cassell.
Maclaren-Ross, Julian. 2005. *Bitten by the Tarantula and Other Writings*. Black Spring Press.
Silver, Alain, ed. 1999. *Film Noir Reader 2*. Limelight Editions.
Spicer, Andrew. 2002. *Film Noir*. Longman.

Woody Haut

Fleming, Ian (1908–1964)

Ian Fleming was the creator of the most famous – and durable – spy in all fiction: James Bond, 007.

In the first James Bond novel, *Casino Royale* (1953), Fleming deliberately set out to write the 'spy story to end all spy stories'. He drew on his wartime experience as a backroom boy in naval intelligence for what little detail of secret service-work crept through, but kitted out James Bond, his hero, with his own personal interests (fast cars, fast women) and accoutrements (breakfast omelettes, hand-made cigarettes). Aside from a 'comma of black hair', which sounds like the kiss-curls sported at the time by Superman and Bill Haley, the only description of Bond in the first book is a passing remark that he looks like Hoagy Carmichael. The American jazz pianist and singer is an unlikely model for the dominant thriller hero of the post-war years, but Fleming's author photographs, invariably soft-focus through a haze of cigarette smoke, bear a resemblance to the Carmichael of *To Have and Have Not*, albeit a Hoagy who might aspire to usurp Humphrey Bogart's station at the centre of the screen, with his arm around Lauren Bacall.

It seems probable that *Casino Royale* was initially intended to be a stand-alone. Fleming set out to evoke and then dispel the pre-war world of **Maugham**'s Ashenden, **Buchan**'s Richard Hannay or Sapper's Bulldog Drummond. Bond earned his license to kill in the Second World War, but later in the book, he is tied naked to a wicker chair with the bottom removed and saved from genital mutilation by an anonymous Soviet functionary, who kills the ostensible villain (the larger-than-life LeChiffre) and upbraids the helpless Englishman for being a hopelessly anachronistic hold-over from earlier times which have been swept away by the drab, new cold war of the 1950s. Even Bond's status as a British spy is nebulous: the CIA agents are also on the case and pose the only real threat to those of SMERSH. In the emphasis on sexual torture (not to mention Bond's active promiscuity), Fleming copped a few licks from the then-phenomenal crime writer Mickey Spillane – 'sexing up' a formula that might otherwise have done for writers like Sax **Rohmer** or Dornford Yates. The book's closing line ('Yes, dammit, I said "was". The bitch is dead now.') echoes the violent misogyny of Spillane's Hammer (when asked 'how could you?' by a duplicitous dame he has just shot in the gut, Hammer cracks 'it was easy').

If there's a 'high concept' to *Casino Royale* it is that Bond is a spy who gambles – albeit at baccarat, one of the simplest games imaginable. Before his knack for killing or even his sex life is established, Bond is reputed as 'the best gambler' in the British secret service, and Fleming began his soon-to-be trademarked habit of presenting the insider details of a world beyond his readers' experience. He has a still-unparalleled flair for writing about games: the bridge and golf contests which stretch over many chapters in *Moonraker* (1955) and *Goldfinger* (1959) are on a par with the pool of Walter Tevis's *The Hustler* or the poker of Richard Jessup's *The Cincinnati Kid*. The success of *Casino Royale* set Fleming and Bond on course to create a franchise, but the original mission went unfulfilled. Rather than end all spy stories, Fleming unleashed an entire library of **espionage**, inspiring fanciful imitations (even Fu Manchu came briefly out of retirement in the late 1950s) and eventually more sombre counter-programming in the 'realistic' fictions of John **le Carré** and Len **Deighton**.

Bond's second literary appearance was in *Live and Let Die* (1954), leaving behind the claustrophobic confines of the casino and making its hero, if not a free agent, at least a free-range agent. The plot covers communist-backed heroin pushing in New York's Harlem and voodoo worship in Jamaica (Fleming's wintering-ground, frequently explored in the books). After his tragic, traumatising affair with double agent Vesper Lynd (the 'bitch') in *Casino Royale*, Bond moves on to Solitaire, a white seeress who defects (as did Vesper, as would many later ladies) from the villains' cause. Like Honeychild Rider of *Dr No* (1958), Solitaire ought logically to be black – but though Fleming would allow Bond to bed (indeed, marry) a Japanese girl in *You Only Live Twice* (1964), he never let his hero come to grips in any real way with his less-Caucasian island neighbours. Felix Leiter, Bond's CIA agent buddy from the previous book, gets dumped into a tank with a shark and is left to die with a note reading 'he disagreed with something that ate him'. Leiter would survive, with prostheses, into later books, but the proprieties were restored – Johnny Yank was Bond's subordinate, and the ineffably British Bond (actually, half-Scots, half-Swiss) was promoted to superhero. This signalled a turn into fantasy. *Moonraker* (1955) brings in science-fictional elements with a mad millionaire (Hugo Drax, who reads like a nightmare prophecy of Robert Maxwell) plotting to launch a nuclear V-weapon at London under the guise of a patriotic space-shot. Readers were not sure about *Moonraker* – half clubland drama about cheating at cards, half runabout in Kent (which pointedly was not Jamaica) with a policewoman who flounces off to an unseen fiancé rather than be bagged by Bond.

Fleming tried a sort of docu-thiller in *Diamonds Are Forever* (1956), written in parallel with his non-fiction paperback *The Diamond Smugglers* (1957), which has Bond following a smugglers' trail from Africa to America and pits him up against mobsters who read like an outrageous parody of Mickey Spillane's villains (Fleming simply could not write Americans). However, the series clicked suddenly into focus with *From Russia with Love* (1957), which Fleming felt to be his best novel. This book convinced admirers (President Kennedy included) of Bond's status as a pop culture hero and signalled 007's rise to franchise status. Part of the trick was to change the format: after four novel-length exploits, Bond has risen to prominence within the series' fictional world, and the Moscow plotters of SMERSH are motivated to frame a complex plot to lure him within range of their top assassins (Irish serial killer Red Grant and frumpy female Russian torturer Rosa Klebb). Opening a Russian intelligence dossier on Bond, Fleming reveals more about his sketchy hero than previously – at once building up his legend and letting slip a few personal hints. The author was canny enough to leave some things vague for later books – a couple of threads are picked up in the agent's obituary in *You Only Live Twice*.

In the last pages, Bond has bested Grant in a fight on the Orient Express and convinced the lovely Tatiana Romanova to defect – but Klebb kicks him in the shins with a poison-dipped knife that extrudes from her shoe. It seems certain that he will die. Like all creators of successful heroes, Fleming had a complex love-hate creation with the paper man who was already more famous than he was and would become exponentially so when Bond went into the movies. *From Russia with Love* was never intended to push 007 over the Reichenbach Falls, but its final chapter was a major surprise and the cliffhanger caromed the reader straight into *Dr No* and *Goldfinger*. Here, Fleming is having as much fun as his audience and there is a genuine exuberance about the adventures as Bond twice pulls the Americans' fat out of the fire, thwarting attempts by villains grotesque enough for Dick Tracy or Batman (the metal-handed slug-like Dr Julius No, the tubby gold fetishist Auric Goldfinger) to destroy the American space program at Cape Canaveral or loot the gold reserves at Fort Knox. The women, too, are more fantastical creatures – wild child Honey Rider, emerging naked from the waves, and leather-clad lesbian Pussy Galore, converted to heterosexuality by a proper British seeing-to in bed.

Fleming, whose primary motive was always to fund a lifestyle as extravagant as his villains' (let alone his hero's), actively pursued other media since the publication of *Casino Royale*. A live television adaptation was aired on *Climax!* in 1954, with Barry Nelson as an American 'Jimmy Bond' and Peter Lorre perfect as LeChiffre and a television series was in development for a while, prompting the author to outline stories that would have been episodes but eventually got recycled as the collection *For Your Eyes Only* (1960). Collaborating with other hands, Fleming worked out a movie pitch that he turned into *Thunderball* (1961) when the project cooled; as with rogue *Casino Royale* rights, this would cause legal problems for the movie franchise after Fleming's death. Bond made it to newspaper strip cartoon form just before *Dr No* (1962) launched bodybuilding Scots ex-milkman Sean Connery as a cool, sexy, classless, ruthless 007. Fleming mostly kept quiet but would have preferred David Niven or Cary Grant. The existence of the film phantom, who overlaps with the character in the books but somehow is not him, starts to haunt the novels. After the rote *Thunderball*, which reads exactly like a screen treatment, Fleming delivered the bizarre *The Spy Who Loved Me* (1962): two-thirds a middle-aged toff's idea of a modern young girl's sexual experiences capped by a cat-and-mouse suspense scene at a motel (was Fleming thinking of Bogart in *Key Largo*?) that now reads like a small-scale précis for *Die Hard*.

Back on track, Fleming tried to wind the whole thing up in style, with *On Her Majesty's Secret Service* (1963) and *You Only Live Twice*. The Cold War backdrop of the 1950s books has been shunted aside, and the Soviet SMERSH has been replaced by the more fanciful SPECTRE, an apolitical international bad guy organisation introduced (along with cat-stroking villain Ernst Stavro Blofeld) in the film of *Dr No* and the book *Thunderball*. In *On Her Majesty's Secret Service*, Bond finally works through his problems with women and marries, but Blofeld murders his wife Tracy just after the wedding. *You Only Live Twice* has Bond on a personal mission of revenge to Japan – the book winds up with the hero officially dead (his obituary runs in the *Times*) and an amnesiac Bond leaving his Japanese wife when exposed to the trigger-word 'Vladivostock'. By now, the screen Bond was going from strength to strength and Connery was universally accepted as an epitome of supermacho self-confidence. In contrast, the books present a character who is emotionally wracked to the point of becoming a basket case. Fleming, after a lifetime of martinis and high-cholesterol breakfasts, was not a healthy man, and the novels have an unhealthy corpse-light about them. Blofeld's garden of venomous flora and fauna – available to any Japanese who wishes to avail himself of the opportunity for honourable (and agonising) suicide – is a memorable, unholy creation that goes further than anything in the Sax Rohmer canon (of course, it was left out of the film).

The Man with the Golden Gun (1965), unfinished at the time of Fleming's death, opens with a brainwashed Bond on the point of assassinating M – then witters on through a feeble plot about a three-nippled hit-man and winds down ingloriously with a miniature train-wreck. Like Fleming, Bond was exhausted, though there were enough leavings for a posthumous collection (*Octopussy and The Living Daylights*, 1966). Robert Markham (Kingsley Amis), John **Gardner**, Charlie Higson, Sebastian Faulks and others have turned out 'authorised' further (or untold) exploits. But, since 1964, the real Bond action has been in the cinema: Connery stayed with the franchise until *You Only Live Twice* (1967), and came back twice on his own terms (once in an independent redo of *Thunderball*, *Never Say Never Again*, 1983); David Niven (in the spoof *Casino Royale*, 1968), George Lazenby, Roger Moore, Timothy Dalton, Pierce

Brosnan and Daniel Craig (in the more serious re-make *Casino Royale*, 2006 and *Quantum of Solace*, 2008) have taken over the role, with varying degrees of success. The spy-mania of the 1960s – to which Fleming also contributed ideas (at least the character names 'Napoleon Solo' and 'April Dancer') for *The Man from U.N.C.L.E.* – was fuelled by Bond, and has never completely evaporated.

The third screen *Casino Royale* returns to Fleming's plotting (which had long since been abandoned by the series) but roots its hero in a post–Cold War world, and shows the franchise can be reinvented, probably to infinity (surviving even parodies as vicious as Austin Powers or films as thin as *A View to a Kill*, 1985). 'Ian Fleming's James Bond', however, remains in his literary time-capsule: a secret agent who leaves unique cigarette ends wherever he goes and lives a fantasy life for the benefit of every post-war schoolboy. *See also* Film and Crime: Page to Screen.

Selected Works by the Author
Casino Royale (1953; also published in the United States as *You Asked for It*)
Live and Let Die (1954)
Moonraker (1955; also published in the United States as *Too Hot to Handle*)
Diamonds Are Forever (1956)
From Russia with Love (1957)
Doctor No (1958)
Goldfinger (1959)
For Your Eyes Only (stories, 1960)
Thunderball (1961)
The Spy who Loved Me (1962)
On Her Majesty's Secret Service (1963)
You Only Live Twice (1964)
The Man With the Golden Gun (1965)
Octopussy and the Living Daylights (novellas, 1966)

Kim Newman

Fleming, Joan (1908–1980)

In the ranks of British detective novelists, Fleming was once regarded as one of the most reliable practitioners in the field, though her work has now virtually disappeared from view. She was twice the recipient of the **Crime Writers' Association** Gold Dagger (in 1962 and 1970) and prided herself on her reluctance to be tied down to any one crime genre. Observing that such straitjackets had vitiated the talents of many of her contemporaries, she switched between a dizzying variety of styles, periods and locales. Her Turkish detective Nuri Iskirlak was cannily characterised, and the problems she devised for him were suitably challenging for this quirky addition to the sleuthing ranks – but although Iskirlak had his admirers, he steadfastly refused to join the hall of fame (much to Fleming's disappointment). Nuri Bey Iskirlak appears in two of her books, *When I Grow Rich* (1962) and *Nothing is the Number When You Die* (1965).

Joan Fleming was Lancastrian-born and educated at Lausanne University. In 1932, she married Norman Bell Beattie Fleming. She was always a genre-hopper when it came to her crime fiction. Her entries in the Victorian crime genre pulled off the difficult trick of seamlessly incorporating well-researched details of the period into the narrative without ever neglecting the key storytelling impulse.

As a professional writer, she prided herself on her ability to tackle a wide variety of idioms and showed herself to be particularly adroit at writing horror stories: her Gothic *contes cruelles* have been much anthologised and demonstrate a well-honed refinement of her craft which is not always apparent in the novels. At the beginning of the twenty-first century, Joan Fleming's work is largely neglected, but her best books may well find an audience again in an enterprising reissue programme. And her Gothic short stories may similarly demonstrate that there is life after death.

Selected Works by the Author
The Gallows in My Garden (1951)
You Can't Believe Your Eyes (1957)
Malice Matrimonial (1959)
The Man from Nowhere (1960)
When I Grow Rich (1962)
The Chill and the Kill (1964)
Nothing Is the Number When You Die (1965)
How to Live Dangerously (1974)
Day of the Donkey Derby (1978)

Barry Forshaw

Follett, Ken (b.1949)

The extensive output of this best-selling author includes wartime **espionage** stories, historical epics, high-tech **thrillers** and action adventures.

Kenneth Martin Follett was born on 5 June 1949 in Cardiff, Wales, to fundamentalist Christians who forbade him from watching television. The family moved to London ten years later, where Follett read philosophy at University College London. In 1970, he returned to his birthplace as trainee reporter for the *South Wales Echo* before becoming a fully fledged journalist for the *London Evening News* three years later.

He then became deputy managing director for Everest Books, who published his first forays into fiction under the pseudonym Simon Myles. *The Big Needle* (1974) was a bold start featuring a father who avenges his drug-addicted daughter by pursuing the dealers. His books appeared from other publishers under further pen names, Bernard L. Ross and Zachary Stone. The Stone books were issued by Collins Crime Club and included a well developed story of forgery and intrigue in the art world, *The Modigliani Scandal* (1976).

Learning his trade with other self-confessed 'hack work' – such as the *King Kong* clone, *Amok: King of Legend* – he finally shot to fame with his coming-of-age novel, *Storm Island* (title soon changed to *Eye of the Needle*) in 1978. Set during the Second World War, with British agents trying to find a German agent before he leaks news of the D-Day landings to Hitler, it went on to win the 1979 Edgar Award for Best Novel.

The story was based on a real Second World War counter-intelligence operation, seen through the eyes of a Nazi spy on a remote Scottish island. Praised by critics and readers, it propelled him into the limelight, with a film starring Donald Sutherland appearing in 1981. He followed this with four more meticulously researched novels: *Triple* (1979), *The Key to Rebecca* (1980), *The Man from St Petersburg* (1982) and

Lie Down with Lions (1986). Although the settings ranged from Edwardian England to then-contemporary Israel, Iran and Afghanistan, they could all be classed as espionage thrillers, very much in the gritty, semi-documentary style of *Eye of the Needle*.

After a three-year gap, Follett surprised his readership by switching genres and penning a weighty historical epic about the construction of a fictitious twelfth century English cathedral: *The Pillars of the Earth* (1989). It has since proved to be his most popular novel, with the author recently writing a loose sequel, *World without End* (2007), set two centuries later during the terrible events of the Black Death.

Further historical novels followed, before 1996s *The Third Twin* signalled a return to the action-orientated thrillers for which he was originally known.

A keen supporter of the Labour Party, his wife Barbara is Labour MP for Stevenage, Herts.

Selected Works by the Author
The Shakeout (1975)
The Bear Raid (1976)
Storm Island (1978; also published in the United States and in the UK as *Eye of the Needle*)
The Key to Rebecca (1980)
The Man from St Petersburg (1982)
A Place Called Freedom (1995)
The Third Twin (1996)
Jackdaws (2001)
Hornet Flight (2002)
Whiteout (2004)

As Simon Myles
The Big Needle (1974; also published in the United States as *The Big Apple*)
The Big Black (1974)
The Big Hit (1975)

As Zachary Stone
The Modigliani Scandal (1976)
Paper Money (1977)

Website
http://www.ken-follett.com

Mark Campbell

Forsyth, Frederick (b.1938)

A journalist by trade, Frederick Forsyth achieved astonishing worldwide success with his first novel *The Day of the Jackal*, in 1971, and he followed that with a string of huge-selling **thrillers** set largely in world trouble spots. His work as a foreign correspondent and, at times, as a war correspondent left him with a clear predilection for first-hand reporting. His novels are full of fastidiously detailed facts – about little-visited countries, complex weaponry and dangerous professions – of which little seems to be mere desk research. Forsyth, one feels, has been there; the places are too real, the detail too precise. At times, what he reveals seems both startling and unobtainable from any other source. He has talked with terrorists, met gun-runners and stalked at night with mercenaries, and he reinvests this exciting material in his books. He has the journalist's knack of clarity. Reading *Jackal* one feels that this is how an assassin would operate; in *Dogs of War* (1974), one feels that one understands, perhaps for the first time, what might motivate and drive a mercenary to risk his life for a cause that, one would have thought, meant no more to him than money; in *The Fist of God* (1994) one becomes a fly on the wall at Saddam's war cabinet.

Frederick Forsyth was born the son of a shopkeeper in the small town of Ashford in Kent and, world traveller that he is, still retains a fondness for 'the old Kent, the Kent that is the garden of England'. His father, with whom young Frederick had a warm and affectionate relationship, had the vision to send him to France and Germany for a year to study modern languages. The boy, typically, became fluent within the year and returned to win a scholarship to Tonbridge School. He joined the RAF in 1956 – National Service was still in operation – and learnt to fly, but after the required two years, he quit to achieve his ambition of becoming a foreign correspondent. For a decade it was his trade. He was a journalist for Reuters and a diplomatic correspondent for the BBC. But ten years later, after a two-year stint in Africa as a war correspondent, Forsyth returned to England and wondered what to do next. His African project finished, and he was temporarily without a task – but that is a situation familiar to many journalists, and, as journalists tend to do, he sat down and wrote. 'With no projects on my plate', he said, 'I thought I'd write a novel. It turned out to be *The Day of the Jackal*. I didn't realise as I wrote it that it was going to be this big blockbuster which would change my life.'

For such a professional writer, it is odd that he did not realise how revolutionary his book was. *The Day of the Jackal* solicits our sympathy (practically our complicity) for a professional assassin hired by the OAS to kill General de Gaulle. The set-up intrigues instantly because we know (or we knew when the book came out) that de Gaulle was very much alive. So how could Forsyth sustain our interest in an attempted assassination which was bound to fail? He did it in part by writing in an apparently documentary style and packing the book with so much factual detail that we could not fail to believe that what he wrote was true. He peppered the plot with real people, people we had heard of, people who *seemed* real (indeed, some were real, although their names were changed), and we were forced to wonder how far this plot (it must surely be a real-life plot, we thought) had actually progressed. We were also deeply interested in his anti-hero. Some fellow-writers were also deeply interested in Forsyth's subsequent claim that he had written the book in just thirty-five days. Most writers, they felt, would need a year. But Forsyth – reminiscent perhaps of another journalist turned author, Arnold Bennett, half a century or so before – was dismissive: twelve pages a day, he retorted, multiplied by thirty-five, and there is your novel.

It was Voltaire who warned that the only reward a writer can expect is 'hatred if one succeeds'. Knowing this to be true, Forsyth might be accused of having gone out of his way to get his defence in first and take the fight to the enemy. From the outset he has been a combative writer and equally combative in presenting himself. Having seen practically all the critics praise and express amazement at his first novel, Forsyth must have heard muskets being loaded and filleting knives sharpening on the stone. Few denied the brilliance of that first book, but what of those that would come after? *Jackal* was a book which could not be revisited. It was a stand-alone novel, surely. Many an author would have struggled to find a follow-up.

His next book was *The Odessa File* (1972) in which, with similar in-depth knowledge, he created a plot cooked up by Arab militants in association with ex–SS Nazis against Israel. It could have been a far-fetched plot – others have written such – but the wealth of supporting detail made the story credible. *The Dogs of War* (1974), equally factual and convincing – especially in its portrait of military mercenaries – was a more personal book for the author whose research in Biafra (which had led to his first book, *The Biafra Story*, 1969) had pushed him to support the Biafran independence fighters against Nigerians seeking their extermination. Not content with merely fictionalising reality, Forsyth dreamt up a plot in which a rich and ruthless tycoon learnt of a mountain of platinum hidden away in the remote African republic of Zangaro. Rather than attempt a conventional purchase, the evil tycoon hired an army of bloody mercenaries with instructions to topple the government and replace its dictator with his own puppet president. *Fourth Protocol* (1984) told of an audacious plan hatched in a remote dacha in the forest outside Moscow in which crude nuclear weaponry would be used to blast Britain into revolution. A crack Soviet agent, whom Forsyth typically made quite likeable, was placed under cover in a quiet English town where, in his rented bedroom, he put together a home-made nuclear bomb made from material he had walked into the country with, lashed together with a few easily acquired components. The construction of the bomb was one of Forsyth's most famous set pieces, leaving the reader doubly chilled: firstly at how easy the process seemed and secondly that any would-be terrorist could use the book as his own Anarchist's cookbook. The way Forsyth exploits contemporary concerns means that inevitably some of his conceits have dated: in *Icon* (1996) he has the West try to prevent a potential fascist dictator coming to power in the collapsing Soviet Union of 1999; *Negotiator* (1989) is set in a world now forgotten by us, when *Glasnost* had a relevance and we were convinced the planet's supply of oil was about to run out. But *The Day of the Jackal* was equally impossible and became his greatest best-seller. He makes fantasy convincing.

Book after book displayed his canny grasp of international politics and grubby subterfuge. To make his plots work usually requires Forsyth to lay out a strong clear ground-plan of genuine fact, into which he can slip one essential fabrication – as in *Avenger* (2003), where he invented a genuine-sounding South American country and told us exactly where to find it on the map. In *The Fist of God*, he plunged his readers into a highly topical world of political assassination and high-tech military might, behind the scenes of the Gulf War. The action took place as coalition forces prepared for battle against the Iraqi Army – that much we recognised – but Forsyth placed a Western spy (fictional, we assume) in Baghdad on a mission to find a mysterious traitor who might hold the key to locating Saddam Hussein's secret weapon. As we now know, the weapons too were fictional.

It should be no surprise that in 2006 Forsyth's subject became al Qaeda. In *Afghan* (2006) he took a topical, all too likely, subject (western intelligence seeking to thwart a new threat from al Qaeda) and laced it with his hallmark thriller element. In notorious Guantanamo Bay is a man who was once a senior Taliban commander – but he has been held there for five years and much has changed in his old terrain. Might it be possible for another man, a western agent, to pass himself off as the long-lost leader? Surely not – except that Forsyth can overlay such an apparently preposterous plot with a thick skin of surface detail and impedimenta which creates a world in which it might be possible. One step forward, Forsyth proposes, an army colonel who for twenty-five years has honed his skills in war zones, but who was born and raised in Iraq. He can pass as an Arab. But can he be passed off as one of the Taliban's lost commanders? Clearly, there is more than a touch of a *Boy's Own Paper* adventure story here, but unlike those stories, this one, as with all the Forsyth oeuvre, is swamped with credibility, an effect achieved in the classic Forsyth way: by writing not as a novelist but as a journalist, reporting from a partly real and partly imaginary frontier.

Although he achieved immediate success with his first novel, Forsyth continues to take himself off to troubled, often dangerous, locations and seek out active, often dangerous, protagonists. He has carried out research in Israeli and Palestinian combat zones, the battlefields of Nigeria, volatile South American states and, in effect, anywhere trouble lurks. Forsyth is the kind of author who happily interrupts the narrative to insert a detailed four-page explanation of how to manufacture a home-made nuclear bomb from basic materials, using a hotel bedroom as a weapons factory. He has showed us how to assemble an effective car bomb out of easily acquired materials which can be mounted beneath the car – he told us exactly where – using nothing more sophisticated than a condom. (He also told us why the condom was an ideal container.) Most famously of all, he showed in terrifying detail how a lone terrorist or mercenary could trick and bypass a massive security operation and assassinate the president of France. Where a criticism often levelled against his rival thriller writers is that their plots, though entertaining, are incredible, the worry with Forsyth's plots is that they can seem *too* credible.

Forsyth the man has always presented himself as unapologetically right-wing, acerbic and certain of his facts, conclusions and importance in the world – an old fashioned English gentleman, in fact. All of his books achieve high sales, even if, understandably, none can rival the sales of his first. Forsyth is a consummate story-teller of deeply researched but fast-moving adventures covering an impressively wide range of subjects – and indeed he has dug out many of those subjects himself and established them as fertile ground for later writers to harvest in his tracks. Forsyth can justifiably claim that he got there first. But will his critics forgive him for that?

Selected Works by the Author
The Day of the Jackal (1971)
The Odessa File (1972)
The Dogs of War (1974)
The Devil's Alternative (1979)
No Comebacks (stories, 1982)
The Fourth Protocol (1984)
The Veteran and Other Stories (stories, 2000)
Avenger (2003)

Russell James

Fowler, Christopher (b.1953)

Christopher Fowler is the author of the quirky, highly imaginative Bryant and May detective novels. Although he is busy with film work, he still finds time to write novels, has published ten volumes of short stories so far (not to mention comics) and has won several nominations and awards. Fowler also reviews and writes for magazines, newspapers, film, television and radio.

His fiction details urban decay and (from 2003 onwards) is principally in the crime arena, but includes elements of horror or dark fiction with some science fiction/ fantasy tropes. Fowler's first four novels have a miasmically described **London** as the

33. Christopher Fowler.

backdrop. He debuted in 1988 with the novel *Roofworld*, which details a story of rival gangs who live on the rooftops of London, fighting arcane battles while the city sleeps. *Red Bride* (1992) chronicles a modern marriage made hell by a couple who cannot trust each other – even though their lives finally come to depend on it.

His essential crime and mystery work is found in his ongoing Bryant and May detective series, but even these have a characteristically surreal flavour. They feature two unlikely detectives investigating unlikely crimes in urban London. Arthur Bryant is rude, depressive, and a Luddite with a bookish nature, while his associate John May is the reverse – likeable, sociable, a man of the future with a weakness for women. They form the backbone of The Peculiar Crimes Unit and their chemistry ignites the tension and humour in these tales of the unexpected. The duo first appeared in 2003 in *Full Dark House*, a remarkably accomplished mystery. The third in the series, *Seventy-Seven Clocks* (2005) is, in fact, a reworking of one of Fowler's earlier novels, *Darkest Day* (1993), and probably the most interesting of the series. Detectives Bryant and May investigate the mysterious death of lawyer Maximillian Jacob, who dies, gasping for breath, at the London Savoy. His death is linked to the aristocratic Whitstable family. Tackling notions of class divisions in British society as well as a cabal of bizarre and surreal characters, the novel moves from the darkness of London under blackout to a secret society called the Alliance of Eternal Light. The murders feature strange methods which make linking them to a single source more complex. Later entries in the series include the impressive *White Corridor* (2007).

Fowler's *American Waitress* won the British Fantasy Society Best Short Story of the Year 2004. His novella *Breathe* won BFS Best Novella 2005 and his short story *The Master Builder* became a CBS movie starring Tippi Hedren and Marg Helgenberger entitled *Through the Eyes of a Killer*, while *Left Hand Drive* won Best British Short Film of 1993.

Selected Works by the Author

Bryant and May Novels
Full Dark House (2003)
The Water Room (2004)
Seventy-Seven Clocks (2005)
Ten Second Staircase (2006)
White Corridor (2007)

Other Novels
Psychoville (1995)
Menz Insana (1997)
Disturbia (1997)
Soho Black (1998)
Calabash (2000)

Ali Karim

Francis, Clare (b.1946)

Following an MBE in 1978 for her achievements as a round-the-world yachtswoman, Clare Francis changed track completely to become the author of several highly successful **thrillers**.

Born Clare Mary Francis on 17 April 1946 in Thames Ditton, Surrey, the author spent five years at the Royal Ballet School before obtaining an Economics Degree at University College, London. After three years in marketing, she embarked on a five-year sailing career, beginning with an unsponsored solo voyage across the Atlantic. It was during the inevitably long periods of inactivity that she first started to write.

Sponsorship quickly materialised for her next trip, the 1974 Round Britain Race partnered with Eve Bonham. This was soon followed by the Azores and Back Singlehanded Race, the Observer Singlehanded Transatlantic Race, and the Whitbread Round the World Race, as part of an eleven-person crew.

These voyages were captured in print in three autobiographical books: *Come Wind or Weather* (1977), *Come Hell or High Water* (1977) and *The Commanding Sea* (1978). Each one described in vivid detail the discomfort, pain and fear of the long days at sea and the extraordinary courage needed to overcome adversity and isolation. She would later point to these experiences – along with her childhood holidays in the Yorkshire Dales – as providing the inspiration for her fiction.

Her first novel, *Night Sky*, appeared in 1983. Spanning the duration of the Second World War, the book had four interlinked stories, of which the principal one concerned single-mother Julia who escapes her mother's disapproval by fleeing to Brittany. One of the most memorable sequences is her perilous journey back home across the Atlantic, following the Nazi's invasion of France.

Two more historically set novels followed. *Red Crystal* (1985) dealt with leftwing terrorist groups in the 1960s, while *Wolf Winter* (1987) was set in the wastes of northern Norway at the height of the Cold War. With 1989s *Requiem*, Francis turned her attention to present-day concerns, in this case the risk caused by illegal use of pesticides.

It was not until *Deceit* in 1993 that the author moved firmly into the crime genre with a story about an ambitious businessman with a shady past who goes missing at sea. Echoing the real-life death of Robert Maxwell two years earlier, the novel was eventually filmed by the BBC in 2000, and later remade, somewhat pointlessly, as an American television movie in 2004.

Among the best of her recent crime output has been *Betrayal* (1995), in which a body is discovered stabbed and bound in a Devon river, and *A Dark Devotion* (1997), wherein a solicitor returns to her childhood village to investigate the disappearance of a friend's wife.

Francis is currently president of the charity Action for ME, having suffered with the illness for many years. *See also* Historical Crime.

Selected Works by the Author
Night Sky (1983)
Red Crystal (1985)
Wolf Winter (1987)
Requiem (1989; also published in the United States as *The Killing Winds*)
Deceit (1993)
Betrayal (1995)
A Dark Devotion (1997)
Keep Me Close (1999)
A Death Divided (2001)
Homeland (2003)
Unforgotten (2008)

Website
www.clarefrancis.com

Mark Campbell

Francis, Dick (b.1920)

With *Dead Cert* in 1962, the former steeplechase jockey Dick Francis began writing a string of racing-set **thrillers** that simultaneously created and colonised a genre. From modest beginnings, the annual Francis tome became a firm favourite with crime aficionados. More than any other writer of his generation, Francis made the action-suspense-detective story extremely popular and arguably forged the widest fan base of any similar writer before or since.

Dick Francis is read for his narrative style, appealing backgrounds and the modest heroism of his protagonists. He learnt his taut prose style as a journalist, and with the assistance of his wife Mary (a consummate researcher and devotee of English literature), Francis utilised his personal experiences as a jockey and countryman to create *non-pareil* generic thrillers. Essentially, the racing world was for Francis a template for an organic view of the English countryside, combined with a robust defence of conservative altruistic values (being rolled back in the second half of the twentieth century – as Francis perceived it – by the blandness of modern life, a loosening of traditional values and the emergence of what seemed like an amoral 'get-rich-quick' society). His books are a charming and thoughtful diversion based on much older pastoral, romanticist, patriotic assumptions. At the heart of many a Francis novel is this secure picture, made vibrant by a questing hero – a protagonist who stood not only for decency and honour but acted out these values even to the extent of physical injury and inner pain.

As a boy, Dick Francis rode his first race in a gymkhana and looked after his father's stable of hunters. He always wanted to be a race jockey, but on the outbreak of the war, he joined the Royal Air Force and several times had his request to be trained as a pilot denied. His persistence was rewarded and towards the end of the conflict, he flew in fighters and bombers. Shortly after that, he met and married Mary Brenchley, a resourceful and cultured woman, who later would gain experience in the publishing world. In 1948, Francis became a professional jockey, was Champion jockey in 1953–1954 and was retained to ride for Queen Elizabeth, the Queen Mother; becoming a nationally known figure on the occasion of his mount, Devon Loch collapsing close to the finish of the Grand National Steeplechase. He decided to retire following another serious fall, and worked as a racing columnist for the *Sunday Express* (a post he held for sixteen years). When an agent asked for consent to a ghostwritten autobiography (published as *The Sport of Queens*, 1957) to exploit his fame, Mary firmly resisted; instead they would undertake the task themselves.

If this beginning was somewhat fortuitous, the transformation from the author of sound thrillers to one of growing stature and appeal was a task accomplished in stages – by trying different literary elements, refining the mix and drawing more on a wealth of sources from as far back as the Victorian ethos. Dick Francis thus became a popular writer of entertainments, but one that few critics could categorise without seeming trite. While the novels always have thriller elements – action-adventure, crime, and suspense – as Francis became a more mature writer the focus was less on physical action and exhibited a greater interest in melodrama and a delight in the many shades of humanity. This talent for compassionate insight marries well with the aforementioned social standpoint and his depreciating hero figures.

The world of Dick Francis is one of a clash between old values and new ones, between decency and honour on the one hand and truculence and rakishness on the other. Often it is presented as a kind of insidious disease eating away at the social fabric, with devious bookmakers, greedy gamblers, rich owners, corrupt stable lads or criminal gangs perpetuating violence for gain. However, the clash seems all the more real at times because Francis often places it at home in the form of family rifts and feuds. On the surface, it may be the future of a racecourse, the business or family fortune that is at stake, but the real issue is that the old values are more than ever under attack from an acquisitive and assertive money-status-power orientated generation. The means by which the old values were protected is through a series of courageous, but surprisingly ordinary, flawed heroes.

Throughout the body of Dick Francis's work we find a variety of heroes. There is the aristocratic and debonair Kit Fielding whose telepathic skill enables him to communicate with his mounts. However, the majority are middle- or working-class figures whose self-worth is deflated, whose life is meaningless or without direction and whose acceptance of a quest can turn this around. A good example is Matt Shore from *Rat Race* (1970). When we meet him at the start of the book, he is totally burnt-out and disillusioned, divorced and unable to form an attachment. His change in outlook and character is gradual through the story. In *For Kicks* (1965), prosperous Daniel Roke accepts the challenge for family reasons to become a scruffy, dishonest, down-on-his-luck stable lad to solve a doping fraud.

The most interesting variation in Francis's recasting of heroism is surely the use of the old code of chivalry whereby the protagonists suffer physical discomfort and pain. Not only do they frequently suffer humiliation, anguish and mental torture but also undergo horrific physical pain – Sid Halley in *Whip Hand* (1979) suffers fear and confusion, Kendall in *Longshot* (1990) is shot with arrows while Roland Britten in *Risk* (1977) is crucified. Characters such as Kendall and Britten are, as we say, victims of circumstance, and unwittingly become targets for others' spite, jealousy and desire to bury the truth. Yet they grow stronger despite these adversaries.

The adventure aspect of the Francis oeuvre was originally centred on the jockey investigator and the colourful world of racing; gradually he and Mary began to explore other occupations – pilot, painter, photographer, toy maker, glass-blower etc – notably with a high degree of craft or skill. The first instance of this was in *Flying Finish* (1966) where Henry Grey rejects his family's wishes (to settle down and find a rich wife) and looks for work which involves his joy of horses *and* love of flying. The dexterity of piloting a plane, the serenity of controlling a machine in motion, has romantic connotations similar to riding a horse. As the mystery reaches the exciting denouement, Grey uses all his skill to engineer an escape which brings to mind the adventure romances of the yesteryears. In *Smokescreen* (1972), film stuntman Ed Lincoln faces a race against time as he tries to escape from a gold mine that has been dynamited. There were other suspense mysteries with a little adventure on boats, trains and aeroplanes, but the other direction that his books increasingly took in the 1980s and 1990s was towards melodrama.

The early Francis novels do have languorous love interest between action scenes but this gives way to other tricks from romantic fiction such as the 'scandalous woman' and the 'woman in jeopardy' trope. The surprising twist is that Francis consistently not only plays this scheme in the standard 'damsel in distress' mode but persists with it in inverting the sex and the role so that it is the protagonist that is in jeopardy. The hero's quest is now to find his feminine side and his soul while outwardly often taking a beating: the man in jeopardy is both the hero and the person who does the soul searching.

The earliest hero of this kind was in a story that was extremely personal to Francis. James Tyrone, in *Forfeit* (1969) is a racing correspondent (like the author) and this character is devoted to his invalid wife (Mary was once invalided). Tyrone is industrious, but spends most of his income on making his invalid wife comfortable – not just in the material sense, but to make her existence more bearable. The villain in the story repeatedly puts pressure on Tyrone as he tries to find out where Tyrone has hidden a horse and muzzle his racing column. *Forfeit* thus has a woman in jeopardy – literally, for the villain threatens to end her life – and her husband is also in real jeopardy through much of the tale. He faces one threat after another, physical beatings and he realises that his soul is on the line (e.g. he asks himself if he should give in to muzzling his newspaper column).

Forfeit is a thrilling read because of the clever combination of action and melodrama. It is similar in structure to another highly rated Francis novel, *The Danger* (1983). A story of multiple kidnapping, it features Andrew Douglas, insurance man, who gets involved in advising not only on the risks but in counselling too. Here too we have a damsel in distress (left shivering and naked by her kidnappers) and Douglas plays the role of comforter (a female role) and, in his dealings with young race jockey Alessia, has to hold his affection in check. The story also brings into sharp relief quite negative aspects of human nature through examining the differing

disabling effects of abduction and ransom demands on members of the families –
offering us a spectrum of responses ranging from anxiety, avarice, guilt and so on.
The Danger involves a cat-and-mouse struggle in which the hero must hold his nerve.
At the same time, the tension mounts with each successive abduction and round
of negotiations with the kidnappers. Inevitably, the villain sets out to trap Douglas.

Melodrama can be exciting and it often has a social message. In *Forfeit*, someone
of modest means does not give in to pressure; in *The Danger*, the hero is wise and
kind despite other pressures. Yet commercialism is destroying the old values, and
the prosperity and the growth of the middle classes is the drama that is increasing
played out in *Decider* (1993) and *Hot Money* (1987). The boardroom struggle to
control the destiny of a racecourse is really about a clash of outlooks on life – both
sides misunderstanding each other. And in the same way, in *Hot Money*, a wealthy
gold trader who fears for his life suspects the culprit may be from his raft of in-laws;
all are upwardly mobile middle class and are unable to accept that Malcolm
Pembroke has a right to spend his own money. The social target of *Hot Money*
is not the cigar-smoking, champagne drinking millionaire who has gold bullion
in his walls, but those whose only ambition is the higher social status that access
to Pembroke's fortune will bring. The redeeming quality of these books is almost
always how the heroes deal with thorny issues: Lee Morris must come to terms with
choosing between self-interest and wider social responsibility, both in his dealings
with the warring Strattons and in his own family of six children. Pembroke's son Ian,
a steeplechase jockey, repairs the distant relationship with his father and in solving
the mystery brings the whole family more into balance with a chance of healing.

Dick Francis decided to stop writing in 2000, and soon after his beloved wife Mary
died. An unauthorised biography, by Graham Lord, published in 1999, had suggested
that Mary had played a significant role in the writing, and Francis himself stated
that she helped both in the research and in polishing his prose. However in 2006,
now aided by his son Felix, Francis returned with a new thriller, *Under Orders*,
followed by *Silks* in 2008.

In general terms, Dick Francis's books do provide us with a romantic reflection
back to a much earlier age. This vision is threatened by a degraded humanity and
it falls primarily to the heroes of the tales to work out some kind of salvation in the
present. The difficulties they face, the challenges and privations they must meet, often
against their own best interests, show them to possess (as we the reader would wish
to share) 'endurance, courage and persistence'. The early stories of villainy and
adventure gradually give way to melodrama and the feelings of romanticism are
evoked not by racing backgrounds but through interesting artistic occupations.
Francis achieved one of the widest followings in crime literature because he
developed as a writer and delivered to the reader a nostalgic sense of solace and
well-being in changing times. *See also* Francome, John.

Selected Works by the Author
For Kicks (1965)
Flying Finish (1966)
Forfeit (1968)
Whip Hand (1979)
Banker (1982)
The Danger (1983)
Break In (1985)
Hot Money (1987)
Straight (1989)

Francis, Dick

Longshot (1990)
Decider (1993)
To the Hilt (1996)

Further Reading
Barnes, Melvyn. 1986. *Dick Francis*. Ungar.
Johnson, Michael. 2006. *Masters of Crime: Lionel Davidson & Dick Francis*. Scorpion Press.
Lord, Graham. 1999. *Dick Francis: A Racing Life*. Little Brown.
Swanson, Jean, and James Dean. 2003. *The Dick Francis Companion*. Berkley.

Michael Johnson

Francome, John (b.1952)

Like Dick **Francis** before him, John Francome's career as a champion jockey has formed the basis of a series of best-selling **thrillers** set in and around the world of horse racing.

The son of a railway fireman, Francome was born in Swindon on 13 December 1952 and educated at the town's Park Senior High School, where he left with few qualifications. Having persuaded his parents to buy him a horse, he enjoyed a short but successful stint as a show jumper before becoming an apprentice to famed Lambourn trainer Fred Winter at the age of sixteen and moving into the more lucrative world of horse racing.

He first raced publicly in 1969 at Worcester, and after a brief setback when he broke his wrist at Cheltenham, his intuitive skills on the turf led to seven National Hunt Championship wins in ten years, with an unbroken run from 1981 to 1985. By the time he retired in 1985 he had notched up a record-breaking 1,138 wins out of 5,072 mounts, although success in the Grand National always eluded him. In 1986, he was made MBE and became a popular racing pundit for Channel 4, a job he is still doing to this day.

While penning his 1985 autobiography *Born Lucky*, Francome discovered a taste for fiction; his first novel, *Eavesdropper* (1986) was co-written with James MacGregor and featured a racing journalist turned amateur sleuth investigating a murder at Newbery races. Three more co-authored books followed, until he struck out on his own with *Stone Cold* in 1990.

Adopting the well-worn epithet 'write about what you know', Francome's plots never stray far from the racecourse. They usually involve the discovery of a body of a prominent racing figure in a public place, leading to a labyrinthine murder enquiry involving trainers, businessmen and jockeys. Often, money is the key to solving the crime, a theme that accurately reflects the huge sums of cash regularly poured into the UK's gambling industry.

Rarely straying from the bestseller lists, Francome's final novel of the last century, *Lifeline* (2000), seemed to turn a corner stylistically. Many consider it his best, and most personal, offering to date. In it, honest jockey Tony Byrne faces seemingly insurmountable problems both domestic and professional, while his rival Freddy Montague has no such worries in a career characterised by corruption and womanising. Francome's sometimes derided sex scenes appeared more plausible here, while the tone of the book allowed its main characters to show previously unseen emotional depths.

His next book, *Dead Weight* (2001), continued the upward trend: Phil Nichols, a jockey scarred mentally by a horrendous fall, overcomes his personal anxieties to uncover the identity of a mysterious assailant who appears to hold a personal grudge against his colleague.

After Dick Francis's decision to cease writing following the death of his wife Mary in 2000, Francome held the lead position in the equestrian thriller stakes, though Francis has opened up competition again by resuming writing with the aid of his son.

Selected Works by the Author
Eavesdropper (1986)
Stone Cold (1990)
Break Neck (1994)
Dead Ringer (1995)
Lifeline (2000)
Dead Weight (2001)
Free Fall (2006)

Mark Campbell

Fraser, Anthea (b.1930)

Anthea Fraser's writing has moved from romance (she sold her first book to Mills and Boon in 1971) to romantic suspense, with a foray into supernatural fiction, before settling in the crime genre with her adroitly written crime series featuring Detective Chief Inspector (DCI) David Webb and his sidekick Detective Sergeant Ken Jackson.

Most of the Webb/Jackson series is set in Shillingham in Broadshire, a fictional Wiltshire town. Those outside the police have a major role in the story each time, so such protagonists are always well-rounded and detailed characters. DCI David Webb is a traditional and methodical detective, persistent in his search for clues and helpful information and is empathetic to those caught up in his cases. He does take leaps of faith to get his man (or woman) but as these mostly pay off, it is a utilitarian modus operandi. The first in the series is *A Shroud for Delilah* (1984), in which the police team helps Kate, who works in the local antique shop. Webb has a romantic interest in Hannah, and the two really come together in the fourth book in the series, *Death Speaks Softly* (1987), when Hannah helps Webb by acting as translator when he investigates the murder of a young French girl. DCI Webb travels to Peru in *The Nine Bright Shiners* (1987), rescues undercover police officer Nina Petrie from a cult she is infiltrating – and shows signs of being brainwashed by the cult– in *The Gospel Makers* (1994) and has to help his friend and colleague DCI Bennett when two members of his family are killed in *One is One and All Alone* (1996). The many entries in the Webb series include *The Twelve Apostles* (1999), in which Webb delves into an old mystery that is opened by the dying words of a clergyman. From the fifth in the series (*The Nine Bright Shiners*, 1987) the titles were memorably taken from the old English song 'Green Grown the Rushes-O'.

Fraser's more recent series features Rona Parish, a journalist who first appears in *Brought to Book* (2003). She agrees, despite the misgivings of her artist husband Max, to take on the biography of a best-selling author who has just died, and naturally there are those who would rather she did not spill the beans. Rona then goes back to writing articles and finds murder with each subject she tackles, while dealing with her sister's bad run of boyfriends, her parents' separation and a worry about Max's involvement with a student in *A Family Concern* (2006). The most recent is *A Rogue in Porcelain* (2007), in which Rona writes about a family business manufacturing bone china and uncovers a tragedy that goes back to the firm's founder.

Fraser's literary strength lies in her dramatic twists that usually spring up at the end of the novels – even if the reader has correctly identified the murderer, there may still be some unpleasant (but plausible) deus ex machina about to put in an eleventh-hour appearance. From 1986 to 1996 she was the **Crime Writers' Association** secretary.

Selected Works by the Author

David Webb Series
A Shroud for Delilah (1984)
A Necessary End (1985)
Pretty Maids All in a Row (1986)
Death Speaks Softly (1987)

Rona Parish Series
Brought to Book (2003)
Jigsaw (2004)
Person or Persons Unknown (2005)
A Family Concern (2006)
A Rogue in Porcelain (2007)

Thalia Proctor

Fraser, Antonia (b.1935)

Antonia Margaret Caroline Pakenham is the daughter of Elizabeth Pakenham and Lord Longford (famous for his campaigning on behalf on the Moors Murderess, Myra Hindley). Fraser was educated at St Mary's School, Ascot and Lady Margaret Hall, Oxford. In 1956 she married the Conservative MP Sir Hugh Fraser, but her most celebrated marriage is that to the playwright Harold Pinter. Her career as a major historical biographer was established with *Mary, Queen of Scots* (1969) and consolidated with such books as *Cromwell, Our Chief of Men* (1973). Her crime novels featuring Jemima Shore have acquired perhaps the author's most devoted following. In her thirty-something heroine, Antonia Fraser has created a post-feminist Everywoman-cum-fantasy figure.

As a television presenter with *Jemima Shore Investigates*, Jemima has the fame of a well-loved national treasure as well as a high salary and the favours of a superior cat, Midnight. She is officially single yet sought out by lovers and has a long-term relationship with devoted lawyer Cass Brindley.

Jemima's investigations spill over from television to life because her public persona seems to encourage confidences and solicit calls for help. Or perhaps the life of a single professional woman runs up against violence in ways less likely than in that of an attached woman. A good example of this syndrome occurs in *A Splash of Red* (1981), when Jemima agrees to flat-sit for her friend, Chloe Fontaine, only to end up dealing with her murder. Elsewhere, in *Oxford Blood* (1985), a dying midwife calls upon the television Jemima to help her make restitution for the sin of switching babies at birth. Jemima wisely refuses to meddle in affairs long over, until her monstrous and engaging employer, C.Y. Frederick of Megalith Television, pushes her into making a television programme about gilded Oxford youth. Television is often a harbinger of death in Fraser. In another example, *Your Royal Hostage* (1987), boardroom politics make a sacrifice of Jemima who is fired for misplaced loyalty to Fredericks. She is then hired by American TV to cover the sumptuous wedding of royal princess Amy. So when animal rights extremists kidnap Amy, implicated persons in the royal household turn to Jemima.

The detective in this series is an experiment in the pleasures, pains and limits of a free woman in the late twentieth century. Jemima is without living family and although loyal to her friends, acknowledges no relationship that limits her choices. Her liberated enjoyment in sexual opportunities is explored both negatively and positively. It threatens to remove her long-term lover permanently and puts her at risk from the murderous dangers stalking her life, yet her liberty is usually contrasted positively with the stifling restrictions of traditional relationships. Moreover, Jemima's sexual adventurousness is directly linked to her detecting success, both practically and metonymically.

What Jemima detects is a version of her own psychological makeup. Fraser is fascinated by the primal contrast between stability, order and self-control and passion, chaos, lack of self-control, refusing to observe limits and boundaries. It is a contrast fundamental to the detective story itself. The detective restores the order wrecked by the chaos of crime. However, for Fraser's novels, this dichotomy is innate in her vision of society and human nature. Indeed, characters veer between those, like Jemima, who can limit their own capacity for chaos in their sexuality and those who cannot, so extreme passion spills over into madness and crime. Sometimes it is extended into a historical vision of the British state, such as the soldiers parading at a royal wedding. Beneath their ornate *ordering* of war, Jemima sees their savage past, a human quality always just beneath the surface. *See also* Sexuality in British Crime Fiction.

Selected Works by the Author
Quiet as a Nun (1982)
Tartan Tragedy (1978)
A Splash of Red (1981)
Cool Repentance (1982)
Oxford Blood (1985)
Your Royal Hostage (1987)

Further Reading
Gamman, Lorraine, and Margaret Marshment, eds. 1988. *The Female Gaze: Women as Viewers of Popular Culture*. The Women's Press.
Munt, Sally R. 1994. *Murder by the Book? Feminism and the Crime Novel*. Routledge.

Susan Rowland

Freeling, Nicolas (1927–2003)

Although born in England, Nicolas Freeling's love of all things European led to the creation of his celebrated Dutch detective van der Valk, along with the less well-known, although arguably superior, French policeman Henri Castang.

Freeling, Nicolas

Born Nicholas Davidson in London on 3 March 1927, the author adopted his mother's maiden name from an early age, with the family moving to Brittany, Southampton, and finally the Irish Free State (now the Republic of Ireland) shortly before the outbreak of the Second World War. This latter location was not a happy one for the family, and his parents soon split up. After the war, Freeling dropped out of university and trained as a chef in various European cities.

While working as a senior chef in an Amsterdam hotel, he was given a three-week jail sentence for allegedly stealing food. Inspired by the smooth-talking detective who interviewed him, he began writing a crime novel in prison, using sheets of paper purloined from his job of wrapping soap bars.

He was then deported, along with his wife Cornelia Termes (whom he married in 1954), but he continued work on the novel back in England, now entitled *Love in Amsterdam* (also known as *Death in Amsterdam*). It was eventually published in 1962 and became the first in a series featuring the laconic Inspector Piet van der Valk (literally 'rock of the falcon').

Van der Valk was a hard-bitten Dutch detective based in Amsterdam, dealing with cases such as drug trafficking, prostitution and murder. Although ostensibly similar to Simenon's Parisian detective Jules Maigret, Freeling consciously aimed his series at a younger, more modern audience: the crimes were often tawdry and lacking in sensation, while the detective was cynical, outspoken and a frustrated intellectual (he would often recite Proust or Dickens during the course of his investigations). *Gun before Butter* (1963) was nominated for a **Crime Writers' Association** Gold Dagger Award, while *The King of the Rainy Country* (1967), van der Valk's sixth outing, won him an Edgar from the Mystery Crime Writers of America.

These enormously popular van der Valk stories appeared on an annual basis until, in 1972, Freeling followed in the footsteps of Conan **Doyle** and consigned his creation to oblivion halfway through *A Long Silence*. Like Sherlock **Holmes**'s creator, he cited gradual disinterest in the character as the chief reason for killing him off and, like Conan Doyle, he eventually bowed to public pressure to resurrect the character, in 1989s *Sandcastles*. In the meantime, van der Valk's widow Arlette, now remarried, took up where her husband left off, in *The Widow* (1979) and *One Damn Thing After Another* (1981, also known as *Arlette*).

Shortly after van der Valk met his fate, Freeling's new series character, French police inspector Henri Castang – a more obvious ancestor of Maigret – debuted in *A Dressing of Diamonds* (1974). Castang was a Parisian exile in Brussels who investigated major international crimes, from business fraud to murder, each with a quintessentially European tinge. Of particular note are *Cold Iron* (1986) and *The Pretty How Town* (1992), both highly descriptive tales with very strong characterisations of the main players.

Freeling also wrote several stand-alone novels, including *Valparaiso* (1964) as 'F.R.E. Nicolas', as well as three autobiographical cookery books. His final novel, *The Janeites* (2002), a meditation on death and the nature of evil set in Strasbourg and Paris, was possibly his most eccentric book. He died of cancer on 20 July 2003 in Mutzig, France.

The van der Valk books were adapted into four French–German TV movies between 1972 and 1975, starring Frank Finlay. For UK audiences, urbane English actor Barry Foster played the title character in thirty-two episodes for Thames Television and Euston Films from 1972 to 1992. *See also* TV Detectives: Small-Screen Adaptations.

Selected Works by the Author

Piet van der Valk
Love in Amsterdam (1962; also published in the United States as *Death in Amsterdam*)
Gun before Butter (1963; also published in the United States as *Question of Loyalty*)
The King of the Rainy Country (1966)
A Long Silence (1972; also published in the United States as *Au pres de ma Blonde*)

Henri Castang
A Dressing of Diamonds (1974)
What Are the Bugles Blowing For? (1975; also published in the United States as *The Bugles Blowing*)
Cold Iron (1986)
The Pretty How Town (1992; also published in the United States as *Flanders Sky*)

Mark Campbell

Freeman, R. Austin (1862–1943)

Richard Freeman (he added the 'Austin' himself), one of the most celebrated of **Golden Age** crime writers, was born in London and came from a fairly humble background – his father was a tailor and his mother was a dressmaker. He gained medical qualifications and secured a colonial appointment as a doctor in West Africa. Fever forced his early return to Britain where he served in less-strenuous medical posts. While he was a student, Freeman had become interested in the legal aspects of medicine and the medical aspects of law. Cases of poisoning and the processes of identifying bodies fascinated him, and so when his failing health finally caused him to give up medical practice, he turned his hand to writing crime stories. His first foray into the genre was with the Romney Pringle adventures. Collaborating with J.J. Pitcairn, a prison surgeon, he created a series of tales featuring a gentleman thief, very much in the A.J. Raffles mode. *The Adventures of Romney Pringle* was published in 1902 under the name of Clifford Ashdown. A second series of Pringle tales appeared in *Cassell's Magazine* in 1903, but these were not collected in book form until 1970.

Pitcairn was never acknowledged by Freeman as a contributor to these stories. His involvement only came to light after Freeman's death when it was divulged by Freeman's widow.

However, it was Freeman's creation of one of the best scientific detectives, Dr John Evelyn Thorndyke, that assures the author a well-deserved place in the crime fiction hall of fame.

Thorndyke is a physician and a barrister, a wonderful combination of the medical and legal, which equips him admirably to solve crime. He uses facts and scientific data, clearly explained, to track down murderers.

John Thorndyke is tall, athletic in bearing and good looking with a fine Grecian nose and classical features. Freeman claimed that this was in reaction to some of his mystery writing contemporaries who made their detectives 'monsters of ugliness'. Thorndyke's brilliance comes from his specialised knowledge and the painstaking application of it rather than from a superhuman intellect. He carries a miniaturised portable laboratory around with him so that he is fully prepared should he stumble across a crime – and he does so on many occasions – instead of waiting to be consulted.

He is assisted by his Watson, Dr Christopher Jervis; by a solicitor, Mr Broadribb, who on occasion brings cases to Thorndyke's attention; and by his factotum, Mr Polton, a genius in the workshop or the laboratory.

No one can claim that Thorndyke is a charismatic fellow with colourful or unusual personality traits. We miss the excitement of genius and passion that one feels in the presence of Sherlock **Holmes**, for example, but Thorndyke's methods are clever and stand up to close scientific scrutiny.

Freeman was a great believer in the idea that reading crime fiction was an intellectual pursuit. He observed that, 'the disputant enjoys the mental exercise, just as a muscular man enjoys particular kinds of physical exertion'. It is a viewpoint expressed many years earlier by Edgar Allan Poe.

In around thirty books from *The Red Thumb Mark* in 1907, in which Thorndyke makes his debut, to *The Jacob Street Mystery* in 1942, Freeman demonstrates his skilful mastery of clever plots and a strong sense of the possibilities of forensic science, long before this was widely practised. Today this approach is the mainstay of many crime novels.

Freeman also maintained that the author of crime fiction should play fair with the reader and he laid out three rules to ensure this:

1. The problem must be susceptible of at least approximate solution by the reader.
2. The solution...must be absolutely conclusive and convincing.
3. No material fact must be withheld from the reader. All the cards must be honestly laid on the table.

Aside from creating Thorndyke, Freeman invented what has come to be known as the 'inverted' detective story. He first used this format in the Thorndyke story 'The case of Oscar Brodsky' (*Pearson's Magazine*, December 1910; included in the collection *The Singing Bone*, 1912). With this inverted approach, the reader is given all the details of the crime and its perpetrator early on in the story and so the interest and suspense centres not on whether the criminal will be caught but how will he be found out. One American critic referred to these stories as 'not whodunits but howcatchems'. Freeman stated that, 'The interest focuses on the unexpected significance of trivial circumstances', adding that, 'the reader should pause after all the facts are laid out, to assess them.'

The inverted approach was demonstrated with great aplomb in the highly regarded novel *Mr Pottermack's Oversight* (1930). In this case, Mr Pottermack murders the man who has been blackmailing him and then sets about laying a false trail. The reader's interest in events is wonderfully sustained as we watch how Thorndyke gradually uncovers his deception. Because of Freeman's cunning approach to presenting the story, by the conclusion we have full sympathy with Mr Pottermack and we almost do not want him to be found out.

Freeman loved to experiment with form. In 1911, he wrote *The Exploits of Danby Croker* (1916), which told events from the viewpoint of the villain. One of his most outrageous books was *For the Defence: Dr Thorndyke* (1934). This was another inverted crime story in which an innocent young man ends up – after a series of extraordinary incidents – standing trial for murdering himself!

Perhaps Freeman's oddest book, a stand-alone novel, is *A Savant's Vendetta* (1914, US title *The Uttermost Farthing*) in which a scientist maddened by the death of his wife at the hands of a burglar turns his house into a death trap for such intruders whom he lures to the premises, kills them and then forms a collection of their skeletons and shrunken heads.

Freeman was a clever and inventive writer who constantly challenged the reader to keep up with him. His Dr Thorndyke stories hold up very well today, and although they may lack a certain amount of colour, emotion and suspense, they certainly keep the brain ticking over.

Selected Works by the Author
The Red Thumb Mark (1907)
The Eye of Osiris (1911; also published in the United States as *The Vanishing Man*)
Dr Thorndyke's Casebook (stories, 1923; also published in the United States as *The Blue Scarab*)
The Shadow of the Wolf (1925)
Mr Pottermack's Oversight (1930)
For the Defence: Dr Thorndyke (1934)
Mr Polton Explains (1940)
The Jacob Street Mystery (1942; also published in the United States as *The Unconscious Witness*)

David Stuart Davies

Freemantle, Brian (b.1936)

After publishing his first novel in 1973, Brian Freemantle, an erstwhile newspaper journalist, rapidly established himself as one of Britain's foremost **espionage** writers of the late Cold War period with a series of books chronicling the exploits of memorable MI5 operative and anti-hero Charlie Muffin.

Having produced almost fifty books in a fecund four-decade period, Freemantle – who also occasionally writes under the pseudonyms Harry Asher, Jonathan Evans, John Maxwell and Jack Winchester – remains at the cutting edge of spy fiction and, as his crime **thriller** about identity theft (*The Namedropper*, 2008) illustrates, is able to keep abreast of the many technological developments that shape contemporary life. In 1986, the Mystery Writers of America nominated Freemantle for the prestigious Edgar Allan Poe award.

Freemantle was born in Southampton and trained as a journalist. Later he became a foreign correspondent for the *Daily Mail*. He was in Vietnam when the war reached its climax in 1975 and was responsible for co-ordinating an airlift of ninety-six orphans in Saigon only a short while before the city fell into communist hands. After this, Freemantle quit journalism to become a full-time novelist. Utilising his background in investigative reporting and expert knowledge of foreign locations to good effect, Freemantle made a significant commercial breakthrough with the Cold War spy thriller *Charlie Muffin* (1977). Boasting vivid characterisation, razor-sharp dialogue and a labyrinthine plot, *Charlie Muffin* proved a hit with the public and kicked off a popular series that ran to thirteen books over twenty-four years.

The key to Muffin's enduring appeal is his ordinariness. He is the complete antithesis of the James Bond–style secret agent. Unlike most of his fellow members in British intelligence, Muffin does not come from a privileged public school background. With his Mancunian accent, brusque manner and well-worn Hush Puppies, he is patently an outsider. A loner and maverick, Muffin is an expendable foot soldier forever compromised by his seemingly inadequate social and educational background – but he always survives. Without any hint of becoming formulaic, this hugely entertaining series evolved via subsequent novels like *Clap Hands, Here Comes Charlie* (1978) and *The Inscrutable Charlie Muffin* (1979). Muffin's clandestine adventures continued in the 1980s and 1990s, with Freemantle seemingly unaffected by the Cold War thaw that stymied many a fellow espionage writer. After a brief hiatus in the late 1990s, Muffin was resurrected in the more recent novels *Dead Men Living* (2000) and *Kings of Many Castles* (2001).

Although espionage remains Brian Freemantle's undoubted métier – and Charlie Muffin his most individual creation – this versatile author has also penned historical novels (*HMS Bounty*, 1977) and laudable non-fiction exposés (*The Fix: Inside the World Drug Trade*, 1985). Freemantle has even written about Sherlock **Holmes**'s son, Sebastian, in the Jonathan Evans–credited novels *The Holmes Inheritance* (2004) and *The Holmes Factor* (2005).

Latterly, the author has continued to demonstrate that he has not been left behind by hi-tech developments in the contemporary thriller genre. He remains a consummate storyteller with a gift for avoiding clichés and presenting well-plotted novels featuring tense action scenes and adroitly etched characters.

Selected Works by the Author
The November Man (1976)
Charlie Muffin (1977; also published in the United States as *Charlie M*)
Clap Hands, Here Comes Charlie (1978; also published in the United States as *Here Comes Charlie M*)
Madrigal for Charlie Muffin (1981)
Comrade Charlie (1989)
Charlie's Chance (1996; also published in the United States as *Bomb Grade*)
Kings of Many Castles (2001)
Ice Age (2002)
Dead End (2006)
The Namedropper (2007)

Charles Waring

Fremlin, Celia (b.1914)

A highly regarded writer in her time, now out of fashion, Celia Fremlin began writing in her forties, achieving success with her first book *The Hours before Dawn* (1958) which won an Edgar from the Mystery Writers of America. Between 1958 and 1994, she wrote sixteen novels and three volumes of short stories. Her novels fit no straightforward category, having been variously labelled as 'domestic suspense', 'domestic mystery' and 'psychological **thriller**'. Fremlin was more of a mystery or suspense writer than a crime writer.

The 'domestic' label was attached early, partly because her first three books contained no actual murder or no murder that moved beyond being attempted. Her settings certainly were domestic, often based around a large house and its residents, where the families living in the house might be supplemented by lodgers who could add an unsettling insubstantiality to the cast. The stories were suspenseful and almost sinister, and each built to a satisfying climax. But the second label to her books, 'psychological', fitted also, in that, Fremlin always seemed more interested in the motivation and inevitability of her crimes. In several books, a psychiatrist was the main character. (Her first husband was a psychiatrist.)

Her own life was marred by tragedy: in 1968 her nineteen-year-old daughter committed suicide, and a month later, Fremlin's husband killed himself as well. Subsequently, Fremlin took herself away to Geneva for a year. After that sabbatical, her novel *Possession* (1969) was published, although the manuscript for this had been delivered to Gollancz earlier, shortly after the tragedies of 1968. Elements of the book – such as the nineteen-year-old girl having a considerably older fiancée, the mother's troubled relationship with the daughter and a father's suicide – have been seen as a fictional retelling of her own real-life tragedy, but the timing of the manuscript's completion leaves this uncertain. Clearly, these events had a permanent effect on Fremlin, who did not bring out another novel until 1972 and that novel, *Appointment with Yesterday*, began with a main character who, after a period of absence, invented a new name and persona for herself. Perhaps the link between Fremlin's fiction and real life continued in her next book, *The Long Shadow* (1975), which explored widowhood. Whatever the truth, Fremlin's books should not be seen as therapy; they remain fine and original examples of the psychological crime novel, informed perhaps by real life but in no way overwhelmed by it. Celia Fremlin left various mysteries about her own life. Did she – as was famously reported – actually go for long walks in London streets many a night, like **Dickens**, without fear, or was this simply a tale she once told a gullible journalist, as friends suggest? We will never know, which is probably just as Celia Fremlin would have preferred.

Selected Works by the Author
The Hours before Dawn (1958)
Prisoner's Base (1967)
With No Crying (1980)
Listening in the Dusk (1990)
King of the World (1994)

Russell James

French, Nicci

Nicci French is the pseudonym for the husband and wife partnership of Nicci Gerrard (b.1958) and Sean French (b.1959). Both journalists, they began writing as a team in 1995, producing their first novel *The Memory Game* in 1997. They made no secret of their having co-written the book – indeed, the fact that 'Nicci French' comprised a husband and wife team was an essential part of their early publicity – and their first book was an immediate success. They followed it with a line of stand-alone psychological **thrillers** as Nicci French as well as others under their individual names.

Although Nicci Gerrard graduated with a first class honours degree in English Literature from Oxford University, she began her first job working with emotionally disturbed children in Sheffield. She switched into publishing in 1985, working initially on *Women's Review* and then, in 1989, becoming acting literary editor at the *New Statesman*. She then moved to *The Observer*, where she was deputy literary editor for five years. Sean French also studied English Literature at Oxford University, graduating with a first class degree, and in 1981, he won *Vogue* magazine's Writing Talent Contest. From 1981 to 1986 he was their theatre critic, and during that time, he also worked at *The Sunday Times* as deputy literary editor and television critic.

He was also film critic for *Marie Claire* and deputy editor of *New Society*. Before the Nicci French partnership, Sean had had two novels published, *The Imaginary Monkey* (1993) and *The Dreamer of Dreams* (1995), and non-fiction books including biographies of Jane Fonda and Brigitte Bardot. He and his wife continue to write both together and separately. The Nicci Gerrard novel *Things We Knew Were True* came out in 2003, and *Solace* in 2005. Sean French's *Start from Here* came out in 2004.

Sean and Nicci have always been open about their collaboration. People were fascinated to learn how the couple worked – and Nicci and Sean were happy to tell. They wrote about it and spoke to interested groups throughout the country. They do not sit and write side by side, they said; they begin by discussing the shape of the novel, clarifying its theme and how it will be developed, and they talk about the characters – in particular, which narrative voice they should use to tell the story. Only then do they begin to write. (They write separately.) Their broad approach – which they freely admit they vary – is that either one of them will produce a first draft for a chapter, then hand it to the other who is free to edit, erase and change as they see fit. They each take different chapters, though who will write which is not predetermined, and by the time the book is finished, they believe the blended text, chapter by chapter, belongs to both of them – to Nicci French.

The theme behind their first novel *The Memory Game*, highly topical in the late 1990s, was 'recovered memory', a pseudo-psychological craze of the time where credulous victims were willingly hypnotised to 'recover' memories said to be lost due to trauma. As the book displayed, most of these supposedly recovered memories tended to be of childhood sexual molestation, which can then be used for potential financial recompense. At the time the book came out, this dubious theory was trusted and much in vogue, and *The Memory Game* was part of the vanguard to defeat it. For this novel, the narrative voice and viewpoint chose itself: it had to be that of the manipulated woman. And for this reason, say Sean and Nicci, they elected to define the author as female too: they became Nicci French.

Their subsequent novels retain a female point of view. *The Safe House* (1998), 'a superior psychological thriller', said *The Times*, was a complex but gripping mystery assembled and unravelled with professional expertise by the pair – but again, it was easy to believe that it had been written solely by a woman. In *Secret Smile* (2003), they hit upon a theme which struck another popular chord: that of a chance reunion with a childhood sweetheart. It was a topic that had been explored before, but the French twist was to make the old flame one that could not be extinguished. In most such scenarios, the old flame is female; here the old love was male – and worse, he refused to go away. For the heroine, none of her old romantic feelings for him remained; she disliked his voice, his mannerisms and above all his present-day behaviour. He would not accept that things had changed, nor that she no longer cared for him. She meanwhile failed to realise that he had a deeper motive: revenge.

The scenario for *The Red Room* (2001) might again seem familiar: a psychologist with expertise in particular forms of mental instability is called in by the police to help them on a case. The twist this time (or the first twist) is that she is asked for advice on a disturbed drifter who previously attacked her. The man is now suspected by the police of having murdered a young homeless woman – but did he? Nicci Gerrard's early career probably influenced this novel – though the pair do seem drawn to psychological topics – but the novel develops into more than a 'did he, didn't he?' mystery. It examines those we dismiss as 'drifters', asking how they became that way and why they are or have made themselves homeless. It also, through the tenacity of its heroine, insists we look at the world around us with a fresh pair of eyes and do not accept too readily the conventional or convenient view. It is an approach common to most of the French books, to present people and situations in ways that at first seem familiar and common place but which on closer, perhaps painful, examination turn out not to be as we thought they were at all.

Selected Works by the Authors
The Memory Game (1997)
The Red Room (2001)
Losing You (2006)
Until It's Over (2008)

Nicci Gerrard
Solace (2005)

Sean French
Start from Here (2004)

Russell James

Frenzy (film, 1972)

Alfred Hitchcock, director

In 1972, Alfred Hitchcock returned to Britain to collaborate with playwright Anthony Shaffer on *Frenzy*, the film of Arthur La Bern's novel *Goodbye Piccadilly, Farewell Leicester Square* (1966) which is almost a gloss on the plot of his first hit, *The Lodger* (1926). Again, **London** is plagued by a Jack the Ripper–like serial murderer and the leading man does himself few favours by acting so suspiciously that he becomes the prime suspect. Hitch evokes a precise mix of prurient fascination and genuine horror in the English attitude to murder with pub chatter that echoes the gossip of the amateur criminologists in his favourite American film, *Shadow of a Doubt* (1943). Embittered ex-RAF officer Blaney (Jon Finch) is an alcoholic working as a barman in a Covent Garden pub, reduced to cadging off his sensible ex-wife (Barbara Leigh-Hunt), who in an ironic stroke runs a dating agency that hopes to bring together better-matched couples. In one of the creepiest, most explicit scenes the master ever directed, Mrs Blaney is visited by cheery cockney fruit-market trader Bob (Barry Foster), whose unstated but perverse special requirements she does not want to fulfil professionally; Bob reveals himself as the notorious Necktie Murderer by raping the woman and strangling her with his paisley tie. The film proceeds to cut between the antisocial, unpleasant, degraded hero – who is reduced to dossing in a homeless shelter at one point – and the charming, engaging, successful villain, who further inconveniences Blaney (who was more blatantly called 'Blamey' in the novel) by murdering his sometime girlfriend (Anna Massey), a chirrupy barmaid.

As in *Psycho* and *Strangers on a Train*, Hitchcock even manages a suspense sequence by enlisting our sympathies in a murderer's attempt to cover up his crime, as Bob fumbles about with a nude corpse in a potato sack in the back of a van to retrieve an incriminating tie-clip. Hitchcock takes advantage of the laxer censorship of the 1970s to be more explicit with the sex and violence (almost as if he had kept up with the 'Hitchcockian' *gialli* of Italian directors like Dario Argento) – but he also knows when a long, slow pull-back away from a murder and downstairs out of the house onto the street will convey more horror than yet another close-up of rapine and strangulation. Much was made at the time of Hitch's 'first British film' since his departure for Hollywood in 1939 – though he had shot films or parts of films in Britain in the 1950s (*Stage Fright, The Man Who Knew Too Much*). The British milieu here is not quite frozen in earlier decades, but these pub bores and degraded officers are preserved well past their time – it is hard to imagine them as the contemporaries of the characters in, say, *Blow-Up*. Typically Hitchcock, and typically British is a streak of comedy of social embarrassment (almost in the Mike Leigh manner) as a police inspector (Alec McCowen) keeps finding excuses to leave the table and get back on the case when his wife (Vivien Merchant) confronts him with hideous gourmet meals. *See also* Film and Crime: Page to Screen.

Kim Newman

Frightened City, The (film, 1961)

John Lemont, director

A lesser achievement than, say, Val Guest's **Hell Is a City** or Joseph Losey's **The Criminal**, this is still an entertaining and flavourful Soho noir – though probably best remembered as an early credit for Sean Connery, playing a character whose dilemma vaguely echoes Marlon Brando in *On the Waterfront* (1954).

Paddy Damion, a conscience-stricken former cat burglar who has given up the game following the on-the-job crippling of his sidekick (Kenneth Griffith), is recruited as an enforcer by spivvy club-owner Harry Foulcher (Alfred Marks) and crooked accountant/criminal mastermind Waldo Zhernikov (Herbert Lom) when they broker a treaty which organises the formerly messy London protection racket business into a syndicate. Inspector Sayers (John Gregson), one of the numberless middle-aged and miserable coppers in British crime films, is on the case, trying to get the victimised restaurateurs to talk. He eventually convinces the conscience-stricken Paddy to turn informer when Harry uses him to set up a troublesome partner for a hit at a Turkish bath. *The Frightened City* (the published book was credited to Vance Leigh) is almost proud of its sleazy, exploitation credentials: it was originally released through Anglo-Amalgamated, one of Hammer's lower-rent rivals and director/co-writer John Lemont would go on to deliver the astonishing mad science/giant ape epic *Konga*. It is a jazzy London movie with flamboyant characterisations and performances, especially from a loudly dressed, cast-against-comic-type Marks as the glad-handing bully and suave, sly Lom as a collector of mediaeval torture devices (naturally, after the final fight, Foulcher ends up skewered on one of these improbable bits of set dressing). There is also a lot of titillation, with familiar starlet Yvonne Romain as a chanteuse sponsored by Waldo and coveted by Paddy, and it all plays out to a poppy score from Soho legend Norrie Paramor, who has a bit-part as a choreographer. The cast is packed with familiar faces, from John Stone as a thug to the likes of George Pastell (always an oily foreigner, whether invoking mummies' curses or running a vice den), Patrick Holt (one of nature's Chief Superintendents), bald Australian Kenneth J. Warren, David Davies, Arnold

Diamond, Vanda Godsell and Marianne Stone. The wallowing in sleaze is naturally accompanied by a high-minded tone of disgust worthy of the *News of the World* as Gregson's copper whines about pampering crooks ('what we wants are laws designed to catch villains and not hamper the police!') even as the camera shifts to ogle more showgirls or get an act of violence centre-frame. The cutting edge of disreputability inevitably becomes quaint with the passage of time – just as the £5-a-week 'protection' gouged out of various publicans and club-owners sounds almost reasonable fifty years on.

Kim Newman

Frost, Inspector

R.D. **Wingfield**'s waspish Detective Inspector William Frost is a much-loved television copper, surly in the strangely winning fashion of John Thaw's equally short-tempered Morse. Beneath the gruff exterior, his colleagues know that he is a man capable of much generosity, and many of the newer recruits look up to him as a hero (although anti-hero might be more appropriate). But if Frost senses the slightest whiff of complacency or incompetence in his officers, he is quick to berate them for it – despite his own slapdash and disorganised work practices that are often just as inadequate. Juggling several disparate cases at once, he is a man who seems intractably wedded to his job, yet perpetually scornful of the mountain of paperwork he has to deal with (which he often files in his wastepaper bin anyway).

Comic actor David Jason of *Only Fools and Horses* fame seemed an odd choice to play the ill-tempered detective for Yorkshire Television's *A Touch of Frost*, yet it seemed clear from the opening moments of 1992s *Care and Protection* that he was ideally cast. Like the television version of Morse before him (a series that *Frost* seemed groomed to replace), his character was a little watered down for the viewing public, but happily his acerbic sense of humour transferred effortlessly to the small screen.

His wife having died of a protracted illness in the first episode, Frost's quest for someone to share his loneliness with ran through several episodes, while the constant change of sidekick was a genuinely innovative concept that kept the stories - based only loosely on the books – constantly fresh and engaging. In 1999, Jason became executive producer of the series, which enjoyed multiple seasons. *See also* Inspector Morse *and* TV Detectives: Small-Screen Adaptations.

Mark Campbell

Fullerton, John (b.1949)

John Fullerton, who covered many wars in twenty years as a Reuters journalist, has used his knowledge and experience to write bitterly realistic novels about the conflicts of the late twentieth and early twenty-first centuries.

He was born in Dorset in the west of England to a naval father and a South African mother, who brought him up in Cape Town. He was educated at Monterey

Preparatory School and Diocesan College, better known as 'Bishops'. After compulsory military service, he became a journalist, reporting from thirty-eight countries over thirty years. For two of those years, during the Cold War, he also worked undercover for MI6, spying on the Soviets.

These experiences all inform *White Boys Don't Cry* (2006), which is set in South Africa in 1994, just after the end of apartheid, when the wounds caused by that regime were still raw. The first-person narrator, Sebastian Palfrey, is a British journalist. He becomes embroiled in a murder investigation when the police interview him about their prime suspect, an Afrikaner, who was his best friend in childhood. In those days, the two played war games with a boy classed as 'coloured'. Fullerton writes: 'All three of us were fascinated by weapons.... For boys of that age edged steel and the mechanism of a firearm have a fascination that's almost sexual'.

It is this precision of observation and clear description of the emotions that propel men into danger that lift Fullerton's novels above the general run of macho **thrillers**. Never glamorising violence, they are well plotted, well informed and full of the moral ambiguities to which international intrigue gives rise.

The first, *The Monkey House* (1996), deals with the corruption and cruelty of civil war in Sarajevo. *A Hostile Place* (2003) covers a desperate journey in the mountains of Afghanistan in search of Osama bin Laden. *Give Me Death* (2004), which was re-titled *This Green Land* for its paperback publication, offers a chilling but broadly sympathetic portrait of a woman suicide bomber in Lebanon. In each novel a fundamentally good man finds himself crossing the line that divides the absolutely right from the absolutely wrong for what seem at the time to be good reasons.

Seb Palfrey of *White Boys Don't Cry* is typical. Detesting the cruelties perpetrated in the name of apartheid, he worked secretly for the Communists for many years, using his journalism as cover. Once the horrors and injustices of apartheid have been successfully overcome, Seb is left to look back at what he did. The only way he can bear what he sees is to drug himself with large amounts of marijuana.

In Fullerton's work, no character would ever claim his actions were justified because his intentions were good. These novels show that no one of any race, religion or political ideology has a monopoly of virtue and that just about everyone is capable of violence.

Selected Works by the Author
The Soviet Occupation of Afghanistan (non-fiction, 1983)
The Monkey House (1996)
A Hostile Place (2003)
Give Me Death (2004; later reissued as *This Green Land*)
White Boys Don't Cry (2006)

Natasha Cooper

Fyfield, Frances (b.1948)

Frances Fyfield is best known as the creator of two remarkably adroit series both featuring female lawyers: Helen West, the London-based Crown Prosecutor (which has been successfully televised with Juliet Stevenson and then Amanda Burton playing West) and Sarah Fortune.

Frances Fyfield (also known as Frances Hegarty) was born and raised in Derbyshire. After reading English at Newcastle University, she studied law in the Midlands. Soon after qualification, Fyfield started to work for the Metropolitan Police and then The Director of Public Prosecutions. As a criminal prosecutor she acquired an inside knowledge of crime, beginning with minor cases, but later progressing onto serious investigations involving abuse, rape and homicide. She continued to practise law in London, which forms the backdrop for many of her books. She claims: 'After a long diet of criminal law, including dangerous dogs, rape, mayhem and much, much murder, the indigestion of pity and fury provoked me to write. I wanted to write romance, but the domestically macabre always got in the way.'

Fyfield's novels have been critically acclaimed internationally with *A Question of Guilt* (1988) nominated for an Edgar Award, while *Deep Sleep* (1991) was the winner of a **Crime Writers' Association** Silver Dagger Award. *A Clear Conscience* (1994) was nominated for the Gold Dagger Award and won the Grand Prix de Littérature Policière in 1998. Her last Sarah Fortune novel *Safer than Houses* was nominated for the inaugural Duncan Lawrie Dagger. Her books are also widely translated and published throughout the world.

Fyfield has also written three novels of dark suspense as Frances Hegarty (Hegarty being her father's name, Fyfield her mother's).

Her work consists of disturbing psychological **thrillers** in the 'whydunit' as opposed to 'whodunit' style, with alienated characters in a stunningly realised contemporary milieu. A classic example is *The Playroom* (2003), written under her Hegarty name, featuring a seemingly happy middle-aged couple with two children living the middle-class dream, until the husband, David, starts to suspect that he may not be the father of one of their children. Soon cracks form in their life and relationship as David's behaviour becomes more erratic. This seems to be a theme Fyfield enjoys exploring – the relationships between individuals and how they simultaneously liberate and constrict the protagonists. This theme is explored in her unnerving *The Art of Drowning* (2006), which explores the relationship between two women who appear as polar opposites but become friends, with one harbouring a tragic family secret that draws the other one to her aid. Added to the mix is Fyfield's fascination with dysfunctional marriages and abuse. Her work follows the same dark psychological pathways as those of P.D. **James**, Minette **Walters** and Ruth **Rendell**/Barbara Vine, but with a leaning towards the workings of the law and plenty of dry humour. An additional facet of Fyfield's talent is her ability to define characters from sketches, mannerisms, and behaviour, without relying on masses of detail, perhaps a result of her legal training, where perception and a swift eye for detail is essential.

Latterly, Fyfield has concentrated on darker psychological territory than the Helen West series which carved out her literary reputation. In fact, the last West novel was published over a decade ago (*Without Consent*, 1996) and, interestingly, showed her work becoming more astringent, with a particularly difficult case for West when a rape case is not all it seems; while the Dagger-nominated Sarah Fortune thriller *Safer than Houses* (2005) similarly moved into more uncompromising territory.

Her most adventurous and challenging work appears outside of the confines of her series novels, and of particular merit are *The Art of Drowning* (2006), *Seeking Sanctuary* (2003) and *Undercurrents* (2000), novels that pose difficult moral questions by putting their protagonists into situations that rigorously challenge their value systems. Her 2008 novel *Blood from Stone* demonstrates an ever-more-complex approach to the genre she has so enriched. *See also* TV Detectives: Small-Screen Adaptations *and* Women Crime Writers.

Selected Works by the Author
Let's Dance (1995)
Blind Date (1998)
Undercurrents (2000)
The Nature of the Beast (2001)
Seeking Sanctuary (2003)
The Art of Drowning (2006)
Blood from Stone (2008)

Helen West Series
A Question of Guilt (1988)
Trial by Fire (1990) also known as *Not That Kind of Place*
Deep Sleep (1991)
Shadow Play (1993)
A Clear Conscience (1994)
Without Consent (1996)

Sarah Fortune Series
Shadows on the Mirror (1989)
Perfectly Pure and Good (1994)
Staring at the Light (1999)
Looking Down (2004)
Safer Than Houses (2005)

Ali Karim

G

Gadney, Reg (b.1941)

The author of several densely plotted and cerebral **espionage thrillers**, Reg Gadney cites Raymond **Chandler** as a key inspiration for his bleak, often dystopian, stories.

Reginald Bernard John Gadney was born in the village of Cross Hills in West Yorkshire on 20 January 1941. His father was the headmaster of a private school, but Gadney was sent away to study at the famous Buckinghamshire boarding school, Stowe. Describing his childhood as miserable, and his time at Stowe especially so, Gadney cultivated a fearful dislike of the establishment from an early age, a theme that would later feature prominently in his fiction.

He was commissioned in the Coldstream Guards from 1959 to 1962 and served in London, Libya, France and Norway, finally working for the British Embassy in Oslo as assistant to the Naval, Military and Air Attaché. He immediately went on to study English, Fine Art and Architecture at St Catharine's College in Cambridge and married Annette Margot Kobak in his final year, 1966. A post as Research Fellow and Instructor at the Massachusetts Institute of Technology (MIT) took him briefly to the 'other' Cambridge, but in 1967, he applied for the job of Deputy Controller at the National Film Theatre in London, which saw him serving in the box office, selling ice-creams and even projecting the films.

It was there that he became friends with the American film actor/director John Cassavetes who suggested that he should write a novel. Gadney's first novel appeared in 1971 as *Drawn Blanc*, the story of a young Czech student in London who is hounded by the authorities for killing a KGB agent. Gadney's debut was generally well received – with a particularly favourable review by playwright David Hare – leading to several more novels during the early 1970s, on a variety of themes. In 1968, he became an art history tutor at London's Royal College of Art, eventually becoming a fellow of the college in 1978.

In the early 1980s, Gadney wrote an exhaustively researched television script about the Kennedy administration, which was made into an acclaimed 1983 Central TV–NBC co-production starring Martin Sheen as JFK. The success of the series prompted the author to take up writing full-time, and he resigned his teaching job to work on a number of television and film scripts by other writers. He also penned the espionage novel *Nightshade* (1987) and a 1993 episode of *The Young Indiana Jones Chronicles*.

His writing career went up a gear in 1995 when Faber and Faber published, and heavily promoted, his post–Cold War terrorist thriller *Just When We Are Safest* (1995). Detailing a customs officer's quest to hunt down an IRA bombing unit, the book's fusion of fact and fiction showcased the author's unerring ability to tap into the then-current unease about terrorism and the apparent inability of world governments to deal with it. It also introduced undercover investigator Alan Rosslyn, a character who would later reappear in *Mother, Son and Holy Ghost* in 1998. In this deliberately provocative thriller, Gadney explored his distrust of religious cults by detailing the millennial prophecies of a group called the Trinity Chapter who believed that their leader, Trinity the Divine, will be reborn on 1 January 2000. Combining horror with crime, the book's complex conspiracy plot stretched into the upper echelons of the American government and the British intelligence services.

Rosslyn returned in *Strange Police* (2000), this time involved in a rather unlikely plot – the theft of the Elgin Marbles. His last case to date, *Immaculate Deception* (2006), witnessed the return of the psychotic assassin Klaas-Pieter Terajima from *The Scholar of Extortion* (2003), a book that was far less well received than most of his other works (being further sabotaged by inadequate proofreading).

Gadney's teleplay, *The Murder of Princess Diana*, based on research by Noel Botham, and co-written with Emma Reeves, was broadcast in 2007. Gadney has also penned non-fiction books on the painter Constable and the 1956 Hungarian Uprising. A keen artist, his work is displayed in several Oxford and Cambridge college collections; he had his first one-man show in 2004.

Selected Works by the Author
Just When We Are Safest (1995)
The Achilles Heel (1996)
Mother, Son and Holy Ghost (1998)
The Scholar of Extortion (2003)

Mark Campbell

Gangster No. 1 (film, 2000)

Paul McGuigan, director

Utilising a narration whose tone echoes that of the novels of Jake **Arnott**, Paul McGuigan's *Gangster No. 1* (which can read as Gangster Number One or Gangster No One), adapted by Johnny Ferguson from his own play, is a bare-knuckles mix of class and crime with a storyline which evokes *All About Eve* or *Persona* as much as **Brighton Rock** or *The Krays*. The film is almost an essay on the stature of British screen icon Malcolm McDowell, who is introduced puffing a big cigar, dominating a tableload of old-time mugs at a boxing match. The former *Clockwork Orange* boy, now scarfaced and crop-topped, is inspired by the news that old boss Freddie Mays (David Thewlis) is just out of jail after a thirty-year stretch, to reminisce about his rise to the top. McDowell dominates the film, though well-matched smoothie Paul Bettany takes over the Gangster in flashbacks which run from 1968 through to the cocaine-fuelled Thatcher years. Gravelly, profane narration gives this clubland Macbeth a turbulent inner life as he schemes to get in with Freddie, but then works just as hard to replace him. Influenced by *Goodfellas* and *Casino* in its bursts of operatic high-style (some flash-forwards are seen in bursts of flame) and use of a slippery narrator, this finds a specifically British (even more specifically London) identity and indulges in the performance (indeed, **Performance**) aspect of criminality.

Bettany does interrogations and tortures that are little music hall turns, laying out his array of killing tools like a conjurer and keeping up a constant patter as he teaches terminal lessons to his victims. This is a world of concrete estates where an Elisha Cook-like squealer (Eddie Marsan) is terrified into confession by the sheer force of Bettany's feral eyes, crowded Dansette parties (Englebert Humperdicnk's 'Ten Guitars') and smoky 1960s pubs and clubs (with Saffron Burrows as the singer who cops off with Mays and makes him go soft in Gangster's jealous eyes). The height of its narrator's ambition is a luxury penthouse, equipped with sunken leather couches, in a brutal tower block. 'Who'd want to be him?' says the ex-ganglord of his dressy, pratty, violent younger self, a vicious dig at Gangster, who has become a self-destructive monster to assume the outward semblance of that same Freddie Mays. Most gangster movies end with a triumph of morality as the hood lies dead in the dirt: this is more offhand about the obsolescence of its criminal protagonist, who drops quietly off the top of his tower leaving a cloud of burning banknotes after Freddie has refused to put him out of misery. Judging from Gangster's fate, to go for the big bankroll, the Italian suits, free 'n' easy 'birds' (though, like many British gangster films, there is a broad gay streak) and the respect that comes with sitting in a mess of someone else's guts is simply to choose death over life.

Kim Newman

Gardner, John (Edmund) (1926–2007)

Although he published many successful **thrillers** during the 1960s and 1970s, Gardner is primarily associated with a long-running series of officially sanctioned James Bond novels.

The son of a school chaplain, John Edmund Gardner was born on 20 November 1926 in Northumbria. He was educated in Berkshire, and having joined the Home Guard band, found himself training volunteers on how to use a Lewis gun at the tender age of fourteen. At seventeen, he travelled around the country doing magic tricks with the American Red Cross entertainment department, and in 1944, he was called up for the Royal Navy, transferring to the Royal Marines, serving briefly in the Middle East and Asia during the closing stages of the Second World War.

On returning to Civvy Street, Gardner finished his education at Cambridge and Oxford and, following in his father's footsteps, was ordained as an Anglican priest. After marrying Margaret, he became vicar of a church at Evesham for seven years and then a chaplain in the Royal Air Force. Eventually, following serious doubts about his faith and an ongoing struggle with alcoholism, he resigned from the clergy and became a theatre critic for the *Stratford-upon-Avon Herald*. In 1959, he came under the care of pioneering specialist Dr Lincoln Williams whose treatment involved hypnosis and aversion therapy. The treatment was a complete success, and in 1964, Gardner wrote of his harrowing battle with addiction in his first (and only autobiographical) book, *Spin the Bottle*.

For his first novel, Gardner chose to mimic the then fashionable trend in spy thrillers with a full-blown James Bond spoof entitled *The Liquidator* (1964). Introducing the cowardly secret agent Boysie Oakes, played by Rod Taylor in a 1965 film adaptation, the book spawned seven further entries, concluding with *Killer for a Song* in 1976. Police inspector Derek Torry appeared in two **police procedurals** – *A Complete State of Death* (1969), incompetently filmed as *The Stone Killer* (1974) and *Corner Men* (1974) – while displaced German spy Herbie Kruger featured in five books, beginning with *The Nostradamus Traitor* in 1979.

Gardner's skills at pastiche were evident from two novels he wrote featuring Sherlock **Holmes**'s arch nemesis, Professor Moriarty, who returns to ruin Holmes's reputation in *The Return of Moriarty* (1974) and *The Revenge of Moriarty* (1975).

In 1980, Ian **Fleming**'s production company Glidrose Publications chose Gardner to write a series of novels starring James Bond, which would follow on from Fleming's last 007 novel, *The Man with the Golden Gun* (1965). The first of these, *Licence Renewed* (1981), although unpopular with diehard Bond aficionados, proved a big money-spinner. Gardner's tentative three-book deal evolved into a mammoth fourteen-book series, equalling Fleming's original run. He also wrote novelisations of *Licence to Kill* (1989) and *GoldenEye* (1995).

In 1995, Gardner was diagnosed with cancer and, following the death of his wife in 1997, he disappeared from the literary scene until his 2001 comeback thriller, *Day of Absolution*, was published to great acclaim. He also began a new 1940s-set series featuring WPC Suzie Mountford. However, he died of heart failure on 3 August 2007. *See also* Espionage Fiction.

Selected Works by the Author
The Liquidator (1964)
The Nostradamus Traitor (1979)
Licence Renewed (1981)
Icebreaker (1983)
Nobody Lives Forever (1985)
Scorpius (1988)
Day of Absolution (2000)

Garve, Andrew (1908–2001)

It has been said of Andrew Garve that he never wrote the same book twice – a summary of his variety and the fact that he almost never uses the same character in two different books. With a few exceptions, like *No Tears for Hilda* (1950) and *Frame-Up* (1964) which approximate to the classic detective story, his work mostly comprises of **thriller** adventure stories.

Garve was a pseudonym for Paul Winterton (who also used the names Paul Somers and Roger Bax when writing crime fiction); he was a journalist for much of his active life as a fiction writer (1938–1978, up to 1950 under the Bax name) and this is reflected in several books, which are either set in a newspaper office or feature press reporters as major characters, like *A Press of Suspects* (1951), *The Galloway Case* (1958), *The Riddle of Samson* (1954) and three books of the four that use the Somers byline: *Operation Piracy* (1958), *Beginner's Luck* (1958) and *The Shivering Mountain* (1959). These latter are the only Winterton novels that employ some of the same characters successively, the hero and heroine being bright, intrepid young journalists from different newspapers whose relationship may be summed up as affectionate rivalry.

The outstanding feature of Garve's work is its exceptional readability (as all good press copy should be); his books convey very interesting, well-researched material about a variety of background subjects. Further, we visit a fair variety of geographical locations, paralleling Winterton's own travels perhaps. *Murder in Moscow* (1951) and *The Ashes of Loda* (1965) take place in Russia, *A Hero for Leanda* (1959) off the coast of Africa, *Boomerang* (1970) in Australia, *No Mask for Murder* (1950) in the Caribbean, *The Late Bill Smith* (1971) partly on a Greek island cruise and *The Ascent of D13* (1969) on the Russo-Turkish border, where rural mountaineer teams try to reach a hijacked NATO plane which has crashed (only one, of opposite sexes, from either side survive the harsh conditions – the predictable ending is not quite conventionally worked out).

Even the Garves set in the British Isles are not stereotyped as to place. *The Far Sands* (1961), *A Very Quiet Place* (1967), *Murderer's Fen* (1966) and *The Cuckoo Line Affair* (1953) all feature East Anglia, but the reader is taken to the Channel Islands and North Wales in *The Galloway Case* (1958), the Scillies in *The Riddle of Samson* (1954), the Pennines in *Counterstroke* (1978), southern Ireland in *The House of Soldiers* (1962), a lighthouse in *The Sea Monks* (1963), canals in *The Narrow Search* (1957) and various sailing backgrounds.

On several occasions, as in *The Megstone Plot* (1956), *A Hole in the Ground* (1952), *Boomerang* (1970) and (the fourth and last Paul Somers) *The Broken Jigsaw* (1961), the viewpoint character is a villain, but Garve's skill compels a reader's empathy with him. In *The Broken Jigsaw*, we see a murder and the evidence hidden in a northern reservoir, but nature foils the murderer when a drought causes the dam's waters to recede.

Even where they are not criminals, Garve's characters' situations are often unusual. In *The Far Sands*, the viewpoint character sees his once happy marriage go downhill when it becomes apparent that his wife's identical twin has callously murdered her husband before being accidentally killed. In *A Very Quiet Place*, a woman sees and photographs a robbery and has to hide from the culprits trying to silence her. In *Death and the Sky Above*, a man awaiting trial for the murder of his estranged wife escapes and, helped by his new girlfriend, proves an alibi by rerunning a telecast of a Test match.

Andrew Garve's books are page-turners, well written, exciting in incident, varied in plot and never dull.

Selected Works by the Author
No Mask for Murder (1950; also published in the United States as *Fontego's Folly*)
A Press of Suspects (1951; also published in the United States as *By-line for Murder*)
Murder in Moscow (1951; also published in the United States as *Murder Through the Looking Glass*)
The Riddle of Samson (1954)
The Narrow Search (1957)
The Ashes of Loda (1965)
Murderer's Fen (1966; also published in the United States as *Hide and Go Seek*)
A Very Quiet Place (1967)
The Ascent of D13 (1969)
Home to Roost (1976)
Counterstroke (1978)

Philip Scowcroft

Gash, Jonathan (b.1933)

Jonathan Gash (real name: John Grant) is famous for his long-running series of mystery novels featuring the roguish antiques dealer Lovejoy. The popularity of the books was cemented by Ian McShane's charismatic portrayal of the title role in a hit BBC television series.

Grant was born in Bolton, Lancashire, on 30 September 1933. He was educated at the University of London and the Royal College of Surgeons and Physicians and became a general practitioner in the early 1960s. He later served as a pathologist in England and Germany and became a lecturer for the University of Hong Kong. From 1971 to 1988, he headed the bacteriology unit at the London School of Hygiene and Tropical Medicine.

In the mid-1970s, he sought relief from the daily stress of his medical career by penning a book about a loveable antiques dealer called Lovejoy (whose first name still remains a mystery). Written under the pseudonym of 'Jonathan Gash', this appeared as *The Judas Pair* in 1977 and featured the wily East Anglian dealer on the trail of a priceless pair of antique flintlock pistols, now in the possession of a dangerous murderer. Permanently broke, Lovejoy was a surly, bad-tempered bachelor who distrusted women (especially pretty ones, whom he used and abused whenever he felt like it) and was always happiest in the company of other disreputable characters. He was also a master of the dodgy deal and not beyond a bit of artful forgery – a talent he combined with an expert's eye for the genuine article. But try as he might, he never seemed to acquire that elusive fortune he was so desperate for.

The Judas Pair won the John Creasey Memorial Award for best first novel and was swiftly followed by *Gold from Gemini* a year later. While not considered among the author's best works, it was sufficient to further establish Lovejoy as one of crime's most interesting detectives, with the author's exhaustive knowledge of the antiques business providing a fascinating and unique backdrop to the stories.

The series gathered pace in the 1980s, with such entertaining tales as *The Vatican Rip* (1981) and *The Gondola Scam* (1984), but it was the BBC television series first transmitted in 1986 that really saw Gash hit the big-time. Ian McShane was cast as a significantly more suave Lovejoy, with much of the misogyny and implied violence toned down for the small screen (as it had been with *Morse*). Teamed with Chris Jury as Eric Catchpole and Dudley Sutton as Tinker Dill, the one-off series was resurrected in 1991, with a further five following until 1994. Based only loosely on the novels, the scripts were overseen by comedy writer Ian La Frenais and proved tremendously popular. Two Christmas specials were also commissioned: *The Prague Sun* (1992) and *The Lost Colony* (1993).

The author had little involvement with the series but continued to steer Lovejoy's literary excursions right through the 1990s. The final novel – for now – saw Lovejoy on the run for stealing one of his own forgeries in *Ten Word Game* (2003).

Grant is also the author of four medical **thrillers** set in Manchester and featuring Dr Clare Burtonall. *Different Women Dancing* (1997) was the first in a series that was deliberately less homely than the Lovejoy adventures. With its emphasis on prostitutes, hit men and gigolos, it was clear that Grant was writing for a completely different market, although his pen-name remained unchanged. However, his 1982 novel, *The Incomer*, about an imprisoned killer who returns to his home village, was written as 'Graham Gaunt'. *See also* TV Detectives: Small-Screen Adaptations.

Selected Works by the Author
The Judas Pair (1977)
The Vatican Rip (1981)
The Sleepers of Erin (1983)
Pearlhanger (1985)
Moonspender (1986)
Prey Dancing (1998)

Mark Campbell

Gay and Lesbian Crime Fiction

Sexuality has always been an integral part of crime fiction, even in traditionally repressed Britain. Physical desires have been the undoing of characters in novels from the era of Wilkie **Collins** to that of Colin **Dexter**, but it is probably in hard-boiled narrative that the force of sexuality has been most clearly evident. More recently, the most interesting developments have been in gay and lesbian crime fiction.

It is necessary, even in the context of British-oriented fiction, to look at the American model. The figure of the femme fatale, a hyperbolic expression of female sexuality whose deadly charms lure red-blooded heterosexual men to a sublime death (or in the detective's case, to the point of coitus interruptus), is central to the work of both Raymond **Chandler** and Dashiell Hammett in the United States, and to later imitators such as Mickey Spillane. The femme fatale had a significant formal function, in that she was customarily deployed to distract the detective from whatever he was pursuing, but she was also the embodiment of a set of deep-rooted prejudices and anxieties regarding the independent woman and her desires. This woman is evasive and uncontrollable – she is about surface rather than depth – and this dangerous mutability is made explicit by her shifting name and her capacity for performance. In Hammett's *The Maltese Falcon*(1930), for example, Brigid O'Shaughnessy is also Miss Wonderly and Miss Leblanc, while in Chandler's *Farewell, My Lovely* (1940), Little Velma graduates to the status of Mrs Grayle – surely the perfect name for an unobtainable object over which men might go to war. Ultimately, the detectives Sam Spade and Philip Marlowe are saved only by their loyalty to a higher calling – the homosocial bond. Spade feels a moral, if not a personal, obligation to avenge his seedy partner Miles Archer, while Marlowe is revealed to owe his allegiance to the men Little Velma has betrayed: Moose Malloy and the spectral Mr Grayle, an 'old man who had loved not wisely, but too well' (1940/1949, 253).

Contemporary crime fiction has, however, found more innovative ways to explore the stereotype of the deadly woman. In Sara Paretsky's *Bitter Medicine* (1987), for example, the figure is inverted to produce an *homme fatal*. Peter Burgoyne replicates the structural purpose of his female predecessors, but achieves only limited success in the role. He briefly distracts V. I. Warshawski from her investigation into medical malpractice, but is ultimately dismissed as a 'lightweight'. Paretsky was a key figure in the development of feminist detective fiction in the 1980s and 1990s, and like many of her contemporaries, she struggled to find a mode through which to incorporate female heterosexual desire into the structure of the hard-boiled crime novel. Frequently, the female protagonist solves the crime only at the expense of her relationship, as lover after lover is proved incapable of accommodating female agency.

Yet while the heterosexual female investigator has struggled to escape from patriarchal gender assumptions, her lesbian counterpart has enjoyed a more unfettered relationship with desire. Sally Munt's authoritative account of feminism and the crime novel *Murder by the Book* (1994) cites M.F. Beal's *Angel Dance* (1977) as the first example of what has become the highly successful sub-genre of lesbian detection. Beal's book was typical of the first wave of lesbian detection in that it was published by a small press for a clearly defined readership, but by the 1990s the number of lesbian professional investigators had enormously increased. According to Priscilla Walton and Manina Jones, lesbian detectives increased from fourteen in 1986 to forty-three in 1995, with a significant number appearing under the imprint of mainstream publishing houses (1999, 41). With such a large number of practitioners it is difficult to generalise about the lesbian detective but, like her heterosexual feminist counterpart, she runs the gamut from accidental amateur to the institutional authority of the police. Barbara Wilson's printer sleuth Pam Nilsen typifies the first category. Introduced in *Murder in the Collective* (1984), Nilsen disrupts conventional constructs of the detective hero by being utterly uncertain of herself. As a number of critics have observed, her indecisiveness throws the moral complacency of the genre into question, while her rape in the second novel *Sisters of the Road* (1986) radically deconstructs the boundary between victim and detective. Although very different in style and setting, Stella **Duffy**'s novels featuring London-based private eye Saz Martin undertake a similar assault on the concept of detective agency. By the time of the fourth novel *Fresh Flesh* (1999), Saz's detective experiences have left her physically and emotionally scarred. Duffy's novels persistently challenge values supposedly central to the genre; in the case of *Fresh Flesh*, the novel suggests that the detective's dogged pursuit of 'the truth' is almost as destructive as the original crimes.

In spite of their serious subject matter, both Wilson and Duffy's novels also operate as lesbian romances. For Pam Nilsen, the first novel is a coming-out narrative, while the later Saz Martin books chart her ongoing relationship with her lover Molly and the couple's decision to have a child. The erotic is central to the sub-genre. From Sarah Dreher's *Stoner McTavish* (1985) to Mary Wings' *She Came too Late* (1986), lesbian detective fiction resurrects and celebrates the figure of the *femme fatale*. There is frequently an element of parody to these encounters, and Wings provides an excellent example of a writer adopting a Chandleresque style to create fiction that simultaneously pays homage and deconstructs the form. Yet probably the best example of lesbian crime fiction's capacity for generic play is provided by Barbara Wilson's *Gaudí Afternoon* (1990). Introducing a new detective, translator and traveller Cassandra Reilly, Wilson creates a world of endlessly deferred desires in which nobody and nothing is what it seems. From its inauthentic *femmes* to its illusory quest, *Gaudí Afternoon* is as much about detecting the enigma of sexuality and gender identity as it is about solving crimes – but it always remains acutely aware of the tradition it is adopting and adapting.

Lesbian detective fiction is also characteristically political. Val **McDermid**'s Glasgow journalist Lindsay Gordon, who first appeared in *Report for Murder* (1987), is very much a product of Thatcherism, and her investigations expose the social cost of a government dedicated to market forces. Other detectives, however, are more interested in sexual politics, and Barbara Wilson's third Pam Nilsen mystery, *The Dog Collar Murders* (1989) debates the politics of lesbian sexuality by situating the crime at a conference where the participants are at loggerheads over lesbian sadomasochism. Pam, as indecisive as ever, listens attentively to both sides of the argument, which challenges the myth of an essential lesbian identity and an unquestioned political solidarity. Similar tensions characterise Kate Allen's *Tell Me What You Like* (1993), the first in a series of novels featuring policewoman Alison Kaine who is gradually seduced by the appeal of s/m, particularly as manifest in the form of dominatrix Stacey.

Although small in number in comparison with private investigators, and arguably a contradiction in terms given the lesbian's outsider status within patriarchal society, lesbian policewomen are an important dimension of the genre. Well-established examples include Claire McNab's Sydney-set series featuring Detective Inspector Carol Ashton and Laurie R. King's San Francisco homicide detective Kate Martinelli, but probably the most influential version of the lesbian police officer is Katherine V. Forrest's Detective Kate Delafield. First introduced in *Amateur City* (1984), Delafield is an exemplary homicide detective whose investigations expose the American Dream to be a myth built on repression, abuse and lies. Yet, ironically, her capacity to fight for justice for the victims of this society is contingent upon the public repression of her sexuality – in a force as homophobic as the LAPD, Detective Delafield's agency depends upon the closet.

In manifestations as diverse as Ellen Hart's cosy restaurateur Jane Lawless, Manda Scott's therapist Kellen Stewart and Sandra Scoppetone's streetwise PI Lauren Laurano, the lesbian investigator has become a significant force within crime fiction. The gay male detective, by comparison, is a rare species. Joseph Hansen's Dave Brandstetter, a middle-aged homosexual insurance-claims investigator, broke new ground in his debut novel *Fadeout* (1970), but in spite of considerable critical acclaim, this was not the beginning of a publishing phenomenon. Hansen, like Forrest, exposes the myth of the American family and establishes liberal patriarch Dave as the custodian of moral and cultural values. Time and again, the detective recognises the signifiers of repression, discovering dysfunctional heterosexuality (and resultant criminality) to be built on the shifting sands of inarticulable desires. As with much lesbian detection, the detective's relationships are integral to the novels. *Fadeout* begins with the detective almost paralysed by grief for his lost lover, and it is the support of his friends that sustains him until he meets Cecil, the young black media student who will become his companion for the remaining books in the series. In marked contrast to Hansen's emphasis on sexuality and its repression, Dan Kavanagh's *Duffy* (1980) – see Julian **Barnes** – focuses on sex and its expression, as the bisexual ex-policeman detective takes the reader on a bleak and dispassionate tour of London's Soho. Duffy has few friends and is haunted by the failure of his ideal sexual relationship with his ex-fiancée Carol – and this, combined with his serial erotic encounters, locates him closer to traditional hard-boiled narrative than to the revised formula of writers such as Hansen, Forrest and Wilson.

The emergence of lesbian detective fiction as an influential and successful sub-genre in the 1980s, however, should not obscure the presence of gay and lesbian characters in earlier crime fiction – but in these former incarnations, they frequently appeared as pathologised figures whose 'deviant' sexuality was a mark of wider criminal tendencies. Yet even now, the stereotype of the homicidal lesbian lingers, as is evident from Quintin **Jardine**'s *Fallen Gods* (2003). In a remarkable throwback to the **pulp** fiction of the 1950s, the detective's career is threatened by 'Black Agnes', Machiavellian councillor, criminal mastermind and, predictably, lesbian sadist.

The demonising of sexual non-conformity that characterises Jardine's thriller remains a staple of the genre, albeit in more subtle form. The attitude to this syndrome (and to the authors' own sexuality) varies from writer to writer. Chaz Brenchley, for instance, has never described himself as a gay writer. 'There are too many variables there. I'm gay and I'm a writer, and the two facts are of course intimately linked, but not at all contiguous. To call myself a gay crime writer would be ridiculous; not everything I write is crime, not everything I write is gay. Sometimes, subjects and forms intersect.' Christopher Fowler, author of The Bryant and May series, adduces other influences for his writing than his sexuality. 'It was London that shaped me as a writer. I'm very patient with annoying people, but is that the gay gene or just being a Londoner? I write gay characters, but only in context of every other kind of character, because that's how life is lived; you're never just one thing. Life would be far too dull.'

Victoria Blake has said that she can't imagine writing a book which doesn't have a lesbian or gay character in it. 'With me, I think it comes pretty close to a feeling of moral duty – but this is not to say that I write exclusively for a gay and lesbian audience, because I don't. Nor do I think other gay and lesbian writers should do the same. For me that feeling of duty comes from knowing how important gay and lesbian writers were for me when I was younger. Reading writers like Val McDermid, Stella Duffy, Jeanette Winterson and Armistead Maupin made me want to be a writer and allowed me to dream that that was a possibility.' Natasha Cooper, however, feels that her sexuality is no more relevant to her work than her gender or the fact that she has green eyes – proving that that the gay sensibility in crime fiction is an amorphous thing.

In the psychological landscapes of much contemporary detection, pathological sexuality is both a motivating force for the killer and a source of fascination for detective and reader alike. While Thomas Harris's *The Silence of the Lambs* (1989) connects sexual and social dysfunction, Val McDermid's *The Mermaids Singing* (1995) uses desire to bring detective and killer into uncomfortable proximity. Rather than the detective curing society of the affliction of crime, *The Mermaids Singing* sees its investigator, Tony Hill, receiving illicit sexual therapy from the murderer. McDermid pushes the inversion of roles to its logical limit, forcing Hill to kill the voice that had seduced him, and thus – in the new guise of psychological complexity – we are returned to the hard-boiled genre's traditional equation of death and desire. Lesbian and gay detectives may have succeeded in disrupting this paradigm, but their influence is yet to have a serious impact on the representation of heterosexuality within the genre. For the most part, then, women are still deadly, and crime fiction continues to suggest that desire and the detective make uncomfortable bedfellows. *See also* Male Crime Writers, Feminist Readings in British Crime Fiction *and* Women Crime Writers.

Selected Works
Allen, Kate: *Tell Me What You Like* (1993)
Duffy, Stella: *Fresh Flesh* (1999)
Forest, Katherine V.: *Murder at the Nightwood Bar* (1987); *Murder by Tradition* (1991)
Hansen, Joseph: *Fadeout* (1970); *Gravedigger* (1982)
Kavanagh, Dan: *Duffy* (1980)
King, Laurie R.: *A Grave Talent* (1993)
McDermid, Val: *The Mermaids Singing* (1995)
Scoppetone, Sandra: *Everything You Have Is Mine* (1991)
Wilson, Barbara: *Murder in the Collective* (1984); *Gaudí Afternoon* (1990)
Wings, Mary: *She Came Too Late* (1986)

Further Reading
Betz, Phyllis M. 2006. *Lesbian Detective Fiction*. McFarland.
Markowitz, Judith A. 2004. *The Gay Detective Novel*. McFarland.
Munt, Sally R. 1994. *Murder by the Book?* Routledge.
Plain, Gill. 2001. *Twentieth-Century Crime Fiction: Gender, Sexuality and the Body*. Edinburgh University Press.
Walton, Priscilla L., and Manina Jones. 1999. *Detective Agency: Women Rewriting the Hard-boiled Tradition*. University of California Press.

Gill Plain

Get Carter (film, 1971)

Mike Hodges, director

Writer–director Mike Hodges made his big-screen debut with this adaptation of Ted **Lewis**'s tough-guy novel *Jack's Return Home*. In 1971, the film was received coolly as just another tough action film – a hard-boiled star vehicle along the lines of many vehicles for Clint Eastwood, Lee Marvin or Charles Bronson then being made in America. Gradually, over the years, its reputation has risen – to the point when it is often hailed among the greatest of all gangster films, and a highlight of the British version of the genre. *Get Carter* is an essay in the kind of stripped-down movie-movie world found in films by Seijun Suzuki (*Tokyo Drifter*), Jean-Pierre Melville (*Le Samourai*) and John Boorman (*Point Blank*). The movie benefits from Caine's blank, wry reading of exceptionally tough dialogue ('You're a big man, but you're in bad shape...with me it's a full-time job'), Roy Budd's melancholic jazz music, a range of interestingly cast character actors (Terence Rigby, George Sewell, Glynn

Edwards, Bernard Hepton, Tony Beckley, Alun Armstrong, Bryan Mosley, John Osbourne) and relatively unfamiliar but distinctive Newcastle locations (the novel, oddly, is set in Scunthorpe). Gangster Jack Carter (Michael Caine), who works as strong-arm man for a London mob, returns to his Northern home town (though it is inconceivable that anyone with Caine's accent comes from the North) to avenge the death of his brother and finds himself genocidally involved in a complicated series of faction fights between local crooks and set up to take a fall because he has unwisely been having sex with his boss's girlfriend (Britt Ekland). Eventually, Carter latches onto his long-time nemesis – chauffeur Eric Paice (Ian Hendry), memorably described as having eyes 'like pissholes in the snow' and whose venomous dislike of the protagonist might spring from the fact that Hendry was originally cast in the lead but bumped by the attachment of a bigger star. Blunt and forceful, Hodges makes no concessions to morality and yet hardly condones the brutalities of its characters, with Carter getting a shock as he discovers his niece (who might be his daughter) has starred in a credibly amateur porno movie and has come to a bad end. By the end of the film, Carter is extracting rough justice on a deserted beach by a forgotten factory. Memorable scenes: a stark-naked Carter with a shotgun ejecting a couple of thugs from his bed and breakfast, a car going into the docks with an unnoticed passenger in the boot, a mob boss taking a dive from a multi-storey car park. The film was almost instantly remade by George Armitage (*Miami Blues*, *Grosse Pointe Blank*) as *Hit Man*, a blaxploitation movie starring Bernie Casey – for the most part, this follows the original closely, but with some of the grit removed (Casey beds a gorgeous babe while Caine gets a quick shag from a middle-aged landlady) and a happier ending. Even further from the original was the 2000 American-set remake, with Sylvester Stallone as Carter and Caine significantly returning as the 'big, out-of-shape' gangster who takes the fall off a building. *See also* Film and Crime: Page to Screen.

Kim Newman

Gilbert, Michael (1912–2006)

In a career that spanned over fifty years, Michael Gilbert's works reached a wide audience. Whether the genre he attempted was that of the **thriller**, mystery, **police procedural** or **espionage** novel, Gilbert provided well-plotted stories peopled with engaging characters, and his accurate legal details granted plausible authenticity.

Gilbert was born on 17 July 1912 in Lincolnshire and was educated at St Peter's School, Seaford, Sussex, Blundell's School (1926–1931) and at the University of London, attaining LL.B. with honours in 1937.

Both Gilbert's early attempts at writing and his career as a solicitor were halted by the outbreak of the Second World War. While serving in the Royal Horse Artillery in North Africa, he was captured in 1943 and sent to a military prison near Parma in Italy. Gilbert managed to escape from the camp, and this experience he later used in the novel *Death in Captivity* (1952), which also inspired the film *Danger Within* (1959). Gilbert states that, while a prisoner, he found a copy of Cyril **Hare**'s *Tragedy at Law* which inspired his crime writing.

By the time his first novel, *Close Quarters* (1947), was published, Gilbert was achieving success as a solicitor in a London law firm. He would later become a senior partner and represent Raymond **Chandler**, whom he would always call 'Ray'. The novel introduced Inspector Hazelrigg, who was to be one of the very first realistic portrayals of a British policeman and a template for many future characters. Hazelrigg is clearly part of the establishment, with thirty years worth of experience, dedicated to the 'job' and a cat lover. Hazelrigg struck a chord with the readers of the time and became a considerable success. The narrative revolves around a murder mystery set in a cathedral close in Salisbury, where Gilbert had worked as a teacher. Gilbert brought back Hazelrigg for a further six novels, of which *Smallbone Deceased* (1950) achieved classic status as the Inspector investigates the death of a law firm's client sealed in a locked box – a neat variation on the locked room mystery. The character of Harry Bouhn, a young solicitor who appears in the book, proved so popular that Bouhn went on to feature in many short stories, which were collected in *Stay of Execution and Other Stories of Legal Practice* (1971).

Although many of Gilbert's novels were inspired by his legal background, his work was not bound by it. *Trouble* (1987) deals with terrorism and the petty rivalries between the Metropolitan police and Special Branch; *Paint, Gold and Blood* (1989) tackles international art smuggling. Clearly, Gilbert enjoyed writing about recurring characters such as the Spanish–English policeman Patrick Petrella, whose literary career spanned over forty years, twenty-eight short stories, the first of which was 'Source Seven' (1953), but only two novels, *Blood and Judgment* (1959) and *Roller-Coaster* (1993). Similarly, the short stories featuring Calder and Behrens may be found in two collections, *Game without Rules* (1967), which the *New York Times* critic Anthony Boucher called the best collection of spy stories ever written, and *Mr Calder and Mr Behrens* (1982). The protagonists were counterspies, congenial gentlemen on the surface but, in fact, very efficient killers, indicating a darker edge to Gilbert's customarily urbane writing. As did *The Queen against Kari Mullen* (1991), in which Gilbert continues to explore the judiciary system when a South African secret police torturer comes to Britain to try to get a prominent black activist extradited. He utilised the Siege of Sydney Street and London's East End as background in *Ring of Terror* (1995), introducing Luke Pagan and Joe Narrabone of MO5 who went on to feature in *Into Battle* (1997) and his final novel, *Over the Top* (1998), both set in the Second World War.

In celebration of his career, he was made a Commander of the Order of the British Empire in 1980; in 1988, he was named as a Grand Master by the Mystery Writers of America; he received the Life Achievement Award at the 1990 Bouchercon in London; and he was honoured with the Cartier Diamond Dagger (1994) from the **Crime Writers' Association**, of which he was a founding member. His voice was one that resonated with many readers and will always be regarded as one of England's most durable mystery writers. He died on 8 February 2006 at his home in Kent. *See also* London in Crime Fiction.

Selected Works by the Author
Close Quarters (1947)
Smallbone Deceased (1950)
Blood and Judgement (1959)
The Crack in the Teacup (1966)
Game without Rules (stories, 1968)
Mr Calder and Mr Behrens (stories, 1982)
The Queen against Karl Mullen (1991)
Over and Out (1998)

Further Reading
Pike, B.A. 1998. 'The Short Stories of Michael Gilbert' (an annotated checklist covering the period 1948–1997). *CADS* Supplement 7.

Mike Stotter

Goddard, Robert (b.1954)

Robert Goddard is the master of a distinct and individual style of crime fiction. Quintessentially English, his stories of intrigue and mystery often concern family history, forgotten tragedies unearthed and assiduously concealed dirty deeds, mostly set in the English countryside with occasional excursions to exotic locations.

His first novel, *Past Caring* (1986), is a classic example of a genre he went on to define and make his own. His hero, Martin Radford, a young history graduate, unemployed and down at heel, is enlisted to look into the mystery of why a leading Edwardian politician resigned at the height of his power.

At first glance, the constitutional crisis of the Asquith Liberal government before the First World War may not seem promising ground for a crime novel, but Radford's enquiries take him to the island of Madeira where he finds not just dark buried secrets but a threat to his own life.

Goddard followed up his initial success with *In Pale Battalions* (1988) – a twisting family intrigue set off by a pilgrimage to the Somme battlefield memorial – and *Painting the Darkness* (1989), the story of a man thought long dead suddenly returning to haunt a Victorian family. The latter would turn out to be something of an anomaly in the Goddard canon as it is set in the 1880s and therefore should be considered as an historical novel rather than the present day narrative with an historical background which has since become his trademark.

Into the Blue (1990) introduced us to Harry Barnett, the closest thing Goddard has to a serial character, who has appeared in three novels. Like many a classic Goddard figure, he is down on his luck when an exotic encounter – in this case, a young woman whom he meets while caretaking a friend's villa on Rhodes – changes his life.

Into the Blue won the W.H. Smith Thumping Good Read award and was a landmark in introducing Goddard to a wider audience. Barnett returned in *Out of the Sun* (1996) in which he discovers he has a son he never knew, a brilliant mathematician currently languishing in a diabetic coma in hospital. Bumbling beer-drinking Barnett wants to know why and soon finds himself involved with a series of sinister deaths and echoes of the paranormal that come straight from the X-files.

An older Barnett features again in *Never Go Back* (2006), when he (of course) does just that: he goes back to a reunion from his National Service days, which takes him to a Scottish castle and a series of deaths that suggest something that happened fifty years ago refuses to lie buried.

Other classic Goddard figures include a retired west country archaeologist descended from the last Byzantine emperor (unsurprisingly with a skeleton in his closet), a Eurocrat called home to save the family cricket-bat company who gets caught up in a rape and murder investigation, a photographer on assignment in Vienna who falls for a woman obsessed with ghosts, and a historian who witnesses the abduction of a child and is never allowed to forget it.

Goddard, Robert

A Robert Goddard novel is instantly recognisable: a well-crafted piece of classic storytelling laced with twists and turns aplenty and a dose of exotic history. *See also* Historical Crime.

Selected Works by the Author
Past Caring (1986)
Into the Blue (1990)
Borrowed Time (1995)
Out of the Sun (1996)
Caught in the Light (1998)
Days without Number (2003)
Never Go Back (2006)
Name to a Face (2007)

Peter Millar

Godfathers of British Crime Fiction: The Impact of Dickens, Collins, Conrad and Buchan

Several literary godfathers have each contributed deep seams of imaginative resources to British crime fiction's future writers: the key novelists were Charles **Dickens**, Wilkie **Collins**, Joseph **Conrad** and John **Buchan**.

Dickens bequeathed the desire to portray a whole society undermined by a criminal fraternity. For him, the neglect of the poor bred endemic lawlessness and perverted the aspirations of the middle classes. Wilkie Collins wrote some of the great novels of plotting and detection in the nineteenth century. In works such as *The Woman in White* (1860), the ordinary are forced to become heroic and extraordinary when faced with a villain of genius. Moreover, the literary forms of Collins's novels encourage the reader to quest for knowledge. Reading *is* detection in a world of powerful psychological deception. In turn, Joseph Conrad may be said to build upon Collins's revelation of a world of uncertain truth and virtue. For Conrad portrays societies disconnected from their own beliefs, and analyses a growing gulf between action and meaning. His characters confront the horror that there is no 'solution' to their crimes in the form of a society able to adequately condemn or forgive. Finally, John Buchan can only provide heroes rooted in the past and the 'outside' in the form of nature. Buchan's heroes are engaging insofar as they are recognised as outdated. The question of what constitutes heroic masculinity in British crime fiction is never more acute than at its inception.

From the start, Charles Dickens wanted to write crime fiction that examined the whole society. His interest was not primarily in individual motives but in the endemic corruption of class snobbery and the pursuit of money above other values. For Dickens, a society primarily motivated by financial greed promoted crime at all levels. Crucially, he saw that in such a world the respectable classes could not morally insulate themselves from the misery below. Respectable Victorian England relied upon an underclass of crime allied to its capitalist enterprise. This is splendidly represented in *Great Expectations* (1861), where the rise of the impoverished child, Pip, to become a 'gentleman' stems from the transported criminal, Magwitch. Pip has assumed that his fortune stems from the respectably upper class, Miss Havisham. He has to learn Dickens's moral lesson, to love Magwitch who has risked everything for him.

The early *Oliver Twist* shows how Dickens will use coincidence in a crime plot to make a moral point, despite its implausibility. What Dickens wants to achieve are the scenes where this child of the criminal underclass becomes incorporated into a middle-class home. Moreover, what is on the one hand a moral argument about the poor has a greater impact because of a psychic dimension about class. Famously, Dickens as a child experienced demotion from lower middle class to poor working boy when he was sent to a blacking factory. Ruth **Rendell** is the later novelist who most picks up the notion of social class as an ingredient of crime for the anxiety it provokes.

As the critic Juliet John has shown, Dickens's villains are studies in 'psychology', where his heroes are not. Dickens regarded romanticism, and its descendant in modern psychology of the unconscious, as a source of social decay. To him, psychology meant egoism and that was villainy, while the good in art should be portrayed as elements of a moral social order. So in *Bleak House* (1853), the evil Krook, meeting a most spectacular end in spontaneous combustion, is far more memorable than Inspector Bucket, one of the first police detectives in fiction. Bucket's name gives us a clue about him for he is only one of many piecing together events and is more a recipient of information than a character generating the reader's interest. Unlike the generic core of detective fiction, Dickens does not regard the detective as the possible saviour of society. Indeed, the detecting of lady Dedlock's secret ensures her death. For Dickens, the act of detecting is not in itself a moral good. Secrets are not always better revealed. He was a pioneer in British crime fiction in exploring the horrors of the criminal self and the crimes of the horrible parts of society.

Unlike his friend Charles Dickens, Wilkie Collins (1824–1889) was interested in human psychology, both good and bad. His key works are more recognisably precursors to British crime fiction as they centre on a close-knit group who are vulnerable to evil machinations. As a result, great harm and injustice is done. There is nothing to save these people, no help from society, so someone is forced into becoming a detective. This is not a world of pre-existing heroes so much as one in which it takes heroic effort to resist evil.

Collins's first bestseller was *The Woman in White*, containing the haunting mystery of two similar looking women who grip the imagination of the young Walter Hartright. Crucially, though, this promising narrator is displaced, and the heroic role of protecting the frail heroine Laura passes to a woman, her sister Marian. Despite Marian's watchfulness, Laura apparently dies. Thereafter, much of the novel is devoted to the joint agency of Hartright and Marian in 'resurrecting' Laura and in repairing her damaged mind. Here, metaphorically, the powers of the saviour detective are displayed in 'solving' death and healing the trauma of crime. At the last, the gaps in the story are filled, to restore trust in the world. Much here foreshadows later crime fiction in the construction of the detecting and the way the narrative highlights anxieties about knowledge. Moreover, the chief villain, Count Fosco, is granted his own engaging appeal to the reader.

Another prefiguring occurs in Collins's use of the middle-class home as a location for crime. Just as Sir Percival Glyde imprisons Laura at home in *The Woman in White*, Rachel Verrinder suffers an even more intimate invasion in the form of a theft from her bedroom in *The Moonstone* (1868). Novels *Armadale* (1866) and *No Name* (1862) have plots originating in family secrets and involve stupendous female impostures in the heart of domestic life. Rather than specific social criticisms as in Dickens, Collins's works tend towards the unreliability of material signs of truth.

If writing and persons are deceiving and can be manipulated as part of a monstrous plot, then cracks appear in the security of reality itself.

Born Josef Konrad Korzeniowski in Russian ruled Poland, Joseph Conrad became a naturalised British subject in 1886, writing all his works in English. Now considered a modernist, Conrad depicts worlds in which society has lost belief in its own ideals and in its own language for them. In such places, moral restraints are loosened and crime attains savage proportions. The human group is forced to function amidst random violence with a growing conviction of meaninglessness. Conrad offers male protagonists who no longer have the social, moral and epistemological means to be heroic in western society's penetration of South America, Africa and contemporary Europe. The result is the despair of the good man or the blank mindlessness of those who have succumbed to the seductions of empty rhetoric. All these characters need an honest detecting job to give them a meaningful achievement, a coherent persona and hope for making sense of the world.

Heart of Darkness (1899) is perhaps Conrad's most famous tale of the breaking of Europe on the wild otherness of Africa. Three sorts of crimes haunt the narrative. Firstly, the story takes place in the context of vicious enslaving of Africans. Secondly, Marlow, the thoughtful narrator, sees cannibals. Thirdly, their civilised adherence to custom even in the face of death, contrasts with Kurtz, whose 'unspeakable' atrocities break the rules of both Europeans and Africans. No wonder Marlow finds the European language of Empire meaningless and even the so-called good ideals corrupting.

In complete contrast, *The Secret Agent* (1907), set in London is based upon an actual explosion in Greenwich Park in 1894. Here the decay in society is viewed from within as small groups of estranged men who find themselves in terrorist cells without really connecting to the violent revolutionary ideas they think they espouse. So when the emissaries of a foreign power (Russia) decide that Britain is too comfortable, they order a bomb plot. *The Secret Agent* puts ordinary emotions among political machinations and the result is terrorism and a breakdown in social bonds. No one group preserves innocence. Even the police know enough about the plotters to resemble them. Conrad's work demonstrates the need for a plot and a hero who can figure wholeness or comprehensibility. He anticipates the political, terrorist or spy **thriller** on an international as well as national scale.

Where Conrad's characters plunge into terrifying modernity with naivety that can be fatal, John Buchan (1875–1940) prioritises the preservation of male heroism by avoiding urban life and placing faith in an imaginary imperial past and male bonding. With Richard Hannay, his most famous hero, he *begins* life in *The Thirty-Nine Steps* (1915), by evincing distaste for modern London and nostalgia for a past life in colonial Africa. Unsurprisingly, when told of a criminal plot to betray England, Hannay insists upon turning the story into a rural gentleman's sport, a hunt, by taking to the northern moors. Indeed, Hannay's or Buchan's model of the crime narrative is deeply archaic as the hunt for a doomed quarry of often the literal or metaphorical core. In *The Island of Sheep* (1936), the first half of the novel consists of Sir Richard and his son stalking game, while the second half merely includes more characters and switches the chase to humans.

Buchan's narrator-hero is a transition figure. He can bear to be an Englishman in England because his identity is founded on an all-male comradeship in the colonies. This comradeship extends to 'fair play' for the natives, who, in this fantasy, accept such enlightened guidance. Then Hannay's English persona is protected by his mediation of another hero, one even less realistic and whose exotic powers exceed the parameters of the story. Sandy, Lord Clanroyden, fulfils the role of the impossible romantic hero, whose learning, network of friendships, skill in fighting, acting ability and sheer charm are *never at a loss*. By structuring stories around male loyalty, Buchan can hang onto the idea of a hero detecting and saving England, if only by taking the story into male romance. Interestingly, *The Three Hostages* (1924) subjects Hannay to the worst violation of modernity by having the villain attempt to control his mind. The frightful possibility that the detective might merge with the villain will be explored later in crime fiction. Meanwhile, this novel simplifies corrupt modernity by ending a tale of an urban predator in the simple spectacle of hero versus villain out on the moor. Later crime writers will be able to keep the romantic masculinity for the detective who, despite all appearances, continues to believe in justice. Buchan's heroes model their social vision on hunting practices and personal loyalty. It is Buchan's achievement that he can make these stand for England and colonies. Later writers cannot. *See also* The Detective in British Fiction, Literature and Crime Fiction *and* Origins of British Crime Fiction.

Further Reading

John Buchan
Kimball, Roger. 2003. 'Realism Coloured by Poetry: Rereading John Buchan'. *The New Criterion* (September): 16–23.
Woods, Brett F. 2007. 'The Last Victorian: John Buchan and the Hannay Quartet'. *The California Literary Review*, 26 March, http://calitreview.com/2007/03/26/the-last-victorian-john-buchan-and-the-hannay-quartet/.

Wilkie Collins
Allan, Janice M. 1996. 'Scenes of Writing: Detection and Psychoanalysis in Wilkie Collins's *The Moonstone*'. *Imprimatur* 1: 186–193.
Heller, Tamar. 1992. *Wilkie Collins and the Female Gothic*. Yale University Press.
Pykett, Lyn. 2005. *Wilkie Collins, Authors in Context*. Oxford University Press.

Joseph Conrad
Carabine, Keith, ed. 1992. *Joseph Conrad: Critical Assessments*, 4 vols. Helm Information.
Hampson, Robert. 1992. *Joseph Conrad: Betrayal and Identity*. Macmillan.
Sherry, Normal. 1971. *Conrad's Western World*. Cambridge University Press.

Charles Dickens
Ackroyd, Peter. 1990. *Dickens*. Mandarin.
John, Juliet. 2001. *Dickens's Villains: Melodrama, Character, Popular Culture*. Oxford University Press.
Miller, J. Hillis. 1958. *Charles Dickens: The World of His Novels*. Harvard University Press.

Susan Rowland

Golden Age Crime Fiction

The classic stories of the so-called Golden Age of British crime fiction appeared between 1920 and 1945 by authors as diverse as Agatha **Christie**, Dorothy L. **Sayers** and Freeman Wills **Crofts**. The Golden Age story, also known as the 'clue-puzzle' or 'cosy', is famous now for certain key characteristics. It was set in an English country house or a sleepy English village or, sometimes, on a train or a cruise liner. The **detective**, male or female, tended to be a civilised amateur, not a professional policeman. The plot was a highly complex puzzle (such as a 'locked-room' mystery) which displayed the author's ingenuity while teasing the readers' credulity. It was intellectual, rather than realistic, a complete contrast to the 'hardboiled' style from the United States. As time has passed, Golden Age stories have been viewed with nostalgia, and, especially as films or television dramas, they have become very popular with audiences all over the world.

It is interesting, however, to examine Golden Age fiction more closely and to tease out some of the features which are not so immediately apparent. What of the typical male detective of the Golden Age, for example – Hercule **Poirot** or Lord Peter **Wimsey**? Golden Age fiction offers a range of men who variously parodied, playacted or simply failed to live up to heroic models of masculinity. And to these playful versions of the previously self-assured male investigator was added a variety of female sleuths from the ageing spinster to young working women and even those modelled on the crime authors themselves as in **Sayers**'s Harriet Vane and **Christie**'s Ariadne Oliver. All these types show a self-conscious, parodic quality. The authors, in collusion with their knowing readers, were playing, in sophisticated ways, with ideas.

Above all, English classic crime is ambivalent. It seems reassuring about the restoration of social stability, yet it can provide an atmosphere of lingering menace. It has rules of construction which form an implicit contract with the reader, yet these are famously broken as in the narrative of Christie's *The Murder of Roger Ackroyd* (1926). Moreover, the typical settings of the serene country house, the hotel, the ordered graceful homes in metropolises such as **London**, which seem to celebrate the status quo, are the sites not only of crime but unease, ambiguity and social criticism too. As Lee Horsley argues, classic crime contains anxieties while demonstrating that the very act of containment may be corrupting.

War

English classic crime was written in the shadow of war. From the First World War and then leading-in to the Second World War, plus its duration, indicates how war features significantly at the beginning with Christie's *The Mysterious Affair at Styles* (1920). This story introduces Hercules Poirot as a Belgian refugee during the First World War. Far from a confident professional, the detective is elderly, shabby and dependent upon the kindness of the local lady of the manor, Mrs Inglethorp. It is gratitude to her, Poirot says, that makes him determined to find her killer. Hastings, Poirot's 'Watson' figure, notes that while mass atrocities are committed over the channel, the death of one elderly lady is pursued with vigour at home. Here explicitly, is the murder story as a displacement of war. Where the slaughter of thousands and millions can hardly be comprehended by the culture, detective fiction processes killing. It transforms senseless death into a coherent narrative – absorbs the dead into the community's story. Where war cannot restore its dead, detective fiction can re-story the end of the person into the ongoing life and history. The critic Gill Plain has pointed out how much classic crime, and Agatha Christie in particular, presents a sanitised body to stand in for, to re-place, those horribly mangled bodies of the First World War trenches.

So one of the ambivalences of classic English crime is the way the world wars are both absent and doubly present. It is absent because crime fiction of this period focuses on individual acts, usually murder, which usually occur in tight-knit groups around a particular house, family or occupation. The notion of 'murder' and war are kept separate. On the other hand, it is present, firstly because the dead body of the story can stand for the war dead and secondly because the effects of war often seem to seep into the plots, as if from a flood that could not entirely be kept at bay. For example, the less-than-macho male detective may be afflicted by war neurosis, as is Sayers's Lord Peter Wimsey. He cannot keep war and detecting wholly separate because he succumbs to shellshock every time he sends a murderer to be hanged. Perhaps Sayers's most radical move is to permit her detective to suffer from (allowing us to see the similarities in) these two forms of state killing. In some stories, of course, war directly impinges on the narrative. In Margery **Allingham**'s *Coroner's Pidgin* (1945), the detective Albert **Campion** sees his 'man' secreting a dead body out of a bombed house during the London Blitz. In *Traitor's Purse* (1941), the same sleuth has to search for his own identity when he discovers himself in wartime England with only a few days to save the country from a dastardly German plot. Christie too is adept at adapting murder contained in a small place to wartime imperatives by using her married adventurers, Tommy and Tuppence. In *N or M?* (1941), the gallant Beresfords have to discover who, in a seaside boarding house, is the traitor. This typical hunt for a killer is explicitly part of a greater whole of chaotic violence that cannot be resolved by the story itself.

Self-consciousness

If the proximity of war threatens the ability of the fictional form to solve and so resolve violence, then the self-conscious nature of classic crime is one of its most powerful characteristics in favour of reassurance. Classic crime is conscious of its own status as fiction and shares this knowingness with its readers. Either it will refer to detective fiction outright, as the Vicar and his wife discuss their reading in *The Murder at the Vicarage* (1930), or they will reference Sherlock **Holmes** as the model for the detective, or the very theatricality of the detective (Hanaud in A.E.W. **Mason**'s *The House of the Arrow*, published in 1924, is an example) will present the story as an explicitly fictional process in which the reader is invited to join. Here is to be found much of the sophistication of the form. When Christie uses titles such as *The Murder at the Vicarage* or *The Body in the Library* (1942), she did not write a cliché, but she wrote a parody of a cliché which she expected her readers to appreciate. Self-conscious fictionality performs many functions. It is used to distance male protagonists from a cited narrow version of heroism, sometimes linked to Holmes; it shifts the story from a dangerous proximity to war; it forms a bond with the reader; and it makes death itself as narratable, part of a game. In this final device, we see the typical ambiguity which both reassures and disturbs. For making death into a story is also the promise of being saved from death as the 'end' of a story. Self-conscious fictionality makes this fabulous promise possible and at the same time denies it, by its own advertised status as fiction, a fantasy.

Moreover, the self-conscious fiction in classic crime spills over into the settings, making them both playful and sinister. English classic crime is popular as the era of the 'country house' mystery: murder occurs within a tightly knit group of people staying in a large grand house. In fact, the majority of stories are not country house mysteries. Christie, in particular, is more forward looking in her settings. When she does offer a house party crime scene, such as in *The Hollow* (1946), it is to emphasise the decadence of such a life where so many have murderous impulses to defend it. The country house is not just a focus of fantasy and nostalgia for later readers; within the genre it is a fantasy of a never-so-golden past and a dream of Eden, which is betrayed time and time again by the primal crime of killing.

Domesticity

An extension of the theme of country house is the domestic focus of the crime and the detection. Classic English crime occurs at home. If it is so vulgar as to happen in the workplace, such as in *Inspector French's Greatest Case* (1925) by Freeman Wills **Crofts**, then it will prove to be a peculiarly domestic workplace full of employees about to become sons-in-law, etc. In such domestic settings, the detective is feminised by being akin to the housewife or the maid. 'He' cleans up the mess. The proper starching of linen or the correct time to serve coffee become vital clues. Sometimes only a woman can provide the necessary information for the male detective – as Miss Climpson does in Sayer's *Unnatural Death* (1927) and *Strong Poison* (1930). Whether male or female, the detective is often placed in a feminine position. His or her scrutiny of domestic routine serves to convert this marginalised area of life into meaningful action. Classic crime, by focussing on the domestic, makes modern family lives narratable and hence meaningful. It does so as part of its generic mission to make modernity comprehensible. The irony of the form is, of course, that it requires a murder to make domesticity signify something beyond itself such as order and stability. It is the greatest violation of domesticity that guarantees it. Hence the self-conscious nature of the stories is vital to playfully restore and undercut domestic ideals.

Classic crime at home does not preclude foreign adventures. Indeed, the stress on the domestic and the English is often pointed out by foreign locations and characters. Whereas some locate criminality in those lacking the benefit of pure English blood, such as the femme fatale in *Inspector French's Greatest Case*, others are careful to indict the rot within. In Christie's *Death on the Nile* (1937), the temptation of the English party to blame Egyptian crew members for a fatal shooting is quickly quashed. The threat to the wealthy English and American tourists comes from themselves, not the exotic landscape. With eligible British males turning to crime or communist agitation, the ancient beauties of Egypt form a backdrop to the collapse of Englishness as an identity with moral pretensions.

Ngaio **Marsh** was a classic writer who tended to maximise the country house flavour in part because she observed it from outside as a New Zealander. Her snow-bound parties often have a foreigner, who is suspected, but rarely guilty. In *Death and the Dancing Footman* (1941), the Austrian doctor endures suspicion and hostility, only to be morally validated among a dubious group of ancient enemies. Symptomatically, the guilty one proves to be a soldier on leave who is reluctant to return to war. Margery Allingham's early works specialise in international criminal gangs. Here it is the rootless capitalist nature of the opposition that she indicts. These gangs will do anything for money and particularly violate what is sacred and long lasting about England. In *Look to the Lady* (1931), England is not represented by detective Albert Campion or the crime story. Rather its essence is contained in a myth and the sacred objects that it is Campion's mission to preserve from the gang. With England a mystical construct, Campion has to decide whether he will kill for it. Fortunately, the novel lets him off this dilemma, but the point is well made. In a modern world where England is not embodied by her youth, the preservation of Englishness may come at the price of her soul.

Detectives of the Golden Age

The previous paragraphs emphasise the role of reading a mystery till the end where the detective wraps up the details and throws light on the truth. One way of looking at the process is in the shape of the stories. Crime fiction offers two types of stories. There is the physical search for clues, interviewing of witnesses etc. and there is the development of the crime in the mind of the **detective**(s). Much Golden Age crime fiction has these two processes echo each other by either staging the hunt for clues as a quest or by a form of 'cooking' the evidence. The typical detective's quest differs from that of the mythical hero in that it is not linear. Whereas the hero fights to leave his childhood home, sets out on adventures, kills the monster, rescues the princess and marries her, finally returning home in triumph, the typical detective's quest for truth goes in circles. In *Inspector French's Greatest Case*, the eponymous hero is pleasantly surprised to get a trip to Europe during his investigation. Yet, surprise turns to frustration when he comes to a dead end in terms of understanding the crime. Yet another long journey begins when he seeks to study the passengers of a ship. More stops and starts occur before the European answer to the brutal murder of a gold dealer becomes a Brazilian one. Conversely, 'cooking' the detecting process refers to the confinement of characters to houses, schools, theatres etc. and their repeated interaction with the detective. Here progress occurs by teasing out details and provoking the suspects to reveal more about themselves. Here the quest for truth emphasises psychic space more than physical space.

Linked to the stress on detection through relating to suspects, for classic English crime, gender is a real issue. Just as the space of the crime and the methods of detection become more marked by the feminine in the domesticity of both, so the detectives, still predominantly male, are distanced from the physically heroic masculinity of predecessors such as John Buchan's Richard Hannay. In particular, women writers of the period tend to contrast their sensitive or flamboyant sleuths to the cerebral Sherlock Holmes. Poirot, Albert Campion, Lord Peter Wimsey and even Marsh's policeman Roderick Alleyn are more willing to probe relationships than the heroes of the pre–First World War genre. For male writers, the classic detective may be a policeman whose intelligent empathy makes him stand out. Or the detective function may be split between a genius, whose theatricality demonstrates a parodic distance from Holmes, and a nice young Englishman, a representative of the reader. *The House of the Arrow* offers an example of the latter with the contrasting masculine characters closing in on the warped emotions of an evil beautiful woman.

The detective's sidekick is often crucial in bringing out such issues as gender, nationhood and the role of the reader. Following on from Holmes and Watson, the detective's dimmer friend mediates the reader's incomprehension, either by providing a role for the reader to identify with or by giving the reader the pleasure of 'beating' the baffled one to the answer. Such a device allows the main detective to keep many of his ideas concealed, or even to disappear from the story for a while as Campion does in *Sweet Danger* (1933). It can be an essential part of the 'game' or contract with the reader. The detective announces that the sidekick has all the material clues, merely not his thoughts about them. This alerts the reader to the challenge of decoding the evidence before the final revelation. Again, the old pattern of male heroism is modified. Where traditionally the male hero slays the monster alone and returns to claim that he has saved the community, classic English crime is more communal. Within the story, typically the detective receives significant help from friends or spouses, or tacitly extends this detecting community to the reader. It is an important part of the genre's appeal that heroism is no longer clearly demarcated as to gender, is no longer singular and is identified with relatively sedentary pursuits such as reading the evidence for clues. Classic English crime makes the mundane domesticity of its crime scenes a space for constructing heroic knowledge on a more egalitarian scale. It offers the readers a more heroic and morally decisive construction of themselves in a complex world.

Josephine **Tey** is a particularly interesting writer about gender. In *The Man in the Queue* (1929), a mundane title if ever there was one, Inspector Alan Grant tirelessly pursues a suspect of a seemingly inexplicable murder in a London street. However, conventional success nearly destroys the sensitive policeman. Grant believes the suspect's story of innocence and suffers near breakdown at the prospect of the wrong person being hanged. Although the guilty person is eventually convicted, Grant can take no credit, for she gives herself up voluntarily. Similarly unable to secure justice is Tey's Lucy Pym in *Miss Pym Disposes* (1946). Ironically the bestselling author of a psychology book, Lucy Pym is forced to conclude that as an expert in psychology she is a good teacher of French. While staying in a physical education college for young women, she witnesses the stress of the examination system pervert passionate friendships and rivalries. Ultimately, despite her self-sufficient independence, she is forced into the feminine role of confidante without being able to switch to the masculine role of freeing the innocent from the consequences of crime.

Of course, it is Miss **Marple** who highlights issues of gender and domesticity so obviously as to create a sort of comedy within the genre. In works such as *The Body in the Library* (1942) and *The Moving Finger* (1942), she insists upon interpreting dire events according to the template of human nature from her small English village of St Mary Mead. She therefore maps the cultural sphere of the English spinster (a prominent social 'problem' after the First World War) onto the morality play territory of murder. St Mary Mead stands for a feminine space, marginalised from urban modernity, yet ironically representing it in narratives which might be interpreted as attempts to redeem the (fallen) modern world – if the detective can solve the crime, in a sense she re-solves death, and space and time are redeemed, made sacred. England is restored as Eden. As a somewhat elderly virgin deity, Miss Marple takes on the darker as well as the benevolent character of justice, as the later title *Nemesis* (1971) shows. So while all classic detectives, with some success, mimic a divine figure dispensing justice, classic English crime also shows such an ambition to be fraught with difficulty, embedded in society and requiring skills associated with both genders.

Above all, classic English crime involves the reader in making sense of a complex social group. England 1920–1945 was not yet multicultural, but Englishness was much more problematic due to the effects of global wars, increasing industrialisation, declining empire and the shifts in genders and families.

Conservatives and Radicals

While the overall tendency of the genre was conservative, in favour of keeping the *status quo*, a closer look at the stories reveals a crucial ambivalence. If crime fiction is simply about uncovering the 'truth' of a crime and the subsequent punishment of the guilty, then the essential form is conservative. Murder, or another serious crime, creates chaos and instability within a social group. The detective removes the instability, which is moral and epistemological as well as physical, and all returns to the way it was before. However, Golden Age English crime rarely operates so cleanly. Take the particularly 'closed' example ('closed' meaning tying up the loose ends and removing the criminal so that previous conditions can be restored) of Sayers's *Gaudy Night* (1935). Perhaps because the crime is not murder, there seems nothing to prevent Shrewsbury College Oxford from returning to normal once the source of poison pen letters and malicious assaults is discovered. Yet the whole episode of the crimes and investigations has taken their toll. The independent woman detective discovered some limits to her self-sufficiency and agreed to marry the vulnerable hero, Lord Peter Wimsey. Sayers allows the criminal to address the company of female dons she has so grievously afflicted. That outpouring of venom is conspicuously not assuaged by anything the detective and victims can do. Justice, in the form of the actual law may be satisfied. Yet chaos and darkness are not healed. English classic crime frequently discovers that the law and the restoration of an (imagined) harmony do not go together. Yes, these stories do discover criminals, yet they also discover that Eden can only be restored ironically or parodically. To the extent that English classic crime locates the source of continuing darkness in social problems, these works are not unproblematically conservative. For example, anxieties attendant upon gender difference and its social consequences have a large part to play in the crimes of *Gaudy Night*.

At first glance, Margery Allingham does not appear to be a social radical. Yet, several times she portrays a rural peasantry so sunken below social inclusion as to embody the occult. The witch in *Look to the Lady* (1931) is not only terrifying to Campion's lugubrious sidekick, Lugg, but also shown to be suffering from her society's neglect. Allingham tends to portray evil as stemming from a modernity corrupted by machines and money, as against virtue based on rural hierarchies. Nevertheless, this conservative stance is belied by both the occult decay in the feudal villages and the necessity for reinvigorating the upper classes. So Amanda Fitton, sister to an Earl and later Campion's wife, becomes an aircraft designer, and later, a delicate aristocratic lady marries working-class policeman Charley Luke because he has a 'manor'. While Allingham is clearly trying to maintain the old class divisions, the humour and parody accompanying their reinvention arguably does more to undermine the fixity of social class than outright hostility.

In genre terms, much of how Golden Age crime fiction represents ambivalence and challenges assumptions about truth and knowledge is bound up with its connection to the Gothic. The Gothic novels of the late eighteenth and nineteenth century, from *The Castle of Otranto* (1764) by Horace Walpole to *Wuthering Heights* (1847) by Emily Brontë served simultaneously to create and make ambivalent categories such as natural and supernatural, good and evil, hero and villain and feminine and masculine. Insofar as anxiety about knowledge, truth and guilt remains unpurged in classic crime, a Gothic legacy remains. Classic English crime stories are an attempt to 'solve' the fears provoked by the modern world. Instead they offer a comic theatrical 'solution' to modernity at best, frequently signalled by a pair of lovers uniting at the conclusion of the mystery. Often what lingers in the reader's mind is the detective's failure to provide a complete answer to the irrational dimension of crime. In repeatedly revealing the gaps in social and literary structures in containing the 'other', as unconsciousness, death, criminal genius and the foreign, classic English crime is a potent form of art for its own time and still for ours. Classic English crime fiction demonstrates that the great solid fictions of empire, gender, soldier heroes and impermeable class barriers are over. They provide a new model for the crime solving hero and for the imaginary detecting passions of the reader. *See also* Death in Academe; Feminist Readings in British Crime Fiction; Male Crime Writers *and* Women Crime Writers.

Further Reading

Horsley, Lee. 2005. *Twentieth-Century Crime Fiction*. Oxford University Press.
Knight, Stephen. 2004. *Crime Fiction, 1800–2000: Detection, Death, Diversity*. Palgrave.
Oleksiw, Susan. 1988. *A Reader's Guide to the Classic British Mystery*. G.K. Hall.
Plain, Gill. 2001. *Twentieth-Century Crime Fiction: Gender, Sexuality and the Body*. Edinburgh University Press.
Priestman, Martin. 1997. *Crime Fiction from Poe to the Present*. Northcote House.
Rowland, Susan. 2001. *From Agatha Christie to Ruth Rendell*. Palgrave.

Susan Rowland

Goodchild, George (1888–1969)

There have been some remarkably prolific producers of crime fiction, notable among them being John **Creasey**, Edgar **Wallace** and William **le Queux**. Another is George Goodchild, whose published output rivals Wallace's and le Queux's, if not Creasey's.

Goodchild, born in Kingston-on-Thames in 1888, went into publishing with various firms and began writing. After wartime service on the Western Front, he was invalided in 1918 and went into authorship full time. From then on his story is the story of his books, which probably number 178 (with twenty-six different publishers) plus others written jointly. As was the case with Wallace, not all were crime. His output comprised adventure novels set in a variety of locales (including thirty under various pseudonyms), war memoirs, Westerns, children's stories and plays; his first crime volume was *The Barton Mystery* (1916).

Goodchild's series heroes include Nigel Rix, John Trelawney and, the most popular, Inspector Robert McLean of Scotland Yard, who figures in fifty books, forty-four including his name in the title. As about half these were short-story collections with maybe twenty investigations in each, McLean's cases must easily outscore those for Freeman Wills **Crofts**'s Inspector French and even Creasey's Inspector West. At an early stage in the McLean saga, he left the Yard to become a private investigator, though he soon returned.

Goodchild was a workmanlike and a prolific writer; his mysteries are usually convincing, with a plethora of incident and excitement. In *McLean Takes a Holiday* (1942, set in 1939) McLean rounds up a Nazi spy ring, in the process rescuing a girl who later becomes his wife. In *Double Acrostic* (1954) McLean and his Sergeant Brook are themselves shot at and then kidnapped. As such a big producer, he inevitably writes in clichés at times; even McLean and his charming wife Valerie are little more than pasteboards. The same could be said of many **Golden Age** writers, among whom Goodchild may be reckoned, even though he lived until 1969 and wrote much post war. His passion for adventure has ensured that he has been reprinted – about a dozen volumes in recent years, albeit in a large-print series (the latter fact suggesting an elderly readership).

Selected Works by the Author

The Barton Mystery (1916)
Ace High (1927)

Philip Scowcroft

Gooden, Philip (b.1948)

Before becoming a full-time writer in 2001, Philip Gooden read English at university and taught for many years. His intriguing, evocative **historical** mysteries are set in England in the late Elizabethan times (for his Nick Revill series) and further back in history (to the mid-fourteenth century) for those novels featuring Geoffrey Chaucer as protagonist.

34. Philip Gooden.

The never-ending fascination with the 'history mystery' genre has almost been taken to breaking point, but on closer inspection, the late Elizabethan period had not been over-subscribed – Gooden's literary excavations are among the most unusual and intelligent. Readers are introduced to Nick Revill (moving in Shakespeare's world), an upcoming, inexperienced actor from the West Country – a wonderfully characterised choice as the Gooden's amateur detective. While Gooden is not the only novelist to utilise the Elizabethan theatre as backdrop, his decision to set the series after the early 1590s – beyond the well-trodden ground featuring Kit Marlowe – marked the series out as something different.

In *Sleep of Death* (2000), there is something rotten in the house of Elliot. Revill, newly recruited to the Chamberlain's Men, is drawn into solving the murder of a man under circumstances that parallel Shakespeare's play *Hamlet*, with the finger of suspicion pointing to the bard himself. Having Revill narrate the story and recreate Elizabethan London, its theatre and its characters through his eyes proves to be an ingenious strategy, as is utilising the narrative device of the murderer articulating his thoughts throughout. *Romeo and Juliet* features in the excellent *Mask of Night* (2004) which is also a locked-room mystery, but also encapsulates the nation's feelings as Queen Elizabeth I nears her death and the capital is ravaged by the bubonic plague. Revill's further adventures are based around Shakespearean plays. Although the series has finished, the character continues in the medieval anthologies written with the fellow authors who constitute the Medieval Murderers.

Seemingly at odds with the Elizabethan series, Gooden decided to write about a well-known historical character, Geoffrey Chaucer, an English poet and diplomat, under the pseudonym of Philippa Morgan. Chaucer's *Canterbury Tales* is well-known, but perhaps not the character of Chaucer himself, and this is one of the series' strengths. *Chaucer and the House of Fame* (2004) borrows its title from Chaucer's own poem *House of Fame* and is set midway (1370) through the Hundred Years War between England and France; as John of Gaunt's emissary, Chaucer is to deliver a message to Henri, Comte de Guyac in the Dordogne. A seemingly straightforward diplomatic mission soon turns to a murder scenario. This sets the template for the following books in the series, which on the surface can be read as a mystery or adventure novel, but which artfully conceal vigorously researched plotting and stories with an edge. The best of the series is *Chaucer and the Doctor of Physics* (2006); brimming with suspense and intrigue, it follows directly from Chaucer's period in Italy as the writer is called upon to investigate the theft of an Italian ship's cargo and the acrimony between its captain and the mayor of Dartmouth. Chaucer's master, John of Gaunt, fears that the newly found détente between England and Italy could implode if the incident is not resolved amicably. Add to this the classic country house murder situation and the reader is presented with a dark, threatening atmosphere and the intertwining of historical facts and fictional mystery: the ingredients which Philip Gooden synthesises so admirably. With *The Salisbury Manuscript*, Gooden has switched to a Victorian setting to commence a series set amongst the cathedrals of England.

Selected Works by the Author
Sleep of Death (2000)
The Pale Companion (2002)
Mask of Night (2004)
Chaucer and the House of Fame (2004)
Chaucer and the Doctor of Physics (2006)
The Salisbury Manuscript (2008)

Mike Stotter

Gorell, Lord (Ronald Gorell Barnes) (1884–1963)

Lord Gorell was a polymath. He excelled in (first-class) cricket, was a minister of the Crown and was interested in flying and military education and, among much else, literature. He was a prolific journalist and published around fifty books, including eleven volumes of poetry, travelogues, biographies of Keats and Christ, straight novels – and detective fiction. This latter he wrote over a period of nearly forty years. Little of his work is truly distinguished in a literary sense and not much more shows unusual ingenuity. But his eleven crime novels have many points of interest. His first, *In the Night* (1917), and a later one, *Red Lilac* (1935), introduce a lady detective, Evelyn Humberthorne.

The Devouring Fire (1928) sprang a surprise with its whodunit and invoked the spectre of the supernatural only to dispel it. *Earl's End* (1951) is better written. The victim's body is discovered in the House of Lords, a locale with which the author was long familiar, having succeeded to the barony in 1917. A Scotland Yard Superintendent investigates competently; the bungling, well-intentioned efforts of an amateur provide comic relief, and tension is well sustained to the end. It was one of four detective novels Gorell published between 1949 and 1954. They made little impact at the time, and it may be that Gorell's detective fiction was by then (and with some justification) perceived to be old fashioned. It is, however, not without interest, especially in the context of his astonishingly varied general literary output.

Dorothy L. **Sayers** was familiar with at least his earlier detective novels and her fictional sleuth Lord Peter **Wimsey** has some remarkable parallels with Gorell. Both read history at Balliol, both played cricket for Oxford University and both served with distinction in the Rifle Brigade during the Great War. Was Wimsey's 'career' influenced by Gorell's example? Possibly; but the latter was not blue-blooded and he held political views which were, if anything, left of centre. *See also* Golden Age Crime Fiction.

Selected Works by the Author
Venturers All (1927)
He Who Fights (1928)
Murder at Mavering (1943)
Let Not Thy Left Hand (1949)
Where There's a Head (1952)
Murder at Manor House (1954)

Further Reading
Scowcroft, Philip L. 1984. 'Lord Gorell: Prototype of Lord Peter Wimsey?' Pp. 9–10 in *Sidelights on Sayers*, vol. IV. Dorothy L. Sayers Society.
Scowcroft, Philip L. 1988. 'Six Neglected British Writers of Crime Fiction'. *CADS* 8 (May): 7–12.

Philip Scowcroft

Gothic and Penny Dreadful

Gothic fiction, with its emphasis on ghostly visitations, inexplicable events and fatalistic revenge (arousing feelings of fear and dread), is usually seen as the precursor to supernatural fiction – but it is equally the progenitor of crime and mystery fiction. The word 'gothic', which originally meant barbarous and uncivilised, was adopted for a style of architecture which in turn converted the meaning of the word into dark and ominous and, by association with the architectural usage, medieval. Thus, when Horace Walpole (1717–1797), who was a devotee of the gothic style, admitted authorship of *The Castle of Otranto* in its second edition in 1765, he called it 'a gothic story' because it was dark, ominous and medieval. In time, the name was given to a whole genre of fiction that flourished at the start of the nineteenth century and continues, in its imagery, today, in many mysteries and romances.

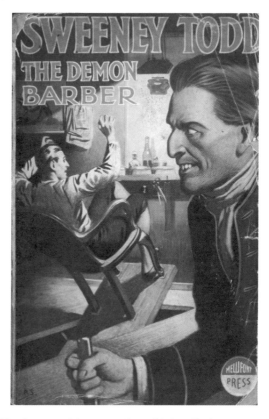

35. Cover of Mellifont Press's *Sweeney Todd* from the 1930s.

Alongside those gothic mysteries which relied upon genuine supernatural manifestations for their sensationalism were those that rationalised the supernatural as caused by human intervention, and these stories usually involved some investigation into the cause and motive. The best of these early novels were those by Ann Radcliffe (1764–1823), in particular, *The Italian* (1797). Unlike earlier Gothic novels, this is not set in the Middle Ages but only a generation before its composition. It has minimal faux-supernatural manifestations and instead involves the kidnapping and planned murder of a young girl and the framing of her lover. It has all the hallmarks of an early mystery-thriller and is the godfather of all those many subsequent gothic romances that focus on a threatened heroine.

The Gothic mystery became the literary rage of the period, so much so that Jane Austen (1775–1817) was able to parody it mercilessly in *Northanger Abbey* (1818) where the young heroine, Catherine, believes real life is as depicted in gothic novels. The storyline includes an imagined murder mystery when Catherine becomes convinced that her host, General Tilney, had murdered his wife. The gothic mood pervaded much fiction – *Wuthering Heights* (1847) by Emily Brontë (1818–1848) is a perfect recreation of a gothic romance – but though stories were filled with murders, crimes and unexplained mysteries, they were not, for the most part, what would be classified today as crime fiction.

Nevertheless, as literature evolved, or in this case degenerated, it was the gothic strain that encouraged the rise in what became known as the Newgate novel. This merged the gothic atmosphere with the sensationalisation of notorious criminals, with characters and plots drawn from the compendium of crimes later dubbed the Newgate Calendar, named after the notorious Newgate prison on the site of what is now the Central Criminal Court. The first compilation to be called *The Newgate Calendar* appeared at the same time as the early gothic novels, between 1774 and 1778, and it continued to be embellished and updated throughout the nineteenth century. The Newgate novel tended to glorify the adventures of criminals, and the key link between the Gothic and the Newgate novel is W. Harrison Ainsworth's (1805–1882) *Rookwood* (1834), which he noted as being directly inspired by Ann Radcliffe's work. It is an historical gothic in form, without the supernatural agencies, but includes a sub-plot involving the highwayman Dick Turpin. *Rookwood* must also owe some credit to *Paul Clifford* (1830) by Edward Bulwer (later Lord Lytton) (1803–1873), which similarly shows how society makes a criminal out of a young boy who becomes a highwayman. Lytton's best-known Newgate novel was *Eugene Aram* (1832) which retold the story of the eponymous convicted murderer and sought to show his innocence. Ainsworth went on to write *Jack Sheppard* (1840), arguably the definitive Newgate novel. It is full of gothic atmosphere, with storms and boys of mysterious parentage, and charts the descent into villainy of Jack Sheppard who falls under the influence of the scheming Jonathan Wild. The book was immensely popular and the murderer Courvoisier, who was executed for killing his employer, Lord Russell, claimed that he had been incited to murder by reading the novel. **Dickens**'s *Oliver Twist* (1838) is also often cited as a Newgate novel.

This glorification of crime was the main reason for the popularity of the 'penny dreadful' – a story of violence and crime, inexpensively issued, often in instalments, for a mass audience – which came to prominence in the late 1830s. Its best-known and most notorious example remains *The String of Pearls* (1846), generally attributed to Thomas Peckett Prest (1810–1859). This was the novel that gave the world Sweeney Todd, the demon barber, who turned customers into meat pies. Todd was not a criminal drawn from the Newgate Calendar but from popular tradition: the idea that an unscrupulous cook steals children for pies dating from at least a Venetian pantomime of the 1790s.

Prest's great rival among the penny hackers was James M. Rymer (1814–1884), who was once also credited with *The String of Pearls* and is now best known for *Varney the Vampire* (1847). Rymer's best crime novel was *Ada, the Betrayed* (1845), about a baby rescued from a burning smithy in which her father has been murdered. Her rescuer, Gray, later kidnaps her in the hope of gaining a hold over the man who instigated the murder, her wicked uncle Learmont, but his plans fall apart. Although the police are involved, the story lacks any detailed investigation of the crime, but it is nevertheless a fascinating study of the criminal underworld. The plot owes much to an earlier penny dreadful, the anonymous *Eliza Grimwood, a Domestic Legend of the Waterloo Road* (1838), which used as its basis the actual murder of a prostitute the previous year. In the fictional version, Eliza is an heiress whose parents have been murdered and she is brought up on an estate where she is seduced by the wicked Lord of the Manor, Rakemore. He takes her to London, drugs her and leaves her to survive in the streets and we follow her general degradation and ultimate murder. The real murder was investigated by Inspector Field, upon whom Charles Dickens later based Inspector Bucket in *Bleak House* (1853), and Dickens also retells the Grimwood story in 'A Pair of Gloves', one of his detective anecdotes published in *Household Words* in 1850.

All of these novels were derivative of the gothic romance with its wronged heroines, villainous relatives and stolen legacies. The most popular of them among all the penny dreadfuls was *The Mysteries of London* (1844) by George W.M. Reynolds (1814–1879), which sold 40,000 copies a week when it first appeared in weekly parts. Reynolds depicts another young lady, duped into impersonating her believed-dead brother, who falls into the hands of a criminal gang. Throughout the book, Reynolds explores the various levels of society in London from the rich to the poor and questions the inequality. Reynolds was a leading light in the Chartist movement of the 1840s and may be considered a revolutionary. His novel was written to highlight the problems of the poor and especially the fate of those cast into prison, often falsely accused or without adequate trial.

It was inevitable that the popularity of this plot would find its way back into the mainstream, which it did via the 'sensation' novels of the 1860s, most notably *The Woman in White* (1860) by Wilkie **Collins** and *Uncle Silas* (1864) by Sheridan Le Fanu (1814–1873). It continued to cast its influence on the emerging detective novel, notably Collins's own *The Moonstone* (1868), and in many of Conan **Doyle**'s Sherlock **Holmes** stories.

Both the penny dreadful and the gothic romance continued to prove popular throughout the Victorian era. The penny weeklies became increasingly confined to juvenile literature, and it was with the intention of ousting the corruptive influence of this fiction on the young that Alfred Harmsworth introduced his halfpenny weeklies, including the *Halfpenny Marvel*, where the adventures of Sexton **Blake** first appeared. The *Union Jack*, in which the Sexton Blake stories subsequently took form, was also a penny weekly but may be seen as the reformation of the former penny dreadful, setting it on a new and morally improving road away from ruin.

The gothic romance has scarcely gone away. It continues to have occasional moments of glory, most popularly in the works of Daphne du Maurier (1907–1989) of which *Rebecca* (1938) repeats all the gothic formulae with dexterous skill. More recently, Basil **Copper** created a moody detective novel set among a vast Victorian cemetery in *Necropolis* (1980), which he described as a 'Gothic mystery'. The American-born but British-based Charles **Palliser** admirably recreated the urban gothic and sensation novel in *The Quincunx* (1989) while the Italian Umberto Eco gave us all the atmosphere of the gothic mystery in *The Name of the Rose* (1983) which, in translation, contributed to the growth in popularity of the historical mystery – which is where the gothic novel started. *See also* Godfathers of British Crime Fiction, Magazines *and* Origins of British Crime Fiction.

Further Reading

Haining, Peter. 1975. *The Penny Dreadful*. Gollancz.
Howells, Coral Ann. 1978. *Love, Mystery and Misery: Feeling in Gothic Fiction*. Athlone Press.
James, Elizabeth, and Helen R. Smith. 1998. *Penny Dreadfuls and Boys' Adventures*. British Library.
James, Louis. 1963. *Fiction for the Working Man*. Oxford University Press.
Mighall, Robert. 2000. *A Geography of Victorian Gothic Fiction*. Oxford University Press.
Summers, Montague. 1938. *The Gothic Quest*. Fortune Press.

Website

Woller, Jack G. 'The Literary Gothic', www.litgothic.com/index_fl.html.

Mike Ashley

Graeme, Bruce (1900–1982)

Bruce Graeme is the pseudonym of a prolific British writer best known for his series featuring gentleman-crook 'Blackshirt'.

Graeme was born Bruce Graeme Montague Jeffries in Barnes, London. He took up a career as a journalist and film writer–producer after returning from the First World War in 1918, but with mixed success. However, in 1924, he began a series of stories about gentleman thief Richard Verrell, rather in the style of **Hornung**'s Raffles, except that Verrell, who is a highly respected and best-selling writer by day, dresses at night all in black (complete with black mask) and becomes a burglar, purely for the fun of it. He acquires the nickname 'Blackshirt', and when his identity is discovered by a mysterious woman, he reforms and becomes something of a Robin Hood rogue. The series ran in *The New Magazine* (1924–1925) and proved extremely popular. Publisher T. Fisher Unwin acquired the stories and published them as the first in a new series of cheap novels. *Blackshirt* (1925) sold over a million copies over the next ten years. The success led to nine further books through to *Blackshirt Strikes Back* (1940) plus three books featuring Blackshirt's son, Anthony Verrell, starting with *Son of Blackshirt* (1941), who becomes Lord Blackshirt. There were four more books starting with *Monsieur Blackshirt* (1933) (under the alias David Graeme) featuring Blackshirt's seventeenth-century French ancestor.

Graeme clearly liked the idea of the villain-cum-hero. He selected 'The Empty House' for the anthology *My Best Mystery Story* (1939) which involves another reformed cracksman who uses his skills to rescue an abducted child. The success and, alas, repetition of this formula – which was continued by Graeme's son Roderic Jeffries (b.1926) with a further twenty *Blackshirt* books – has overshadowed Graeme's other works, of which there were a further seventy novels and several dozen short stories.

Among his best books are the international **police procedurals** that began with *A Murder of Some Importance* (1931) and feature Superintendent Stevens of Scotland Yard assisted by Inspector Allain of the Sûreté. Although the characters are stereotypical for the period, the plots are often ingenious, especially in *The Imperfect Crime* (1932). The series ran to thirteen novels and include the fascinating shipboard puzzle, *The Mystery on the Queen Mary* (1937) and an attempt to resolve the ending of Charles **Dickens**'s *The Mystery of Edwin Drood* in *Epilogue* (1933). Graeme enjoyed stories of international intrigue and included several in his later police series involving Detective Sergeant Robert Mather such as *Two-Faced* (1977), which involves the fate of an Arab sheikh. Of late, Graeme's most collectable series has become his cosy bibliomysteries featuring antiquarian book dealer Theodore Terhune, which began with *Seven Clues in Search of a Crime* (1941).

Graeme wrote several **historical** mysteries set in nineteenth-century France. These include two, written under the alias Peter Bourne, featuring the renowned detective Vidocq, *Fall of the Eagle* (1967) and *And Bay the Moon* (1975) and two with Inspector Jantry, *Cherchez la Femme* (1951) and *Lady in Black* (1952).

Graeme also produced many non-series books, frequently including novel plot devices. He had entered Gray's Inn as a barrister in 1930 before writing became a full-time career and he used his knowledge in two courtroom dramas, *Through the Eyes of the Judge* (1930) and *Cardyce for the Defence* (1936), while *The Undetective* (1962) has a mystery writer's alter-ego become the suspect in a murder.

Graeme, Bruce

Graeme's prolific output, which includes further work under the pseudonym Roderic Hastings, Fielding Hope and Jeffrey Montague, has worked against him and none of his books has remained in print. Some have seriously dated with the racial and social outlook of the period, but his best include examples of ingenious plots and unusual ideas.

Selected Works by the Author
Blackshirt (1925)
Through the Eyes of the Judge (1930)
The Imperfect Crime (1932)
Epilogue (1933)
Mystery on the Queen Mary (1937)
House with Crooked Walls (1942)
The Undetective (1962)

Mike Ashley

Graham, Caroline (b.1931)

It is for both her narrative skills and her judicious evocation of English village life that Caroline Graham, the author of the much-loved Inspector Barnaby novels, has been identified (in the words of a *Sunday Times* critic) as 'simply the best detective writer since Agatha **Christie**'.

Caroline Graham was born in 1931 into a working-class family in Nuneaton, Warwickshire, and educated at Nuneaton High School for Girls and the Open University. She went on to do an MA in theatre studies at Birmingham University. She has written very successfully for radio, television and the theatre but is best known for her series of crime novels featuring detectives Barnaby and Troy, televised as the perennially popular *Midsomer Murders*. The first of these novels, *The Killings at Badger's Drift* (1987), won the Macavity Award for Best First Mystery Novel in 1988 and was also listed in Hatchard's Crime Companion as one of the best 100 crime novels of all time. The television adaptation of her thriller, *Death of a Hollow Man* (1989), was runner-up in the Edgars (US) television awards.

Encomiums for her work are plentiful ('A wickedly deft pastiche of the Agatha Christie school of village whodunnits: updated, witty, full of character and characters'; 'acid, yet sympathetic'; 'Richly, often affectionately, characterised'; 'Well written, witty and elegantly plotted'), but what counts is the unshakeable affection which Graham's work inspires in her admirers; they will be the first to maintain that the books are much more accomplished than the rather anodyne television adaptations. The latter have finessed the author's bank balance rather than increase admiration for the books – and the novels will undoubtedly be her most lasting legacy.

Selected Works by the Author
The Killing at Badger's Drift (1987)
Death of a Hollow Man (1989)
Death in Disguise (1992)
Written in Blood (1994)
Faithful unto Death (1996)
A Place of Safety (1999)
A Ghost in the Machine (2004)

Barry Forshaw

Granger, Ann (b.1939)

A writer who deliberately places herself within the so-called 'cosy' mystery tradition, Ann Granger is the author of a successful series of detective novels featuring Alan Markby, superior policeman, and Meredith Mitchell, a Foreign Office diplomat trying to make a home in the country. They first appeared in *Say it with Poison* (1991). Markby is divorced and Mitchell traumatised by a love long past. The slow romance of these two middle-aged lovers is a satisfying device uniting the sleuths from different backgrounds. Indeed, the Mitchell and Markby detecting union solves a number of generic problems for the modern whodunit. This duo has the resources of the police with the gossipy techniques of the amateur detective. Mitchell is technically single with the independence of a professional woman, yet her loneliness is assuaged as her presence softens the harshness of Markby's official detecting persona.

Granger shows an abiding interest in the single woman in an institutional, mostly masculine, environment. Once Meredith is near marrying Markby, Granger introduces a new policewoman to Markby's team. Jess Campbell arrives in *That Way Murder Lies* (2004). Her difficulties are explored as she investigates the death of the spoiled daughter of a businessman at his country estate. With Mitchell and Markby previously invited to help with a poison-pen mystery, Granger has her country house filled with 'amateur' sleuths *and* police procedural elements. The modern mystery is a hybrid of sub-genres; Granger is evoking the **Golden Age**.

Crime in these attractive settings thrives on the margins of families. It stands for what they cannot quite shut out, even in their large, secure homes. For the past is inescapably woven into the present through long-lived hurts. So many of Granger's works rely on untangling a history in which the repressed past has to re-surface. A particular characteristic is the revelation of how passion from the family's past leads to murder.

Granger's second series is a new departure. The Fran Varaday novels start with *Asking for Trouble* (1997). Set mainly in a **London** of run-down streets, this single woman making her way in the world is young, penniless and virtually friendless. Fran wants to be an actress but quite often finds herself sleeping in her friend Ganesh's uncle's garage. The police regard her as trouble, yet her position on the margins means that she sees crime that the police miss, such as the strange death of a young woman in her squat, or the racket bringing Eastern Europeans illegally into London. Fran, too, has a story of unresolved connection to her past. Believing she is an orphan when her father is murdered, she is astonished to be told of her dying mother who wants Fran to find the daughter she gave away. These mysteries emphasise Fran's desperate struggle to find the true story of her identity. The Varaday novels satisfy because they take modern urban multicultural Britain and weave myths of belonging out of crime fiction. Indeed, Granger's work here suggests a role for murder mysteries in simultaneously representing and fictionally healing the violence we sense in today's world.

Selected Works by the Author

Mitchell and Markby Series
Say It with Poison (1991)
Cold in the Earth (1992)
Candle for a Corpse (1995)
Beneath the Stones (1995)
Shades of Murder (2000)
That Way Murder Lies (2004)

Granger, Ann

Fran Varaday Series
Asking for Trouble (1997)
Running Scared (1999)
Risking It All (2001)
Watching Out (2003)

Further Reading
Irons, Glenwood, ed. 1995. *Feminism in Women's Detective Fiction*. University of Toronto Press.
Mann, Jessica. 1981. *Deadlier than the Male: An Investigation into Feminine Crime Writing*. David & Charles.

Website
www.twbooks.co.uk/authors/agranger1.html

Susan Rowland

Grant-Adamson, Lesley (b.1942)

Having originally made her name as a journalist (with *The Guardian*), Lesley Grant-Adamson became a crime novelist, dividing her fiction between quirky and highly individual series and non-series books. Her best-known series characters are Rain Morgan, Jim Rush and Laura Flynn.

36. Lesley Grant-Adamson.

She was born in London but spent much of her childhood in the Rhondda Valley. Her journalistic experience ranges from *The Guardian* to local and trade papers, and her range of writing extends from journalism and crime stories to poetry, short stories and 'how-to' writing guides. She was the first British crime writer to be appointed Writer in Residence to a British university (Nottingham Trent in 1994). As a cub journalist she was covering crime and living in Gloucester when the Fred West murders came to light. Although the case affected at least two of her books, her first,

Patterns in the Dust (1985), was a relatively conventional whodunit about a gossip columnist cum amateur investigator, Rain Morgan. There were five Morgan books, each of which gave an interesting stretch to the genre, and of particular note is *Curse the Darkness* (1990), more mainstream than genre, a biting attack on the debased values of the 1980s.

The detective Laura Flynn was promising in establishing a series, but after *Flynn* (1991), there was only a novella, *Music to be Murdered By* (2001), and a short story. This surprised many, since *Flynn* had been well received and seemed set for a good run. But the following year, Grant-Adamson brought out the first Jim Rush book, *A Life of Adventure* (1992). Rush was an American conman working in the United Kingdom and after his first 1992 'biography' he reappeared in *Dangerous Games* (1994). The fact that neither he nor Flynn became long series – and that the decision to stop them seems the author's rather than arising from poor sales – suggests that her preference is for stand-alones alternating with non-fiction. The second Rush book was followed by a steady flow of strong stand-alone novels, among which both *Wish You Were Here* (1995) and *Evil Acts* (1996) seem to recall the author's experiences covering the Fred West affair. (Both concern a woman's relationship, witting or unwitting, with a serial killer.) But a more common theme in her books is the lingering effect of past crimes. Her stand-alone *The Dangerous Edge* (1994) is haunted by the disappearance of a child twenty years before, while in *Lipstick and Lies* (1998), another stand-alone, the woman at the heart of the novel cannot shake off responsibility for the murder of her mother four decades before.

Selected Works by the Author
Flynn (1991)
The Dangerous Edge (1994)
Wish You Were Here (1995)
Writing Crime and Suspense Fiction (non-fiction, 1996; new edition 2003)
Threatening Eye (1998)
Undertow (1999)

Rain Morgan Series
Patterns in the Dust (1985)
The Face of Death (1985)
Guilty Knowledge (1986)
Wild Justice (1987)

Jim Rush Series
A Life of Adventure (1992)
Dangerous Games (1994)

Russell James

The Great Detectives: The Mass Appeal of Holmes, Poirot and Wimsey

'There's a scarlet thread of murder running through the colourless skein of life, and our duty is to unravel it, and isolate it, and expose every inch of it' (Sherlock **Holmes**, *A Study in Scarlet*, 1887).

The great detectives are a considerable imaginative creation. They possess such longevity and impact that their authors longed to be free of them. Indeed, perhaps part of their greatness is that they refused to die: their bond with public consciousness was so intense that they became more than literary characters. Bored with the affectations of Lord Peter **Wimsey**, Dorothy L. **Sayers** tried to marry him off in *Strong Poison* (1930). Unfortunately, in Harriet Vane she had created too vital a woman to meekly accept the detective who had saved her from the gallows. Wimsey was now in a situation that demanded psychological realism. As his painful romance continued, he absorbed more and more erotic power until Sayers could never entirely let him go.

Bored with **Poirot**, Agatha **Christie** sensibly attempted no drastic measures. She developed other contrasting detective figures in the uxorious Tommy and Tuppence, the scatty intuitive Ariadne Oliver, and of course, the deadly Miss **Marple**. Perhaps Christie had learned from the struggles of Arthur Conan **Doyle** (1859–1930) with the fiendishly slippery, Sherlock Holmes. With literary ambitions beyond the detective story, Doyle sent Holmes over the Reichenbach Falls with the evil Professor Moriarty in 'The Final Problem' (1893). 'Thank God, I've killed the brute', Doyle is reported to have said. Unfortunately for Doyle, the exuberance of Holmes in the public mind eventually overcame his reluctance. After returning with *The Hound of the Baskervilles* (1901–1902) set prior to the confrontation with Moriarty, Doyle acknowledged the return of Holmes to the world with further stories and novellas, ending with *The Case-Book of Sherlock Holmes* (1924–1927). Like the most potent mythical heroes, Sherlock Holmes returns from the dead and has a powerful afterlife in the literary identity of **London** in particular. So what makes these detectives stronger than their authors, more long lasting and arguably more necessary to modern life?

Sherlock Holmes

Sherlock Holmes solves mysteries; in doing so he seems to offer himself as another. It is not his astonishing powers of deduction, his network of contacts in different walks of life or his combination of closed-in reticence with a desire to tell but his singular attitudes to humanity that mark him as an *outsider*. In the two early novellas, *A Study in Scarlet* (1887) and *The Sign of Four* (1890), Watson notices not only his brilliance but also his reluctance to accept human limitations in himself and others. Holmes offers no story of origins. He puts himself outside relationships with women by declaring, in *The Sign of Four*, that none of them are to be trusted. He disdains sleep when a problem lingers and knows where to lay his hands on a dog with preternatural talents for sniffing out creosote.

Yet, as Watson records to his concern, Holmes's desire to set himself outside human weakness does not altogether succeed. Holmes may reject women, but he shows a great need for admiration. Holmes will not accept a role as part of a team, however much the less-gifted police officers, Gregson and Lestrade, wish to incorporate him. Nevertheless, Holmes is annoyed when the police grab the glory. He does want to be part of society, but only on his own terms that go beyond accepted conventions. In this we have the great detective establishing the paradox of the role: the detective is an outsider by nature; in becoming a detective he finds a role (almost) adequate to his need to serve and his desire to escape conventions. The detective is an outsider who is dedicated to healing the social body. He must retain part of himself in the inhuman twilight if he is to banish the spectre of murder from his peers. By nature of the almost occult genius for detection, the detective is someone who finds it incredibly difficult to conform to personal or professional relationships.

Holmes is almost supernaturally full of energy when engaged upon a case. When idle, he suffers depression and turns to cocaine and morphine. Only a criminal case locks Holmes into the world. Without one, he has no human connection capable of sustaining his vulnerability, his need for applause. *The Sign of Four* provides an astounding opening with Dr Watson observing Holmes taking drugs and feeling unable to contain his frustration. Holmes arouses strong emotions while defending against them for himself. When Holmes is lured into treating a watch produced by Watson as a piece of evidence, Holmes swiftly ascertains that it was the property of Watson's elder brother who died drunk and indigent. His 'abstract' manner touches Watson on the raw, and Holmes has to apologise for forgetting that a brother might have feelings. These two minor episodes, the cocaine and the exercise of the watch, precede the real start of the case with the announcement of the arrival of a client, Miss Mary Morstan. In effect, the opening of the story divides Holmes and Watson into one who is a man of family and feeling and one who insists upon placing himself outside social convention. Unsurprisingly, the story will prove to be one of families and brothers, before giving way to a tale of desperadoes who by murder and treasure hunting have placed themselves outside society in prison in India.

Watson, the man of family pieties, falls in love with Mary Morstan, who is likely to inherit half a great fortune in Indian jewels. While stoically pursuing Miss Morstan's interest, Watson's great fear is that huge wealth will remove Mary to *outside* his social reach. That sense of social estrangement within England is, of course, an echo of the way the story turns on the English colonial relationship with India. An Indian Rajah sends his great fortune away during the Indian mutiny and his trusted servant is robbed by an Englishman with one leg, Jonathan Small, and three Indians, hence the sign of four. The four are rightly convicted of murder and spend long years in prison. Among their guards are Miss Morstan's father and a Captain Sholto, who double-crosses everyone and steals the treasure home to London. Small comes after him with a savage native friend, Tonga. Soon Holmes and Watson are after Small. After a tense boat chase down the Thames to its obscure reaches in the Plumstead marshes, Tonga sinks below the water with the treasure. Small lives to tell his story of betrayal and revenge.

In very broad terms, *The Sign of Four* is an ironic story of colonial enterprise. Treasure belonging in India ends up in the Thames. It seems to be a metaphor for both the greed and the futility of colonialism. The wealth of other lands will remain illusory, while seeking it will degrade the parties into violence and killing. Indeed, in bringing Tonga to London, Small has literally brought home violence engendered by the operation of the Empire. While the portrayal of Tonga as inherently savage appears racist today, his brutality is made evident largely because he is out of place in a strange world. When compared to Doyle's Tonga, we must note Small's insistence on the honourable nature of his Indian co-conspirators whom he refuses to betray. The person of bad faith in the story is, of course, the wholly English Captain Sholto.

So, running through *The Sign of Four* is the motif of the outsider, detective, killer and the victim, Sholto, isolated from most society by his secreting of the treasure. Another class of outsiders is utilised by Watson to keep Holmes away from the streets. The Baker Street Irregulars arrive for orders. These ragged boys are explained by Holmes as his eyes and ears. Typically, the nearest we see Holmes in a parent role is as a semi-military figure giving orders to his child troops. Again, there is a relationship structure that sustains Holmes and distances him from the possibility of being a parent, just as his enlisting of Watson distances him from being officially attached to one person.

If *The Sign of Four* shows fascination with the complications of the English in India, *A Study in Scarlet* evokes anxieties about the rough uncultured state of America. It is this work that introduces Watson to Holmes. First of all, we hear of Watson's past. War wounded in Afghanistan, he faces a long recovery in London and searches for someone to share rooms. A friend introduces him to a strange man in a chemical laboratory who has been beating corpses to research bruising. Holmes is therefore heralded as a man of science, medical research, and *not* of a squeamish or sentimental disposition. When Watson comes upon him, Holmes has eyes that 'glittered' at the prospect of discovering a test for bloodstains that might make him famous. Moreover, Watson soon discovers that Holmes is not a polymath. He has no use for general knowledge. If he deems it relevant to his work then his research is second to none. If not relevant, then he will be ignorant of facts such as the solar system, to Watson's surprise.

Although Watson is frequently surprised throughout the stories, he is more than just Holmes's witless sidekick. More significant than helping Holmes with the cases, Watson's real job is to detect the detective. He discovers both the amazing heights of Holmes – in his deductive reasoning, his definitive monograph on cigar ash – and also the detective's fallibility in drug use, depression, turning away from relationships, refusal to engage with the world, need for adulation and petty desire to outsmart the police. Watson is a good deal more intelligent and humane than he is usually given credit for.

So it is not untoward that in *The Hound of the Baskervilles* Watson is left alone to manage affairs for large parts of the story. Typically, it is Watson who is installed at the heart of the mysterious dwelling, Baskerville Hall, to protect young Americanised Sir Henry Baskerville. Of course, he does soon find himself out of his depth, crying to fatal beauty, Miss Stapleton: 'Life has become like that great Grimpen Mire, with little green patches everywhere into which one may sink and with no guide to point the track.' Fortunately, another outsider is at hand as a dirty old wanderer of the moor. After a comic confrontation, Holmes puts off his disguise and becomes again the detective as guide to a labyrinthine landscape of clues. Finally, it is the villain who lands in Grimpen Mire, not the detectives. Sherlock Holmes organises the reading of space until it becomes a map to the solution of the puzzle. Lord Peter Wimsey will pay subtle tribute to the Holmes of the Baskervilles when he detects *through* immersion in the bog and not by avoiding it in *Clouds of Witness* (1926).

Holmes is notable by what he cannot do and refuses as much as by his genius in re-storying death. He sets the standard for the great fictional detective as a hero who is apart from life as well as utterly dedicated to the solution of its greatest enemy, murder. He sees the importance of absences such as the dog that did not bark in the night time – *that* was the curious incident! Holmes solves the most unbearable of mysteries, the gaps, silences and chaos, surrounding death. His heroic confidence is a mythical promise of solving the incomprehensibility of the modern world. No wonder the public could not let him go.

Hercule Poirot

Rather than heroic, Hercule Poirot strikes a mock heroic note, whether he enters as a drab Belgian refugee during the First World War in his first case, *The Mysterious*

Affair at Styles (1920) or by his more delightful expedient of throwing marrows over his garden wall in *The Murder of Roger Ackroyd* (1926). With a first name denoting mythic strength, Poirot has a typical narrative arc in the novels. To begin with, he is anti-heroic – a 'little' man with an egg-shaped head, elaborate moustaches, heavily accented English, fussing over small, often domestic, details. After being patronised by the range of English types deployed around a dead body, Poirot starts to make insightful connections. From being regarded as a buffoon, he is quickly a confidante, gaining authority from his knowledge of the group from inside out. Finally, Poirot will unveil the killer. His method is often theatrical, a reconstruction, either narrated by himself or by manipulating the suspects into recreating their guilt. He ends as a hero, one who cleanses a community by removing the canker at the heart.

So Poirot is a detective hero surrounded by ironies. He has the heroic success of Holmes in his deductive capacities, but he adds a liking for talking to suspects, regarding 'psychology' as equally important. Like Holmes, he is an outsider, here signalled by his 'foreignness' and un-English obsession with neatness of dress. However, unlike Holmes, Poirot is an outsider who comes inside in the course of detecting the plot. To Poirot, detecting means getting to know a group of people intimately. He will often become a confessor or a comforter to the innocent and guilty alike, such as his support of the English doctor, Sarah, in *Appointment with Death* (1938) and his penetrating words about evil to distraught Jacqueline in *Death on the Nile* (1937). At the end of *The Hollow* (1946), Poirot predicts to Henrietta, whom he has come to admire, that the murderess' son, now a child, will one day come to him and ask the truth. For Poirot has connived at concealing the full extent of the crimes in the Christow family. As elsewhere, by the end of the case, Poirot becomes a figure dispensing mercy and sometimes overriding the precepts of the law. Indeed, much of the drama of the second half of the typical Poirot novel is his negotiation of legal and police requirements on the one hand and his own standard of justice, tempered with empathy, on the other. The most extreme version of Poirot's heroic rewriting of the law occurs in *The Murder on the Orient Express* (1934). This is an explicit case where the law has failed. A brutal killer will forever escape justice and will probably kill again. Poirot decides that this time justice resides outside the law. Yet when reminded of this case when faced with the murder of a family tyrant in *Appointment with Death*, Poirot refuses to make it a general rule. The tension between the detective as the dispenser of justice and as upholder of the law, between a quasi divine figure of truth and heroic champion of society's truth, haunts Poirot's cases up to and including the last, *Curtain: Hercule Poirot's Last Case* (1975).

In effect, Poirot is a detective who spans serious meditation about justice as communal or individual, with social comedy, and a theatrical dimension to the action. Poirot is a detective in novels where the solution of death is a ritual, requiring constant re-enactments, while Holmes is closer to the status of myth. Explicitly, Poirot arrives in England to solve a country-house murder in the midst of war. By constructing the story that explains the death, he theatrically (because it can only be done fictionally) 'solves' death at a time when it never seemed less possible or more necessary. In this, Poirot is a truly great detective, answering the deep needs of the reading public post–First World War.

The great detectives have been accused of exerting a conservative influence on storytelling. A heinous crime takes place, one that rips apart social bonds. The social group, whether it is as large as London or as small as a country house, is in chaos. After the detective has done his work, chaos is banished and order restored; *society continues as before*. So in this reading, heroically successful detectives are fundamentally about social stability and conformity. This is true apart from two factors, the detective role and the literary nature of his text. The great detectives are great because they do not follow expected procedures. In Holmes's slumping over the Hansom Cab in a trance and in Poirot's inconsequential conversations is a *resistance to conformity* that is very strong in the stories because it is shown to succeed. Moreover, in part because of the unusual and surprising behaviour of the detective, this genre has an inbuilt self-consciousness. It refers to itself as a fiction, either by the conscious use of heroic male romance (treasure stories in Holmes) or by Poirot's reference to his predecessor such as cunningly roping in a suspicious person by making him his 'Watson'. The result is that the stories of the great detectives do assert social continuity, *as a fiction*. They satisfy their readers because they seem to heal modernity, by solving death and re-making the world as coherent *and* by showing the modern world to be only understandable by a conscious effort of telling stories. The great detectives stand for the story-making partly successful capacity of negotiating modern life. No wonder, they attract such psychic investment. Hercule Poirot is the most humane.

Lord Peter Wimsey

If Hercule Poirot shows an un-Holmesian liking for people, shifting the insider/outsider status of the detective, then Lord Peter Wimsey, stepping onto the page in 1923 in *Whose Body?* is positively prepared to embrace humanity. He is immediately placed in a familial group by receiving his first case from his mother. The Duchess rings to tell her son, whose detecting hobby she pretends not to notice, that 'little' Mr Thipps, the architect, has a spot of bother. He has discovered a dead, almost naked, body in his bath. Wimsey responds with enthusiasm. In this first story he is to learn two things about his role as a detective. In the first place, he cannot always do his detecting encased in the class barrier of being a Duke's son. He learns not to patronise 'little' Mr Thipps and get beyond class to a sense of being 'inside' a human group. On the other hand, he discovers a second point about not detecting as a Duke's son that places him 'outside' the group; that solving murders is not a game subject to the 'fair play' of his special upbringing. Here the professional detective, Parker, shows what he contributes to 'amateur' Wimsey when he tells him: 'You want to be consistent, you want to look pretty, you want to swagger debonairly through a comedy of puppets or else to stalk magnificently through a tragedy of human sorrows and things. But that's childish. If you've any duty to society in the way of finding out the truth about murders, you must do it in any attitude that comes handy.' Parker's point is that you cannot detect murderers for sport because murder is too serious; society needs the protection. Moreover, a murderer will be hanged and so a detective is a kind of killer!

Wimsey is the classic detective whose creator takes the death penalty seriously. All detectives resemble criminals because they follow their footsteps and try to reconstruct their mindsets. However, British detectives, until the 1960s, faced another forced resemblance in the death of the convict they captured. Wimsey suffers, even when he does play the gentleman and allow the guilty to spare their families a trial by committing suicide. In *Whose Body?* the strong bond between Wimsey and manservant/ detecting assistant Bunter is explained when the latter cares for his master as he sleepwalks back into a nightmare in the trenches. Almost the last we see of Wimsey, in *Busman's Honeymoon* (1937), is a similar breakdown as the murderer is hanged.

The Wimsey novels are a careful balance of this serious evocation of death and the law against Wimsey partly inhabiting his anomalous role by theatricality and references to fiction. Wimsey is given to mimicking Holmes, calling for his pipe and announcing himself as Sherlock Holmes in disguise. Like Holmes and Poirot, Wimsey too offers the promise of solving death *fictionally*. Unlike Holmes and less like Poirot, Wimsey is offered to the reader as an attractive engaging persona with whom to form a bond while hunting for clues. Yes, Wimsey and, by extension, the reader have been told to develop an ethics of detection, but that is extended, not negated, by *relating* to the detective and feeling a part of his quest.

Of course, the main way by which Wimsey becomes more related to the reader is by his big difference to Holmes and Poirot, his romance and subsequent marriage to Harriet Vane. Arriving in *Strong Poison* (1930) on trial for her life accused of killing her lover, Harriet first appears to be an example of the detective falling for the murderer, a variation of the detective resembling one. Naturally, Wimsey believes that Harriet is innocent. The pressure to prove her so lest she be hanged gives *Strong Poison* urgency and suspense. Perhaps it was the combination of erotic tension under the imminence of death, but at the end of the novel both characters effectively outgrow the genre. In the next few years, Wimsey will be most purely the great detective when drawn away from his reluctant beloved, in such works as *Murder Must Advertise* (1933) and *The Nine Tailors* (1934). The detective genre has always been an *alternative* to romance as the centre of interest is the fusion of the detective with the clues, not the union of two people. However, in *Gaudy Night* (1935) and *Busman's Honeymoon* (1937), Sayers sought to marry the two popular forms. What results is something rather special. Wimsey becomes a detective who surpasses Poirot in detecting through emotion and passion rather than mostly by deduction and reason. He draws on what he intuits through love of Harriet, and what that enables him to understand about an all women's college in Oxford. Married, Wimsey is able to make his delicate psychological state a lens by which to examine a close yet troubled rural community.

All three detectives are great because their grip on the public imagination remains strong. Each brought something new to the genre, while paying tribute to predecessors. Holmes, Poirot and Wimsey all demonstrate the ambiguities, pleasures and pains of detecting. They bring the reader intimations of divine heroism while insisting on moral fallibility of their incarnations in the tales. Above all, the great detectives stand for the ability to tell stories to make sense of modern life. For this they inherit readers' gratitude, generation after generation. *See also* The Detective in British Fiction, Golden Age Crime Fiction, Holmes's Rivals, Male Crime Writers, Origins of British Crime Fiction *and* Women Crime Writers.

Further Reading
Haining, Peter. 2002. *The Classic Era of Crime Fiction*. Chicago Review Press.
Knight, Stephen. 2004. *Crime Fiction, 1800–2000: Detection, Death, Diversity*. Palgrave.
Light, Alison. 1991. *Forever England: Femininity, Literature and Conservatism between the Wars*. Routledge.
Plain, Gill. 1996. *Women's Fiction of the Second World War: Gender, Power and Resistance*. Edinburgh University Press.
Rowland, Susan. 2001. *From Agatha Christie to Ruth Rendell*. Palgrave.

Susan Rowland

Greene, Graham (1904–1991)

Had Graham Greene not written the 'serious' novels (such as *A Burnt Case*, published in 1961, and *The Heart of the Matter*, in 1948) which marked him out as one of the greatest of all English writers, his 'entertainments' (as the author rather dismissively described them) would constitute a body of crime and **thriller** fiction almost without equal in the field.

Greene originally worked as a journalist, becoming sub-editor on *The Times* before he risked writing full-time, following the relative success of his first novel *The Man Within* (1929). Early in his career, Greene introduced an element of the spy story into *The Confidential Agent* (1939), in which D, the agent of a Latin government (Republican Spain in all but name), figures in a narrative that was clearly influential on such later writers as John **le Carré**. The latter has long acknowledged Greene's considerable influence on his work. Greene's most celebrated crime novel, of course, is *Brighton Rock* (1938, with its psychotic young anti-hero Pinkie), which the author decided to move out of his 'entertainments' category. This sometimes slippery shifting of genres by the author was always a rather arbitrary endeavour: the moral concerns of the thrillers were often precisely those of the more serious books, while the pursuit narratives of the serious books (such as the whisky priest on the run in *The Power and the Glory*, 1940) had precisely the same visceral trajectory as the thrillers. But all the books have that dark and sardonic view of existence which quickly became identified as 'Greeneland', a queasy admixture of the seedy, the surrealistically funny and the dangerous. Two other crucial ingredients need to be identified in the Greene mix: the author's uneasy relationship with Catholicism (he converted under the influence of his wife's piety, but was never an unquestioning believer after the fashion of his correspondent and colleague Evelyn Waugh (1903–1966), who chastised Greene for his doubts). Greene's work is also distinguished by its frank and realistic depiction of the sexual relations between men and women – not, that is to say, in any graphic fashion, but with an unblinking assessment of the joys and despair concomitant with sexual passion.

Brighton Rock, with its brilliantly realised picture of a violent seaside underworld, is as strong a starting point for those new to Greene as anything he wrote, but such superbly honed thrillers as *The Ministry of Fear* (1943) demonstrate an authority and mastery of the narrative form that makes most practitioners look mere journeymen. Despite the writer's long association with the cinema, the number of first-rate films associated with his work is relatively few (Carol Reed's *The Third Man*, of course, and Fritz Lang made a creditable stab at *The Ministry of Fear*), but re-reading such exemplary novels as *The Quiet American* (1955, in which CIA doubledealing is the mainspring of the plot, and the Vietnam conflict was introduced to many readers as a significant subject for a novel) is a salutary reminder that the best way to approach the writer is (unsurprisingly) through the books rather than the hit-or-miss films (the first cinematic version of *The Quiet American* downplayed the anti-American underpinnings of the book, and even though a later version did more justice, the author's particular tone of voice was once again lost). It might be argued that John le Carré and the playwright Harold Pinter (b.1930) adopted Greene's once-controversial (and sometimes over-splenetic) mistrust of all American foreign policy.

Greene's crime and thriller novels offer a wide panoply of pleasures, such as the wonderfully mordant humour of *Our Man in Havana* (1958, which drew on Greene's own experiences in the intelligence services), and it is notable that even in the twenty-first century all of his novels remain as vivid and involving as they were when first published. *Stamboul Train* (1932), for instance, is an exhilarating Hitchcockian adventure shot through with moral ambiguity, while *A Gun for Sale* (1936, with its chillingly drawn killer, Raven, and a political assassination that generates the threat of war) is far more than a period piece.

Of course, there are those readers who will find difficulties arising from the author's self-torturing Catholicism (a trait replicated in several of his protagonists), but Greene (unlike Waugh) was never an apologist for the Catholic Church. The acquisition of faith in his books is rarely a life-enhancing, positive experience. In fact, the overriding impression that the reader receives is that most of his heroes would be far better off without the dubious consolations of religion. And Greene himself was far too much of a self-confessed sensualist to be at ease with the anti-sex asceticism of the Catholic Church (it is possible to imagine Greene's wry response to the host of recent scandals involving priests), so the agnostic reader need not allow these religious elements to prevent them from tackling one of the most considerable bodies of work (both the thrillers and literary novels) in English literature. And thriller readers will be doing themselves a considerable disservice if they read only the 'entertainments' – such books as *The Comedians* (1966) generate quite as much suspense as Greene's more avowedly generic novels (the latter may be in fact the best book for the novice Greeneian to tackle – this is the novel that made Haiti's dictator Papa Doc Duvalier very hot under the collar, a testament to its persuasiveness). *See also* Literature and Crime Fiction.

Selected Works by the Author
Stamboul Train (1932; also published in the United States as *Orient Express*)
A Gun for Sale (1936; also published in the United States as *This Gun for Hire*)
Brighton Rock (1938)
The Confidential Agent (1939)
The Ministry of Fear (1943)
Our Man in Havana (1958)
The Comedians (1966)

Barry Forshaw

Gregory, Susanna (b.1958)

Susanna Gregory is the crime-writing pseudonym of botanist Liz Cruwys, who works for the Scott Polar Research Institute at Cambridge University, specialising in the study of marine pollution. Gregory is best known for her series of **historical** mysteries featuring Matthew Bartholomew, a physician living in the mid-fourteenth century and who has advanced thoughts on diseases and cures. He serves as the Master of Medicine at Cambridge University. The series began with *A Plague on Both Your Houses* (1996). Bartholomew's unorthodox approach to medicine allows him to develop forensic skills in the investigation of local crimes. Gregory gained her own knowledge of forensics when working at a coroner's office before undertaking her doctoral studies.

Cruwys's husband, Beau Riffenburgh, is a lecturer on history at Cambridge University and advises on the historical content. He also collaborated directly on the series about Crusader knight Sir Geoffrey Mappestone, published under the alias Simon Beaufort. In the first book, *Murder in the Holy City* (1998), set in 1100, Mappestone investigates the deaths of several knights in Jerusalem. Subsequent books in the series are set in Britain where demands upon Mappestone to investigate crimes continually thwart his plans to return to the Holy Lands.

Gregory's third series, which began with *A Conspiracy of Silence* (2006), is set in the early days of the restoration of the monarchy under Charles II and features Thomas Chaloner, a former spy who knows too much and realises his life may be in jeopardy unless he can prove himself to his new masters.

All of Gregory's novels are steeped in period detail and have complex plots which combine a near seamless blend of historical fact and creative fiction. Gregory is also one of the group known as the Medieval Murderers who give talks and readings and have collaborated on a series of episodic novels starting with *The Tainted Relic* (2005).

Selected Works by the Author
A Plague on Both Your Houses (1996)
An Unholy Alliance (1996)
A Masterly Murder (2000)
An Order for Death (2001)
A Conspiracy of Silence (2006)

As Simon Beaufort
Murder in the Holy City (1998)

Website
www.matthewbartholomew.co.uk

Mike Ashley

Grimwood, Jon Courtenay

A novelist who defies easy categorisation, Jon Courtenay Grimwood is, loosely speaking, a writer who combines post-cyberpunk **science fiction**, noir and crime. Certain themes run through his fiction: a clash between cultures, fragmented families, the corrosive impact of memory, a hero on the edge of power without having power himself and – perhaps most important of all – the potential for redemption. His novels are also marked by a strong sense of place, showing most strongly in the Ashraf Bey mysteries, where the city of El Iskandryia becomes a character almost in its own right. This, combined with the tightness of the writing and Grimwood's refusal to avoid difficult themes, results in his critical reputation.

His early novels – *neoAddix* (1997), *Lucifer's Dragon* (1998), *reMix* (1999) and *redRobe* (2000) – were essentially potboilers that outgrew their format. All of them borrowed heavily from the crime genre, and the first and the third of them featured Lady Claire Fabio, an imperial prosecutor in twenty-second-century France.

It was not until *Pashazade* (2001), his first novel set in El Iskandryia and featuring the half Berber–half American detective Ashraf Bey, that Grimwood began to write novels that are crime fiction first and everything else afterwards. Two other Ashraf Bey novels follow (Effendi and Felaheen), also set in a twenty-first century where the Ottoman Empire still existed.

37. Jon Courtenay Grimwood.

Falsely accused of the murder of his aunt in *Pashazade*, Ashraf Bey (Raf) finds himself chief of police in *Effendi* (2002), tasked with investigating war crimes committed by the father of the woman he refused to marry in the previous book. *Felaheen* (2003) sees Ashraf Bey in disguise in Tunis, investigating the murder of a kitchen hand, while trying to thwart the assassination of a princeling who may be his own father.

Stamping Butterflies (2004) is more complex. Two of its three storylines tie to real-world crimes: one is a murder in 1970s Marrakech and the other a thwarted murder attempt on the US president. It is the third storyline that gives the novel its science-fiction edge. Set half a galaxy away, *Stamping Butterflies* turns on the death of a servant in an analogue of the Chinese Empire. If not for this, the novel could easily stand as an exotic urban noir.

9tail Fox (2005) is Grimwood's most traditional crime novel. Sergeant Bobby Zha works for the SFPD, his marriage is in ruins and his teenage daughter will not talk to him, his lieutenant wants him off the force and younger officers are snapping at his heels. So far so normal.

The twist is in Bobby Zha's early death and reappearance to investigate his own murder. Combined with elements of Chinese myth, this gives a typical Grimwood twist to what is otherwise a standard **police procedural**. The last of the books currently published is *End of the World Blues* (2006), set mostly in Tokyo and featuring Kit Nouveau, ex-guitarist, ex-sniper and ex-lover of Mary O'Mally, a missing art dealer. This time, the hyper-real description of city life is undercut by a far-future backstory, possibly written by one of the characters.

It is this endless playing with the nature of fiction that has led the *Daily Telegraph* to say of *9tail Fox*, 'Messes with time more cleverly than most SF writers could manage in light years of time dilation...'. The later *End of the World Blues* presented an ever-richer, more layered reading experience for Grimwood aficionados.

Selected Works by the Author
Pashazade (2001)
Effendi (2002)
Felaheen (2003)
Stamping Butterflies (2004)
9tail Fox (2005)
End of the World Blues (2006)
Arabesk (2007)

Barry Forshaw

Gumshoe (film, 1971)

Stephen Frears, director

Written by Neville Smith (both screenplay and the novel based on it), this quirky 1971 gem marked a film directorial debut for multiple BAFTA and Palm d'Or winner Stephen Frears. Eddie Ginley, a thirty-one-year-old bingo caller with ambitions to become a stand-up comedian, places an ad in the local paper as a birthday present to himself: 'SAMSPADE, Ginley's the name, Gumshoe's the Game. Private Investigations. No Divorce work.' But the joke is on him when he answers a summons to a plush hotel and ends up with a grand, a gun and a photo of a girl. He thinks it is a joke, until the girl disappears and a body turns up in his flat.

Eddie Ginley, winningly played by Albert Finney, refuses his wealthy brother's demands to pull the ad, and is sacked from his job, which only makes him more determined to solve the case. Billie Whitelaw is effective as the ex-fiancé who ran off with Eddie's odious sibling, and Frank Finlay is suitably despicable as the splenetic older brother who has everything but happiness. Eddie's investigations lead to the discovery of a drugs drop, murder, sanctions-busting, and in the best traditions of noir – treacherous dames. The 1970s Liverpool setting is both edgy and atmospheric, showing the city's crumbling Georgian terraces before the redevelopment boom of the 1990s. As the Liverpool landscape of the twenty-first century is typified by supercranes and commercial tower-blocks, seventies Liverpool was characterised by bulldozers and urban clearance. So, when Eddie is accosted by a hard man demanding the £1,000 fee as his own, the dole office seems an appropriate setting. Frears makes good use of the city's dereliction and social deprivation as a backdrop, while avoiding the political polemic of the novel. Though sometimes episodic, as in a rather puzzling scene in which Eddie meets a former pal by chance on a trip to London, the story arc generally works as well and the comedy is finely balanced against suspense and moments of explosive violence.

Neville Smith's original screenplay won a Writers' Guild of Great Britain award for best comedy screenplay. The film also gained two BAFTA nominations – one for Albert Finney, in the category of Best Actor, and the other for Best Screenplay for Smith, who plays a cameo role in the film. Notable also for its soundtrack by Andrew Lloyd Webber, *Gumshoe* presents an eclectic mix of Raymond **Chandler** and Dashiell Hammett – with a dash of *Casablanca* thrown in. There are plenty of plot twists to keep crime buffs guessing, and the in-jokes will more than satisfy noir aficionados. Finney's Liverpool accent is entirely credible and as the pace hots up, his quick-fire delivery evinces a more-than-passing resemblance to Bogart; an element Finney is happy to play up in this highly diverting and affectionate homage to the film noir genre. *See also* Film and Crime: Page to Screen.

Margaret Murphy

Guthrie, Allan (b.1965)

Allan Guthrie is a Scottish novelist whose roots are firmly planted in American noir fiction. He is a writer of crime fiction as opposed to detective fiction, with police investigations rarely having more than a peripheral role in any of his books. His vivid tales of Edinburgh's underbelly are written from the viewpoints of criminals and victims and told in prose that is spare and hard-hitting. His scabrous and powerful writing contains explicit violence, absurdity and black **humour**.

Guthrie has stated that he is influenced by James M. Cain and his mid-twentieth-century literary descendents such as David Goodis, Jim Thompson and Chester Himes. Guthrie's Scottish influences, however, are clear from his debut novel *Two-Way Split* (2004), eventual winner of the Theakston's Crime Novel of the Year in 2007. The book tells the story of an ex-concert pianist turned armed robber with mental health problems who is secretly off his medication. On the day of a robbery, he finds out his wife and a fellow gang member have been sleeping together. This is modern Scottish Gothic, with more than a passing nod to Stevenson and Hogg.

While personal identity crisis lies at the heart of *Two-Way Split*, Guthrie's second novel, *Kiss Her Goodbye* (2005), looks at the nature of fatherhood. The novel opens with Joe Hope, an enforcer for a loan shark, discovering that his teenage daughter, Gemma, has killed herself. The rest of the book focuses on Joe's attempt to make sense of her death. Joe Hope is hardly a likeable character, but Guthrie stresses empathy over sympathy. *Kiss Her Goodbye* was nominated for an Edgar award, a Gumshoe award and an Anthony award in the United States.

Guthrie does not have a series protagonist, although Gordon Pearce, a benign thug first seen in *Two-Way Split*, re-appears in *Hard Man* (2007). This, Guthrie's third novel, is his most overtly humorous. The plot centres on the dysfunctional Baxter family and their attempts to protect their pregnant teenage daughter from her estranged and extremely violent husband, who has recently found out that he is not the baby's father. Beneath the humour lies a question about the nature of masculinity and about male relationships with other men, their wives, their wives' lovers, their sisters, and even their dogs. *Hard Man* won the inaugural Spinetingler award for Best Novel (New Voice), 2007. *See also* Scottish Crime Fiction.

Selected Works by the Author
Two-Way Split (2004)
Kiss Her Goodbye (2005)
Hard Man (2007)
Kill Clock (2007), also featuring Pearce, is a novella for emergent adult readers

Barry Forshaw

Guttridge, Peter (b.1951)

One of the finest writers of comic crime, Peter Guttridge is the best British exponent of the caper novel, a sub-genre that is generally considered the most difficult to accomplish. Traditionally, caper novels are narrated from the criminal's point of view, but Guttridge has added an original twist by employing, as his protagonist, an amateur investigator of questionable competence.

Born in Burnley, Lancashire, and educated at Keble College Oxford and Nottingham University, Guttridge is a journalist who writes about **literature**, film and comedy for national newspapers and magazines. He is currently the crime fiction reviewer for the *Observer* newspaper.

Similar in style to his American counterpart, Carl Hiaasen, although more wide-ranging in both subject-matter and location, Guttridge's novels are a fast-paced mixture of the staples of stand-up **humour** (one-liners, puns and anecdotes) and the set-piece physical comedy of farce. Unlike Ruth Dudley **Edwards**, he steers clear of overtly political topics, choosing instead to satirise subjects ranging from new-age religion and millennium fever to reality television shows and the film industry. A sceptical liberal, he often targets the paradoxes of modern society, such as the bogus history served up by the heritage industry and the absurdity of a bunch of hard-living musicians doing a 'Rock against Drugs' tour. He also exploits the gentler comic potential of subjects such as animals, cosmetic surgery and yoga.

Guttridge's protagonist, Nick Madrid, is, like his creator, a Lancastrian freelance journalist and devotee of astanga vinyasa yoga. Sceptical, self-mocking, emotionally immature and a self-confessed sexual failure, Madrid, despite his imposing build, is the antithesis of the macho hero. Eking out a hand-to-mouth existence from a small, scruffy flat in London's Shepherds Bush, obsessed by films and music and spouting

38. Peter Guttridge.

trivia at every opportunity, he is the engaging underdog who ultimately triumphs, despite loss of dignity. Madrid's sidekick and foil is journalist Bridget Frost, sardonic, hard-drinking, promiscuous and pushy, with a penchant for tight clothes and killer heels, and surprising athletic ability. In a relationship characterised by unrealised sexual tension, Frost, although constantly belittling Madrid, is nevertheless a firm friend who frequently comes to his rescue when Madrid finds himself in danger.

Guttridge's mysteries are set in a variety of exotic locations where Madrid is sent to write articles: the Montreal Comedy Festival and Los Angeles feature in his first novel, *No Laughing Matter* (1997), his third book, *Two to Tango* (1998), revolves around a trip to the Amazon and the Andes, *The Once and Future Con* (1999) has a spectacular denouement at the Venetian Carnival and *Cast Adrift* (2004) takes place in Mexico, on the film set of a musical about pirates.

Guttridge's work displays great inventiveness and a strong sense of theatre. He has a talent for pastiche, as well as an ability to parody not only the conventions of the murder mystery, but also the work of filmmakers, songwriters and other authors as diverse as Hitchcock, W.S. Gilbert and bluesman Robert Johnson.

Selected Works by the Author
No Laughing Matter (1997)
A Ghost of a Chance (1998)
Two to Tango (1998)
The Once and Future Con (1999)
Foiled Again (2001)
Cast Adrift (2004)

Website
www.peterguttridge.com

Laura Wilson

H

Haggard, William (1907–1993)

William Haggard was one of the most artful practitioners of the Golden Age of spy writing which occurred in Britain between the late 1950s and early 1970s, a period when the country was finally facing up to the loss of the empire. He showed the world of intelligence and counter-espionage to be an inseparable part of the civil service, its management requiring an expert knowledge of bureaucracy and governmental hierarchy. This may sound unpromising, but Haggard created authoritative tales leavened with suspense, intrigue and a dash of violence.

Haggard was a pseudonym taken from his mother (who was a distant relation of Rider Haggard). He was born Richard Clayton in Croydon, the son of a clergyman. Haggard was educated at Lancing and Christ Church, Oxford, and he served in intelligence in India and Burma during the Second World War and, on his return to England, worked in the civil service. He ended his career as controller of the Enemy Property Department, a surprisingly long-lived hangover from the war and one which dealt with the legal and other ramifications of seized enemy property. This gave Haggard experience of both government and finance and contributed to the insider feel of his novels. Coming to writing comparatively late, he produced his first thriller, *Slow Burner*, in 1958 and continued to turn out books more or less at the rate of one a year until the late 1980s. The central figure in all the novels was Colonel Charles Russell, head of the Security Executive, described as 'soldiery but faintly donnish' and even in the early books not far from retirement. It is hard to avoid seeing the mandarin figure of Russell, politically astute yet slightly above the fray, as anything other than a self-projection of his creator. *The Arena* (1961), reputedly Haggard's favourite among his novels, is typical of his best and earliest work. It involves a takeover battle of one merchant bank by another; the target bank has an interest in a hush-hush defence project while the buyer is being manipulated by shadowy foreign interests. Haggard personalises the clash through two characters, one a decent 'old-school' type, the other an unscrupulous tycoon, and his subtlety lies in sympathising with the one while not dismissing the other. A similar contrast is at work in *Venetian Blind* (1959), where two industrialists are the prime suspects in leaking secrets to the enemy. (Haggard was always rather vague about the other side.) Women have a more than marginal role in this gentleman's clubland, often as independent figures though occasionally seen simply as the male's Achilles, heel. If this was characteristic of the period, so too was Haggard's ingenious use of pseudo-science as a plot device: 'negative gravity' in *Venetian Blind*, a new addictive drug in *The Unquiet Sleep* (1962) and a form of biological warfare affecting particular ethnic groups in *The Doubtful Disciple* (1969). Haggard's plots, generally tortuous and oblique, are seen from several viewpoints although always with Colonel Russell as the presiding deity. He does not spell things out for the reader and that, combined with his urbane prose, caused him to be acclaimed as 'the adult Ian **Fleming**'. The comparison was also made with **le Carré**, but Haggard's world is closer to that of C.P. Snow with some of the international flavour of Eric **Ambler** thrown in. What is urbane can become mannered, however, and Haggard's style tends towards the homogenous. (For example, the Chinese villain in *A Cool Day for Killing* (1968) sounds just like the character of an unscrupulous jeweller who, in turn, speaks in the same tone as the fire chief.) The later novels grew increasingly out of touch with the contemporary world and, as a whole, Haggard's considerable output has the charm but also the limitations of a period piece. *See also* Literature and Crime Fiction *and* Male Crime Writers.

Selected Works by the Author
Slow Burner (1958)
Venetian Blind (1959)
The Arena (1961)
The Unquiet Sleep (1962)
The High Wire (1963)
The Antagonists (1964)
A Cool Day for Killing (1968)
The Doubtful Disciple (1969)
The Old Masters (1973; also published in the United States as *The Notch on the Knife*)
The Poison People (1977)

Philip Gooden

Haining, Peter (1940–2007)

As anthology editor, Peter Alexander Haining clocked up an enormous number of titles on varied subjects such as horror (real and imagined), crime (ditto), witchcraft, humour, erotica, fantasy and science fiction. As a non-fiction author, he penned books on all manner of subjects, from Edgar Allan Poe to Sherlock **Holmes**, through *Doctor Who*, *Dracula*, *Sweeney Todd* and James Bond.

Born in Enfield, Middlesex, on 2 April 1940, Haining was keen on writing from an early age. He grew up reading the sleazy adventures of Chicago private eye Hank Janson and cites *The Wind in the Willows* (1908) as his favourite book: 'It uplifts you and depresses you at the same time. I've done nothing which comes within a million miles of that' (Interview, *Crime Time*, 2000). His first published piece was for a racing pigeon magazine, and on leaving school at seventeen, he immediately got a job as a reporter on the local newspaper *West Essex Gazette*. He moved to London and worked on various magazines before becoming editor of the popular New English Library imprint in 1963.

By the end of the decade, he had become editorial director and sought to get the infamous Hank Janson titles back in print. Janson was a fast-talking 1940s Chicagoan gumshoe whose gritty adventures were characterised by myriad 'almost pornographic' sex scenes aimed largely at pre-pubescent boys. Stephen Frances, the English writer of the series, had been charged with obscenity at the Old Bailey in 1954 and was currently residing in Spain. Although he was happy to see his books re-released, he had sold the rights to two men, one of whom vetoed the suggestion. (They were subsequently reprinted by Telos in 2003.)

Although crime fiction always interested Haining, his first anthologies concentrated on horror fiction. Conceived as a rival to the long-running Pan Books of Horror (1959–1988), his first collection of short stories was *The Hell of Mirrors*. Such titles as *Beyond the Curtain of Dark* (1966), *The Craft of Terror* (1966), *Summoned from the Tomb* (1966) and *Where Nightmares Are* (1966) followed soon after. Haining also compiled several anthologies selecting stories from *Alfred Hitchcock's Mystery Magazine* and issued as edited by Hitchcock. These included *Anyone for Murder* (1967), *The Late Unlamented* (1967) and *Anyone for Murder* (1967). Concentrating on specific themes, his anthologies presented the best of horror fiction from a wide cross-section of the genre, with household names rubbing shoulders with less familiar writers. A preface and notes provided background details on the stories and their creators.

Although credited to Haining, and based on his plot outline, *The Hero* (1973) was ghost written by Terry Harknett (b.1936). Set during the Cold War, *The Hero* detailed a secret agent's attempt to get into China and uncover details about a deadly weapon that China was developing. The story had several twists: the agent would have to be an ordinary civilian with no formal training (an **espionage** background may have given him away), and a film company was making a movie of his experiences, which was released after his mission ended in apparent tragedy. In reality, film rights were actually optioned and a script produced, but it never got off the drawing board. Haining is also credited with *The Savages* (1986), exploring what happpens when a primitive South American native is abandoned in New York, though this was also ghosted by Harknett.

Haining gained a considerable following for his compendia bringing together a variety of fascinating details about various literary figures. The first was *The Sherlock Holmes Scrapbook* (1973), a cornucopia of articles, newspaper cuttings and anecdotes relating to the **Great Detective**, with a foreword by Peter Cushing. A similar project on Edgar Allan Poe followed in 1977, while Haining's fascination for **pulp** fiction was reflected in *The Fantastic Pulps* (1975), *Terror! A History of Horror Illustrations from the Pulp Magazines* (1976) and *Mystery! An Illustrated History of Crime and Detective Fiction* (1978), which contained many examples of the sensationalist jacket designs so prevalent in that genre during the 1940s and 1950s.

In 1976, a series of true mystery stories retold for children began with *The Monster Trap*, while his books about Elvis Presley, Raquel Welch and Charlie Chaplin filled publishers' schedules during the 1980s. His *Doctor Who – A Celebration* (1983) was a phenomenal success, thanks in part to its defining status as the first illustrated hardback history of the programme.

In the mid-1980s, Michael Cox, the producer of the Granada TV Sherlock Holmes series starring Jeremy Brett, approached Haining about doing a companion to the programme. This appeared as *The Television Sherlock Holmes* in 1986. In a similar vein were 1990s *Agatha Christie: Murder in Four Acts* (concentrating on film, radio, television and stage adaptations) and 1995s *On Duty with the Chief* (the making of the Anglia TV series), while *The Television Detectives' Omnibus* (1992) was an assemblage of stories from the authors of such famous small-screen detectives as Albert **Campion**, Inspector **Morse** and Perry Mason.

Anthologies and compendia aside, Haining wrote a number of volumes considering historical **true crimes**, especially those of a gruesome nature. These began with *The Legend of Sawney Bean* (1975) under the alias Ronald Holmes. Other under his own name include *The Legend and Bizarre Crimes of Spring-Heeled Jack* (1977), *The Mystery and Horrible Murders of Sweeney Todd* (1978) and *Buried Passions: The Murder of Maria Marteen* (1980).

In recent times, Haining focused on various aspects of the Second World War in his writings, as well as continuing to indulge his love of horror and the occult (a recent anthology *The Mysterious Novice* (2007) selected several tales of terror from the 'Gothic bluebooks' of the nineteenth century). His home in Boxford, Suffolk, in a former brewery, boasted an extensive library of crime, horror and science-fiction titles. A hugely versatile writer – few could follow a book on Lassie with one on cannibal killers – Haining's role as researcher, compiler and anthologist over the past few decades has been invaluable. At the end of 2007, he met Barry Forshaw, the editor of this volume, to discuss his entries as contributor. The two planned a further meeting in January 2008 – but it was not to be. Haining, apparently in good health, died suddenly before the end of the year.

Selected Works by the Author

Non-fiction
The Art of Mystery and Detective Stories (1977)
The Mystery and Horrible Murders of Sweeney Todd (1978)
James Bond: A Celebration (1987)
Agatha Christie: Murder in Four Acts (1990)
Agatha Christie's Poirot: A Celebration of the Great Detective (1995)
The Classic Era of the American Pulp Magazine (2000)

Edited
The Sherlock Holmes Scrapbook (1974)
The Edgar Allan Poe Scrapbook (1977)
The Final Adventures of Sherlock Holmes (1981)
Murder on the Menu (1991)
The Television Detectives' Omnibus (1992; also published in the United States as *Great Tales of Crime and Detection*, and reissued in the UK as *The Armchair Detectives*, 1993)

Hunted Down: The Detective Stories of Charles Dickens (1996)
London after Midnight (1996)
Death on Wheels (1999)

Mark Campbell

Hale, Hilary (b.1949)

Distinguished publisher's editor and anthologist, former editorial director of the Macmillan crime fiction list and editorial director of the Little, Brown Book Group, Hilary Hale is one of the most significant players in the current British crime field.

Born Hilary Watson, she joined Macmillan in 1969 as a secretary but, tiring of the tedium, went to the *Daily Telegraph Magazine* before being tempted back by George **Hardinge** to help in the development of Macmillan's crime fiction list. She also served as editor of *Winter's Crimes*, alternating with Hardinge from volume 8 (1976) and taking over completely from volume 18 (1986). By then she had married Macmillan's fiction publisher James Hale in January 1983, and the byline Hilary Hale first appeared on volume 16 (1984).

Hale sustained the crime list developed by Hardinge, seasoning it with further names including Alanna Knight (b.1923), Janet **Laurence**, Jill **McGown**, Gwen Moffat (b.1924) and Graham Ison. She likewise kept *Winter's Crimes* on the same course, acquiring new stories by major authors including Peter **Lovesey**, Ellis **Peters**, Ted Willis (1918–1992), Colin **Dexter**, P.D. **James**, Antonia **Fraser**, N.J. Crisp (1923–2005) and Desmond **Bagley**. From volume 18 onwards, she introduced work by Robert **Barnard**, Michael Z. **Lewin**, Haydn Middleton (b.1955) and Ian **Rankin**. In addition to the British crime list, Hale established the American hard-boiled crime list including Sue Grafton, Lawrence Block and Loren Estleman.

In 1990, she moved to Macdonald to create a crime list for their Scribner imprint, which, after the death of Robert Maxwell, eventually re-emerged as Little, Brown. For Scribner, she began *Midwinter Mysteries* which was similar to *Winter's Crimes*, with many of the same contributors, though with new name Mike **Ripley** in volume 1 and Reginald **Hill**, Gillian **Linscott** and Peter **Tremayne** in subsequent volumes. While she brought with her several authors from Macmillan, when establishing the new crime list, including Paula Gosling, Graham Ison, Gillian Linscott and Peter Lovesey, she also soon attracted Christopher **Brookmyre**, Margaret **Yorke**, Frances **Fyfield**, Susanna **Gregory** and Mark **Billingham** and, from America, Patricia Cornwell, Linda Fairstein and Caleb Carr.

Hale is held in high esteem by her authors and is regarded as one of the most influential crime fiction editors who has done much to develop and encourage new writers. She was promoted to editorial director in 1992, and the *Midwinter Mysteries* series ceased owing to her increased responsibilities. Following the death of her husband in 2003, she stepped down from her full-time role to concentrate on her special group of authors but remains publishing representative of the Harrogate Crime Writing Festival and is a member of the General Committee of the Royal Literary Fund.

Edited Works
Winter's Crimes volumes 8, 10, 12, 14, 16, 18–22 (1976–1990)
Midwinter Mysteries volumes 1–5 (1991–1995)

Mike Ashley

Hall, Patricia (b.1957)

Patricia Hall – pseudonym of journalist Maureen O'Connor – sets her gritty crime novels in and around West Yorkshire, her birthplace.

Born in Bradford, West Yorkshire, in 1957, the author was surrounded by books from an early age, her father being a Latin teacher, and later a headmaster, of a nearby grammar school. From the age of thirteen, she knew she was keen on following a journalistic career, and after leaving Bradford Girls' Grammar School, Hall worked at the prestigious *Yorkshire Post* in Leeds. A year later, she reluctantly took up a place at Birmingham University to read English, but spent as much time as possible on the student newspaper, *Redbrick*, which she eventually edited. While there, she met her future husband, John O'Connor, and they moved to London, marrying shortly afterwards.

For sixteen years, the author wrote for and edited the education section of *The Guardian*, a demanding job that took most of her time and energy. In the late 1980s, she decided to try her hand at fiction, and chose the pseudonym 'Patricia Hall', a combination of her middle name and her grandmother's surname, in order to distinguish herself from her journalist alter ego. Her first attempt was swiftly consigned to the bottom drawer, but her second, *The Poison Pool*, was accepted by the first publisher she sent it to, HarperCollins and appeared in 1991.

Set in a small town on the edge of the Yorkshire Dales, *The Poison Pool* featured Inspector Alex Sinclair investigating the death of a local man, Tom Carter, in a mugging incident. But social worker Kate Weston believes the suspected assailant is innocent and, faced with a conspiracy of silence, the couple attempt to eke out the truth behind the seemingly open-and-shut case.

Hall's third book, *Death by Election* (1993), was the first to feature newspaper reporter Laura Ackroyd and Inspector Michael Thackeray; they have appeared in eleven books to date. Set in the fictitious Bradfield, a thinly disguised version of Bradford, the story's blend of political scandal and murder played out against a backdrop of interracial urban tension proved extremely popular. The next Ackroyd and Thackeray story, *Dying Fall* (1994), took place in the equally grim confines of a Bradfield housing estate where joyriding was rife and teenage gang violence the order of the day. Praised for its unflinching depiction of the realities of inner-city life, the book received rave reviews, which convinced O'Connor that she should forego her journalism to concentrate on her new crime-writing career.

Subtitled 'A Yorkshire Mystery' in the United States, the series has since expanded locations to include **London** (*Dead on Arrival*, 1999) and Oxford (*Skeleton at the Feast*, 2000), although each time, the emphasis has been on contemporary social issues.

Now retired from journalism, Hall shares her time between her home in Oxford and her family in Bradford. *See also* Realism and Crime Fiction.

Selected Works by the Author
The Poison Pool (1991)
The Coldness of Killers (1992)
Death by Election (1993)
Dying Fall (1994)
The Italian Girl (1998)
Skeleton at the Feast (2000)
Deep Freeze (2001)

Website
www.patriciahall.co.uk

Mark Campbell

Hamand, Maggie

With her debut novel, *The Resurrection of the Body* (1995), Maggie Hamand established herself as a crime writer of unusually wide-ranging interests.

Hamand was born in London and spent much of her childhood in Hong Kong and Singapore. She is currently a freelance journalist and the author of twelve non-fiction books. In 1994, she won the first World One-Day Novel Cup. Hamand is also the co-founder of Maia Press, an enterprising independent publisher of original fiction by new and established authors. She lives and works in East London.

39. Maggie Hamand.

It is her debut novel, however, an assured piece of work with ambitions beyond the customary remit of the crime novel, which has won her such a reputation. In the past, it was possible to believe in miracles and to lead a life of faith, but for Richard Page, vicar of a poor East End community in a more confused, cynical time, faith does not come in so straightforward a fashion, and the experience he endures during the celebration of Easter proves how fragile his devotion really is. The Good Friday service is shockingly interrupted when a man staggers in, bleeding from wounds inflicted during a vicious knife attack. There is no identification on him, and when he dies, no one comes forward to claim the body. Then on Easter, even more bizarrely, his corpse disappears from the morgue, leaving the police baffled but suspicious. The events which follow are even more disturbing and draw Page into a bruising quest to uncover the man's identity and explain the unexplainable. His obsession will bring him in conflict with the police, his superiors, his congregation and even his wife. As reality slips beyond his control, Page's faith is battered almost beyond endurance. *The Resurrection of the Body* provocatively addresses notions of love, religion and madness within the context of the mystery novel.

The Rocket Man (1995) was a change of pace for Hamand, but equally striking.

Selected Works by the Author
The Resurrection of the Body (1995)
The Rocket Man (1995)

Barry Forshaw

Hamilton, Patrick (1904–1962)

One of the most gifted and successful writers of his generation, Patrick Hamilton was described by J.B. **Priestley** as 'uniquely individual...the novelist of innocence, appallingly vulnerable, and of malevolence, coming out of some mysterious darkness of evil' (Introduction to *Hangover Square*, 1972). His work includes some of the earliest examples of the psychological thriller.

Hamilton worked briefly as an actor in repertory and wrote several plays, including the murder mysteries *Rope* (1929) and *Gaslight* (1939), and the melodrama *The Duke in Darkness* (1943), as well as twelve novels, which include *Hangover Square* (1941) and *The Slaves of Solitude* (1947). He also wrote several mystery plays for radio. Hugely popular in his lifetime, but largely forgotten after his death in 1962, Hamilton's work is once more gaining the recognition it deserves.

Hamilton was born in Hassocks, Sussex, into a family of writers. His mother, Ellen, wrote two romance novels; his sister, Lalla, was heavily involved with the theatre; his brother, Bruce (1900–1974), wrote several legal and murder mysteries; whilst his father, Bernard, a notorious womaniser who squandered a family fortune on drink, wrote several execrable **historical** sagas. He spent most of his childhood in Hove, where the family moved to when he was four, and was educated at a local school, Holland House, and later at Westminster. He left school at fifteen, and after a period of time spent at a commercial school, an army crammer in London and a succession of lodging houses which were to furnish material for his books, his brother-in-law, Sutton Vane, gave him a job in the theatre.

His first novel, *Monday Morning*, written when he was twenty, was published in 1925, and his second, *Craven House*, the following year. Both books deal with the theme of the boarding house, and, to a lesser extent, the pub. These were milieus that Hamilton described more eloquently than any writer of his generation, picturing, in the words of J.B. Priestley, 'a kind of No-Man's-Land of shabby hotels, dingy boarding houses and all those saloon bars where the homeless can meet'. The spectacular success of the thriller play *Rope* (1929, filmed by Alfred Hitchcock in 1948), based on the case of Richard Leopold and Nathan Loeb, two American students who attempt a perfect murder, brought Hamilton fame and financial independence. His 1929 novel, *The Midnight Bell*, the first book in what was to become the **London** pub-and-streets trilogy *Twenty Thousand Streets Under the Sky* (1935), brought critical acclaim. The other titles, *The Siege of Pleasure* (1932) and *The Plains of Cement* (1934) were similarly well received. It was in this series, with its unsentimental portrayal of rootless lives, the sleazy vitality of prostitutes and pub studs, the effects of drink, and self-deluded people who torment and manipulate each other, that Hamilton developed the subjects that he was to make his own. They were reflections of his life: his addiction to alcohol (which caused his death at the age of fifty-eight); his obsession, in 1927, with a prostitute, Lily Connolly (who provided the template for the object of Bob the barman's desire, the capricious tart Jenny Maple, in *The Midnight Bell*). *Twenty Thousand Streets Under the Sky* was filmed by the BBC in 2004.

In 1932, while walking in Earl's Court with his first wife, Lois, Hamilton was hit by a car. The impact broke his arm and leg, and almost ripped off his nose. It left him with extensive facial scarring (all subsequent photographs were heavily touched up) and prevented him from working for almost two years. The trauma of this incident was re-created in *The Siege of Pleasure*, where a drunk driver knocks down a cyclist.

The 1938 play *Gaslight*, a Victorian melodrama about a villain who marries a rich woman and tries to drive her mad in order to get his hands on her money, gave Hamilton another success on the London stage. The play ran for almost three years in America, before being filmed by Thorold Dickinson in 1940 and again by George Cukor in 1944. *Impromptu in Moribundia* (1939), Hamilton's most overtly political novel – he was a Marxist – was also his least successful, both critically and commercially. It was followed in 1941 by his classic murder novel, *Hangover Square* (filmed in 1945 by John Brahms). The protagonist, schizophrenic George Harvey Bone, is infatuated by selfish, worthless Netta Longdon, a failed actress, similar in character to Jenny Maple. Bone, who gets transformed from a passive man into a murderer by the (admittedly rather clumsy) device of a snapping sensation inside his head, is a superb study of an indolent, directionless man who becomes prey to a murderous obsession, and the novel is second only to Malcolm Lowry's *Under The Volcano* (1947) as a study of alcoholism. *Hangover Square* was followed by *The Slaves of Solitude* in 1947, in which Hamilton created Mr Thwaites, his ultimate 'monster-bore'. Like the unreliable tart, the bore, a character based originally on his father and praised by Michael Holroyd as 'that terrible mixture of the banal and the sinister' (Introduction to *The Slaves of Solitude*, 1999), appears in several of Hamilton's novels.

In 1952, the first book in what was to become *The Gorse Trilogy*, entitled *The West Pier*, was published. The first two books in this series are undeniably better than the third, *Unknown Assailant* (1955), which was written when Hamilton's powers were waning and is little more than a padded-out short story. However, the character of the con man Ralph Gorse, is magnificently drawn; this is dark comedy coupled with a pitiful inevitability. Graham **Greene** described *The West Pier* as 'the best book written about Brighton'. The BBC series *The Charmer*, based loosely on these three novels, was aired in 1987.

Throughout his work, Hamilton's handling of suspense is masterly, and his ear for dialogue, grasp of nuance and ability to create atmosphere – the glittering allure of the saloon bar at opening time, the dreary torture of a suburban boarding house or the brass-filled bungalow of a Colonel's window – are beyond compare. *See also* Literature and Crime Fiction.

Selected Works by the Author
Craven House (1926)
Twenty Thousand Streets under the Sky: A London Trilogy (1935), containing *The Midnight Bell* (1929), *The Siege of Pleasure* (1932) and *The Plains of Cement* (1934)
Hangover Square (1941)
The Slaves of Solitude (1947)
The West Pier (1951)

Mr Stimpson and Mr Gorse (1953)
Unknown Assailant (1955)

Further Reading
French, Sean. 1993. *Patrick Hamilton: A Life*. Faber.
Jones, Nigel. 1991. *Through a Glass Darkly*. Little, Brown.
Hamilton, Bruce. 1972. *The Light Went Out: A Biography of Patrick Hamilton*. Constable.

Laura Wilson

Hannah, Sophie (b.1971)

Sophie Hannah writes highly adroit contemporary **thrillers**, set in a fictional UK town, that blend the psychological suspense genre with the police procedural. She is quoted as saying: 'I wanted to combine the direct, visceral appeal of the first-person woman-in-peril narrative with recurring police characters whom readers would get to know better with each book.'

Hannah's detectives are DC Simon Waterhouse, who has never, to his colleagues' knowledge, had a romantic or sexual relationship, and Sergeant Charlotte Zailer, who is mouthy, promiscuous and in love with Waterhouse. Their relationship evolves over the course of the books.

In *Little Face* (2006), Hannah's first crime novel (a debut that effortlessly rose above the plethora of first crime books), a woman claims her newborn has been swapped for another baby, and nobody believes her. *Little Face* was longlisted for the International IMPAC Dublin Literary Award and the Theakston's Old Peculier Crime Novel of the Year Award and described by the Spectator as 'fascinating and original, beautifully written, outstandingly chilling'. Hannah's second thriller, *Hurting Distance* (2007) ('confirms Sophie Hannah as a rivetingly original arrival in crime fiction' – *Sunday Times*), is the story of a woman who, to persuade the police to search for her missing lover with the urgency she feels is required, pretends he is a sadistic psychopath, thinking they will look for him urgently if they believe he is a danger to others. In *The Point of Rescue* (2008), a woman watching the news with her husband hears the name of a man she recently had a fling with, but the face on the screen is not his face, and his wife and daughter have been brutally murdered.

The protagonist of Hannah's fourth crime novel, *The Other Half Lives* (2009), confesses to the murder of a woman who is still alive. Hannah's twisty plots have been described as 'genius' and 'unguessable', and she has declared herself obsessed with unusual plotlines: 'In crime fiction, what I love most is unfathomable mysteriousness – not just "Which of these suspects killed this dead body?", but the sort of mystery that makes readers think, "What can possibly be going on here?" ' The book represented a deepening of Hannah's already considerable psychological acuity.

Hannah is also a best-selling poet. Her collection *Pessimism for Beginners* (2007) was shortlisted for the 2007 T.S. Eliot Prize.

Selected Works by the Author
Little Face (2006)
Hurting Distance (2007)
The Point of Rescue (2008)
The Other Half Lives (2009)

Barry Forshaw

Hardinge, George (1921–1997)

George Hardinge was a publisher's editor noted for his work in developing the Collins crime list and establishing the crime fiction list at Macmillan. He was also instrumental in helping develop the Booker Prize in 1969. On his father's death in 1960, he became the third Lord Hardinge of Penshurst.

Son of the second Lord Hardinge and grandson of Lord Edward Cecil, Hardinge was born on the Balmoral Estate where his father was assistant Private Secretary (later Principal) to King George V. He served in the navy during the Second World War, when he was twice torpedoed. He retired from the navy in 1947 and after a brief but unsuccessful period as a market gardener joined Collins in 1951, where, because of his interest in detective fiction, he was put in charge of their crime list. This was a huge responsibility. The Collins Crime Club had been established in 1930 and included among its many major authors Agatha **Christie**, Ngaio **Marsh**, Mignon G. Eberhart, Miles Burton/John Rhode (1884–1964), G.D.H. & M. Cole and Rex Stout. Hardinge sustained the list, demonstrating a quality that marked his career in publishing and that was never to lose traditional values in the wake of progress. In further developing the Collins crime list in the 1950s and 1960s, Hardinge was able to introduce Julian **Symons**, Nina Bawden (b.1925), Catherine **Aird**, Reginald **Hill**, Patricia Moyes (1923–2000), Ellis **Peters**, Roderic Jeffries (b.1926), Sara Woods (1922–1985) and John **Wainwright**, as well as lure H.R.F. **Keating** away from Gollancz.

Hardinge was not averse to publishing his own work, disguised under the alias George Milner. His first two books, *Stately Homicide* (1953) and *Shark among Herrings* (1954), which feature his impeccable if flamboyant Private Investigator Ronald Anglesea, who betrays some of Hardinge's traits and views, are imbued with a rich and laconic wit. Of Hardinge's other novels, all as Milner, only two are traditional crime novels, *Your Money and Your Life* (1957) and *The Crime against Marcella* (1963), though all are well-plotted **thrillers** with an element of the absurd.

When Hardinge moved to Macmillan in 1968, several authors moved with him, including Ellis Peters, Laurence Meynell (1899–1989) and John Wainwright, but he otherwise had to establish a new crime list from scratch. Previously, only Miles Tripp (1923–2000) had been a regular writer in an otherwise lacklustre list. Hardinge's approach was two-fold. He launched a £1,000 competition for the best first crime novel and began a regular anthology of all-new fiction, *Winter's Crimes*. The winner of the contest was Peter **Lovesey** with *Wobble to Death* which was announced at the same party held to launch *Winter's Crimes* in October 1969.

With a new list to create, Hardinge was prepared to be more experimental than at Collins. From America, he attracted Tony Hillerman, George Baxt and E. Richard Johnson, while from Britain, he published Celia Dale (b.1912) and P.M. **Hubbard**. Hardinge, with his assistants Virginia Whitaker and Hilary Watson, helped develop the sub-genre of historical crime fiction publishing not only Ellis Peters's Brother Cadfael books but also the Bow Street Runner stories by Ben Healey (1908–1988) (writing as Jeremy Sturrock), the LeStrade novels by M.J. **Trow** and the **historical** novels of Gwendoline **Butler** and John Buxton Hilton (1921–1986). Other writers whom Hardinge discovered or developed include Gordon Williams and Terry Venables writing as P.B. **Yuill**, Colin **Dexter** – whose Inspector **Morse** novels began with *Last Bus to Woodstock* (1975) – Jessica **Mann**, Paula Gosling and Gillian

Linscott. He also saw *Winter's Crimes* through seventeen volumes before he retired in 1986, though he left the editing of volume 5 to his assistant Virginia Whitaker and alternate volumes from volume 8 on to Hilary Watson (later Hilary **Hale**). Most of his authors contributed short stories to *Winter's Crimes* making it the one of the most prestigious crime fiction anthologies in the world. He assembled a two-volume *The Best of Winter's Crimes* (1986).

Another of Hardinge's passions was angling, and the book in which he took most pride was his autobiographical *An Incompleat Angler* (1976).

Selected Works by the Author
Stately Homicide (1953)
Shark among Herrings (1954)
The Crime against Marcella (1963)

Edited by George Hardinge
Winter's Crimes volumes 1–4, 6, 7, 9, 11, 13, 15, 17 (1969–1985). The first two volumes were combined as *The Mammoth Book of Modern Crime Stories* (1987).

Mike Ashley

Hare, Cyril (1900–1958)

Cyril Hare's comparatively small body of work captures the spirit of the period often referred to as the **Golden Age** of British crime fiction.

Alfred Alexander Gordon Clark was born in Surrey and educated at Rugby and New College, Oxford. In 1924, following the family tradition, he was called to the bar and he worked mainly in the criminal courts from chambers in Hare Court. This address, together with his home in Cyril Mansions, Battersea, provided Clark with his pseudonym.

In 1950, Hare became a County Court judge, hearing only civil cases, and his link with criminal activities continued only in his fiction. He wrote several sketches and short stories before the publication of his first novel, *Tenant for Death*, in 1937. This investigation into the disappearance of a shady financier – a popular character in crime novels at the time – introduced Inspector Mallett, who was to feature in several more books, including *Death Is No Sportsman* (1938), though his role is not central in *Suicide Excepted* (1939), which is a more accomplished novel than the previous two.

Hare's other regular sleuth, Francis Pettigrew made his debut in *Tragedy at Law* (1942), an acknowledged classic of the genre. Pettigrew, an elderly barrister, joins Mallett to solve a mystery whose solution turns on an obscure legal point. The novel was listed in *The 100 Best Books* (1987) by H.R.F. **Keating**, who called it 'a beautifully unguessable murder story'. Pettigrew is on his own in *With a Bare Bodkin* (1946), notably less for its plot than for its entertaining depiction of wartime bureaucracy – Hare had worked in the Ministry of Economic Warfare – and for Pettigrew's falling in love with his young secretary, whom he eventually marries. He has another solo performance in *The Wind Blows Death* (1949), a clever mystery with a musical background. *An English Murder* (1951) is a traditional country-house whodunit, which Dr Wenceslaus Bottwink, a Czech refugee, investigates, and it was made into a two-part television film in the Soviet Union in 1975. *He Should Have Died Hereafter*

(1957) brings Mallett, now retired, and Pettigrew together for the last time in a skilfully plotted story which was reissued in 1987 as *Untimely Death*.

Mallett is not one of fiction's great detectives, but Hare does not spend a great deal of time on detection. Pettigrew, who is one of those amateurs who stumble upon mysteries, openly admits to not enjoying detective work, but he is an endearing personality, whose passionate dislike of the death penalty was unfashionable at the time. While not all the books are first-rate, they often show the author's dry wit, the characters are sympathetically drawn and the courtroom scenes are particularly well done, as we might expect.

Selected Works by the Author
Tenant for Death (1937)
Suicide Excepted (1939)
Tragedy at Law (1942)
With a Bare Bodkin (1946)
When the Wind Blows (1949; also published in the United States as *The Wind Blows Death*)
An English Murder (1951; also published in the United States as *The Christmas Murder*)
He Should Have Died Hereafter (1958; also published in the United States as *Untimely Death*)

Susanna Yager

Harris, Herbert (1911–1995)

Herbert Harris's contribution to British crime writing is unusual, being confined almost entirely to short stories. At one time, he was the holder of the record as Britain's most prolific writer of short stories.

Harris trained as a journalist, working for the World's Press News from 1929, before turning a freelancer. He served as a press officer during the Second World War and continued in publicity for various organisations, including launching and editing the magazine *Red Herrings* of the **Crime Writers' Association** (CWA) from 1956 to 1965. He also edited the CWA annual anthology *John Creasey's Mystery Bedside Book* from 1966 to 1976 and its successor *John Creasey's Crime Collection* from 1977 to 1989. He was chairman of the CWA from 1969 to 1970.

Harris began writing short stories in the late 1920s. He liked the punch of the ultra-short story of 2,000 words or less and stated that his training as a journalist allowed him to cut all extraneous words and concentrate on the essentials. As a result, his stories can often be read like a synopsis or like the final chapter of a novel with everything summarised for the reader and the denouement delivered. Harris wrote when several daily and evening papers ran short stories as did many weekly papers, so there was no shortage of markets. As a consequence, he was able to write and sell six or seven stories a month. Harris entered the *Guinness Book of Records* in 1969 as the most prolific writer in Britain. By 1975, 3,000 short stories were published in Britain and twenty-eight other countries. Some appeared under the pen names Frank Bury, Michael Moore, Peter Friday or Jerry Regan. Not all his stories were crime fiction, though this remained his favourite field. Such a relentless output consumes ideas, and it was common for Harris to rework the same plot in various ways. For instance, both 'Poison Trail' (1955) and 'A Swig of Strychnine' (1980) use the motif of revealing that the apparent near-victim of poisoning is actually the murderer of a seemingly innocent third party. Most of his stories – many of which are told in the first person by a police inspector's assistant – take the form of a quick overview of a crime and the surprise revelation of some simple clue that the perpetrator overlooked, like fingerprints left on the inside of gloves in 'Concealed Evidence' (1963) or how a murderer forgot that a photograph he had taken of the girl he had killed revealed the evidence needed to convict him in 'Picture of Guilt' (1972).

Harris did not like the dedication needed to complete a novel and only wrote three, two of which were novelisations of the television series *Hawaii Five-O: Serpents in Paradise* (1975) and *The Angry Battalion* (1976). His one solo suspense novel was *Who Kill to Live* (1962).

The ingenuity of Harris's ideas and the shortness of his stories made them ideal one-pagers for newspapers or radio slots, but too many at once become repetitious in their formulaic construction. As a consequence, despite his enormous output, not a single collection of Harris's stories has been compiled, and only a few have been anthologised. He may well be the most prolific but least read of all British crime-fiction writers.

Mike Ashley

Harris, Robert (b.1957)

Robert Dennis Harris was an established non-fiction writer before *Fatherland* (1992) – his debut novel in fiction writing – which imagines what would have happened if Germany had successfully invaded Britain during the Second World War. It became a bestseller with widespread critical acclaim, and he continued to write bestsellers, all of which hit top spot in *The Sunday Times* Bestseller List.

Harris's best-selling fiction – to date he has had no other kind – include *Enigma* (1995), *Archangel* (1998), *Pompeii* (2003) and *Imperium* (2006). His non-fiction works include *A Higher Form of Killing* (1982) – co-authored with his friend Jeremy Paxman – an investigation into chemical and biological warfare; *Gotcha!* (1983), a spotlight on the British Press during the Falklands crisis; and *Selling Hitler* (1996), about the scandal of the fake Hitler diaries. Harris would, in due course, write the official biography of John **le Carré**, which he is authorised to publish after le Carré's death.

Harris was born in Nottingham and grew up there and in neighbouring Leicestershire. He contracted polio as a child and spent much of his childhood in sanatoria, educating himself on Arnold Bennett, Graham **Greene** and John **Buchan**. His father, Dennis Harris, a well-known Leicestershire printer, was what would once have been called a self-taught artisan, intelligent and well-read, the backbone of the labour movement. Upbringing was to have a significant effect on the adult Robert Harris. He says that much of his political writing was influenced by his father and he dedicated his novel *Archangel* to him – since Stalin, the villain of *Archangel*, was the cruel 'father' of the Russian state, this was perhaps an unfortunate book to choose. Harris was educated at King Edward VII School, Melton Mowbray, and then went on to Selwyn College, Cambridge, where he had a BA Honours in English. At Cambridge, he became president of the union and found himself a job with the BBC before he left. A television reporter in his early twenties with *Newsnight* and *Panorama*, he joined *The Observer* as political editor in 1987. He was a columnist for *The Sunday Times* and *The Daily Telegraph* and, in 2003, was named Columnist of the

Year in the annual British Press Awards. He lives in Berkshire with his wife, Gill Hornby (sister of novelist Nick Hornby), and has four children.

Yet Harris had another life, one ingrained in him from childhood, a life in politics and, specifically, the Labour Party. These were the years when the old, tired party went through several transformations before settling on the utterly different if deceptively labelled 'New Labour'. At the 1997 election, Harris flew with Tony Blair in his private aircraft and sat with him in his constituency as results came in. At the time, he was a friend of fellow media specialist Peter Mandelson, who is godfather to one of Harris's daughters. Harris was elected to the Garrick Club, sported double-breasted blazers and cravats and drove around town in a Jaguar convertible. But by the time of the next election, as a writer for *The Daily Telegraph*, he expressed his distaste for the party he had had high hopes for. In *The Sunday Times*, he wrote, 'There is something truly loathsome about the modern Labour Party.... It is a dream come true. It is a nightmare.' The article made it plain that he had put New Labour and politics behind him.

Before his thirtieth birthday, Harris had published several books, all non-fiction, including those mentioned above, and a short biography of Neil Kinnock. As a successful journalist, he had already achieved much that any man might hope for – except for writing a best-selling novel. In his early thirties, he began precisely such a work, a large and imaginative 'alternative history' called *Fatherland*, which took as its concept that Hitler's Germany had won the Second World War. What would have happened to island Britain? Would the stubborn islanders have holed out in their woods and fought an interminable guerrilla war or would they, like Vichy France, have collaborated with the victors? Many Britons at the time thought they had more in common with Germany than France. Perhaps if the war had ended soon enough, there might never have been millions of Jewish deaths in concentration camps. Alternative history is attractive; we look back to imagined forks in the paths of our past lives and wonder, what would have happened if we had taken that other path? *Fatherland* was reputed to have earned Harris four million pounds. *Enigma*, considered by many to be his best novel, followed that first success before a third big hit, *Archangel*.

In 1994, *Fatherland* became a television movie starring Rutger Hauer, Miranda Richardson and Michael Kitchen. Where the audacious concept behind *Fatherland* had been to imagine a world in which Germany won the Second World War and Hitler lived, Harris stayed with the Second World War theme for his second novel *Enigma*. But this time, he created a story around the real-life code-breaking centre at Bletchley Park with its large team of undercover puzzle buffs seeking to crack the Nazi Enigma code. Into this cryptic setting, Harris slipped a further mystery (the girlfriend disappears). His plot became a riddle wrapped in a mystery inside an enigma, and the book was the nearest Harris came to writing a puzzle mystery. In 2001, *Enigma* came out as a film produced by Mick Jagger, written by Tom Stoppard and starring Dougray Scott and Kate Winslet.

Archangel represented another change. Harris spent more than a year researching and shaping the subject matter so it would not only retell an exciting story but explore how past events left a legacy for the present world. Set for the most part in present-day Russia, the story began with a hunt for Stalin's lost diary, a danger-ously tale-telling journal which might expose old men still living. Memory and fear of the dead Stalin – and of his one-time partner in evil, Beria – loom across the narrative, and the hero meets those who warn him that Stalin never dies. His search

takes him to the frozen wooded wilderness of Archangel where he meets not just
a violent and exciting climax but potential nemesis. To write a thriller in which
the villain is already dead is a challenge, but Harris swept it away superbly in an
audacious and haunting end. When the book was first published, Mel Gibson's
company optioned the film rights, but *Archangel* never went into production.
It was filmed as a BBC drama instead.

Pompeii (2003) tells the story of the final hours of the Roman city when it was
obliterated by the famous eruption of Vesuvius in AD 79. In the book, a young
engineer, Marcus Attilius, has promised Pliny that he can solve an unexplained
failure of the great aqueduct. His career depends on solving the problem before public
unrest breaks out. But the man working on the project before has disappeared and
Marcus has come to the notice of a shady self-made millionaire. He has also fallen
for the beautiful Corelia, a love we realise is unlikely to be consummated, because
everything will be swept away when Vesuvius explodes. This, of course, is part of the
challenge Harris set himself: everyone knew the ending of the story, so how could
he keep his readers interested? (It was a challenge met most famously in Thornton
Wilder's *The Bridge of San Luis Rey*.) Harris has said that a news report in *The
Telegraph* in 2000 prompted the idea for *Pompeii*. According to that report, new
research has revealed that rather than everyone in the town dying instantly as had
been supposed, what actually happened was more complex and extended. Harris read
into that a broader political theme with modern parallels, where the Roman water
supply symbolised the empire. 'I was interested in power, and those who seek power,'
he explained. The politics of ancient Rome showed him similarities to the modern-day
superpower America, and it was those parallels which he used to great effect in the
book. To Harris, the luxurious lifestyles around the Bay of Naples in the Roman era
were like present-day Palm Beach or Malibu. Ancient Romans shared with modern-
day Americans the concept of a dynamic society in which people could rise up by their
own efforts. His character Ampliatus, a freed slave who makes his money from shady
property deals, flaunts his wealth with all the ostentation of today's *nouveaux riche*.
Harris discovered that, extraordinarily, many of the richest people in the Roman
empire were freed slaves, and he painted Pompeii as a boom town, trembling with
new money and reconstruction.

By now, ancient Rome had gripped him – as he hoped it would grip his readers –
and in his next book *Imperium*, he turned to the city of Rome itself. Rome was 'a city
of glory built on a river of filth', to which came Marcus Cicero, idealistic and cynical,
proud but insecure. The famous Cicero was by no means, according to Harris, a
charismatic military and sexual conqueror: he had to lose a stutter before he become
'the most famous voice in the world', and Harris presents him as a prudish and
workaholic lawyer, too squeamish even to attend the games. Although the book was
not written as a thriller – it has little sex and no battle scenes – Cicero's story is made
genuinely exciting. Every reader, not merely historians, will enjoy these portraits
of the ancient city and its famous residents: Pompey; the plutocratic Crassus; stern
Cato; Catiline the killer; and Julius Caesar, young and still to grasp what would
become his ultimate office of power – the Imperium.

The book is clearly that of a man who is steeped in politics, for all that Harris
claims to have left politics behind, and critics studied the text eagerly for veiled
portraits of Blair and Mandelson. Their search was in vain – the later *The Ghost*
(2007) explored this territory. In truth, it is not Harris's best book. The prose,
surprisingly, admits lazy clichés which would not have been allowed in earlier books.

But it remains a fine story, worthy to be told, and is the precursor to two more novels to complete the Roman tale. Harris has not written a poor book yet, but the verdict of time seems unlikely to place these Roman novels first. *Enigma* and *Archangel* will take some beating, and *The Ghost* is a political thriller of scabrous, sardonic appeal.

Selected Works by the Author
A Higher Form of Killing (non-fiction, 1982, revised 2002)
Gotcha! (non-fiction, 1983)
Good & Faithful Servant (non-fiction, 1990)
Fatherland (1992)
Enigma (1995)
Selling Hitler (non-fiction, 1996)
Archangel (1998)
The Ghost (2007)

Russell James

Harrod-Eagles, Cynthia (b.1948)

Harrod-Eagles's early reputation was as a writer of historical fiction, but since the early 1990s, she has produced a highly accomplished series of crime novels featuring police detective Bill Slider. Born and raised in London's Shepherd's Bush, she wrote her first novel at the age of ten (it was not published), continued to write in various genres and had her first success with the non-crime novel *The Waiting Game* (1972), winning the Young Writer's Award. In 1979, she began *The Dynasty Series* – not related to the television drama, but a family saga spanning British history from the Middle Ages and running to over thirty volumes. Not until 1991 did her first Bill Slider novel – *Orchestrated Death* – appear.

When we first encounter Slider, he seems a middle-aged cop going nowhere, on a case involving a naked female corpse, a Stradivarius and an oversize can of olive oil. The victim has the letter 'T' carved into her toe, but Slider decodes a more significant clue: the callus on her neck shows that she played the violin. Nevertheless, he is not acute enough to avoid a romantic entanglement with a suspect. The second in the series, *Death Watch* (1992), sees Slider entangled again – in red tape and government guidelines – and in the third, *Necrochip* (1993), Harrod-Eagles places her protagonist beneath the last man he would choose to have as boss. This time, however, it seems his boss may bear investigation as much as does the case, a seedy little murder with a body dismembered in a chip shop – in flagrant contradiction of hygiene regulations. Harrod-Eagles's wry humour permeates all her Slider stories, but the books impress with sharp pace, expert plotting and clever resolutions. Few of her characters are walk-ons.

Harrod-Eagles returned to classical musicians in *Dead End* (1994), with a conductor shot dead in a church. No one liked the victim, and in this book, no one much likes anyone. Slider certainly does not like his boss. In *Blood Lines* (1996), a music critic seems to have killed himself – and if Slider seems too often involved in musical cases, it is because thus far into the series he has become romantically involved with a violinist. It is not a harmonious case for Slider, and we are reminded that, amusing as she can be, Harrod-Eagles is no mere cosy writer. She can deliver violence. *Killing Time* (1996) takes Slider out of the music world into one of poison-pen letters, table-dancers, prostitutes, pimps and cabinet ministers. *Shallow Grave*

(1998) plunges him into the rough terrain of the building trade, with his personal life almost reduced to rubble. In *Blood Sinister* (1999), the obligatory corpse is of a journalist – one loathed by Slider's colleagues because of her attacks on them in print. *Gone Tomorrow* (2001) introduces a crime baron behind a stew of debts, drugs and dodgy deals, while in *Dear Departed* (2004), Slider investigates the case of a young woman stabbed to death while jogging in a west London park. She was richer than she ought to be, not that it helped. The Slider series is a highly accomplished one, probably improved by Harrod-Eagles being equally adept in other genres. When she is playing at crime, she plays to win.

Selected Works by the Author
Necrochip (1993)
The Bill Slider Omnibus (1998)

Russell James

Harvey, John (b.1938)

John Harvey is one of the most popular and accomplished British crime novelists working in the field. He is equally successful in France: *Le Monde* called him, 'one of the leading writers of crime fiction alive today'. For his excellent body of work, Harvey was awarded the **Crime Writers' Association** (CWA) Diamond Dagger in 2007.

40. John Harvey.

Harvey was a teacher for twelve years before jumping ship and turning full-time writer, producing at first (among much bread-and-butter work in various popular genres) a series of short **pulp**-fiction works. Among them was a quartet of novels featuring an English private investigator, Scott Mitchell. It was his first attempt at British noir.

Harvey returned to university to obtain a degree in American Studies and then became a part-time lecturer in film and **literature** at Nottingham University. It was here that he began his love affair with the city and created the first of his critically acclaimed Resnick novels, *Lonely Hearts* (1989). This has been named by *The Times* as one of the 'Hundred Best Crime Novels of the Last Century'. The second novel in the sequence, *Rough Treatment* (1990) was shortlisted for the CWA Gold and Silver Daggers, and the tenth and final entry in the series, *Last Rites* (1998) won the first-ever Sherlock Award for best detective created by a British author. Resnick, a detective with the Nottingham force, is part Polish, part English and lives alone, while trying to come to terms with his wife having left him. He is a melancholic soul who combines the wayward independence of a Marlowe, while operating from the official position of a Wexford. These are dark novels featuring a damaged soul who has to investigate the most depressing of crimes in what appears to be a crumbling city: child abuse, rape, prostitution and vicious murders. He is a wonderfully realised character and is as much an attraction of these books as is the mysteries he investigates.

Besides being a novelist, Harvey is a scriptwriter and poet. In 1992, his screenplay for *Resnick: Lonely Hearts* won a bronze medal in the Best TV Drama Series section at The New York Festivals.

More recently, Harvey completed a trio of novels featuring retired policeman Frank Elder. The first novel, *Flesh and Blood*, won the CWA Silver Dagger and the Barry Award in the States for Best Crime Novel of 2004. Elder is another loner with baggage who is reluctantly drawn back into the world of police work by his personal connections with the mysteries that need to be unravelled.

Harvey then produced a novel set in Cambridgeshire and the surrounding Fens and, once again, the familiar landscape of Nottinghamshire. *Gone to Ground* (2007) features Detective Inspector Will Graham and Detective Sergeant Helen Walker, who first saw the light of day in the short story, 'Snow, Snow, Snow' (2005). Their investigation into the murder of Stephen Bryan, a film historian and academic, sees them caught up in a morass of corrupt business practices, family secrets and 1950s film noir. But 2008 had Harvey fans celebrating the return of Resnick in *Cold in Hand*. Of this novel, Barry Forshaw wrote in *The Independent*: 'As in so much of the best crime fiction, what we have here is basically a state of the nation novel, and Harvey repeatedly suggests that his own vision may have become as nihilistic as that of the sociopathic characters that populate *Cold in Hand*. But this is no hand-wringing tract – the book is quite possibly Harvey's most authoritative in years: visceral, engaged and, yes, unputdownable.'

Selected Works by the Author
Lonely Hearts (1989)
Rough Treatment (1990)
Cutting Edge (1991)
Cold Light (1994)
Living Proof (1995)
Easy Meat (1996)
Flesh and Blood (2004)
Ash and Bone (2005)
Darkness and Light (2006)
Gone to Ground (2007)
Cold in Hand (2008)

David Stuart Davies

Haslam, Chris (b.1965)

Chris Haslam is the author of a number of highly distinctive, blackly comic crime novels.

One of the quirkiest talents in current British crime writing, Haslam cites a childhood spent in rural isolation with no television as the probable cause of his twin desires to write and to see the world. After an adolescence spent slipping out of school for illicit jaunts across Europe, he travelled further afield after graduation, paying his way through unusual occupations, including pipe laying in Africa, working as a scrap metal broker in Laos, selling bibles in Sicily, teaching weapon handling in Alabama and volunteering in El Salvador.

41. Chris Haslam.

His first novel, *Twelve Step Fandango* (2003), was a jet-black literary crime thriller set among the drug dealers of Spain's Costa Del Sol. Described as 'a classy debut caper' by the *Daily Mail*, it introduced Haslam's comic anti-hero Martin Brock and was shortlisted for the Edgar Award.

Brock reappeared in Haslam's second book, *Alligator Strip* (2005), a tale of grifters working the coin fairs of Florida on a 'sure-fire' plan to scam six million in six months. Described as 'a seriously funny, truly engrossing thriller' by *The Guardian*, it earned him the accolade of 'the nearest thing Britain has to Carl Hiaasen'.

El Sid (2006) marked a departure from the first-person picaresque of the Brock adventures and a return to Spain, the land Haslam clearly loves best. Seamlessly switching between the 1930s and the present-day El Sid chronicles, it was a tragic-comic quixotic quest by an aged veteran of the Spanish Civil War and his two ne'er-do-well sidekicks for seven tons of Republican gold stolen and lost in 1938. Described as 'a rare and wonderful book' by the *Irish Examiner*, it was chosen by *The Independent* as Crime Book of the Year.

On crime writing, Haslam has said 'plots are like statements and readers are like prosecutors, so if your story isn't absolutely watertight they'll get you bang to rights'. *See also* Humour and Crime Fiction.

Selected Works by the Author
Twelve Step Fandango (2003)
Alligator Strip (2005)
El Sid (2006)

Barry Forshaw

Hayder, Mo (b.1962)

Mo Hayder exploded onto the crime-writing scene on 2001 New Year's Day with *Birdman*, a grittily realistic first novel of gruesome serial killings in south-east London, remarkable first and foremost for its vividly evoked milieu.

42. Mo Hayder.

Hayder has since developed into one of Britain's most adroit commercial exponents of the grisly crime novel, testing the strengths of her readers' stomachs with gruesome descriptions of atrocities not just produced by her vivid imagination but plucked from the litany of war crimes.

Hayder, Mo

Lacking much formal education in her early years, Hayder has literally profited from the clichéd 'university of life': she left school at fifteen and worked as a barmaid, security guard and hostess in a Tokyo club – all those experiences are reflected in her writing – before taking an MA in film from The American University in Washington and MA in creative writing from Bath Spa University.

It might have been a canny move on Hayder's part, given the millennial timing of *Birdman*'s publication, to have her first corpse discovered on wasteland close to the Millennium Dome. But it was her skill at recreating the seedy pubs, clubs and back streets of East Greenwich on the cusp of much-needed regeneration that brought the novel to life.

Her lead character, Detective Inspector Jack Caffery, was vividly portrayed as a rounded, flawed character with a troubled past, revealed more deeply in her second novel *The Treatment* (2002), which similarly centred around the streets of South **London**.

The Treatment scored highly by building strongly on Caffery's troubled psychology while maintaining a remarkable feel for the grim realism of life in some of the bleaker parts of British cites. However, its central issue, child abuse, confirmed a tendency, which has become a trademark of Hayder's writing, to flirt with the darker side of human **sexuality**. The serial killer's motive in *Birdman* was also sexual.

Her third novel *Tokyo* (2004), shortlisted for three **Crime Writers' Association** Dagger Awards, was a radical change in location, although it once again confirmed, controversially, Hayder's obsession with the darkest elements in human nature. The lead character is a young female British film-maker, Grey who has an unhealthy obsession with a piece of footage taken during the bloody Japanese 'Rape of Nanking' in 1937, allegedly showing a baby ripped live from its mother's womb. Her attempts to find it lead her to become a hostess in a Tokyo nightclub which introduces her to a geriatric gangster allegedly kept healthy by a gruesome 'elixir of life' but not before we have plunged the dark depths of her own obsession. A trenchant and powerful novel, it was definitely not for the squeamish.

Pig Island (2006) saw Hayder return (almost) to UK shores with a story of a mysterious religious cult living on a remote Scottish island and allegedly dabbling in diabolical practices. Her hero is a sceptical hard-nosed journalist determined to find the truth behind the disappearance of his charismatic leader.

Ritual (2008) is one of her most uncompromising (and most sheerly compelling) novels in a career notable for its audacity.

Like her work or loathe it, Hayder has taken a strong female grip on a particularly bleak sub-genre of the crime novel, verging on horror, and made it very much her own. *See also* Women Crime Writers.

Selected Works by the Author
Birdman (2001)
The Treatment (2002)
Tokyo (2004; also published in the United States as *The Devil of Nanking*)
Pig Island (2006)
Ritual (2008)

Website
www.mohayder.net

Peter Millar

Hazell (television series, 1978–1980)

'Down these mean streets a man must go' is Raymond **Chandler**'s famous dictum for his hero, private detective Philip Marlowe. But it might just as well apply to James 'Jimmy' Hazell. However, in the latter's case, the streets are not in Los Angeles but in **London**. Adapted from the novels jointly written by Gordon Williams and Terry Venables (best known for his sports connection) under the pseudonym P.B. **Yuill**, Thames Television made twenty-two one-hour (less advertisement breaks) episodes between 1978 and 1980, starring Nicholas Ball as Hazell, Roddy McMillan as 'Choc' Minty (his policeman nemesis) and Desmond McNamara as Cousin Tell (his ever-present accomplice), plus the usual cast of character actors who seemed to materialise in every drama series of the period, including *The Sweeney* (whose time slot in the schedules *Hazell* filled admirably). Overseen by Verity Lambert, head of drama at Thames, and a mover and shaker of the period, the series was written by some of the strong dramatists who worked in popular drama at that time, such as Tony Hoare and Trevor Preston. Great things were expected of the series, which never seemed to realise its full potential. But viewed today, the episodes have a wonderful, quirky take on the days before mobiles, the Internet and global warming.

Invalided out of the Met due to a troublesome ankle, and recently divorced because of a love of the bottle, tab-collared and shiny-suited Hazell sets up a shop in a seedy office where he offers his services as a cockney-style private eye. Complete with deadpan voice-overs, Nicholas Ball was magnificent as the weary loser shadowed by his police contact Minty, who often used him as a patsy when officialdom was thwarted. Their constant bickering was presented as a marriage of opposites who stayed together more out of habit than love, although the detective's use of a Triumph Stag as a vehicle in which to work undercover, often meant 'Cousin Tell' appropriating a more non-descript vehicle. Sadly, the locations of London were few and far between, most of the series being studio bound.

Violent for the time, *Hazell* was cancelled early. The first series has been made available on DVD, although the sudden jumps from tape to film and back again (a distinguishing mark of filming in that period) can be disconcerting. The second series, although advertised, has never appeared.

Crime-writer Mark **Timlin** is quoted as saying: 'Without Hazell there would have been no Nick Sharman'. In fact, on closer examination, the comparison with Timlin's London private eye seems more like daylight robbery than a *homage*. Perhaps, Timlin was remembering the maxim 'Talent borrows, genius steals'. Subsequently, Nicholas Ball never seemed to enjoy the successful post-Hazell career that many felt he deserved, but the television work still came regularly, even though the actor was rather more rotund than in the days of *Hazell*. *See also* TV Detectives: Small-Screen Adaptations.

Brian Ritterspak

Heald, Tim (b.1944)

Simon Bognor, the invention of Tim **Heald**, is no James Bond or Lord Peter **Wimsey**. Bognor – journalist, speaker, editor of anthologies and prolific author of novels, short stories and non-fiction – appears as anti-hero in ten satirical novels. After graduating in Oxford, he inadvertently becomes a civil servant in the Special Operations Department of the Board of Trade. Mostly, he works with codes and ciphers but also has to investigate aspects of trade and industry. Bodies appear wherever he goes, making him wonder if he is the Angel of Death.

Unlike Wimsey, Albert **Campion** and other heroes, Bognor is overweight, unfit and not very attractive, largely due to a high-cholesterol diet, sloth and gin. His investigative approach is 'highly intuitive and unorthodox', as he bumbles from hunch to hunch. The biggest cross he has to bear is his unsympathetic and dismissive boss, Parkinson. Monica, his girl friend (later his wife) often agrees with Parkinson but is mostly loyal and supportive. Bognor concedes that she is cleverer than he is. His relationships with both are often funny. So, too, are the attempts to seduce him by attractive young women. Frequently, he encounters hazards which would be no problem to Bond. Apart from receiving frequent blows to the head, he is shot at, chased by a herd of bison, trapped in a lift likely to plummet to the ground at speed, locked in a cold store at freezing point and has to swim across a lake pursued by ravenous dogs.

Heald has fun with the backgrounds to these adventures – satirising modern institutions, manners and customs. Even the honey export business of a Friary is a cover for sinister activity. Disputes and disagreements cause havoc in the stately home industry, as they do in the gossip column of a national newspaper. Amazing things happen in the worlds of dog breeding, *haute cuisine* and book production. Murder and international **espionage** are not uncommon. Even Bognor's Oxford college is not exempt. In Canada, the death of an international businessman starts him on another trail of murder and mayhem. His last two cases, back in England, portray a small town riddled with corruption and an idyllic village seething with crime. Murder methods and motives are often ingenious, with plentiful red herrings. Improbable situations and characters add to the comedy. Bognor gets the right answer, even if Monica and Parkinson have to rescue him at the last moment. After nearly twenty years, he reappeared in a short story as Sir Simon, head of his department, but otherwise little changed.

In 2004, Heald published the first of a new series, concerning Dr Tudor Cornwall, head of the Criminal Studies Department at Wessex University. In two novels and a short story (published in *Ellery Queen's Mystery Magazine*), Cornwall's study of real and fictional crime enables him to solve the mysteries of two deaths and a kidnapping. Again, Heald has used his background and experiences to create amusing characters and intriguing plots laced with gentle satire.

Selected Works by the Author

Unbecoming Habits (1973)
Deadline (1975)
Just Desserts (1977)
Masterstroke (1982; also published in the United States as *A Small Masterpiece*)
Brought to Book (1985)
Death and the D'Urbervilles (2005)
'Bearded Wonders' (short story, 2006) in *The Verdict of Us All*, edited by Peter Lovesey

Christine Simpson

Hebden, Mark (1916–1991)

Mark Hebden was the pseudonym of John Harris, the author of sixteen highly efficient **police procedurals** set in France featuring Chief Inspector Evariste Clovis Desire Pel.

Born in Rotherham, Hebden attended Rotherham Grammar School. He also wrote a number of books under the name of Max Hennessy and John Harris. He held a number of different jobs including that of an airman and a journalist. During the Second World War, he served in two air forces and two navies.

The first book in the series, *Pel and the Faceless Corpse* (1979), introduced readers to the irascible, quirky Burgundian Inspector of Police. When an unidentified and faceless corpse is discovered near a memorial dedicated to villagers killed by Nazis, it is up to Pel to discover its true identity. His investigations take him from Burgundy to the borders of France. The book also introduced readers into a number of other characters who go on to play significant roles in the series – initially, the canny Sergeant Darcy and the shy but resourceful Sergeant Nosjean and, later on, the delightfully handsome Sergeant Misset and the aristocratic De Troquereau. Pel's home life is also not easy one especially with the constant troubles that he has with his difficult and tyrannical cook. This relationship is an added bonus to the series.

In *Pel and the Bombers* (1983), five murders on Bastille night, a terrorist group at work and a State visit by the President means that Pel has his work cut out.

By the eighth book in the series, *Pel and the Predators* (1984), Pel has been promoted to Chief Inspector and is occupied by a number of murders that have taken place in his beloved Burgundy; he has also been sent a letter bomb. The two events soon threaten his plans to marry his long-suffering girl friend Mme Genevieve Faivre-Perret.

The books in this series are classic police procedurals, which follow Pel as he pursues the criminals of Burgundy. Pel is an unusual character for a police officer. He is clever, testy, crotchety, chain-smoking and has a distinct lack of respect for authority. He has a loyal cadre of officers working for him despite his rather lamentable behaviour. Hebden has created a likeable group of people, and in each book, he reveals a bit more of their private lives and the politics of a provincial French town.

The dialogue is spare and Hebden's dry humour is one of the things that make this series such an enjoyable one, which is entertaining to read, timeless and a must for readers who enjoy classic police procedurals with a hint of Gallic charm. Following his death, his daughter, writing as Juliet Hebden, went on to write eight more books in the series.

Selected Works by the Author
Pel and the Faceless Corpse (1979)
Pel under Pressure (1980)
Pel and the Staghound (1982)
Pel and the Pirates (1984)
Pel among the Pueblos (1987)
Pel and the Picture of Innocence (1988)
Pel and the Missing Persons (1990)
Pel and the Sepulchre Job (1992)

Ayo Onatade

Hell Drivers (film, 1957)

Cy Endfield, director

'Roaring Down the World's Deadliest Roads!' *Hell Drivers* is a rare British crime/
action movie with a lorry-driving theme (and an acknowledged influence on several
British crime writers), directed and co-written by American exile Cy Endfield (fleeing
the Hollywood blacklist). It offers Stanley Baker, then Britain's leading hard man
star, and once-in-a-lifetime cast of future cult personalities and favourite British film
faces. The ensemble includes the original Doctor Who (William Hartnell), the first
James Bond (Sean Connery), the Prisoner (Patrick McGoohan), a Man from UNCLE
(David McCallum), a Professional (Gordon Jackson), a Carry On star (Sid James) and
Clouseau's boss (Herbert Lom), plus Alfie Bass, the excellent Peggy Cummins (in
a run of cult greats from *Gun Crazy* to *Night of the Demon*), the inimitably befuddled
Wilfred Lawson, sylph-like Jill Ireland and you've-seen-them-a-hundred-times faces
Wensley Pithey, George Murcell, Robin Bailey, Vera Day and Marianne Stone. Just
out of prison, Tom Yateley (Baker) pitches up at a dodgy firm and joins a motley crew
of brawlers who rush loads of gravel ('ballast') dangerously fast through winding
English roads. Red (McGoohan), the brutal foreman, is a 'pace-setter', offering
a gold cigarette case to anyone who can beat his daily record of eighteen runs but
using every trick to make sure no one does. He works a scam with the sneaky boss
(Hartnell) to keep the undermanned crew working at a murderously dangerous rate
while pocketing money that should be going to extra drivers. Trying to keep his nose
clean to avoid going back to prison, Tom stays out of a fight between the drivers and
the local lads at a rowdy dance and gets ostracised in the workplace, with more and
more dangerous pranks played to hinder his bid to break Red's record. Lom overdoes
his role as the sentimental, religious Italian obviously doomed to become a plot
sacrifice, but the rest of the hairy-knuckled blokes are spot on: Connery and James
make a surprisingly good double-act (forking water into Baker's glass); a thickly
Irish-accented McGoohan is memorably vicious as the psychopath who quaffs
Guinness from the bottle at the wheel and always has a half-smoked cigarette gripped
in his teeth (even throughout a fist-fight, though he finally loses the gasper as his
truck goes over a precipice); and Cummins is a rare well-spoken British 1950s leading
lady with onscreen sex appeal (she is introduced with an ogling shot of her bottom
in tight jeans). It offers the blazing excitement and the working-class grit of the best
American hardboiled thrillers (cf. *Thieves Highway*) along with some of the absurdism
of artier foreign films (cf. *La Salaire de la Peur*), as the trucks bomb back and forth
to perform an essentially absurd, repetitive task shifting endless unromantic loads
of grit from one site to another ten miles away. Endfield, who would stick with Baker
for bigger pictures (most memorably *Zulu*), casts a foreign eye on Britain and pits
an unfamiliar but convincing milieu on screen: pull-in cafes, village dances, works
huts, backstreet newsagents, rowdy boarding houses, battered lorries, rural lay-bys
and desolate quarries.

Kim Newman

Hell Is a City (film, 1960)

Val Guest, director

Adapted by writer-director Val Guest from a novel by Maurice Procter, this tough British crime picture makes excellent, distinctive use of Manchester as a backdrop. It was made at a particular point (1959) in the history of Hammer Films when the studio scion Michael Carreras thought their success in revitalising the gothic horror genre ought to prompt them to give the 'Hammer treatment' to other genres, including the war movie (*Yesterday's Enemy*) and the swashbuckler (*Pirates of Blood River*). *Hell Is a City* was their stab at serious police drama, far more ambitious than the tatty B mysteries they had shovelled out before hitting big with *The Curse of Frankenstein*. It is significantly darker than *The Blue Lamp* (1949), showing a policeman not as a saintly martyr or kindly uncle but a driven, haunted noir figure torn between tedious respectability and the violent underworld. Stanley Baker, the leading hard man of British cinema, is Inspector Harry Martineau, who flees from his loveless suburban home and frigid shrew of a wife (Maxine Audley) to spend as much time as possible on the job, or down at the pub, where he is repeatedly at the receiving end of come-ons from blowsy barmaid 'Lucky' Lusk (Vanda Godsell). The plot motor is the jailbreak of armed robber Don Starling (imported Yank thug John Crawford), a vicious nutcase who is no sooner in town than he has coerced lesser felons into a daylight raid which leaves a nineteen-year-old girl clerk dead and prompts a citywide manhunt. Martineau and Starling shake up everyone they come across, and the film works in smart little portraits of fringe figures, with bookmaker Donald Pleasence robbed and cuckolded by the gangster; Billie Whitelaw as his slutty trophy wife; and a gallery of familiar British film faces as villains and victims (Joseph Tomelty, Warren Mitchell, Peter Madden, George A. Cooper, Dickie Owen, Joby Blanshard and Marianne Stone). Manchester remains an underfilmed city and was practically virgin territory then – Guest hares all over town with his characters, making a trip out onto the misty moors to break up an illegal shove ha'penny meet. Few of the accents are broad Mancunian, because Hammer Films wanted an overseas market which resisted allegedly incomprehensible dialogue – but everyone is just about credible for the region. As often in docu-crime movies, part of the fascination is the everyday clothes, slang, manners and milieux: we visit pubs and snooker halls, while the contrasted stay-at-home and out-to-party wives inhabit supposedly aspirational homes which offer less comfort than the cluttered demi-monde of copper and crook. A touch unique to Britain and the period is that the final rooftop shoot-out ends not with Starling falling to his death but arrested and taken off to be tried, convicted and hanged. The final scene shows a copper's uncomfortable feeling on the day a felon he has brought in goes to the gallows, and Baker brilliantly plays a strange spasm of sympathy ('well, nobody's perfect, you know') for the man he has spent the whole film obsessively tracking down.

Kim Newman

Henderson, Lauren (b.1966)

Though Lauren Henderson's novels have the structure of crime fiction from the **Golden Age** of the 1920s and 1930s, they very much reflect the culture and society of the 1990s, the decade in which they were written. With the wit of a modern-day Dorothy Parker, and a liking for recreational drugs and casual sex, her heroine Sam Jones is more Ms than Miss Marple.

43. Lauren Henderson.

After obtaining a BA degree in English literature from Cambridge, London-born Henderson worked for a variety of publications such as *The Observer*, *Marxism Today!* and the 'indie' music magazine *Lime Lizard*. After the latter two folded, she decided to move to Italy and try her hand at fiction. An avid reader of crime fiction, the aspiring writer felt the genre would allow her to write about the role of women in society in a light-hearted way. Though Henderson found the contemporary female sleuths she encountered strong and independent women, she disliked many of them for being copies of their male counterparts, or negative and deliberately self-pitying. Sam Jones would be happy and successful, and though she is initially single, she has friends and is not alone. The books reflect the lifestyle of the author's social circle and are largely based in **London**. (Notable exceptions are *The Strawberry Tattoo*, 1999, and *Pretty Boy*, 2001, where Sam enters the New York art scene and the English countryside, respectively.) Instead of being a struggling journalist like her creator, Sam would be a sculptress on the brink of success. This would allow her to be comfortable both partying in squats and attending receptions in exclusive galleries. Another practical reason for Sam to be an artist was the physicality of being a sculptress: the required strength, together with her cunning, made it realistic for her to successfully defend herself in a fight. Encountering murder and mayhem wherever she goes, Sam begins as a struggling artist in *Dead White Female* (1995) and supplements her income by working part-time as a gym instructor in *Too Many Blondes* (1996). Following her first major artistic success in *The Black Rubber Dress* (1997) – one of her sculptures is unveiled in the vast atrium of a City bank – Sam is plunged into the world of theatre in *Freeze My Margarita* (1998). Commissioned to create a series of mobiles for a play, she finds love in the form of Hugo, an actor with a Lord Peter **Wimsey** drawl, only to be kidnapped as he is shooting a television series in *Chained!*

After *Pretty Boy* (2001), Henderson turned away from the crime genre, instead writing a succession of highly successful 'chick-lit' novels as well as best-selling non-fiction titles such as *Jane Austen's Guide to Romance: The Regency Rules* (2005). She briefly returned to crime fiction, writing a short story for *Tart Noir* (2002), an anthology she edited with Stella **Duffy**. Though no further Sam Jones escapades are scheduled for the foreseeable future, Lauren **Henderson** does plan to return to crime fiction. *See also* Sexuality in British Crime Fiction, Tart Noir *and* Women Crime Writers.

Selected Works by the Author
Dead White Female (1995)
Too Many Blondes (1996)
The Black Rubber Dress (1997)
Freeze My Margarita (1998)
The Strawberry Tattoo (1999)
Chained! (2000)
Pretty Boy (2001)

Adrian Muller

Hewson, David (b.1953)

Much of the background for Hewson's Italian crime novels comes from his having been a travel writer and journalist for *The Times*. Among other novels, he has written the Nic Costa series, Costa being a maverick cop in Rome whose tenure in the force becomes shakier with each new escapade.

Though the books read as if Hewson were an Italian writer translated, he was in fact born in Yorkshire and now lives in Kent. He joined *The Times* in 1978 and is now a weekly columnist for the *Sunday Times*. He began writing thrillers in the mid-1990s and had his first, *Epiphany*, published in 1996. Four more thrillers followed before the first Nic Costa, *A Season for the Dead*, appeared in 2003. This dark and complex opener rammed the troubled cop through the mangle to such an extent that he ought to have left the force for good – except for a little teaser at the end, inserted perhaps to turn a stand-alone into a series. Without this scene, the story was of an initially idealistic cop soured when confronted with an excess of corruption within the forces of supposed good. It opens with a serial killer whose imaginative approach to slaughter recreates the martyrdom of saints. Soon it becomes clear that there is more to these grisly episodes than the solitary amusement of a madman. The Mafia and the Vatican are bedfellows, the female love interest seems a cold-hearted whore and absolutely no one can be trusted. What seems a simple story becomes increasingly dark and matted – perhaps too complex to be believed. Yet, when one looks back, the whole astonishing conspiracy hangs together.

In *Villa of Mysteries* (2004), a girl is found in a peat bog outside Rome with her throat cut. She wears a ceremonial dress and has a coin inside her mouth – to ease her passage to the next world? But as she has been dead for eighteen years and no one knows of a similar case, there seems no need to hurry the investigation. Except, bizarrely, her death might be linked to the recent abduction of another girl: one with the same tattoo, the same blonde hair and a powerful mother raising hell. *The Sacred Cut* (2006) is set in the Christmas after the second Gulf War, again in Rome, and is permeated by the clamour around Iraq and the fallout it caused, sometimes among friends.

Hewson's modern Roman cops are as richly disparate as in any longer-running series and the atmosphere is as densely layered as cold lasagne. He writes well, and the Rome he describes is a venous and breathing city – if not the one you recognise as a tourist. His characters are individuals, freshly drawn, and his Rome, cops, bureaucrats and criminals shine hard and clear as sunlight bouncing off the Trevi fountain.

Selected Works by the Author
A Season for the Dead (2003)
The Villa of Mysteries (2004)
The Sacred Cut (2006)
The Seventh Sacrament (2007)
The Promised Land (2007)
Garden of Evil (2008)

Russell James

Heyer, Georgette (1902–1974)

Better known for her historical romances, Georgette Heyer also wrote mysteries. In her twelve detective novels, she took the traditional English murder mystery, shifted its emphasis away from an intellectual puzzle and turned it into a series of sharply observed drawing-room comedies.

Heyer's focus is usually on the effects of murder upon a largely dysfunctional family group. She explores this theme through witty dialogue and unforgettable characterisation. The murder itself sometimes takes place before the story even opens, and the police investigation is largely peripheral. This theme reaches its climax in the powerful *Penhallow* (1942), an uncharacteristically dark and brooding story in which the reader knows who murdered the tyrannical Adam Penhallow, but the characters remain in ignorance.

The shy, retiring Heyer will forever be associated with the Regency Romance, a sub-genre of romantic fiction that she created in forty five novels. Romantic entanglements, with the outspokenly rude male character usually assuming the role of amateur detective, figure largely in her crime stories. This rudeness acts as a mask for a keen intelligence and as a counterpoint to the polite social hypocrisy of the other characters, puncturing their pretensions to good comic effect. The best of the early books is *The Unfinished Clue* (1934), which has a least likely culprit and one of Heyer's finest comic creations – the flamboyant Lola de Silva. With an increasingly mature style, these elements are played down in favour of an official police investigation.

With her fourth novel, *Death in the Stocks* (1935), Heyer introduces her series detectives Superintendent Hannasyde and Sergeant, later Inspector and then Chief Inspector, Hemingway. This is a good example of Heyer's ability to capture her readers in the first few pages with a dramatic opening: a moonlit night, a village green and a corpse in the stocks. Although Hannasyde is the nominal detective, these are transitional novels; in the first three of the four Hannasyde books, it is the amateur sleuth, who is one of the suspects, who cracks the case. Only in his last story, the excellent *A Blunt Instrument* (1938), does the superintendent catch his man through his own efforts.

The irreverent Hemingway, with his interest in psychology and his self-proclaimed flair, firmly takes centre stage with *No Wind of Blame* (1939), a story centring on a remote method of murder. *Envious Casca* (1941) is a locked-room mystery set at a Christmas gathering. *Duplicate Death* (1951) involves a garrotting at a bridge party, and *Detection Unlimited* (1953) is a full-blown English village murder mystery in which every inhabitant of the village has their own theory about whodunit.

Heyer's novels, particularly the early ones, demonstrate that the puzzle need not be the main focus in a traditional English mystery and that the story can be carried by character and dialogue.

Selected Works by the Author
The Unfinished Clue (1934)
Death in the Stocks (1935; also published in the United States as *Merely Murder*)
A Blunt Instrument (1938)
No Wind of Blame (1939)
Penhallow (1942)
Detection Unlimited (1953)

Further Reading
Hodge, Jane Aiken. 1984. *The Private World of Georgette Heyer*. Bodley Head.

Nick Kimber

Higgins, Jack (b.1929)

Jack Higgins is the pseudonym of the prolific thriller writer Harry Patterson, one of several he has used over the course of a long and highly successful career.

Born in Newcastle on 17 July 1929, Patterson was brought up in Belfast, Northern Ireland, during a time of religious and political upheaval. After leaving Leeds Training College, he served for two years as an NCO in the Household Cavalry on the East German border. Graduating from the University of London with a degree in sociology, he turned to teaching, during which time he wrote his first novel, *Sad Wind from the Sea*, in 1959.

A series of brisk, workaday thrillers followed, written under various aliases – James Graham, Hugh Marlowe and Martin Fallon – until he struck gold in 1975 with *The Eagle Has Landed*, under his Jack Higgins pseudonym. Based partly on fact, it told the seemingly far-fetched story of a Nazi plot to kidnap Winston Churchill during the Second World War. The huge success of this novel spawned a 1976 film adaptation with a starry cast headed by Michael Caine and Donald Sutherland.

The book's protagonist, Irish gunman and philosopher Liam Devlin, reappeared in three further escapades: *Touch the Devil* (1982), *Confessional* (1985) and *The Eagle Has Flown* (1990), a belated sequel to the original novel. Other returning characters included MI5 agent Paul Chavasse (first appeared in *The Testament of Caspar Schultz*, published in 1962 under alias Martin Fallon; reissued in 2006 as *The Bormann Testament*), detective Nick Miller (*The Graveyard Shift*, 1965) and hired assassin Sean Dillon, who featured in thirteen novels beginning with *Eye of the Storm* in 1992.

Dillon is similar in many ways to the character of Liam Devlin, and his recruitment to British Intelligence in his second outing, *Thunder Point* (1993), allowed Patterson to explore a wide-ranging international and political backdrop for increasingly more action-packed adventures, often with IRA overtones. *The President's Daughter* (1997) dealt with a scandal in the White House; *Day of Reckoning* (2000) was a Mafia story based in London, Beirut and Ireland; while *Bad Company* (2003) saw the rediscovery of the Hitler diaries threatening to destabilise US President Jake Cazalet, another ongoing character.

Patterson's longevity as a thriller writer has been cemented by his almost annual book offering, but recent years have seen the author broaden his writing style to include romance (*Memoirs of a Dance Hall Romeo*, 1989) and the lucrative teenage market (*Sure Fire*, 2006, with Justin Richards).

Since the early 1980s, Patterson's books have all been rebranded under the Jack Higgins name. A fellow of the Royal Society of Arts, he is an expert scuba diver and marksman and currently resides in Jersey. *See also* Historical Crime.

Selected Works by the Author
The Keys of Hell (1965)
A Fine Night for Dying (1969)
A Game for Heroes (1970)
A Prayer for the Dying (1973)
The Eagle Has Landed (1975)
Eye of the Storm (1992, also known as *Midnight Man*)
Thunder Point (1993)
Day of Reckoning (2000)
Without Mercy (2005)

Mark Campbell

Hill, Reginald (b.1936)

Reginald Hill's first book, *A Clubbable Woman*, was published in 1970. It boasted three features that were to be characteristic of the fabulously successful Dalziel and Pascoe series: a reworking of Falstaff and Prince Hal in the protagonists, a sympathy with what women were trying to achieve through feminism and a focus on creative experimentation within the police procedural/detective form.

Dalziel and Pascoe are Falstaff and Hal in the partnership straining under the challenges of remaking social order with energy devoted, trickster-like, to overturning convention. Dalziel is Falstaff the corpulent sly wit, but it is he, not Hal in Pascoe, who holds ultimate power. In turn, Pascoe is a liberal intelligence, a best possible policeman in conventional terms, who is tested to the limit by Dalziel's antics – which get results. Consequently, the title of an early novel, *An Advancement of Learning* (1971), is a key

44. Reginald Hill.

to the series. Although Dalziel is not really a scholarly figure, his anarchic energy is harnessed, through a murder case, to the aim of learning something about an enclosed social space. That is true of the society of the college in *An Advancement of Learning* or the bereaved McIver family in the later *Good Morning Midnight* (2004). Crucially, though, the opening up of a small social landscape is always seen as being connected to wider social and political pressures. While the college suffers from the opening up of higher education, the McIvers feel the effects of the Iraq war.

So, while Hill is always interested in the limitations of the police force in securing justice, his novels variously discover these limits in human psychology, such as the near-schizophrenic killer in *Dialogues of the Dead* (2001) or sexual deviance in *On Beulah Height* (1998) or in the betrayals and compromises of politics such as surround the arms trade in both *Arms and the Women* (2000) and *Good Morning Midnight*. Indeed, another way to regard the main detective partnership is as a dual version of the medieval knight errant, seeking the grail of truth that might heal the wounds of this world. Pascoe wants to believe that there is enough strength in the law and in how it is implemented for him to fulfil this role. Dalziel knows there is not. He is a trickster knight errant who wields semi-divine powers over his subordinates. As trickster, Dalziel oscillates between being a god figure, trying to right the fallen world, and Pascoe's partner in the quest. Sometimes he takes on the role of Pascoe's tempter, his bad angel, with Pascoe's splendid feminist wife, Ellie, as good angel. But this medieval structure is too rigid, too clear cut for the complexities of modernity, even for Pascoe and Ellie, let alone Dalziel.

The construct of the detective as a fallible god is most apparent in *Bones and Silence*, where the author is also a trickster, showing his hand to the reader. For Dalziel is cast as God in a street production of a medieval morality play. Appropriately enough, the chief suspect in a criminal case plays opposite him as the devil, and continues baiting him. Dalziel as God achieves much in *Bones and Silence* but fails to save a despairing woman who has been writing to him of her intention to commit suicide. Pascoe works out too late who she is. She falls from a tower, a fall from grace that indicts this world for failing to be the paradise where pain and evil are eliminated by a just God.

Hill's novels are not primarily 'whodunits', although there is plenty of excitement for the reader here. Rather, Hill is keen to explore the metaphysic of detective fiction, whether the detective has the (divine) powers to restore paradise, and whether human beings could live there if he or she did. Two novels explore this ambivalence about paradise. In *Pictures of Perfection*, the reader is horrified by an apparent mass killing at the start. Little is exactly what it seems in Hill's Yorkshire. In fact, this is the novel where the loyal, gay Sergeant Wield finds happiness and helps to right the structural wrongs in a beautiful village. The nearest place to paradise is restored. Symptomatically, detective knights Dalziel and Pascoe decide to leave well alone. Another paradise is described in *On Beulah Height*. However, this Elysium is gone, literally, underwater in a new reservoir. Also, it was more effectively and cruelly destroyed by the unexplained disappearance of several young girls years before. Now, in a hot summer, the water in the reservoir recedes to yield its secrets. Similarly, memories are stirring from other depths; Pascoe has to face the possibility of losing his own daughter to something that the police cannot heal. *On Beulah Height* is a powerful hymn to the limits of police powers to heal the pain of crimes.

Hill wrote a second, shorter series of stories featuring Joe Sixsmith, a black former lathe operator from Luton turned amiable private investigator. It is Joe who most explicitly explores Hill's detecting metaphysic and the psychological mood that goes with it. In *Singing the Sadness*, where his presence in a church choir while visiting Wales provokes religious comment, he affirms that there is 'something' out there, beyond human understanding that can sometimes put the pieces together. Indeed, he reflects that his detecting needs that 'something'. In particular, Joe needs the 'something' because of the pain of life in this fallen world. It is explained to him that the Welsh sing the sadness as a way of trying to make something of it, not to escape it. Avoiding the sadness of humanity is not possible, as every Hill novel demonstrates. In a way, what all Hill novels detect are those who sing the sadness and those who become the sadness and those who inflict it on others. *See also* Police Procedurals.

Selected Works by the Author
A Clubbable Woman (1970)
An Advancement of Learning (1971)
A Killing Kindness (1980)
Exit Lines (1984)
Underworld (1988)
Recalled to Life (1992)
Pictures of Perfection (1994)
On Beulah Height (1998)
Death's Jest Book (2003)
Good Morning Midnight (2004)
The Death of Dalziel (2007)

Further Reading
Knight, Stephen. 2004. *Crime Fiction 1800–2000: Detection, Death, Diversity*. Palgrave Macmillan.
Ling, Peter J. 2006. Identity, Allusions and Agency in Reginald Hill's Good Morning Midnight. *CLUES: A Journal of Detection*.
Mandel, Ernest. 1984. *Delightful Murder: A Social History of the Crime Novel*. University of Minnesota Press.

Susan Rowland

Hill, Susan (b.1942)

Susan Hill's novels are characterised by their brooding atmosphere of heightened emotion, coupled with strong, sometimes supernaturally inclined, Gothic themes.

Born in Scarborough, North Yorkshire, on 5 February 1942, Susan Elizabeth Hill was educated at the town's convent school. At an early age, she found herself drawn towards the dramatic arts, spending much of her spare time visiting Scarborough's Repertory Theatre and the Stephen Joseph Theatre in the Round. In 1958, her family moved to Coventry, and she graduated in English from King's College, London, in 1963. At university, she wrote her first novel, *The Enclosure* (1961). The book presciently depicted the life of a middle-aged female novelist, Virginia, who had to choose between her career and her marriage. A second novel, *Do Me a Favour* (1963), dealt with similar issues but from a younger perspective.

Hill's early prolific period was between 1968 and 1973, in which she produced six novels. The most famous of these was *I'm the King of the Castle* (1970), a disturbing story about the cruelty of children in the same vein as William Golding's *Lord of the Flies* (1954). Charles Kingshaw is forced to live with Edmund Hooper in his father's lonely Victorian home, but Hooper's animosity to the unwelcome newcomer is chillingly demonstrated in a campaign of bullying that leads to a conclusion as tragic as it is inevitable. The novel's realistic depiction of a borderline psychotic child won it many accolades, most notably the Somerset Maugham Award in 1971.

After university, Hill returned to Coventry where she wrote for a local newspaper. In 1975, she married the prominent Shakespeare scholar Dr Stanley Wells, and they moved to Stratford-upon-Avon. Three years later, they moved to Oxford, where Wells had been made a Fellow of Balliol College, and thence to a cottage in a rural village 5 miles from the city. From here, she produced a series of countryside memoirs, including *The Magic Apple Tree* (1983) and *Through the Kitchen Window* (1984), as well as the world-famous ghost story *The Woman in Black* (1983) – her first work of fiction in a decade. Inspired by the eerie and suspense-laden stories of M.R. James, the book was adapted into a phenomenally successful stage play by Stephen Mallatratt, premiering at Hill's birthplace in 1987.

After moving to a farmhouse in the Cotswolds in 1990, several stand-alone novels followed, including another ghost story, *The Mist in the Mirror* (1992), and a sequel to Daphne du Maurier's *Rebecca*, *Mrs de Winter* (1993). From 2004, with *The Various Haunts of Men*, Hill has embarked on a series of mainstream crime novels set in a small cathedral town and featuring genial detective Simon Serrallier. *The Various Haunts of Men* (2004) deals with a grisly murder that disrupts the status quo, while *The Pure in Heart* (2005) is a strangely low-key examination of child abduction. None of Hill's crime novels are in any way conventional – and while her crime books have received a more mixed response than her other work, they are intriguing entries in the field. *See also* Literature and Crime Fiction.

Selected Works by the Author
The Enclosure (1961)
I'm the King of the Castle (1970)
Strange Meeting (1971)
In The Springtime of the Year (1973)
The Woman in Black (1983)
Air and Angels (1991)
The Various Haunts of Men (2004)
The Pure in Heart (2005)

Mark Campbell

Hines, Joanna (b.1949)

Joanna Hines writes penetrating, psychologically acute novels that revolve primarily around family secrets. All families have secrets, as does each individual within that family, though as a general rule, these are a subject for embarrassment or minor scandal. In Hines's novels, however, family secrets ignite a slow-burning fuse, which smoulder unseen until the moment they flare up in tragedy and confusion. There are no mean streets in these stories but rather the hidden deceptions and cruelties that are acted out in 'ordinary' homes.

Fern Miller is the catalyst in Hines's first book, *Dora's Room* (1993). An orphan, she has had no contact with her father's family until she unexpectedly inherits her grandfather's estate and is forced to confront her other relatives, including her uncle, author of the cult book, *Dora's Room*. The claustrophobic atmosphere of the Chatton Heights, the huge but grim family home, is vividly portrayed; so too, the persistent murmurings of a long-buried memory which does not become clear until the identity of Dora and the location of her mysterious room are explained.

Memory and a strong sense of place are again evident in *Improvising Carla* (2001), perhaps Hines's most commercial book to date. Helen North, of whom the reader is told almost nothing in the course of the novel, hooks up with another solitary traveller, Carla Finch, on an idyllic Greek island. As both women are escaping from their everyday reality, they reach an unspoken agreement not to bore each other with the mundane details of their normal lives. The consequence is that when Carla dies, suddenly and violently, Helen knows almost nothing about the friend she has lost. Worse, although she was with Carla when she died, Helen can remember nothing about it. Haunted by guilt, she returns to England and tries to piece together the fragments of Carla's world, a journey that proves dangerous but ultimately revelatory.

Two novels deal with a group of young people whose friendship was shattered by violent death. In *Surface Tension* (2002), one member of the group has gone on to found a weird cult, and at first it appears to be another 'cult' novel, in which the foolish and unwary are lured by power-crazed leaders to abandon their loving families. But as the masks are peeled away, the truth is revealed to be very different. *The Fifth Secret* (1995), which is narrated by the cynical Jane Baer, is perhaps the most humorous of these books, describing the events that follow from a violent attack on Esmé Drummond, whom she knew during magical childhood holidays at Glory Cottage.

The Murder Bird (2006) focuses on two families united by marriage. Kirsten Waller, a renowned American poet, is separated from the eminent barrister Ralph Howes. When she is found dead in a lonely Cornish cottage, the official verdict is suicide, but Sam, her daughter, knows she would never kill herself and that her death could not have been an accident. Sam's search to find out the truth opens ancient family wounds and brings her to the brink of destruction.

Hines has also written a contemporary novel, *Autumn of Strangers* (1997) that is about the impact of a group of travellers on the inhabitants of a small English village, and a historical trilogy set in seventeenth-century Cornwall.

Selected Works by the Author
Dora's Room (1993)
The Fifth Secret (1995)
Improvising Carla (2001)
Surface Tension (2002)
Angels of the Flood (2004)
The Murder Bird (2006)

Barry Forshaw

Historical Crime

Historical crime stories are those where both the crime and its investigation are set in the past. Some definitions include those stories where the crime is in the past but the investigation is in the present, a concept employed with considerable influence by Josephine **Tey** in *The Daughter of Time* (1951) which re-investigates the deaths of the princes in the Tower. When the Crime Writers Association established the Ellis Peters Historical Dagger award for the year's best historical mystery in 1999, it defined the category as 'any period up to the 1960s' but otherwise there is no agreed definition as to when the 'past' begins.

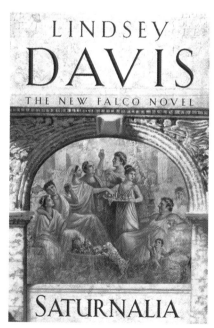

45. Cover of the paperback edition of *Saturnalia* (2008) by Lindsey Davis.

The historical crime genre is relatively new as a marketing niche, establishing itself with the popularity of the Brother Cadfael books by Ellis Peters in the early 1980s. There had been earlier stories and novels that qualify as historical mysteries, both in Britain and America, but they were mostly regarded as mystery stories with the historical setting little more than a gimmick. There is a case to argue that the theme goes back as far as the gothic novels of the late eighteenth century, especially those where the supernatural trappings were rationalised, such as Ann Radcliffe's *The Mysteries of Udolpho* (1794), as these were frequently set in a medieval period and involved crimes that were resolved. However, the crime novel as such had yet to develop its accepted form so that even though Charles **Dickens**, who did much to popularise detective fiction, wrote two historical novels containing murders and trials – *Barnaby Rudge* (1841) and *A Tale of Two Cities* (1859) – neither are regarded as historical crime novels.

The form as it is now recognised, began to emerge in the United States with the stories by Melville Davisson Post featuring Uncle Abner, a god-fearing preacher in nineteenth-century Virginia whose sharp observations helped solve (and even prevent) many local crimes. The stories appeared in the *Saturday Evening Post* from 1911 and were collected in *Uncle Abner: Master of Mysteries* (1918). Britain was not far behind. Jeffery Farnol (1878–1952), noted for his Regency swashbucklers, introduced the character of Jasper Shrig, the Bow Street Runner, in *An Amateur Gentleman* (1913), though Shrig did little detecting in that volume. He moved centre stage in *The Loring Mystery* (1925), investigating a murder in Sussex, and thereafter became a feature character. Of particular interest is *Murder by Nail* (1942), in which Shrig is obsessed by a case that happened seventy years earlier – making it an historical within an historical.

Farnol was not alone in producing such books. Georgette **Heyer**, perhaps Farnol's best-known disciple, produced many novels of period intrigue right from her first, *The Black Moth* (1921), in which a highwayman foils an abduction plot and becomes involved in a chain of mystery. Perhaps her best is *The Talisman Ring* (1936), set in 1794, in which a man is framed for murder and his friends do all they can to prove his innocence. Bruce **Graeme**, whose books about the gentleman thief Blackshirt had proved exceptionally popular in the late 1920s, wrote a series about his seventeenth-century ancestor, starting with *Monsieur Blackshirt* (1933). Into this grouping we could gather the long-running series of books by Baroness Orczy (1865–1947) about the Scarlet Pimpernel and Russell Thorndike's (1885–1972) series about the smuggler-hero Dr Syn. All of these are about crime and criminals, though they are not stories of historical detection as has since become the mode.

Occasionally, authors would select a genuine historical murder and rework it as fiction. Thomas Burke (1886–1945), for instance, based *Murder at Elstree* (1936) on the notorious Radlett murder of 1823. Robert Graves (1895–1985) sought to show the innocence of William Palmer, the 'Prince of Poisoners', who was hanged in 1856, in *They Hanged My Saintly Billy* (1957).

Agatha **Christie** had attempted one historical mystery, *Death Comes at the End* (1945) set in ancient Egypt, though she had not pursued the genre. If one author popularised historical crime fiction before Ellis **Peters**, it was John Dickson **Carr**, British by adoption. Carr became something of a champion of the not-quite historical novel during the 1950s and 1960s. In *The Devil in Velvet* (1951), *Fear is the Same* (1956, as by Carter Dickson) and *Fire, Burn!* (1957), among others, Carr used the idea of a present-day individual slipping back into the past to become involved in solving a mystery. Carr's best historical novel, *The Bride of Newgate* (1950), is set in 1815 and involves a man who escapes the hangman's noose and proves his innocence. Carr's fascination for historical mysteries remained to his last novel, *The Hungry Goblin* (1972), which includes Wilkie **Collins** as the detective.

In the years just before Ellis Peters created Brother Cadfael, there were others making their mark. Peter **Lovesey** had already established a reputation with his series featuring Victorian detective Sergeant Cribb, starting with the wildly idiosyncratic *Wobble to Death* (1970). Lovesey later developed a series around the life of the Prince of Wales (the future Edward VII) with *Bertie and the Tinman* (1987). Barbara Mertz, writing as Elizabeth Peters, began her popular series featuring the archaeological detective Amelia Peabody, set in the late Victorian period, with *Crocodile on the Sandbank* (1975). Jeremy Potter (1922–1997) had also written several novels re-evaluating noted historical mysteries, including *A Trail of Blood* (1970), which again considered the Princes in the Tower, and *Death in the Forest* (1977), about the death of William II. Derek Lambert (1929–2001), writing as Richard Falkirk, penned six books featuring Bow Street Runner Edmund Blackstone, starting with *Blackstone* (1972).

All of these books, though, were marketed as mysteries, and it was left to the popularity of Brother Cadfael, which began with *A Morbid Taste for Bones* (1977), to establish a new 'historical mystery' genre. The most likely reason is that Peters's contemporaries were already known for their mystery novels and thus continued to be marketed as mysteries. While Peters was also known for her mystery novels featuring Inspector Felse, she was equally well known (under her real name of Edith Pargeter) for her historical novels. The emphasis of the Cadfael books was as much on the historical setting – the civil war between King Stephen and the Empress Matilda in the mid-twelfth century – as on the crime, and it was a difficult decision whether to label them as historical novels or mysteries. The result was a merger of the two fields and the establishment of one of the most popular categories of fiction of the last quarter-century.

Another factor made the Cadfael books different: the twelfth-century setting was uncommon, even in historical fiction. Victorian and Regency novels – and their equivalent cinema costume dramas – were well known, as were the Sherlock **Holmes** pastiches, but for many readers, Cadfael was entirely new territory. Furthermore, the stories were not set in London but in Shrewsbury, on the Welsh borders, and Cadfael himself was Welsh. The books were true to their period and Peters introduced many unfamiliar names. As a consequence, the stories felt different to any other mystery series. In fact, Peters not only gave substance to a new genre of historical mystery but created a sub-genre within it – the medieval mystery. As the genre grew, so the medieval mystery remained both prominent and popular, especially after the success of Umberto Eco's *The Name of the Rose* (1980), translated in 1983.

The first to benefit from this was Paul **Doherty**. His area of expertise was the reign of Edward II, and his first novel, *Death of a King* (1985), is an investigation into that king's death. With *Satan in St. Mary's* (1986), he began what has become his longest running series featuring Sir Hugh Corbett, who investigates on behalf of King Edward I. Doherty has since written many novels covering a wide range of historical periods, including ancient Egypt and Greece, but the core of his work remains in the English Middle Ages.

Besides Doherty's work, and the Huy the Scribe series by Anton Gill (b.1948), Ancient Egypt and Greece have attracted few British writers, unlike the Roman world. Lindsey **Davis** is the best known and most popular with her books featuring Marcus Didius Falco, which began with *The Silver Pigs* (1989), set in AD 70. Davis recreates Rome in the vernacular, bringing it alive for modern readers, yet keeping the integrity of the ancient world. Others who have rebuilt Rome include Philip Boast (b.1952), Jane Finnis, Mike **Ripley**, Rosemary **Rowe**, Marilyn Todd (b.1958) and David **Wishart**, while British-born Mary Reed and her husband, Eric Mayer, have recreated the Byzantine world in their John the Eunuch series, starting with *One for Sorrow* (1999).

Bridging that middle ground after the downfall of the Roman Empire and before the growth of the European empires stands Peter **Tremayne**'s unique series, which began with *Absolution by Murder* (1994), featuring Sister Fidelma, an Irish *dalaigh*, who upholds the rule of law in the seventh century.

The medieval period remains popular, especially among British writers. In fact, it is possible to follow English history through the various mystery series. Keith Miles, writing as Edward **Marston**, has the earliest post-Conquest series with his novels about Norman soldier Ralph Delchard and his lawyer companion Gervase Bret and the crimes they encounter during the compilation of the *Domesday Book*. Bernard **Knight** set his Crowner John series in twelfth-century Devon while Michael **Jecks**'s Simon Puttock series, also in Devon, is set some 130 years later. Ian **Morson**'s Master Falconer series takes place in the fledgling Oxford University in the mid-thirteenth century, while Susanna **Gregory**'s Matthew Bartholomew is set in the early years of Cambridge University, a century later. Knight, Jecks, Morson and Gregory have teamed with Philip **Gooden** and, more recently, C.J. **Sansom** to form The Medieval Murderers, providing talks and readings and also collaborating on a series of books starting with *The Tainted Relic* (2005).

We enter the fifteenth century with Kate Sedley's Roger the Chapman series, which begins with *Death and the Chapman* (1991) at the start of the Wars of the Roses. The Tudor dynasty, including the Elizabeth period, has become as popular as the medieval. C.J. Sansom won the Ellis Peters Historical Dagger for *Dark Fire* (2005), the second of his novels featuring Matthew Shardlake, a lawyer during the reign of Henry VIII. Valerie Anand (b.1937), writing as Fiona Buckley, introduced Ursula Blanchard in *The Robsart Mystery* (1997). Blanchard is believed to be Henry VIII's illegitimate child and becomes a spy for Queen Elizabeth. Patricia Finney (b.1958), both under her own name and as P.F. Chisholm, has set several novels in the Elizabethan age, and her Becket and Ames secret-agent series, set at the time of the wars with Spain, has earned her the epithet as the 'Elizabethan John le Carré'.

The Elizabethan and Jacobean theatre, at the time of Shakespeare, is an obvious setting for historical mysteries and has been used by both Keith Miles (as Edward Marston), with his Nicholas Bracewell series, and Philip Gooden, with his stories about Nick Revill. Marston has also written a series set in England soon after the Restoration of the monarchy in 1660 and featuring architect Christopher Redmayne. This was also the period used by Iain **Pears** in his intriguing novel *An Instance of the Fingerpost* (1997), which considered a murder from the viewpoint of several characters.

With the eighteenth century, and the dawn of the novel, there is a feeling that historical crime fiction is entering the modern period. Whereas the pre-Georgian periods have a distant, genuinely historical feel, there is more of an affinity with the characters and settings of stories taking place from the 1700s on. The authors are able to move away from royalty towards artists and craftsmen and, indeed, the dawn of the police force. Deryn **Lake**, regarded as the 'Queen of the Georgian Mystery' has written a long series featuring Sir John Fielding, the 'Blind Beak', the magistrate who helped establish the Bow Street Runners in the 1750s and who, in books from *Death in the Dark Walk* (1995) on, is assisted by John Rawlings in investigating crimes. Janet **Laurence** took advantage of the fact that the Italian painter Canaletto settled in London in 1746 for her historical mysteries which began with *Canaletto and the Case of Westminster Bridge* (1997). Janet Gleeson has created a series of whodunits around the artisans and craftsmen of the period, starting with Thomas Chippendale and his apprentice in *The Grenadillo Box* (2002). Robert **Barnard**, writing as Bernard Bastable, created a world in which Mozart did not die but lived on in London and is forced to become a government agent in *Dead, Mr Mozart* (1995) and its sequels.

Royalty is never far away, however. In *The King Cried Murder!* (2000), Gwendoline **Butler** depicts Fanny Burney in her younger days when she was lady-in-waiting to a mentally declining George III and comes under scrutiny following a series of murders. Also in the novel are two special agents in the intelligence service set up by William Pitt, and that same service features in the George Keene series by Derek Wilson, starting with *Keene's Quest* (2000), during the French Revolutionary War. David Donachie (b.1944) uses the Napoleonic wars as the background for his Privateersmen series featuring Harry Ludlow, where we encounter shipboard crimes, starting with *The Devil's Own Luck* (1991). Bernard Cornwell (b.1944), renowned for his Sharpe novels, has a former soldier turned government investigator in *Gallows Thief* (2001).

The Victorian and Edwardian period is synonymous with Sherlock Holmes, and the many Holmes pastiches that have appeared since Conan Doyle's death are historical mysteries in their own right but are so numerous and specialised as to be treated separately. Anne **Perry** is generally regarded as the doyen of the Victorian crime novel with her two long-running series: the Inspector Pitt novels, starting with *The Cater Street Hangman* (1979), and the William Monk books, starting with *The Face of a Stranger* (1990). Both emphasise the psycho-social issues arising from the era's cultural problems that the upper-levels of society preferred to ignore. In similar vein are the Harriet Unwin stories by H.R.F. **Keating**, writing as Evelyn Hervey, which began with *The Governess* (1983). Julian **Symons** likewise explored the underbelly of the Victorian class system in three novels, *The Blackheath Poisonings* (1978), *The Detling Murders* (1982) and *Sweet Adelaide* (1980), the latter based on the Adelaide Bartlett case, which had led to one of the most famous trials of the Victorian age.

The most notorious criminal of the period was undoubtedly Jack the Ripper, whose reign of terror has prompted many stories and novels. Of special interest is *The Cry from Street to Street* (1992) by Hilary Bailey (b.1936), which explores the problems of trying to survive in London's East End through the eyes of the Ripper's victims.

Donald Thomas, who has also written a Jack-the-Ripper novel, featured several celebrities in his Inspector Swain books which included *Belladonna: A Lewis Carroll Nightmare* (1984) and *Jekyll, Alias Hyde* (1988). Gyles Brandreth (b.1948) has turned Oscar Wilde into a sleuth in *Oscar Wilde and the Candlelight Murders* (2007). Frank **Tallis** entered the world of Sigmund Freud in *Mortal Mischief* (2005) and its sequels. Gillian **Linscott** had explorers clash in the aftermath of the death of David Livingstone in *Murder, I Presume* (1990), while she has used the suffragette movement for a series of novels featuring Nell Bray, which began with *Sister beneath the Sheets* (1991) and included the award-winning *Absent Friends* (1999).

Joan Lock's forte is on the workings of the police force in the nineteenth century which has resulted not only in several excellent non-fiction studies but also in a series featuring Detective-Inspector Ernest Best, which began with *Dead Image* (2000). What Lock did for London, so Alanna Knight (b.1923) has for Edinburgh, with her long-running series about Inspector Faro, starting with *Enter Second Murderer* (1988).

The First World War has come under increasing re-evaluation in recent years. Anne Perry wrote a series in which former college professor turned war chaplain, Joseph Reavley, together with his brother and sister, become involved in various intrigues from just before the outset of the war, in *No Graves as Yet* (2003) to the approach of Armistice in *We Shall Not Sleep* (2007). Ben Elton (b.1959) produced a thought-provoking novel about how one ascertains the truth on the front line in *The First Casualty* (2006). Michael **Gilbert**'s character Luke Pagan is a police constable involved in investigating an anarchist plot just before the outbreak of war in *Ring of Terror* (1995), and subsequent novels take him into war as part of military intelligence. Graham Ison's Detective Inspector Hardcastle finds himself at odds with military intelligence in *Hardcastle's Spy* (2003), which takes place in Britain at the time of the Somme.

The aftermath of the war, especially its psychological impact upon the survivors, has been explored in two excellent series, one by the American mother-and-son team writing as Charles Todd, and the other by South-African born Rennie Airth, whose *River of Darkness* (1999) introduced Inspector John Madden trying to solve the death of an entire family in the months following the war and the flu epidemic.

The 1920s and 1930s are becoming increasingly popular as historical settings. Barbara Cleverly's series featuring Commander Sandilands was set in India for the first four volumes but returned to England in *The Bee's Kiss* (2005), contrasting the glories of the Raj with England's strife. British-born Carola Dunn, though now resident in America, remains true to her roots in her series featuring the Honourable Daisy Dalrymple, which began with *Death at Wentwater Court* (1994). Though superficially cosy country-house mysteries, Dunn does not overlook how society changed after the war and its effect upon the class system. David **Roberts** also considers the transition in the class system between the wars in his series featuring Lord Corinth and Verity Browne, which began with *Sweet Poison* (2001).

Series set during the Second World War include the television series *Foyle's War*, created by Anthony Horowitz (b.1955), which began in 2002, and follows the attempts by Chief Superintendent Foyle, based in Hastings, to uphold law and order. Perhaps the most acclaimed wartime series in book form is by John **Gardner**, featuring Suzie Mountford, a young policewoman who at the outset, in *The Bottled Spider* (2002), is promoted beyond her capabilities into CID, but who in later books grows in experience to meet the demands of the time.

The master author of stories in the post-war years is Andrew **Taylor** who has won the Ellis Peters Historical Dagger twice. His books, which include the Roth trilogy and the Lydmouth series, bridge the gap between the historical and the present.

British historical crime fiction does not have to be rooted in Britain. Simon **Levack** has recreated the Aztec empire under Montezuma in *A Demon of the Air* (2004), and the world of Machiavelli and the Borgias in *The Swarm of Heaven* (1999), while Michael **Pearce** depicts the British control of Egypt prior to the First World War in his sharply delineated Mamur Zapt series, starting with *The Return of the Carpet* (1988). Pearce has also set books in Tsarist Russia and, starting with *A Dead Man in Trieste* (2004), takes readers on a tour of European embassies. These, and many more, show that history provides an almost infinite array of settings for creating crime. A good selection of historical crime short fiction will be found in various anthologies compiled by Mike **Ashley** and Maxim **Jakubowski**.

The profusion of such books belies how difficult they are to write, as the author has to create an authentic and believable historical world and convey the differences in culture and attitude to the reader while still producing a story accessible to the modern mind. The advantage of such books, though, is that they can reinterpret history to modern sensibilities and show how attitudes towards both crime and its detection have grown and changed over the centuries, a dimension that cannot be explored so thoroughly in contemporary fiction.

Further Reading

Browne, Ray Broadus, and Lawrence A. Kreiser, eds. 2001. *The Detective as Historian: History and Art in Historical Crime Fiction*. Popular Press.

Burgess, Michael, and Jill H. Vassilakos. 2005. *Murder in Retrospect*. Libraries Unlimited.

Website

The following provide details on a wide range of historical crime fiction and are not limited to British authors.

Bishop, Alan J. 'Criminal History' at www.criminal-history.co.uk/index.html

'Crime Thru Time' website and discussion group at www.crimethrutime.com/index.htm

Gaslight Books. 'Historical Mystery Fiction' at www.gaslightbooks.com.au/checklists/histmyst.htm

James, Dean. 'Historical Mystery Bibliography' at www.twbooks.co.uk/authors/bibliographies/historic.html

Mike Ashley

Holmes, Sherlock

Dr John Watson first meets Sherlock Holmes in the bar of the Criterion restaurant in Piccadilly Circus, in the opening chapter of *A Study in Scarlet* (1887). The mystery man rattles off a few of his shortly-to-be-trademarked observations ('you have been in Afghanistan, I perceive') and, in no time, has enlisted Watson as co-tenant in his rooms at 221B Baker Street. At first, Watson does not even know the profession of his eccentric flatmate and is given to making lists of his qualities and areas of expertise and ignorance, but no sooner had Holmes revealed he is a 'consulting detective' than the pair are involved with Inspector Lestrade of Scotland Yard and investigating the murder of American Enoch Drabber, stabbed in a room in Laurelton Gardens, with 'Rachel' scrawled on the wall in the victim's blood. Lestrade assumes that there is a lady named Rachel in the case, but Holmes leaps to the conclusion – despite his confidence and explanation of his methods, it is a long-shot guess – that the graffito is German for 'revenge'.

Holmes is not the first 'consulting detective' in literature (he acknowledges Poe's Dupin as a predecessor, even though in a somewhat snide manner) and his methods and manners remain utterly fantastical in many particulars, but he is the Great Detective. Sir Arthur Conan **Doyle** followed *A Study in Scarlet* with three more novels and five volumes of short stories – his ambivalence about his most successful creation became obvious early, but despite several attempts (at least one – 'The Final Problem' – seemingly definitive) to shut Holmes off, he was irresistibly drawn back to Holmes and Watson. Public pressure and money had a lot to do with *The Hound of the Baskervilles* (1902), the best of the novels, but it was produced while Holmes was officially dead. Originally presented as an 'untold case' before Holmes's death at the Reichenbach Falls, *Hound* exists because Doyle had ideas which demanded the presence of his fictional sleuth not because editors dangled an enormous cheque in front of him – as they did with 'The Empty House', in which Holmes turns out not to be dead.

Other authors, even contemporaries of Doyle, came up with mysteries as puzzling and melodramas as vivid. The Holmes canon outlasts its rivals because of the characterisation. Holmes is presented at first as a series of eccentricities (the business about not caring whether the earth revolves around the sun or the other way round – no wonder a gastro-mathematician like Professor Moriarty despised him) and traits (the pipe, the violin and the needle). *The Sign of Four* (1890) is Watson's book: he has an arc from bereaved and damaged war veteran (the deduction from Watson's brother's watch is among the best passages Doyle ever wrote – clever and heartfelt) to happy husband. 'A Scandal in Bohemia', which reintroduces the pair for a new magazine audience, is explicitly constructed around the reason why Holmes will never be able to go this route and must remain eternally detached. Despite the gap-filling imaginations of later writers, we know Holmes's admiration for Irene Adler is not sexual – he is celibate, a man apart from life. His profession is singular, in that he is neither an official detective (though Lestrade calls him in) nor one of those know-it-all amateurs who came to the fore in the early twentieth century (Vance, **Wimsey** and **Marple**). He is not even a private eye; in theory, he supplies the intellectual rigour that would lead Philip Marlowe to solve chess problems between cases, but the rest of the **Chandler** package – the devotion to the client, to higher justice, to going down mean streets without being afraid – rests on the true amateur in the team, Watson. Holmes operates by his own moral code and on more than one occasion, much to Watson's disquiet, he is prepared to let the perpetrator go free, as in 'The Boscombe Valley Mystery' (*The Strand Magazine*, October 1891).

One reason for our lasting devotion to Holmes is that we, like Watson, have to assemble our own detailed portrait of the man, and we have nine books' worth of clues to play with. Doyle doles out scraps about Holmes's background (a family background in Yorkshire – would anyone dare play the role with a Brontë-style accent?), two early cases from his university years, surprise introductions of his sluggish but even cleverer brother Mycroft and his nemesis Moriarty, a few stories narrated by the detective to make up for the cutting remarks about Watson's published accounts, occasional bursts of real feeling and an awareness of the hero's growing celebrity and sense of himself as a public figure (in later tales, he all but speechifies – as Basil Rathbone would do, quoting Churchill to sign off those wartime quickies). When William Gillette whipped up *Sherlock Holmes* (1899) as a stage vehicle for himself, he famously asked Doyle if he could 'marry Holmes' and Doyle responded 'you may marry him or murder him' – justifying later fictions he could not have imagined, from Nicholas Meyer's *The Seven-per-Cent Solution* (1974), in which Holmes consults Freud to be cured of cocaine addiction and recover memory of a childhood trauma, to Michael **Dibdin**'s *The Last Sherlock Holmes Story* (1978), in which Holmes is a split personality who (taking on the persona of Moriarty) is also Jack the Ripper. Holmes has been a vampire and vampire slayer, a clone from the future, a robot, a homosexual, the father of Nero Wolfe, a dullard, an arch-fiend, a time-traveller and a mentor to Batman, Eliot Ness and Mr Spock. There are as many scholarly, speculative, argumentative biographies of Holmes as of, say, Disraeli. There are solo adventures for Watson, Mycroft, Lestrade, Mrs Hudson and Moriarty, not to mention Basil of Baker Street and Sherlock Hound.

Holmes characterisation escaped Doyle's influence when elements from Sidney Paget's illustrations (the deerstalker) became accepted as part of his image; Gillette added the catchphrase 'elementary, my dear Watson', and a long line of actors, authors and parodists has contributed to the creation of a vastly contradictory, but rounded figure. Holmes is the first true popular culture superhero, with his distinctive uniform, lair, methods, gadgets and resolute stand against chaos, fog and deviltry. Doyle established that Holmes retired 'to Sussex to keep bees' in 1903, and the stories he wrote up until 1927 became increasingly imbued with nostalgia for the pre–First World War world. Certainly, the rattle of hansom cabs, the setting aside of the violin and a cry of 'the game's afoot' have become as comforting and promising as 'once upon a time' or 'are you sitting comfortably?'. There is a real darkness in the stories, which are shot through with hideous cruelties and injustices wrought on the other side of the world coming home to roost in complacent England, but Holmes is untouched. He conquers his weaknesses – his *humanity* – and becomes a rock, a beacon and an archetype. Every other detective in literature and film defines himself or herself by how similar and how different he or she is from Holmes. In all probability, if he had never existed, neither would this book. *See also* Film and Crime: Page to Screen; The Great Detectives: Sherlock Holmes, Hercule Poirot, Lord Peter Wimsey; Holmes on TV; Holmes's Rivals; London in Crime Fiction; Male Crime Writers; and *The Strand Magazine*.

Further Reading

Baring-Gould, William. 1962. *Sherlock Holmes of Baker Street: A Life of the World's First Consulting Detective*. Clarkson N. Potter.
Dakin, David. 1972. *A Sherlock Holmes Commentary*. David & Charles.
Karlson, Katherine, and Patrica Guy. 2007. *Ladies, Ladies: The Women in the Life of Sherlock Holmes*. Aventine.
Keating, H.R.F. 2006. *Sherlock Holmes: The Man and His World*. Castle.
Klinger, Leslie, ed. 2005. *The New Annotated Sherlock Holmes*. W.W. Norton.
McQueen, Ian. 1974. *Sherlock Holmes Detected: The Problems of the Long Stories*. David & Charles.
Rennison, Nick. 2005. *Sherlock Holmes: The Unauthorized Biography*. Atlantic Books.
Riley, Dick. 2005. *The Bedside Companion to Sherlock Holmes*. Barnes & Noble Books.
Thomson, June. 1995. *Holmes and Watson*. Constable.

Kim Newman

Holmes on TV

Sir Arthur Conan **Doyle**'s Sherlock **Holmes** moved from the page to the theatre and the cinema within the author's lifetime. Among the most recognisable and often-exploited characters in fiction, Holmes surpasses even Tarzan and Dracula in the number and variety of his media manifestations. His television appearances date back to the infancy of the medium and stretch to international productions as afar afield as France, Germany, Belgium, Italy, the Soviet Union and Japan.

The great detective's television debut was in *The Three Garridebs* (1937), with Louis Hector (Holmes) and William Podmore (Watson). It was an American show, transmitted live (six times in a week, like a play) by NBC to the few owners of the television apparatus in New York. Fourteen years on, there was a flurry of Holmes television activity. *Sherlock Holmes: The Man Who Disappeared* (1951) – with John Longden (Holmes) and Campbell Singer (Watson), an adaptation of 'The Man with the Twisted Lip' – was a British–American pilot for a series that was not made. The BBC's first Holmes adaptation (an episode of an anthology series called *For the Children*) was 'The Adventure of the Mazarin Stone' (1951), with Andrew Osborn (Holmes) and Philip King (Watson). Then, the corporation mounted the first Holmes series, the

46. Jeremy Brett and Edward Hardwicke star as Holmes and Watson in *The Return of Sherlock Holmes* (Granada Television, 1987).

six-episode *Sherlock Holmes* (1951), with Alan Wheatley (Holmes) and Raymond Francis (Watson). Unusually, this chose to kick-off with the detective returning from the dead in 'The Empty House'. Bill Owen and Iris Vandeleur were regulars, as Lestrade and Mrs Hudson.

Basil Rathbone – who played the role on stage, screen and radio – partnered with Martyn Green (Watson) in an episode of the US anthology series **Suspense** ('The Adventure of the Black Baronet', 1953), based on one of the Holmes pastiches by John Dickson **Carr** and Adrian Conan Doyle. The first non-anglophone television Holmes also showed up in the 1950s, from Germany: 'Sherlock Holmes liegt im sterben' (1954), an episode of *Der Galerie der Grossen Detektive* based on 'The Adventure of the Dying Detective', with Ernst Fritz Fürbringer (Holmes) and Harald Mannl (Watson), and the small screen debut of *Der Hund von Baskerville* (1955), with Wolf Ackva (Holmes) and Arnulf Schröder (Watson). More lasting, if only because it is the first television Holmes to survive and has fallen into a copyright limbo that makes it a much-issued public domain video and DVD release, was *Sherlock Holmes* (1954–1955), a series of half-hour episodes with Ronald Howard (Holmes) and Howard Marion-Crawford (Watson). Oddly filmed in Paris, passed off as period London and with Archie Duncan as a Scots Lestrade, this show turned out a few favourites ('The Red Headed League') but mostly neglected the canon to come up with new stories, which was criticised at the time but makes the program seem fresher after every single Doyle story has been done over and over. Typical episodes were 'The Case of the Belligerent Ghost', 'The Case of the Night Train Riddle' and 'The Case of the Careless Suffragette'. Howard and Marion-Crawford are a middle-of-the-road team, but are pleasantly warm: Howard is a kindlier, more amusing sleuth than some other artists who played

Holmes, while Marion-Crawford sometimes drops the comic relief to raise his fists to reveal Watson's bruiser side in defence of a passing heroine or his best friend.

From 1964 to 1969, the BBC mounted a series called *Detective*, which afforded various sleuths a shot at the limelight. Simenon's Inspector Maigret (in the 'official' form of Rupert Davies) introduced the episodes, which (like those of *Comedy Playhouse*) were obviously backdoor pilots for possible series. Competing with Edward Woodward (as Poe's proto-Sherlock Chevalier Auguste Dupin), Richard Wordsworth (as Edmund **Crispin**'s Gervaise Fen), David Horne (as John Dickson Carr's Sir Henry Merrivale) and Geoffrey Keen (as Ngaio **Marsh**'s Inspector Alleyn) were Douglas Wilmer (Holmes) and Nigel Stock (Watson) in 'The Speckled Band' (1964). This dark and gothic adaptation led to *Sherlock Holmes* (1964–1965), with Wilmer and Stock, and then – after recasting and a decision to make the show in colour – the slightly re-titled *Sir Arthur Conan Doyle's Sherlock Holmes* (1968), with Peter Cushing (who had played Holmes in Hammer's *Hound of the Baskervilles*) partnering the suitably bluff and stalwart Stock. The Wilmer and Cushing series have a tendency to the horrors and benefit from sterling supporting casts – including Peter Madden and William Lucas as Lestrade, Derek Francis and Ronald Adam as Mycroft Holmes and Enid Lindsey and Grace Arnold as Mrs Hudson. The black-and-white Wilmer episodes are grimmer and less shaky than the Cushing shows – which include a two-part 'Hound of the Baskervilles'. The German *Sherlock Holmes* (1967), with Erich Schellow (Holmes) and Paul Edwin Roth (Watson), used translations of the scripts prepared for the first BBC series. There were also 1960s Holmes shows from Belgium (*Het avontuur van de drie studenten*, 1966) and Italy (*Il Mastino dei Baskerville*, 1968).

In the 1970s, *The Rivals of Sherlock Holmes* (1971–1972), based on Sir Hugh Greene's anthologies of vintage detective stories, began a decade of revisions and ever-odder adaptations. *The Hound of the Baskervilles* (1972), with a miscast Stewart Granger (Holmes) and Bernard Fox (Watson), was a cheap, shoddy US television movie that might have hoped to have sequels, but did not. William Shatner did it. *Sherlock Holmes in New York* (1976), with Roger Moore (Holmes) and Patrick MacNee (Watson), was an early attempt to add 'depth' to the character by giving him some sort of an emotional life – in this case, a long-standing attachment to Irene Adler (a well-cast Charlotte Rampling). Moore's saintly, handsome sleuth is a bland reading, but the plot is surprisingly satisfying and John Huston makes a splendidly vicious, Irish-accented Professor Moriarty. Otherwise, there was a tendency to treat Holmes as a joke, with John Cleese taking two (fairly weak) stabs at the part, in 'Elementary, My Dear Watson' (*Comedy Playhouse Presents*, 1973), with Willie Rushton (Watson), and *The Strange Case of the End of Civilisation As We Know It* (1977), with Arthur Lowe (Watson) and Connie Booth (Mrs Hudson and Moriarty). Subtler, but still a jape, was *Dr Watson and the Darkwater Hall Mystery* (1974), scripted by Kingsley Amis, with Edward Fox's Watson blundering through a case while his friend is on holiday. *The Return of the World's Greatest Detective* (1976), a television imitation of *They Might Be Giants* (1971), offers Larry Hagman as 'Sherman Holmes', a purportedly amusing lunatic who *thinks* he is the great detective. A rare straight 1970s Holmes was the British 'Silver Blaze' (*Classics Dark and Dangerous*, 1977), another pilot which did not go to series, with Christopher Plummer (Holmes) and Thorley Walters (Watson); Walters had played Watson several times before, and Plummer (one of a surprising number of Canadian Holmeses) would return to the role in depth in the film *Murder By Decree* (1979). Germany and France offered *Das Zeichen der Vier* (1974) and 'Le Chien des Baskerville' (*Au théâtre de soir*, 1974).

Holmes on TV

Arthur Conan Doyle died in 1930, which meant that under British copyright law as it stood in 1980, his work passed into the public domain at the start of 1981. (This differed in the United States, and revisions to British copyright later muddied the waters by putting Doyle's work back into copyright until the start of 2001.) Consequently, the 1980s saw more Holmesian television than any other decade. *Sherlock Holmes and Doctor Watson* (1980), with Geoffrey Whitehead (Holmes) and Donald Pickering (Watson), was made in Prague and scarcely seen in the United Kingdom or the United States; rather surprisingly, many episodes were remakes of the Ronald Howard shows from the 1950s. Patrick Newell and Kay Walsh appeared as Inspector Lestrade and Mrs Hudson, and some Hammer horror names (Peter Sasdy, Freddie Francis, Roy Ward Baker, Val Guest) handled the direction. The American *Sherlock Holmes* (1981), with Frank Langella (Holmes) and Richard Woods (Watson), and the French *Sherlock Holmes* (1982), with Paul Guers (Holmes) and Philippe Laudenbach (Watson), were both adaptations of the William Gillette play of the same name, which had enjoyed several successful revivals since its 1899 debut. ITV's *Young Sherlock: The Mystery of the Manor House* (1982), with Guy Henry (Holmes), was a children's tea-time serial in which a teenage Holmes embarks on his life's work over eight somewhat-attenuated episodes. In contrast, the BBC's *The Hound of the Baskervilles* (1982), with Tom Baker (Holmes) and Terence Rigby (Watson), was a plodding, straight version of the book. *The Baker Street Boys* (1983), with Roger Ostime (Holmes) and Hubert Rees (Watson), was a more imaginative BBC children's show, with the detective as a supporting character to the street urchins who run his errands. The kids were somewhat outclassed up against Professor Moriarty (Colin Jeavons), but managed four multi-part adventures.

Peter O'Toole, who dropped out of the lead role in Billy Wilder's *The Private Life of Sherlock Holmes* (1970), voiced the detective in four Australian made-for-television cartoons in 1983 (*The Baskerville Curse, The Valley of Fear, The Sign of Four* and *A Study in Scarlet*). That same year, Ian Richardson's Holmes teamed with David Healy and then Donald Churchill as Watson in lavish, but fairly redundant television films based on the best-known books (*The Sign of Four* and *The Hound of the Baskervilles*). Made in Britain, but intended for the international market, they are less memorable than a couple of fanciful television movies. *The Masks of Death* (1984), with Peter Cushing (Holmes) and John Mills (Watson), is set during the First World War and finds the elderly sleuth tackling German spies (including an inevitably fiendish Anton Diffring) and poison gas in the sewers. This elegiac case finds room for Anne Baxter as Irene Adler and Jenny Laird as Mrs Hudson. Directed by Roy Ward Baker, it is a makeshift effort, with fine work from Cushing but tatty in all departments. *The Return of Sherlock Holmes* (1987), with Michael Pennington in the lead, is lifted from the BBC's *Adam Adamant Lives!* (1966–1967). It shows a defrosted detective who awakes in modern times to adventure anew. Before memories could fade, the premise was recycled as *Sherlock Holmes Returns* (also known as *Baker Street 1994*, 1994), in which Anthony Higgins goes through the same shtick to less effect. *Meitantei Holmes/The Amazing Adventures of Sherlock Hound* (1984) is a Japanese anime in which Sherlock and his regular support cast are all dogs; some episodes were directed by anime master Hayako Mayazaki.

All this activity was easy to overlook because the 1980s had an official Sherlock Holmes: Jeremy Brett – who first took the role, with David Burke as Watson, in a series of faithful Doyle adaptations, *The Adventures of Sherlock Holmes* (1984–1985). Brett returned, with Edward Hardwicke replacing Burke, in further series (*The Return of Sherlock Holmes*, 1986; *The Case-Book of Sherlock Holmes*, 1991; and *The Memoirs of Sherlock Holmes*, 1994) and feature-length 'specials' (*The Sign of Four*, 1987; *The Hound of the Baskervilles*, 1988; *The Master Blackmailer*, 1992; *The Last Vampyre*, 1993; and *The Eligible Bachelor*, 1993). Also featured over the run were Colin Jeavons (Lestrade), Gayle Hunnicutt (Irene Adler), Rosalie Williams (Mrs Hudson), Eric Porter (Moriarty) and Charles Gray (Mycroft). At first, Brett's incisive, elegant, wired portrayal of the detective seemed refreshingly close to the literary figure, and the series took great measures to match ***The Strand Magazine*** illustrations. However, as the saga wore on, the leading performance became more and more erratic, stressing the detective's neuroses and failings to the point where the hero ceased to function as a sleuth or a human being. Brett's own illness and production problems meant that two episodes of his final series had to bring on Gray's Mycroft – a hold-over from the film *The Seven-per-Cent Solution* (1976) – to handle the heavy lifting and to take lines written either for Sherlock or Watson. Nevertheless, the first two series – which benefit from excellent, contrasting Watsons – are among the best Doyle adaptations ever mounted for television, and Brett's Holmes casts as long a shadow over those who came later as Gillette's or Rathbone's.

At the same time as Brett was re-establishing Holmes on TV, a similar, perhaps even more accomplishment was achieved on BBC Radio 4. Between 1989 and 1998 the entire Holmes canon was adapted for radio, primarily by Bert Coules, and featured Clive Merrison as Holmes and Michael Williams as Watson. This is the only time the complete Holmes stories have been dramatised featuring the same actors in the lead roles, parts that they fitted perfectly. Coules added further stories to the canon in later radio plays though the untimely death of Williams (he was replaced by Andrew Sachs) meant that the ideal partnership had been sundered.

Outside the English-speaking world, there was another 'definitive' Holmes in a long-running *Sherlok Kholms* series (1979–1986), with Vasili Livanov (Holmes) and Vitali Solomin (Watson), made in the Soviet Union. Though these shows, which adapt all Doyle's major stories and novels, seem strange outside their country of origin, they are charming, respectful and ingenious. Made in the spirit of Russian anglophilia, these stories are uniquely fond of their lead characters and stress the comradely friendship of Holmes and Watson at a time when most other depictions of the pair were intent on presenting them as darker, spikier, far less likeable folks. They certainly offer more entertainment value than various other efforts which flounder in the wake of Jeremy Brett: 'My Dear Watson' (*Alfred Hitchcock Presents*, 1989), with Brian Bedford (Holmes) and Patrick Monckton (Watson); *Hands of a Murderer* (1990), with Edward Woodward (Holmes), John Hillerman (Watson) and Anthony Andrews (Moriarty); *The Crucifer of Blood* (1991), with Charlton Heston (Holmes) and Richard Johnson (Watson); *Sherlock Holmes: The Golden Years* (1992), two long adventures (*Incident at Victoria Falls*, *Sherlock Holmes and the Leading Lady*) with Christopher Lee (Holmes) and Patrick MacNee (Watson) plus parts for Raffles, Eliot Ness and Irene Adler (Morgan Fairchild); and *The Hound of London* (1993), with Patrick MacNee (the first Watson-to-Holmes since Reginald Owen) and John Scott Paget (Watson). More fun was to be had, again, from children's shows: *The Adventures of Shirley Holmes* (1996–1999), with Meredith Henderson as Sherlock's grand-niece, and *Sherlock Holmes in the 22nd Century* (1999), a cartoon with another defrosted Holmes (voiced by Jason Gray Stanford) and a robot Watson (John Payne) pursuing a clone Moriarty (Richard Newman).

Getting back to business as usual, Matt Frewer (Holmes) and Kenneth Welsh (Watson) starred in a quartet of unexceptional, made-in-Canada television movies – inevitably including largely redundant remakes of *The Hound of the Baskervilles* (2000) and *The Sign of Four* (2001). Slightly more interesting are *The Royal Scandal* (2001), which melds 'A Scandal in Bohemia' with 'The Bruce-Partington Plans' and 'His Last Bow' (featuring Liliana Komorowska as Irene Adler and R. Thomson as Mycroft), and *The Case of the Whitechapel Vampire* (2002), a distant derivation from 'The Sussex Vampire' but with a Ripper-like mad monk stalking the fog wielding a garden implement as in the vintage Rathbone case *The Scarlet Claw* (1944). In the twenty-first century, Holmesian television has tended to be more revisionist. *Sherlock* (also known as *Case of Evil*, 2002), with James D'Arcy (Holmes) and Roger Morlidge (Watson), is a 'sexed-up' look at the early days of the partnership, with the callow young Holmes enjoying a three-way with some nineteenth-century sleuth groupies before settling down to the life of celibacy and restraint. Morlidge's Watson is a working coroner (and boxing blue) and a more equal partner in the detective team, but the best thing on offer is Vincent D'Onofrio (channelling James Mason) as Professor Moriarty, who is credited with revolutionising the illegal-drugs trade by refining opium into something much more addictive ('it's called dy-hydro-morphine, but I'm looking for a "street name"...something *heroic*').

Richard E. Grant, Mycroft in *Sherlock* and a lunatic who believes he is Holmes and sets about persecuting Sir Arthur Conan Doyle (Frank Finlay) in 'The Other Side' (*Encounters*, 1992), turned up as Stapleton in the umpteenth *Hound of the Baskervilles* (2002). This dreary BBC production, with Richard Roxburgh (Holmes) and Ian Hart (Watson), again plays up the miserable side, with Holmes as a neurotic, unreliable drug addict who is estranged from his best friend while working on his greatest case. Hart was back, with a louche Rupert Everett (Holmes), in the marginally better *Sherlock Holmes and the Case of the Silk Stocking* (2004), which pits Holmes against a sexual sadist – and dares, in the twenty-first century, to use an evil identical twin as a plot resolution. *Reichenbach Falls* (2007), from the Ian **Rankin** short story, is a musing on the tendency of authors to murder their successful characters – it features Richard Wilson as the ghost of Arthur Conan Doyle; though not very good, it opens up possibilities for more oblique Holmesian television far more interesting than yet more remakes of the Baskervilles. *Sherlock Holmes and the Baker Street Irregulars* (2007), with Jonathan Pryce (Holmes) and Bill Paterson (Watson) is a reprise of *The Baker Street Boys* – this Holmes is not a maniac, but merely melancholy, and spends most of his time under house arrest while some stage-school urchins set about foiling a robbery plot masterminded by an unusually ruthless Irene Adler (Anna Chancellor). It seems highly unlikely that Pryce will be the last television Holmes, but – as most post–Jeremy Brett productions have demonstrated – it is becoming harder and harder to find fresh ways of interpreting the character and his world without tampering with Doyle so much that the detective becomes unrecognisable.

Odd Sherlockian television footnotes include the following: 'Elementary, Dear Data' (*Star Trek: The Next Generation*, 1988), with a hologram Professor Moriarty (Daniel Davis) gaining self-awareness on the *Enterprise*; 'don't worry, the dead man in the deerstalker is just a guest at a fancy dress ball' in *The Murder of Sherlock Holmes* (1984), the pilot for *Murder, She Wrote* (1984–1996); and 'Who Shot Sherlock' (*CSI: Crime Scene Investigation*, 2005), in which a Holmes obsessive is found mysteriously dead in a recreation of the detective's study. Besides straight dramatic productions, many television documentaries have been made about Holmes and his creator (e.g. *True Stories*, 'Sherlock Holmes', 2003; *Timeshift*, 'A Study in Sherlock', 2004). Several dramatic productions have presented biographies or biographical fantasies about Doyle, often focusing on his real-life interest in criminal cases (e.g. Nigel Davenport in *The Edwardians*, 1972) or his association with Harry Houdini (e.g. Peter Cushing in *The Great Houdini*, 1976). David **Pirie** scripted the ingenious *Murder Rooms: The Dark Beginnings of Sherlock Holmes* (2000) – with Ian Richardson as Dr Joseph Bell, the purported real-life inspiration for Holmes, and Robin Laing as the medical student Doyle – is set in Edinburgh with a serial murderer. In 2001, Charles Edwards replaced Laing in four further feature-length cases with Richardson as Bell. Pirie raked over the subject again in *The Strange Case of Sherlock Holmes & Arthur Conan Doyle* (2005), with Douglas Henshall (Doyle) and Brian Cox (Bell); this dropped the crime angle to concentrate on Doyle's relationships with his father, mentor, wives and fictional characters. *See also* TV Detectives: Small-Screen Adaptations.

Kim Newman

Holmes, The Rivals of

The Rivals of Sherlock Holmes is an influential phrase concocted by Hugh Greene for his anthology *The Rivals of Sherlock Holmes* (1970), which showcased detective stories that appeared at the time that Conan **Doyle** was writing the **Holmes** stories, particularly in the period after Holmes's apparent death in 'The Adventure of the Final Problem' (***The Strand Magazine***, December 1893). The stories are to some degree imitative of Holmes, to the extent of a detective investigating unusual crimes, though they are not Holmesian pastiches or parodies. In his anthology, Greene restricted his selection to stories set in **London**, as another defining factor of the Holmesian world, but the success of the book led to three further **anthologies** (and a television series) which removed that restriction, expanding to other cities in *More Rivals of Sherlock Holmes* (1971), the rural counties in *Further Rivals of Sherlock Holmes* (1973) and America in *The American Rivals of Sherlock Holmes* (1976). The phrase has since been used on two further anthologies compiled by Alan K. Russell (1978 and 1979) and a third by Nick Rennison (2007), though David Stuart **Davies** showed originality with *The Shadows of Sherlock Holmes* (1998).

The popularity of the Holmes stories in *The Strand* meant that other **magazines** sought their own equivalent, as did *The Strand* after Conan Doyle ceased writing them. The demand for Holmesian-style detectives continues to this day, but the true rivals are confined to Victorian and Edwardian England, the age of Sherlock Holmes. By the 1920s, a new generation of detectives had emerged as successors to Holmes rather than rivals, most notably Hercule **Poirot**.

The first true 'rival', commissioned by *The Strand* especially for that purpose, was Martin Hewitt, created by Arthur Morrison (1863–1945). Hewitt was a lawyer who became a consultant detective with offices in London and undertook similar unusual cases. However, Hewitt had little of the depth of character of Holmes, a problem with several of the 'rivals'. Loveday Brooke, a female detective created by Catherine L. Pirkis (1839–1910), had appeared in *The Ludgate* in 1893. She was observant and astute but had none of Holmes's ratiocinative deduction. Few of the rivals did. Only a handful came close to walking truly in Holmes's footsteps and satisfying the public for his ability and ingenuity. These include Sebastian Zambra, created by Headon Hill (1857–1927), who had stories in *The Strand*'s companion paper, *The Million*, in 1893; Dr John Thorndyke, the first true scientific detective, created by R. Austin **Freeman**; Paul Gilchrist, the 'Man of Science' in stories by L.T. Meade (1844–1914) and Clifford Halifax; the Old Man in the Corner, one of the first of the armchair detectives, by Baroness Orczy; Paul Beck who relies heavily on his 'rule of thumb', by M. McDonnell Bodkin (1850–1933); and Addington Peace created by Doyle's friend B. Fletcher Robinson (1871–1907). All of these apply themselves to the problem as an intellectual challenge using a variety of skills to reach conclusions. One can also squeeze into that list the stories about Eugene Valmont by Robert Barr (1850–1912). Barr was one of the first to write a Holmes parody in 'The Adventures of Sherlaw Kombs' in his magazine *The Idler* (May 1892). Valmont, though, was a rather vain Frenchman, who was not always successful in his investigations, but who was nevertheless highly perceptive.

Sexton **Blake** is also regarded as a Holmes clone, though in the earliest stories by Harry Blyth and W. Shaw Rae, he bore little comparison. It was not until W. Murray Graydon (1864–1946) moved him into offices in Baker Street and gave him a Holmesian profile that the similarities emerged.

Rather curiously, rogues and villains who outwit the police but who also solve crimes are counted among the rivals, most notably A.J. Raffles by E.W. **Hornung**, Simon Carne by Guy Boothby (1867–1905) and Colonel Clay by Grant Allen (1848–1899). In a growing need to make their detectives distinctive, writers created further abilities. Ernest Bramah's (1868–1942) Max Carrados was blind but used more heightened other senses. Richard Marsh's (1867–1915) Judith Lee could lip read, while Fergus Hume's (1859–1932) Hagar Stanley was a gypsy with special intuitive skills. Then there were the occult investigators among whom Carnacki by William Hope Hodgson (1877–1918) and John Silence by Algernon Blackwood (1869–1951) have clearly recognisable Holmesian traits.

With the passing of Conan Doyle in 1930 and the end to the original Holmes canon, there could only be successors, no more rivals, though imitators and clones continued to appear, showing just how remarkable a creation Sherlock Holmes had been. *See also* The Great Detectives: The Mass Appeal of Holmes, Poirot and Wimsey *and* Origins of British Crime Fiction.

Selected Works
Hugh Greene: *Rivals of Sherlock Holmes* (1970); *More Rivals of Sherlock Holmes* (1971); *Further Rivals of Sherlock Holmes* (1973)
Alan K. Russell: *Rivals of Sherlock Holmes* (1978); *Rivals of Sherlock Holmes 2* (1979)

Mike Ashley

Holms, Joyce (b.1935)

Joyce Holms is the author of a series of accomplished novels set in Edinburgh featuring Scottish solicitor Tam Buchanan and his assistant Fizz Fitzgerald.

Educated in Glasgow, Holms has held a number of different jobs including that of managing a hotel on the Isle of Arran, running a bed-and-breakfast hotel in the

Highlands to working as a private investigator in Edinburgh. She is also the author of three historical romances.

Payment Deferred (1996), Holms's first book, introduced readers to the long-suffering and rather staid solicitor Tam Buchanan and his guileless but ambitious legal assistant Fizz Fitzgerald. When he first meets Fizz, Buchanan is disappointed as she appears much too young for the job. However, Fizz has a knack for getting people to talk and she uses this to good effect. When Murray Kingston comes to see Buchanan, he has already served a three-year sentence for the alleged abuse of his daughter following his wife's death. Kingston hopes Buchanan can persuade the procurator fiscal to reopen the case and prove that he was framed. Holms's narrative skill here is immediately apparent.

In *Thin Ice* (1999), the fourth book in the series, Buchanan is cornered by his cousin Mark, a general practitioner (GP), and persuaded to look into the kidnapping of a young child by his drug-addict father. They do not want to involve the police, and it is left to Fizz with her foolhardy ways to use her ingenuity and intuitiveness to find a way to rescue the child. Like the earlier books, *Thin Ice* crackles with snappy dialogue and witticisms.

In *Hot Potato* (2003), the seventh book in the series, Fizz and Buchanan's attempt to go on a walking holiday is disrupted when they observe a horrendous car crash. They soon find themselves looking after an elderly gentleman with a price on his head. Plotting, always Holms's strong suit, is beautifully turned here.

With the rise of the comedic crime novel, Holms's books established themselves as one of the best from a UK perspective. There are two very different characters in this series: Buchanan, who can be seen as sedate, unexciting and very set in his ways, and Fizz, who is an antithesis, in fact, to Buchanan. Despite this, Fizz does have considerable virtues. She is the type of person who will indulge in disreputable thoughts and opinions that most want to but do not. Fizz and Buchanan are a perfect foil for one another.

The series has real momentum, and characterisation is enriched from book to book. Along with the tight plotting, the black **humour** in the series is dispensed in steady measure but with a lightness of touch. *See also* Humour and Crime Fiction *and* Scottish Crime Fiction.

Selected Works by the Author
Payment Deferred (1996)
Bad Vibes (1998)
Mr Big (2000)
Bitter End (2001)
Hidden Depths (2005)
Missing Link (2006)

Ayo Onatade

Hornung, E.W. (1866–1921)

Although the majority of E.W. Hornung's novels and short stories have not stood the test of time, his relatively few Raffles adventures remain hugely popular.

Ernest William Hornung was born on 7 June 1866 in Marton-in-Cleveland in Middlesbrough. The third son of a Hungarian coal merchant, Hornung (affectionately known as 'Willie') was educated at Uppingham School in Rutland, where he contributed many articles for the school magazine. However, due to ill health, caused partly by severe childhood asthma, he left school at seventeen before completing his studies.

Deciding that a spell in warmer climes might help his recovery, Hornung travelled to Australia in 1884 where he became tutor to the large family of Cecil Joseph Parsons, owner of the 250,000-acre Mossgiel station sheep farm in New South Wales. He stayed there for two years, and his experiences in teaching and working on the farm formed the backbone of his first novel, *A Bride from the Bush*, published in 1890. Concerning the cultural clash caused by an Australian woman on English soil, the novel sought to point out hypocrisies in British society, a theme revisited in his third novel, *Tiny Luttrell* (1892).

Hornung returned to England in February 1886 to care for his sick father (who died later that year). He bought a house in Marylebone and worked as a journalist on various newspapers and periodicals, soon becoming acquainted with such leading literary figures as Jerome K. Jerome, J.M. Barrie, George Gissing and Rudyard Kipling. His most significant friendship, however, was with Arthur Conan **Doyle**, creator of Sherlock **Holmes**. It was this iconic character (together with his trusty colleague Watson) who would become the antithesis of Hornung's celebrated upper-class thief.

Hornung became a member of the Society of Authors, as well as the esteemed Reform Club, and was a tolerable batsman (when his asthma allowed) for the Marylebone Cricket Club. On 27 September 1893 – shortly before Holmes fell from the Reichenbach Falls – he married Conan Doyle's sister, Constance Aimée Monica, in a Catholic wedding service in London, thus becoming Doyle's brother-in-law. They had one son, Arthur Oscar, who was tragically killed in the First World War at the age of twenty-one.

In 1896, Hornung featured an Australian upper-class thief, Stingaree, in his novel *Irralie's Bushranger*. Two years later, in June 1898, an Anglicised incarnation appeared in his short story 'The Ides of March' in *Cassell's Magazine* – and Arthur J. Raffles was born. Reflecting many of the author's own interests, Raffles was a debonair gentleman bachelor of independent means whose apartment in one of Piccadilly's most famous residences, the Albany, showcased his high social status. However, under the cover of darkness, and aided by faithful ex-fag Harry 'Bunny' Manders, Raffles's true self as a criminal mastermind was revealed.

Referring to himself as an 'amateur cracksman' (rather than the more demeaning 'professional criminal'), Raffles was a deliberate inversion of the amateur consulting detective of his brother-in-law. His status as an affluent gentleman (although he was generally penniless) allowed him free access to all the wealthiest homes in London, so that he could burgle those very houses by night that he had visited as a guest by day. Like Holmes's, his exploits were narrated in the first person by his faithful friend Bunny, a former schoolmate rescued from an insolvent lifestyle and now Raffles's strong-arm man in times of trouble. And like Holmes's, Raffles's personal moral code dictated his actions, above and beyond the law: he never took a life (unless it was a foreigner or a blackmailer) and never, ever burgled his host. That just wasn't cricket.

The Ides of March detailed the pair's first crime – a fairly straightforward jewellery robbery – and was followed by seven more stories for *Cassell's*, each more sensationalist than the last. These were collected in a single volume in 1899 as *The Amateur Cracksman* (also known as *Raffles*) and prefaced with a generous dedication to Conan Doyle. The final story, 'The Gift of the Emperor' (November 1898), saw Raffles apparently throwing himself to his doom from a ship rather than facing the ignominy of capture by the authorities.

But, like Holmes before him, Raffles proved so popular that he was resurrected in *The Wrong House* (1899), which bears more than a passing resemblance to Conan Doyle's similarly titled 'reunion' story, *The Adventure of the Empty House*. After eighteen months in jail for Bunny and a mysterious trip to Italy for Raffles, they are brought together once more by way of a forged telegram and a personal notice in *The Daily Mail*. Raffles is noticeably older, having aged 'twenty years' after his watery escape, but the pair are soon up to their old tricks, this time in the less palatial confines of a cottage adjoining Ham Common. Seven stories followed, forming a 1901 collection called *The Black Mask* (also known as *Raffles: Further Adventures of the Amateur Cracksman*).

A third collection, *A Thief in the Night* (1905), consisted of ten stories that brought the Raffles legacy to an end for good. Volunteering for the Boer War under an assumed identity, he is killed in action and his companion left seriously wounded. It is a poignant moment, but by this time, the character had nowhere left to go. A later novel, *Mr Justice Raffles* (1909), set before Raffles's death, didn't quite recapture the happy-go-lucky spirit of the original stories.

Over the years, various actors have played the quintessentially English Raffles, including Ronald Coleman, David Niven, Anthony Valentine and Nigel Havers, while the character was incisively deconstructed by George Orwell in his famous 1944 essay 'Raffles and Miss Blandish'.

During the First World War, Hornung joined the Anti-Aircraft Corps and wrote two volumes of war poetry and a 1919 memoir based on his experiences. In 1921, while holidaying in the picturesque fishing village of Saint-Jean-de Luz on the Basque coast, he contracted pneumonia and died, aged only fifty-four, on 22 March.

Selected Works by the Author
Irralie's Bushranger (1896)
The Amateur Cracksman (1899)
The Black Mask (1901; also published in the United States as *Raffles: Further Adventures of the Amateur Cracksman*)
A Thief in the Night (1905)
Mr Justice Raffles (1909)

Mark Campbell

Horton, Lesley (b.1939)

Lesley Horton's **police procedurals** are set in the complex cultural mix of urban West Yorkshire. Gritty and realistic, they confront the issues and conflicts that arise within multicultural communities.

The books form a series set in Bradford in which the working relationship between Detective Inspector John Handford and Detective Sergeant Khalid Ali reflects the complexities of the community in which they work: a socially deprived urban community with a complicated cultural mix. Religious, cultural and racial issues underlie the books, as do the social problems that confront this community and any modern urban community: interracial and intercultural marriage, the tensions of different sexual mores, child trafficking and child prostitution, racism and the rise of the political extreme right.

Her first novel, *Snares of Guilt*, was published in June 2002 after Horton retired from teaching in order to fulfil her ambition to write. It was recognised as the debut novel of a talented new voice in the field of crime fiction. The book is set in the aftermath of severe racial tension and involves the murder of Rukhsana Mahmood, a young woman in a mixed marriage. The book is not simply a crime novel: it explores the deep hostilities and tensions that such marriages cause within the families and between the communities involved.

Horton's second novel, *On Dangerous Ground* (2003), confronts the issues of child murder and child prostitution, and continues the exploration that began in her first book of the frequently edgy working relationship between Handford and Ali.

Devils in the Mirror (2005) explores the very current issue of false accusations of child abuse when a young girl, Shayla Richards, who has accused her teacher of abusing her is found sexually assaulted and murdered on Druids Altar, a beauty spot on the moors above the city.

The Hollow Core (2006) addresses the rise of the far right in socially deprived UK cities with large ethnic minority communities, as a series of crimes are committed that may be politically or racially motivated. It also explores the ways in which concepts of honour and shame can obstruct the progress of an investigation.

The books trenchantly anatomise the development of the characters in their private relationships, their career paths and the professional relationships the central characters have with each other. Horton makes use of her own career background in these books. She taught in a predominantly Muslim inner-city comprehensive in Bradford for many years and earlier was the head of a unit for pregnant schoolgirls and schoolgirl mothers. The theme of the different identities women have to assume within the context of a multicultural society is one that Horton returns to repeatedly. Her books use the conventions of the police procedural to explore a range of issues confronting modern urban society, within the context of compelling narrative. *See also* Realism and Crime Fiction *and* Social Comment in Crime Fiction.

Selected Works by the Author
Snares of Guilt (2002)
On Dangerous Ground (2003)
Devils in the Mirror (2005)
The Hollow Core (2006)

Carla Banks

Household, Geoffrey (1900–1988)

One of the earliest examples of the 'high concept' thriller, Geoffrey Household's remarkable 1939 novel *Rogue Male* has overtaken in popularity many of the author's other, equally interesting works.

Born in Bristol on 30 November 1900, Geoffrey Edward West Household was the son of a lawyer who later became Secretary of Education for Gloucester. Household was educated at Clifton College in his hometown, and then went on to study English at Magdalen College, Oxford, where he received a BA degree in 1922. For the next thirteen years, he worked abroad in a variety of jobs: as an assistant secretary for the Bank of Romania in Bucharest, as marketing director for a fruit exporter in Spain, as a children's encyclopaedia contributor in America and as a travelling salesman for a printing-ink manufacturer across Europe, the Middle East and South America.

In Spain, Household taught himself to speak and write in the country's native language, while his wide-ranging international travels allowed him to build up a huge storehouse of knowledge that would be of immeasurable use to him as a novelist. In the early 1930s, he had his first taste of professional writing when, during his stay in America, he was asked to compose some children's radio plays for Columbia Broadcasting System (CBS); a few years later, his first published story, *The Salvation of Pisco Gabar*, appeared in the January *The Atlantic Monthly*. Together with eleven other stories, it was included in a collection of the same name in 1939.

His debut novel was a fantasy adventure for children: the luridly titled *The Terror of Villadonga* (1936, also known as *The Spanish Cave*) in which courageous young Dick Garland battles a terrifying prehistoric sea serpent in present-day Spain. His second novel, *The Third Hour* (1937), continued the theme, with its fantasy-orientated search for a legendary Utopia in the jungles of South America. However, it was with his next novel, *Rogue Male*, that he cemented his reputation as a contemporary thriller writer of great skill.

Written in commendably lean prose, *Rogue Male* describes what happens when an unnamed English hunting enthusiast utilises his well-honed marksmanship skills to assassinate a European dictator bent on world domination. The dictator, of course, is a thinly disguised Adolf Hitler, while the protagonist is the sort of lantern-jawed upper-crust hero familiar from such spy novels as John **Buchan**'s *The Thirty-Nine Steps* (1915). What sets *Rogue Male* apart is the sheer bravado of its rugged, no-nonsense narrative style and the brutality of its controversial torture scene, neither rarely attempted again – at least, in such depth – until Ian **Fleming**'s *Casino Royale* a decade and a half later. Household's gentleman assassin has a higher moral code than, say, Raffles, but his 'means to an end' philosophy inevitably invokes the cold, emotionless killing machine that is James Bond. Both Bond and the nameless assassin have a further thing in common – they endure a journey of extreme personal hardship, physically as well as emotionally, and despite the first-person narratives, we never quite know how they are going to survive their terrible predicaments.

The hunter fails to kill his quarry, is captured and thrown from a cliff, but manages to escape to England where he is hunted down like a rabid dog by the ruthless German henchman Major Quive-Smith. Seeking refuge in Dorset, where the hunter once found true love, he is literally brought to ground in an underground den with apparently no means of escape. Tense, thrilling and full of well-researched detail, it's hard not to see Household's novel as providing the inspiration for Frederick **Forsyth**'s equally documentary-like assassination thriller *The Day of the Jackal* in 1971.

Rogue Male was made into a film in 1941 by German director Fritz Lang. Retitled *Man Hunt*, it starred Canadian actor Walter Pidgeon as the English protagonist, here named Captain Alan Thorndike, while the quintessentially English George Sanders played Quive-Smith. Odd casting aside, it was an effective mood piece, although more of a springboard for Lang's expressionist tendencies than a straightforward adaptation. A more accurate version was Clive Donner's 1976 television movie, co-written by Eric **Ambler**; it featured Peter O'Toole as Captain (Robert) Thorndyke – a restrained performance – and John Standing as his evil nemesis.

After *Rogue Male*, there was a gap of nearly ten years before Household wrote the spy caper *Arabesque* (1948), which was soon followed by two books in which ex-soldier Roger Taine battles against secretive East German gangs: *A Rough Shoot* and *A Time to Kill* (both 1951). A welter of assorted thrillers materialised from 1960 onwards, the most significant of these being the well-crafted *Watcher in the Shadows* (1960, filmed as *Deadly Harvest* in 1972) and *Dance of the Dwarfs* (1968, filmed as *The Adversary* in 1983). Both of these depicted nail-biting chases not a million miles from the plot of *Rogue Male*, so it was no great shock to see Household attempt a belated sequel to it in 1982s *Rogue Justice*, where the hunter, now called Raymond Ingelram, sets off to Poland to rescue his lover from the clutches of the Nazis.

Household lived in Dorset, and then Buckinghamshire, and continued writing until his death on 4 October 1988. His final book, *Face to the Sun* (1988), was a picaresque adventure set against the political turmoil of South America.

Selected Works by the Author
Rogue Male (1939)
Arabesque (1948)
A Rough Shoot (1951)
Watcher in the Shadows (1960)
Dance of the Dwarfs (1968)
Red Anger (1975)
Hostage: London (1977)
Rogue Justice (1982)

Mark Campbell

Hubbard, P.M. (1910–1980)

For a decade and a half, P.M. Hubbard was a prolific exponent of quintessentially English literary mysteries that dwelt as much on murder as they did on vivid characterisations, gloomy, brooding horror and sharply defined *genius loci*.

Philip Maitland Hubbard was born in 1910 in Reading, Berkshire, but moved to Guernsey when he was a boy. He was educated at Elizabeth College, a boys' public school in the island's capital, Saint Peter Port. He studied Classics at Jesus College, Oxford, winning the Newdigate Prize in 1933 for his poem *Ovid Among the Goths*, and went straight into the Indian Civil Service in north-west India until its independence in 1947.

On returning to England, he worked for the British Council before becoming a freelance writer, contributing various articles and poems to *Punch* magazine from 1950 onwards. He eventually settled down to writing novels, and his first book – *Flush as May*, a quotation from *Hamlet* – appeared in 1963. Ostensibly a murder story set in a sleepy English village, the story is infused with Hubbard's love of pagan mysticism, and there is a tangible sense of suspense that belies the lack of any obvious horror.

His next book, *Picture of Millie* (1964), recounted the deliberate drowning of a vamp at a genteel seaside resort. In this book, the author gives exhaustive descriptions of the flora and fauna of the place that, depending on one's point of view, are either deeply engrossing or painfully slow. It was to be his third book, *A Hive of Glass* (1965), that proved to be one of his best remembered. Set in a run-down English seaside town, the story is about glass-collector Johnnie Slade's obsession for a rare Venetian goblet which leads him to a remote house and a mysteriously alluring woman. The novel mixed sex, death and greed with – for its time – graphic scenes of violence.

Hubbard's predilection for atmosphere over plot, coupled with his often relentlessly dour prose style, led to some critics calling his later books dull, specifically *The Tower* (1967) and *A Rooted Sorrow* (1973). But his obsessions with water, isolation and the underlying amorality of the main characters led to some memorable tales. *The Causeway* (1976) has all these, with its setting of an island cut off from the Scottish coast at high tide, a strange couple in a mysterious house and the selfish actions of its protagonist, Peter Grant.

Hubbard died on 17 March 1980. Long out of print, his richly evocative mystery novels are well worth seeking out by discerning readers of both literary crime and gothic mysteries.

Selected Works by the Author
Flush as May (1963)
A Hive of Glass (1965)
The Tower (1967)
High Tide (1970)
The Dancing Man (1971)
A Thirsty Evil (1974)
The Quiet River (1978)
Kill Claudio (1979)

Website
http://www.mysteryfile.com/Hubbard/Worlds.html

Mark Campbell

Humour and Crime Fiction

Some readers and critics believe that fictional crime should not be treated humorously. Fortunately, many writers have disregarded this view. Instead, they have followed the examples of such great literary predecessors as Shakespeare, who balanced tragedy and comedy, and **Dickens** and Wilkie **Collins**, whose humour lightens their plots.

The rules for detective fiction devised by Ronald **Knox** in the 1920s do not exclude humour, even though it can be distracting. Knox used it in his own writing, as did other **Golden Age** authors. Dorothy L. **Sayers** created comic characters and situations, and introduced witty repartee and satire. Similarly, Margery **Allingham**'s fertile imagination devised unforgettably amusing characters and episodes. This convention continued, particularly with comic characters in **police procedurals**, like Joyce **Porter**'s Dover and H.R.F. **Keating**'s Inspector Ghote. In the works of Reginald **Hill** and Catherine **Aird**, the **humour** is partly in the interplay between senior and junior police officers: Dalziel and Pascoe, and Sloan and Leeyes, respectively.

Although Nicholas **Blake** and other male authors in the 1930s and 1940s conformed to this pattern, some rejected it. Between the wars, Michael **Innes** produced his early works. His enormous output of crime fiction includes humour ranging from academic wit and satire to pure farce. Innes regarded detective fiction as amusement combined with a puzzle, using crime as a background to the comedy. Edmund **Crispin**, master of farcical set pieces, used the same approach. He was adept at creating comic or witty scenes and characters, and attacking human foibles. In Colin **Watson**'s writing, the plot is sometimes almost overwhelmed by the comedy, which is generally much earthier than that of Innes and Crispin. Equally irreverent, and often a wickedly funny satirist, is Robert **Barnard** – at his best when targeting academics. Ruth Dudley **Edwards** is one of the few women whose plots and investigations are subordinate to humour. Like Watson and Barnard, she creates bawdy and uproarious situations whilst satirising different aspects of the establishment.

A number of other contemporary crime writers have constructed their humour around an amateur detective. The adventures of Tim **Heald**'s anti-hero, Bognor, Board of Trade investigator, form a background to comedy and biting social satire. Similarly, Simon **Brett**'s seedy actor, Charles Paris, reveals the comic failings in the world of performing arts. For his investigative journalist Jack Parlabane, Christopher **Brookmyre** was awarded the Sherlock Award for Best Comic Detective in 2000. Peter **Guttridge** combines thrills and comedy for his journalist sleuth Nick Madrid, while Mike **Ripley**'s Angel has never been very keen to work at anything. Angel's investigations are usually entangled in hilarious incidents.

The outcome of most investigations is a court case, which might involve Horace Rumpole, John Mortimer's barrister creation. Though he frustrates his wife and colleagues, Rumpole's great success lies in defending the downtrodden.

Although all readers do not appreciate the same kind of humour, and some might prefer David **Williams**'s witty Treasure to the coarse Dover, the introduction of humour has done much to enrich crime writing. A good cross-section of humorous short fiction will be found in Maxim **Jakubowski**'s anthology, *The Mammoth Book of Comic Crime* (2002).

Further Reading
Jakubowski, Maxim. 2002. *The Mammoth Book of Comic Crime*. Constable Robinson.

Christine Simpson

Hunter, Alan (1922–2005)

In just under fifty novels, Alan Hunter's Chief Inspector (later Superintendent) George Gently's thorough investigations form the basis for a solid series of **police procedurals**. The humanity with which Gently does so has drawn comparisons to Georges Simenon's Inspector Maigret.

Alan Hunter, a passionate advocate for his beloved Norfolk countryside, made a mark as a poet in the Second World War and began writing crime fiction in 1955. He was a stalwart of the East Anglian Chapter of the **Crime Writers' Association**. Hunter died in 2005, just before his character achieved success in a series of television adaptations with Martin Shaw.

When Chief Inspector George Gently made his first appearance (in 1955 in *Gently Does It*), he is in his early fifties and ages little in the subsequent instalments. He works for the Criminal Investigation Department (CID) and is called in on unsolved cases for local authorities. Inevitably, this leads to an antagonistic relationship with the police officers who were previously in charge, and George often has to remind them that they are all working for justice. To ensure a tight narrative, Hunter introduces Gently onto the scene after a situation has arisen over a period of time, becoming the catalyst that brings it to an end. Hunter has said that he based his policeman on the characteristics of four top-ranking detectives described in Anthony Martienssen's *Crime and the Police* (1951). Some of these traits were phased out in later books, and some of the Hunter's own added. The author tends to set his books in the East Anglia that he was familiar with. However, three novels were set in **London**; a further three in Scotland; one in Wales; and one, *The Honfleur Decision* (in which George meets Gabrielle Orbec, his future wife), in France. (It takes Gently a few further instalments, however, before he can convince her to marry him.) In many books, both Gently and the reader are aware of the culprit long before the end. The remainder of the story is focused on the gathering of evidence, allowing the police to make a fully informed arrest. In building his case, Gently will familiarise himself with the surroundings of the crime and those affected by it, followed by a close examination of the facts and evidence. Only this will allow Gently to successfully interrogate the suspects and identify those responsible for the crime. Though Hunter made an occasional foray into narrative experimentation, the vast majority of his novels are written in the third person.

In 2007, Martin Shaw, having previously played P.D. **James**'s Commander Dalgliesh for the BBC, played the title role in their feature-length drama *George Gently*. Loosely based on *Gently Go Man* (1961), this pilot for a subsequent series has George about to leave the police force when a case with personal ties and police corruption sees him travelling to northern England.

Selected Works by the Author
Gently Does It (1955)
Gently down the Stream (1957)
Gently Go Man (1961)
Gently with the Ladies (1965)
Gently Continental (1967)
Gently with the Innocents (1970)
The Honfleur Decision (1980)
The Unhung Man (1984; also published in the United States as *The Unhanged Man*)
Gently Mistaken (1999)

Adrian Muller

Hurley, Graham (b.1946)

In the crowded genre of the **police procedural**, Graham Hurley's ever-more-impressive Portsmouth-based series has been widely hailed as an authentic depiction of modern-day policing, with authentic detail matched by highly adroit plotting.

Hurley was educated at a boarding school in London and went on to read English at Cambridge. His ambition was to be a novelist, but after several rejection slips, he went to work at Southern Television, first as a promotion scriptwriter, then as a researcher, before becoming a director and producer of documentary films, several of which won awards. His first novel, *Rules of Engagement*, published in 1990, was based on a six-part drama series commissioned for ITV. Having lost his job when TVS lost its franchise, he embarked on a career as a full-time writer, publishing a further eight novels and two factual books before producing the first of what was to be a series of police procedurals.

The series, which begins strikingly with *Turnstone* (2000), describes an over-stretched police force fighting a rising tide of violence and petty crime. *Turnstone*'s

47. Graham Hurley.

central character is Detective Inspector Joe Faraday, and the centrality of his role is made clear on the book's jacket: 'A Joe Faraday novel'. Among the dramatis personae is Detective Constable Paul Winter, a volatile maverick whose personality immediately stands out. Winter went on to play an increasingly important part in the books that followed, and the Faraday tag line was eventually (and wisely) dropped. Theirs is not the traditional partnership in police procedurals, in which the inspector or chief inspector has a junior officer, usually a sergeant, as his assistant. The new approach in Hurley's books adds a certain piquancy to the relationship of his protagonists when their paths cross. Faraday is an intuitive detective, self-contained, solitary. Winter is a copper in the old style, a thief catcher who knows all the regular criminals in his area and is impatient with rules if they get in his way. By the third book, *Angels Passing* (2002), he has seen his wife die of cancer. Faraday, a widower for many years, relaxes by birdwatching, on his own or in the company of his deaf son, but Winter, once a serial womaniser, now has only his work. They follow separate paths in the kinetic *Cut To Black* (2004), in which Faraday leads a squad in an ambitious operation to try to bring down the city's chief villain, a man with whom Winter has his own scores to settle. In the fifth book, *One Under* (2007), Winter, recovering from a near-fatal brain tumour, has softened slightly and for the first time, the two men work closely, if not always comfortably. *The Price of Darkness* (2008) freighted in extra layers of complexity and ambiguity.

Not unexpectedly from an experienced film-maker, the books have an almost cinematic quality, and this enables Hurley to include minute detail of the police investigations without slowing the narrative. His books intelligently explore some of the fundamental problems of contemporary British society. Grimly realistic, they utilise violence only when relevant to the plot and are above all examples of well-paced storytelling.

Selected Works by the Author
Turnstone (2000)
The Take (2001)
Angels Passing (2002)
Deadlight (2003)
Cut to Black (2004)
Blood and Honey (2006)
One Under (2007)
The Price of Darkness (2008)

Susanna Yager

Hutchinson's Mystery Story Magazine

The **pulp** magazine *Hutchinson's* has acquired a legendary status, not so much because of its quality, but because of its rarity and its association with the American pulp magazine *Weird Tales*. It ran for fifty-five issues from February 1923 to September 1927. No editors are credited, but research has shown that E. Charles Vivian (1882–1947) was editor for the first two years, followed by Oscar Cook (1888–1952), Meredith Dixon and Miss G. Gilligan. Only one complete run is known.

48. Cover of *Hutchinson's Mystery Story Magazine*.

It was produced by the publisher Hutchinson and was a companion to Britain's first specialist magazine, *Adventure-Story*, launched in September 1922. Hutchinson relied heavily on exchange arrangements for stories with American publishers, initially with Bernard Macfadden for his magazine *Midnight Mysteries* (and later *Ghost Stories*) and also Street & Smith for various publications, including *Detective Story Magazine*. As a consequence, most of the magazine's content was American, and in the vein of suspense, mystery and horror rather than crime and detection. In the early issues, British authors tended to contribute supernatural stories, though there were some straight detection stories. Francis D. Grierson (1888–1972) contributed a series, 'The Professor's Problems' (April to November 1923), much in the style of Dr Thorndyke, whilst Ronald Newman created a Holmes-like detective in 'Concerning Mr Rumm' (April 1923). Editor Vivian contributed several of his own stories including a serial about an accursed jewel, 'The Tiger's Tear' (November 1923 to April 1924), under the pseudonym Galbraith Nicholson.

Only a few well-known writers appeared, with most other contributors being reliable second-tier authors such as F.A.M. Webster (1886–1949), Edmund Snell (1889–1972) and E.R. Punshon (1872–1956), and, most of the stories by major names (Sax **Rohmer**, Mrs Belloc Lowndes, Edgar **Wallace** and William **Le Queux**) were reprints. There were, though, a handful of new stories by names that were becoming better known or later earned reputations. There was an early story by Peter **Cheyney** ('A Double, Double Cross', May 1924), a now-classic horror story by Michael Joseph ('The Yellow Cat', June 1924) and three brief macabre tales by Ursula Bloom (1893–1984).

Under Oscar Cook, the magazine ran a high level of *contes cruel*, whilst under its final editors, it reprinted heavily from the American magazine *Ghost Stories*, including staged photographs of hauntings. The magazine was combined with *Adventure-Story* in October 1927 and renamed *Adventure & Mystery-Story Magazine*; ironically, it was the mystery element that strengthened, with the magazine reprinting Agatha **Christie**'s 'Tommy and Tuppence' stories from *The Sketch*, but before they appeared in book form, as well as a higher quota of stories from American detective pulps.

During its existence, *Mystery-Story* opened up a small British market for strange and unusual stories but did little to advance British crime fiction.

Further Reading
Miller, Stephen T., and William G. Contento. 2006. *Science Fiction, Fantasy & Weird Fiction Magazine Index (1890–2005)*. Locus Press.

Mike Ashley

List of Illustrations

1. John Thaw as Inspector Morse in the ITV television series. Carlton TV. Ronald Grant Archive.
2. Margery Allingham at her desk. The Margery Allingham Society.
3. Lisa Appignanesi. Credit Isabelle Boccon-Gibod.
4. Steve Aylett. By permission of the author.
5. Carla Banks. By permission of the author.
6. Simon Beckett. By permission of the author.
7. Mark Billingham. Credit Charlie Hopkinson.
8. Cover of *The Sexton Blake Library*.
9. Victoria Blake. By permission of the author.
10. Nicholas Blincoe. By permission of the author.
11. Stephen Booth. By permission of the author.
12. Chaz Brenchley. By permission of the author.
13. Actors William Hartnell, Richard Attenborough and Harry Ross in *Brighton Rock* (1947). Ronald Grant Archive.
14. Christopher Brookmyre. By permission of the author.
15. Tom Cain. By permission of the author.
16. Ramsey Campbell. Credit Peter Coleborn.
17. A newspaper of 1 January 1926 reports Christie's mysterious disappearance. Hulton Archive. Getty Images.
18. William Wilkie Collins, photographed c.1870. World History Archive. Alamy.
19. Natasha Cooper. By permission of the author.
20. Cover of *Creasey* Mystery Magazine for July 1958.
21. Cover of *Crime Time*, issue 52, 2007.
22. Charles Cumming. Credit Neil Cooper.
23. David Stuart Davies. By permission of the author.
24. Carol Anne Davis. By permission of the author.
25. Lindsey Davis. Credit Michael Trevillion.
26. Autograph fair copy of 'The Adventure of the Missing Three Quarter', first published in *The Strand* magazine in August 1904. The British Library/HIP. Topfoto.
27. Stella Duffy. By permission of the author.
28. Cover of the second issue of the *Edgar Wallace Mystery Magazine,* in September 1964.
29. Martin Edwards. By permission of the author.
30. Ruth Dudley Edwards. By permission of the author.
31. R.J. Ellroy. Copyright 2007 riverstudio.co.uk.
32. Director Alfred Hitchcock contemplates Robert Donat and Lucie Mannheim on the set of *The 39 Steps* (1935). Ronald Grant Archive.
33. Christopher Fowler. By permission of the author.
34. Philip Gooden. By permission of the author.
35. Cover of Mellifont Press's *Sweeney Todd* from the 1930s. Mary Evans Picture Library. Alamy.
36. Lesley Grant-Adamson. By permission of the author.
37. Jon Courtenay Grimwood. By permission of the author.
38. Peter Guttridge. By permission of the author.
39. Maggie Hamand. Credit Philip Wolmuth.
40. John Harvey. By permission of the author.
41. Chris Haslam. By permission of the author.
42. Mo Hayder. By permission of the author.
43. Lauren Henderson. By permission of the author.
44. Reginald Hill. By permission of the author.
45. Cover of the paperback edition of *Saturnalia* (2008) by Lindsey Davis. The Random House Group Ltd.
46. Jeremy Brett and Edward Hardwicke star as Holmes and Watson in *The Return of Sherlock Holmes* (Granada Television, 1987). Granada TV/Album. AKG-Images.
47. Graham Hurley. By permission of the author.
48. Cover of *Hutchinson's Mystery Story Magazine*.
49. Bill James. By permission of the author.
50. Russell James. By permission of the author.
51. Cover of *When Dames Get Tough* (originally published in 1946). Telos Publishing Ltd.
52. Quintin Jardine. By permission of the author.
53. Paul Johnston. By permission of the author.
54. Portrait of Ronald Knox by caricaturist Powys Evans ('Quiz'), 1922. Mary Evans Picture Library. Alamy.

55. Janet Laurence. By permission of the author.

56. Stephen Leather. By permission of the author.

57. Police Constable Neil finds the body of Ripper victim Mary Ann Nicholas in Bucks Row, Whitechapel, in the East End of London. Mary Evans Picture Library. Alamy.

58. Cover of *The London Mystery Magazine*, 1950.

59. Peter Lovesey. Credit Kate Shemilt.

60. Paul McAuley. Credit Georgina Hawtrey-Woore.

61. Val McDermid. Credit Andy Peebles.

62. Cover of *Mackill*'s Mystery Magazine in September 1952.

63. John McLaren. By permission of the author.

64. Cover of a war-time issue of *The Strand* magazine.

65. Cover of the first issue of *Mystery Stories* in 1936.

66. Jessica Mann. By permission of the author.

67. Joan Hickson as Miss Marple in *A Pocketful of Rye* (BBC Television, 1985). BBC. Ronald Grant Archive.

68. Ngaio Marsh (right) and Agatha Christie (left) meet at a party at the Savoy Hotel, June 1960. Evening Standard/Hulton Archive. Getty Images.

69. Margaret Murphy. By permission of the author.

70. Barbara Nadel. By permission of the author.

71. Cover of the Modesty Blaise novel, *A Taste for Death* (1969)

72. Gilda O'Neill. By permission of the author.

73. Charles Palliser. By permission of the author.

74. Stuart Pawson. By permission of the author.

75. Portrait of Hercule Poirot by Smithson Broadhead, published in *The Sketch* in 1923. Illustrated London News. Mary Evans Picture Library.

76. James Ellis and Arthur Slater star in *Z Cars* (BBC Television). Ron Spillman. Rex Features.

77. Ian Rankin. By permission of the author.

78. Robert Richardson. By permission of the author.

79. Phil Rickman. By permission of the author.

80. Michael Ridpath. By permission of the author.

81. Mike Ripley. By permission of the author.

82. David Roberts. By permission of the author.

83. Rosemary Rowe.

84. Nicholas Royle. By permission of the author.

85. Cover of the magazine when it was still called *The Saint Detective Magazine*.

86. Zoë Sharp. Credit Andy Butler, ZACE Photographic.

87. Cover of *Wycliffe and the Cycle of Death* (1990), one of W.J. Burley's novels set in Cornwall. Orion Publishing Group.

88. Cover of P.D. James's *A Shroud for a Nightingale* (1971), set on the Sussex-Hampshire border. Faber and Faber.

89. Cover of John Harvey's *Wasted Years* (1993), a Charlie Resnick story set in Nottingham, in the Midlands. The Random House Group Ltd.

90. Cover of Graham Hurley's *Blood and Honey* (2004), set in Dorset. Orion Publishing Group.

91. Cover of *Shots* magazine, Summer 2001.

92. Chris Simms. By permission of the author.

93. Iain Sinclair. By permission of the author.

94. Joan Smith. By permission of the author.

95. Michelle Spring. Credit Mary Bernard.

96. Cath Staincliffe. By permission of the author.

97. Veronica Stallwood. By permission of the author.

98. Cover of *The Strand* magazine for February 1936, advertising a new story by Agatha Christie. Mary Evans Picture Library. Alamy.

99. Cover of *Suspense* magazine, July 1959.

100. Frank Tallis. By permission of the author.

101. Elizabeth Mackintosh, also known as Josephine Tey, photographed in April 1934. Sasha/Hulton Archive. Getty Images.

102. Cover of *The Thriller* magazine, August 1935.

103. James Twining. By permission of the author.

104. Cover of *Union Jack* magazine, advertising a Sexton Blake feature, in January 1931.

105. John Williams. By permission of the author.

106. Laura Wilson. By permission of the author.

Select Bibliography

Books

Benstock, B., and T.F. Staley, eds. 1988. *British Mystery Writers, 1860–1919*. Gale.

———. 1989a. *British Mystery and Thriller Writers since 1940*. Gale.

———. 1989b. *British Mystery Writers, 1920–1939*. Gale.

Binyon, T.J. 1989. *'Murder Will Out': The Detective in Fiction*. Oxford University Press.

Breen, J.L., ed. 1981. *What about Murder? A Guide to Books about Mystery and Detective Fiction*. Scarecrow.

———. 1993. *What about Murder? 1981–1991: A Guide to Books about Mystery and Detective Fiction*. Scarecrow.

Chernaik, W., M. Swales and R. Vilain, eds. 2000. *The Art of Detective Fiction*. Macmillan.

Chibnall, S., and R. Murphy, eds. 1999. *British Crime Cinema*. Routledge.

Church, R., and M. Edwards, eds. 1995. *Anglian Blood: An Anthology of East Anglian Crime Writing*. Rampant Horse.

Earwaker, J., and K. Becker. 2002. *Scene of the Crime: A Guide to the Landscapes of British Detective Fiction*. Aurum.

Forshaw, Barry. 2007. *The Rough Guide to Crime Fiction*. Penguin.

Haycroft, H. 1941. *Murder for Pleasure: The Life and Times of the Detective Story*. D. Appleton-Century.

———. 1946. *The Art of the Mystery Story: A Collection of Critical Essays*. Biblo and Tannen.

Herbert, R., ed. 2000. *The Oxford Companion to Crime and Mystery Writing*. Oxford University Press.

Johnson, T.W., and J. Johnson, eds. 1981. *Crime Fiction Criticism: An Annotated Bibliography*. Garland.

Kestner, J.A. 2003. *Sherlock's Sisters: The British Female Detective, 1864–1913*. Ashgate.

Klein, K.G., ed. 1994. *Great Women Mystery Writers: Classics to Contemporary*. Greenwood.

Knight, S. 2003. *Crime Fiction, 1800–2000: Detection, Death, Diversity*. Palgrave Macmillan.

Lehman, D. 2000. *The Perfect Murder: A Study in Detection*. University of Michigan Press.

MacDonald, G., ed. 2003. *British Mystery and Thriller Writers since 1960*. Gale.

Maguire, S., and A. Hargreaves, eds. 1999. *Something Wicked, Something New: New Scottish Crime Writing*. Polygon.

Mandel, E. 1984. *Delightful Murder: A Social History of the Crime Story*. Pluto.

Mann, J. 1981. *Deadlier Than the Male: Crime Writing – the Feminine Touch*. David and Charles.

Murch, A.E. 1958. *The Development of the Detective Novel*. Philosophical Library.

Murphy, B.F. 1999. *The Encyclopedia of Murder and Mystery*. St Martin's Press.

Ousby, I. 1976. *Bloodhounds of Heaven: The Detective in English Fiction from Godwin to Doyle*. Harvard University Press.

Panek, L.L. 1979. *Watteau's Shepherds: The Detective Novel in Britain 1914–1940*. Popular Press.

Pederson, J.P., ed. 1996. *St. James Guide to Crime and Mystery Writers*, 4th ed. St. James Press.

Penzler, O., ed. 1978. *The Great Detectives*. Little, Brown.

Priestman, M., ed. 2003. *The Cambridge Companion to Crime Fiction*. Cambridge University Press.

Roth, M. 1995. *Foul and Fair Play: Reading Genre in Classic Detective Fiction*. University of Georgia Press.

Rowland, S. 2000. *From Agatha Christie to Ruth Rendell: British Women Writers in Detective and Crime Fiction*. Palgrave Macmillan.

Salwak, D. 1991. *Mystery Voices: Interviews with British Crime Writers – Catherine Aird, P.D. James, H.R.F. Keating, Ruth Rendell and Julian Symons*. Borgo Press.

Swanson, Jean and Dean James. 1994 (revised, 1996). *By a Woman's Hand*. Berkley.

Symons, J. 1962. *The Detective Story in Britain*. Longmans, Green and Company.

———. 1992. *Bloody Murder: From the Detective Story to the Crime Novel*, 3rd ed. Mysterious.

Thoms, P. 1998. *Detection and Its Designs: Narrative and Power in Nineteenth-Century Detective Fiction*. Ohio University Press.

Watson, C. 1971. *Snobbery with Violence: Crime Stories and their Audience*. Eyre and Spottiswoode.

Winks, R.W., ed. 1988. *Detective Fiction: A Collection of Critical Essays*. Foul Play Press.

Winn, Dilys. 1979. *Murderess Ink*. Workman Publishing. Revised 1981, Bell.

Journals

Baker Street Journal Steven Rothman, editor
  (www.bakerstreetjournal.com)
CADS Geoff Bradley, editor
CrimeSpree Jon & Ruth Jordan, editors
  (www.crimespreeemag.com)
Crime Time Barry Forshaw, editor
  (www.crimetime.co.uk)
Deadly Pleasures George Easter, editor
  (www.deadlypleasures.com)
Mystery File Steve Lewis, editor (currently
  in blog format)
Mystery News Lynn Kaczmarek & Chris
  Aldrich, editors (www.blackravenpress.com)
Mystery Readers Journal Janet Rudolph, editor
  (www.mysteryreaders.org/journal.html)
Mystery Scene Brian Skupin & Kate Stine,
  publishers (www.mysteryscenemag.com)
Over My Dead Body (www.overmydeadbody.
  com)
Thriller UK (www.thrilleruk.fsnet.co.uk)

Websites

Classic Crime Fiction: www.classiccrimefiction.
  com
Crimespot – RSS Feed to all main Crime Blogs:
  www.crimespot.net
Crimesquad: http://crimesquad.com/
Crime Time: www.crimetime.co.uk
The Crime Writers' Association:
  www.thecwa.co.uk
A Guide to Classic Mystery and Detection:
  www.members.aol.com/MG4273/classics.htm
A Guide to Classic Mystery Novels and
  Detective Stories: www.mysterylist.com
January Magazine: www.januarymagazine.com
Murder in the Stacks: www.springfieldlibrary.
  org/stacks
The Mystery Reader: http://www.
  themysteryreader.com/
Mystery Writer: http://writemystery.
  blogspot.com/
A Pathfinder on the Evolution of the English
  Detective Novel: www.unc.edu/~rdtowery/
  detective_novel.htm
Tangled Web UK: www.twbooks.co.uk
Thrilling Detective: http://www.
  thrillingdetective.com/
Thrilling Detective Blog: http://
  thrillingdetectiveblog.blogspot.com/
Web Mystery Magazine: http://lifeloom.com/
  webmysterymagazine.htm

About the Editor and Contributors

Editor

Barry Forshaw is the author of *The Rough Guide to Crime Fiction* (Penguin, 2007) and a contributor to *Film Noir* (Penguin, 2007). He has written for *The Independent, The Express* and *The Times*. His book on Italian cinema was published in 2006, and he edits the fiction review *Crime Time*. Besides his specialist area of crime fiction, he writes on film for a variety of magazines and creates booklets for special-edition DVDs. He has contributed to books on literary fiction and film noir. He has acted as a judge for the Crime Writers' Association Dagger Awards.

Contributors

Mike Ashley is a freelance writer and researcher, primarily in the fields of crime fiction, science fiction and fantasy, but exploring all avenues of literary and ancient history. His books include *Starlight Man*, the biography of Algernon Blackwood, *The Age of the Storytellers*, and *The Mammoth Encyclopedia of Modern Crime Fiction* which won the MWA's Edgar Award. He has also written books on the British monarchy and the seven wonders of the world.

Robert Barnard was brought up in Brightlingsea, Essex, and educated in Colchester. After Oxford, he lectured in English at Antwerp during 1961–1962. Moving to Norway, he was professor of English Literature at Tromsø. In 1983, he went full time as a crime writer and moved back to Britain; his celebrated novels include *Sheer Torture* and *Out of the Blackout*. He has published books on Dickens, Christie and Emily Brontë, and in 2007, he and his wife published their *Brontë Encyclopaedia*. He is the recipient of a Cartier Diamond Dagger.

Graham Barnfield is a senior lecturer in journalism at the University of East London. He has a PhD in cultural studies and is a fellow of the Wolfsonian-FIU in Miami Beach, Florida. He is an affiliate editor of *Reconstruction: Studies in Contemporary Culture* and has contributed to numerous publications, webzines, broadcasts and documentaries, including a column on film for *TES New Teacher*.

Leslie Blake is a lecturer in Law at the University of Surrey. A qualified barrister, he specialises in criminal law, public law, housing and environmental health law and notable British trials. He wrote the articles on William Roughhead and Oscar Slater for the *Dictionary of National Biography*.

Geoff Bradley is the editor and publisher of *CADS*, an irregular magazine devoted to the publication of articles about the crime and detective story; the coverage in the magazine is both comprehensive and eclectic. He has been a key administrator for the Crime Writers' Association.

Mark Campbell has written for *Time Out, The Independent*, the *Bookseller* and *Sherlock*. He has contributed interviews, articles and reviews for *Crime Time* magazine since 1998 and is the author of *Sherlock Holmes* and *Agatha Christie*. A keen film-maker, he is also artistic director of the Edward Alderton Theatre, Bexleyheath.

Michael Carlson has reviewed for the *The Spectator, Daily Telegraph, Financial Times* and *Crime Time* (for which he edits the film section) and has written books on Sergio Leone, Clint Eastwood and Oliver Stone. His online column, *American Eye*, appears in *Shots*, and his features on crime writers have appeared in *Bookslut, Headpress, USA Today* and the *Perth Sunday Times*. As Mike Carlson, he presents sport on television.

Natasha Cooper worked in publishing for ten years, winning the Tony Godwin Memorial Trust Award, before leaving to write her first novel. After six historicals published under another name, she found her natural home in crime. She chaired the Crime Writers' Association from 1999 to 2000. She has judged several literary prizes, broadcasts, speaks at conventions and festivals and reviews for a variety of newspapers and journals, including *The Times Literary Supplement* and the *Toronto Globe and Mail*.

Bob Cornwell is an eclectic and lifelong reader of crime fiction. His reviews, interviews and articles have appeared in *Crime and Detective Stories (CADS)*, on the Tangled website and in *Shots, Crime Time* and *Deadly Pleasures*. He edited *Private Passions, Guilty Pleasures*, a supplement to *CADS* to celebrate its fiftieth issue.

David Stuart Davies is an author, editor and playwright. For ten years, he edited the crime-fiction magazine *Sherlock* and has written two books on the movies of Sherlock Holmes as well as five Holmes novels. He is the supervising editor of Wordsworth's Mystery & Supernatural series. He is on the committee of the Crime Writers' Association and edits their monthly magazine, *Red Herrings*. His wartime detective John Hawke features in three novels, *Forests of the Night*, *Comes the Dark* and *Without Conscience*.

Carol Anne Davis is the author of true crime books such as *Women Who Kill*, *Couples Who Kill*, *Children Who Kill* and *Sadistic Killers*. She is also the author of several realistic crime novels, including *Sob Story*, in which an alienated student teenager is persuaded to write to a long-term prisoner, unaware that he is an about-to-be-paroled killer who plans to kill again.

Martin Edwards has written such Lake District mysteries as *The Coffin Trail* (short-listed for the Theakstons prize for best British crime novel), *The Cipher Garden* and *The Arsenic Labyrinth*. Twice short-listed for CWA Daggers, he has written seven other novels about lawyer Harry Devlin (including *Waterloo Sunset*), plus a stand-alone, *Take My Breath Away*. He completed Bill Knox's last book, *The Lazarus Widow*, and has edited sixteen anthologies. He has published eight non-fiction books, including *Urge to Kill*, a study of homicide investigation.

Terry Fountain founded the crime magazine *ThrillerUK* in 2000 and still edits this, as well as the magazine's website www.thrilleruk. fsnet.co.uk. He has written numerous articles on crime fiction as well as having work published in magazines in Europe and the United States.

Philip Gooden read English at Magdalen College, Oxford, and taught for many years before becoming a full-time writer in 2001. He writes historical mysteries, principally a series featuring Nick Revill, a player with Shakespeare's acting company at the Globe theatre, including *An Honourable Murder*. He also produces reference books on language, most recently *Name Dropping?* and *Faux Pas?*, which won the Duke of Edinburgh's English-Speaking Union Award for the best language book for 2006.

Peter Haining was a Fleet Street journalist and publishing executive before becoming a full-time author in the early 1970s. He wrote biographies of several notorious killers, including *Thomas Corder: The Murder in the Red Barn* and *Sweeney Todd: The Real Story of the Demon Barber of Fleet Street*; a series of books about Sherlock Holmes – *The Sherlock Holmes Scrapbook*, *The Television Sherlock Holmes* and *The Final Adventures of Sherlock Holmes*; as well as a number of best-selling anthologies of crime fiction, notably *The Television Detectives' Omnibus*, *The Crimebusters' Omnibus* and *The Orion Book of Murder*. Peter died in 2007, shortly after delivering his final entries for this book.

Woody Haut was born in Detroit, Michigan, but noir historian Haut has lived in Britain since the 1970s. He is the author of *Pulp Culture: Hardboiled Fiction and the Cold War*, *Neon Noir: Contemporary American Crime Fiction* and *Heartbreak and Vine: The Fate of Hardboiled Writers in Hollywood*. He has also contributed to a variety of periodicals, including *The Observer*, *Financial Times*, *Sight & Sound*, *Crime Time*, *Paradoxa* (US), *Rolling Stock* and *Rolling Stone*. He divides his time between London and the south-west of France.

Lauren Henderson has written seven books in her Sam Jones mystery series (which has been optioned for American television), many short stories and three romantic comedies: *My Lurid Past*, *Don't Even Think About It* and *Exes Anonymous*. Her book *Jane Austen's Guide to Dating* has been optioned as a feature film. She is currently finishing *Kiss Me Kill Me* – the first novel in a YA series. Lauren's books have been translated into over twenty languages. Together with Stella Duffy, she has edited an anthology, *Tart Noir*.

Steve Holland grew up an avid reader of comic strips, children's stories and crime novels and has since spent most of his career writing about them. He is the author of over 1,400 articles and a dozen books relating to crime fiction, comics and pulp culture, including the definitive study of crime paperbacks *The Mushroom Jungle*, nominated for the Anthony Award for non-fiction, and *The Trials of Hank Janson*, nominated for the Silver Dagger Award by the Crime Writers' Association.

Maxim Jakubowski is a former publisher who now writes and edits in both the mystery and the erotica field. He has published over fifty anthologies, and his crime novels include *It's*

You That I Want to Kiss, Because She Thought She Loved Me, On Tenderness Express and *Confessions of a Romantic Pornographer*. He has been the crime reviewer for *Time Out* and *The Guardian*. He runs London's Crime Scene festival and owns the Murder One bookshop.

Russell James is the author of dark multi-layered underworld thrillers largely set in contemporary London. James – 'an acknowledged British master of hard-edged crime' as the *Mail on Sunday* described him – has also compiled and written *The Great Detectives*. He was chairman of the Crime Writers' Association from 2001 to 2002 and is also a crime-fiction critic and journalist.

Michael Jecks is the author of the Templar series of medieval murder stories. He is a judge for the CWA Ian Fleming Steel Dagger and, in the past, organised the CWA Debut Dagger for unpublished authors. He founded the performance group Medieval Murderers and contributes to their annual anthology of linked novellas. He was the chair of the Crime Writers' Association during 2004–2005.

Michael Johnson has run Scorpion Press since 1991, a successful small press publisher of crime fiction in fine bindings. He has friendly contacts with many writers and wrote the overview on crime writers in *Breese's Guide to Modern First Editions* (2000 edition). He devised and contributed to *Masters of Crime: Lionel Davidson and Dick Francis* and has written a study of the espionage novels of Ted Allbeury.

Stephen Jones is the winner of three World Fantasy Awards, four Horror Writers Association Bram Stoker Awards and three International Horror Guild Awards as well as being a seventeen-time recipient of the British Fantasy Award and a Hugo Award nominee. A former television producer/director and genre movie publicist and consultant, he is one of Britain's most acclaimed anthologists with almost 100 books to his credit.

Ali Karim is an assistant editor at *Shots eZine*. He is also a contributing editor to *January Magazine* and *The Rap Sheet* and writes for *Red Herrings*, *Deadly Pleasures* and *Crime Spree* magazines. He is an associate member (and literary judge) for the Crime Writers' Association, International Thriller Writers Inc. and *Deadly Pleasures*' Barry Awards. Karim has contributed to *Dissecting Hannibal Lecter* (edited by Benjamin Szumskyj) and has written *Black Operations*, a violent science-fiction–tinged thriller.

Nick Kimber has written for *CADS*, *A Shot in the Dark*, *Keeler News* and *Notes for the Curious*. He has contributed to *Locked Room Murders* (Crossover Press) and *Wild about Harry* (Ramble House).

Joel Lane is the author of two novels, *From Blue to Black* and *The Blue Mask* (Serpent's Tail), as well as two collections of short stories and two collections of poems. His article on the noir fiction of Cornell Woolrich appeared in the review journal *Wormwood*. He and Steve Bishop have edited an anthology of crime and suspense stories, *Birmingham Noir* (Tindal Street Press).

Jessica Mann has published twenty crime novels, most recently *The Mystery Writer*. She is the author of *Deadlier Than the Male*, a study of feminine crime writing (1981), of *Out of Harm's Way*, the history of the wartime evacuation of children from Britain, and of numerous articles and book reviews. She is the crime fiction reviewer for *The Literary Review*.

Susan Massey is currently at St Andrews University, researching the representation of masculinity in contemporary crime fiction for her PhD, focusing in particular on the work of Ian Rankin, Henning Mankell and George Pelecanos. She is also interested in 'masculinity' in female detectives, such as those created by Sara Paretsky and Stella Duffy.

Val McDermid grew up in a Scottish mining community then read English at Oxford. She was a journalist for 16 years, becoming Northern Bureau Chief of a national Sunday tabloid. As one of Britain's leading crime novelists, she is a winner of The Gold Dagger and many more literary awards throughout the world. In 2007, she won The Stonewall Writer of Year Award, in 2008 saw the 6th series of the ITV series *Wire in the Blood* based on McDermid's books, along with a 3-part ITV drama based on *A Place of Execution*.

Farah Mendlesohn lectures in creative writing at Middlesex University. She was editor of *Foundation* – the international review of science fiction from 2001 to 2005 – and won a Hugo Award for the co-edited *Cambridge Companion to Science Fiction*.

Peter Millar was born in Northern Ireland and read French and Russian at Magdalen College, Oxford. He has been a correspondent for *Reuters*, *The Sunday Telegraph* and *The Sunday Times* in Brussels, East Berlin, Warsaw and Moscow, and was named Foreign

Correspondent of the Year for his reporting on the fall of the Berlin Wall in 1989. He is the author of one non-fiction book and four novels, as well as the translator of several books, fiction and non-fiction, from German. He continues to write for *The Sunday Times* and is a thriller reviewer for *The Times*.

Adrian Muller is a journalist and events organiser specialising in crime fiction. His articles and profiles have been published in books and magazines internationally. Adrian co-founded Britain's Dead on Deansgate convention, and he was one of the originators of *The Times*' crime-fiction supplements. He helped in founding the International Thriller Writers Association, co-hosted Left Coast Crime in Bristol and is the organiser of CrimeFest, an international crime-fiction convention.

Margaret Murphy has written nine psychological crime novels. The grittier themes and faster pace of her more recent books, *The Dispossessed* and *Now You See Me*, are set against the urban landscape of Liverpool. Shortlisted for both the First Blood Award and the CWA Dagger in the Library, she is founder of www.murdersquad.co.uk, CWA Dagger Liaison Officer and former chair of the CWA Debut Dagger. She lectures on writing at LJMU.

Heather O'Donoghue is reader in Old Norse at the University of Oxford and a professorial fellow of Linacre College. Her academic work focuses on Old Norse literature, especially its influence on later poets and novelists, and on the way authors – both medieval and modern – handle complex narratives. She is a regular reviewer of crime fiction in *The Times Literary Supplement* and has acted as a judge for the Crime Writers' Association Duncan Laurie Dagger Awards.

Ayo Onatade has been reading crime and mystery fiction for over thirty years. She helps run the group Mystery Women, and writes for *Reviewing the Evidence*, *Shots eZine* and *CrimeSpree* magazine. She has presented a number of papers on various crime-fiction topics and has a fondness for historical crime fiction as well as books set in Italy and Spain. She has acted as a judge for the Crime Writers' Association Dagger Awards.

Gill Plain teaches English at the University of St Andrews. She is the author of *Twentieth-Century Crime Fiction: Gender, Sexuality and the Body* (Edinburgh University Press) and *Ian Rankin's Black and Blue: A Reader's Guide*

(Continuum). She has also written a critical study of the film career of John Mills and edited a special issue of the journal *Clues* on Scottish crime fiction.

Thalia Proctor gleaned her crime-fiction knowledge from working in every crime bookshop in London during 1989–2004 (Murder One, Crime in Store and Goldsboro Books). She then turned to publishing, first working at Van Lear literary scouts and then moving to Orion. She was then asked to work on the crime list at Little, Brown, where she is currently a desk editor.

Brian Ritterspak is a mainstay of *Crime Time* magazine, where his enthusiasms stretch from the flintiest of hard-boiled fiction to the cosiest of Home Counties mysteries. He writes under a variety of names and bears a strong physical resemblance to another alumnus of this encyclopedia.

Susan Rowland is author of *From Agatha Christie to Ruth Rendell: British Women Writers in Detective and Crime Fiction* and of articles on authors such as Dorothy L. Sayers, Georges Simenon and Sue Grafton for *Crime Time*. She teaches English literature at the University of Greenwich and also publishes on CG Jung and literary theory. She recently made a presentation on myth and detective fiction at St Andrews University.

Nicholas Royle, born in Manchester, is the author of five novels – *Counterparts*, *Saxophone Dreams*, *The Matter of the Heart*, *The Director's Cut* and *Antwerp* – and one short-story collection, *Mortality*, and a novella, *The Enigma of Departure*. Widely published as a journalist, with regular appearances in *Time Out* and *The Independent*, he has also edited twelve anthologies.

Philip L. Scowcroft was for thirty-four years a solicitor in local government service before retirement in 1993. He specialises in crime fiction, military history, sport, transport history and music and has written and lectured extensively on all these subjects. On crime fiction alone, he has written around a thousand articles for ten crime periodicals on both sides of the Atlantic, for societies devoted to crime authors and for partworks on the subject. His *Railways in British Crime Fiction* appeared in 2004.

Chris Simmons is a well-known face on the British crime- and thriller-fiction scene. He has been an über-fan of the genre for many years and is a keen collector of hardbacks and first editions. He co-founded and edits the highly successful UK-based crime and thriller website www.crimesquad.com and is a respected authority on classic crime writers and an active supporter of new writing.

Christine Simpson is an authority on Dorothy L. Sayers and Margery Allingham and has written and lectured on her subjects, as well as acting as editor of The Sayers Society's serial publications for ten years. From 1987, she has contributed to Geoff Bradley's *Crime and Detective Stories* (*CADS*) magazine and has contributed to *The Oxford Companion to Crime and Mystery Writing*.

Mike Stotter is the editor of the website (www.shotsmag.co.uk) for crime and thrillers, *Shots*. Besides working for the Crime Writers' Association, he is member of International Thriller Writers Society and has served as a judge for the Ian Fleming Steel Dagger and the prestigious CWA Gold and Silver Daggers. He is an award-winning children's author for his non-fiction title *The Wild West* and has contributed to various anthologies and encyclopedias covering crime, westerns and science fiction.

Andrew Taylor has won three CWA awards, one of them for the international bestseller *The American Boy* (published in the United States as *An Unpardonable Crime*), a Richard and Judy Book Club selection. His other books include *The Roth Trilogy*, televised as *Fallen Angel* starring Charles Dance and Emilia Fox, the Lydmouth Series set in the 1950s and the Dougal Series. He reviews crime fiction widely, mainly in *The Spectator* and *The Independent*.

Mark Timlin is the creator of the Sharman series of crime novels (which comprises sixteen novels and one collection of short stories) and television series (a pilot and four ninety-minute episodes screened on ITV in 1995/96 and starring Clive Owen as Sharman). He has also written thirteen other novels in various genres and under various noms de plume, plus a number of short stories in magazines and anthologies. He is a feature writer for, among others, *Arena* and *Mojo* magazines, and a crime-fiction reviewer for *The Independent on Sunday*, *Shots* and *Crime Time* magazines and *The Good Book Guide*.

Charles Waring has been the television and music editor of *Crime Time* since 1999. He was born in Evesham, Worcestershire, and educated at Leeds University, where he studied English and music. He began writing professionally in 1996 and now writes regularly for several publications – in addition to being a regular album reviewer for *MOJO* magazine, he is the jazz columnist for *Record Collector* and recently became an editor at *Blues & Soul*. He has also written countless CD liner notes and put together several compilations for record companies.

Laura Wilson has worked as an editor of non-fiction books and written history books for children. Her psychological thrillers have been critically acclaimed, and the first, *A Little Death*, was shortlisted for the Anthony Award for Best Paperback Original in America and the CWA Ellis Peters Award for Historical Crime. Her fifth novel, *The Lover*, was shortlisted for the CWA Gold Dagger for Fiction and the Ellis Peters Award and won the Prix du Polar Européen in France. Her novel, *A Thousand Lies*, was shortlisted for the Duncan Lawrie Dagger. She also reviews crime fiction for *The Guardian*.